Parents and Their Children

Seventh Edition

Verdene Ryder
Family Life Education Consultant
Houston, Texas

Dr. Celia A. Decker
Professor of Family and Consumer Sciences, Retired
Northwestern State University of Louisiana
Natchitoches, Louisiana

Publisher
The Goodheart-Willcox Company, Inc.
Tinley Park, Illinois
www.g-w.com

Library of Congress Catalog Card Number 2007041002
ISBN 978-1-59070-926-9

3 4 5 6 7 8 9 10 — 10 — 15 14 13 12 11

Library of Congress Cataloging-in-Publication Data
Ryder, Verdene.
  Parents and their children / Verdene Ryder,
Celia A. Decker. -- 6th ed.
    p. cm.
  Includes index.
  ISBN 978-1-59070-926-9
1. Parenting. 2. Parent and child. 3. Child psychology.
4. Parenthood. I. Decker, Celia Anita. II. Title.
HQ755.8.R93 2010
649'.1--dc22   2007041002

Introduction

Do you love children? Have you thought about becoming a parent someday? Perhaps you are excited about a career working with children, parents, and families. If any of these peak your interest, *Parents and Their Children* is written for you!

Because most people become parents, this book focuses on the decisions and skills related to effective parenting. It explores various family forms and functions, the cycle of family development, and how the parenting role changes as children grow and develop. When and why to have children, what health practices to follow before and after pregnancy, and how to prepare for childbirth are just a few early decisions prospective parents must make.

From the moment of birth, parents and their children constantly learn, grow, and change. Parents move from imagining what their child will be like to the realities of day-to-day parenting. Learning about children's stages of development and how parental interactions can promote optimum development are crucial for successful parenting. Positive parental attitudes and behaviors powerfully impact how well children develop and succeed in the world. This text shows you how to promote enjoyable, supportive, encouraging, and rewarding parent-child interactions.

Along with a strong emphasis on effective parenting practices, this revised edition of *Parents and Their Children* includes up-to-date information on pregnancy, prenatal care, and childbirth. Important topics, such as moral development and character in children and ways for families to work through challenges and crises, lead to strong parenting skills and children who are capable of making their way in the world.

Your future success as a parent (or in a child and family-related career) requires important skills and personal qualities, such as guiding children, communicating effectively, and loving children unconditionally. *Parents and Their Children* offers the foundation knowledge you need on the pathway to effective parenting.

About the Authors

Verdene Ryder is a nationally recognized author and family life specialist. In addition to authoring *Parents and Their Children*, she is also the author of the popular family living texts *Contemporary Living* and *Human Sexuality: Responsible Life Choices*. Added to her written accomplishments are several booklets and a newspaper column for teens. She is often consulted in interviews on radio and TV relating to family life issues. Mrs. Ryder has extensive teaching experience at both the high school and university levels. She is a member of several professional organizations and has received numerous academic and leadership awards. A scholarship has been named in Mrs. Ryder's honor to enable women in financial need to attend college.

With her extensive teaching experience at Northwestern State University of Louisiana, Texas A & M at Commerce, and the University of Arkansas at Fayetteville; **Dr. Celia A. Decker** brings a wealth of background information in authoring *Parents and Their Children*. In addition to teaching courses in early childhood education, child development, and family relations, Dr. Decker has also been a key presenter on many early childhood topics at over 30 state, regional, and national professional-association conferences, including the National Association for the Education of Young Children (NAEYC). Throughout her career, Dr. Decker has also done consultation work for Head Start and military child care programs. Along with authoring this text and *Children: The Early Years*, she and her husband, Dr. John R. Decker, wrote *Planning and Administering Early Childhood Programs*.

Contents in Brief

Contents

Part Three
The Beginning of Parenthood 156

Part Four
Understanding Children's Growth and Development 268

Part Five
The Challenges of Parenting 466

Part One
Decisions About Parenting

Your Potential Career

Human Services in Demand

Are you a helper? Do you like to see people maximize their independence and succeed in the world to the best of their abilities? Are you a person of character who lives by high ethical standards? Can you communicate well and show compassion to others? Are you detail oriented, organized, and technology savvy? If you answered yes to any of the above, a career in human services may be for you.

With many job opportunities growing at a *faster than average* rate, careers related to helping others are in *high demand*.

How can you prepare for a human-services career? First, build your career plan with a solid academic foundation—science, math, and communications supplemented with family and consumer sciences, health, and humanities. Some careers, such as a *personal care assistant*, require a high school diploma and on-the-job training.

Other careers—such as a *child, family, or school social worker*—require at least a four-year degree and some work experience.

Depending on skill level and education, wages for human services careers range from low to moderate. As with many careers, a person with more education, training, and experience will command a higher wage.

Build a Portfolio

Begin creating a well-organized collection of items that reflect your education and work experience. You might include your résumé, photographs of work experience, written descriptions or a DVD of a community service project along with many other accomplishments. Choose your best work. Use your portfolio when seeking further education or employment.

Learn and Serve

Plan an ongoing service-learning project related to human services with your class. Projects should relate to serving children and parents and may involve a community organization, such as the Boys and Girls Clubs, Big Brothers and Sisters, YMCA, Habitat for Humanity, or child and family services. Use effective decision-making steps to develop and execute your plan. At the end of the course, write a detailed summary about the effectiveness of your class service-learning project. How did this project personally impact your life?

FCCLA

Develop an FCCLA STAR Events project for a human-services career related to parenting and children. Consider a project idea from FCCLA National Programs, such as *Career Connection, STOP the Violence, Dynamic Leadership, Community Service, or Power of One* as the foundation for your project. Obtain necessary STAR Events forms and guidelines from your family and consumer sciences teacher.

You can read more about planning your career in Chapter 22.

Career Cluster—Human Services

Cluster Pathways

Early Childhood Development and Services	Counseling and Mental Health Services	Family and Community Services	Consumer Services
Sample Careers			
Child Care:	*School:*	Human and Social Services Worker	Consumer Credit Counselor
Nanny	Counselor	Human and Social Services Assistant	Financial Advisor
Teacher	Psychologist	Emergency Relief Worker	Consumer Advocate
Teachers' Assistant	Career or Employment Counselor	Dietitian	Insurance Representative
Principal	Marriage, Child, and Family Counselor	Community Food Service Worker	Customer Service Representative
Director		Community Housing Worker	Event Specialist
		Personal Care Assistant	Buyer
Elementary School:			Small Business Owner
Counselor			
Parent Educator			
Teachers' Assistant			
Child Care Worker			

Chapter 1

Parenting: A Rewarding Choice

Objectives

After studying this chapter, you will be able to

- contrast the terms *parent*, *parenting*, and *parenthood*.
- describe the personal qualities and knowledge needed for effective parenting.
- recognize popular myths about parenthood.
- relate the overall job responsibilities of parents to the parenting needs of children.
- summarize the rewards of parenting.

Key Terms

parent
parenting
role
parenthood
nurturance
realistic expectations
unconditional love
dedication
flexibility
myth
moral development
morals
structure
ethnic groups
cultural traditions
ethnic identity
heritage
diversity
stress

Look at the titles of this textbook and this chapter. You see the terms *parents* and *parenting*. Between these two words in the dictionary, you will find the related term *parenthood*. What do the three terms mean?

When you look up **parent**, you will find that the meaning has two parts—a person who gives birth to offspring *and* brings up and cares for a child. Does the term parent include grandparents or other family members who raise a child, too? What about nannies, child care teachers, school teachers, scout leaders, coaches, and countless other leaders of children's programs who help care for and raise a child? Although they are not called *parents*, they do help raise a child. When considering all these aspects, the term *parent* applies to the following:

- the mother and father responsible for their child's birth

- the actions of a mother and a father in caring for and raising a child

- other people who care for a child by serving the role of mother or father, such as adoptive parents and foster parents

Related to the term *parent* is the word *parenting*. **Parenting** is the act or process of raising a child. It involves meeting the child's needs to age 18 or sometimes longer. Parenting also means guiding a child toward the goal of becoming a competent adult. Biological, adoptive, and foster parents, as well as family members, teachers, and others can handle the process of raising children.

A **role** is a set of behaviors related to a certain function you assume in life. **Parenthood** refers to the role of parenting in society. Parenthood is a highly valued role that involves legal rights and responsibilities. Because of these rights and responsibilities, parents can make many decisions about how to raise a child. It is their legal right to make responsible decisions. Responsible decisions are those considered to be good for the child by moral and legal standards. When parental decisions are thought to be harmful to the child, the child can be removed from the family and those legal rights ended. Examples include cases of neglect or abuse.

At some time in life, most people become parents. Of those who remain childless, many handle parenting tasks for other family members or friends. Sometimes they hold careers that involve parenting tasks, such as child care or teaching.

As you study parenting, think about how you were raised. Also consider your observations of parents and their children, and your thoughts about ideal parenting. Compare these views with what is known about competent parenting. Consider the challenges and the opportunities of parenthood.

In this chapter, you will learn about the job of parents, myths about the job of parenting, and the responsibilities and rewards of parenthood. This chapter will also explain why parenting education is needed and how to make the most of your studies.

The Job Description

Parenting is a series of related jobs and work experiences. In this sense, parenting is often called a *career*. It is probably the most exciting and challenging career a person can have.

Suppose you were reading the want ads online or in your local newspaper and discovered the ad in 1-1. Would a job like this interest you? Why or why not?

You would probably not accept a job, even one that looks interesting, before knowing its responsibilities and salary. Likewise, you should not become a parent before learning about that career's qualifications, responsibilities, and rewards.

While reading the job description, did you notice the qualifications for parenting? Several factors determine whether a person is qualified to handle a given job. These include the individual's personal qualities, knowledge of the subject, and past experience.

Personal Qualities

Personal qualities are most important because parenting duties mainly involve interactions with the child. Parents also interact with their child's friends and with other adults, such as teachers, on behalf of their child.

Parenting demands a special maturity—a person who is willing to put his or her needs after the child's. Because social maturity usually blooms in the young-adult years, teen parents are at high risk for finding parenthood overwhelming. Although parents should find time to meet their needs as individuals and couples, children's needs must never be neglected. The following personal qualities are part of the special maturity needed for parenting.

Class activity → make students design wanted ads

describe all details of perfect parent.

WANTED: PARENT

Full-time position available for mature individual. Job requires nurturance, dedication, and flexibility. Must be willing to work seven, 24-hour shifts per week. No experience required, but child development knowledge is a definite plus. Responsibilities include: changing diapers, fixing meals, cleaning up messes, and answering questions, as well as teaching, loving, and guiding a child from infancy to adulthood. A minimum 18-year commitment is required.
Salary: You pay thousands.
Fringe benefits: Excellent, including the opportunity to hear a child's first words, help a child learn to ride a bicycle, and watch with pride as your grown-up son or daughter receives a college diploma.
For application, contact:
The Stork Company

Call Today!

1-1 Does this sound like the job for you? Parenting is hard work, but it has many rewards.

Nurturance

Nurturance means loving care and attention. To nurture children is to love, teach, and guide them. From the very beginning of their lives, infants need to be assured they are surrounded by love. Infants feel love through the parents' touch, tone of voice, and facial expressions. Holding children close and soothing them also conveys love. Parents need to continue to love and nurture their children even into adulthood.

A parent is a child's first and most important teacher. Having **realistic expectations**, or knowledge of developmental skills children have at a certain age, helps parents provide an atmosphere for growth and learning. Nurturance involves challenging children to do their best at developing skills appropriate for their age. Through help and encouragement from parents, children gradually develop important physical, intellectual, emotional, and social skills.

Above all, nurturance involves giving **unconditional love** to children. This type of love sets no conditions or boundaries. Children need to know that parents love them even when they make mistakes, disobey, or fail to live up to what parents expect. If you choose to parent, your children will need to know they can always count on your love. Never, under any circumstances, use love as a reward or threat. Do not tell children you will love them more for eating their vegetables, or less for getting bad grades. Parents should give their children constant love in large doses, 1-2.

Dedication

Parenting demands **dedication**, or a deep level of continued commitment. It is a 24-hour-a-day, everyday job. When you become a parent, you must devote yourself to your new role. You can't punch a time card and go off duty. If your baby needs to be fed or changed, it is your job to see those needs are met. When your child comes to you with a bloody knee, you can't say, "Sorry, I'm on my break." You can't resign—or even take a vacation—from parenting when the job is difficult. You have to hang in there, giving whatever help and support your child needs.

Flexibility

Parents need flexibility to survive the many challenges they face. **Flexibility** means being ready and able to adapt to new and different circumstances. When you become a parent, you must be able to adjust easily and quickly to many different situations.

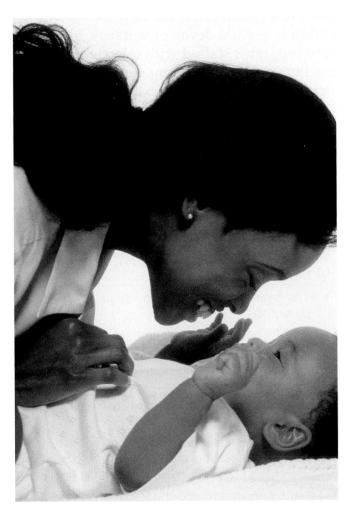

1-2 Giving lots of love to a child is an important part of nurturance.

As children grow and develop, they may pass through phases during which they display undesirable behaviors. Common examples include getting into mischief, tattling, or playing practical jokes. Flexibility allows you to adjust to these passing phases and the behaviors your child displays. Often, your child will grow out of a phase just as you learn how to handle behavior in that phase. You have to stay alert to keep up with growing children.

A parent's daily plans often change, even at the last moment, due to the child's activities or needs. For example, as a parent, you may have to skip an adult social event to watch your child play in a soccer match. You may have to postpone a business meeting to stay home with a sick child. You may have to push back mealtime when, with your child's "help," preparing dinner takes longer than planned. In cases like this, a good sense of humor is just as important as flexibility.

Being flexible in your daily routine will allow you to enjoy children's spontaneous nature. You can share their delight when they first play in water or see themselves in the mirror. You can marvel at their first words and first steps. You can smile proudly as they show you a new music or dance skill. Sharing such moments with your child is one of the most precious fringe benefits of the job of parenting, 1-3.

Knowledge and Experience

Do people get much *knowledge* about parenting before having their first child? If they take a course like this, they do. Do people get much *experience* with parenting before their first child? Generally, the answer is no. People who cut hair for the public or provide manicures must have knowledge and a license. You must have a license and on-the-road experience to drive a car. Yet, acquiring knowledge and experience with parenting is not a condition for becoming a parent—and babies do not come with instructions.

1-3 Flexibility in your daily routine allows you time to share special moments with your child.

In the past, young women were raised to be mothers. They developed skills by caring for younger family members. When they became mothers, their mothers and other women in the family helped them with child rearing. Parenting, therefore, was learned through years of experience and tradition.

Times have changed. Today's parents have fewer child-care experiences before their first child. Grandmothers and older family members are often employed outside the home. Others may live too far away to

help new parents. Yet, there has never been a better time in history to be an informed parent. Reliable information on parenting can be found everywhere—in bookstores, on Web sites, at newsstands, in libraries, and on television programs.

Still, most adults are not prepared for parenting. Why not? Many adults are overwhelmed by the wealth of information available to parents. Busy adults may have little time to read many materials or the knowledge to choose the best. They may feel even less confident about parenting.

Without a doubt, parenting is complex. Some basic knowledge can take you a long way toward becoming a competent parent, 1-4. Experiences with children are helpful, too. The best experiences are working with children in child development labs, in child care programs staffed with experienced teachers, or from any competent parent or person who has had rich experiences with children. They can help you learn what to expect and how to respond as children grow and develop.

What Parents Need to Know

- The general concepts and methods of effective parenting.
- How these concepts and methods apply to children's developmental stages.
- Common problems children face at each stage and how these problems might be worked out.
- How parents will likely react to children's developmental stages.
- How parents and their children can adapt to stressful events and crises.

1-4 Basic knowledge about parenting can help make you a competent parent.

Parenting Myths and Realities

As with other careers, some people may think of parenting as the "perfect" career. Because of this thinking, they may believe and spread myths about parenting. A **myth** is a half-true or untrue story or notion used to explain certain traditions, practices, or beliefs.

Myths about parenting come from several sources, such as society and families. Society has had a long history of cultural and traditional thinking. These thoughts contain many truths as well as myths. Until rather recently, experts in family life and child development rarely studied parenting. Because parent education was not available, people relied on information passed down to them through generations about how to raise children. This information was based on *family* culture and traditions. Although some of this traditional thinking was correct, and continues to be, other ideas are now known to be incorrect. For example, such notions as "You'll spoil babies if you pick them up" are now known to be false. The reality is that babies need to be held and comforted in order to build trust and feel secure, 1-5.

Second, society often promotes a *romantic complex*—an ideal view having no basis in fact—about parenthood. For example, think about how the media represents children and their families. Is it realistic or a misrepresentation of reality?

Third, not all experts agree on every aspect of parenting. This problem may confuse some parents. Parenting is a highly complex and individual process. Experts will continue to do research and provide more knowledge about parenting, but myths may still exist until facts replace them.

Why is it important to address parenting myths? Believing false ideas about the role of parenthood may harm the parent-child relationship. Having unrealistic or impossible role expectations may lead to stress for both

1-5 Holding and comforting babies is essential in order for them to feel secure in their world.

parents and their children. Understanding myths for what they are will help you know what the parenting career is *really* like. Here are some common parenting myths you may have heard.

Myth #1:
All parenting skills are instinctive.

Some people say all parenting skills are *instinctive*, or based on a natural skill or capacity. They say people are born knowing how to be parents; it just comes naturally. Many mothers and fathers do seem naturally well suited to being parents. This doesn't mean they instinctively know it all or have nothing to learn. No one is born with all the preparation needed to be an effective parent. Parenting takes hard work and practice.

What skills seem to be the most instinctive? Some people are skilled observers of others. This skill allows them to quickly recognize their children's needs and respond. Other less-instinctive qualities are the personal qualities you have studied—nurturance, dedication, and flexibility. Even these skills can be improved with knowledge, training, and experience. *All* parenting skills are not instinctive, however. This is a myth because many parenting skills must be learned through gaining knowledge and experience.

Myth #2: A mature adult can be a perfect parent.

Parenting is a human role. Humans are not perfect so no one can be a perfect parent. Even mature adults lack some parenting knowledge and skills. Mature adults make mistakes, too. Parenting involves children who are also imperfect people.

Trying to be perfect parents is not good for parents or their children. When parents make mistakes, they may feel as though they are failures. Lack of confidence often results in more parenting mistakes and robs parents of the joys of parenting. If parents try too hard to be perfect, children pick up on their parents' anxiety. Parental anxiety lowers children's self-confidence, too.

Mature adults should strive to become competent parents, not perfect parents, through parent education and real-life experiences, 1-6. Competent parents will make mistakes but will also learn from them. At times, they will even need to say "I'm sorry" to their children. Yet, they can be confident they are responsible parents who handle most parenting tasks well.

Myth #3: Good parenting guarantees "good" children.

This myth closely relates to Myth #2. In the past, much pressure was put on parents to perform the "right" parenting actions in order for children to grow into healthy adults. This myth is based on the idea that personality is completely formed in the early years. Early experiences are most important, but personality continues to develop throughout life. Influences outside the family, such as peers, adults other than parents, and media, affect children in healthy or unhealthy ways.

Parenthood does not come with any guarantees. However, effective parenting highly increases the chance of having children grow to be responsible adults. It also leads to positive relationships with parents and their adult children.

Myth #4: Parenting is always fun.

From the outside looking in, it is easier to see the rewards of parenting than the challenges and responsibilities. People who are not yet parents cannot foresee all these less-positive aspects. Parents who have raised children sometimes look back and remember the good times more easily than the bad.

Like any other job, parenting can be fun, sad, exciting, boring, satisfying, and frustrating. The point is you need to have *realistic* expectations. You will soon be disappointed if you believe parenting is just one fun day after another. You may even grow to resent your child for not fulfilling your dreams of parenting bliss. On the other hand, if you can accept that bad times occur, too, you will probably enjoy parenting.

1-6 Parents must be prepared to accept the reality that their children can have difficult moments.

Parenting is not fun all the time, but many parents have lots of fun as they raise their children. An important influence is a person's attitude toward parenting. Keeping a sense of humor can help parents through difficult times. Overall, many people genuinely enjoy being parents.

Myth #5:
Children are always cute and sweet.

Many people daydream about having a baby. They look forward to holding a sweet, cuddly bundle of joy. It is not as easy to anticipate times when babies are not so cute and sweet. The reality is that babies also cry, scream, and squirm, 1-7. They are sick and unhappy at times. Parents must be able to handle the noise and mess babies create. Toddlers can be downright stubborn. It can be a big adjustment if parents have unrealistic expectations about what babies and toddlers are really like. While children can be adorable, parents should be prepared to accept reality.

Even the cutest and sweetest babies grow quickly into school-age children and teens. Older children can be just as enjoyable, if not more so, than babies. However, some parents are not ready to handle older children's needs and demands. They may not find older children as cute and sweet as babies. Babies cannot start an argument or run all over the house. People will be disappointed if they become parents simply to care for cuddly babies. Parents who look forward to all the stages of growth are more prepared for the realities of parenting. They will find satisfaction throughout their lives as parents, not just during the first few years.

The Responsibilities of Parenting

Every job has its responsibilities, and parenting is no different. Just like most

1-7 Although babies are generally cute and sweet, the reality is they also cry, squirm, and scream.

jobs, parenting is complicated. It has basic requirements in caring for children. In addition, parenting involves complex tasks in figuring out the best way to help children grow and develop based on parents' values and what is known about competent parenting. Parents cannot know in advance all the parenting duties they will have, but several are common to all parents. The following duties are the main responsibilities of parenting.

Wanting and Being Ready for Children

A parent's first responsibility is deciding if he or she wants children and is ready to have them. People should think carefully about whether they really want children and are ready to be parents. Every child deserves proper care and guidance. Making rational decisions about parenting is best for adults and children.

Becoming a good parent also means recognizing when it is *not* the right time to start (or add to) a family. Family planning decisions are described more fully in later chapters.

Fulfilling Legal Responsibilities and Rights

Regardless of parents' marital status, parents have a legal responsibility to support and supervise their children. Parents have corresponding rights to make many decisions about their children's lives, 1-8. For example, parents have the right to choose where a child lives and the responsibility to make sure children are safe in this environment.

A parent's legal responsibility continues until the child reaches the *age of majority*. This is the age, usually 18, when a person is considered an adult by the legal system. The law in each state sets the age of majority. When children reach this age, they are free to live on their own, make their own decisions, marry, and financially support themselves. With this freedom, comes the taking of responsibility for their actions.

Meeting Children's Needs

Children have many needs from birth to adulthood. Babies are totally dependent on parents for satisfying their physical needs. As children grow, they can meet some of their needs, but parents must assist and supervise their efforts. Because meeting needs is critical to children's development, parents must be prepared to give the required help. Here are some ways that parents meet children's needs.

Need for Unconditional Love

First, and foremost, children need unconditional love. Children need to know they are loved for who they are and for their own special qualities. Constant, unconditional love helps children feel good about themselves, self-confident, and secure.

Physical Needs

Loving parents provide for children's food, clothing, and shelter and ensure their health and safety. These needs change as children grow and develop so parents must

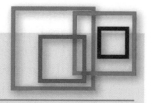

Parents' Legal Responsibilities and Rights

Responsibilities

Support children by providing life necessities (food, clothing, shelter), medical care, and education.

Supervise and control children's behavior. Parents are liable for children's accidental or intentional injury of others, destruction of property, stealing, truancy, and curfew violations.

Examples of Corresponding Rights

Determine where children will live, what medical care they will be given, and which school they will attend.

Control children as they see fit as long as they do not neglect or abuse children or ask children to do something illegal.

NOTE: Courts may intervene on behalf of children if parents' do not adequately support, supervise, and control their children's behavior.

1-8 Parents are legally required to meet basic responsibilities in parenting, but can make choices in how to fulfill this role.

continually adjust how they meet these needs. For example, living space for a newborn can be a small area in the parents' bedroom or a nursery. By school age, a child needs more and different spaces. These include a private place to sleep, dress, and study, in addition to storage space for clothing and other items. The child also needs a place to pursue quiet activities and outdoor space for active play. Abraham Maslow, a psychologist, felt that a person's physical needs must be met before any other needs, 1-9.

Intellectual, Emotional, and Social Needs

Children are born ready to learn. Babies learn through their "home schooling" as they are carried, cared for, talked to, read to, and played with by loving parents. Parents also promote their learning outside the home by taking them on trips to a library,

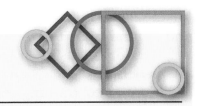

Maslow's Hierarchy of Human Needs

Psychologist Abraham Maslow studied how the fulfillment of different human needs affect thought, behavior, and personality. He organized human needs into five levels according to priority, with the highest-priority needs at the bottom. This arrangement is called *Maslow's Hierarchy of Human Needs*.

Maslow's theory shows that helping children meet their needs can help make them feel complete. Read the pyramid from the bottom up. The hierarchy follows this order:

- **Physical needs.** Air, food, shelter, water, clothing, and any other life-sustaining needs
- **Safety and security needs.** Feeling safe from danger and secure in daily routines
- **Love and acceptance needs.** Feeling secure in relationships with family and friends; praise, support, and encouragement help people feel a sense of love, affection, and belonging
- **Esteem needs.** Self-respect, self-esteem, and the esteem or admiration of others necessary for confidence
- **Self-actualization needs.** The realization of a person's full potential

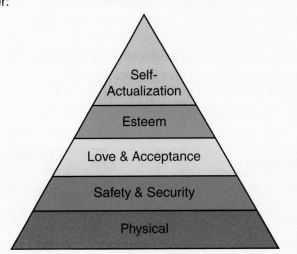

1-9 According to Maslow's theory, all needs have a certain priority. The needs of one level must be at least partially met before a person can realize higher needs.

nature preserve, zoo, or museum. Children tend to imitate their parents' desire to learn. As children grow, parents meet children's intellectual needs by supporting their learning in child care programs and schools.

Showing love to children and responding to their needs is the backbone of good emotional development. Parents must help children recognize and name their emotions. They must teach their children to express intense emotions that are not hurtful.

From the beginning, parents need to be social teachers. They encourage social interactions with babies through the loving exchange of smiles, cooing sounds, and first words, and by playing such games as peek-a-boo. As children develop, they need to share experiences with family members of all ages

and play and visit with friends. Through these interactions, children learn valuable lessons in sharing, communicating, and compromising.

Need for Moral Development

Loving parents want their children to become mature, responsible, and happy adults. For this to happen, children need to learn to behave in ways that are acceptable to society and the family. This process, called **moral development**, is gradual and reflects a child's understanding of the difference between right and wrong. However, children are not born knowing the difference between right and wrong.

Very young children cannot understand **morals**. These are the beliefs people have that help them discern between right and wrong. Parents can begin this learning by having a home filled with warmth, affection, respect, and mutual trust, 1-10. A home such as this helps children trust their parents' judgments and beliefs.

More direct training begins between the ages of two and three. At this time, parents need to provide **structure**. Structure sets behavioral limits (home rules) that teach children how to get along in the world. It involves guiding children to develop personal boundaries that do not infringe on others' needs and rights. Structure also means providing children with experiences that promote self-worth and a sense of safety and security. When children reach the school years, they can talk with their

1-10 Providing an atmosphere of warmth, affection, and mutual trust helps build the foundation for moral development.

parents about right and wrong decisions and the consequences of certain actions. These combined elements form the foundation for moral development.

Heritage and Culture Awareness Needs

Each family belongs to one or more **ethnic groups**. These are groups of people with a common racial, national, tribal, religious, or cultural origin or background. Members of ethnic or cultural groups have shared customs, beliefs, and behaviors, or **cultural traditions**. Children learn from and enjoy participating in traditions that involve food preparation, clothing, or religious practices of a family's ethnic background. Children also want to hear stories and see items from their own family history.

All of these experiences help children form an **ethnic identity**. This refers to the way a person views himself or herself as a member of a particular ethnic group. Children develop pride in their family background by knowing about their **heritage**, or all that has been passed down through the generations. As children learn of their cultural heritage, they learn that others may also have a different cultural heritage. Parents can help their children learn about **diversity**, which is a condition of differing from one another. By helping children learn about and respect other customs, beliefs, and behaviors, they promote appreciation of cultures that are different.

Maintaining Good Health

Parents have a responsibility to take care of themselves physically, intellectually, socially, and emotionally. Maintaining good health helps parents take good care of their children. Parents need a balanced diet, regular exercise, plenty of sleep, and interaction with others. Because the parenting role is ever changing, all parents feel **stress**. This is the tension caused by a condition or situation that demands a mental or physical adjustment. Mild and short-lived stress is not harmful. Severe and long-term stress harms parents' physical and mental health.

Parents need to find ways to cope with their stress. Outlets for stress relief can include time to themselves (to read or pursue other interests) and time for activities they enjoy with other people who can provide emotional and social support. A satisfying marriage is a major source of emotional strength, too. Many authorities say parents should view their marriage as their primary relationship and work to keep it strong and healthy. Such a marriage creates positive feelings and it enhances parent-child relationships, 1-11.

The Rewards of Parenting

Why do so many people choose to become parents and accept all these responsibilities? For most parents, parenting has rewards that far outweigh the challenges. No other job offers the satisfaction that parenting does. Nothing can compare to the opportunity to watch your children grow and develop. Here are some examples of rewards that parents often feel.

- **Parenting sparks a wide variety of emotions.** Parents feel content when they rock a baby to sleep. They feel happy when they hear "mama" or "dada" for the first time. They feel proud when their child learns to read.

- **Parenting can help people experience new or deeper emotions.** They may feel a new tenderness within themselves when they care for a sick child. Parents are often amazed at how much they are able to love their children. Parental love is a unique kind of love, unlike any other love. After becoming parents, a couple may grow closer and find they

1-11 Parents can be better parents by maintaining good health. Keeping their marriage strong and healthy is also important.

love and respect each other even more. This type of personal growth is a unique opportunity of parenting.

- **Parenting offers a sense of satisfaction in children.** As parents watch their children grow and succeed in the world, they often experience a sense of personal satisfaction in how they have parented their children. This satisfaction comes from knowing that they are loving, competent parents.

- **Parenting offers the reward of constant adventure.** Every stage of development brings new experiences for parents and child. Parents learn how to make an infant smile and how to help a baby build a tower of blocks. They learn to answer questions, such as "Where do stars go during the day?" Later, parents may learn to coach a Little League team or referee a soccer game.

It is impossible to describe all the rewards of parenting. They differ from day to day and from child to child, 1-12. Many people feel the special love their children have for them is the best reward of all.

At some time in life, many people choose to become parents and accept all of the responsibilities and rewards the job involves. Of those who remain childless, many are involved in parenting tasks with the children of other family members or friends.

As you study parenting, think about your parents and other parents you've observed. Also consider your own ideas about parenting. Compare these views with what you know about responsible parenting. Consider the challenges and the rewards of a parenting career.

1-12 The rewards of parenthood are many and differ day to day.

Summing It Up

- The terms *parent*, *parenting*, and *parenthood* have interrelated meanings in regard to the care and support of children.

- Parenting can be compared to a career because both require commitment, involve responsibilities, present challenges, and offer rewards.

- Nurturance, dedication, and flexibility are three important personal qualities of parents.

- Parenting is complex. Knowledge, training, and experience are needed, but rarely happen before a couple's first child is born.

- Myths about parenthood should be recognized for what they are—half-true or untrue stories or notions used to explain certain traditions, practices, or beliefs.

- People should understand the responsibilities and rewards of parenting before they become parents. Parenting responsibilities include wanting and being ready for children, fulfilling legal responsibilities and rights, meeting children's needs, and maintaining their health.

- Children have physical, intellectual, emotional, social, and moral needs that parents must meet.

- The rewards of parenthood far outweigh the challenges for most people.

Recalling the Facts

1. Contrast the terms *parent, parenting,* and *parenthood.*

2. Describe the personal qualities of nurturance, dedication, and flexibility for effective parenting.

3. Describe two myths about parenthood. Explain why each is considered a myth.

4. List four responsibilities of parenting.

5. Why is a child's need for love considered the most important need?

6. What are children's physical needs?

7. Name two ways that parents can promote their children's intellectual growth.

8. How can parents encourage social development in their children?

9. Why is moral development important for children?

10. How does structure in the home help children develop morally?

11. Contrast *ethnic identity* and *diversity.*

12. Why do parents have the responsibility of maintaining their good health?

13. Name two actions that parents can take to maintain good health.

14. What are two ways that parents can reduce their stress?

15. List two rewards of parenting.

Applying New Skills

1. **Parent interview.** Interview a parent about the importance of being a nurturing, dedicated, and flexible parent. Ask if this person always finds it easy to display these qualities. Are there things about being a parent that make parenting more difficult? What advice would the parent give others about developing nurturance, dedication, and flexibility before they become parents? after? Write a summary of your findings to share with the class.

2. **Picture wall.** Gather pictures from magazines and newspapers that depict parenting. Working in small groups, sort the pictures according to which parenting responsibilities they most represent. Share your group's thoughts about the pictures with the rest of the class. Then, as a class, create a picture wall depicting the responsibilities of parenthood. Mount pictures in groups by type of responsibility.

3. **Brainstorm.** On a piece of paper or on the board, write these two headings: *Responsibilities of Parenting* and *Rewards of Parenting.* As a class, brainstorm a list for each heading. Do the lists seem to balance, or does one list seem much longer than the other? What conclusions can you draw about the rewards and responsibilities of parenting?

Thinking Critically

1. Do you accept or reject the parenting myths presented in this chapter? Why? Draw conclusions about other misconceptions you think people have about parenting. What conclusions can you draw about the realities of parenting?

2. Analyze how a person may know when he or she is ready to have children. Discuss your analyses in a small group. Then share your group's ideas with the rest of the class.

3. Assume you are a parent. Assess the morals you feel are important for your children to develop and make a list. Explain why you selected each moral.

Linking Academics

1. **Writing.** Write an essay describing what your parents have taught you about your heritage and culture. Or, write about other parents you know and what they have taught their children about heritage and culture. (Be sure to avoid using real names.) End the paper by writing what you think you will want to teach your children about their heritage and culture.

2. **Social Studies.** Use Internet, print, or interview resources to investigate one or more cultures that exist in your community. Find out at least five positive facts that you didn't know about this ethnic or cultural group and list them on a sheet of paper. How can you use these facts to help build better relationships between cultures in your community? Write a summary of your conclusions.

Chapter 2

Families and Parents

Objectives

After studying this chapter, you will be able to

- explain ways that families may be formed.
- describe the five family structures and the unique characteristics of each.
- list the functions of the family.
- describe the stages of the family life cycle.
- identify six parenting stages.
- explain how the family operates as a social system.
- describe how other factors affect parents' goals and interactions with their children.
- summarize the effects of parenting practices for children, parents, and society.

Key Terms

family
adoption
adoptive families
foster family
guardians
nuclear family
single-parent family
stepfamily
extended family
family functions
values
gender role
family life cycle
socioeconomic status
lifestyle
technology

In all societies, the family is the social group within which the child is nurtured and rooted. The family ensures the consistent care that is not broken by changes for the child. The parent-child relationship is primary for the child—above all others. The family also manages the child's interactions outside of the family, such as those with peers and in child care programs and schools.

In this chapter, you will learn how the family influences parenting. You will also see how the community and the culture at large impact parenting. Finally, you will see the major effects of parenting on children, families, and society.

Parenting Occurs in a Family

What makes a family? Do people have to live in the same home to be family? Do they have to have a biological link? Does a family need a certain number of people to be a family? Does everyone in a family have the same last name?

As you answer these questions, compare answers with a classmate. Did your classmate have all the same answers? Your classmate probably sees family a little differently from the way you do. No two families are the same. People define the word *family* in many different ways.

Basically, a **family** is a group of two or more people who are related by birth, marriage, adoption, or other circumstances. When family is mentioned, many people immediately think of the members of their household. A family also includes relatives who do not live in the same home.

Your *family of origin* includes the family members with whom you lived during your childhood, 2-1. You may have grown up with one or both of your biological parents, adoptive parents, or foster parents. If you have brothers and sisters, they are also included in your family of origin.

2-1 This child's family of origin includes her biological mother and father. Some families of origin include adoptive parents or foster parents.

Families, like individuals, come in all shapes and sizes. This is why the word family has different meanings to people. Families vary in the way they are formed and in their structure.

How Families Are Formed

As you learn about how families are formed, think about the circumstances that bring people together to form a family. The ways some families are formed result in special parenting challenges, such as blending lifestyles and routines when a stepfamily forms. Perhaps you can think of some challenges as you read through the paragraphs that follow. The common ways families are formed include marriage, birth, adoption, inclusion in foster families, and with guardians.

By Marriage

People become related to one another by marriage. When a man and woman marry, they create a new family. Their marriage is the foundation of their family. The couple may or may not choose to add children to their family by birth or adoption. In marriages in which one or both spouses have children from a previous relationship, the family includes the newly married spouses and their children.

By Birth

A baby is biologically related to the man and woman who gave him or her life. These people are the baby's *biological parents* or *birthparents*. The baby is also related to members of the biological parents' families, including brothers, sisters, grandparents, aunts, uncles, and cousins. All children are related to their birthparents although the family of origin may differ for some children, such as adopted children.

By Adoption

Adoption also creates family relationships. **Adoption** is a legal process of transferring a child's parental relationship from his or her birthparents to adoptive parents. **Adoptive families** include adoptive parents and one or more adopted children who may have the same birthparents, 2-2. Adoptive parents are legally the child's parents and have the same responsibilities as birthparents.

People may choose adoption for various reasons. Some couples are unable to have biological children. Adoption can allow them to experience parenting. A couple may also adopt if one spouse has a hereditary condition that would likely affect their future biological children. Other couples adopt simply to offer loving homes to children who need them. They may adopt infants or

2-2 This couple became parents when they adopted several children who needed a loving home.

older children. Because they have chosen to become parents, adoptive parents are usually very dedicated to parenting.

Through Foster Families

Another circumstance that creates family relationships is foster care. *Foster care* is temporary care provided for a child who needs a loving home. *Foster parents* are adults who volunteer and are trained to provide a temporary home for a child who needs one. Each state directs the care of children placed in this temporary care. Basically, a **foster family** provides a child with a substitute family. While the child is in their care, foster parents have the similar legal rights and responsibilities as biological parents. Foster parents assume the parenting role. They take care of their foster child as if he or she were their own. However, foster parents must consult with their caseworker before making decisions that affect the foster child. They also cannot move out of the state when a child is temporarily in their care.

No matter how long foster care lasts, it can be rewarding for both foster parents and foster children. Foster parents have the satisfaction of helping children grow and develop. They can experience parenting and contribute to a foster child's life in positive ways. Foster children can gain a loving home and quality care until a permanent arrangement is made.

With Guardians

Related or unrelated adults, or **guardians**, also raise children, but never legally adopt them. The child's last name is not changed in a guardianship relationship. Unlike foster parents, guardians provide a permanent home. Often the adults are close relatives or friends of the birthparents. They are generally chosen by children's biological parents as guardians in case of the deaths or prolonged absence of the birthparents. These arrangements, like adoption, are legally approved. The guardians will have some custodial and parenting responsibilities, but may have to follow some of the decisions, such as the use of monies, made by birthparents and upheld by the court. The court supervises guardians and may hold some decision-making power over the child.

Because guardians are closely tied by blood or friendship to the child's biological parents, they may feel a very close emotional bond to the child. The child, in turn, will likely consider these adults part of his or her family. The guardian-child relationship ends when the child becomes a legal adult or the court terminates the relationship.

How Families Are Structured

Another way families differ is by their structures. A family's structure tells how it is organized. The structure tells how many people live in a household and how they are related. How many adults and children are in the family? How are they related to one another? By answering these questions, you can identify the family's structure.

Five basic family structures are common in America today. These include nuclear families, single-parent families, stepfamilies, extended families, and couples without children. Each family structure has its advantages and disadvantages, 2-3. Each person may prefer one family structure instead of another. The family structure that works best for one family may not work well for another. Families in each structure can be loving, nurturing, and strong. A family's well-being depends much less upon the family structure than upon how well the family meets its members' needs.

Nuclear Families

A **nuclear family** includes a husband, wife, and the children they have together. These children may be biological or adopted. At one time, nearly all American families were nuclear families. Today, the nuclear family is becoming less common. Yet, many experts consider this structure the most stable and secure setting for parenting.

In nuclear families, spouses generally share parenting responsibilities. Since neither spouse parents alone, parenting is often less stressful. These couples often have more time and energy to enjoy their children and each other. Children who live with both parents have both male and female role models.

Advantages and Disadvantages of Basic Family Structures

Advantages	Disadvantages
Nuclear Families	
• Income is usually higher than in other family structures, especially when both spouses are employed, so more child care options are available.	• Rate of divorce is high. Families often have to adapt to new family structures.
• Both parents split the burden of parenting tasks.	
Single-Parent Families	
• Children are likely to have more and earlier opportunities to become self-reliant.	• Single parent carries the burdens of all the parenting tasks. This can be overwhelming.
• Children may be better adjusted and happier with a well-adjusted single parent than with two parents who are in conflict.	• With less income, child care options are limited.
	• Single parent may expect too much from children and give them tasks they are too young to handle.
Stepfamilies	
• Family members often develop patience, cooperation, and creativity in their new roles.	• Roles, responsibilities, and schedules often change.
• Various child care options are available. Father or mother may stay at home or work at home and take care of children. Center care is often discounted for families enrolling more than one child. Larger families with lower incomes may qualify for not-for-profit centers or programs funded with government monies.	• Children may resent discipline by the stepparent.
	• Family members must learn to share attention and space.
	• Income may be limited if several children are part of the new family. One or both spouses may have to pay alimony, child support, and possibly debts of a former spouse.
Extended Families	
• Children develop closer relationships with family members of several generations and learn to respect and appreciate aging family members.	• Instead of being able to help, elderly family members may need care themselves. This may put time, financial, and emotional strains on the family.
• Older family members can provide good child care and parenting advice.	• Living space may be crowded.
• Older family members often help children develop family pride and ethnic identity.	• Adjustments in lifestyle take time and patience.
• Children often have more emotional security.	• With more adults in the family, children may have problems in knowing "who's in charge" and may feel over-supervised.
Couples Without Children	
• Without the challenges of parenting, couples can focus more time and energy on their careers, hobbies, and interests.	• Unplanned pregnancy can be traumatic.
• Couple often finds the spouse relationship more satisfying.	• Long postponed pregnancy can result in physical complications for mother and baby, and adjustment problems for parents.
	• Couple does not have the rewards of parenting.

2-3 Each family structure has its advantages and disadvantages.

Single-Parent Families

A **single-parent family** includes one parent and his or her biological or adopted children. Single-parent families can be formed in a variety of ways. Many single-parent families consist of a once-married parent and his or her children. The other parent is gone from the family as a result of death, divorce, desertion, or legal separation. Other single parents have never been married. Today, it is more common for never-married adults to give birth or adopt children. These single parents may not have had the chance or the desire to marry.

Although married-couple families still outnumber them, single-parent families are the *fastest* growing family structure in America. More and more adults are raising children alone. One-fourth of all children in the U.S. will spend at least part of their childhood living with a single parent.

The reasons for single parenthood can be traumatic. A parent may not have planned to raise children alone. Despite these factors, parent-child relationships in this structure are often very close, 2-4. These families often develop strong relationships with relatives and friends.

Stepfamilies

When two people marry, one or both of them may bring children from a previous relationship into the marriage. The new family they create is called a **stepfamily**. In a stepfamily, one or both spouses may have been married before.

As the number of single parents increases, the formation of new stepfamilies becomes more common. For example, a single parent may meet a new partner and decide to remarry, creating a stepfamily. Each spouse becomes a stepparent to the other spouse's children. Stepparents are related to stepchildren by marriage instead of biologically. In their new marriage, the

2-4 Although single-parent families often face many challenges, they can feel happy, secure, and loved.

parents may decide to have a child of their own. This child is a half brother or half sister to the other children in the family.

Stepfamilies may include the following relationships: parent and child, stepparent and stepchild, brothers and sisters, half brothers and half sisters, and stepbrothers and stepsisters. Each set of stepchildren also has another parent outside the stepfamily. This parent may or may not be remarried and head a stepfamily of his or her own.

As with nuclear families, spouses can share parenting tasks and responsibilities. All the family members can develop new relationships, even though some relationships may become more complicated than others. At the beginning of these new families, all family members experience some level of difficulty adjusting. It takes work and commitment to blend the lifestyles of two families, 2-5.

Extended Families

An **extended family** includes all the relatives in a family, such as grandparents, aunts, uncles, and cousins. In contrast, a family of origin, which may also be called an *immediate family*, includes only parents and their children. In general, all people have extended families.

In the *extended-family structure*, more relatives than an immediate family live in one home. Any mixture of grandparents, parents, children, aunts, uncles, and cousins may live in one residence. These living arrangements may be temporary or permanent, depending on the family's situation. The extended-family structure is more common in other countries than in the United States. Many American families do share their homes with extended family members, however.

Extended family members may live together for various reasons. Adult children may move back into their parents' homes following college, while they are searching for a job. Newlyweds may live with one spouse's parents until they find a separate living space. Following divorce, a parent and his or her children may move into a relative's home temporarily.

Another type of extended-family structure includes aging parents who move in with an adult child's family. Sometimes older adults move in with family members to assist in caring for the children. Older people may also move in with an adult child if they become unable, for health reasons, to live alone.

Couples Without Children

The fifth family structure includes married couples without children. People may not always think of childless couples as families, but spouses are related to one another by marriage. This makes them a family even if they do not have children.

A married couple may be unable to have biological children or may choose to remain

2-5 A stepfamily includes each spouse's children from previous relationships and any children they have together.

childless. Some couples delay parenthood until they have been married several years. They remain in this family structure until they have children and enter the nuclear family structure, 2-6.

How Families Function

Why do people need families? What purposes do families serve? These questions can best be answered by looking at how families function in society. **Family functions** refer to the responsibilities a family has for its members and how the family carries out these responsibilities. The family's main purpose is to take care of its members. Although families may differ in the way they are formed and in their structure, today's families all perform these same basic functions. These functions include procreation, economic support, emotional growth and well-being, socialization and education, and assignment of social roles.

2-6 Couples without children are able to develop their relationship and spend more time alone together.

Procreation. Through the couple, children are conceived and born. As discussed earlier, children may not be raised by their biological parents. In these cases, the family of origin meets all of the family functions except procreation.

Economic support. The family provides shelter, nourishment, and protection. Each family must decide who helps with economic support. These decisions may change over time. For example, a parent may stay home while the children are young, but may return to work as the children enter school. Older children may even work to pay some of their expenses.

Emotional well-being. All people need to feel their family members love and accept them for who they are as individuals. The way each person feels about himself or herself is affected, positively or negatively, by being part of a family. Family members support each other as they cope with the stresses of life. This function is critical in parenting children. Through nurturance, parents provide the foundation for positive interactions with others throughout life.

Socialization/education. All family members strive to grow and change. Although this function is often shared with child care programs and schools, it is a major parenting function. Parents need to transmit positive **values**—their ideals and beliefs about what is important and how to act on them. They also need to transmit positive attitudes. In addition, they must provide knowledge and skills in many areas. Parents must also promote self-discipline in children. Helping children grow and develop enables them to become competent adults.

Assignment of social roles. Family members have roles. The titles of the roles are basically the same in all families, such as wife/mother, husband/father, son and daughter. Each role has certain tasks. Family tasks within social roles help define a person, such as mother as a wage earner, family cook, and scout leader. These tasks show how she fits into the family. For each family role, the tasks will vary from family to family. For example, in some families the father may stay home and care for the children while the mother works outside the home.

Similar, Yet Different

Although all families share the same functions, no two families are alike. Why do tasks differ for the same role in two different families? Customs, including social roles, come from a family's background, such as its racial, ethnic, religious, or socioeconomic group. Social roles, like other aspects of heritage, are passed down within a family from generation to generation. For example, in some families the husband/father takes on the traditional role of wage earner. As the family leader, he makes major family decisions including how to raise children. In these traditional families, however, the wife/ mother (or perhaps the grandmother) does the day-to-day parenting. Children develop their **gender role**, or a person's behaviors, attitudes, and beliefs about men and women in society.

Tasks also differ from family to family due to family structure. For example, mothers who are single parents usually take on all the family roles. If this same mother becomes a wife/mother in a stepfamily, she will need to adjust her tasks to fit the way the new family functions.

Tasks may also change due to decision-making power in a given family. For example, career families may decide to share parenting tasks and decisions even if these were not the roles they saw in their childhood homes. Shared decision making often results in more positive attitudes.

Families Develop in Stages

A family grows and changes over the years, just as the individual members do. In most families, these developmental changes occur in what some experts call the *family life cycle*. The **family life cycle** represents the stages of family development over a period of time from marriage through old age. As children are born, the family expands. As children leave home as young adults, it contracts. The eight stages of the family life cycle include the following:

- *Beginning stage.* The first stage of the family life cycle begins with a couple's marriage, which establishes a family unit. During this stage, their main goal is adjusting to married life. Each person must learn to share life with the other while maintaining his or her own individuality. The length of this stage varies from one couple to another. Some couples shorten this stage and enter the childbearing stage right away. Other couples enjoy this stage longer while they postpone parenting. Couples without children remain in this first stage, continuing to mature in their marriage, until the middle-age years.

- *Childbearing stage.* The second stage begins with expectant parenthood. As this stage begins, the couple focuses on the coming birth. As they prepare for the arrival of their first child, the couple realizes nothing will ever be quite the same. Primary attention is focused on the baby, 2-7. The couple now has dual family roles—husband/father and wife/mother. Parents must learn how to manage extra responsibilities and conflicting demands on their time and energy. This stage ends when the first child reaches age 3.

- *Parenting preschoolers stage.* Primary attention is focused on providing for the child's growth and development in the preschool years. Parents develop firm thinking about how to support, guide, and discipline their children socially and emotionally in this stage.

- *Parenting school-agers stage.* This stage begins when the first child is age 6. Parents adjust to other parents within the school community and must encourage their children's school achievements.

2-7 Parents in their childbearing years focus their attention on nurturing their children.

Children are also expected to internalize the "rules" of home and school and become more responsible. The stage ends when the first child reaches age 13.

- **Parenting adolescents stage.** Parents must now focus on the adolescent who wants to become more independent of the family system. Parents have to reason with children about decisions they are making within and outside the family setting.

- **Launching stage.** Parents now prepare each child in turn to be independent of the family. Parents assist their children in becoming established in homes and careers. The launching stage is a process of letting go of day-to-day parenting tasks.

- **Middle-age years stage.** During this time, parents can focus on each other again. Many assume the role of grandparents and prepare for the retirement years. Couples without children gradually transition to this stage while others are in their parenting years. They mature in their marriage relationship and prepare for their retirement years as do people who have children.

- **Aging family stage.** The couple must adjust to changes brought on by retirement. For many couples, this means having more time to spend with each other and with new activities. This time offers couples opportunities to learn new skills or take on new hobbies. For many older adults, this also means dealing with declining health and making changes in how they handle daily activities of living. Adult children often play a greater role in caring for their parents during this stage. The stage ends with the death of both partners.

Experts in family life development hold differing views on the concept of *family life cycle*. Some feel the "circular" view of the family life cycle is somewhat misleading for two reasons. First, a *cycle* refers to repetitions that happen over a period of time. Generally, there are no repetitions in this "cycle." Other experts call these same stages a *family life career*. They view the stages that families go through in a *linear*, or straight-line arrangement that has a specific beginning and ending. Second, some people do not follow these stages in sequence or go through all of the stages. For example, some people have children and then marry at a later time. Some launch their biological children and then begin the parenting stage again with their grandchildren or even foster children. Some people do not have children and gradually mature into the later stages. Once again, you can see how unique families really are! Figure 2-8 gives you a graphic example of both views. Throughout this text, you will find these stages referred to as the *family life cycle.*

Children Develop in Stages

Competent parents recognize each stage of their child's development. They adapt their parenting goals and methods to fit the child's current stage. Adapting parenting to meet a child's current stage shows respect for the child as a person. Responsible and supportive parents promote a child's healthy development. By using the "best fit" parenting goals and methods for each stage, parenting is made easier and more rewarding. As you read later chapters, you will learn more about how children develop and the role of parents at each stage.

Parenting Happens in Stages

Just as families and children develop in stages, so do parents. According to Ellen Galinsky, a highly respected parenting

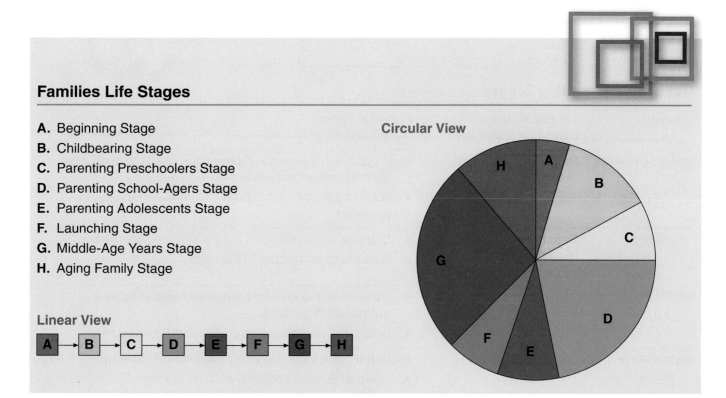

Families Life Stages

A. Beginning Stage
B. Childbearing Stage
C. Parenting Preschoolers Stage
D. Parenting School-Agers Stage
E. Parenting Adolescents Stage
F. Launching Stage
G. Middle-Age Years Stage
H. Aging Family Stage

Circular View

Linear View

A → B → C → D → E → F → G → H

2-8 The stages of family life can be examined as points around a circle or steps along a straight path. Some families go through all stages, but others do not.

expert, parents go through six parenting stages, 2-9. Galinsky says parents can be in several stages at the same time. Each stage is described from the parents' view and correlates to the parenting stages of the family life cycle. For example, Galinsky's *image-making* and *nurturing* stages for parents relate to the child-bearing stage. The *authority* stage for parents relates to the preschool stage. The *interpretive* parenting stage relates to school-age stage. The *interdependent* parenting stage relates to the adolescent stage while the *departure stage* relates to the launching stage. All other stages of the family life cycle are non-parenting stages.

Families Operate as a System

As you draw together the facts you have learned about how families are formed, structured, and function, you'll begin to see

a pattern, or system, evolve. According to Webster, a *system* is an interacting group of parts (in this sense, family members) that form a unified whole. Extend this definition to your understanding of parenting. Think about families as a *social* system. In this system, families work together to make decisions and set and achieve family goals. The family system also governs the behavior of each family member.

Thinking about the family as a system explains why each family is different, yet still works together as a whole. Factors that are both inside and outside the family influence the system. Factors *inside* the family include any changes in the family structure and the family life cycle. Factors *outside* the family include the physical and social environment in which the family lives. These include the neighborhood, community, schools and other youth-related organizations, and the economy.

Galinsky's Parenting Stages

Stage	Timing of Stage (based on child's age)	Parental Tasks
Image-making	Beginning of pregnancy to birth	• Prepare for changes in their relationship with each other and with other family members and friends. • Form images of their unborn child and of themselves as parents.
Nurturing	Birth to 18 or 24 months (Ends when the child begins to say "no.")	• Struggle to balance their baby's and their own needs. • Give much loving care to the child.
Authority	2 to 4 or 5 years	• Recognize that love for child goes hand-in-hand with "rules" about behavior. • Help child see and comply with what is expected.
Interpretive	5 or 6 to 12 years	• Share more facts and information about the world. • Interpret authority figures, such as teachers. • Teach values and morals. They guide children's behavior. Through guidance children learn to interpret social reality.
Interdependent	Teen years	• Share power with their children, but still maintain authority. • Monitor teen's behavior and provide guidance.
Departure	Later teens or early adult years	• Evaluate themselves as parents. • Identify they are pleased where they have succeeded in parenting. • Note ways in which they might have parented in a different way and been more successful.

2-9 Parenting stages show changes in the parent-child relationship from the parents' view.

In a family system, parents and children do not behave independently of one another. In order to fully understand parenting, look beyond the parent-child relationship. This relationship can be influenced by each family member's characteristics. These include age, health, and personality. It can also be influenced by the way a family communicates. Other family relationships, such as the parent's marriage, may impact the family system. As you read the following, you will discover there are several parts in understanding family systems.

Parenting Goes Two Ways

In the past, it was thought that parenting went one way, or only toward the children. This belief held that the parents taught children facts, values, and skills. Children absorbed these teachings like a sponge. Current research shows that parenting is really a two-way process. Parents do influence children, but the children also influence parents, 2-10. For example, a fussy baby may cause parents to feel less confident about their parenting skills. Some parents seek help, but others may see themselves as failures.

2-10 Parenting involves both parent and child.

Patterns of Behavior Evolve

Patterns of behavior evolve in a family. These patterns may include family role functions, rules, and communication styles. Healthy behavior patterns help families maintain balance in the family system. Unhealthy patterns of behavior can be difficult to change. These patterns can harm family members' relationships. For example, getting into the habit of using negative communication can cause family members to feel low self-worth.

Family Systems Have Boundaries

Boundaries are limits that control the degree of closeness between family members. They also control the closeness between the entire family and influences outside the family. Family members and the family as a whole determine whether they will operate as an "open" or "closed" system or somewhere in between.

Boundaries within the family have major effects on how parents interact with their children. For example, families with *closed* boundaries may value emotional closeness, togetherness, and a sense of belonging within the family. They are more likely to place restrictions on children's behavior, friendships, activities, and time away from the family. These families are less likely to be open to others outside the family, information, or new ideas. In times of challenge or crises, families in a closed system tend to rely on each other. They are less likely to reach beyond the family boundaries. For example, they may reject counseling during a crisis. Each person's identity is linked to how he or she fits in the family.

Families with *open boundaries* operate a little differently than those with closed boundaries. These families value independence more than a sense of belonging. They want an exchange of information and interactions outside their family. They see new points of view as ideas to discuss within the family, a way for each member to grow and develop. In an open system, each family member is free to be his or her own person and may pursue his or her own interests. Families with open boundaries view this as a positive way to promote individual growth and development. In times of crisis, these families tend to reach outside the family for support services. Generally, no family system is entirely open or closed.

Events Can Challenge Family Systems

The strength of a family system can be challenged. Sometimes challenges come from within the family, such as a severe illness or disability of a family member or divorce of the parents, 2-11. At other times, challenges come from outside the family, such as a job loss or a natural disaster that threatens the family's home and belongings. Challenging events also put stress on all family relationships, including parenting. The stability of the family system is often threatened by severe challenges. Flexible

2-11 Changing jobs and adjusting to a new home can stress everyone in the family unless parents and children work together.

families can often work through the challenge and restore stability to the family systems. For other families, the challenges may be too great, and the family system fails. Then new family systems must be formed and new adjustments made that may take years. For example, some parent-child relationships are forever damaged by divorce.

Factors That Impact Parenting

As you have learned, families differ in form, structure, and function. Just as each family is unique in the way members interact and meet each other's needs, parents are unique, too. However, most parents express similar overall goals for parenting. They want their children to

- have happy and fulfilling lives
- possess knowledge and skills that allow effective functioning as adults
- become people who function independently but who can get along well with others

Families and parents are unique in the way they try to achieve these goals. Besides children's characteristics and development, family life and parenting are mainly shaped by many other factors. These include cultural backgrounds, socioeconomic status, lifestyle, the parents' own family relationships as children, community agencies and events, the media, and technology influences.

Cultural Background

Parenting in various ethnic groups is more alike than different. All parents form relationships with their children and guide children's behaviors to conform to the group's standards. Families are influenced significantly by their ethnic and cultural backgrounds, however.

Some families strive to mirror their cultural background. These families model their values after those of their extended family members. They may also mirror the values of neighbors of similar cultural background. More families, however, are unique because parents absorb behaviors that fit their own beliefs and discard other beliefs and practices of their culture.

Culture is the framework for the lives of all people. Because of this, culture has profound effects on everyone. Some of these effects may seem subtle, but others are more obvious. For instance, it may be easier to identify the influence of cultural holidays and traditions than the influence of cultural beliefs and values.

A group's attitudes, beliefs, and values affect how families in that group perform their family functions. Cultures and ethnic groups also vary in the ways family members relate to one another. For example, in many cultures, extended family relationships are very important.

Parenting goals, roles, and styles differ among cultural groups, 2-12. Cultural learning begins in infancy. For example,

Cultural Differences in Parenting

Area	Individually Oriented Culture	Group-Oriented Culture
Goal of parents	Raise *independent* adult child (child does tasks alone for the most part)	Raise *interdependent* adult child (child views self as member of the group)
Communication during childhood	Child speaks for himself or herself Parent asks for child's viewpoint Parent is expressive with words	Parent speaks for child Parent gives directives Parent uses nonverbal cues, such as making deep, long eye contact or touching the head
Parent discipline style	Parent and child negotiate the rules and consequences of breaking the rules as age-appropriate	Parent uses authority and control to set rules and consequences to the rules
Consequences of misbehavior	Parent reasons with child Older children may have privilege withdrawn	Parent punishes misbehavior Misbehavior dishonors the family; consequences can be severe
Parents helping children as adults	Personal choice	Moral obligation
Adult child's relationship with parents	Personal choice	Obligation to parents

2-12 Parenting differs among cultural groups. Parenting differs even more among families of the same cultural background.

individually oriented cultures provide children with their own cribs, strollers, and play yards (play pens). Babies go to sleep by themselves. They also play for a few minutes without the parent present. Drinking from a cup and eating finger foods occur early. Babies cry or call out to get attention. Babies are often cared for at times by nonfamily members. On the other hand, *group-oriented* cultures carry their babies most of the day. Babies sleep with mothers. They are often breast-fed on demand through the toddler period. Babies cry less because parents respond to their needs before crying begins. Babies are most often cared for within the extended family.

Through parenting, children learn their family's cultural values. Pride in family

cultural values is a vital aspect of children's healthy development. There is no "best" child rearing method. Some families, in fact, are *bicultural,* meaning that they promote the teaching of two or more sets of family cultural values. Children with parents from different cultural backgrounds often are bicultural because they want their children to have the family's "full heritage." Other families teach their children to be bicultural so they can fit into the world of work as well as the family.

In American society, most children are exposed to many cultures. All children need to appreciate other cultures. Parents often begin teaching about diversity in the late toddler or preschool years.

Socioeconomic Status

A family's **socioeconomic status**, or position within society based on social and economic factors, such factors as parents' occupation, education, and level of income influence this position. These social and economic factors are often related. For example, people with more education often have higher paying jobs and vice versa. Sometimes, however, income may drop suddenly due to unemployment.

Income level can influence parenting practices. When you compare families with poverty-level incomes to families with higher incomes, you may find that families with lower incomes have less time and energy to spend with their children. This is because so many hours are spent working to provide basic needs. In contrast, families with middle or higher incomes have more time to spend with their children. They seek ways to best meet their children's needs and spend more time daily talking with their children.

Why do low income and poverty affect parenting in negative ways? Income pressures make parents more irritable and sometimes depressed. Parents' emotions affect interactions with their children. Poverty is also high in single-parent families. Poverty in single-parent families increases stress beyond other problems, such as parents having too many responsibilities and less time in which to meet their children's needs.

Lifestyle

Each family has a **lifestyle**, or way of living. Today, there are many more lifestyles available than in the past. Families adapt to many of these changes. Here are just a few lifestyle factors that impact many families.

Location

A major component of lifestyle is *where* a family lives. Families may live in cities, where their lives may take on a hectic pace. Other families live in smaller towns or suburban areas. Some people live in rural areas, where their activities revolve around a smaller community and the pace is slower.

Work Life

The parents' jobs or careers also affect the family's lifestyle. In some families, both parents work. These families may have a different lifestyle from families with only one wage earner. If one or both parents work at more than one job, this can also affect the lifestyle the family leads. Parents' jobs or careers also determine the family's earning potential. Families with higher-paying jobs may be able to afford a lifestyle different from those with lower-paying jobs.

Leisure Time

Another factor that reflects lifestyle is how a family spends its *leisure* time. Some families spend time together, but in other families parents have their separate activities. Choices about leisure events, such as athletic, music, theater, craft, travel, and volunteer or community work, are lifestyle choices, too, 2-13.

Impact on Children

Children are affected by the lifestyle choices their parents make. Their lives, attitudes, beliefs, and values are shaped by the lifestyle of their family of origin. When children leave home, they may choose a lifestyle that is similar to, or quite different from, their parents' lifestyle.

Early Relationships

Parents' early interactions with their own parents shape how they in turn respond to their own children. Childhood family experiences provide the mental blueprint for parenting the next generation. Parents, who were close to their own parents and had a good relationship with them, tend to be emotionally supportive of their own children.

2-13 Families can enjoy many types of leisure activities.

They are apt to be open and direct and to set clear and reasonable limits.

Parents who had problems with their own parents tend to carry feelings of conflict into their parenting role. They often think negatively about their children's behavior and blame them for family problems. These parents often waver between being gentle and angry; some even become explosive and abusive.

Community

The communities in which they live influence families. For example, families who live in an urban area have different concerns from families who live in rural areas. People in urban and rural areas may worry about high rates of crime and violence. In a rural area, people may worry about isolation from others and opportunities for their children.

Each community differs in the amount of resources available to meet its citizens' needs, 2-14. In larger cities, for instance, many more social service agencies and programs might be offered; however, some people may find them inaccessible due to distance or lack of public transportation. Smaller towns may have fewer resources, but their services are sometimes more personalized. A family might already know and trust the people who work in these agencies and programs.

Each community passes regulations and laws that reflect the needs of its members. These laws may affect individuals and families within that community. For instance, a community may determine what schools

Types of Community Resources

- Parks
- Recreational facilities
- Education (schools, museums, libraries, special events)
- Youth organizations (YMCA, Scouts)
- Child care (all types of programs)
- Children's protective services
- Counseling services
- Child health and welfare
- Foster care and adoption
- Economic assistance programs
- Employment training
- Community development projects
- Mental health facilities
- Correctional facilities
- Special needs services (services for immigrants, housing assistance, services for people with disabilities)

2-14 Community resources can lessen the stress of parenting.

children must attend, where houses can be built, and what the penalties are for certain offenses. Communities also regulate the activities of their local businesses.

A family's level of involvement with its community can also make a difference. In small communities, people may have more say in local government. Large cities may have more political groups and organizations that people can join. In small towns, every family may know one another. In larger areas, people do not know everyone in their community well, but may have a wider variety of acquaintances.

No matter where families live, their communities will influence them. Living in each type of community has advantages and disadvantages. When selecting the community where they will live, parents should weigh these factors carefully before making a decision.

Media

The media has powerful influences, both positive and negative, on today's families. Families are affected in different ways by the media. Some families are better able than others to use the media in beneficial ways and limit its negative effects. Forms of the media include the television, movies, radio, magazines, and newspapers. Families use media in the ways that follow.

- *Information and learning.* Families can learn vast amounts of information about weather, world news, sports, science, nature, and history. Parents can also use TV programs to open family discussions about important societal issues such as AIDS, hunger, poverty, and violence.

- *Entertainment.* Families may spend time together watching TV, going to the movies, or listening to music. Sharing these activities can make families closer. It can also be a lot of fun. Families need to spend time enjoying one another's company.

When used responsibly, the media can be very useful. Dangers exist, however, when parents do not monitor their children's exposure to the media, 2-15. For example, unsupervised children may watch shows or listen to music that condones violence. Also, TV programs or music with adult language and themes are not suited for children. Children are too young to understand what they see and evaluate its content. These programs and music can send damaging messages to children.

Another danger is overexposure to the media. The average child watches about four hours of TV daily. Time spent viewing TV is time taken away from other activities, such as reading, hobbies, and exercise. Families should balance their viewing time with other activities that will help children grow. Parents who set standards for their children's exposure to the media help their children profit from the positives the media offers while limiting negative effects.

2-15 Television can be a source of family entertainment; however, it is important for parents to monitor what their children watch.

Technological

Technology involves using scientific knowledge for practical purposes. Technology is created in the search for new ways to improve life. Inventing new devices or improving current ones can make tasks easier or faster. In years past, technological advancements included the invention of the lightbulb and the airplane. Think of ways new technologies benefit family life as you read the following.

Home Technology

Most people depend on electricity and heating and cooling systems in their homes. Telephones, cell phones, cable TV or satellite dishes, Internet service, and home entertainment centers are also common.

Home appliances speed up cooking, cleaning, and other household tasks that once took a great deal of time. These appliances make it easier for families to manage their homes. New materials for the home, such as stain-resistant upholstery and unbreakable dishes, are also the result of technology. Think how each of the following has made family life easier: refrigerators, ranges, dishwashers, vacuum cleaners, trash compactors, and lawn mowers. These timesaving devices also allow families to spend more leisure time together.

Technology also provides security systems that can make homes, businesses, and cars safer. Smoke and carbon monoxide detectors and home security systems also increase a family's safety. Television and radio stations monitor weather and issue warnings directly to homes.

Computer Technology

Advancements in computer technology have revolutionized the communication process. Computers can provide access to the Internet. Via the Internet, families keep in touch with e-mail. Internet access also allows families to use timesaving online services, such as banking and shopping, 2-16.

2-16 Computer technology helps families separated by distance maintain communication.

Inventions such as cellular phones, pagers, voice mail, and fax machines also make it easier for family members to stay in touch despite their busy schedules.

Health Technology

Health care technology enables doctors and other health care providers to enrich, lengthen, and even save lives. Advancements in laser surgery, organ transplants, and diagnostic equipment provide new hope for people with diseases or injuries. Today people live longer, which means family members can spend more time with older relatives.

Drawbacks of Technology

Technology has many benefits for families. It can also have drawbacks. Families can invest in the technology they want and can afford, but they should be careful. Relying too heavily on technology can make families dependent upon it. When families adjust to technology, they may find it harder to adapt if it becomes unavailable.

The newest trends in technology can be costly. This means technology may not be equally available to everyone because not everyone can afford it. When use of a certain technology is commonplace, people who don't have access to the technology are left behind.

For example, as home computers become more common, children whose families don't have them will be at a disadvantage. These children may not develop the same computer skills as children with home computers. People need computer skills to compete in the job market. As a result, many public libraries and schools are working to make computers more accessible to the general public.

Families must be careful to use communication and entertainment technology in moderation. Spending long hours in front of a TV or computer takes time from other activities, such as exercising and spending time with family and friends. Families must balance their time among various activities.

Connecting Parents, Children, and Society

Parents, children, and society all have critical, interacting roles in the parenting process. As you read through the following information, look at Figure 2-17 to gain understanding about these connections.

- *Importance of parents to children and society.* As part of the parental role, parents provide for their children's needs. They nurture them and teach children valuable skills needed by adults. They also teach society's values. While fulfilling these responsibilities, parents also prepare their children to be responsible citizens for society.

- *Importance of children to parents and society.* Without any effort of their own, children give meaning to the lives of their parents. They help parents feel mature and responsible. Children also impact what resources (food, clothes, toys, or services) parents may need from society.

From society's view, children ensure that society continues. They become the workers and consumers that keep the economy running. In addition, children pass on society's values and traditions to the next generation.

- *Importance of society to parents and children.* In addition to expressing gratitude for the role of parents in society more often and directly, society informs parents of the skills children need. It provides support services for parents who need them. Likewise, society provides for children's needs through community resources and the media. When families have problems that interfere with how children grow and develop, society intervenes on behalf of the children to protect their rights. Society makes sure that children have everything needed to grow into mature, responsible citizens.

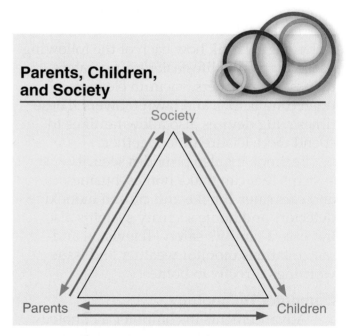

2-17 Important consequences come from the interacting roles of parent, child, and society in the parenting process.

Summing It Up

- The word *family* has many different meanings, but basically *family* describes two or more people who are related by birth, marriage, adoption, or other circumstances.

- Five basic family structures are common in America today. Each structure has both advantages and disadvantages.

- Regardless of their structure, all families perform five basic functions. A family's ability to perform these functions is an indication of its strength.

- Families are in different developmental stages as described by the *family life cycle*. Within the family's developmental stages, children and parents go through their own developmental stages, too.

- Families operate as a social system. In doing this: the parenting role is a two-way process; patterns (roles, rules, and communication styles) evolve; boundaries between family members and between the family as a unit and the outside world are set up; and family systems can be challenged resulting in family stress.

- Parenting is affected by other sources, including cultural background, socioeconomic status, lifestyle, parents' childhood experiences with their parents, community resources, and media and technology influences.

- The effects of parenting are significant and far-reaching. The roles of parents, children, and society are connected. Each affects and impacts the other two roles.

Recalling the Facts

1. What is a *family of origin*?

2. Name three of the ways a family can be formed.

3. Explain the differences between adoptive parents, foster parents, and guardians.

4. Name two advantages of the nuclear family structure.

5. Identify the family structures described as follows: (A) husband, wife, and their biological or adopted children; (B) an immediate family unit plus other relatives; (C) husband and wife with children from previous relationships; (D) husband and wife; (E) a man or woman raises his or her child or children

6. Describe five functions of the family.

7. What are the stages of the *family life cycle*?

8. Briefly describe the parenting stages of the *family life cycle*.

9. Explain the family systems concept that parenting goes two ways—parent to child and child to parent.

10. What are parents' three overall goals for children? Explain what causes parents to be unique in the way they achieve these goals.

11. Name one way each of the following factors influences families: (A) culture; (B) socioeconomic status; (C) early relationships; (D) community; (E) media; (F) technology.

12. What effect do parents have on children and society?

Applying New Skills

1. **Oral report.** Research foster care laws in your county or state. Who can become a foster parent and how are children placed in foster homes? Present your findings to the class in an oral report.

2. **Parenting interview.** Interview a parent or parents who head a family structure different from your own. Ask about the roles of family members and the pros and cons of the family structure. Then write a summary of your findings.

3. **Picture wall.** As a class create a picture wall depicting families in various stages of the family life cycle. For each stage, list key points that are unique to the stage on note cards to mount with the pictures.

4. **Researching services.** Use Internet or print resources to research preventive or supportive services in your community. Find out what services they provide for families, especially children. How can families receive these services? Inquire about the benefits. Then put your information into a pamphlet to give to classmates and others you know.

Thinking Critically

1. Write a creative story about a family in one of the parenting stages of the family life cycle. As you tell the story, be sure to weave the following information into the story:

   - How did the family form?
   - Who are the members and how are they related to one another?
   - Which family structure represents the family?
   - How does this family operate as a system?
   - Does this family have open or closed boundaries?
   - How might the family structure and functions change if the family faces a life-altering challenge?
   - How do culture; socioeconomic status; lifestyle; early relationships; and community, media, and technology influences impact this family?

   Share your story with someone you know.

2. Watch a TV program based on family life. Identify the family structure and functions represented. Analyze the relationships of the family members. How did family members work together in this family system? Do you think the program realistically represents that family structure and function? Write a summary of your analyses.

Linking Academics

1. **Writing.** Write a one-page essay on how you influenced your parents and your parents influenced you in the parenting process. As an alternative, write about someone you know and his or her parents.

2. **Reading.** Use library resources to select a book about building strong families. Read the book. Write a short report on the key concepts presented in this book. Which concepts might you prefer to use in building a strong family of your own? How do the book concepts relate to your personal knowledge or experience related to building strong families?

Chapter 3

The Decision to Parent

Key Terms

goal
short-term goals
long-term goals
time/life line
dual-career families
hereditary
infant mortality rate
decision-making process
alternatives
consequences

Objectives

After studying this chapter, you will be able to

- explain why some unplanned pregnancies are generally unfair to the couple and to the children.
- describe factors that influence parenting decisions.
- identify parenting factors to consider before marriage and parenting.
- analyze a couple's readiness for marriage.
- describe challenges and risks faced by teen parents, "older" parents, and grandparents who are raising grandchildren.
- demonstrate how people can use the decision-making process to decide about parenting.

Becoming a parent is one of the most significant events that can occur in a person's life. Someday, you may discuss marriage with a future spouse. The two of you will want to consider many issues, including the decision to have children.

Deciding whether or not to become a parent is one of the most difficult and important decisions a person can make. Couples must deal with societal pressures, family pressures, and peer pressures. They must also question their own abilities, wants, and needs. After deciding about parenthood, couples must live with the choice.

In years past, almost all married couples had children. They relied solely on biology to determine their family size and spacing. For the most part, married couples did not choose if, or when, they would have children.

Today, most couples can decide whether or not they want to have children. If couples choose to have children, they can plan how many children they want and when to have them. Planning also allows couples to decide not to have children. Yet, among married couples, 31 percent of first babies are unplanned and 5 percent of all second babies are unplanned. Among teens, 85 to 90 percent are unplanned.

Much of what happens in the early stages of parenting is shaped by what happens to the couple before the birth of the first child. The way the couple goes about deciding whether to become parents is very important. Couples vary in the ways they make decisions.

Fortunately, most unplanned children are welcomed at the time of birth. Some unplanned and unwanted children, however, show severe problems by their school-age years. As teens and adults, they have even more severe problems. For example, school-age children may have achievement problems in school, fewer friends, and more behavior problems. Teens and young adults may have more conflicts with others. They may also be less happy with their jobs, marriages, and friendships. Couples should discuss their views of parenting prior to marriage because couples with conflicting views have the most unplanned and unwanted children.

In this chapter, you will learn about the parenting risk of unplanned pregnancies. You will also learn what influences pregnancies and what factors couples should consider as they make parenting decisions. You will learn risks associated with parental age. Finally, this chapter also presents a decision-making process you can use for parenting.

What Influences Parenting Decisions?

A variety of factors influence couples' decisions about parenting. Couples should be careful not to make these decisions for the wrong reasons. Considering why they want, or don't want, to be parents will help them decide if parenthood is for them. Think about the factors that follow and the way they influence parenting decisions.

Desire to Express Marital Love

When a husband and wife love each other and want to be parents, having children can be a wonderful experience, 3-1. Becoming parents can be a natural extension of a couple's love for one another.

New emotions develop as a man and woman become parents. They feel parental love for the first time. Parental love is based on concern for the well-being of the child. Parental love does not replace other forms of love. In fact, it can enhance other types of love.

Couples can express their marital love in ways other than by having a child, such as enjoying activities together. A desire to express marital love should not be the only

3-1 Love may be the best reason to have a child.

reason a couple chooses to have a child. This is especially true for couples that really do not want to have a child or be parents.

Desire to Be Parents

Another common reason couples have children is quite simple—they wish to be parents. A person may feel he or she would be a good parent. This person may strongly desire to nurture a child and raise him or her to adulthood.

Couples may have children because they wish to add to their families. They may really enjoy the lifestyle of a family with children. These parents genuinely like children, and enjoy being around children of all ages. They look forward to sharing their lives with their children, 3-2.

Some couples choose parenting out of curiosity. They may wonder what their children would be like. Couples may be curious whether their children would resemble them in appearance and personality. Prospective parents may be curious about themselves as well. They might wonder if they would be good parents. They may wonder how their parenting skills compare to their own parents' skills. It is natural to be curious about these things, but curiosity by itself is not a good reason to have children. It is also important for couples to want their child and be prepared to take care of their child.

Expectations About Parenthood

People may decide to become parents based on expectations they have about parenthood. Some couples may mistakenly think parenthood will prove their masculinity or femininity. Others grow up expecting that one day they'll be parents. Parenting, they may reason, is the natural thing for married couples to do. For these couples, the expectation they will be parents is reason enough. The decision should also include other positive reasons.

Other married couples become parents as a way to feel fulfilled as adults. Although there are many rewards in parenting, being completely focused on these rewards is not enough. Competent, loving parents consider the well-being of the child first. However, couples should not choose to become parents if they do not have positive expectations of parenthood, too.

3-2 Parents enjoy sharing special activities with their children. This father, son, and daughter spend time together on the beach.

Expectations About Children

Some couples decide to become parents based on expectations they have about children. People who choose to have children based on realistic expectations about them will be well prepared for parenting. What are realistic expectations? People need to know that parenting is a big responsibility. They should also have a real understanding about how children grow and develop. Successful parenting brings many rewards, such as enjoyment of parenting tasks and the joy of seeing your child grow from a helpless newborn to a competent adult.

Parents with unrealistic expectations about children will face a more difficult time. They may be very disappointed. Worse yet, their children may suffer if the parents cannot overcome these expectations and become effective parents. What are unrealistic expectations? Parents may believe if they love their children, the children will love them in return. They may think children will bring love and happiness to their lives. Other people have children because they expect their children to be companions for them in their old age. These people may assume their children will take care of them and keep them company. There are no guarantees that these things will happen.

Pressures from Family and Friends

Many people assume when a couple marries, they will have children. Because this assumption is so common, newly married couples may feel pressured to have children. This pressure may come from their families, their friends, or both.

Family may be the primary source of this pressure. Some pressures are indirect, such as relatives who ask about the couple's parenting plans. Other family pressures may be more direct, such as a couple's parents who want grandchildren to carry on the family name or to provide them with enjoyable times, 3-3.

Friends more often apply pressure indirectly than directly. Friends may not understand why a couple would not begin having children right away. Some couples have children because it seems as though many people their age are having children.

Becoming parents due to pressure from others is not a good idea. Couples should have children only if they genuinely want them. Family and friends may make parenting sound like the perfect choice. However, they are not the ones who will be responsible for the children's care. This responsibility belongs to the couple.

Desire to Influence the Partner

Parenting is a serious commitment that should be based on a couple's mutual desire to have a child. Yet, some people use parenthood to "trap" a partner. An attempt to "trap" a partner often does not work. In some dating relationships, one partner may

3-3 This couple has planned for their aging years. They find companionship in each other, not in their children.

think pregnancy would cause the other to stay in the relationship and marry him or her. Today, many people would not automatically marry due to a pregnancy. This is especially true in relationships where the couple was not thinking about marriage before the pregnancy occurred. Marriages that occur solely because of pregnancy are likely to fail.

For similar reasons, having a child does not strengthen a shaky marriage. Although some people may say that "children make marriages work," research shows that this is not true in most cases. If spouses are already drifting apart, adding the pressures of parenting will probably cause even more problems between them. In fact, research shows parenting stress causes a short-term decline in marital happiness even when a couple has a strong marriage.

Using a pregnancy to influence your partner to marry you is manipulative and unfair to both partners. It is most unfair to your child. Using children as the glue that holds their parents' marriage together is too much pressure for children. This motivation considers the parents' desires first and doesn't ensure if a child were born, he or she would be wanted. As you read earlier in this chapter, children who are unwanted may have serious problems.

Factors to Consider Before Parenting

In the future, you will probably think about marriage. Before you and your partner marry, you should carefully discuss your goals, including your views about parenting. You should choose a future spouse who shares your views because these decisions will greatly affect your life together. Before marriage, you and your partner should be able to agree about parenting decisions. In addition to goals, also discuss the impact of careers and finances on the marriage and on parenting.

Your Goals

As you approach adulthood, you will begin to set goals for your future. A **goal** is a direction or end toward which you work. Your goals may include further education, career plans, and parenting hopes.

Only you and your partner can decide what individual goals you want to achieve in your lifetime. You must also decide what goals the two of you want to achieve as a married couple. Sample questions you need to discuss are shown in 3-4.

Individually and as a couple you can set both short-term and long-term goals. **Short-term goals** are goals you hope to accomplish soon, within a few days or months. **Long-term goals** are those you want to accomplish later, perhaps years from now. Considering all these questions at once can seem confusing. Many people find it helpful to list their goals. Making a written plan can show a couple how certain goals fit together or conflict. Some individual or couple goals may conflict with parenting goals. Some people may choose not to have children for these reasons. Others may decide to compromise their travel desires, for example, so they can experience parenting.

You can use your long-term goals to create a time/life line that represents your married life. A **time/life line** is a graph that gives a visual picture of the goals a person or couple plans to reach throughout life. A time/life line allows you to visually see your goals five years from now or forty years from now.

Impact of Careers

In the past, after a couple married, a wife's career was housekeeping and parenting, and her husband was the wage earner. Today, many women get an education and enter careers equal to those of men. Like men, most women find their careers rewarding for personal fulfillment, financial reasons, or both. In most families today,

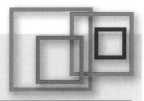

Thinking About Individual and Couple Goals

Type of Goal	Questions to Ask
Individual goals	• Do I plan to continue my education? If so, for how long? How much will it cost? Will I have any income while working toward this goal?
	• What career plans do I have? How many hours per week will I work, including commute time? Will I travel as part of my job? If so, how often and for how long? Will I be asked to work overtime or at home beyond work hours? Does the employer provide for leave time at the birth or adoption of a baby, or during severe family illness? Does the employer have any form of child care help?
	• What leisure activities are important for my personal growth? What time and expenses are involved?
Couple goals	• Do we both expect to work after marriage? If so, do we plan to continue being a dual-career family with children? What will our combined earnings be?
	• What major consumer purchases do we want to make? How will these affect our income? What are our plans for savings? for gifts and contributions? for retirement?
	• What are our goals for social life? How important are these goals? What time and expenses are involved?
Parenting goals	• How do we feel about children? Do we both want children? If so, how many children do we want?
	• Have we decided when we want to start a family?
	• What kind of child care would we have? prenatal care? relative care? non-relative care? For how long would child care be needed? at what cost? (Remember parents who do not work during the parenting stages forego an income. However, they pay less taxes and do not pay child care expenses.)
	• How would our plans for having children change our social life? Would we have less time to spend with family and friends? Would we be willing to give up plans for leisure activities if we had children?

3-4 Couples need to think about their long-term goals, including the choice of parenthood.

married couples are **dual-career families**, families in which both spouses work outside the home.

Before marrying, a man and woman should discuss their feelings about balancing work and parenting goals. As couples consider parenting, they should think about resolving child care issues and having enough quality time for children. Some child care options include the following:

• A parent staying home with children until the last child enters school

• Parents working during different shifts, or one parent working at home

• Parents finding quality child care in the home or out of the home

Parents must solve this dilemma in the way that works best for them. No single choice is best for every couple. Almost any situation can work if both spouses are happy with the arrangement and genuinely interested in their child's well-being. See 3-5 for a close look at how two couples dealt with this decision.

Balancing Career and Parenting Roles

Jermaine and Suzanne

Jermaine and Suzanne have been married four years and they want to have a child. They both have good, steady jobs. Two years ago, they bought a small house. Jermaine and Suzanne need both paychecks to pay the mortgage and other living expenses. Therefore, both plan to continue working after the child is born. They realize their situation may be difficult. Jermaine and Suzanne have the following concerns:

- Worry they may feel guilty about not spending enough time with their child
- Difficulty in finding quality child care
- Strain on their budget, even with both paychecks, for child care expenses
- Potential stress about trying to fulfill too many different roles (They will need to remember expecting one another to be loving spouses, caring parents, skilled housekeepers, and valued employees is asking a lot.)

Jermaine and Suzanne have identified the following ways they can make the best of their situation. These include:

- Finding satisfaction in their work
- Having satisfaction in caring for their child when they are not working
- Locating quality child care at an affordable price
- Working out alternate plans for times when their child care may not be available, such as holidays and illnesses
- Sharing the responsibilities of child care, running the household, shopping, cooking, cleaning, and doing repair and maintenance chores

Mike and Angelica

Mike and Angelica have been married two years and want a child. Mike has high goals for his banking career. Angelica enjoys her job as a nurse, but wants to be a full-time homemaker once their child is born. They realize the potential difficulties in this situation. Mike and Angelica have the following concerns:

- Possible feelings of alienation for Mike if the child develops a closer relationship with Angelica since she will be at home
- Possibly growing apart if Mike's main interest is work and Angelica's main interest is their child
- Meeting their expenses on one paycheck
- Difficulty in reentering the workforce for Angelica once their child is grown

Mike and Angelica believe the situation will work if they keep the following factors in mind:

- Developing a close relationship with their child is a priority for both (especially Mike during his off-work hours)
- Communicating so their relationship stays strong (Mike needs to know what is happening at home; Angelica needs to know what is happening with Mike at work.)
- Finding satisfaction with the division of labor and their work and family roles
- Tightening their budget since they will only have one paycheck
- Realizing the benefits gained by having a parent as the primary source of care, nurturance, and guidance for their child
- Maintaining other interests so they can continue enjoying life even as their lives change

3-5 This chart offers two examples of ways couples can balance their careers and parenting roles.

Couples need to be aware that some parenting and career goals do not mesh well. For example, careers that require travel, long or irregular work hours, or dangerous job duties may not fit well with parenting tasks. A couple may decide against parenting if their careers would not combine well with parenting responsibilities. Even when parenting and careers, such as teaching, mesh well, the couple must find a workable balance between the two.

Impact of Finances

The cries of a newborn are not the only things that keep parents awake at night. The sudden weight of new financial responsibilities, such as rent or a mortgage, life insurance, and the costs of a child may add to the couple's concerns about parenting. Added to marriage debts may be debts acquired prior to marriage—student loans, cars, wedding expenses, and possible money follies resulting in high credit card debts. Families with or without children need to follow good consumer advice, 3-6.

Prospective parents should realize having a child involves huge financial commitments. Parents often get their first taste of child-expense reality when they start buying things for their new baby. The bills do not end because the baby quickly outgrows furniture, clothing, toys, and other baby items.

Parents may wonder how they will pay all these bills and when they will end. Parents may hope that, as children grow, child-related expenses will eventually decrease. However, the opposite is true. Overall, as children grow older, they cost more money. Older children eat more, need more clothes, go more places, and participate in more activities. They also need more space, so families may have to move to larger homes. See 3-7 for a summary of the costs involved in raising a child.

Child-related expenses make up a sizable percentage of a family's yearly income. For

Some Good Financial Advice

Control spending.

Use income in this order:

- Save first.
- Pay bills second.
- Spend on extras last.

Pay debts. Especially pay those debts that are not tax deductible as quickly as possible. Above all, do not increase these debts.

3-6 Most couples need to follow "tried and true" methods of saving and spending.

example, the U.S. government estimates middle-class family pretax income ranges from $44,500 to $74,900. A yearly cost of $11,660 per child is a serious sum. Families with higher incomes may spend a total of $338,370 per child over the 18-year period. This amounts to about $18,798 per year child cost.

The costs of raising a child through the college years are much more expensive. Children born today will likely face college costs three to four times the current prices. For parents who pay these costs, they may expect to pay more than 50 to 66 percent of their children's college costs. Colleges often contribute to paying the balance of these costs through scholarships. Parents should save early for their children's college expenses. Waiting until later can harm a couple's savings for their own future. Banks lend money for college, but not as often for retirement.

Prospective parents should answer these questions as they decide about parenting. Is their income adequate to pay the costs of raising a child? If both spouses work, will one quit to stay home with the child? If so, can they manage on one salary? If both continue working, can they afford child care costs?

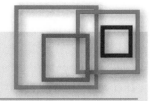

What It Costs to Raise a Child

The total cost to raise a child from birth to age 17 for middle-income parents averages $260,700 (2006 figures, USDA). The following categories of household expenses are affected by child-rearing costs. Approximate percentages of the total dollar amount are shown.

Housing (33 to 37%): Parents and their new baby can live comfortably in a cozy apartment or small house. The family may need more room, however, as the child grows or more children are added to the family. If so, parents face the increased cost of renting or buying a bigger home. Their rent or mortgage will vary depending on the size and cost of their new home. Housing expenses also include taxes, utilities, furniture, and equipment.

Food (15 to 20%): Food will take a big bite out of the parents' budget. If a baby is breast-fed, the mother will have extra nutritional needs. If a baby is bottle-fed, parents will need to purchase formula and feeding equipment. When the baby begins eating solid food, this will add to the grocery bill. As they grow, children eat more food. Food expenses can be quite large, especially if families eat many meals in restaurants.

Transportation (14 to 15%): Parents will need to buy a stroller and a good car seat for their new baby. If parents work outside the home, they may need to transport their child to and from child care. In cities, parents may use trains or buses. If they don't have a car, parents may decide to buy one, which can be expensive. As their family grows, parents may invest in a second car to meet the family's transportation needs. Transportation costs also include gasoline, maintenance and repairs, and insurance.

Clothing (6 to 8%): The cost of baby clothes varies, but the cost for diapers adds a substantial amount. Disposable diapers cost up to $960 a year. Cloth diapers you wash at home can be less costly. Babies grow quickly. Parents must replace children's clothing and shoes as often as needed to ensure a proper fit. School-age children and teens grow less quickly than babies. Parents may not have to replace their clothes as often, but their clothing usually costs more.

Child Care and Education (7 to 10%): This cost is the biggest variable. It may include child care tuition and babysitting costs. If children attend private elementary and secondary schools, education costs will be high. Another consideration is whether parents will pay for any education and training their children need after high school, such as college or technical training. (This is not included in the total cost since it occurs after a child is 17.) If parents pay for tuition and books at a state university, expenses for four years will be about $24,000. Tuition and books at private universities for four years may be more than $80,000. These costs do not include living expenses while in college.

Health Care (5 to 7%): During pregnancy and delivery, the costs involved with bringing a baby into the world become a reality for new parents. These initial costs are just the beginning. The American Academy of Pediatrics estimates babies visit a pediatrician an average of 10 times during their first two years. Over the next few years, children generally visit the doctor less. However, the average child still requires about $650 or more a year for various medical expenses, including dental services. When children become teens, parents may have additional medical expenses, such as braces, contacts, and sports-related injury expenses. With continually rising health and medical costs, parents may spend more than expected.

Other Expenses (10 to 13%): Raising a child involves more than providing necessities. Music and sports lessons, camps, toys, books, software, and entertainment for children can be very costly. Regardless of their income level, most parents tend to spend as much as they can on their children's extra activities.

3-7 Raising a child is a big financial responsibility. This chart gives some of the costs involved in raising a child. Costs will vary depending on where a family lives.

Couples should think about ways to reduce child costs. For example, parents might take advantage of all government tax breaks, accept hand-me-down clothes or shop at yard sales, trade babysitting services with friends, or clip coupons for needed products. Even with these cuts, parenting is a major financial commitment. Some may not be able to afford these high costs or may need to limit the number of children they have due to costs.

Financial reasons influence some couples not to become parents. When some people discover the large financial commitment of parenting, they decide against parenthood. They may not be able to afford the high costs. Other people may prefer to spend their money on their own activities and expenses. They may want to have a luxurious lifestyle.

Readiness for Parenthood

When considering parenthood, you need to determine whether you are ready for the role of parenthood. As you have learned, a role is a set of behaviors related to a certain function you assume in life. You already have several roles, such as student, employee, son or daughter, and brother or sister.

Readiness for parenthood involves many different factors. It is important to carefully consider these factors before having children. If either spouse does not feel ready to have children, the couple should delay parenting until both spouses are ready. To determine your readiness, review the information that follows.

The Marital Relationship

Although single-parent families can be strong, most experts agree that a nuclear family structure is ideal for parenting. Before bringing children into your lives, take an honest look at your marriage. Thinking about the following questions can help:

- ***Is our marriage strong and secure?*** A solid marital relationship can provide the foundation needed for creating a strong family, 3-8.

- ***Are we willing to work to keep our marriage the primary relationship in our lives?*** Couples should decide if they are ready to focus much of their attention on parenting. They may decide they need more time to develop their marital relationship before parenting. Once children come along, it can be harder for couples to focus on their own relationship.

- ***How well do we communicate?*** Solid communication skills can help you and your partner make a smoother transition into parenthood.

3-8 Being happy in their marriage gives couples a firm foundation for raising children.

- ***Do we generally agree or disagree?***
  Couples who usually disagree may spend a lot of time arguing about their children's care and guidance. They should work together to solve problems in their relationship. This will improve their marriage and help them become better parents.

Acting with Responsibility

Parents must accept responsibility for another human being's life. They should be mature enough to understand what children need and how to provide for these needs. Parents need to be able to guide their children as they grow and develop. They must also be willing to make personal sacrifices in order to meet the needs of their children. For example, getting less sleep and going without some items you might like to have (a new DVD or trendy clothes) are just some ways that parents take responsibility in providing for their children.

Acceptance of Lifestyle Changes

Once you have a baby, your lives will never be the same. If you say *yes* to parenting, it may mean saying *no* to some aspects of your social life as a couple. You may not be able to go as many places or participate in as many activities as you once did. You and your spouse cannot be as spontaneous in your own or couple plans.

Children change a couple's lifestyle in some very important ways. Instead of always having individual and couple activities, couples must shift their focus to activities they can enjoy with their children.

Maturity for Parenting

Erik Erikson, a noted psychologist, has divided a person's life span into eight stages.

In each stage a person faces certain conflicts and challenges. If they are successful, they are mature for that stage and move on to face the tasks of the next stage.

Biologically, parenting could occur in Stages 5, 6, or 7 of Erikson's theory, 3-9. (See Appendix A for "Erikson's Theory of Personality Development" for detailed information on the characteristics for Stages 5, 6, and 7.) The best stage for parenting is Stage 7. In this stage adults are trying to contribute to society, and this can be done through parenting. Later in this chapter, you will read about the risks of teen parenting (Stage 5). You have already read that couples need time for adjustments to each other before parenting (Stage 6).

Knowledge About Parenting

Realistic expectations about parenting come from knowledge. You can learn about parenting and child development by taking classes, reading books, and observing parents interacting with their children. For example, prospective parents may want to learn about child care, guidance, and discipline before making the decision to parent.

Your Age and Health

Biologically, some ages are better than others for women to give birth. The ages of 20 through 32 are considered best for childbearing. Prospective parents also need to consider whether their health would affect their ability to parent. Ideally, both prospective parents should be in excellent health. They should be capable of handling the physical and emotional stress of raising children, 3-10.

When a couple is trying to have a child, the woman's health is an important consideration. A woman who wants to become pregnant needs to evaluate her health habits. Does she eat healthfully and get enough exercise and rest? Does she

Erikson's Theory of Personality Development

Stage	Approximate Age	Step Toward Stable Personality	Step Toward Unstable Personality
1	Birth to age 2	Trust	Mistrust
2	Ages 2 and 3	Autonomy	Shame and doubt
3	Ages 4 and 5	Initiative	Guilt
4	Ages 6 to 11	Industry	Inferiority
5	Ages 12 to 18	Identity	Role confusion
6	Early adulthood	Intimacy	Isolation
7	Middle age	Generativity	Stagnation
8	Late adulthood	Integrity	Despair

3-9 Parenting best meshes with Erikson's Stage 7.

avoid alcohol and other drugs when trying to become pregnant? Once pregnant, she needs to seek quality prenatal care. The baby's health is directly related to how the mother cares for herself before and during pregnancy. Couples should think about how any health problems they have would affect their ability to care for their children. Health concerns should be shared with your doctors.

Some health problems are **hereditary**, or genetically passed from parent to child. Couples should be aware of the statistical odds of their child inheriting a genetic disorder or condition from them. Couples may decide against having children if it is very likely they would pass a genetic disorder to their child. People with serious health problems may decide not to have children for fear that their health may affect their parenting abilities.

High-Risk Parenting

People of all ages have many factors to consider before deciding to become parents. Becoming a parent is a big responsibility— one many adults find difficult to accept.

3-10 Couples should consider their health when making parenting decisions. Regular exercise is essential to good health.

Parenting is an even bigger challenge for teens. Sometimes older parents (especially those over age 35) and their babies can have problems. Grandparents who serve as parents also have many challenges in parenting.

Teen Parenthood

In the United States, more than a million teens become pregnant each year. The vast majority of teen pregnancies are unplanned. An unplanned pregnancy can drastically alter the lives of everyone involved, including the child, 3-11.

Most teens make responsible decisions that allow them to reach their future goals. Other teens are drawn into risk-taking behaviors involving drugs, alcohol, and sexual activity. These behaviors are often linked. For instance, using alcohol and drugs decreases a teen's ability to make responsible decisions concerning sexual activity. Some teens mistakenly think pregnancy can never happen to them. Every year, over a million teens and their partners face the sobering reality that teen pregnancy can, and does, occur.

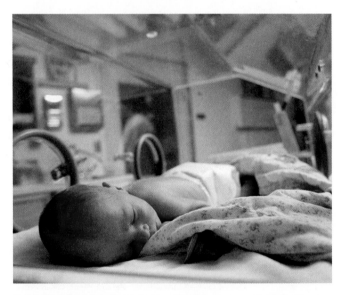

3-11 Babies born to teen mothers are at risk for a number of health problems.

Becoming pregnant during the teen years creates health risks for both mother and baby. Teens who are pregnant often have poor eating habits and may not get enough rest and exercise. According to the **infant mortality rate**, the rate of infant death per 1,000 live births, almost 13 infants in every 1,000 born to teen mothers die in infancy. Pregnancy also causes many changes in teens' social relationships. Finally, teen pregnancy can jeopardize young people's educational plans and career goals, 3-12.

Teen parents often need outside support. Financial help may come from various federal assistance programs. The TANF (Temporary Assistance for Needy Families) Bureau provides food, money, and child care assistance for those who qualify. Families in the Medicaid program receive free or low-cost medical services. Local social service agencies may be able to provide additional help, such as needed counseling. Education and career risks may be lessened if teen parents take advantage of school programs that allow work time and/or provide child care while the parents take high school classes.

Teen parents face many challenges and risks. Teens should consider these challenges and risks before placing themselves in a situation where pregnancy might occur. Teen pregnancy can dramatically alter a teen's life plan. This does not mean, however, that teens cannot be good parents. Teens can be effective parents if they can overcome these hurdles. Some teen parents finish their education and reach their career goals while raising healthy, happy children.

Delayed Parenthood

The average age at which American women have their first child has climbed to an all-time high of 25.1 years. This average is primarily due to the birthrates among women ages 35 to 39 (41 births per 1,000 women) and those ages 40 to 44 (8 per 1,000). Why is

Special Risks for Teens and Their Babies

Factors	Reasons
Health Risks	
Teens have a higher rate of complications than women who are in their twenties.	• Their bodies are still growing and developing. • Teens often do not get enough nutrients for themselves and their babies. • Teens often do not get enough rest and sleep. • Teens may have engaged in high-risk behaviors (alcohol, drugs, and sexual activity). • Less than two-thirds of teens receive early prenatal care.
Babies of teens are often born too early or too small.	• These babies have not completed normal growth before birth. Their organs and body systems may not be fully developed or function properly, reducing their chances of survival. • Those babies who live often have disorders of the brain, heart, liver, and respiratory system. • Babies of teen mothers who have engaged in high-risk behaviors are apt to have more health problems. • Teens and their babies face even greater health risks if teens become pregnant again too soon.
Social and Emotional Problems	
The future becomes more uncertain for teen parents. They face many decisions about themselves and parenting.	• Single teens must decide whether to get married. Due to stress, teen marriages are more apt to end in divorce than other marriages. • Teen parents have to decide whether to keep their baby or give it up for adoption. Some fathers do not accept responsibility for their babies. Because of this, teen mothers must make this decision without support. • Many other decisions must be made, too, such as continuing one's education, paying the costs of having a baby, and finding and paying for child care.
According to Erikson, teens are working toward a clear identity of who they are and where they are headed in life. Due to teen parents uncertain futures, they are apt to experience role confusion.	• Teens may feel trapped by their large responsibility. They may have little time to be with friends. • Teens may feel isolated from peers because of their soon-to-be roles as parents. Many teen mothers feel they have less in common with their friends than before becoming parents.
Education and Career Risks	
Almost 70 percent of teen parents do not graduate from high school.	• Teen fathers may quit school to provide financial support. • Teen mothers may quit school to work and/or care for their babies. • Career achievement is highly limited without a high school education. A person with a college degree will earn about one million more over a lifetime than a person without one.
Financial Risks	
Teens faced with an unplanned pregnancy have not planned how to pay the costs of raising a child.	• Teen fathers may not take financial responsibility. If so, teen mothers and their families will have to bear total costs. • If teen mothers (or fathers) are dependent on their parents, the costs may jeopardize the family's financial well-being.

3-12 Teen parents face great risks when parenthood occurs too soon.

delayed parenthood occurring? Americans are marrying later in life. One-third of men and nearly one-fourth of women have never been married when they reach age 34.

Careers are becoming more of a goal than marriage and parenting for some well-educated women. About a third of women who earn $65,000 or more a year are childless at age 40. Many of these women believe they can wait until this age to think about having children. The reality is that at this age a woman has a 3 to 5 percent chance of having a baby. This is true even if she has *fertility treatments*—medical treatments that increase the chance of having a baby. These treatments are costly (easily $10,000 per attempt at pregnancy and not covered by most insurance) and often fail.

Career women are not the only ones who delay parenthood. Remarried men and women often want children in their "new" marriages. These couples are often older than first-time married couples, 3-13.

There is also an increase in the number of unmarried, highly educated women over the age of 30 deciding to have children, too. By

3-13 People delay parenthood until they are older for a variety of reasons.

this age, some single women often feel they have lost the chance to have children within a marriage. Many of these women adopt children, but some become pregnant with medical help.

Biological Risk Factors

Older parents have some risks related to delayed parenthood. The decision to parent may be easy for couples, but actually becoming pregnant may be difficult. Here are some of the biological challenges

- As women get older, they become less fertile. For example, women over 40 years of age are 20 times less fertile than those women at peak fertility.

- Fertility treatments raise the odds of having multiple children; however, these births result in more complications for the babies. Parenting multiples is also more difficult and more costly.

- Down syndrome, a condition causing mental and physical disabilities, occurs more often in children of older moms. Other birth defects may be more common, too.

- Older parents may not have the physical health or stamina to keep up with a toddler or "pick up" after a teen.

Financial and Emotional Stress

Along with biological challenges come some financial risks and emotional stress. Although they may be better off financially when children are born, the most costly time of child rearing comes later in life. When the child reaches college age or begins a new life away from the parents, costs peak. At this time, parents may be living on retirement income and have fewer flexible resources.

Many older parents find themselves part of the "sandwich generation"; that is, they may be caring for older parents with health problems while raising young children. The emotional stress of caring for two generations while keeping a marriage strong can be overwhelming for couples. Other emotional stresses older parents may encounter include

- *Fear of parenting.* Due to their ages and experiences, they almost expect to be *perfect parents.* Striving for parenting perfection may cause a fear of failure.

- *The loss of privacy, quiet, and order.* Adults often find that having privacy, quiet, and order does not mesh well with parenting.

- *Feelings of isolation.* Older parents may feel isolated from friends who are either childless or have much older children.

Older couples also have some parenting benefits. Research shows they are better off financially, spend more time with their children, and have a closer connection to their children's friends than younger parents.

Grandparents Raising Grandchildren

In recent years, the number of children who live without their parents has skyrocketed. Half of these children are under the age of 6. Most often this results from what is called the *Four Ds*: drugs, divorce, desertion, or death. Grandparents are often left to raise their grandchildren. Experts state that the situation is so common that any grandparent might be faced with this decision, 3-14.

Close to eight million children are raised by grandparents, with different degrees of parenting help from social-service agencies. In 75 percent of these families, grandparents, not parents, are heads of these households. This means that these grandparents are providing the finances and taking on the responsibilities for minor children. About 50 percent of these children are raised by two grandparents. Grandmothers alone raise the other 50 percent. Half of all grandparents care for two or more children.

3-14 Many grandparents are raising their grandchildren due to an array of circumstances.

When parents are ill or their lives are in turmoil, grandparents may care for grandchildren on a short-term basis. For most grandparents, though, parenting grandchildren is long-term. This is often due to the parent's death, serious substance abuse, or incarceration (in jail).

Risks

Parenting grandchildren is a high risk for grandparents. Some have poor health and may not be physically able to care for their grandchildren until they are grown. They also may experience financial difficulties. Emotional adjustments can be difficult due to change in lifestyle. Raising grandchildren often occurs when grandparents are looking forward to fewer responsibilities and more leisure time. The health and emotional adjustments of the grandchildren may also be a concern. For example, grandchildren may have addictions, be malnourished, or have disabilities due to their parent's neglect.

Benefits

With support, many grandparents do an excellent job raising their grandchildren. They are often mature, experienced in parenting, and dedicated to their grandchildren. In return, grandparents often receive loving praise from their grandchildren.

Decision Making

Deciding about parenting may be even more difficult than deciding about marriage. When considering marriage, you will already know your potential spouse. While dating, you will find out if you are really compatible. If it doesn't work out, you can date someone else.

Parenting is different. You can't try out a child or practice being a parent. You will not meet your child until he or she is born. Once you become a parent, you can't change your mind and decide you don't want to be one anymore without major consequences for you and for your child. (Note that under extreme circumstances some parents do surrender their parenting rights making their child available for adoption. This is not an ideal situation.) That's why you need to think about parenting so carefully beforehand. It will change your life forever.

One way to make parenting decisions is by using the decision-making process. The **decision-making process** involves several steps that can help you make careful, responsible, and informed decisions. They include:

1. Identify the decision to be made.
2. List all possible alternatives. **Alternatives** are the available options from which you can choose.
3. Evaluate the consequences of each alternative. **Consequences** are the results of each alternative. Some will be good and others will not. Some consequences will affect the present, while others will affect the future.
4. Choose the best alternative. Make your decision based on the evaluation of each alternative.
5. Act on the decision.
6. Evaluate the results.

Following this six-step process can help you make the best decision possible. You will be more satisfied with your decision than if you make a hasty choice. When making parenting decisions, carefully consider how having children will influence every aspect of your life. Think about the consequences and the responsibilities.

When you and your partner begin thinking about marriage, talk honestly about your views on parenting. Perhaps the most important decisions you will make together are those concerning parenting. Any decision you make prior to becoming pregnant can be reversed. Once a child is born, however, your choice of parenting can't be changed.

A decision-making chain for parenting is shown in 3-15. This chain may help you identify the available alternatives and the consequences of each decision. As you study the diagram, assess your feelings about parenting. This may help you decide whether parenting is right for you.

Decision-Making Chain for Parenting

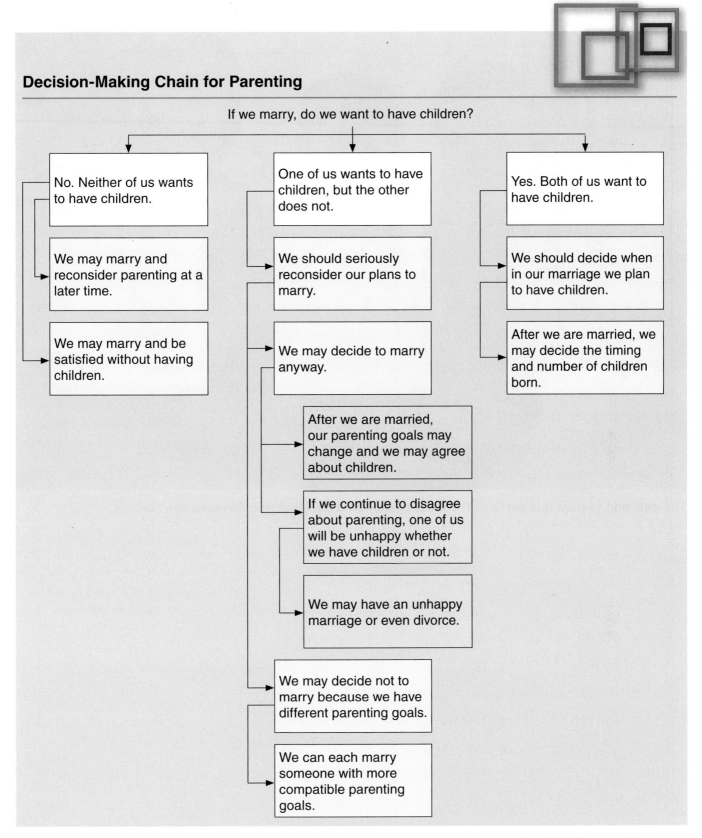

3-15 Couples can use the decision-making chain to think logically about parenting decisions as they consider marriage.

The decision to parent is perhaps the most challenging decision people make in a lifetime.

Summing It Up

- Today's couples have many important choices regarding parenting.

- Unplanned children are a parenting risk. Unless the couple comes to accept the baby, the couple's relationship and the baby's future are in jeopardy.

- Several factors may influence a couple's parenting decisions. These include: the desire to express marital love, the desire to be parents, expectations about parenthood, expectations about children, pressures from families and friends, and the desire to influence a partner.

- Parenting factors to consider before marriage include individual and couple goals, the impact of careers on parenting, and the impact of finances on parenting.

- Parenting readiness factors to consider after marriage include: the marital relationship, how responsible the couple is, how willing they are to give up some social activities and accept a new lifestyle, how mature they are, what they know about parenting, and how their age and health will affect parenting.

- Parenting is a much bigger challenge for teens, older couples, and grandparents. These groups have all the challenges of "ideal-age" couples, but they have additional risks due to age and special circumstances.

- Couples can use the decision-making process to make responsible decisions about parenting.

Recalling the Facts

1. Name two reasons why unplanned pregnancies are unfair to couples and their children.

2. What may be the best reason for having a child?

3. Describe two negative reasons for having a child.

4. Name three factors a couple should consider before marriage when making decisions about parenting.

5. What is the purpose of designing a time/life line?

6. How does the cost of raising a child change as the child grows older? Why?

7. How should a couple's marital relationship relate to their parenting decisions?

8. Besides their marriage, describe two other factors a couple should consider before beginning a family.

9. For each of the following risks caused by teen pregnancy, list one example for the parent and a corresponding one for the baby: (A) health risks; (B) social and emotional problems; (C) education and career risks; (D) financial risks.

10. Name two parenting challenges faced by couples that delay parenthood.

11. Identify three risks that grandparents may face when raising grandchildren.

12. List the six steps of the decision-making process.

Applying New Skills

1. **Parent interview.** Interview the parents of an infant or a toddler about the financial impact their child has had on their lives. Ask them how they expect their child's expenses to change in the coming years. Write a summary of your findings and share them with the class.

2. **Time/life line.** Design a time/life line that shows the goals you have for your life and when you hope to achieve them. To make a time/life line, draw a horizontal line that stretches across a piece of paper. Divide the line into five-year segments from age 15 to 85. Write down two goals you have achieved or hope to achieve by each five-year milestone. Save your time/life line to review at regular intervals. Revise your goals as needed.

3. **Decision-making demonstration.** In small groups, discuss how couples can use the decision-making process to make parenting decisions. Then, through role-play, demonstrate a couple using this process as they decide whether to become parents.

Thinking Critically

1. Analyze the following statement: If you say yes to parenting, you are saying *no* to other things. Give examples of what people might say *no* to if they choose parenting. Write your responses on a separate sheet of paper. Discuss the pros and cons of these choices in a small group. Does the group agree or disagree?

2. Create a two-column chart on a separate sheet of paper. Write these two headings (one at the top of each column): *What I Like About Children* and *What I Don't Like About Children*. Draw conclusions about how each item listed might affect parenting decisions. Then discuss your responses in a small group.

3. Select one of the factors mentioned in the chapter that people should consider when making parenting decisions. Analyze how you think this factor might affect your future parenting decisions. Then write a paragraph summarizing your views in a journal for future reference.

Linking Academics

1. **Writing.** Examine the pros and cons of having a dual-career family. On a separate sheet of paper, suggest ways parents in dual-career families can share child care responsibilities and balance their work/home lives effectively. Use Internet or print resources for background information as needed. Write a summary of your findings.

2. **Reading.** Choose a novel written about a teen parent. Read the novel. In a brief written summary, describe the challenges that the teen parent faced. How did he or she overcome these challenges?

3. **Math.** Use Internet or print resources to locate information on using disposable versus cloth diapers for an infant during the first year. What is the cost of using each type of diaper per month? per year? If a couple's net income is $38,000 per year, what percentage of their income will be spent on diapers?

Part Two

Positive Parenting

Your Potential Career

Hot Jobs in Hospitality and Tourism

Are you a "people" person? Do you enjoy working varied hours and with many different people? Are you friendly, organized, and physically fit? Are you a skillful communicator? Think about your personal qualities in relationship to a career in *hospitality and tourism*.

Because families need time for leisure and recreation, many careers in hospitality and tourism are in *high demand*. More and more families eat meals out and spend vacation time at destinations far from home. The wages for these careers range from low to moderate. People in management positions command higher wages based on experience and education. Review the chart on the next page to identify hospitality and tourism careers that interest you.

The range of skills and education needed are as varied as the careers in this cluster. For example, a high school diploma and on-the-job training are all you need to obtain work as a cook in a foodservice kitchen. In contrast, a cruise-ship fitness trainer or hotel manager may need a 4-year degree. Many jobs require a two-year associate's degree and on-the-job training. Since peoples' health and safety are of utmost concern, some hospitality and tourism careers require *high skill* and special certifications, such as those in foodservice or fitness industries.

Build Your Portfolio

Create a photo essay or video clip of your involvement in a community service event or on-the-job experience related to hospitality for parents, children, and families. Add your photo essay or video clip to your portfolio.

FCCLA

Display your management skills by participating in an FCCLA STAR Event competition related to hospitality and tourism. Family and child related projects might include *Early Childhood, Focus on Children, Hospitality, Entrepreneurship, or Culinary Arts.* Be sure to obtain all necessary forms and guidelines from your family and consumer sciences teacher.

Get Connected

Many community service organizations offer hospitality-related events for their programs, such as fund-raising dinners, fairs, bake sales, walkathons, or auctions. Investigate a group that serves families, parents, and children to find out about volunteer areas in which you could serve.

You can read more about planning your career in Chapter 22.

Career Cluster—Hospitality and Tourism

Cluster Pathways

Restaurants and Food/Beverage Services

Recreation, Amusements, and Attractions

Sample Careers

Catering Manager	Executive Chef	Parks and Gardens Director	Family Centers Equipment Operator
Banquet Manager	Chef	Parks and Gardens Activity Coordinator	Fitness Worker
Caterer	Cook	Parks and Gardens Ranger	Physical Trainer
Banquet Set-Up Employee	Specialty Chef	Festival Event Planner	***Exhibit Developer:***
Kitchen Manager	Server	Theme Park Manager	Museums, Zoos, Aquariums
Baker	Bus Person	Family Centers Manager	***Animal Trainer:***
	Counter Server		Museums, Zoos, Aquariums

Chapter 4

Becoming a Competent Parent

Objectives

After studying this chapter, you will be able to

- recognize how family relationships and parenting impact children, including marriage and the characteristics of strong families.
- describe how the parenting role supports the child's development.
- distinguish between the physical, intellectual, emotional, and social forms of development.
- distinguish between the influences of heredity and environment on a child's development.
- explain how parents influence a child's development by promoting attachment, using direct and indirect teaching, and managing nonfamily experiences.
- analyze key elements for using guidance and positive discipline.
- identify resources for parents, including sources of parenting support and assistance.

Key Terms

growth
development
physical development
intellectual development
emotional development
social development
maturation
environment
temperaments
attachment
socializers
guidance
self-control
positive discipline
punishment
imitation
identification
positive reinforcement
negative reinforcement
delay of gratification
support system
support group

Most family members find their greatest happiness in life comes from their relationships within the family. These relationships give meaning that can last a lifetime. Although the family is the most meaningful relationship in peoples' lives, it is also the most demanding. Parents may tell you that having a baby is easy, but raising that child is difficult! Becoming a caring parent requires more dedication, patience, persistence, and control than anything else people do. Yet, this work is often the most rewarding.

To become competent with any skill requires study and experience. Parenting competence is no different. Becoming a competent parent requires learning what is needed to become a good parent. Studying this chapter will help you learn how to become a competent, caring parent.

Family Relationships and Parenting

Though families have changed over the years, the family remains the foundation upon which most societies are built. Regardless of a family's structure, it has tremendous influence on its members. The family serves as a foundation upon which children build their own lives.

Marriage Affects Children

The couple's relationship should be the *primary* relationship in the family. A strong marriage supports both spouses and helps them be better parents. A good marriage can provide solid ground upon which to build strong parent-child relationships.

Children are greatly influenced by their parents' relationship. A couple that loves one another and openly shows affection impacts children in positive ways. Children can sense their parents' happiness. These children feel secure in their families and free to grow and pursue their own goals.

Children can also sense if their parents have a weak marriage. They may feel threatened by a division that exists between their parents. Children's concern about a possible divorce leads to stress. Stress, in turn, may cause schoolwork and relationships with siblings and peers to suffer.

Strong Families, Strong Parents

Children who grow up in a strong family may be better prepared than other children to succeed as adults. Strong families pull together and overcome difficulties while others may fall apart. Researchers have identified several characteristics commonly found in strong families, 4-1. Continue reading to find out more about these characteristics.

Support and Appreciate

In strong families, members are dedicated to each person's welfare and happiness. They support each other in good times and bad. Family members show their affection with words and actions. Here are some ways that families show support and appreciation.

4-1 Strong families are the foundation of society. They take time to have fun.

- *Needs and goals.* Strong families recognize each member's needs and goals. Parents understand each child is a unique individual with strengths and weaknesses. Parents also support one another in achieving individual goals and working together to achieve family goals.

- *Contributions.* Strong families acknowledge each person's contribution to the family. Children thrive and develop healthy personalities when they feel loved and valued. Adults feel worthwhile and successful when they feel appreciated.

- *Respect.* In strong families, members show their support by respecting one another. They respect each person's rights, opinions, privacy, property, and decisions. When children learn to respect family members, they learn to respect people outside the family, too.

- *Trust.* When family members support one another, they develop trust. Children learn they can depend upon their parents and look to them for love, support, and nurturance. Through this trusting relationship, children learn to trust others. Parents who trust their children give them increasing responsibilities.

Spend Time Together

Strong families spend time together. Feelings of appreciation, support, trust, and respect develop when family members spend time together. It is important that family members try to find time to be together. Couples need time to foster their relationships. Children need time to be with their families. One of the lasting memories of childhood should be of time spent together as a family, 4-2.

Family members work together to complete household chores. They eat meals together and share concerns with one another. They spend some of their leisure

4-2 Strong families spend time together sharing activities they enjoy, such as having a cookout.

time together. Strong families have fun together. Humor allows family members to relax after stressful situations and enjoy the pleasures of family life.

Work demands and the personal pursuits of adults and children sometimes interfere with time available for family life. Families need to learn how to balance competing demands. The quality of time spent together is more important than spending large amounts of time together.

Communicate with One Another

Communication is a key component to developing strong family relationships. In strong families, members feel free to share their joys and their sorrows. Communication helps family members know and feel closer to each other. This promotes a sense of family unity.

Good communication is the basis for solving the problems that occur within every family. In a strong family, members understand the importance of communication to help them solve these problems. Instead of ignoring a problem, strong families talk about it. They are open and truthful with each other about how they feel and what they think. Members listen to one another's thoughts and feelings with respect. This promotes a sense of closeness and understanding.

Manage Resources and Share Responsibilities

Strong families may not have all the resources they need, but they make the most of what they have. In a strong family, members work as a team and share their resources. If one member has items or talents the family needs, he or she shares these with the family. Members of strong families help one another in normal circumstances, as well as in times of need. Family members work together to find ways to solve their problems, meet their needs, and reach their goals.

Members of strong families also feel a certain responsibility to help their families, such as sharing household responsibilities. All family members, including children, pitch in and do their part. Not only does the family profit from sharing responsibilities, each member can learn certain life skills.

Share Moral Standards

Strong families share moral standards. Moral standards may be an expression of religious faith; however, they also stem from a natural concern for other people and the world in which they live. For example, some of these standards (also called *universal values*) are compassion, respect, justice, honesty, integrity, equality, and responsibility. Such moral standards are common in families from all cultures or walks of life.

Moral standards provide families with measures by which they judge behavior. Strong families teach children to differentiate right from wrong. The moral standards children learn from their families influence them as they develop relationships with others.

Share Rituals and Traditions

A sense of family identity comes from family rituals and traditions. For instance, children learn very early that their families have special ways of doing things. This may be something as simple as serving the same meal on a certain night of the week. It may

be a way of celebrating special holidays. Children remember from year to year the little things that make celebrations special, such as a holiday decoration or menu.

Through marriage, new family members share in these traditions, too. Newlyweds may disagree about whether to retain his or her family rituals. With communication and flexibility, the couple will reach a solution and establish their own rituals that include traditions from both families. This ties the young family together.

In addition to holiday and other family celebrations, family reunions are good for children. At such gatherings, children learn about their ancestors as relatives share family stories. Children enjoy hearing about their family's history and heritage. They develop a sense of pride, increasing their own self-esteem. How can families establish their own rituals and traditions? See 4-3 for some ideas.

Parenting Supports Child Development

When new mothers and fathers cradle their newborn in their arms, they view their baby as a miracle. Very quickly, however, the coos of a newborn may change to the nonstop, piercing cries of a baby in distress. The soft, warm cheeks of a tiny baby change to the sticky, gooey skin of a toddler eating an ice cream cone. Babies grow up. This is a reality of parenting.

Why do parents need to know about child development? Parents need to support development by having realistic expectations and attitudes. Research shows many parents do not know enough about child development. For example, "older" parents often overestimate the ages at which most of the developmental milestones of infancy occur, such as rolling over, crawling, or saying the first word. Teen parents usually underestimate these same milestones. Do

Building Family Strength Through Family Traditions

- **Recognize your family history.** Even a young family has a past. Keep a family history by saving photos and mementos in a special place. Videotapes, photos, and birthday cards allow families to record the family's past. Recognizing past traditions allows you to repeat them. Children love to look at old photos and videos and talk about how their family is special.

- **Take cues from your children.** Children may be quicker than adults to recognize the potential for turning a routine into a tradition. Children often say, "But we always do it this way." Children feel a sense of security when family routines are repeated. Doing something together is an opportunity for a child to bond with his or her family. Family rituals or traditions also give a child a sense of safety and control.

- **Give traditions a name.** You may want to designate a traditional family supper, and call it "Spaghetti Monday." A pet rabbit's addition to a family may be designated as "Harvey the Rabbit Day." These special days, even though they are very simple, can be very meaningful. They give an event a distinction that sets it apart from the ordinary.

- **Remain committed to your family rituals.** Let your family know these are special events for your family. Rituals and traditions prompt a sense of "us" or "we" for families. It provides a feeling of connection, and this is important.

4-3 Building family traditions can strengthen family relationships.

you see problems for both children and their parents due to a lack of knowledge? As you read the following, think about children you know and how they are changing.

Know Your Child

Effective parents need to understand how children grow and develop. **Growth** is a process that begins with pregnancy and continues through adulthood. Growth refers to an increase in size, strength, or ability. Physical growth includes increases in weight (measured in pounds or kilograms) and height (measured in inches or centimeters).

Development means a change of function as a result of growth. Development refers to progress in skills and abilities. Development is measured in stages, because it occurs in an orderly sequence. Most development requires growth, too. For example, the development of motor skills requires the growth of muscles and brain cells. Several types of development exist.

- **Physical development** includes the biological changes in a person. Some of these changes are growth of the entire body, such as bones and muscles, internal organs, and the brain. Physical development also includes changes in hormones and motor skills.

- **Intellectual development** involves changes in a person's thinking, intelligence, and language. Intellectual development includes the many brain activities, such as memory, problem solving, and imagining.

- **Emotional development** involves recognizing feelings or emotions such as love, hate, fear, happiness, or anger. Another part of emotional development is learning to express emotions and learning to control certain responses to emotions. Emotions or feelings play an important role in personality development. Children learn to experience and express their feelings through their interactions with parents, siblings, and others.

- **Social development** involves changes in a person's relationships with other people. Children first learn about relating to others by observing, and interacting with their parents. A child's social development is also greatly affected by contact, or lack of contact, with other children and adults, 4-4.

Although you can study social and emotional development separately, they are really interwoven or blended. As you just read, many feelings arise from and are expressed through social relations. For this reason, many researchers express this blend as "socioemotional development." Parenting involves the whole child—all aspects of growth and development blended together.

Each Child Is Like Most Others

All living things—plants, animals, and humans—grow and develop in an orderly way. This is due to each living thing's special genetic blueprint. **Maturation** is the orderly sequence of developmental changes shaped by human genes, 4-5. In a few cases, the "sameness" of development can be changed by extreme conditions. These include a severe defect present before birth or a profound problem during or after birth.

Because of maturation, children around the world are much more alike than different. They share most of the same physical characteristics. Children also develop along the same general patterns. These patterns are often referred to as *principles of growth and development.* You will explore these principles in Part 4.

4-5 Most babies follow an orderly sequence of development called maturation.

How does understanding the patterns of growth and development help parents? First, parents will be better able to support their child's current stage of development as a way to prepare for the next stage. For example, babies need "tummy time" in the very early months. This helps them gain strength in their necks and backs and gain control over their heads. These skills lead to the ability to sit.

Second, parents can get ready for the next stage. For example, a baby who can sit without support will soon pull up using furniture. How should parents childproof their homes for this stage? Why would parents need to do this before the child enters a stage?

Third, parents will have more realistic expectations for their children. Knowing the age-range for various behaviors helps parents avoid putting too much pressure on their children. It also helps them to see possible lags in development and to ask for expert help when needed.

As parents get to know their child, they will soon discover that their child is like other children in basic needs. Parents need to find ways to help their children meet those needs. The way in which needs are met can

4-4 Participating in playgroups can help children develop social skills.

differ somewhat. For example, the nutrition needs of children can be met with many different foods from various cultures.

Each Child Is Like No Other

Hereditary traits do not act alone to form the total person. Environment also plays a role. **Environment** consists of everything in a person's surroundings. The environment affects people from the beginning of life to death. People have a physical environment (nutrition, exercise, medical care, and physical accidents) and a social environment (family, peers, schools, community, media, and culture).

People's genes and environment interact all of the time. Together they make each person unique, 4-6. Even children who have the same genes (identical twins) and who are raised in the same family are unique from birth. This happens because identical children, as all people, filter the environment in unique ways. For example, the same parent behavior or even the same toy can have a different impact on each child.

4-6 Although children follow predictable patterns of development, parents must keep in mind no two children are exactly alike.

Parents need to recognize the uniqueness of their children from birth. Children are born with certain **temperaments**, or tendencies to react emotionally in certain ways to events. Parents who adjust parenting behaviors to their child's temperament are less stressed and more successful. As you learn more about children, you will find that there are generally three broad types of temperaments, 4-7. They include the following:

- *Easy children.* These children generally have a positive mood and an easy-going nature. At most times, they are happy, adaptable, calm, and interested in new things. They tend to have regular eating, sleeping, and elimination habits. Children with an easy temperament are not fussy.

- *Difficult children.* Children with a difficult temperament can provide some parenting challenges. These children may be fussy. Their eating and sleeping habits are often irregular. They become upset easily and react with strong emotions. They may not respond well to unfamiliar people.

- *Slow-to-warm-up children.* At first, slow-to-warm-up children may respond negatively to new experiences and new people. They tend to watch the activity around them before getting involved. They gradually warm up to new people and experiences around them.

Because parenting goes two directions, parents' temperaments affect the parent-child relationship, too. Due to their own temperaments, parents may encourage or discourage their child's traits. Parents often encourage traits similar to their own and discourage traits less like their own. For example, an active parent may play vigorously with an active child. The same parent may be impatient with an inactive child. Parents need to be more aware and accepting of their child's temperament.

Parenting and the Child's Temperament

Temperament	Traits	Parenting Needs
Easy child	<ul><li>Adapts to change</li><li>Likes new experiences</li><li>Is easy to distract</li><li>Displays moderate activity</li><li>Has a happy disposition</li></ul>	<ul><li>Follow the child's lead.</li><li>Enjoy parenting.</li></ul>
Difficult child	<ul><li>Does not easily adapt to change</li><li>Does not like new experiences</li><li>Is difficult to distract (appears to be stubborn)</li><li>Displays high activity levels</li><li>Seems to be out-of-sorts most of the time</li></ul>	<ul><li>Provide a consistent environment; make all changes slowly.</li><li>Be patient with the child.</li><li>Remain objective. (Realize temperament is inborn, not something parents cause.)</li></ul>
Slow-to-warm-up child	<ul><li>Is resistant or hesitant at first</li></ul>	<ul><li>Be patient.</li><li>Encourage child to try new things.</li></ul>

4-7 Parenting methods should be adjusted to a child's temperament.

With each passing year, a child shows more and more individual traits. Family, peers, the schools, the community, and the media all influence a child's traits. This encourages the child to become more and more like no other.

Nurturing Promotes Attachment

Nothing is more important to children than parents who nurture them by being sensitive and responsive to their needs. T. Berry Brazelton and Stanley D. Greenspan, who are nationally known doctors and parenting experts, say that an "ongoing nurturing relationship" is one of the seven bottom-line basic needs of children.

Through nurturing, attachment develops. **Attachment** is the lasting emotional relationship that begins in infancy and ties the child to his or her parents and later to other important people. Attachment is a two-way process in which adults "attach" to infants and infants to adults.

Attachment is a result of a significant relationship. It begins with adults, especially parents, who meet children's needs. Children need loving care, freedom to grow, and steady guidance. They need close family ties to serve as the basis for security and trust. Children need structure in their lives to help them develop a sense of order and purpose. They need consistency and reasonable limits placed on their behavior.

When children feel unconditional love and have their needs met, they are generally willing to comply with their parents' wishes. They learn their behavior affects people other than themselves. They become self-disciplined. As they reach adulthood and become parents, this cycle is repeated.

Attitudes held by a family create a lasting influence upon children from one generation to the next.

Without attachment, children feel distressed and insecure. All areas of their development suffer. As you will learn throughout this text, attachment has profound effects on children.

Parents Are Primary Teachers

Not only are parents the first nurturers, they are the first **socializers**—family and nonfamily members, as well as all aspects of the environment, that transmit knowledge, skills, and traits to others and enable them to be fit for society. They are also their children's first teachers. Nonhuman influences, such as the media, are also socializers. Children's early experiences affect their development for the remainder of childhood and as adults. There are many ways parents can teach, 4-8. They influence children's growth and development by

- *providing sensory stimulation.* Sensory stimulation is essential to normal development. A baby needs sensory experiences during the first few weeks of life. This includes seeing the parent's face, hearing the parent's voice, and feeling the parent's gentle touch. As movement skills develop, a baby needs new things to explore in a safe home. Still later, a young child's needs include being read to, having countless questions answered, and visiting community sites, such as the zoo, library, and parks. Many new experiences and good conversations stimulate the child in the school years.

- *doing direct teaching.* Children learn much through the direct teaching of parents and other adults. Direct teaching means an adult deliberately instructs a child how to do something. To prevent children from being overwhelmed and frustrated, tasks should be broken into child-size steps.

- *encouraging children to try new things.* Feeling confident about trying something new is vital to getting the most out of life as a child. Being willing to try new things also makes children more flexible to changes as adults. Parents can encourage this attitude in many ways. For example, to encourage independence a preschooler might help put the flatware on the table for the family meal. A child might also help sort socks when a parent is folding the family laundry (this helps build confidence and math skills, too).

4-8 This mother is explaining how to measure ingredients and allowing her daughter to practice. She is using direct teaching.

Managing Nonfamily Experiences

Children develop and learn in many social settings besides the family. Three of the most important nonfamily social settings are child care and school, peer contacts, and the media. Other highly important socializers not discussed in this chapter include religious settings, health care settings, and community and neighborhood settings, such as recreational centers or parks. Along with the family, these nonfamily settings directly influence children's knowledge, skills, and traits. These socializers prepare children to become competent citizens, 4-9.

For most children, contacts with these socializers begin very early in life. When infants enter child care, socialization begins soon after birth. Almost all toddlers, including those not in child care, have had experiences with playmates and the media.

In these settings, parents are not with their children all the time. Parents, however, can have major impact on their child's socialization in these settings. The impact depends on the links between the parents and the settings, 4-10. Parents can enhance the impact of their child's experiences when they approve of the setting.

Some nonfamily experiences are not in the best interest of children. For example, some television programs show violence and use language that is not suitable for children. Parents are still responsible for their children and must make decisions for their welfare. This requires careful monitoring and management of the setting. For example, parents can counteract some of a socializer's negative influence by limiting their child's contact.

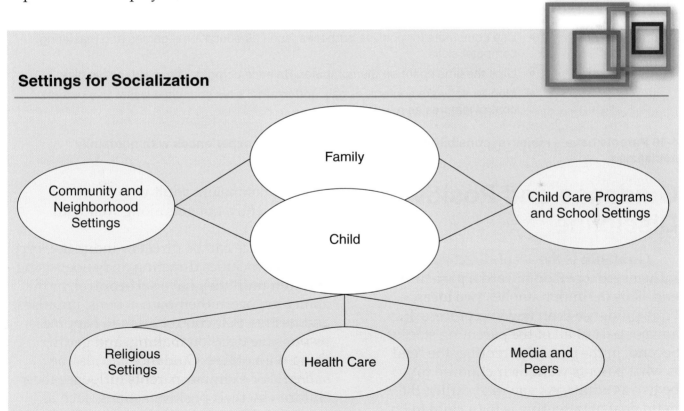

Settings for Socialization

Family

Child

Community and Neighborhood Settings

Child Care Programs and School Settings

Religious Settings

Health Care

Media and Peers

4-9 The family is the primary socializer, but other face-to-face settings can have major impacts on children.

Linking Parents and Nonfamily Socializers

Socializers	Parent Involvement
Child care programs and schools	• Choose a quality program. • Communicate with staff and teachers frequently. • Be involved with program activities.
Peers	• Know the families of your child's friends. • Teach your child how to be a good friend. • Encourage visits from peers after getting to know the families. • Use caution in some situations, such as aggressiveness in peers.
Television	• Use television for positive purposes, not as a babysitter. • Limit the amount of time children watch television. • Review the content of programs for violence and other issues that conflict with family values. • Note the effects of television on your child. If you see negative effects, such as aggressive behavior or fear, make changes immediately.
Music	• Listen for appropriate lyric content. • Check CD labels for parental advisories. • Monitor volume. Loud sounds can damage hearing even at a young age.
Computers and the Internet	• Use computers for positive purposes, such as educational games and mastering computer skills. • Limit the time spent on the computer. Balance computer time with active play. • Monitor software content, e-mail, and Internet sites your child visits. Use parental control features as needed.

4-10 Parents have a major responsibility in supporting their child's experiences with nonfamily socializers.

Guidance and Positive Discipline

Guidance is the act of directing and influencing a person toward a particular end. This definition implies two ideas. First, guidance is an ongoing process. It is a major part of all of the parenting stages. Second, in the case of parenting, the "end" is what parents want their children to be like as adults. As you read earlier, the main goal of parenting is for a child to be a happy, competent adult who functions independently, but gets along well with others.

Guidance can be direct or indirect. *Direct* guidance includes directing and supervising children until they have **self-control**, or the ability to govern their own actions, impulses, and desires. Self-control leads to happiness, responsible decision making, and getting along with others. Guidance can also be *indirect*. For example, parents influence their children by their positive actions, such as parents' self-control.

Positive discipline is the process of intentionally teaching and training a child to behave in appropriate ways. Unlike, guidance, positive discipline is *always* direct. Guidance and discipline should not be confused with punishment. **Punishment** is a penalty for something a person has done wrong. Punishment is a consequence for inappropriate behavior. Parents control punishment.

How Children Learn Positive Behaviors

Parental control begins in a child's life with the parents' efforts to schedule and to teach certain physical behaviors, such as sleeping through the night, weaning, and toilet learning. These efforts produce tensions between the child and parent. Between 18 and 24 months, a child begins to develop a sense of self and may directly challenge parent control. At this time, guidance becomes a parenting issue.

Parents must help their children learn positive behavior. *Positive behavior* is behavior that is acceptable, healthy, and satisfying for the child and those around him or her. Children feel best about themselves when they use positive behavior. Positive behavior promotes harmony between the child, family, and society. In order to guide children's behavior, parents need to understand how children learn behaviors. Although children learn in countless ways, the main ways include direct teaching, imitation, identification, trial and error, and reinforcement, 4-11.

Direct Teaching

Parents use direct teaching to teach their children about proper ways to behave. The adult explains why the child should act a certain way. The parent may also show the child how to behave. For example, a parent may tell a child not to hit the family cat, but

4-11 Children learn in many different ways.

then show the child how to gently pet the cat. Direct teaching begins at an early age and continues into adulthood.

Imitation

When children intentionally copy the behavior of others, they are learning by **imitation**. Children constantly observe their parents and others. They then wait for a chance to experiment for themselves. Children learn positive behaviors, such as touching younger siblings and pets gently, through imitation.

Similarly, children learn by imitating the negative behaviors of their parents. Parents should be aware of the examples they are setting. If parents' actions conflict with their direct teaching, children will often imitate the behavior rather than follow the direct teaching.

Identification

Identification is another way children learn behavior. **Identification** means children unconsciously adopt the behavior patterns of people they like and admire. Behavior patterns are internalized. The child actually "feels like" the other person. He or she may begin to look and act like the person admired. Because of this, parents need to ask, "What kind of model am I?"

Trial and Error

Children also learn by trial and error. Trial and error means choosing behaviors through a process of testing. They learn from their mistakes. If children try a behavior that doesn't work well, they abandon this behavior and try another. When they find a behavior that works, they will repeat it.

Reinforcement

Reinforcement is a response to a behavior learned in any way that encourages or discourages a person to use the behavior again. There are two types of reinforcement—positive and negative. **Positive reinforcement** describes a response that makes repeating a behavior more likely. A simple word for positive reinforcement is *reward*. The reward may be the child's own feeling of pride or a positive parent response, such as encouragement, praise, or a treat, 4-12. **Negative reinforcement** describes a response that makes repeating a behavior less likely. This type of reinforcement is always unpleasant. *Punishment* can be one form of negative reinforcement. Ignoring behaviors and broken toys that result from temper tantrums are also forms of negative reinforcement.

Reinforcements can be rather tricky to use, however. For example, parents who give treats may cause the child to use bribery. For example, a child may say, "I'll clean my bedroom if you give me _____," or "I'll yell if you don't give me _____." Punishment can be a positive reinforcement for a child who wants parent attention.

Guiding as a Parenting Team

No job is more invested with a sense of self and values than parenting. Learning to parent as a team provides a solid foundation on which children grow and develop. When parents disagree on how to raise their children, and they often do, emotions may run high. These clashes can affect all relationships in the family system.

Understanding what causes parents to clash can help you avoid some pitfalls when you parent children of your own. Here are some reasons why parents may clash.

- *Parents may have different temperaments.* For example, some parents are patient and others react quickly with strong emotions. Some are easy going, and others are rigid. Temperaments **affect** discipline techniques, especially those that are not well thought out. For example, some parents may immediately explode and give a harsh punishment for a child's minor misbehavior.

4-12 Encouraging children when they behave appropriately makes it more likely they will repeat the behavior.

- ***Parents come from different family and cultural traditions or beliefs.*** Some traditions believe in very strict discipline along with physical punishment. Other parents believe in trying to create a perfect childhood free from any tensions between parent and child. Discipline may consist of only a few "suggestions" and misbehaviors are not punished.

- ***Parents tend to parent as they were parented.*** Their childhood family life was their training ground in parenting. Parents tend to use the same techniques as their parents used. Couples are likely to clash if their childhood family lives greatly differed.

Areas of Disagreement

Intense bickering in front of children is not healthy. Almost any difference can become an issue if parents allow this to happen. Some of the major areas of disagreement include

- having different standards for tolerable behavior. For example, one parent may want everything neat and clean, while the other parent accepts some house clutter with children.

- having different ideas about the timing and methods of getting children to reach certain milestones. For example, parents may disagree about when and how to get their child to sit through a family meal or to sleep alone in his or her bedroom.

- viewing the other parent as taking control of the child while he or she is "disciplining." This happens most often when both parents have been "in control" at their place of work or when the "disciplining parent" is seen as too harsh.

- looking at what the "experts" say in different ways. For example, parents may agree that sugary foods are not good for a child's nutrition. However, one parent sees sugary foods as strictly off-limits, while the other parent allows "sweet treats" for special occasions.

Parents should solve most conflicts over discipline issues away from children's hearing. Children's negative emotions come from listening to their parents' frequent fighting or "silent treatments."

When angry episodes occur between parents, children show distress, 4-13. Distress is more acute if children think they are the cause of the conflict. Many children try to end their parents' fighting. Younger children's pleas may reduce the conflict. Older children's pleas for calm are often ignored.

Besides the distress, children learn destructive patterns of behavior. Some children become aggressive in childhood.

4-13 Children may show distress when conflict occurs between parents.

When these children become adults, many are still aggressive and unhappy. Those who are happy as adults say they found happiness outside of their families.

Working Toward Agreement

Some parental differences are not bad for children to hear. It is healthy for children to be exposed to differences in opinion. Children can see how parents work together to find a solution. More importantly, they can learn that parents can love and respect each other even if they do not always agree.

When parents differ a great deal in their rule making and rule enforcement, children do not learn positive behaviors. By finding the weak links, children often do as they wish.

Parents need to work together to resolve child-rearing issues. They will likely never agree on all issues. Parenting experts now say that total agreement, or a *unified front*, on every issue is unrealistic. They believe parents should have a compatible front, or be willing to back each other on decisions that they can both accept without resentment. Careful listening is key to agreeing on parenting issues. Here are some ways that parents can use to work toward agreement on guidance and discipline issues.

- *Discuss values and goals for child rearing.* Considering what is important in life, what parents want for their children, and how they hope to achieve these goals contributes to competent parenting.

- *Discuss overall views of guidance and discipline.* Parents should examine themselves to determine whether they are "lenient" or "strict." Do they want to befriend their children, or do they want to be in control of them? What fears do parents have about parenting failure? How do parents see their guidance and discipline techniques changing as their child grows older?

- *Anticipate problems.* As parents discuss values, goals, and views on guidance and discipline, they need to take note of any differences in their views. Are there patterns of discipline about which either spouse disapproves? Do you think that certain techniques might have a negative impact on a child? Recognizing that many patterns of disciplining begin early can help parents avoid inconsistent enforcement of house rules and harsh discipline.

- *Compromise, if possible.* It's unlikely that parents will agree on every parenting issue or discipline technique. When disagreements occur, parents should clearly state their reasons. Rather than either parent "giving in," they need to work together to find a new way to deal with a child's behavior problem, 4-14. It takes time to think over these issues and come up with a decision. Once a decision is made, parents should always back each other when dealing with a child.

When parents cannot reach agreement on parenting issues, it may be time to seek professional help. Issues such as a child's depression or dishonesty or parent's harsh, explosive punishment by a parent may indicate that help from professionals is needed. Most communities offer parenting programs and assistance to families in which parents desire to learn constructive ways to parent.

Setting a Positive Parenting Tone

Research shows that parental discipline is sometimes far from positive. Many parents admit to losing their tempers, making empty threats, and criticizing children's minor mistakes. Some parents do all three on a regular basis. Losing patience and yelling at their children happens frequently with a large percentage of parents.

4-14 Parents need to work together to deal with a child's problem behavior.

What causes a negative tone in disciplining children? The daily challenges of parenting often trigger a negative tone, not major challenges with children. These challenges fall into two groups that include

- the effort needed to parent, such as cleaning up children's messes and running errands to meet their needs

- dealing with children's negative behaviors, such as demanding, whining, and fighting with siblings

The amount of stress parents experience depends upon their temperaments and coping skills. It also depends on the amount of support they receive, especially spousal support. Parent emotions, in turn, determine how they perceive their child's actions. For example, a toddler getting into drawers might be seen as "curious" by a parent in a good mood. However, a parent in a bad mood might view this action as "trying to aggravate." An angry or frustrated parent is more likely to use harsh punishment methods than a parent who is happy and confident.

Parents' emotions mirror the health of the parent-child relationship. Parents need to set a positive parenting tone with their children. Read further to discover some ways to establish a positive parenting tone.

Keep Control

Parents, who love their children, take it personally when their children misbehave. They may see this misbehavior as a failure. Because they sometimes feel helpless in a situation, many parents become frustrated, angry, and emotionally out of control, 4-15. This breakdown in self-control is often called a *meltdown*. Frustration, anger, and parental fatigue may lead to a meltdown. Yelling at children and making idle threats indicates a loss of self-control. Meltdowns do not solve problems and can have very negative results. The results of losing control impact the parent-child relationship in several ways. These include

- losing sight of the goals of guidance and positive discipline. A meltdown does not cause a child to behave as parents wish.

- negative results for the child. Young children are often frightened and feel insecure around the parent. Older children become resentful and defensive (blame others for their misdeeds).

- feeling drained and guilty once parents have time to "cool off." Some parents who feel guilty "give in" to their children's demands as a way to make up for the parents' behavior.

4-15 Parents need to set a positive tone by not becoming too frustrated or angry about a child's misbehavior.

Maintaining self-control is an important element of positive parenting. What can parents do to help prevent meltdowns as they parent their children? Here are a few ideas.

- *Find ways to stay calm.* Parents can physically walk away from their child and breathe deeply. They should avoid talking at this point. Parents might also say *no* to activities that are not priorities to eliminate stress.

- *See the humor.* Sometimes it helps to step back and look at the humor in a tense situation. Parents can try writing a funny story about their parenting day or talking with a friend.

- *Act firmly and quickly on discipline issues.* Letting anger build only increases the likelihood of a loss of self-control. Parents should deal with discipline issues as they arise.

- *Seek help.* Parents should be sure to regularly take time for themselves as individuals and as a couple. They should be sure to seek professional help if they feel out of control on a regular basis.

Be a Positive Model

Children learn by observing models and imitating them. Children prefer to imitate models who are warm and nurturing more than cold and detached. Parents need to create a nurturing environment and also be positive models.

Modeling can be a part of *direct* teaching. Parents can tell children what they want them to do and show them. For example, parents can tell their child to pick up the toys and then show how to put them on toy shelves. Direct modeling also includes using stories to model desired behaviors, 4-16. For example, Johnny Gruell's characters, Raggedy Ann and Andy, are kind, unselfish, generous, and friendly. Like stories, puppets are effective in direct modeling of behaviors. *Mister Rogers' Neighborhood* is a good example of how to use puppets to model desired behaviors.

Modeling is mostly an *indirect* way of learning. Children watch and listen to everything parents do and say. If parents' actions do not match their teachings, children will model their actions. It is important to consider the impact of everything you do as a parent. For example, suppose your child comes home from school and uses a negative word he or she picked up on the school bus. You tell your child that it is impolite and wrong to use words like this. If the child uses the word again, he or she will be punished. Several days later your child overhears you using the same word in conversation with a friend. What will your child think? What kind of model have you been?

Use Positive Words

Young children are in the beginning stages of learning social skills, or socialization. Although they make many learning mistakes, they try to please. Instead of supporting and encouraging their efforts, some parents become frustrated with their children as well as with life outside the parenting role. Parents' words are a major contributor to children's perceptions of themselves. Children often act in the manner in which they've been labeled and treated. For this reason, positive words can help improve the quality of children's lives. They come to act as they have been labeled and treated. Positive words can literally "light up" your child's eyes. You can reduce negative words by

- *thinking of children in positive terms.* Regrettably, language is filled with negative terms for children. To avoid this

4-16 Children will watch and listen to everything their parents do. What kind of model are you?

pitfall, try new ways of thinking about young children, such as *alert* instead of a *light sleeper; a good communicator* instead of *a fussy baby; an independent thinker* instead of *stubborn; curious* instead of *a menace;* and *terrific twos* instead of *terrible twos.*

- *greeting children in positive ways.* If people greeted friends in the same manner they greet their children, they would soon be friendless. Perhaps you've heard a parent say, "Where in the world have you been? Look at your clothes! How did you get so dirty?" Parents should try a smile and discuss the child's play before talking about the condition of the clothing.

- *finding better ways of saying "no."* Most children from the toddler years on hear the word *no* repeatedly each day. Some safety situations call for a quick *no.* The purpose of *no* is to establish authority and to set firm limits on behaviors. Too many *no's* either inhibit children or cause them to tune parents out. Parents can use other words and actions to get better results, 4-17.

- *showing respect to your children.* When parents are most frustrated, they often express it with a gibe. *Gibes* are hurtful phrases that label, shame, threaten, and compare. If children hear these regularly, they lose respect for their parents and are less likely to internalize the rules. Parents should focus on more positive alternatives to make their points.

- *sticking to core issues.* When parents are frustrated, they often look for other issues while venting their frustrations. For example, the parent says, "You forgot to wash your snack dishes. You didn't remember to take off your muddy shoes before you walked into the house either." Children feel hurt because parents appear to be looking for faults.

Better Ways to Say "No"

Strategies	Examples
Substitute body language.	• Shake your head. Frown. • Raise your eyebrows.
Try some new words.	• Enough! • Not polite! • Too far! • Stop! • Don't! • Will hurt! • Unsafe! • Wait! • Not now! • Will break!
Make "no" sound positive.	• Yes, you can have a cookie after dinner. • First, clean your room; then play outside.
Remove forbidden objects.	• Move breakable objects out of reach. • Childproof your house. • Cover easy to soil upholstery. • Serve only nutritious food products.
Ignore silly requests.	• Say nothing. • Say, "Save it for later." Later play a verbal game with your child with both of you making outlandish wishes in a back-and-forth style. Laugh at each other's wishes.

4-17 Parents should have firm limits but use alternatives to the word, *no*.

• *saying "I'm sorry."* Parents are not perfect. They make mistakes. When you make a mistake, apologize. Children are very forgiving.

Helping Children Meet Realistic Expectations

Parents want children to learn specific behaviors. The desired behaviors may vary due to the parents' cultural backgrounds. Desired behaviors may also vary due to family needs, such as staying away from a busy street or self-care during nonschool hours.

Although parents may believe that children do not like rules, children thrive when they grow up in a home that has structure, limits, and rules. Children need parents who not only impose limits to their behaviors, but who will not back down from them.

What is the best way to do this? Parents need to help their children feel as though discipline is a team effort—between parents and child. Although you will read much more about guidance and discipline in the next two chapters, these eight strategies are basic to all teamwork.

Establish and Maintain Realistic Expectations

Realistic expectations begin with considering rule priorities. Rules often fall into these three groupings

• health and safety

• better social living (taking care of property, being sensitive to other people's feelings, and being considerate of others)

• conventional norms, such as manners and proper attire

Most families make rules in the above order. Realistic expectations must also take into account the child's developmental level and his or her family, 4-18. Rules are most effective when they match the child and the family.

Provide Structure

How does establishing structure help parents? Structure helps prevent problems by getting children's cooperation. Structure involves:

Creating an atmosphere of cooperation. If parents respond to their child's needs in a nurturing environment, children hear parent requests as fair. Children fulfill these requests without feeling a loss of self-respect.

Structuring the environment. Removing tempting objects from a young child's reach and child proofing reduce the number of "nos." Having enough space and making children's play and sleeping areas child-sized helps children meet expectations, such as putting things away and self-care.

Having a daily routine. Children have less stress and behave better when they have a regular routine of eating, sleeping, and exercising.

Monitoring the amount of stimulation. Behaviors become a problem when children are either overly tired, overly excited, or bored. Parents can take action to help eliminate problem behaviors. They can reduce the amount of noise or eliminate active play when a child is overly tired or stressed. Children can be "too tired to sleep," so play quiet music, read a story, or bathe the child in warm water. When a child is overly excited, parents can try toy rotation. Also restrict the number or length of activities. Bored children need an enriched environment. Be imaginative! For example, if weather does not permit the child to play outside with his or her favorite ball, give the child an inflated balloon as an "indoor ball." Think of a new building project with the child's "old blocks." Try a parent-child craft project.

4-18 Explaining and enforcing rules is part of parenting.

Preparing for a change. When changes are planned or expected, prepare children. For example, talk about the event, read stories, and even rehearse expectations. Remember that the child's temperament affects his or her ability to readily cope with changes.

Stay Connected

Parents sometimes do not get their child's attention when they are trying to state a rule or get compliance. Like adults, children can be totally involved in what they are doing and block everyone out. If parents have been somewhat ineffective in their disciplinary methods, children may have been "trained" not to respond on the first call. These children respond after many requests or when the parent's voice is raised.

What can parents do? With older infants and toddlers, connect by taking the child's hand or holding gently, 4-19. Parents with older children should go to their child rather than calling from a distance. Control is best at five feet or less. After calling his or her name,

4-19 Holding and playing with a child helps parents keep connected, which leads to better control over a child's behavior.

wait until your child has looked up before talking. Getting on eye level and looking at each other helps, too.

Distract and Redirect

Distract and *redirect* is a technique used with older infants and toddlers who are not mentally ready to handle any form of disciplinary reasoning. To distract, the parent simply changes the child's focus. For example, if a baby is grabbing for the feeding spoon, you can give the baby two other spoons or small washable objects—one for each hand. Toddlers can often be diverted with a toy, book , song, or a walk with the parent. When the child begins the new activity, they are said to be *redirected*. Often they forget what they originally wanted.

Preschoolers seldom forget what they wanted, so they cannot really be distracted. However, their behaviors can be redirected. For example, a preschooler may be throwing his or her blocks. The parent redirects the throwing by saying, "You are having fun throwing your blocks. Those blocks are just for building. Would you like to toss beanbags in a box or throw balls outside?" (Note the parent acknowledges the child's emotion, states the rule, and offers alternative behaviors.)

Set Limits

All children need limits set by their parents. These limits are often communicated as rules. Because a parent may have more rules than a child can learn and comply with at one time, parents do better by limiting the number of "new" rules. This is why rule priorities within families are important. Some parent experts say, "Pick your battles." Parents must learn to state their rules effectively, too, which takes practice. Here are some examples.

- *State rules clearly.* For example say, "Carry your coat so it doesn't touch the floor" or "Wash your hands before we eat."

- *State rules in the positive.* Children cannot mentally turn a negative statement into a positive one until they are about school age. Instead of saying, "Do not run" say "Walk."

- *State rules impersonally when possible.* Leave the words "You must" out of statements when you can. Say "Bedtime is at 9:00 p.m." instead of "You must be in bed by 9:00 p.m."

- *State rules simply, especially for younger children.* Say "Buckle up" rather than saying "Please buckle up your seat belt."

- *Give options when possible.* Say, "Pick up your toys before or after dinner." Options create less resistance.

Positively Enforce Limits

Limits must be positively and consistently enforced. If not, children will be confused and not know what is expected of them. If a rule is enforced one day but not the next, the child's behavior will also be inconsistent, 4-20. If only one parent enforces the rules, children soon learn what they can and can't do with each parent. When limits are consistent, children are more likely to respect them. How do parents enforce rules? Read the following for some helpful ways.

4-20 If this girl's parents are not consistent with their rule about not playing on the playground unsupervised, she may not pay much attention to the rule.

- Watch your own reactions to your child's misbehaviors. For example, chuckling or winking about misbehavior is quickly "read" by your child to mean, "Mommy says this is naughty, but she thinks I'm funny."

- Use gentle reminders about your house rules. These reminders say, "The rule is still in force."

- Use positive reinforcement when a child follows the rule. Reinforcement should never be a bribe. Children need to know when parents are pleased with their behavior. Tell your child that you are confident about his or her ability to follow the rule. Say, "I know you will remember what to say when your friends give you a birthday present."

- If the child does not comply, use consequences. Some examples include: Take away a problem object, such as a toy, or remove a privilege. Give a kind, but firm command such as, "Do _____ now. We'll talk about it tomorrow." Give a reprimand such as, "No splashing in the bathtub. It makes the floors wet, and we might slip and fall. If you keep splashing, you cannot play in the tub. Here's a boat you can float." (Here the parent gives the rule, an explanation of the rule, the consequences of not complying, and an alternative action.)

- When a child argues, accept the child's wish without argument and state the rule again. For example, say, "I understand you want to _____. You know the rule is _____." Ignore any resentment without further comment.

Use Delay of Gratification

Delay of gratification is the postponement of an immediate reward for an even greater reward. For example, you work many years for a diploma. Through the delay of gratification, you also control impulsive behaviors that you can later regret. Thinking things through results in better decision making.

A child begins to see waiting is worthwhile between two and three years of age. This is when the frontal brain lobes, the center of reasoning, begin to develop. The development continues until the teen years. Studies show that good impulse control at age 4 is related to impulse control in the late childhood and teen years, 4-21. Parents can begin training for the delay of gratification in the early preschool years. This can be done by

- telling the child he or she must wait. Say, "I'm sorry, but you'll just have to wait until (time) for (whatever is wanted)."

4-21 Older children and teens show good impulse control when this behavior is encouraged in early childhood.

- suggesting the child wait. Say, "If you don't eat your cookies now, we can all have a tea party as soon as grandma arrives."

- helping the child mark off calendar days until a special event. This teaches calendar skills, too!

- encouraging the child to save money for a "big" purchase rather then spending each time money is given.

- modeling delay. Comment when you see opportunities. For example, say, "Dinner smells so good. We are so hungry. We'll need to wait for Daddy. He should be here soon."

- waiting with your child. Each day you can check for a rose to bloom, a tomato to ripen, or eggs to hatch.

Use Reasoning and Problem Solving

Reasoning and problem solving cannot be used effectively before the preschool years. Both skills require the ability to see from another person's viewpoint and to communicate. These suggestions will help:

Ask questions. Instead of blaming the child for misbehaving, ask him or her questions, such as: Why do you think (name) cried? What can you do differently next time?

Why do you think I am upset with you right now? Why do we have a house rule about treating our pets gently?

Resolve problems. Try to resolve problems with school-age children this way: Identify wants. "What do you want? What do I want?" Restate the problem. "You want _____ and I want _____." Think of ideas to solve the problem. Ask, "What can we do about this problem?" Decide on one idea acceptable to both parent and child. Try the idea. Then ask, "How did it work out?" If the idea is not working, brainstorm for another idea.

Support and Encourage

People are social beings. Children desire to belong to the family and other social groups. Support and encouragement are words and deeds that give children a sense of belonging and self-fulfillment. How do parents provide support and encouragement? Some basics include

- using gentle nurturing to show child that he or she is a worthwhile person and a valued member of the family.

- permitting the child's self-sufficiency—or providing for one's own needs and feeling worthwhile—in all possible situations, such as self-care, learning tasks, and chores.

- doing "we" tasks with the toddler. For example, instead of saying, "Go put on your coat," say, "Come, let's get your coat," as you lead the toddler by holding his or her hand.

- teaching the "older" child to ask for help when he or she needs and wants it. Parents should not start off by helping with the task. If the child asks for help (by words or by actions showing intense frustration), the parent should call attention to the challenge of the task. Say, "It's hard now, but you'll learn how with practice." Then tell the child how you can help by saying such phrases as: "We can fix this together." or "Let's find a way to make this work."

- giving verbal encouragement, 4-22. (Note that the word *encouragement* is better than *praise*.) Praise can be manipulative. Praise as manipulation tends to stifle children's natural desire to learn. Encouragement, on the other hand, helps build a child's confidence. It allows the child to own his or her accomplishments. This creates a desire within the child to do his or her best.

Keeping Your Perspective

It is easy for parents to allow guidance and discipline to take over the parent-child relationship. However, life with a child must be more than saying "no," scolding, and punishing. Parents should not dwell on the ways their children misbehave.

Improving the parent-child relationship often improves the child's behavior. Children and parents need activities to drain off tensions and provide other sources for feelings of belonging and competence. Family bonds anchor children to the family. Children often remember their parents more for the times they played and laughed together than for the times they had to be disciplined. What are some things parents can do? Parents can

- love their children unconditionally and express that love in many ways. As a parent, use your imagination for ways to express your love, 4-23.

Encourage Instead of Praise

Encouragement	Praise
Do be specific. Describe the encouragement in concrete terms of what you see. "You caught the ball, threw it, and made the out for your team."	**Don't praise by comparison.** It may encourage unnecessary competition or fear of failing the next time. Don't say "You're the best player on the team!"
Do describe behavior and its consequences. For instance, "Thanks for putting the dishes away. When we all work together, we can get done faster and have time to spend at the park."	**Don't praise constantly.** If everything your child does is wonderful and terrific, you may run out of superlatives, and your child may become immune to praise.
Do focus on the child's effort—not the end result. "You practiced hard for your piano recital."	**Don't praise indiscriminately.** Children know when something they have done is really not so great. Parental praise over average performance can make children cynical.
Do point out how your child has progressed. "Three cartwheels in a row! You couldn't have done that last year."	**Don't praise so extravagantly children feel pressured to go on shining.** Overenthusiastic applause destroys a good motive for activity (to please oneself) and substitutes a poor one (to please parents).
Do give control back to the child. Let your child do his or her own thing. Instead of saying, "I'm so proud of you," say, "You must feel very proud that you did that all by yourself."	**Don't use backhanded praise.** For instance, don't say, "It's nice to see you being good for a change." This takes away from any good feelings a child has from earning praise.

4-22 To be most effective, parents should encourage rather than praise their child.

Some Ways to Say "I Love You"

- Smile and hug your child often—even for no special reason.
- Celebrate small events, such as finishing a music book or earning a Scout badge, by putting a birthday candle in a cupcake at a family meal.
- Send a "love note" in your child's lunch box or put one under his or her pillow.
- Have a snapshot of you and your child laminated for taking to child care programs. (This eases the stress of separation and is similar to having family photos on your office desk.)
- Kiss your young child's palm during a stressful time. Tell your child to touch that hand to his or her cheek and "feel" the kiss when lonely or sad.
- Make a cuddle blanket to be used when the child is sick or stressed. Tell your child that you "stitched your love into it."
- Surprise your child with a special weekend or vacation treat, such as a trip to a museum, park, or special event.
- Put photos in the child's room of people he or she loves.
- Give your child "cuddle time" when leaving and picking up from child care, putting to bed, and sensing stress.

4-23 The ways you say "I love you" are not as important as doing it regularly. Your child will get the message.

- play with their children. Playing together says to the child, "You are worth my time." How a person had fun in childhood is more predictive of good long-term mental health than is the presence or absence of negative events in childhood.
- enjoy family rituals with your child. These can be anything you and your child enjoy doing together. They can be done daily, weekly, or monthly. They are done no matter what else is going on in your family and are never withdrawn as a privilege.

Resources for Parents

Raising children can be a tough job. One of life's realities is that problems and crises will occur. Even the most stable and self-sufficient families may need to ask for help. No parent can do it all alone.

Parents need help for many reasons. Perhaps parents need someone to care for their children during an emergency. Possibly health care is needed quickly, and no funds are available for a doctor's care. Maybe a parent under stress is beginning to abuse a child. Perhaps children are having trouble adjusting to their parents' divorce. These and many other problems may be too much for parents to handle alone.

Many services are available to assist families in times of need. Too often, however, parents don't use the services available to them. They may think asking for help is a sign of weakness. Parents may be embarrassed to admit they have problems. They may feel they should be able to solve their own problems. Other parents don't realize when they need help or may deny a problem exists. Asking for assistance when it is needed is not a sign of weakness or failure, but a sign of strength. It shows parents truly care about their children and want what is best for them. Good parents know when to seek and accept help from others.

Parent Support Systems

The people, institutions, and organizations parents turn to in times of need make up their **support system**. Parents' primary support comes from the people they know and trust. A parent may be able to turn to various people for support.

Many times family members can solve problems themselves. Relatives can also help. Today, people may live far away from relatives who could help them in the midst of a crisis.

Now, more than ever, families depend upon people outside the family. Friends, neighbors, teachers, and coworkers can be important members of a parent's support system. During a difficult time, a parent may just need a good friend who can listen and give advice, 4-24. Neighbors may be able to provide short-term child care if parents are called away during an emergency. Sometimes coworkers or teachers can offer advice or support. A person's religious organization may offer counseling and referral services.

Today's families also have a wide range of public and private agencies available to provide needed support. These agencies can be an important part of a parent's support system. Agencies provide many different kinds of services, such as health care, financial and legal assistance, recreation, child care, and parent education.

Finding Help

As you think about parenting, acquaint yourself with resources for parents in your community. It may take effort to locate these resources because they may not be easy to find. These resources exist to help people feel less isolated and frustrated in a crisis and help solve the family's problems. The available resources depend on the size of your community. Resources include the following:

- 911 telephone number for emergencies, which even young children should know how to dial

- toll-free hot lines that provide information or assistance for specific problems, such as domestic violence, sexual assault, child abuse, and drug addictions

4-24 Friends, neighbors, and relatives can be good support to parents in difficult times.

- agency listings in your telephone directory

- *Helpline* by United Way, which also links people to appropriate agencies

- local library, which will have materials on many topics of concern as well as helpful librarians

Local agencies are listed under the city, county, or state government listings. (They are often alphabetized as: "Chicago, City of.") An agency can often refer you to other government agencies or private organizations and support groups for better or faster service.

Support Groups

Sometimes parents need to add a support group to their support system. A **support group** is a group of people who share a similar problem or concern. Members of a support group hold regular meetings at which they discuss their concerns. These meetings may or may not be facilitated by a professional counselor. See 4-25 for a list of support groups that exist in many communities.

In a support group, members find support by talking to one another about their common concerns. They can listen as others share their experiences. Members of a support group encourage each other as they learn new ways to cope with their own problems. People may attend a support group for a short period of time, or for many years.

Support Groups for Families

Support Category	Organization	Who Is Served
Grief support	GriefShare	Bereaved adults
	Child Grief Education Association	Children and families who are grieving the loss of a loved one
	Share: Pregnancy & Infant Loss Support, Inc.	Parents who have lost a newborn through miscarriage, stillbirth, or infant death
Addictions	Al-Anon	Family members and friends of alcoholics
	Alateen	Teens (ages 11–18) affected by another person's alcoholism
	Alcoholics Anonymous® (AA)	People who want to stop drinking and recover from alcoholism
	Cocaine Anonymous (CA)	Cocaine addicts who still suffer, but are trying to recover
	Gamblers Anonymous® (GA)	People who gamble compulsively and want to recover from their addiction
	Families Anonymous (FA)	Families and friends who have been adversely affected by a loved one's drug or alcohol addiction
	Nar-Anon Family Groups™	Family members and friends of drug addicts
	Narcotics Anonymous® (NA)	Drug addicts who seek to recover from their addiction
Health and disabilities	Alzheimer's Association	Family members of people with Alzheimer's disease
	American Diabetes Association	Diabetics and their families
	American Cancer Society	Cancer patients and their families
	Mended Hearts	People who have had heart surgery
	National Association of People with AIDS	People who have tested positive for HIV/AIDS
	Resolve: The National Infertility Association	Infertile couples who are trying to become parents
	TOUGHLOVE® International	Parents who are dealing with children and teens with out-of-control behavior
	National Alliance on Mental Illness (NAMI)	Families and friends of persons with serious mental illness

(Continued on next page)

4-25 In many communities, these and other support groups and agencies can help families in times of need.

Support Groups for Families

Support Category	Organization	Who Is Served
Health and disabilities	National Dissemination Center for Children with Disabilities	Provides state listings of support groups for parents of children with disabilities
	Autism Society of America	Families who have children with Autism and Autism Spectrum Disorders
	National Down Syndrome Congress	Parents of children who have Down syndrome
	National Organization of Parents of Blind Children	A division of the National Federation of the Blind that provides support for parents
	Lion's Clubs International	Provide vision support services to people with vision loss or who are blind
	American Society for Deaf Children	Families with children who are deaf or have hearing loss
	Parent to Parent	Families who have children with special needs
	Pathways Awareness Foundation	Parents who have children with early motor delays
Missing children	Child Find® of America, Inc.	Parents trying to find missing children and teens
	National Center for Missing and Exploited Children® (NCMEC)	Parents trying to locate missing children or teens
	National Runaway Switchboard	Children or teens that have run away from home
Violence, abuse, and neglect	Parents Anonymous® Inc.	Parents and children seeking prevention of child abuse
	Parents United International	Individuals and families who have experienced child sexual abuse
	National Network to End Domestic Violence	Provides state listings of support groups and counseling services
	National Domestic Violence Hotline	Provides support, resources, and referrals for families experiencing domestic violence
Single parents	Parents Without Partners (PWP)	Single parents and their children
Financial services	Consumer Credit Counseling Services™	Offers help to people and families with budgeting, money management and credit issues
	American Consumer Credit Counseling	Offers confidential credit counseling and financial management education to consumers

4-25 Continued.

Summing It Up

- The parenting role is affected by all relationships within the family system.

- Strong marriages and families influence children in positive ways.

- Parents need to understand children's physical, intellectual, emotional, and social development as children grow, develop, and mature.

- The influence of heredity and environment makes each child unique.

- Children are born with different temperaments that influence how they react emotionally to events in their environment.

- The family, as the primary nurturing unit, is a tremendous influence on children.

- Attachment is the emotional relationship with parents and others that results from loving care, freedom to grow, and steady guidance.

- As the first socializers of their children, parents provide their children experiences within the family and support and manage their children's experiences in nonfamily settings.

- Guidance or positive discipline is a major responsibility of parents.

- To guide their children parents must work as a team.

- Parents' emotions mirror the health of the parent-child relationship. Because of this, parents need to set a positive parenting tone with their children.

- Several parenting strategies help parents establish and maintain realistic behavioral expectations for their children.

- Many resources exist to help parents and children. These include family and friends, community resources, and support groups.

Recalling the Facts

1. Name two ways family relationships affect parenting.

2. Name an example of each of the following types of development:
(A) physical, (B) intellectual, (C) emotional, (D) social.

3. What are three broad categories of temperament that children may display?

4. How does a child's temperament impact the parenting role?

5. How is nurturing related to children's compliance with their parents' wishes?

6. As *socializers*, how can parents influence their children?

7. Contrast *guidance* and *discipline*.

8. List five ways children learn positive behaviors.

9. What is the difference between a unified and compatible front in discipline?

10. List nine strategies parents can use to help children meet their expectations.

11. Describe criteria used for setting limits. Give three limits that meet the criteria.

12. Contrast a *support system* and a *support group*.

Applying New Skills

1. **Observing development.** Observe a group of preschool children and cite examples of physical, intellectual, social, and emotional development. Note similarities and differences among the children. Write a summary of your observation. Share key points with the class.

2. **Observing behavior.** Observe parents and children in public places, such as stores, or at public events, such as a ball game. Listen to their interactions. List some of the negative and positive statements you heard parents say and the effects on their children's compliance. Share your observations with the class.

3. **Community resources.** Use Internet or print resources to locate articles featuring family problems. List resources in your community these families might turn to for assistance. At the library, ask the reference librarian to show you reference materials parents could use to locate needed community resources. If possible, use desktop-publishing software to create a resource brochure that can be used by other students and families in your community.

Thinking Critically

1. Select one of the characteristics of strong families. Draw conclusions about how you think having this characteristic can make families stronger. Write a one-page summary of your conclusions.

2. Write a paragraph explaining whether you think a child's development is influenced more by heredity or environment. Give examples to support your position.

3. Complete the following statement: "Parents can improve a child's guidance by…" Share your responses with the class.

4. Debate whether seeking support outside the family is a sign of weakness or a sign of strength.

Linking Academics

1. **Writing.** In small groups, write case studies depicting problems families might face. Exchange case studies with another group. Identify the problem faced in each case. Then describe a possible support system for each family.

2. **Reading.** Read a book on child guidance and discipline of your choice. Talk with your teacher about possible options. Write a summary about the key principles for guidance and discipline described in the book. Share your findings with the class.

Chapter 5

Developing an Effective Parenting Style

Key Terms

social competence
parenting style
authoritarian
permissive
democratic
communication
active listening
open communication
"you" messages
"I" messages
"we" messages
problem ownership
win/win method
time-out
natural consequences
logical consequences
self-discipline
self-concept
self-esteem
behavioral reflections

Objectives

After studying this chapter, you will be able to

- summarize how nurturance, behavioral expectations, communication, and control impact effective parenting.
- distinguish among three types of parenting styles.
- analyze the influence of effective communication on parent-child relationships, including the use of active listening and verbal and nonverbal communication.
- describe how to handle the three types of problem ownership.
- explain how parents should choose and implement consequences and punishment for misbehavior.
- contrast punishment to natural and logical consequences for misbehavior.
- describe how parents develop self-control and self-discipline in their children.
- summarize how parents encourage healthy self-concept and self-esteem in their children.

From the moment of birth, babies are social beings who engage with other people, especially their parents. The baby's ability to engage with others is the basis for social and emotional learning. Babies are not socially and emotionally competent any more than they are reading or math competent. In fact, not until adulthood do children develop

- knowledge of the values and expectations of the society in which they live

- **social competence**, or the knowledge and use of social skills in all social settings

Parental guidance and discipline techniques greatly impact a child's social competence. Children develop all aspects of this competence through parent-child interactions. Guidance and discipline have lifelong effects.

Good parenting is not all instinct. As with anything worthwhile in life, you have to work at it. To teach society's expectations and to guide a child's developing social competence, parents must have a plan of action. In Chapter 4, you learned some effective discipline techniques. In this chapter, you will learn about strategies that address the long-term goals parents have for their children.

Effective Parenting Strategies

Parenting strategies greatly impact children's behavior either positively or negatively. Strategies that produce socially competent children also tend to prevent behavioral problems in children at all ages. Why do some parenting strategies work better than others? The answer is simple. When parents have a strong commitment to their children, they balance the demand for proper behavior with sensitive care. Effective parents set rules and enforce them. More importantly, they support their children and pay attention

to their needs. To accomplish all these goals, effective parents balance each of the four aspects of parenting: nurturance, behavior expectations, communication, and control.

Nurturance

By nurturing their children, parents show their children they are loved unconditionally. Nurturing helps children to develop good feelings about themselves. It also increases children's willingness to accept parental behavior standards and fulfill their potential. These children generally become competent adults who are able to overcome stressful life events and live life fully.

Nurturance is more than hugs, as important as those are, 5-1. Nurturance is primarily sensitive, loving care and attention. Young children need much direct care. Parents recognize their child's needs and respond to those needs in loving ways. Because of this, young children form trusting bonds with parents.

As children age, parents gradually replace direct care with supportive care. They offer care or assistance at appropriate times, but children are free to accept or decline. For example, the parent might offer to help a child with homework or a project. Once

5-1 Nurturing parents recognize their child's needs and respond with love and care.

the offer is made, the child decides if he or she wants or needs the help. Both direct and supportive care involve observing and listening to children. Most importantly, care is given freely without conditions attached.

Behavior Expectations

Having high, but realistic, behavior expectations helps parents guide children to develop appropriate skills. Realistic expectations are not too high or low for most children of a certain age. For instance, typical three-year-olds are ready to ride tricycles and string large beads. Encouraging a three-year-old to develop these skills will likely lead to success. Parents can nurture their children by helping them master age-appropriate skills.

Studying child development helps people understand what to expect from children. To have realistic expectations, parents need to know how development progresses. Each developmental skill has its own timetable. To be truly realistic, parents need to consider the sequence (stages) of development more than the time range. Most children follow the sequence. Time frames vary widely among children. Parents also need to consider how they communicate with their children about behavioral expectations.

Communication

Communication is vital to all loving and caring relationships, 5-2. It strengthens the family bond. It also plays an important role in how children develop. Effective parents are good communicators. They rely heavily on their communication skills to develop their children's social skills. For example, when parents are clear about their behavior expectations, children are better able to follow through appropriately. As you continue to read this chapter, you will learn more about communication and its vital role in helping children develop social competence.

5-2 Effective communication strengthens the family bond. When parents are clear about behavior expectations, children are more likely to display these behaviors.

Effective Control

All children need and want control—they want to know where their limits are. As you will learn, caring parents control behavior in ways that allow children to learn the social skills they will use throughout life. To be effective, the control methods need to be firm but not harsh. Consequences of misbehavior need to teach, not strictly punish. Parents control behavior using a variety of methods relating to their values for raising children.

The Impact of Parenting Styles

Parents develop certain ways of parenting that are called **parenting styles.** The parents' values about what is important in childrearing determine their practices. Parents determine their parenting style by using the following:

- knowledge of child development
- cultural background
- socioeconomic status
- own childhood relationships

The child's age, gender, and temperament also impact which methods parents choose. Family size and structure also influence parenting styles.

Numerous experts study parenting practices, especially how they differ in terms of nurturance, behavior expectations, communication, and control. By examining these four factors, three basic types of parenting styles are evident. The types of parenting styles are called *authoritarian, permissive,* and *democratic.* All three styles are within normal parenting boundaries, but each reflects a range of values about parenting practices and raising socially competent children.

Authoritarian

Authoritarian is a style of parenting in which behavior expectations are set very high by parents. These parents offer little or no explanation when they give directions. They expect their children to follow directions without question. Children in these families rarely make decisions on their own. These factors combine to make this style low in communication.

Parents who choose this style often have a structured family environment. They value obedience as a virtue. These parents favor using high control and punishment to correct children's misbehaviors. They teach children that obedience to parental standards is highly important. Children in these families know their misbehaviors will likely result in punishment. They may think their parents will love them more if they are "good." These children may not feel unconditional love. For this reason, researchers say that this parenting style, as compared with other styles, is lowest in nurturance.

Permissive

In the **permissive** style of parenting, parents allow children to make their own decisions. Very few limits and very little guidance and consistent discipline are used to help children learn proper behavior. Behavioral expectations, communication, and behavior control by parents are all low.

Because these parents want to make their children happy, their nurturing level is very high. Permissive parents feel that giving their children complete freedom will make them happy. Some research indicates that these children are more likely to feel insecure because they have no boundaries.

Democratic

In the **democratic** style of parenting, parents and their children talk openly as children develop socially. Parents not only use certain limits, but also allow freedom within those limits. They believe that rules and limits give children a sense of security, stability, and consistency. These parents also value such virtues as obedience and respect. However, they talk openly to guide and discipline their children. Parents set high behavior standards for their children. They also express the reasons for these standards, 5-3.

Although they have high expectations, these parents are also high in nurturance, communication, and control. They teach their children how to behave. Children gradually choose their own behavior and make their own decisions. This allows children to develop decision-making skills and independence. If their children choose poor behavior, these parents enforce consequences. They hold their children accountable for their actions. Another name for democratic parenting is *authoritative*. Due to their knowledge and experience, parents have the parenting authority to guide their children. Parents always have the leadership role in this parenting style.

Choosing a Style That Fits

Parenting styles all reflect the choices parents make about how to support and guide their children. As you read, did any of the styles sound familiar? Most families do not perfectly fit any one style just as a child does not exactly fit a specific stage. All three styles involve nurturance, behavior expectations, communication, and control. Parents can combine and use these factors in many ways.

Why do parenting practices differ so much from family to family? You may recall that a family's culture often influences how parents raise their children. Traditions, religion, and a country's politics all reflect culture. Parents often use a given style from one generation to the next. Close friends or neighbors with similar cultural backgrounds may use the same style, too.

A family's structure and social system may affect parenting style. For example, large families may be more authoritarian than small families. This happens because it takes more time to teach decision-making skills to children in a large family. Personalities and temperaments of parents and children also affect parenting style. For example, parents may choose to use stronger control methods with a more willful child. In contrast, parents may use more democratic controls with a child who readily follows their expectations.

5-3 Democratic parents talk with their children about reasons behind the rules.

You may be wondering which parenting style is best. Parenting experts favor the democratic style because it is high in nurturance, communication, behavior expectations, and control. This approach takes the middle ground between the authoritarian and permissive styles, 5-4. The democratic style overcomes the weaker aspects of the other two styles.

Even if parents choose the democratic style, the balance between nurturance, communication, behavior expectations, and control is up to the parents. All parents make many choices. A couple's parenting style clearly shows by the time a child turns three. From that point on, parents' choices can enhance or harm their child's knowledge of society's values and expectations. Although happy, well-adjusted children are the result of many influences, parenting style has a major impact on social competence.

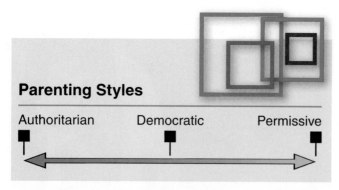

Parenting Styles

Authoritarian   Democratic   Permissive

5-4 Parents' choices about how to support and guide children can be described as authoritarian, democratic, and permissive. Parents' practices can be anywhere between the end points although they tend to cluster near one style or another.

Which style do you think best fits your cultural and family background? How might this impact the way you parent your children? Think about these questions as you read further about effective parenting strategies.

The Importance of Communication

Any means by which people send and receive messages is **communication**. It has two parts: messages sent and messages received. Communication is nonverbal, including body movements, facial expressions, and tone of voice. It is also verbal, including spoken and written words, 5-5.

Children Are Sensitive to Communication

Children are receptive to both nonverbal and verbal communication. Often these two basic types of communication occur together. When they do, words take a back seat to the nonverbal aspect of the message. Nonverbal cues intensify verbal messages. For example, an angry person's tone of voice, facial expression, and gestures may be more important than what he or she says.

Children are not only receptive to, but also sensitive to how their parents communicate with them. Small babies sense warmth, caring, and trust in the way parents hold and talk to them. Babies also communicate their needs. From birth, they cry when their basic needs are not met. The piercing wail of a hungry baby usually brings fast results. Babies communicate contentment with coos, gurgles, and smiles.

Small children quickly learn to sense when parents are pleased with what they are doing. They can also sense when parents are upset by their behavior. Small children have special ways of communicating with their parents, too. Before a child learns to speak, the child may tug at a parent's clothes to get attention. A child may take a parent's hand and pull the parent to a desired location. If these attempts at communication fail, children may intentionally misbehave. Even if it means they will be scolded, these children quickly learn that misbehaving will get their parents' attention.

Older children's ability to communicate with their parents often depends on the communication patterns established in the family. In families where communication is strained or nonexistent, older children may resort to drastic measures to ask for help. When they are troubled, older children are more likely to turn to their parents if they already communicate freely with them. If the lines of communication are open, older children know when and how to seek their parents' advice, 5-6.

Effectively Using Nonverbal Communication

Nonverbal communication is important for emotional understanding. The emotional content of a message is given more accurately by nonverbal communication than by verbal means. In fact, feelings of happiness, anger, and fear can be expressed without a verbal

Parts of Communication

Nonverbal communication	Sender	Receiver
	Body movements, including gestures	Viewer
	Facial expressions	Viewer
	Touch (how rough or gentle)	Person who is touched
	Tone of voice	Listener
Verbal communication	**Sender**	**Receiver**
	Spoken words	Listener
	Written words	Reader

5-5 Communication is an interaction between the sender and the receiver.

message. Social interactions often involve nonverbal communication, such as the nod of a head or a face that means "I'm serious" or "I'm kidding." By school age, some children try to deceive by looking completely innocent and using the "Who, me?" expression.

There are many types of nonverbal cues. How these cues are used depends on a person's culture. For example, in some cultures, the voice is raised in anger, but in other cultures, the voice is lowered in anger. See 5-7 for additional types of nonverbal cues and how they might be used.

For the most part, nonverbal cues are learned indirectly. Expressive adults help children learn these cues. Adults may directly teach some nonverbal behaviors. For example, saying, "During the concert, we sit still and do not whisper" and then modeling this behavior will have a great impact on children.

Children can interpret nonverbal and verbal messages before they can send them. Young children rely on the tone of the voice. Between 7 and 10 years, children can easily interpret facial expressions although they still listen to the voice. Parents use nonverbal communication effectively when they

5-6 This child knows when his parents listen to him, and he seeks their advice when he needs it.

- use warm and caring nonverbal cues, such as positive facial expressions, good eye contact, and soft voice tones

- sit or stand within an arms length of the child

- keep the eyes at the same level as the child's and lean forward

- avoid sending mixed messages, such as using an angry or sad tone of voice while smiling

Types of Nonverbal Cues

- **Body movements**—moving forward or backward, moving suddenly or slowly
- **Head placement**—tilting the head to one side, bowing it
- **Body position**—leaning forward or backward, standing or sitting
- **Gestures**—clenching or pounding fist, nodding, beckoning, shaking hands
- **Touching**—holding gently or firmly, patting or stroking back
- **Facial expressions**—winking, frowning, smiling
- **Eye contact**—looking at, looking away, staring
- **Nonword sounds**—whistling, laughing, crying, humming
- **Changing voice**—louder or softer, higher or lower pitch, talking faster or slower

5-7 There are many types of nonverbal cues. Your culture helps determine what these cues mean to you.

Using Active Listening

Parents communicate most effectively when they listen carefully and observe the nonverbal cues of their child. **Active listening** is hearing the total message, verbal and nonverbal, and making responses to promote mutual understanding. Active listening is also called *reflective listening*. The listener focuses all attention on the receiver. The listener does not just listen passively, but also "listens" with the eyes and the ears. He or she reacts in a way that responds to the message communicated as well as the child's feelings. To be an effective active listener, the parent should do the following:

- *Talk less and listen more.* If you are a parent and your children want to talk, turn off the TV. Put down your newspaper or close your book. Stop what you are doing and pay attention, 5-8. This

shows children you care about them and what they have to say.

- *Acknowledge what is being said.* Nod your head or repeat simple phrases, such as "I see" or "Uh-huh," to indicate you are listening. You can ask questions to summarize points if they become long and drawn out. This helps children know whether you understand.

- *Acknowledge feelings.* Show you understand how the child feels by saying, "You must feel very angry" or something more fitting. Children sometimes do not understand their own feelings. Having a parent acknowledge how they may feel helps children deal with these feelings.

Active listening encourages the speaker to share, and it makes the message clearer. It also makes the speaker feel respected and accepted. With active listening, there is less chance for misinterpretations of ideas.

Using Open Communication

Open communication is the sharing of thoughts and feelings between two people, such as a parent and a child. With open communication, both parent and child

5-8 Giving a child your complete attention as he speaks can make him feel valued and loved.

communicate honestly. They share their thoughts and feelings as best they can and do not hide how they really feel. This sounds simple enough, but isn't always easy. These problems can occur:

- People can't always identify how they feel, much less explain these feelings to someone else.

- The receiver must understand the message in the same way the sender meant it, or miscommunication occurs. This understanding is extremely important, and it plays a major role in effective family communication. Miscommunication can cause conflict and misunderstandings.

- The receiver must be willing to hear and accept the message. If not, open communication will not occur. For instance, if the parent thinks the child's message is silly or wrong, the child will not feel able to openly share thoughts and feelings.

Many problems can be overcome with effort. Success breeds more success. Open communication promotes understanding, sharing, respect, and trust among family members.

Using "I" and "We" Messages

Experts agree that how people use words in their messages impacts how others receive the messages. For example, when people use **"you" messages**, they place all the blame for a situation on others, creating defensiveness and resistance. These statements may cause conflicts instead of improving family relationships. "You" messages tend to create greater distance between people, especially parents and children.

How can parents communicate with their children without creating defensiveness or resistance? They can use "I" and "we" messages. **"I" messages** describe a thought, feeling, or other experience in the singular,

first-person manner. "I" messages give the responsibility for an issue to the person making the statement. "I" messages allow the speaker to declare how he or she feels without attacking the other person.

"We" messages imply that two or more people are jointly involved in a situation. "We" statements increase the togetherness and sense of cooperation in a relationship. "I" or "we" messages related to parenting contain three statements that express

- how the parent feels, such as happy, sad, hurt, or proud

- what behavior by the child caused the parent to feel this way

- why the behavior is pleasing or upsetting the parent

Both "I" and "we" messages are less threatening than "you" messages and do not provoke rebellion or resistance in negative situations. They also promote compliance when parents use them to encourage or praise their children. Parents can use these statements when communicating with their children about specific problems or about events in which children are successful, 5-9.

5-9 By using "I" and "we" messages, children are more likely to listen and respond positively.

Using Communication Techniques for Specific Problems

Thomas Gordon, a psychologist who worked with parents and families, proposed that parents choose communication techniques that fit certain situations. To do this, parents have to define **problem ownership** or determine who owns the problem. The person who owns a problem is the person most concerned or upset by it. Here are the three major types of problem ownership and how to handle them.

Child Owns the Problem

These are problems that affect the child, but do not directly affect the parent. Some problems the child owns include rejection by friends, sibling squabbles, or problems with schoolwork. The parent cannot directly change these problems. Instead the parent should work like a counselor who cares for the child and wants the child to figure out how to resolve the problem.

To do this, the parent engages in active listening and open communication. The parent pays attention to the child who talks about the problem. The parent does not offer possible solutions. Instead, the parent focuses on the child's feelings and restates those feelings using words different from those of the child.

Using active listening and open communication helps keep parents from making costly mistakes when trying to help their children solve problems. Even with good intentions, parents still make mistakes. They may do the following:

- *Take over the problem.* Parents may immediately take over when their child has a problem. This can give the child the message that he or she doesn't know how to handle the problem. Taking over puts parents in the middle of peer or sibling disputes or in the middle of teacher-child relationships.

- *Tell their children what to do.* Children like to feel they can share in the decision-making process. Parents who want to make all their children's decisions for them eliminate children's chances to learn to make decisions. Children may either become very dependent on the parents' control or rebel against it.

- *Give too much advice.* Some parents tell their children how they handled similar problems when they were young. Well-meaning parents may present their solution as the only possible answer.

- *Make light of a problem.* Children need to be treated with respect and deserve to have their problems viewed as important matters.

- *Block communication.* Well-intentioned parents may use words or phrases that block communication. These words or phrases have the same impact as roadblocks on a street, 5-10. Effective communication comes to a halt. For example, assume a child expresses anger about a friend who doesn't play fairly. If the parent says to her angry child, "You've got to get along with your friends," she would be preaching. What reaction would the mother likely receive from the child? How would this block communication?

Parent Owns the Problem

Some problems directly affect the parents. The child's behavior, for example, may be a problem to the parents because it interferes with meeting a need of their own. Some examples include disturbing or embarrassing a parent.

Three solutions are available to parents. First, they can change their positions, such as deciding it is okay if the child's room is not neat. Second, they can modify the

Roadblocks to Open Communication

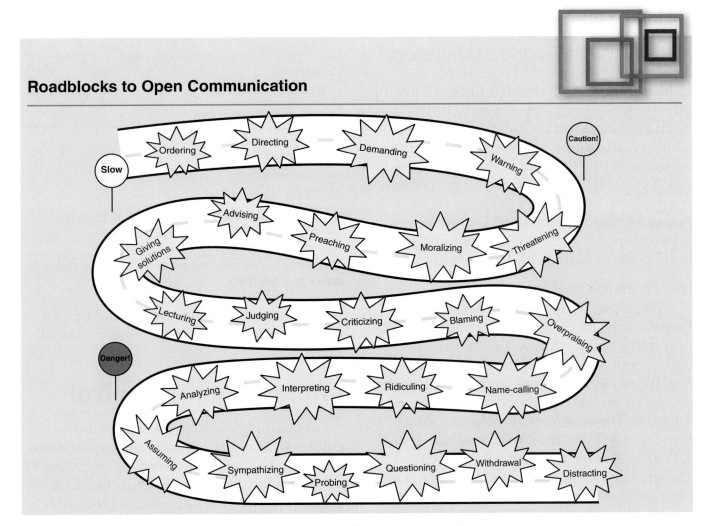

5-10 Keep the lines of communication open by avoiding these roadblocks.

environment to control the child's behavior. For example, having games to play in the car may keep a child from fussing. This resolves the parent's problem. Third, they can send "I" or "we" messages instead of "you" messages.

Think about the following situation. A parent spent an hour cleaning his child's playroom before some guests arrive. Just before their arrival, the parent discovers toys and books scattered throughout the room. The parent says "I feel upset when I look at the playroom and see toys and books scattered on the floor. I worked hard to make our house look nice for our guests. The mess in this room spoils my efforts." How do you think the child responded to the parent sharing his or her feelings by using an "I" message?

"I" and "we" messages replace "you" messages in parent-child communication. As you learned earlier, when parents use "you" messages with their children, they blame or criticize the children for the parents' feelings. When parents use "I" messages and "we" messages, they help children see their problems from others' perspectives. These messages also help children react openly without attacking another person with "you" messages.

In order to solve their problem, parents must examine why the child's behavior bothers them. Is a change in behavior really necessary? Could the problem or emotion come from another source, such as work?

In order to intervene or keep misbehavior from occurring, parents can also send *preventive* "I" messages that express parents' future wants and needs. For example, a mother might say, "I couldn't finish all my office jobs at work today. I need to finish them at home. I want it quiet while I work." Children also welcome the *appreciative* "I" message. A parent might say, "I feel relieved when you call me as soon as you get home from school. I don't want to worry about you as I finish my workday." Preventive and appreciative "I" and "we" messages help build positive parent-child relationships.

Both Own the Problem

These problems are different because they directly affect both parent and child. For example, a child's cluttered room can affect both parent and child. If the child cannot find his or her homework in the morning, the child may be late for school and the parent for work. The solution to problems such as these is called the **"win/win" method**. Figure 5-11 identifies the problem-solving steps that are key to using this method. Here is an example showing how parents and children can use this approach:

1. The parent sends an "I" message to the child (or the child sends it to the parent) identifying the problem.

2. The child and the parent suggest ideas to solve the problem.

3. The child and parent agree to try one solution acceptable to both.

4. The parent and child try the solution for an agreed period of time.

5. The parent and child evaluate how the solution worked.

If the solution works, they continue. If it does not work, they go back to step 2. Sometimes children need reminders about the agreed solution. Using these communication techniques will improve

Steps to Problem Solving

1. Identify the problem.
2. Identify alternative solutions.
3. Choose a solution.
4. Implement the solution.
5. Evaluate the solution.

Note: If the solution does not work, go back to step 2 and start again.

5-11 People can use the problem-solving steps to solve any problem.

family communication. Additional tips for good communication in families are listed in 5-12.

Implementing Control

As parents learn to nurture their children, have realistic behavior expectations, and learn to communicate effectively, they must develop strategies for implementing control effectively. Children need the order and consistency that rules and other controls bring to their lives. How can parents do this? Here are a few methods.

Giving Positive Consequences

Children often comply with their parents' expectations especially when the results are positive. To encourage children to continue fulfilling these wishes, parents need to express positive consequences. Try these methods:

- ***Reinforce the child with a positive personal message.*** This message affirms a child's compliance with a rule. It also reminds him or her of the rule and the reason for it. For example, a parent might say, "I appreciate the way you moved the

Tips for Good Family Communication

- Recognize the feelings of each member.
- Encourage members to express good feelings as well as bad feelings.
- When sending messages, make sure the message is received as you intended. Ask for feedback if you are uncertain.
- When receiving messages, avoid jumping to conclusions.
- Provide feedback using both verbal and nonverbal acknowledgement.
- Watch for nonverbal messages and clues.
- Open the door to communication by inviting members to talk to you. Tell them you are interested and concerned about them.
- Pick a good time to begin a discussion.

5-12 Following these guidelines can improve family communication.

toys out of the hallway to the playroom. Now we all have a safe path to walk from the kitchen to the living room."

- *Acknowledge the benefits of following a rule over a period of time.* For example, the parent can say, "You studied each day and did all your school assignments. Your grade shows all your hard work. Studying really paid off!"

- *Give privileges connected to the desired behaviors.* For example, a parent can say, "You learned boating safety rules. Now you can take a ride in the boat with me. We will practice those rules."

Using Negative Consequences

Despite a parent's best efforts to set behavior limits, children still misbehave. Children experiment with both positive and negative behaviors as they learn how to behave. Misbehavior can be the parents' best chance to guide and direct their children. At times, parents can be so upset by misbehavior that they do not take advantage of this opportunity. How parents handle such situations will influence how children feel about themselves.

Negative consequences, either established by the parent or occurring as a result of misbehavior, reduce the chances that the child will repeat undesired behaviors. Some of these consequences also teach desirable alternative behaviors. Children need to learn to correct their own misbehaviors.

Children need to know that their parents still love them even when they disapprove of the children's behavior. If children must receive punishment, they should understand it is only their behavior that is unacceptable. It is important that parents reassure children they will always love them. Parents should never threaten to withdraw their love to get their children to behave.

Determine the Cause of Misbehavior

Before dealing with problem behavior, parents should try to determine *why* a child is misbehaving. For instance, some children may misbehave to get attention. These children would rather be punished than feel ignored by their parents. Children who feel ignored on a continual basis desperately want to be loved. When good behavior goes unrecognized, they misbehave to get the attention they seek.

If a child who gets regular, positive parental attention misbehaves to get attention, the parents should ignore the misbehavior if possible. If the misbehavior is not reinforced, children are less likely to repeat it. When the child is using positive behavior, the parents should try to give extra attention to the child, 5-13. Doing so will encourage the child to repeat the desired behavior.

5-13 Showing affection with a hug is one of the most helpful kinds of positive reinforcement.

In addition to examining why a child misbehaves, parents need to look at their parenting methods. Sometimes parents undermine their own rules. For example, the child may be seeing differences between parents in beliefs about rules. The child may also pick up on the parents' chuckles at his or her misbehavior. Parents are often inconsistent on enforcing their own limits. They need to ask themselves, "What messages are we sending?" Parents who use the techniques that follow have the most success in helping children learn appropriate behavior.

Use Punishment with Care

If misbehavior requires the parent to take action, the child should see the punishment as the result of his or her *willful* misbehavior. If a child doesn't know he or she is doing something wrong, parents should not use punishment. Instead, the child should be given a chance to explain his or her behavior. This will reveal if the child's misbehavior is due to a lack of understanding or too little knowledge. Parents need to make this distinction when deciding whether to use punishment or another way to guide behavior.

Choose Punishment That Fits

When punishment is necessary, parents should choose one that fits the misbehavior. If it is a minor offense, the punishment should also be minor. Suppose a child repeatedly rides his or her tricycle into the flower garden (breaking the house rule to stay on the walkway). In this case, a punishment that fits would be for the child to park the tricycle in the garage for a time. If the misbehavior is a first offense, only a warning may be needed. Punishment should not be too harsh for the misbehavior.

Sometimes parents handle misbehavior by offering alternate activities. Rather than telling children they can't do something, parents can suggest another activity instead. For instance, if two children fight over the same toy, a parent might invite them to join him or her in a game. If children get rowdy indoors, parents might suggest an outdoor activity.

Use Punishment Infrequently

Parents should carefully balance punishment with positive ways of guiding behavior. In certain cases, parents may need to withdraw privileges when a child does not comply with the rules. For example, if a child skips a required activity to do a preferred activity, the parents can withdraw the preferred activity until the child complies.

Some parents use **time-out** to withdraw their misbehaving children from an activity or the presence of other children, 5-14. Experts believe you should limit this form of punishment. It is not appropriate for children younger than preschool-age and is seldom effective after a child is age 7 or 8. Use time-out when children display aggressive, antisocial, or destructive behaviors. Usually, the time the child spends in time-out is limited to five minutes or less or until the child is calm.

On rare occasions, some parents use physical punishment. However, it is generally the least effective method for changing behavior. Children who receive physical punishment often feel hurt, rejection, humiliation, and anger. They are not likely to remember what they did wrong after they are punished. Instead, resentment begins to build within them. What they do learn is that hitting is an acceptable form of behavior. Physical punishment is more likely to lead to child abuse. It may also lead the child to use physical violence to settle his or her own disputes.

Use Natural Consequences

Children need to recognize the impact their behavior has on themselves and others. A long-term parenting goal is to help children learn to discipline themselves. One of the most effective ways to teach children is for them to experience the **natural consequences**, or common results, of their misbehavior. The misbehavior, not the parent, brings the consequences. Natural consequences show children that actions have results. For example, if a child comes late to dinner, the food will be cold. If a child handles a toy roughly, the toy breaks. In situations such as these, the parents do not need to impose further punishment.

If a child's safety or health is in danger, parents should not use natural consequences. For example, parents cannot allow a child to play in a dangerous street. Although natural consequences would likely occur, the consequences would put the child's safety at risk. Likewise, parents cannot permit a child to forego tooth brushing. The natural consequences would be a health risk. Parents can point out the natural consequences of risky behaviors, such as saying, "The range is hot; it will hurt (or burn) your fingers. Just look at the range."

Use Logical Consequences

Because harmless natural consequences are limited, parents often explain the logical consequences that result from a child's misbehavior. **Logical consequences** are adult-planned consequences that show a direct link between misbehavior and the consequences, 5-15. For example, if a child doesn't put dirty clothes in the laundry basket, the child will not have clean clothes. The child sees the link between the misbehavior and the consequence, and changes the behavior to avoid the consequence.

5-14 One effective way of discouraging negative behavior is to have the child sit alone for a few minutes.

5-15 Parents should discuss and agree on how to handle their child's misbehavior. Time alone helps parents prepare for certain misbehaviors before they occur.

Implementing Consequences

In getting their children to comply with behavior standards, parents should not act impulsively. Careful thought and planning help parents identify how they will respond to certain types of misbehavior. When a child does not comply, parents should implement the consequence in a calm, but firm, way. Many find the following method helpful:

1. *State the rule.* For example, "Play with your toys. I can't let you throw them at your brother when you are angry. Throwing things hurts others." Wait a few seconds for the child to comply.

2. *If the child does not comply, give the "either-or" warning.* For example, say, "Either quit throwing toys, or you'll have to put your toys on the toy shelf." Wait a few seconds, but do not count aloud.

3. *Summarize the situation and repeat the warning.* For example, "I know you are upset at your brother, but I can't let you throw toys. If you don't stop, you will have to put your toys on the toy shelf."

4. *Restate the consequence.* "Put your toys on the toy shelf now!"

5. *Implement the consequence and ignore any pleas from the child.* Accompany the child to the toy shelf. Do not respond to pleas.

Implementing a consequence shows the child there is a limit to his or her inappropriate actions. It also shows that the parent means business! The child may resist, shout, or run. The parent cannot let the child "get by" with these actions because the inappropriate behavior becomes ingrained. If the child breaks another rule, such as kicking the parent, repeat the sequence with a new warning. For example, the child might go to time-out and then return toys to the toy shelf.

Parents as Positive Role Models

Parents are their children's primary role models. Children learn values from observing others. They imitate and identify with their parents' use of language, behaviors, and emotions, and their values. Because of this, it is important for parents to be aware of the positive and negative examples they may set. If parents guide their children in a caring and loving way, children tend to relate to others in the same manner. When a child's parents care about other people's feelings, children will likely model this behavior in their own relationships. When parents follow rules and laws, children are more likely to do the same.

If parents are positive role models, they will help children build an inner voice that helps the children choose positive behavior. Most parents try hard to set a good example—one they hope their children will follow, 5-16.

5-16 When parents model appropriate behavior, such as wearing a bicycle helmet, children are more likely to follow their lead.

Developing Self-Control and Self-Discipline

A continuous task of parents is to transmit society's expectations about behavior to their children. They tell and show their children how to comply countless times. When parents reward good behavior and provide consequences for misbehavior, they help their children learn *self-control* and *self-discipline*. What does it mean for children to have self-control and self-discipline? What can parents do to help their children develop these traits? As you read the following, think about how the youngsters you know

have learned to behave properly. How can this information help set you on the path to encouraging children to develop self-control and self-discipline?

Encouraging Self-Control and Self-Discipline

To fit into their social setting, children must be taught their culture's norms regarding emotional expression. Norms, or general practices, dictate how people may express emotions. They also tell which emotions are acceptable in certain situations and which are not. Learning to control the expression of emotions, or *self-control*, is highly important to children and to society. Self-control relates to positive interactions with family members and friends. It also relates to stress management, moral development, and positive attitude.

Learning to control emotions is a developmental task of childhood and is a gradual process. Parents play a crucial role in helping their children to identify their emotions, understand them, and understand those of others. Children must also be able to separate their feelings from their actions. This is key to learning self-control. It takes time and patience on the part of parents. They do not try to restrict their child's feelings. However, parents *do* try to change the behaviors their child may use in certain intense situations. For example, they may teach a child appropriate words to use as a substitute for physical actions.

Parents desire their children to monitor their emotions, react with appropriate behavior, and take responsibility for their actions. The self-control a child needs for these tasks goes hand-in-hand with self-discipline. **Self-discipline** is judging what behavior is right or wrong and acting appropriately. People with self-discipline feel good about themselves and can control negative impulses.

Like self-control, self-discipline emerges gradually. By the middle childhood years, some self-discipline links more closely to situations (current events) than to age. Even adults may function with different levels of self-discipline, 5-17.

Helping children to develop a sense of control over their lives is an important task for parents. By teaching the reasons behind the rules, children will incorporate the rules within themselves and fit rules to new situations. At some point, children will develop self-control and self-discipline and no longer need their parent's direction.

As in other areas of development, parental attitudes and practices can support the child's development in positive ways. Nurturance, realistic expectations, constructive communication, and effective control methods are the most important aspects of parenting for self-control and self-discipline. Think about how you might use the following information when parenting children.

Provide Nurturance

In happy, well-adjusted families, parents respect and nurture each person. Rules are an expression of family values. Because children want to belong to this warm, loving family, they feel secure in knowing just what parents expect of them and why.

Using patience and support, rather than strictly relying on punishment, helps the children develop self-control and self-discipline. Parents can encourage these traits by

- recognizing their children's emotional state and responding appropriately. Through the parents' response, children

Emergence of Self-Discipline

Age of Child	Characteristics of Self-Discipline
Infants and toddlers	• Child is not ready to learn self-discipline. • Parents rely on physical interventions and brief commands to manage their child's behavior.
Preschoolers and early school-age children	• Parents regulate behavior. • The child follows rules to get a positive consequence and avoid a negative one. • The child knows some rules, but does not understand the "whys" behind them. Until a child can mentally see things from another's perspective, there is no concern for other's welfare. • The child performs the expected behaviors under parents' (and other adults') supervision. The longer this type of supervision continues, the more difficult it is to wean children from direct supervision.
Children in middle childhood years	• The child wants to be like important people in his or her life. The child will follow the rules their models follow. • The child begins to treat some rules as a logical extension of their own values. They now understand the reasons behind the rules and feel a commitment to follow them. This is the beginnings of self-discipline.

5-17 Self-discipline emerges in adolescents who have democratic parents, but its foundation is laid in early childhood.

learn that their feelings are important. Parents teach their children how to cope with their emotions, too. Effective coping skills are essential for developing self-control and self-discipline.

- reducing negative emotions through sensitive and responsive caregiving. In this way, children have more positive feelings and are better able to control negative reactions. For example, by providing a regular schedule for eating, sleeping, and play activities, parents help their children avoid displaying negative emotions.

- avoiding high levels of stress for which children are not yet ready to cope. Children learn to handle stress when their parents set a steady pace for age-appropriate activities and social interactions. For example, parents can limit the number of daily activities or monitor the content of certain TV programs.

- comforting children who are sad or fearful. When children are afraid of the dark, for example, parents must first calmly comfort their children and offer encouraging words. Then parents can take other actions to help eliminate fears, such as turning on a night-light. When children learn to persevere through negative emotions or stressful events, self-control and self-discipline are strengthened.

Set Realistic Behavior Expectations

Realistic behavior expectations go hand-in-hand with developing self-control and self-discipline. Although children do not generally show these traits until school age, parents lay the foundation for them in the preschool years. To develop self-control and self-discipline, children must identify feelings in themselves and in others and know what

events trigger these feelings. Children also need to experience a range of emotions, 5-18. For that reason, children should not be shielded from such common emotions as disappointment or sadness.

As they teach about behavior expectations, parents need to help children see the effects of their behavior (the reasons behind the limits) on themselves, others, and the environment. When children have this understanding, they are more likely to accept there are things they must do regardless of personal desires. As they grow and develop, children learn to separate feelings from actions and take ownership for their actions. They accept that there may be positive or negative consequences for their behavior. When children show commitment to acting

5-18 Allowing children to identify their feelings helps them learn to deal with emotions in positive ways.

properly and following rules without constant supervision, parents know their children are becoming socially competent.

Promote Positive Communication

Along the path to developing self-control and self-discipline, children encounter many challenges. As they develop, children begin to connect language, emotions, and rules with their behavior. When parents communicate positively, children more often react with appropriate behavior. While setting limits and reasoning with their children, parents' positive communication is especially important. For example, when parents explain a behavior and then model it, their children see the desired behavior. When parents link new situations with a certain limit, they help children see that a behavior fits other situations. Not only does positive communication result in children behaving properly, it also results in less family stress. Here are some helpful techniques that parents can use.

- *Name emotions when they occur in their children.* This way the young child gets the connection between an event, a physical reaction, and the name of the emotion. For example, a preschooler might climb to the top of a slide and say, "Look at me!" The parent responds, "You climbed all the way by yourself. That's exciting!" The parent's voice matches the emotion.

- *Encourage their children to talk openly about their emotions.* For example, the parent can say, "You look frightened. What happened?"

- *Describe feelings to others rather than use inappropriate actions.* For example, the parent can say, "You are angry because your brother took your blocks. I cannot let you hit him because hitting hurts, but you can tell him how you feel."

- *See cues that tell how another person is feeling.* The parent may point out a facial expression and say, "Naomi is crying. She is unhappy." The parent may also draw attention to the situation by saying, "Jessica spilled her milk. She looks upset."

- *Discuss how everyday events affect the parent's feelings.* By doing this, parents show their child that everyone has similar emotions. The child also sees the parent's effective coping skills.

- *Validate the child's feelings.* The parent can say, "I see why you feel so (name of emotion)." The parent never denies their child's expressed emotions, such as saying, "You don't really feel (name of emotion)."

- *Empathize with the child's feelings.* The parent can say, "You must feel so (name the emotion)." The parent *never* shames or labels his or her child for the child's emotional response, such as saying, "Big boys aren't afraid. Why are you a scaredy-cat?"

- *State behavior expectations clearly.* For example, a parent might state a behavior limit and the parent's feelings behind it this way: "I see you are in a hurry to play. It upsets me when you leave your dirty school clothes on the floor in your room. I have to pick them up before I can do the laundry. Please put them in the laundry-room basket before you play."

Enforce Reasonable Rules

Enforcing rules consistently is a major parenting task. Parents desire to help their children understand their emotions and those of others. In order to encourage their children to talk openly about feelings, parents should try not to diffuse emotions too quickly. However, parents do need to set clear limits on inappropriate actions resulting from emotions. For example, anger often leads to attempts to hurt. Parents should stop this action and work with their child on more appropriate responses.

Using logical consequences more than punishment and accepting mistakes are important to developing self-control and self-discipline in children. When children remember an expectation without a reminder, it is important for parents to respond with a warm, positive personal message. For example, a parent might say, "I have noticed you have become more careful in completing your schoolwork. I am very pleased." Positive expressions reinforce desired behaviors, 5-19. Parents should never use negative labels to reinforce positive behavior.

Handling Aggression

Aggression is not an emotion, but does show lack of self-control and self-discipline. It is an action that results in physical or emotional injury to a person or animal or damage to property. Aggression often follows anger or frustration and can be a real problem for parents and their children. There are four types of aggression. *Accidental* aggression is unintentional, such as bumping into a sibling while playing. *Expressive* aggression is done for the enjoyment of the act, such as kicking toys just to make noise.

Instrumental aggression is used to achieve a goal, such as fighting over objects, territory, or rights. *Hostile* aggression is a deliberate act of ill will, such as bullying someone.

Accidental aggression can occur as early as infancy. Expressive and instrumental aggression both start around age 2. Hostile aggression is seen in older preschoolers and school-age children as well as adolescents and adults.

It is important for parents to know that *all* children can exhibit aggression. At the same time, they should know it is important to teach children that aggression is unacceptable. Setting firm limits helps children learn how to control anger and use strategies that are not hurtful. Figure 5-20 shows some ways that parents help children curb aggression.

Avoiding physical punishment is also important in handling aggression. Physical punishment tends to teach children that hitting is okay when dealing with problems.

5-19 When parents positively reinforce desired behaviors, children are more likely to repeat them.

Helping Children Curb Aggression

- Model calmness, problem solving, and willingness to compromise.
- Reinforce positive behaviors, such as sharing.
- Reduce frustration in a child's day. Having a regular daily routine and letting children know when changes will occur helps eliminate aggressive behavior.
- Screen media content for violence. Do not allow children to watch violent programs.
- Set clear limits and enforce them consistently.
- Use time-out to let a child calm down before teaching effective ways to handle emotions.
- Teach children to respond verbally rather than physically.

5-20 Dealing with aggression can be a challenge for parents. These ideas can help.

Ignoring aggression also leads to a child becoming more aggressive. The child sees this parental act as a reward for the aggressive behavior.

Increasing Self-Concept and Self-Esteem

Parents' nurturance, reasonable behavior expectations, constructive communication, and effective control, support the child's development in positive ways. Nurturance and communication are most important for the development of self-concept and self-esteem.

Self-concept and self-esteem are aspects of development that have close ties. A child's **self-concept** is his or her mental image of himself or herself. It also includes how the child sees his or her actions, the child's view of how others see him or her, and the child's view about reactions others have to him or her. This self-concept may be healthy or unhealthy. Children may see themselves as they are, or they may have unrealistic ideas about who they really are.

While self-concept describes how a person sees himself or herself, **self-esteem** is how that person *feels* about himself or herself. In other words, the child evaluates his or her self-concept. This evaluation is self-esteem. Self-esteem includes how a person values and likes himself or herself (worth), beliefs about his or her ability to achieve goals (competence), and feelings about his or her ability to influence life events (control).

People with healthy self-esteem think of themselves as likable and competent and think their actions impact what happens to them. They expect to do well with challenges. They expect social interactions to be rewarding. They trust their own ideas and will defend their viewpoints if other people challenge them.

In contrast, people with low self-esteem have opposite feelings. Sometimes they tear others down in order to build themselves up. Underneath their surface confidence, they are most fragile. See 5-21 for indicators of self-esteem.

Many people think self-esteem is an either/or situation. They think you either have self-esteem or you don't. You either feel good or bad about yourself. In reality, everyone has ups and downs, as well as secure and insecure moments. People grow from these experiences if they learn from their mistakes and their successes. A person's self-esteem fluctuates over time, even on a given day.

Stressful situations and events may affect a child's self-esteem. For instance, a child may move with his or her family to a new home and have to go to a new school. The events may be very upsetting. The result may be a temporary loss of self-esteem. As the child becomes more comfortable in this new setting, his or her self-esteem will likely return.

Fostering Self-Concept and Self-Esteem

Self-concept and self-esteem are products of a child's social interactions. Because parents are the most important people in a child's life, their influence is the greatest. Parents have a dramatic impact on their child's self-concept and self-esteem. They are good mirrors through which children see and judge themselves. When parents guide and discipline their children in a positive way, they foster healthy development of self-concept and self-esteem.

Provide Nurturance

As parents show their children affection, they take an interest in what their children are doing and interact with them, 5-22. They are patient in helping children to achieve goals. Showing children encouragement, love, and support helps them develop a healthy, realistic self-concept and self-esteem.

Self-Esteem Indicators

Person with Self-Esteem	Person Lacking Self-Esteem
• Is not afraid of new situations	• Lacks initiative
• Makes friends easily	• Depends on others for direction
• Tries new ideas and projects	• Usually asks for permission
• Trusts teachers or others in authority	• Is not spontaneous
• Cooperates and follows reasonable rules	• Enters few new activities
• Manages behavior responsibly	• Prefers to be alone
• Is creative and imaginative	• Does not say much
• Talks freely	• Is possessive
• Is an independent worker	• May respond to threats by being aggressive or withdrawing
• Is generally happy	• Is easily frustrated

5-21 These signs can help parents identify a child's level of self-esteem.

5-22 Having good relationships with their parents positively influences children's self-concepts.

Set Realistic Behavior Expectations

In order to encourage healthy self-concept and self-esteem, parents should have realistic behavioral expectations. Expectations for developing a child's positive self-concept and self-esteem include

- encouraging the child's independence as appropriate for his or her age/stage.

- helping the child to positively compare traits with those of his or her cultural group and express pride. The child should become aware of differences in the traits of other groups in positive, accepting ways.

- creating a climate in which the child is comfortable in expressing his or her own opinions and feelings. This should be done in respectful ways.

- encouraging the child to work out his or her own problems. Parents should be supportive through active listening.

- encouraging a young child to try many things to see what he or she is "good" at.

By the middle childhood years, parents encourage the child to concentrate mainly on self-selected activities that result in feelings of success and pride.

Promote Positive Communication

How parents communicate with children, affects self-concept and self-esteem. By modeling courteous talk and behavior, parents can create an environment that encourages positive communications. They can engage their children in conversations in which the children take the lead. This shows the parents' interest, acceptance, and caring. Through conversations, parents are a source of information and guidance.

Parents can use **behavioral reflections** as their child works toward goals. These reflections are nonjudgmental statements regarding some aspect of their child's behavior. For example, the parent says "You are working hard on the requirements for your merit badge. That project is interesting and has a lot of detail." In cases such as these, the child notes the parent's interest and does not need to "act out" to get attention. Making the child more aware of his or her own efforts creates feelings of self-esteem, too.

As children face challenges, parents should take a supportive role through active listening. By not offering to solve the problem, the child handles it, thinking "I am capable." Parents express their acceptance of their child's feelings (anger, jealousy, sadness), but do not "take sides" on the problem. Although they may know their child's solution will not work, they allow their child to fail in order to teach. However, they remain supportive of their child by comforting and encouraging the child to "try again."

Enforce Reasonable Rules

Although they have high expectations, parents use their authority to set reasonable limits. They clearly explain limits and the reasons for them to their child. Having limits

says to the child, "You love me. I must be a worthwhile person for you to care."

Children develop self-esteem when they know that loving parents set limits to protect and guide rather than to be harsh, 5-23. In this way, a child also knows misbehaviors are seen by his or her parents as a teaching opportunity. Discipline techniques are fair and never harsh. Parents are careful to use words and actions that do not destroy self-concept and self-esteem even when implementing punishment for misbehavior. The focus is always on the child's behavior.

Avoiding Overindulgence

Indulgent parents will do anything to make life better for their child. They want to create a perfect childhood and believe any upset or setback hurts their child's self-esteem. In many ways, indulgent parents harm their child's self-esteem as much as overly harsh parents do.

5-23 When parents lovingly set limits, children recognize their parent's desire to protect and guide them.

In contrast, most parents believe children can feel too much self-importance. They tend to agree with two psychologists, Laura Smith and Charles Elliott who compare the amount of self-esteem to air used to inflate a balloon. An empty balloon is useless; an overly full one is apt to pop. A well-filled balloon is functional and resilient, or elastic, so it can easily adjust. Effective parents, unlike indulgent ones, believe their children need challenges. They realize this is the way their children become competent adults. These children are well able to find their personal niche in life and true self-concept and self-esteem.

Popular Parenting Methods

Several parenting methods have been devised by psychologists, counselors, educators, and doctors. Each strategy comes from a different perspective, and each has a unique focus. Parents can use these strategies to improve their parenting. They can also learn valuable techniques for interacting with their children. This chapter addresses some of the techniques, such as active listening and "I" messages. See 5-24.

If parents want to learn about well-known parenting methods, they have a few options. First, parents can read books about parenting methods. Second, they could attend workshops or parenting classes on a specific method. They might also ask their doctors, teachers, or counselors what methods they recommend. Another option includes using reliable Web sites for popular parenting information. Whatever source parents choose, they should be sure the information is proven to be reliable and effective. Harm to a child is a high price to pay for not checking out the reliability of parenting information.

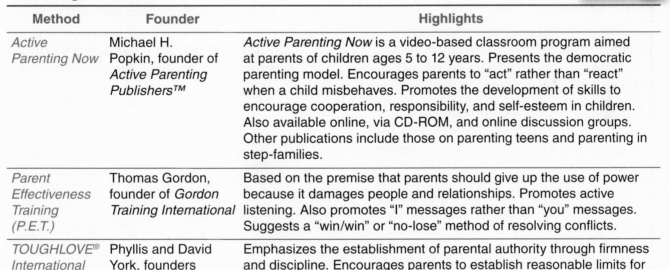

Parenting Methods

Method	Founder	Highlights
Active Parenting Now	Michael H. Popkin, founder of *Active Parenting Publishers™*	*Active Parenting Now* is a video-based classroom program aimed at parents of children ages 5 to 12 years. Presents the democratic parenting model. Encourages parents to "act" rather than "react" when a child misbehaves. Promotes the development of skills to encourage cooperation, responsibility, and self-esteem in children. Also available online, via CD-ROM, and online discussion groups. Other publications include those on parenting teens and parenting in step-families.
Parent Effectiveness Training (P.E.T.)	Thomas Gordon, founder of *Gordon Training International*	Based on the premise that parents should give up the use of power because it damages people and relationships. Promotes active listening. Also promotes "I" messages rather than "you" messages. Suggests a "win/win" or "no-lose" method of resolving conflicts.
TOUGHLOVE® International	Phyllis and David York, founders	Emphasizes the establishment of parental authority through firmness and discipline. Encourages parents to establish reasonable limits for their children's behavior as well as consequences or punishments for violations of those limits. Encourages parents to meet together and support each other during crises.

5-24 Various kinds of parenting programs are available to offer help, support, and training.

Summing It Up

- Helping the child develop social competence is a major parenting goal.

- *Parenting styles* are certain ways of parenting. Three common parenting styles include *authoritarian, permissive,* and *democratic.*

- Strategies focused on nurturance, behavior expectations, communication, and control impact effective parenting.

- Factors such as culture, traditions, religion, politics of a country, family social system, and a child's temperament and personality all impact the parenting style that parents use in raising their children.

- Parents who nurture with unconditional love and sensitive care tend to have realistic behavioral expectations and effective control of their children.

- Communication skills, such as active listening, "I" and "we" messages, and nonverbal communication skills, help build positive parent-child relationships.

- Understanding problem ownership helps parents choose communication techniques that fit situations owned by the child, by the parent, or both.

- Parents may use both positive and negative consequences to get their child to comply with behavioral expectations.

- Parents implement punishment with caution and only for *willful* misbehavior. Punishments should fit the misbehavior and not be too harsh.

- Many parents rely on natural and logical consequences in dealing with their child's misbehavior. The child learns to replace misbehavior with positive behavior.

- Parents nurture and communicate to show concern about their child's feelings and those of other people. This strategy helps children learn self-control.

- Parents view their child's self-control and self-discipline as an ultimate skill leading to social competence.

- Parents encourage self-discipline in their child by linking the current situation to the rule, the rule to the reason for the rule, and the misbehavior to the consequence.

- Setting limits and helping children learn to control anger help curb aggression.

- In fostering self-concept and self-esteem with nurturance and positive communication, effective parents are careful not to overindulge their children.

Recalling the Facts

1. Contrast authoritarian, permissive, and democratic parenting styles for each of the following factors: (A) nurturance, (B) behavior expectations, (C) communication, and (D) control.

2. What factors determine the parenting style that parents choose to use?

3. What is the difference between verbal and nonverbal communication?

4. What should a parent do to be an effective active listener?

5. Explain the difference between *"I" messages* and *"we" messages*.

6. Name five mistakes that parents might make when trying to use active listening when their child owns the problem.

7. When might a parent use the "win/win" method of problem solving? Give an example.

8. What types of positive consequences can parents use to get their children to comply with specific behavior standards?

9. Explain the importance of choosing punishments that fit. What punishment might you consider too harsh for the tricycle incident mentioned on page 122?

10. What forms of punishment should parents use infrequently?

11. Contrast punishment using natural consequences with that of using logical consequences.

12. What must a child be able to do in order to learn self-discipline?

13. Contrast *accidental* aggression with *hostile* aggression.

14. List three effective methods for dealing with aggression.

15. Why should parents avoid physical punishment?

16. What realistic behavior expectations can parents use to foster self-concept and self-esteem?

Applying New Skills

1. **Recognize parenting styles.** In small groups, write and act out short vignettes that involve interactions between parents and their children. Each vignette should clearly demonstrate one of the parenting styles identified in this chapter. After all the groups have presented their vignettes, discuss the parenting styles the class observed. Which parent-child relationships seemed most positive? Which may hinder children in becoming socially competent?

2. **Observe parenting.** For 10 to 15 minutes, observe a preschool or school-age child and parent together in a park, playground, mall, or store. On a sheet of paper, record everything you see and hear. Then respond to these questions: How did the parent handle the child? How often did the parent intervene? How successful were the parent's interventions? What parenting style do you think was being used? (Explain how you came to your conclusion.)

3. **News review.** Collect magazine or newspaper articles of stories about the results of child, adolescent, or adult aggression. Read the articles, analyzing them for reliability of information and bias. What do these articles say about the source of aggression? What implications do these articles have for effective parenting? Write a summary about your conclusions.

Thinking Critically

1. Watch at least three different television shows that involve parents and children. Identify a possible parenting style used in each show. Provide supporting evidence for each parenting style that you identified. Then answer these questions: How does the media influence families and children in regard to parenting style? Are the family portrayals realistic or biased in any way? Share your conclusions with the class.

2. Use a two-column chart to examine the cause and effect relationship of parenting strategies to a child's self-control. Label the left side of the chart "Parenting Strategies (Cause)" and the right side of the chart "Effective Self-Control (Effect)." In the left column, list strategies that parents can use to encourage self-control. In the right column, list the effect that using each strategy will likely have on a child.

3. Distinguish between parenting strategies that enhance a child's self-esteem and those that do not. On a separate sheet of paper, complete the following statement: Parents can improve a child's self-esteem by... Share your responses with the class.

Linking Academics

1. **Quick-write summary.** Summarize the key components of active listening in 10 sentences or less. How does active listening positively influence communication?

2. **Communication.** Write an example of an *"I" message* and a *"we" message* for each of the following problem situations:
   A. A four-year-old constantly asking for things at the store.
   B. Two preschool children fighting over a toy.

Chapter 6

Moral Development and Character

Objectives

After studying this chapter, you will be able to

- summarize moral development, including moral judgments, moral feelings, and moral actions.
- describe the characteristics of moral judgments in the theories of Piaget and Kohlberg.
- explain how both empathy and guilt contribute to moral development.
- describe how Freud's idea of the superego works to make a person moral.
- identify parenting behaviors that help children in developing an internal moral system.
- compare and contrast moral development with character development.
- describe parenting behaviors that encourage the development of responsibility, honesty and integrity, caring, respect, and perseverance.

How do children learn right from wrong? How do they learn what is morally and ethically important in life? How do children develop *ethical values* or moral excellence? Values are absorbed through contact with all socializers, but most of all through family interactions. As children reach adolescence and young adulthood, they often do some soul searching. They define and appraise the values they have grown up with and decide whether to embrace, modify, or completely redefine them. Their decisions will determine their character and the rules they follow.

In this chapter, you will study ideas about moral development and some aspects of character. You will see how these most important elements of development connect to the positive parenting techniques you studied earlier.

Moral Development

Morality is conformity to the ideals of right human conduct. It is important to think about what those ideals include and how parents determine them. Morality includes

- evaluating past, present, and planned (future) actions and events in terms of right and wrong

- holding to and using good (right) conduct consistently

- being aware that moral decisions result in emotional responses, either positive or negative

- having a concern for others' well-being and acting on that concern, such as being just and fair in dealings with others

Moral development is a gradual process of learning to behave in ways that show an understanding of the difference between right and wrong. Moral competence depends on intellectual, emotional, and social development. In general, children fully achieve moral competence in the later stages of their development, 6-1. In fact, some aspects of moral development occur in the adult years.

Reasoning About Right and Wrong

One aspect of moral development involves **moral judgments** or how children reason or think about rules for ethical conduct. Two psychologists, Jean Piaget and Lawrence Kohlberg, created the better-known theories about moral judgments. Piaget, a Swiss psychologist who began his research in the early 1900s, studied children's intellectual development in many areas,

6-1 This child is displaying moral behavior by observing rather than touching the bird's nest.

including moral judgment. Kohlberg, an American psychologist, based his studies of moral judgment on Piaget's research. Unlike Piaget, Kohlberg carried his study of moral judgment into the adult years. Both Piaget and Kolhberg had a major impact on the study of moral development.

Piaget and Kohlberg found that young people between the ages of 10 and 18 develop moral reasoning more rapidly than people at any other stage of life. At this time, there is a developmental change from behavior that is externally controlled (by adults) to behavior that is controlled by internal standards and principles (by self). This internal control is due to intellectual maturity and exposure to a variety of ethical issues. These issues lead children to examine the moral standards of their parents and others.

Piaget and Kohlberg found a strong link between intellectual reasoning and learning moral judgment. Their studies showed that change in moral judgment occurs in stages. Perhaps you can recognize some of these stages in children, in your peers, or even in yourself.

Piaget's Theory

Piaget studied moral judgments of children ages 4 through 12 by interviewing them about rules for the game of marbles. He then observed them play. As they played, he noted their cooperation, fairness (who goes first), mutual action (taking turns), and justice (giving up a marble if they lost).

Based on his observations of game playing, Piaget developed a set of stories about moral conflicts. He used the stories for individual interviews of children. During the interviews, the children heard the stories, made moral decisions, and justified their answers.

Piaget noted two distinct stages of moral reasoning. In the first stage, called *moral realism,* children view rules with high value and as unchanging. They also view justice as whatever the authority figure expects or commands. In the second stage, called *moral relativism,* children weigh the intentions of others before judging their actions as right or wrong. Piaget also noted a period of transition between the two stages. Figure 6-2 explains Piaget's stages.

Kohlberg's Theory

Kohlberg patterned his studies of moral judgment after those of Piaget. Like Piaget, he developed stories in which characters face moral dilemmas. After interviewing children for over 20 years, Kohlberg developed his theory. He believed three levels of moral judgments exist:

- *Level 1—preconventional reasoning.* Children in this level, generally under 9 years of age, behave in ways that allow them to avoid punishment or gain rewards.

- *Level 2—conventional reasoning.* During early adolescence, children alter their behavior to conform to the expectations of others, such as parents, teachers, and society in general.

- *Level 3—postconventional reasoning.* At this level, people base their behaviors more on abstract principles of right and wrong. A person makes moral decisions using internal moral values. This level occurs during adulthood, but not all adults reach this level.

Each of Kohlberg's six levels of moral judgments is divided into two stages. See Figure 6-3 for a full description of these stages.

Feelings About Moral Matters

A second feature of moral development is that it has emotional elements. Child development experts believe that both positive and negative feelings contribute to moral development. Two major emotions

Piaget's Stages of Moral Development

Stage 1—Moral Realism

Age of children	Characteristics of children forming moral judgments
4 through 7 years	• Consider rules as unchangeable • See rules as an extension of all-powerful authority figures, such as parents • Believe everyone should obey rules • Believe in absolute values. All behavior is either *all* right or *all* wrong • Judge fairness in terms of treating everyone the same • Evaluate actions on the basis of consequences, such as the amount of damage, not on the basis of a person's intent • Are generally able to verbalize "good" behavior but do not always act on it • Believe what is right in one situation may not be in another • Do what is right for fear of punishment or loss of approval • Believe that punishment for breaking rules is automatic

Transition Phase

Age of children	Characteristics of children forming moral judgments
7 through 10 years	• Develop some shared give-and-take understandings • Believe that what is fair is more important than the given "rule" • Believe punishment may or may not be fair, depending on the rule violation

Stage 2—Moral Relativism

Age of children	Characteristics of children forming moral judgments
11 years and up	• Are aware that people create rules and laws that are socially agreed upon • Realize that rules can change through reasoning, discussion, and agreement • Judge fairness in terms of *equity* (fair treatment, but unequal treatment because of differing circumstances) • Take intent and consequences into account when assessing wrongdoing • Believe punishment is socially set and occurs only if the relevant person sees the misbehavior

6-2 Young children believe rules are to be obeyed to get approval or avoid punishment by authority figures, especially parents and teachers. As children age, moral judgments become more mature as a result of peer relations. Peers, as socializers, help children understand that rules are made and enforced for the benefit of getting along with others.

contributing to moral development are empathy and guilt.

Empathy and Guilt

Empathy is a deeply felt sensitivity to the emotions, thoughts, or experiences of others. Have you heard the saying "walking a mile in someone else's shoes"? This is an example of empathy. Empathy helps a person to feel that a current or planned action is right.

To have empathy, a person must be able to understand a person's physical and psychological state. When babies mimic the cry of other babies, this is not true empathy.

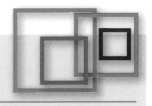

Kohlberg's Theory of Moral Judgment

1. Preconventional Reasoning	2. Conventional Reasoning	3. Postconventional Reasoning
Stage 1: Punishment and Obedience Orientation • The most important value to children is obedience to authority in order to avoid punishment. • Children obey because adults tell them to obey. • Other people externally control moral behavior. *Stage 2: Individualism and Purpose Orientation* • Moral thinking is based on self-interest. Children obey when it is in their best interest to do so. • Moral thinking is based on reward. What is right feels good and is rewarding.	*Stage 3: Interpersonal Norms* • Teens often adopt their parents' moral standards. • Teens believe that behavior is right if it meets the approval of others they admire. *Stage 4: Social System Morality* • Teens base their moral judgments on their understanding of society's need for order, law, and justice. • Teens consider right behavior as doing their duty and showing respect for authority.	*Stage 5: Social Contract or Legalistic Orientation* • Adults believe the rules of society exist for the benefit of all. They also believe rules that do not work should be changed. • Adults believe that rules are established by mutual agreement. • Right actions are defined in terms of individual rights and standards agreed upon by the whole society. *Stage 6: Universal Ethical Principles* • General universal principles determine right and wrong for adults. • Adults choose principles after much reflection.

6-3 Kohlberg's theory shows a developmental change from behavior that is externally controlled to behavior that is controlled from within the person (internalized).

Toddlers can feel empathy in some cases, such as physical hurt. They often respond with a pat on the arm or a hug. In the later preschool years, children have much better ability to perceive the needs of others and respond to them in a variety of ways. By 10 to 12 years of age, children will respond with empathy toward people with whom they have never had contact. For example, they may show empathy after a media account about an ill child or people experiencing a disaster.

Because of empathy, children can consider how their planned actions might affect others positively or negatively. They simply think about how they might feel if someone did this to them. For example, a child might think, "How would I feel if my special toy were stolen?" Understanding the viewpoint of others often leads the child to do what is "right" and to resist what is "wrong." This is part of self-discipline, 6-4.

Guilt is the ability to self-criticize or have remorse. It shows that a person accepts moral principles and enforces those principles within himself or herself. Guilt also indicates a person has a conscience. **Conscience** is the inner sense of the moral goodness that drives a person's conduct, intentions, and character. It combines with a feeling of obligation to do right or be good. Guilt makes a person feel that a past, current, or planned action is wrong.

Freud's Theory

Sigmund Freud, a *psychoanalyst* (a psychologist who works with mental-health patients by studying their childhood years),

Self-discipline and moral development are much alike because they both deal with right and wrong behaviors.

- *Moral development* addresses rules about what people should do in their interactions with others.

- *Self-discipline* sometimes includes morals as well as other values.

For example, a person might have self-discipline in his or her study habits. However, study habits are not moral behaviors.

In contrast, always telling the truth requires both self-discipline and moral development. Because the link between self-discipline and moral development is close, parenting actions impact both in similar ways.

6-4 Self-discipline and moral development are closely related.

proposed in his theory that three features of human functioning are the basis for human personality. These features include the

- *id*—the part of personality that is present from birth and is the source of psychological and physical tension

- *ego*—the part of personality that deals with logic and controlled behaviors

- *superego*—the part of personality that makes up a person's moral code

In his theory of personality development, Freud said that morality is not involved in the id or ego because these aspects of personality do not take into account right or wrong, 6-5. Morality involves the development of the superego.

For the very young child, all resistance to misbehavior exists outside the child. The child is afraid of losing parental approval and receiving punishment. Between the ages of 4 and 6, the child identifies with the parent of the same gender. The superego arises out of this identification. The child now thinks, "I will act as my parents expect me to act."

According to Freud, both the id and the superego try to influence the ego. When the id "wins" the battle, misbehavior occurs, and the person feels guilty. When the superego "wins" the battle, the person is able to resist misbehaviors and avoid the pain of guilt.

Because guilt involves self-punishment, the thought of guilt keeps the child from misbehaving. The situations that cause feelings of guilt change as the child matures in thinking and reasoning ability. Young children can feel guilty when they violate known expectations, such as damaging a toy. They may even feel guilty when their actions were accidental. By the end of elementary school, children can feel guilty when they neglect their responsibilities or fail to act on behalf of others. Children may also feel guilty when they do not live up to their own standards, such as getting good grades or making the team. Teens can feel guilty about dishonest behaviors, inconsiderate behaviors, and events that are not fair. In each of these stages, according to Freud, children conform to societal standards for their ages/stages to avoid guilt.

Actions in Moral Circumstances

Actions are the third feature of moral development. As you learned earlier, morality depends on some ability to reason about right and wrong. A child may endorse moral virtues, but his or her behavior, or actions, may fall short. Based on Kohlberg's stages, people at the higher stages of reasoning tend to take action on right moral behaviors more often than those at lower stages. Because a person can reason about right moral actions, however, does not guarantee that he or she will follow through with positive behavior.

Freud's Concepts of Personality

Id	Ego	Superego
Exists from birth.	Forms during the first years of life.	Forms between ages 4 and 6.
Is the source of wishes and desires.	Deals with the person in the real world.	Is the internal compass for right and wrong behavior.
Wants desires fulfilled without delay. Cannot tolerate delay of gratification.	Satisfies the needs and desires of the id in socially approved ways.	Consists of principles of right and wrong behaviors gathered from interacting with admired others. This is called the *ego ideal*. Compares the ego ideal to actual behavior. *Conscience* develops.
Operates on the pleasure principle. Id's reality is "I want… now."	Operates on the reality principle. Ego understands the world outside the self, or society's expectations. ("I want, but…")	Operates on the morality principle. Superego tries to inhibit the id's drives or urgent needs. ("Nice people don't want…")
When drives or urgent needs of the id are unfulfilled, the person experiences anxiety.	The ego tries to find a compromise between the id and the superego. The ego does this by satisfying urgent needs to the extent it can without violating personal ideals. In doing this, tension is reduced.	Violation of the ego ideal results in guilt.

6-5 The relentless conscience strives to keep the id in check. The ego mediates between the desire of the impatient id and the superego's effort to reach its ideal—perfection.

Empathy and guilt do not always cause a person to resist temptation either. Morality is only moderately consistent across social settings. For example, a child may be honest with peers, but not honest with teachers or vice versa. A child may be honest in English class, but not in math class. This occurs because other factors may be at work.

One factor may be personal motivation. Personal motivation often determines the moral action a person takes. For example, a child may steal a much-wanted toy but would not steal other things. A child who is anxious about grades may cheat on a test, but not in sports. Another factor may involve the demands of the setting. These demands often vary in intensity. People feel pressure when demands are great. For example, more rule violations occur during "big games" than within-team skirmishes. More attempts to cheat occur during high-stakes testing than during a daily quiz.

Developing a Moral System

Children face moral decisions daily. During the school years, cheating, lying, and stealing are commonplace. As children, teens, and young adults try to analyze moral dilemmas, they often receive mixed messages about right behavior from different sources. For example, peer-group codes, religious beliefs, cultural values, and moral standards of parents, teachers, and youth leaders may conflict. The pressures are great and very difficult to handle. Making a wise choice can be a problem, 6-6.

6-6 As children try to analyze moral dilemmas, they often receive mixed messages about moral standards.

The ultimate goal for all people is to develop an internal moral system. When people integrate moral principles into their value systems, they use these principles to guide decision making. Having a well-developed moral system eases the internal pressures regarding ethical choices. A person who has a strong moral foundation will follow these principles without considering other options. Parenting style can impact how a child builds an internal moral system. For example, parents can

- establish a positive home environment that includes warmth, affection, respect, and mutual trust. In this atmosphere, children are more likely to learn from their parents and adopt their parents' morality.

- model the moral standards they expect their children to follow.

- link situations to the rules, rules to the reasons for the rules (effects of the misbehavior on self and others), and misbehaviors to the consequences.

When parents consistently embrace high moral standards in all aspects of life, children generally follow their parents' model, 6-7. People who hold fast to a solid moral foundation are often said to be people of character. As you continue reading, think about what it means to be a person of good character.

Character Development

People develop ethical traits based on their moral decisions. These traits, or virtues, reflect a person's character. **Character** includes the principles, concepts, and beliefs that a person uses as a guide for his or her life. A person often uses this internal guide as a filter in making moral decisions. It reflects moral excellence. For example, a person facing a moral dilemma might ask, "Would it be honest to…?" Ethical traits are so important that people sometimes use them to describe others. For example, descriptions of others might include being a "responsible person," an "honest person," a "caring person," or a "respectful person."

6-7 Children are more likely to adopt their parents' morals when they know their parents value and love them.

Who influences character development? Parents are perhaps the greatest influence over their child's character through their words, actions, and decisions. Children learn much more about values from what their parents *do* than from what their parents *say*. As children watch their parents on a daily basis, they learn to behave as their parents do. A parent's example can guide a child's behavior in both positive and negative ways. Parents who display moral behavior are more likely to raise children who will behave morally. If parents are honest in their interactions, their children will likely learn honesty. In contrast, if children see their parents lie they are more likely to learn to be dishonest.

When parents' actions and words do not match, the child gets a mixed message. Parents should try to be consistent with what they say and how they behave. If parents tell their children one thing and set an entirely different example, this can confuse children. When they often receive such mixed messages, children may stop looking to their parents for guidance.

Because parents are not the only socializers, other people will influence a child's developing character, too. Nonfamily socializers can be a powerful influence, especially in the preteen and teen years. Because of this, parents should carefully monitor their child's nonfamily experiences and practice open communication.

What are the most important character traits? There is no one single list. Although there are many traits of good character, several cross all cultures. They are responsibility, honesty and integrity, caring, respect, and perseverance.

Responsibility

Guiding their children toward responsibility is one of many challenges for parents. **Responsibility** means having a sense of duty to accept and meet obligations without reminder or direction. Children learn this value from their parents, schools, peers, and society. Developing a sense of responsibility begins at young ages. It is an ongoing process for children.

One part of responsibility is being able to recognize and choose appropriate actions. A responsible person knows the difference between right and wrong. This person seeks to use positive behavior, 6-8. He or she avoids negative behaviors and tries to stay out of trouble.

Responsibility also implies reliability and accountability. *Reliability* means that you can depend on a person to be true to his or her word and follow through with the right actions. *Accountability* means a person is able to answer for his or her own actions. Responsible people own up to their actions and answer for them. It's easy to take credit for successes, but much harder to admit mistakes. Too often, people are not accountable for their actions. Instead, they blame others for their mistakes.

Parents can guide their children to develop responsibility. They can offer children chances to feel the satisfaction of a job well done. Enthusiasm helps, too.

6-8 Children show responsibility when they follow through on assigned chores.

Children are likely to have stronger work values if they hear parents say, "Let's see what we can do," more often than "It's no use; we can't do that."

As children grow, parents need to let them accept more responsibility for their own care. Each step toward mastering life skills brings a child one step closer to becoming a responsible person. In addition, taking these steps gives children the satisfaction of feeling self-reliant. One day, children will be adults with total responsibility for themselves. If parents encourage their children to assume this responsibility gradually, the children's transition to adulthood will be much easier.

Some parents set such high behavior standards that their children can never produce satisfactory results. Eventually, these children may think of themselves as failures. In such cases, parents may have to try to lower their standards. For example, some parents demand that their children get all "A's" in school. When a child gets a "B," he or she feels like a failure. If parents encourage their children to do the *best* that they can, children are more likely to see themselves as successful. Parents might also ask their children to do other tasks that the children are able to do well. When children act responsibly and do tasks well, they have feelings of personal satisfaction.

At the other extreme are children who are obsessed with perfection. They work endlessly, but are never satisfied with their results. These children desperately want approval and believe the only way to win approval is through their achievements. Because of this, they are constantly striving to achieve.

Parents can help children strive to do their best, no matter what their different ability levels are. Parents should show appreciation for tasks their children do well. To promote responsibility in their children, parents can

- **Teach self-care.** Part of developing responsibility comes from learning self-care. Parents begin teaching self-care (such as bathing, dressing, and tooth-brushing) from infancy. As soon as children are able, parents encourage them to get themselves up, dressed, and to school on time.

- **Share family tasks.** Children learn responsibility by doing daily tasks, 6-9. Sharing in household tasks can be fun for children—especially if they believe their tasks help the whole family. Ideally, parents should demonstrate a task and then let their children do it. If children can choose from a number of tasks, they usually enjoy the work more.

- **Teach resource management.** From a young age, parents can model responsible resource use to their children. Whether teaching about human or natural resources, parents have a profound effect on their children. For example, parents can talk with children about how to earn, save, and use money. When parents "reduce, reuse, and recycle," they demonstrate how to care for the environment.

- **Participate in community service.** When parents have a passion for "giving back," or serving their community, children embrace this passion, too. In order to develop a responsibility to serve others, it is important for children to choose a project that is worthwhile and interesting to them. When parents join in and support them, children learn a basic democratic principle—people of any age can identify a need or problem and take initiative to help solve it. What type of community service ignites your passion to serve?

Honesty and Integrity

Honesty is one of the most basic ethical values and is the foundation of good character. People who are honest refuse to lie, steal, or deceive others in any way. They are often said to have integrity. **Integrity** means to firmly adhere to a code of moral values. People with integrity are trustworthy and incorruptible. These honest people often receive the admiration and honor of others. They do not waver from what is right and good for all people and situations.

In contrast, dishonest people rarely show other positive character traits. Adults who deceive often destroy family, business, and social relationships. Children who lie and cheat likely have no friends.

How do children learn to be honest? How can they become people of integrity and good character? Here are some ways that parents can guide their children on the path to honesty and integrity.

Through Truthfulness

A reality that parents must know is that all children lie occasionally. It is a part of normal development, although not acceptable behavior. By age 3, telling tall tales is a positive sign of creative development in children. At the age of 4, children love to brag and tell tall tales. They are striving to identify with their world. At age 5, children use tall tales to purposefully fool or deceive others. They may use tall tales to protect themselves or reveal unfulfilled wishes. Children of 5 or 6 years may blame siblings or inanimate objects for their mistakes. Children at this age are often poor losers. They may cheat to win when playing games.

By the age of 7, children are developing a moral sense of right and wrong. They are becoming aware of attitudes as well as actions. They are bothered when friends tell lies or cheat. Most 8-year-olds are basically truthful, but they may exaggerate a story to impress an audience. The words *honesty*

6-9 During the summer, the children in this family must pick the fruits and vegetables that are ripe every day from their garden.

and *truth* have become a part of 9-year-olds' vocabularies. Even when they exaggerate, they quickly set the record straight by saying, "Oh, Mom, you know that isn't real." By the age of 10, most children develop moral standards. They may be very exacting of themselves and others.

Truthfulness is a value children may or may not develop as they mature. Those who find that telling the truth contributes to their well-being are more likely to be truthful in the future, 6-10. Parents are an important influence on children accepting truthfulness as a character trait. To teach their children how to be truthful, parents should

- avoid telling "little lies." When adults use false excuses to decline invitations or end phone conversations, children may try to imitate what they see and hear. This is a mixed message: parents can lie, but children cannot.

- separate the child's fantasy from reality. Parents should deal with the fantasy tales of the young children by sending positive messages. At the same time, they should let their children know that they recognize the story as a fantasy. For example, a parent might say, "You tell fun stories that we enjoy hearing."

6-10 Although parents want their children to be honest, some cheat or act dishonestly if they think they can get away with it.

- avoid confronting a child who lies about a wrongdoing. Just say, "Everyone makes mistakes. It's okay. Let's see if we can fix the problem." Focus on the problem, not the lie.

- tell children they will not be harshly punished for making mistakes. Sometimes children become skillful liars if they find they can escape punishment by telling lies.

- give a child needed attention and reward a child for honesty when compulsive lying is a problem. These children often become deceptive to win parental approval.

- encourage children to play fairly and honestly at board games and other games. Parents should not condone cheating by looking the other way.

- talk with their children about cheating. Children need to know why cheating is wrong and what the consequences can be. Parents should not blame others when a child cheats.

Respecting Others' Property

Early in life, a child needs to learn that some things belong to him or her and other things belong to other people. Parents should allow a child to have a special toy that is his or hers alone. Sharing is a lesson to learn, but there is also a lesson to learn about personal property.

Respecting the property of others involves not stealing. Stealing includes *shoplifting* (stealing from a store), stealing from friends and family, *cheating* (practicing fraud or trickery such as cheating on a test), and *plagiarism* (taking ideas from someone and passing them off as your own). Parents can teach respect for others' property in several ways that include

- modeling respect for others' property. If parents are dishonest, children may think that stealing is all right as long as a person avoids getting caught. If parents justify their dishonest actions, this may weaken their children's character.

- encouraging honesty if they notice toys or objects in their home that do not belong there. Parents might say, "We see a toy that is not yours. Let's take it back to the store." In this way, parents confront the child with the truth. The child can then correct the misdeed. Parents should avoid overreacting with anger or embarrassment.

- building self-esteem. Children who lie or steal often have low self-esteem.

Caring

Caring is a virtue that powerfully affects human relationships. When children and adults are caring, they show understanding, kindness, and compassion to others. Caring people are also generous and willingly express gratitude when it is due. They are unselfish in helping those in need. They also forgive those who treat them poorly.

Children seem to have a natural tendency to be caring and compassionate, 6-11. They tend to be more positive in their interactions with others. Some research shows that children will do eight positive acts to one negative act.

To be caring, a child must recognize another person needs his or her help. The ability to "read" the nonverbal or verbal distress cues of others is a necessary skill for children to develop. If the child perceives someone needs help, he or she must then decide whether or not to help. To do this, a child must know what would be helpful and must have the needed "know-how" to carry it out. There are many ways parents can encourage caring in their children. They can

- show support to other family members daily. This allows children to see caring behavior in action.

- use open communication by responding to family member's thoughts and feelings appropriately. This means demonstrating kindness and compassion in dealing with others.

- use reasoning to focus on others. For example, the parent might say, "Taking turns means that everyone can play."

- act in a caring way within the community. When children see their parents involved in the community, they are more likely to follow this action.

- develop their child's empathy for others. This way, children learn that small things can make a difference. For example, parents might encourage children to walk to raise money to fight a disease, visit someone at a nursing home, or donate a portion of their allowance to a charity.

When children display an attitude of caring to others, they gain competence and feel valued. This enhances self-esteem. It also increases a child's desire to continue caring. Caring children are more successful in social interactions and more apt to receive the kindness of others in return.

6-11 Showing compassion is a natural tendency for children.

Respect

Respect has to do with how you relate to others. It especially shows your high regard for other people, authority, self, and where you live. Respect involves treating others with consideration and courtesy. It also means showing acceptance of people who differ from you. Respect involves using good manners and dealing peacefully with others even when you disagree with them. Respect is such a major part of character that people use such expressions as "gaining respect for" or "losing respect for" a person.

Consideration and Courtesy

Consideration involves reciprocity. **Reciprocity** occurs when people treat others in the same way they want others to treat them. It involves mutual give-and-take. Throughout the world, reciprocity receives great emphasis in relationships. It is also a guiding moral principle in many religions. Kohlberg noted reciprocity emerging in level 2 of his theory, "Conventional Reasoning."

Courtesy is one way that people show consideration. People show courtesy through both words and actions. Parents influence their child's consideration and courtesy through daily interactions, 6-12. They influence these features of respect by

6-12 Children learn how to be courteous through interactions with their parents.

- modeling consideration and courtesy through their daily interactions within and outside the family.

- explaining to their child how words and actions can hurt others, and when this occurs, they teach empathy for the victim.

- showing respect for their child at all times, including when he or she misbehaves.

- using positive affirmations when their child shows consideration and courtesy and using negative consequences when their child shows disrespect.

- taking advantage of a young child's innocent rude remarks as a time for explanation. For example, parents may explain that staring at or talking about the way a person looks or acts can make that person feel bad.

- teaching their child manners and modeling these at home. Some manners are basic, such as saying "please," "thank you," and "excuse me."

Acceptance and Fairness

Because it includes people from more than one culture, the United States is considered a **multicultural** country. Millions of people from many different countries have made this country their home. In fact, many cultural and ethnic groups live here. Parents teach children about their own heritage and culture, but teaching them about other cultures is important, too.

Ethnic diversity occurs in any setting that includes people of more than one ethnic group. When parents teach respect and appreciation for diversity, children are better able to get along with others in this multicultural world. Showing acceptance of others is a sign of good character.

As they grow, most children come into contact with people of different ethnic groups. Differences that children see and hear may make them curious or may frighten or confuse them. Parents can help children understand how people are different from one another and that diversity is positive. They can also encourage children to recognize the uniqueness and value of people from all cultural and ethnic backgrounds, 6-13. Teaching children about diversity can also help them overcome

- *Cultural bias.* A belief that a person's own cultural or ethnic group is better than any other is called **cultural bias**. Someone with a cultural bias might treat people of other cultures differently than people from his or her own culture.

6-13 Getting along with people of other cultures is an important skill children can learn both at home and at school.

- *Prejudice.* Making unfair judgments or opinions about people of another group without getting to know them is called **prejudice**. Prejudice keeps people from knowing what other people are really like.

- *Stereotypes.* Widely held beliefs that all members of a group are alike and share the same characteristics are called **stereotypes**. If children believe stereotypes about an ethnic group, they may think all people from that group are alike. Stereotypes can lead people to form incorrect views about other people.

Parents should teach children stereotypes usually involve untrue statements or myths. They can help children distinguish between myths and the truths about other people. For instance, statements that use the words *all, none, always,* or *never* are often stereotypes. These statements make generalizations about an entire group. Statements that include words such as *some* and *sometimes* are more likely to be true.

Cultural biases, prejudices, and stereotypes are all disrespectful because they do not treat others fairly. These beliefs and attitudes often lead to hurtful words and harmful actions. Through parent modeling and child imitation these negative attitudes often pass from one generation to the next. They keep people from knowing and understanding one another. They divide people instead of encouraging them to get along. Parents need to teach their children respectful acceptance of others. The suggestions in 6-14 can be helpful.

Perseverance

As children grow and develop, teaching them to persevere through challenges is an important parenting task. **Perseverance** is setting and pursuing worthwhile goals and seeing them through to completion. Children

Teaching Children About Diversity

- Examine your attitudes and comments about people from other cultural and ethnic groups. Your example is an important influence.

- Learn more about other cultural and ethnic groups. This will increase your own understanding and prepare you to teach your children more about other groups.

- Correct children's negative statements and incorrect ideas about people from other ethnic groups. Use children's conflicts or problems with children of other cultures as learning experiences.

- Encourage children to meet people from other cultures. Include people from various ethnic groups in your life.

- Provide books, toys, games, and movies that reflect ethnic diversity. Children learn through play. Toys and books that represent other cultures can help them understand, accept, and appreciate ethnic diversity.

- Help children find answers to their questions about people from other cultures. Reading books or talking to people from these cultures (if possible) may help.

- Attend events that reflect a cultural or ethnic group different from yours. Cook foods, wear clothes, or celebrate a holiday as people in another culture or ethnic group do.

- Remind children that being different from one another is positive. Everyone has unique strengths and gifts.

- Discuss children's concerns regarding diversity issues. Be available and show willingness to listen.

6-14 Parents can follow these suggestions for teaching their children about ethnic diversity.

and adults who persevere show courage and strength even when confronted with failure. They keep on trying to meet their goals.

Developing perseverance is an on-going process for children and adults. Parents begin encouraging perseverance when their children are very young. Can you see how helping a child learn to walk lays the foundation for perseverance? As children learn to walk, they may stumble and fall, but generally pick themselves up and try again as parents cheer them on.

Part of the parent's role in guiding their children toward perseverance is to help children set realistic goals. When goals are realistic, children are more likely to succeed. How can parents help their children set goals? First, they should observe how their children might already be using goal-setting skills. This can be a springboard for talking with children about setting goals. Then parents should encourage their children to set short goals they can achieve in a small amount of time. For example, making cookies (with mom or dad) or doing a craft project may not take much time but does lead to a sense of accomplishment, 6-15. As parents look for other ways to infuse perseverance into their children's character, they can

- let children choose their goals. When children have a choice, they make an investment in the goal and are more likely to keep working toward it.

- help children make a plan. Parents may need to show children how to break a goal into parts in order to achieve the goal.

- encourage children if they feel frustrated or discouraged when things don't go as planned. Help them look for alternative ways to meet a goal.

Growing in perseverance takes time and effort for both children and their parents. As with all traits of good character, when parents have positive expectations about their children's ability to persevere, their children most often develop this trait. As parents encourage and reward their children's efforts, their children take on an "I can do this" attitude. This sense of accomplishment gives a real boost to children's self-esteem and desire to persevere.

6-15 Achieving small goals helps young children feel a sense of accomplishment. This leads to developing perseverance.

Summing It Up

- Moral development has three parts: moral judgments, moral feelings, and moral actions.

- Piaget and Kohlberg indicate that learning moral judgments is a long, developmental process. These judgments occur in stages that tie closely to intellectual reasoning.

- Empathy and guilt encourage moral development. *Empathy* allows a person to see how his or her actions might affect others.

- *Guilt* is the ability to self-criticize or have remorse. It shows a person has a conscience.

- Freud's theory includes concepts about three features of personality: the id, the ego, and the superego.

- Freud believed the superego restrains the pleasure-seeking id, and the ego finds a compromise that doesn't violate personal ideals.

- Moral reasoning, empathy, and guilt do not always cause a person to resist temptations and choose right behavior.

- People show internal moral control when social expectations link with moral judgments and moral feelings.

- *Character* is made up of the principles, concepts, and beliefs that a person holds as a guide for life. People use these values as a filter in making moral decisions.

- Character traits include responsibility, honesty and integrity, caring, respect, and perseverance.

Recalling the Facts

1. Summarize the key features of the following three aspects of moral development: (A) moral judgments, (B) moral feelings, and (C) moral actions.

2. Describe the characteristics of children's *moral judgments* in the two stages of Piaget's theory on moral development.

3. How do the moral judgments of children differ in Kohlberg's preconventional and conventional levels?

4. How do the feelings of empathy and guilt contribute to moral development?

5. Describe five ways that parents can help their children develop an internalized moral system.

6. Name two ways that children can develop a sense of responsibility.

7. How can parents help their children learn to value honesty?

8. What does a child learn when parents bring the child to a store to return an item the child stole?

9. Name two ways that parents can teach children to respect others' property.

10. Name five ways parents can help their children develop caring behavior.

11. How can parents encourage consideration and courtesy, including reciprocity, in their children?

12. Contrast *cultural bias, prejudice,* and *stereotypes.*

13. What clues tell a person that a statement about another cultural group is untrue?

14. Why should parents teach respectful acceptance of others to their children?

15. Name two ways that parents can encourage perseverance in their children.

Applying New Skills

1. **Interview.** Interview a security guard or store manager from a local department store about shoplifting. Ask questions about the store's policy concerning shoplifters and the legal consequences of shoplifting. Are the consequences different if the shoplifter is a young child? How might the security guard or store manager respond to a parent who is making a child return an item that the child took from the store?

2. **Book review.** Write a book review about Samuel and Pearl Oliner's book, *The Altruistic Personality* (Free Press). This is especially interesting in times of concern about natural disasters and terrorism. The questions are: "Who can you count on?" "Why?" "Would you be a hero or a bystander?" As an alternative, read two children's books that have themes about caring. Write a review of each and share your reviews with the class.

3. **Observation.** Observe a teacher from a child care center or preschool that serves children from a variety of cultural or ethnic groups. How does the teacher help children learn about the similarities and differences among them? How does he or she promote ethnic diversity and appreciation for other cultures? How does the teacher keep parents up-to-date on teaching respect for other cultures?

Thinking Critically

1. Form small groups, each with three people. Have your teacher call out moral dilemmas for teens, such as eating nutritious foods, sexual abstinence before marriage, and honesty on a final exam. The first person in the group should say what the *id* might "say." The second person gives the *superego's* response to the *id*. The third person responds as the *ego* might.

2. Choose a moral dilemma that many teens face. Briefly describe what each pressure source might "say" to a teen. Pressure sources include peer groups, religious beliefs, cultural values, and moral standards of parents, teachers, or youth leaders. Explain why the dilemma is such a difficult decision. For example, are teens getting mixed messages or are one or more pressure sources silent on the issue?

3. Formulate ways parents can help their children develop responsibility other than those described in the chapter. With a partner, brainstorm your list. Then share the list with another pair of students or the class.

4. Create a poem, story, or collage to represent the concept "Perseverance is a trait of good character." Share your creation with the class.

Linking Academics

1. **Writing.** Write two Piagetian-type stories. Each story should be four to six sentences. In your first story, have a child break one dish while misbehaving. In the second story, have another child break five dishes while trying to help the parent. At the end of the second story, ask these questions: "Which child do you think was naughtier?" "Why?" Have your stories approved by your teacher. Then interview five children between ages 4 and 10 years. (Before interviewing the children, be sure to obtain written permission from their parents to do so.) Try to choose some younger and some older children. Before you tell your stories say, "There are no right or wrong answers. I just want to know what you think about two children." What do your findings tell you about the moral development of children? After questioning the children, write a summary of your findings to share with the class.

1. **Reading.** Collect and read a variety of books for young children that deal with perseverance. Some possible choices include: *The Carrot Seed* by Ruth Krause, *A Chair for My Mother* by Vera B. Williams, *The Little Engine That Could* by Watty Piper, or *Whistle for Willie* by Ezra Jack Keats. Choose one book and share an oral presentation with the class about how the character(s) in the story demonstrated perseverance.

Part Three
The Beginning of Parenthood

157

Your Potential Career

Where's Your Passion? Health Science?

When you think about working with parents and children, what health-science career opportunities kindle your passion? Does working in a hospital nursery, becoming a pediatric physician's assistant, or researching cures for childhood cancer peak your interest?

- **Job outlook.** Many careers in health science will see *high demand* in coming years. Which health-science career pathways do you find most interesting? Choose one and check it out!

- **Education or training.** A degree from a community college or four-year university is required for most health-science careers. Some entry-level careers may require on-the-job training and a high school diploma. What does your desired career require? How much time are you willing to take to further your education?

- **Skills and personal qualities.** Do you work well with people? Can you show great compassion, but still keep your emotions in check in difficult situations? Are you a dedicated person with high integrity? Which skills and personal qualities are most important for your career of interest?

- **Wages or salary.** Along with the *high skill* and *high demand* for many health/science careers come moderate to *high wages*. What are your financial goals? Will a health-science career meet your needs?

Up Close—Job Shadowing

Select a health/science career that interests you. Then contact a person in your community that works in this career. Make arrangements for a job-shadowing experience. During this experience, note foundational and workplace skills needed to perform on the job. What does this person like and dislike about this career? What education or training did he or she need?

FCCLA

Develop an FCCLA STAR Event project such as *Career Investigation, Job Interview, Focus on Children, Illustrated Talk,* or a *Chapter Service Project* for a parenting- or child-related career in health science. Consider using National FCCLA Programs such as *Career Connection, Power of One, Student Body, Leaders at Work,* or *Dynamic Leadership* as the foundation of your project. Obtain all necessary forms and guidelines from your family and consumer sciences teacher.

Get Connected

One of the best ways to learn about potential careers is first-hand experience. Consider volunteering at a children's hospital or getting a part-time job at a health clinic. For the short-term, think about participating in a fundraiser for such organizations as *The March of Dimes* or *St. Jude Children's Research Hospital.*

You can read more about planning your career in Chapter 22.

Career Cluster—Health Science

Cluster Pathways

Therapeutic Services	Diagnostics Services	Health Information	Biotechnology Research and Development
Sample Careers			
Certified Nursing Assistant	Diagnostic Medical Sonographer	Community Services Specialist	Cell Biologist
Certified Nurse-Midwife	Mammographer	Patient Advocates	Toxicologist
Registered Nurse	Medical Technologist	Medical Assistant	Geneticist
Nurse Anesthetist	Geneticist	Health Educator	Genetics Lab Assistant
Child Life Specialist	Clinical Laboratory Scientist	Public Health Educator	Lab Technician
Dietitian	Phlebotomist	Social Worker	Research Assistant
Exercise Physiologist	Nutritionist		
Occupational Therapist	Exercise Physiologist		
EMT/Paramedic			
Dentist			
Physician			
Surgical Technician			
Home Health Aid			

Chapter 7

Planning a Family

Objectives

After studying this chapter, you will be able to

- summarize the advantages of family planning and factors that influence these decisions.
- explain the process of human reproduction, including conception.
- identify two general types of family planning.
- summarize the purpose of assessing health before pregnancy, including possible genetic counseling.
- identify causes of infertility for men and women.
- describe options for infertile couples and the implications of these options.

Key Terms

family planning
sperm
egg
testes
vas deferens
ovaries
ovulation
uterus
endometrium
menstruation
conception
fallopian tubes
zygote
chromosome
gene
contraception
genetic counseling
congenital disorders
infertility
artificial insemination
in vitro fertilization
closed adoption
open adoption

Becoming parents is special for each couple. Some plan for parenthood with much joy and excitement. Other couples experience pregnancy without deciding to do so. Couples are also unique in terms of age, careers, economic situation, and sources of support. All of these factors influence planning a family.

Family planning is a couple's commitment to making decisions about their reproductive capabilities. It includes decisions about the number, timing, and spacing of children born to the couple.

Advantages of Family Planning

Couples should learn about family planning before deciding to have children. The best time for this is before marriage. Then couples can begin marriage with a clear understanding of their parenting goals. Sharing common parenting goals increases a couple's chance for a happy marriage. Family planning has several advantages. Family planning

- *ensures parenthood is by choice rather than by chance.* As you read earlier, planned pregnancies mean couples are often more satisfied with becoming parents and children are born wanted. This has great implications for families and society as a whole.

- *allows couples to achieve the goals they have set for themselves.* A couple may decide never to have children. They may postpone having children until they have met certain goals, such as educational, career, and financial. They may want more time as a couple. Postponing parenthood until they are ready enables couples to be better parents and benefits couples and their children, 7-1.

7-1 A husband and wife may want to take plenty of time adjusting to their marital roles before starting parenthood.

- *offers choices when couples decide to stop having children.* This occurs when couples feel their families are the right size.

Influences on Family Planning

As you read in earlier chapters, couples should think through many factors before parenting. Ideally, a couple will discuss parenting goals before marriage. If not, they should do so before having a child. Talking about parenthood as a goal for some future time is different from discussing it as an upcoming reality.

Planning for the First Child

Deciding when a couple should have their first child is a common question about family planning. The simplest answer is when both spouses feel ready. When couples feel ready to have children, they have likely considered many related factors. Couples who want children should not delay parenting until their future is absolutely secure. This time may never come.

Before bringing a child into the world, take an honest look at your readiness to parent. Asking these questions can help.

- *Have we had enough time as a couple?* As you recall Erikson's theory, a couple needs time to form a stable, close relationship. He described the special closeness as intimacy. In this stage, the couple shares their identities while feeling secure with whom they are. (See Appendix B, Stage 6.) Some experts recommend couples be married at least 18 months before becoming parents. This will allow them to adjust completely to their marital roles before adding parenting roles.

- *Have we looked again at our readiness for parenthood?* As couples talk again about parenting, they need to look at the security of their marriages. Reviewing their personal and couple goals, including career and financial goals, is also an important step. Couples need to consider the possible impact of their ages and health on parenthood. All of these situations may be much different from when they were first married. Their views or opinions about parenting may have changed, too.

Planning for More Children

After the birth of their first child, many couples make further decisions about family planning. Couples may wish to consider the questions in the decision-making chain in 7-2. In making these decisions, both partners should agree.

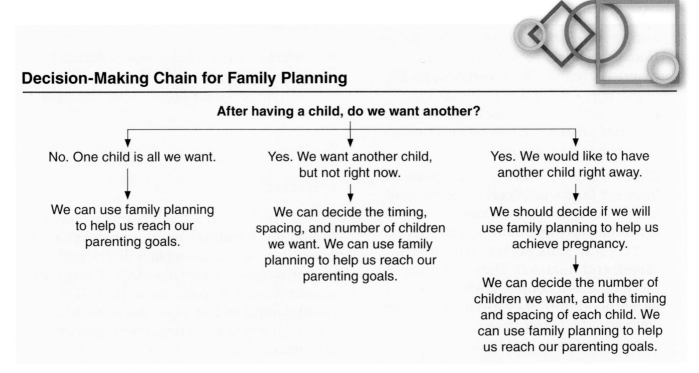

Decision-Making Chain for Family Planning

After having a child, do we want another?

No. One child is all we want.	Yes. We want another child, but not right now.	Yes. We would like to have another child right away.
We can use family planning to help us reach our parenting goals.	We can decide the timing, spacing, and number of children we want. We can use family planning to help us reach our parenting goals.	We should decide if we will use family planning to help us achieve pregnancy.
		We can decide the number of children we want, and the timing and spacing of each child. We can use family planning to help us reach our parenting goals.

7-2 Couples may ask themselves these questions about family planning after having their first child.

A couple may decide to have only one child, or they may want more children. Polls show most families want more than one child, 7-3. Couples may want to have a second child immediately or wait several years. Planning for more children includes decisions on readiness and how far apart their arrivals should be.

Readiness for More Children

Many factors influence parents' decision about having more children. In making this decision, parents must reconsider all the factors that influenced their decision to have their first child. These factors can change with time. Several new factors enter into the picture as well, including

Emotional Factors. If one or both spouses were only children, they may recall a desire to have a brother or sister. In this case, couples may decide to have at least two children. If they were happy as only children, couples may wish the same for their child. Family background can influence couples from large families, too. On one hand, spouses who grew up in large families may want a peaceful home with a small family. On the other hand, they might also choose an action-packed home filled with children.

Planning Family Size

Number of Children Desired	Percent of Families
1	9%
2	42%
3	29%
4	12%
As many as possible	8%

7-3 According to an online poll by American Baby, about 91 percent of families want more than one child.

Financial Factors. More children cost more money. Food, clothing, transportation, entertainment, education, and health care costs keep climbing. They grow with the birth of each child, and continue to increase as children age. Although most couples do not feel they have reached total financial security by the time they have children, they do need to have some degree of financial security, however. This will ensure adding children to the family will not cause great financial problems.

Parenting Factors. If parenting is seen as rewarding, parents often want other children. If parenting is seen as only a challenge, the couple needs to weigh the decision for having more children very carefully. If parenting takes all the couple's time and energy because the child has special needs, plans for more children may be postponed. Couples might also seek medical advice about the chances of having another child with special needs.

Spacing of Children

Spacing of children is an important family planning decision. It has benefits for both the child and the parents. Spacing can even make parenting more rewarding.

Spacing is the timing between births. Although there is not one optimal time for all couples, they need to consider several factors. First, most authorities agree that about three years between children is best. This amount of time allows each child to achieve a separate status in the family. The older child will be better able to accept and understand having a new brother or sister. There may be less sibling rivalry as a result. See 7-4. Of course, multiple-birth children, such as twins and triplets, are never "only" children. The same is true for all additional children unless the firstborn is a teen or an adult when the second child arrives.

A second factor in deciding the spacing of children is the mother's health. It takes about 18 months for a woman to resume her normal health after the birth of a baby. If there is less time between pregnancies, a woman's health and the baby's health may be at risk. The more time between pregnancies, the better chance a woman has to maintain her health and strength.

In a few cases, doctors suggest closer spacing of children. Women who are older will need to have children before the end of their fertility. Some younger women have decreasing fertility due to reproductive problems. A doctor may advise these women to complete their families without waiting too long between children.

A third factor focuses on the family finances. Some parents believe that having children close together saves money. They think about handing down baby furniture, clothing, and toys. This idea is more myth than reality. For example, if children are

7-4 Spacing children about three years apart allows each child to achieve a separate status in the family. It may also lessen sibling rivalry.

born close together, a family may need two cribs because the toddler is not ready for a youth bed. Clothing from the first child may be worn, stained, or not appropriate for the second child's gender. Toddlers may even want to "claim" their outgrown toys. Having two or more children in child care at the same time can cause financial hardships.

As children become adults, their spacing can impact family finances in a major way. The costs of providing a college education increase yearly. The costs of launching children into careers and marriages also continue to rise. If children are born three to five years apart, these events in children's lives will overlap little, if at all.

Lastly, because parenting in the early years is so physically demanding, parents need to consider the impact of having children close in age. Think about the number of times you will lift and carry an infant and a toddler. Think about the number of feeding times and diaper changes each day. Think about getting two children bathed and down for naps or nighttime sleep. Think about monitoring a toddler who is into everything and a baby becoming more mobile and curious each day. Parenting one young child is tiring. Parenting two can leave even the best parents totally exhausted!

If a couple can get past these concerns, parenting children who are close in age can be very rewarding. Siblings are often wonderful playmates as young children. They will likely stay close in the teen and adult years. Having children close together can help stay-at-home moms or dads return to the world of work sooner, too.

Human Reproduction

Many complex and emotional issues are involved in family planning and human reproduction. Each couple's decision is often based on family, religious, and personal beliefs. People who view these decisions as a responsibility say every child has the right to be wanted.

Couples should make reproductive and family planning decisions together. Some people think these choices only belong to women because they feel the full impact of pregnancy. Since these decisions affect both partners, both should take responsibility for making them. As with other decisions, having reliable information helps couples make the best choices for themselves, 7-5.

Learning about human reproduction is a good first step in making family planning decisions. Humans reproduce sexually. Two sex cells—the **sperm** from the male and the **egg** (ovum) from the female—unite to form a fertilized egg. This fertilized egg then divides millions of times to form the new human being. Knowing how babies form helps couples plan pregnancy. Both men and women have important roles in reproduction. Consider the following facts as you think about having children.

The Male's Role

The male's role in reproduction is to produce the sperm he will then deliver to the woman. A man begins producing sperm at puberty and continues throughout his lifetime. At first, sperm are produced in small numbers. By adulthood, men produce millions of sperm each month.

A man's two **testes,** or testicles, are reproductive glands that produce sperm. Next to each testis is a coiled tube called the *epididymis.* Sperm pass through a series of ducts to reach the epididymis. There the sperm mature. Each epididymis attaches to a long, narrow tube called the **vas deferens.** Sperm travel through the vas deferens up into the man's body. Each vas deferens leads to an *ejaculatory duct.* The two ejaculatory ducts are located side by side and connect to the *urethra.* Sperm leave the body through the urethra which extends through the penis.

7-5 Because children impact both spouses, family planning decisions should be made jointly.

When sperm first leave the epididymis, they are relatively inactive. The muscular walls of the vas deferens contract and propel sperm upward. Sperm combine with secretions from three sets of glands as they reach the urethra to form semen. It is this semen that leaves the man's body through ejaculation during sexual intercourse.

The Female's Role

The female's role in reproduction is to provide eggs, or *ova,* and to carry and nourish a fertilized egg within her body until a baby is born. A woman is born with about 400,000 immature egg cells. Her body does not produce any more eggs after she is born.

A female has two **ovaries,** or almond-shaped organs, that store the immature egg cells. When she reaches puberty, one of her ovaries usually releases a mature egg about once a month. This process is **ovulation.** The ovaries release about 400 eggs during an average woman's reproductive years.

The **uterus** is a hollow, muscular organ that holds the baby during pregnancy. The **endometrium** is the inner lining of the uterus. Each month, it thickens and develops a large network of tiny blood vessels in preparation for pregnancy. If the mature egg is unfertilized, it disintegrates in 24 hours. As a result, the endometrium flows from the uterus over the course of several days. This bloody discharge leaves the body through the vagina in the process called **menstruation.**

A different sequence of events takes place when **conception,** or fertilization, occurs. After leaving the ovary, the mature egg passes into one of two tubes called the **fallopian tubes**. Note that one end of each fallopian tube lies close to an ovary. The other end of each tube attaches to the uterus. The mature egg is available for fertilization for about 24 hours after ovulation. Sperm usually meet the egg while it is in the fallopian tube to achieve fertilization. The sperm travel through the uterus and finally into the fallopian tube. Sperm can survive in a woman's body for as long as 72 hours. (For example, this means pregnancy is possible if a couple has intercourse on Monday and the woman ovulates on Wednesday.) Only one sperm enters the outer wall of the egg cell, closing out all other sperm, when conception occurs.

After fertilization, several important events occur during the next few hours. The nucleus of the egg cell combines with the nucleus of the sperm cell to form one cell. Note that these nuclei contain the genetic information from the mother and father. This new cell, or **zygote**, forms when the separate nuclei of sperm and egg merge into one nucleus. The merger of the nuclei takes 24 to 36 hours.

Within hours of formation, the new zygote begins to divide and grow. The zygote usually spends about three to four days traveling through the fallopian tube to the uterus. By the time it leaves the fallopian tube and enters the uterus, it contains many cells. Once in the uterus, the zygote floats free for one or two days after fertilization. By the sixth or seventh day, it begins to attach to the endometrium of the uterus. The zygote embeds completely in the uterine wall by day 11 or 12 after fertilization, 7-6. This entire process is called *implantation.* Cell division continues as pregnancy progresses. The uterus continues to hold and nourish the fertilized egg as it develops into a baby during pregnancy.

The Couple's Role in Heredity

Both spouses contribute to the hereditary makeup of their children. Babies receive 23 chromosomes from their mother's egg and 23 chromosomes from their father's sperm. This gives human babies 23 pairs of chromosomes (46 total) in every cell of their bodies. A **chromosome** is a threadlike structure that contains hereditary information. Each chromosome contains thousands of genes. A **gene** is the basic unit of heredity. *Heredity* includes all the traits that pass from one generation to the next. Genes carry all the characteristics that transfer from parent to child. Genes occur in pairs. In each pair, one gene comes from the mother, and one from the father, 7-7.

The kind of genes a baby inherits from each parent determines his or her traits. Some genes are dominant and others are recessive. Dominant genes mask the effects of recessive genes. For instance, dark hair is a

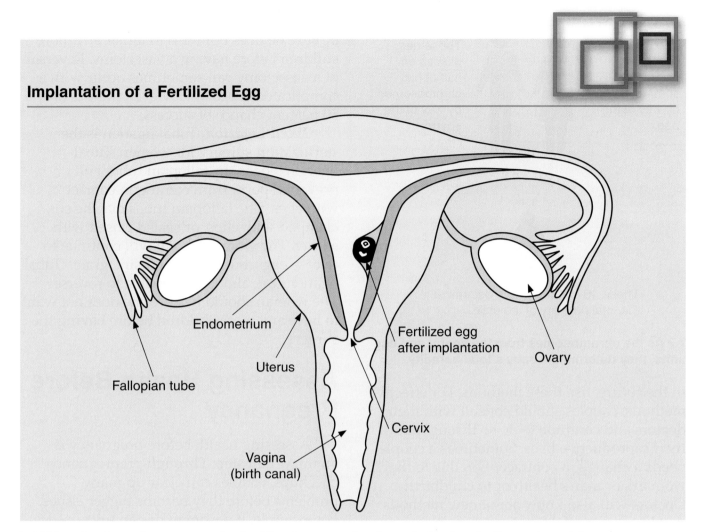

7-6 When implantation occurs, the fertilized egg nestles in and attaches to the endometrium.

dominant gene and blond hair is recessive. A child with two dark-hair genes or one dark-hair gene and one blond-hair gene will have dark hair. A recessive trait will appear only if recessive genes from each parent combine for that particular trait. Therefore, a child who receives two blond-hair genes will be blond.

Family Planning Methods

Couples interested in the timing of the first pregnancy will want to use a family planning method. They will also use a family planning method for spacing any additional children. Couples who do not want children also need to use some form of family planning.

Contraception, or birth control, is the deliberate prevention of pregnancy. Couples can use any of a number of different methods. They should never rely on myths about birth-control methods. Unplanned pregnancies and/or sexually transmitted diseases often result from using these unreliable methods. Couples should, however, rely on their doctor to guide them toward the best choice for their situation. In order to meet different goals and needs, couples can use non-permanent or permanent methods of family planning.

Non-Permanent Methods

Non-permanent birth-control methods temporarily prevent pregnancy. Couples who do not want children now, but do want them

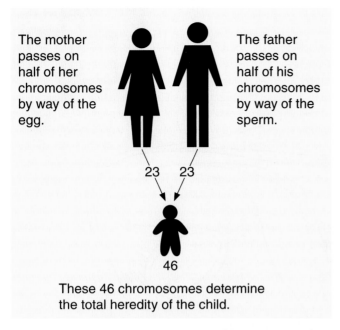

The mother passes on half of her chromosomes by way of the egg.

The father passes on half of his chromosomes by way of the sperm.

23   23

46

These 46 chromosomes determine the total heredity of the child.

7-7 As the chromosomes from the sperm and egg unite, they determine a baby's total heredity.

in the future, use these methods. For effective methods, couples should consult with their doctors and continue to do so throughout their reproductive lives. Sometimes a couple needs a change in contraception due to the woman's or man's health or to childbirth. Doctors will also know about new methods that become available.

Permanent Methods

Couples who do not want to have a child or want more children may choose sterilization. *Sterilization* is surgery that permanently prevents pregnancy. A couple might also choose this option if their genes could cause a congenital disorder in the baby or if pregnancy would threaten the woman's health. Sterilization surgeries are expensive and permanent. Two methods are used.

Vasectomy. A vasectomy is the sterilization surgery for men. During a vasectomy, both vas deferens are cut surgically. Sperm can no longer travel into the penis. The male's body continues to produce sperm, but the body absorbs them.

A vasectomy is permanent. A man should be sure he does not wish to father any more children before having a vasectomy. Reversal of a vasectomy can sometimes occur with a complicated surgery. However, there is only a 50 percent chance of success.

Tubal Ligation. Tubal ligation is the sterilization surgery for women. Tubal ligation blocks the fallopian tubes and prevents sperm from coming in contact with eggs. The fallopian tubes may be cut, clamped with clips, or sealed closed with a laser. The woman's body will continue to release eggs, but they will disintegrate. Tubal ligations are almost impossible to reverse. The woman should be sure she does not want to have any more children before having the surgery.

Assessing Health Before Pregnancy

Assessing health before pregnancy is an important step. Through prepregnancy checkups, couples can clear up many problems before they become bigger issues. For example, if a woman has an untreated disease or is too heavy or thin, dealing with these conditions before pregnancy can lead to fewer pregnancy complications. These preventative checkups are also cost effective. Pregnancy combined with some health problems can lead to hospitalization, which can be expensive. Birth defects resulting from some maternal health conditions may require years of expensive medical care.

Although women carry the baby, they cannot get pregnant alone. A healthy pregnancy is not just the woman's responsibility. Each spouse should have medical tests and take stock of personal and family health history, lifestyle, and any other concerns, 7-8.

7-8 A health assessment before pregnancy is important for both spouses.

General and Reproductive Health

For females, doctors can check blood type and do a pap smear, mammogram, and a urinalysis. They can check for diseases that can affect the mother or the baby during pregnancy. For males, blood tests, blood-pressure check, and prostate and hernia exams are common medical tests. Dental checkups for both spouses are essential because poor dental health can impact overall body health.

Generally, both partners answer health and lifestyle questions. From the results of medical tests and answers to lifestyle questions, doctors can also do an overall risk assessment for the pregnancy. Pregnancy risks may include a family history of certain diseases, obesity, or poor nutrition. In addition, use of caffeinated beverages, cigarettes, alcohol, or drugs can be risky.

Genetic Counseling

Responsible family planning may include genetic counseling. **Genetic counseling** offers scientific information and advice about heredity. Couples may seek genetic counseling to learn how likely it is their baby will be born with certain congenital disorders. **Congenital disorders** are problems resulting from heredity that exist at birth. See 7-9 for a list of common congenital disorders.

Genetic counselors are usually physicians or genetics specialists. A primary doctor may refer a couple for genetic counseling following a general checkup. This is the best time for counseling. The couple has a chance to use the information before becoming pregnant. They can also decide not to have children if the risk of a congenital disorder is high.

Genetic counselors usually begin their work by asking couples for complete family medical histories. Next, couples have physical exams and blood tests. In some cases, the genetic specialist will photograph and analyze the parents' chromosomes. These tests can identify people who carry certain genes that cause congenital disorders. A *carrier* is a person who has genes for a disorder without suffering any of its effects. A carrier might pass those genes along to his or her child. The child might inherit the disorder.

Genetic counseling cannot prevent congenital disorders. It simply tells couples about the statistical chances their children will inherit these disorders. Counselors can also tell couples how a certain disorder may affect a child and the family.

When Infertility Occurs

Some couples wish to achieve pregnancy, but find they cannot. Couples who cannot become pregnant are infertile. **Infertility** is the inability to conceive despite having intercourse regularly for at least one year. Infertility occurs in as many as 10 percent of marriages.

Common Congenital Disorders

Disorder	Symptoms	Cause	Treatment
Cleft lip/palate	A cleft lip occurs when the two sides of the upper lip do not grow together correctly. A cleft palate is an opening that remains in the roof of the mouth. These conditions, visible from birth, interfere with breathing, talking, hearing, and eating.	Variable: often caused by a number of factors working together.	Corrective surgery and speech therapy.
Cystic fibrosis	A chemical failure affects the lungs and pancreas. Thick, sticky mucus forms in the lungs, causing breathing problems. Digestion is affected by reduced amounts of digestive juices. An excess amount of salt is excreted in perspiration.	Recessive gene.	Physical therapy, synthetic digestive hormones, salt tablets, and antibodies can relieve symptoms. No known cure exists. People often have a shorter life span because they are very vulnerable to respiratory diseases.
Diabetes	Metabolic disorders cause high blood sugar, making people feel thirsty, hungry, and weak. Weight loss is common.	A number of factors working together.	Medications and insulin injections, along with careful diet and exercise, can control this disorder. No cure exists.
Down syndrome	Distinct physical features are evident. Common effects are slanting eyes; large, misshapen forehead; oversized tongue; curved fingers; and varying degrees of mental retardation.	Chromosome abnormality. More likely to occur when the mother is over age 35.	Special education, started as soon as possible, can help. Life span may be nearly normal.
Hydrocephalus	Extra fluid is trapped in the brain, making the head larger than normal.	A number of factors working together.	Surgical removal of excess fluid is normal. Without treatment, hydrocephalus is usually fatal.
Muscular dystrophy	A group of disorders which damage muscles, causing progressive weakness that leads to death.	Carried by the chromosomes.	There is no cure, but therapy and braces offer some relief.

(Continued on next page)

7-9 Congenital disorders are inherited and present from birth. This chart lists the most common congenital disorders.

Common Congenital Disorders

Disorder	Symptoms	Cause	Treatment
Phenylketonuria (PKU)	An enzyme deficiency that makes people unable to digest a certain protein. This protein collects in the bloodstream and harms brain development.	Recessive gene.	A special diet that avoids the indigestible protein. If treated within six weeks after birth, effects of the disease can be avoided.
Sickle-cell anemia	Causes red blood cells to be sickle-shaped rather than round. Sickle cells cannot carry oxygen through the body well. The body attacks these cells, lowering the red-blood-cell count, which can cause organ damage and disability. People with sickle-cell anemia may become pale, tired, and short of breath. They have occasional pain and low resistance to infection.	Recessive gene.	No cure exists. Various treatments may relieve some symptoms. Occasional blood transfusions may be needed. Life span may be shorter than normal.
Spina bifida	Baby's backbone does not close during the prenatal period. Paralysis and problems of the bladder and bowels are common.	Cause is unknown.	May require surgery to repair the spinal column. Prenatal tests can detect spina bifida.
Tay-Sachs	No symptoms until about six months of age, when baby stops growing normally. Causes a lack of a blood chemical that breaks down fatty deposits in the brain. Results in blindness and weakening muscles. Nervous system eventually stops working.	Recessive gene.	No known cure or treatment exists for Tay-Sachs disease. People with Tay-Sachs often die in early childhood.

7-9 Continued.

Causes of Infertility

It was once widely believed that infertility was a women's problem. Today, research shows that both men and women can have fertility problems. In about one-fourth of all cases, both the male and the female contribute to the problem. In the remaining cases, about as many men as women experience fertility problems. Maximum fertility requires that both males and females have healthy reproductive systems.

Rarely, psychological stress interferes with a couple's ability to conceive. Much more commonly, the causes of infertility are physical. Here are some major fertility problems in men and women.

Fertility Problems in Men. No sperm production, insufficient sperm production, and the production of weak sperm are infertility problems for men. These problems may be the result of certain diseases, such as mumps. They may also occur after prolonged fever. Other problems with the sperm may be due to physical or metabolic disorders (such as diabetes), some of which may be present from birth. A man's use of alcohol and drugs can also lessen his ability to produce healthy sperm.

Fertility Problems in Women. A number of factors may cause infertility in women. A woman's body must be able to produce and release a mature egg. Problems with egg or hormone production account for many cases of infertility. Ovulation problems may also cause infertility. A woman's ovaries, fallopian tubes, and uterus must be in working order.

If not, this can interfere with conception. For example, physical abnormalities or scar tissue from surgery or disease may block fallopian tubes and prevent conception.

More specific causes of infertility in women and men are given in 7-10. Most fertility problems require some type of medical help. A couple that has trouble conceiving may wish to consult a doctor. The doctor can help the couple discover what is causing their problem and advise them about their options. Knowing the cause of the problem and some possible solutions can greatly reduce the stress associated with fertility problems. Understanding the problem is the first step to solving it.

Options for Infertile Couples

If a couple is unable to conceive, they have several options. First, a couple may decide to accept their infertility and pursue goals other than parenting. More often, however, couples may wish to research

Physical Causes of Infertility

In Women	In Men
• Absence, disease, or disability of the ovaries, which prevents egg production or ovulation.	• Absence, disease, injury, or disability of the testes, which interferes with sperm production.
• Failure to ovulate.	• Absence or blockage of the vas deferens, which interferes with travel of sperm to the ejaculatory duct.
• Hormone imbalance that prevents ovulation.	
• Absence, disease, disability, or blockage of the fallopian tubes, which prevents the sperm from meeting the egg.	• Blockage, disease, infection, or disability of the urethra, which interferes with ability to release sperm during ejaculation.
• Absence, disease, or disability of the uterus, which prevents implantation, nourishment, or development of a fertilized egg.	• Absence of sperm in semen.
• Disease or disability of the cervix that prevents sperm from reaching the fallopian tubes.	• Insufficient amount or strength of sperm in semen.
• Disease or disability of the vagina that destroys sperm or blocks its entrance into the cervix.	• Problem related to erection or ejaculation.

7-10 The physical causes of infertility can be identified, and in many cases, remedied.

options that could help them become parents. These options are either medical treatments or adoption.

Medical Treatments

Many medical treatments are now available for infertility. Some of these options include fertility drugs and surgeries. Assisted-reproductive technologies are medical procedures that can also help a couple conceive. See 7-11. These medical technologies include

- **artificial insemination,** a procedure in which a doctor places sperm-containing semen directly in the upper part of a woman's vagina or uterus

- **in vitro fertilization,** a procedure that involves removing eggs from a woman's ovaries, fertilizing them with a man's sperm in a glass dish, and then placing the fertilized eggs in the woman's uterus

Medical Treatments for Infertility

Type of Treatment	How It Works	Possible Problems
Fertility drugs	Corrects hormone imbalances that can lead to conception (doctor prescribed)	Increases the likelihood that couples will experience multiple births
	Stimulates or regulates ovulation which can lead to conception (doctor prescribed)	Results in more complications for mothers and babies (twins, triplets, or more)
Surgery	Repairs the vas deferens or fallopian tubes so eggs and sperm can travel through these pathways	May result in health risks that exist with all major surgery
	Corrects problems with a woman's vagina, uterus, or cervix that prevent fertilization and implantation	Success in correcting problems may be limited
		May result in financial problems due to expense of surgery
Artificial insemination	Sperm-containing semen is directly placed in the upper part of a woman's vagina or uterus by a doctor	Expensive
	Increases the chances for fertilization	Use of fertility drugs may be required with this procedure
		Use of donor sperm (not father's sperm) may be required, thus raising ethical and legal questions
In vitro fertilization	Requires removal of eggs from a woman's ovaries which are then fertilized by a man's sperm in a glass dish (in vitro)	Expensive
	Requires transfer of some eggs to woman's uterus after fertilization and cell division begins (in one to two days)	Success rate is low—about 10 percent per attempt
	Results in success if fertilized eggs implant in uterus and prenatal development continues	Use of donor eggs or sperm may raise legal and ethical issues
		Unused fertilized eggs may raise legal and ethical issues

7-11 Medical help is available for infertile couples. Yet it comes with a high price tag. Success rates are not very high but are improving.

Adoption Options

Adopting a child is another way couples can become parents. Adoptive children and parents may or may not be biologically related. (For example, adoptive children may be nieces, nephews, or cousins of the adoptive parents.) Some couples choose adoption over biological parenthood. Decisions about adoption are permanent, however, and require careful thought.

Couples wishing to adopt have several choices to make. First, they should research the laws governing adoption in their state. Secondly, adoption counseling may help them clarify their options and choose an adoption situation that is best for them.

If a couple desires to adopt, they may wish to contact several adoption agencies. These agencies are either public or private. Most are nonprofit agencies. Agencies that handle international adoptions are also a choice. All agencies must hold a license in the state in which they function. Whether couples choose a public or private agency, they should be sure to check the state license to make sure the agency meets state requirements. See 7-12 to compare public and private adoption agencies. Couples may also choose *independent adoption*. In this case, the couple works with an attorney or doctor, not an agency, to adopt a child. Independent adoptions are legal in most states.

What can couples expect when they apply for an agency adoption? First, couples must complete a lengthy application. The agency obtains medical records on each spouse. They also obtain personal references for the couple. Then an agency staff member (usually a social worker) interviews the couple, separately and together. Interviews occur at the agency office and at the couple's home. Couples applying for adoption also receive information about fees, agency procedures, and legal procedures for adoption. In the case

Comparing Adoption Agencies

Public Agencies	Private Agencies
• Operate as part of the state government.	• Are run by an organization other than the government.
• Place children who are in the state's custody (children who have been abandoned or surrendered to the state by their biological parents).	• Licensed by the state, that is, they must meet certain state standards.
• Place older children more often than infants.	• May place more newborns than state agencies.
• Have shorter waiting lists for children and more children than private agencies.	• Often specialize in certain types of adoptions, such as newborns, older children, entire families of siblings.
• Have fewer restrictions on who can adopt. For example, single people and married couples usually can adopt.	• Have longer waiting lists for children and fewer children than public agencies.
• Charge lower fees than those charged by private agencies.	• May have many restrictions about who can adopt. For example, the couple's marital status and length of marriage can impact eligibility
	• Charge higher fees than those charged by public agencies.

7-12 Public and private adoption agencies function in different ways, but help couples achieve their goal of parenthood.

of international adoption, couples may also be required to make one or more trips to a child's birth country. Travel expenses and any international fees add to the cost of adoption.

If the agency approves a couple for adoption, agency social workers match the couple with an available baby or older child. Depending on the waiting list, this process can take a long time. The social worker also visits the couple's home between the time of placement and the final court appearance. The agency handles all legal matters for the couple.

When adopting a child, couples may have a choice between a closed or open adoption. With a **closed adoption,** no contact occurs between the birthparents and the adoptive family. In **open adoption,** there is some degree of contact between birthparents and adoptive parents. For example, birthparents and adoptive parents may meet or send letters or e-mail messages with photos. They may talk on the phone or have regular visits. With open adoptions, the birthparents choose the adoptive parents. They read background information on each possible couple. The adoptive parents are often present for the child's birth.

Choosing an Option

No matter how they attempt to resolve fertility problems, couples have these factors to consider: legal, financial, physical, and emotional. Each option may pose one or more implications.

Laws apply to medical treatments and adoptions. Laws cover who is eligible and what procedures to follow. In some cases, when babies are born as a result of assisted-reproductive technologies, the "parent status" can be a legal issue.

Medical treatments are very costly. Couples may go into debt trying to conceive. Adoption requires the couple to be financially stable. Private adoption agencies often charge on the basis of family income. Some adoptions, such as international adoptions, can be costly due to travel expenses and special fees.

Medical treatments involve health risks or side effects. Some treatments have a low success rate. The couple should be aware of any risks they face and weigh them carefully.

With medical treatment and adoption comes emotional uncertainty that can be difficult to handle. There is no guarantee a couple can become parents. For the couples that do become parents, however, the emotional rewards are great. They may feel their success is a miracle, 7-13.

7-13 Couples who have overcome a fertility problem are especially happy about the arrival of a healthy baby into their family.

Whether through natural birth, adoption, or with medical treatment, when a couple decides to parent much planning is needed.

Summing It Up

- Responsible family planning has advantages for both parents and children.

- Several factors influence a couple's reproductive and family planning decisions. Factors may differ somewhat depending on whether planning for a first child or for additional children.

- Understanding human reproduction is an important first step in family planning.

- Doctors can explain family planning options for couples interested in planning their families.

- Each partner should undergo pre-pregnancy health assessments. Genetic counseling is a possibility for some couples.

- Couples who cannot conceive have many options that can help them reach their parenting goals.

Recalling the Facts

1. Name two advantages of responsible family planning.

2. Why do most authorities suggest that parents space children about three years apart?

3. Why is it difficult to parent several young children at the same time?

4. Explain the male's role in reproduction.

5. Describe the female's role in reproduction.

6. Summarize the relationship of dominant and recessive genes to a baby's traits.

7. Name the male and female surgeries for permanently preventing pregnancy.

8. List health assessments that are common for women and for men prior to pregnancy.

9. How can genetic counseling benefit couples before pregnancy occurs?

10. What are congenital disorders? Name two and give a cause and possible treatment for each.

11. What are two causes of infertility in men? in women?

12. Name two options for couples who cannot conceive.

13. List two ways a couple might adopt a child.

14. Briefly explain the differences between public and private adoption agencies.

Applying New Skills

1. **News review.** Collect reliable Internet, newspaper, and magazine articles concerning family planning. Write a brief summary of each article, comparing and contrasting the facts. Then create a bulletin board featuring these articles for others to read.

2. **Research and report.** Use Internet or print resources to investigate one of the congenital disorders described in the chapter. Can this disorder be detected by genetic counseling and prenatal tests? How common is the disorder? Is there a cure? How is the disorder treated? Write a summary of your findings to share with the class.

3. **Role-play.** Role-play a couple discussing the possibility of adopting a child after finding out they are unable to conceive. What factors might they consider?

4. **Interview.** Interview a person who was adopted as a young child and/or a couple who has adopted one or more children. How do they view adoption? How did the adopted child and/or the adoptive parents feel about adoption? What are the pros and cons of adoption? Write a summary of your findings to share with the class.

Thinking Critically

1. Debate the advantages of family planning as compared to "letting nature take its course."

2. Compare and contrast decisions about having a first child with decisions about having more children.

3. Analyze whether family planning is a shared responsibility. If not, which partner should have more responsibility and why? Do males and females in your class have different opinions on this issue? If so, why do you think this is?

4. Draw conclusions about how genetic counseling can benefit couples with congenital disorders in their family histories.

Linking Academics

1. **Quick write.** Summarize the process of conception in 10 sentences or less.

2. **Social studies.** Investigate the legal and ethical issues surrounding assisted-medical technologies for infertile couples. What are the issues? How do the views on these issues vary?

3. **Reading.** Review a book about infertility or adoption from the library. Consider books that include factual information and/or narratives on various couples' journeys through infertility, including the choices they made. Write a brief summary about your book to share with the class.

Chapter 8

Pregnancy

Objectives

After studying this chapter, you will be able to

- summarize the biological processes related to prenatal development and the health of the mother and child.
- identify signs that may indicate pregnancy.
- identify ways to confirm pregnancy.
- explain the physical changes and possible complications that occur during pregnancy.
- describe the feelings wives and husbands may have during pregnancy.
- propose ways couples can support each other during pregnancy.
- identify factors that determine the intensity of the emotional trauma of a miscarriage or stillbirth.

Key Terms

pregnancy
trimester
prenatal development
blastocyst
embryo
placenta
umbilical cord
amniotic fluid
fetus
miscarriage
stillbirth
pregnancy-induced hypertension
gestational diabetes
rubella
Rh factor disorder
sexually transmitted infections (STIs)
AIDS (acquired immunodeficiency syndrome)
HIV (human immunodeficiency virus)

Many couples find pregnancy to be a fascinating time of life. A baby's development seems magical, yet it follows a set biological sequence. Pregnancy can be a very happy time, but it may bring fear and doubt. The months of pregnancy may seem to go by slowly. When labor finally begins, however, couples may still feel unprepared for the birth of their babies. For many couples, no other time of life is as complex or as rewarding as pregnancy.

In this chapter you will be able to describe how babies grow and develop before birth. You will learn about common signs of pregnancy and how to confirm it. You will also learn about the physical changes that occur during pregnancy. Then you will be able to explain pregnancy complications and warning signals. Finally, you will learn about expectant parents' reactions to pregnancy. This includes how parents begin Galinsky's first stage of parenting called the *image-making stage*.

After Conception

As you recall, pregnancy begins with the union of a sperm cell and an egg cell. This union results in conception, 8-1. At the beginning of pregnancy, the mother's egg cell and the father's sperm cell unite to form a fertilized egg. At this stage, the fertilized egg, or *zygote*, is about the size of the tip of a pencil or ballpoint pen.

Pregnancy is the period during which a fertilized egg grows and develops into a human being inside the mother's body. This period lasts about nine months, and is divided into three trimesters. A **trimester** is a period of about three months. By the end of 40 weeks, a newborn baby arrives in the world, 8-2.

Gender Determination

The single-celled zygote contains all the genetic information needed to determine the gender of the developing baby. Whether

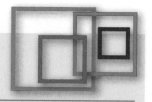

Conception Review

Ovulation Occurs
Through ovulation, the woman's body releases an egg that can be fertilized.

Sperm Enter Female's Body
Through sexual intercourse, the man releases semen, which contains sperm, into the woman's body. These sperm swim up the vagina and through the cervix, uterus, and fallopian tubes. In the fallopian tubes, sperm come into contact with the egg. Conception is likely if sperm are released a few days before, during, or after a woman ovulates.

Union of Sperm and Egg
Only about 200 sperm ever reach the egg. One sperm will penetrate the egg. Immediately following the union of the sperm and egg, the egg forms a hard outer coat that prevents other sperm from entering.

8-1 During conception, the sperm and egg unite.

the zygote will become a boy or a girl depends upon the sex chromosomes it inherits from its parents. Each person possesses two sex chromosomes. One is inherited from the mother, and the other is inherited from the father, 8-3.

Females possess two X chromosomes. Therefore, a mother will always pass an X chromosome to her children. Males possess one X chromosome and one Y chromosome. This means that a father might pass an X chromosome to his child. If so, the child would be a girl because she would have two X chromosomes. Instead, a father might pass a Y chromosome to his child. This child would be a boy because he would have one X chromosome and one Y chromosome.

8-2 This baby developed over three trimesters of pregnancy. He started as two separate cells and developed into a human being.

Prenatal Development

Prenatal development is all development that occurs between conception and birth. *Prenatal* means before birth. Like all other types of development, changes will occur. These changes occur faster than at any other time in a person's life.

Stages of Development

Although growth is continuous, it occurs in stages. Prenatal development has three stages. It includes the germinal, the embryonic, and the fetal stages. Each stage has certain milestones in the development of the baby before birth.

Every cell of a woman has two X chromosomes.

Every cell of a man has one X chromosome and one Y chromosome.

Every egg has one X chromosome.

Half the sperm have an X chromosome: half have a Y chromosome.

If a sperm with an X chromosome enters the egg, the result is a person with two X chromosomes—a girl.

If a sperm with a Y chromosome enters the egg, the result is a person with one X and one Y chromosome—a boy.

8-3 The sex chromosome from the father's sperm determines what gender a baby will be.

Germinal Stage

The formation of a zygote begins the *germinal stage*, which lasts from conception until about two weeks later. The germinal stage is the first stage of prenatal development. Another name for this stage is the *stage of the zygote*.

As you recall, the single-celled zygote begins to grow rapidly. In about 36 hours, it divides into two cells, each of which grows and divides. This cellular division will continue as the new organism travels down the fallopian tubes and into the uterus. By 10 to 12 days after fertilization, the new organism has developed into a hollow ball of cells. This ball of cells, called a **blastocyst**, implants itself into the endometrium (uterus lining). After implantation, the blastocyst will remain in the uterus and continue to grow and develop.

Embryonic Stage

Cells of the blastocyst form the embryo. The developing baby is an **embryo** from two weeks after conception through the eighth week of pregnancy. This is the *embryonic stage* of prenatal development. Because all body systems begin developing, this is the most critical prenatal stage.

Important structures that sustain the pregnancy also develop during this stage. Parts of the blastocyst develop into the placenta. The **placenta** is a special organ that allows nutrients, oxygen, and water to pass from mother to baby. It also allows the baby's waste products to pass to the mother for elimination. The **umbilical cord** is the flexible cord that contains blood vessels and connects the baby to the placenta, 8-4.

Still other parts of the blastocyst develop into the fetal membranes. These membranes are the outer membrane, or *chorion*, and the inner membrane, or *amnion*. Together, they make up the *amnio-chorionic membrane* or "bag of waters." Inside the amnio-chorionic membrane is **amniotic fluid** that completely surrounds the baby. Amniotic fluid has several important functions. It regulates the baby's temperature. It also cushions the baby against possible injury and allows the baby to move around easily.

Fetal Stage

From the ninth week of pregnancy until birth, the developing baby is called a **fetus**. This is the *fetal stage* of prenatal development. During this stage all body systems develop and mature. Body details such as hair, fingernails, and eyelashes also form. The developing baby grows in size.

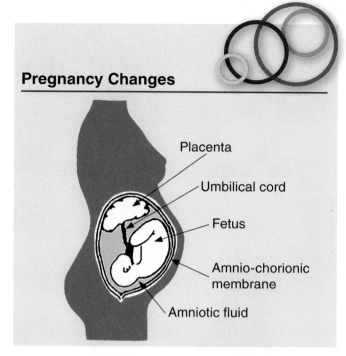

Pregnancy Changes

Placenta
Umbilical cord
Fetus
Amnio-chorionic membrane
Amniotic fluid

8-4 The female body undergoes many changes to provide nourishment and protection of the fetus growing inside her.

Month-by-Month Development

Although it is accurate to describe prenatal development by its stages—the germinal stage, the embryonic stage, and the fetal stage—these basic descriptions do not explain much about *how* the baby is developing. All of these stages begin in the first trimester. The fetal period, for example, lasts about thirty-two weeks, or most of the second and third trimesters. It is difficult to easily describe how much a baby grows and changes during these thirty-two weeks.

It is most helpful to describe prenatal development in smaller segments. For instance, studying this development month-by-month makes it easier to describe how a baby grows and develops before birth. See Figure 8-5 for details on this development.

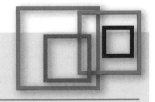

Prenatal Development

First Trimester

First month

- Baby begins as a *zygote*. It grows into a *blastocyst* and then into an *embryo*.
- First signs of the baby's heart, lungs, face, arms, and legs show.
- Heart begins beating and pumps blood through arteries.
- Digestive system is forming.
- Baby's brain and spinal cord develop from the neural tube.
- Ears and eyes begin to form.
- Tissue that will later form the baby's backbone, skull, ribs, and muscles can be seen on ultrasound.
- By month's end, baby becomes an embryo and is ½-inch long and weighs much less than 1 ounce.

Second month

- Body organs and systems that began in the first month are continuing to develop.
- Liver and stomach start to work.
- Head makes up nearly half of the embryo.
- Brain grows quickly and directs the baby's movements.
- Arms and legs become longer and take shape.
- Fingers and toes develop.
- Distinct wrists, elbows, hands, knees, and feet are present.
- Eyes take on color and eyelids form but are sealed shut.
- Ears, nose, and mouth take shape.
- At month's end, embryo is 1-inch long and weighs ⅓ ounce.

Third month

- Baby is now called a *fetus.*
- Bones are growing.
- Kidneys are working.
- Fetus moves often, but cannot be felt by mother yet.
- Tooth sockets and buds for teeth forming in jawbone.
- Fetus can open and close mouth and swallow.
- Fingerprints appear.
- All parts of the baby's body are formed by the end of the month.
- At month's end, baby is 4-inches long and weighs 1 ounce.

(Continued on next page)

8-5 Critical changes take place in the developing baby during each of the nine months of pregnancy.

Illustrations courtesy of the March of Dimes. ©2007 March of Dimes.

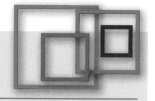

Prenatal Development

Second Trimester

Fourth month

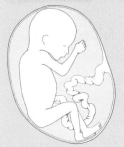

- Baby's heartbeat is strong.
- Baby's airways develop but are not in use yet.
- Skin is transparent and thin.
- Fingernails appear.
- Baby sleeps and wakes.
- Baby moves and kicks. Toward the end of the month, the mother may feel movements.
- Placenta is now formed.
- Umbilical cord grows and thickens to carry enough blood and nourishment to baby.
- By the end of the month the baby is 6- to 7-inches long and weighs about 5 ounces.

Fifth month

- Baby's internal organs continue to grow.
- Blood supply to the lungs increases.
- Eyelashes, eyebrows, and scalp hair appear.
- Silky body hair and a waxy coating protect baby's skin from its watery surroundings.
- Baby sleeps and wakes in a pattern.
- Baby turns from side to side, kicks, and moves a lot.
- By month's end, the baby is 12-inches long and weighs about 1 pound.

Sixth month

- Baby's growth speeds up.
- Baby opens and closes its eyes and can hear sounds.
- Skin is red, wrinkled, and oily.
- Baby stretches, kicks, and sucks its thumb.
- At month's end, the baby is 12- to 14-inches long and weighs about 1½ pounds.

(Continued on next page)

8-5 Continued.

Prenatal Development

Third Trimester

Seventh month

- Baby's brain, nervous system, and lungs have become much more mature.
- Bones are developed, but are soft and flexible. They are beginning to harden.
- Skin is wrinkled and covered with a thick, white protective coating called *vernix.* Fatty tissue begins developing under the surface.
- Lungs have matured and can support the baby outside the uterus.
- Baby kicks and stretches to exercise. The outline of the baby's fist, foot, or head may be seen outside the mother's body when the baby moves.
- At month's end, the baby is 15-inches long and weighs about 2½ pounds.

Eighth month

- Baby continues to grow in weight and length.
- Rapid brain growth continues.
- Skin is no longer wrinkled due to the layer of fatty tissue under the surface. The skin color is pink, not red.
- Baby has less room to move around but kicks strongly.
- Baby may position itself head-down in the uterus.
- At month's end, the baby is about 18-inches long and weighs about 5 pounds.

Ninth month

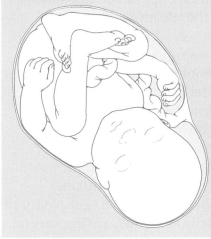

- Baby gains about ½ pound each week.
- Lungs are mature.
- Downy hair that covered the skin disappears.
- During the ninth month, the baby moves into final position—usually head down—and stays there until birth.
- At birth, babies are an average of 19- to 21-inches long and weigh an average of 6 to 9 pounds.

8-5 Continued.

Signs of Pregnancy

The miraculous process of conception occurs within a woman's body without her even knowing it. Most of the time, a woman does not know she is pregnant until several weeks after conception.

Most women initially suspect they are pregnant only after observing certain signs that often indicate pregnancy, 8-6. All of these signs can have other causes. They are not always sure signs of pregnancy.

Missed Menstrual Period

Missed menstrual periods are the most common signs of pregnancy. This is because women do not menstruate during pregnancy. When a healthy woman has had intercourse and her period is more than 14 days late, pregnancy is likely. If she misses another period, this probability is even stronger. If a woman's period is lighter or shorter than normal, this may also indicate pregnancy. The period is not really menstruation. Instead, the spotting comes from the implantation of the blastocyst into the endometrium.

A missed menstrual period is not a sure sign of pregnancy. Women may stop menstruating for other reasons. These include emotional stress; changes in climate, diet, and exercise; rapid change in body weight; and chronic diseases such as anemia. A woman should see her doctor to determine the cause of the missed period. The doctor can advise her what, if anything, she can do to make her cycle more regular.

Breast Changes

Changes in a woman's breasts may also indicate pregnancy. During pregnancy, the breasts become larger to accommodate the production of breast milk to nourish the baby. A woman's breasts begin changing during the first trimester. Generally, these changes start about the same time the woman misses a menstrual period.

A woman's breasts may swell and enlarge during pregnancy. They may also become quite tender or sore. The *areola*, the pigmented area around the nipple, will become darker and wider. Since many women's breasts become tender or slightly swollen just before a menstrual period, changes in the breasts by themselves are not a sure sign of pregnancy.

Nausea

Nausea is another common sign of pregnancy. Another name for the nausea that occurs during pregnancy is "morning sickness." Although it may occur at any time of day, many women experience this nausea upon waking in the morning. About one-third of pregnant women have nausea severe enough to cause vomiting. Another third experience occasional or mild nausea. The remaining third feel no nausea at all.

Morning sickness usually occurs in the first trimester as a woman's body adjusts to being pregnant. Fatigue, a poor diet, or an empty stomach may add to the problem. If a woman experiences nausea during pregnancy, she should be sure to get plenty of sleep and eat nutritious foods. Eating several small meals a day rather than two or three

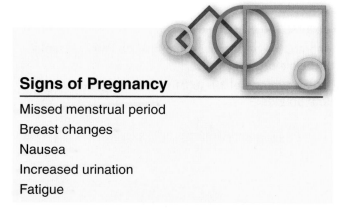

Signs of Pregnancy

Missed menstrual period

Breast changes

Nausea

Increased urination

Fatigue

8-6 Many signs can indicate pregnancy. No single sign is, by itself, a sure sign of pregnancy.

large ones may also help. If the nausea is severe enough to cause routine vomiting, a woman should consult her doctor.

Increased Urination and Fatigue

Increased urination is another sign of pregnancy. During the first trimester, the uterus grows and pushes against the bladder. This pressure on her bladder causes the pregnant woman to urinate more frequently.

Fatigue is another sign of pregnancy. As a woman's body adjusts to pregnancy, she may feel very tired. She may sleep more than usual and need to take naps. For some pregnant women, this fatigue lasts throughout the first trimester. By itself, fatigue is not a sure sign of pregnancy. Fatigue can also occur for many other reasons.

Confirming Pregnancy

If a woman suspects she is pregnant, she should have a pregnancy test to confirm she is indeed pregnant. Home and medical pregnancy tests check for the presence of a hormone called *HCG (Human Chorionic Gonadotropin)*. This hormone is secreted by the blastocyst as early as a week after conception. Pregnancy tests use antibodies that react to the HCG in a blood or urine sample. If a pregnancy test seems to confirm pregnancy, a woman should see her doctor for further medical tests, 8-7. Read the following for more information about home and medical confirmation of pregnancy.

Home Pregnancy Tests

A woman may choose to first use a home pregnancy test. She can buy this test over-the-counter in a supermarket or pharmacy. Home pregnancy tests are generally low in cost.

8-7 Once pregnancy is confirmed, a woman should see her doctor to begin prenatal care.

The way a home pregnancy test works is fairly simple. It requires a sample of the woman's urine. A woman should read the directions and follow them carefully. Some home pregnancy tests can detect pregnancy as early as the first day of a missed menstrual period. The level of accuracy in home pregnancy tests varies from one test to another. Home pregnancy tests are less accurate than lab tests done in a doctor's office.

If a woman is pregnant, her body will produce the HCG hormone. The antibodies in the pregnancy test will cause a chemical reaction to any HCG in the urine sample. Observing this reaction confirms the woman has this hormone and is pregnant.

If the reaction does not occur, the woman is probably not pregnant. If she continues having symptoms of pregnancy, however, she should test again in a few days. Sometimes a reaction does not occur because the woman's level of HCG is too low for the test to detect. This means she has taken the test too soon in her pregnancy for the test to confirm her pregnancy. When she tests again, her level of HCG will have risen if she is pregnant. This second test should indicate whether she is pregnant.

Medical Tests to Confirm Pregnancy

If a home pregnancy test is positive, the woman should make an appointment with her doctor. The doctor will have a lab test done to confirm the pregnancy. The lab test will require the woman to give a sample of her blood or urine to test for HCG. Also, if the lab test confirms she is pregnant, a woman will need to talk with her doctor about the pregnancy and the medical care she will need. Prenatal care is described in Chapter 9.

Some women go directly to their doctor's offices for lab tests instead of using a home pregnancy test. These women may worry a home pregnancy test will be inaccurate. They may feel pregnancy is certain and know they will need a doctor's care. If the lab test is positive, the doctor will do pelvic tests to confirm the pregnancy and begin prenatal care.

Physical Changes During Pregnancy

A woman's body undergoes dramatic changes during pregnancy. The basic changes are much the same for all women. No two pregnancies are exactly alike, however, even for the same woman.

The most obvious changes during pregnancy are the increased size of a woman's breasts and abdomen, 8-8. Many pregnant women have mixed emotions about the changing shape of their bodies. A woman may be very excited when she first notices the tiny bulge in her abdomen. When her pregnancy starts to show, it may begin to seem more real to her. A woman may enjoy the way her body looks as her abdomen grows. She might also feel embarrassed or less attractive. A woman may feel she is growing fat as her size increases. She should remember her shape is changing because the baby is growing inside her, not because she is fat.

8-8 The most obvious physical change during pregnancy is a woman's body shape. A husband's loving support is crucial during this time of change.

As her breasts and abdomen grow, a woman's skin will stretch, too. As her skin stretches, the tissues just below the skin surface may tear. This can cause pink or red marks called *stretch marks* to appear on her skin. After pregnancy, these marks usually fade into faint, silvery lines. A slow, even weight gain within the doctor's recommendations is the best way to prevent stretch marks. Rapidly gaining too much weight will cause more stretching and more stretch marks. Daily massaging with cream or lotion helps keep the skin soft and supple. This may reduce the amount of tearing and stretch marks.

Pregnancy may also affect a woman's digestive system. During the first trimester, she may experience nausea. Toward the end of pregnancy, as the growing fetus exerts more pressure on her stomach and intestines, she may feel heartburn and indigestion. If these problems bother a woman, she should talk with her doctor. Often, changing what she eats can help.

Internal pressure also affects the bladder. Early in pregnancy, the growing uterus pushes against the bladder and causes the woman to urinate more often. In the middle months, the fetus moves out of the pelvic region and into the abdomen, which lessens pressure on the bladder. Late in pregnancy, the growing baby again puts pressure on the bladder, causing a need to urinate more frequently. When the baby drops lower into the pelvis in preparation for birth, this pressure may ease.

A woman's hormone levels change dramatically during pregnancy, which can cause mood swings. Hormones cause many of a woman's emotional changes during pregnancy.

Pregnancy Complications

Most pregnancies proceed normally. Sometimes, however, complications occur. Lack of proper health care during pregnancy or nature can cause these complications. Methods of prevention and treatments exist for some of these complications. Others simply run their course.

In many cases, warning signals precede complications. If a pregnant woman notices any of the warning signals listed in 8-9, she should contact her doctor at once. Proper medical attention and care reduce the risk of serious, untreatable complications.

Two of the most common complications during pregnancy are miscarriage and stillbirth. Others include pregnancy-induced hypertension, gestational diabetes, rubella, and Rh factor disorder. Sexually transmitted infections (STIs) may also complicate a woman's pregnancy and affect her baby.

Miscarriage and Stillbirth

The loss of any pregnancy can be devastating to expectant parents. There is no way to predict who will be affected by pregnancy loss. There are two types of pregnancy loss in which babies die *before*

Warning Signals for Pregnancy Complications

- Bleeding from the vagina
- Severe or continuing nausea or vomiting
- Continuing or severe headache
- Swelling or puffiness of the face or hands, or marked swelling of the feet and ankles
- Blurring of vision or spots before the eyes
- A marked decrease in the amount of urine passed
- Pain or burning while passing urine
- Chills and fever
- Sharp or continuous abdominal pain
- Sudden gush of liquid from the vagina before the baby is due

8-9 Reacting promptly to one of these warning signals may help avoid serious complications during pregnancy.

delivery. **Miscarriage** refers to the death of a baby before the 20th week of pregnancy. Doctors sometimes call miscarriage *spontaneous abortion*. A **stillbirth** occurs when a baby dies after the 20th week of pregnancy but before delivery. Miscarriage and stillbirth are not one and the same. Doctors use various methods to evaluate the cause of death when a baby dies before birth. These evaluations can be helpful for parents while grieving their loss and in planning future pregnancies.

Miscarriages may occur in as many as one-fourth of pregnancies. Most happen during the first trimester, often before a woman even suspects she is pregnant. At other times, a woman may lose her pregnancy to stillbirth as late as 36 weeks. Each year in the United States, approximately one stillbirth occurs out of 115 live births.

No single factor explains all miscarriages and stillbirths. The causes may vary. Many miscarriages and stillbirths are linked to chromosome problems in the embryo or fetus. If the baby is not developing normally, it may not survive. Miscarriage or stillbirth may occur.

Exposure to harmful substances or illnesses can also cause miscarriage of the developing baby. The mother's habits, such as smoking, drinking, and using drugs, can lead to miscarriage. Some sexually transmitted diseases or other infections can result in death of the fetus. Many doctors suggest couples wait three to six months after a miscarriage or stillbirth before trying to conceive again. This time allows the woman's body to recuperate. It also gives the couple time to grieve their loss.

Pregnancy-Induced Hypertension

Pregnancy-induced hypertension (PIH) is a condition that affects a woman's kidneys, heart, or blood circulation. It usually develops gradually during the second half of pregnancy, or after the 20th week. The symptoms of PIH include high blood pressure and too much protein in urine. In severe cases of PIH—or *preeclampsia*—a woman may experience rapid weight gain, swollen face and fingers, headaches, and blurred vision. If a woman notices these symptoms, she should contact her doctor at once, 8-10.

Although the exact cause of PIH is unknown, there are some conditions that may increase a woman's risk of developing PIH. These conditions include the following:

- high blood pressure before pregnancy
- diabetes
- PIH with a previous pregnancy
- kidney disease
- age of mother (younger than 20 and older than 40)
- pregnancy with multiple babies (twins, triplets, or more)

PIH may also result from a lack of proper nutrition and health care during pregnancy. The increase of PIH is disturbing to medical authorities. PIH is very common in teen pregnancies. Pregnant teens are the least likely to receive proper medical attention early in pregnancy. They are also less likely to eat well-balanced meals. PIH may also occur in the pregnancies of women who have abnormally low weight gains or women over the age of 40.

In mild cases, doctors treat PIH with a carefully monitored, nutritious diet and bed rest. Other treatments may include medication for high blood pressure and fetal monitoring to check the baby's condition. Doctors will do regular testing of urine or blood to check for worsening PIH. Severe cases may require hospitalization. If other treatments do not work, early delivery of the

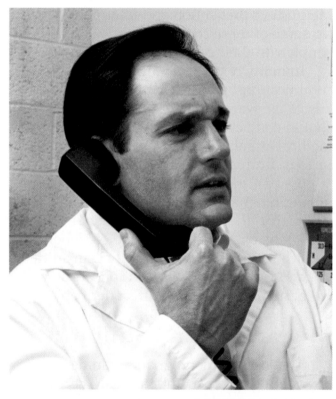

8-10 A woman's doctor wants her to call if she has any questions or concerns about her pregnancy. Obstetricians handle many such calls every day.

baby may occur. If it is not treated, PIH can cause convulsions and the pregnant woman's death or stillbirth of the child.

Gestational Diabetes

With increasing incidence of obesity in women of childbearing age, comes the increasing risk of **gestational diabetes**. High blood glucose (blood sugar) is characteristic of this disorder. When it occurs, a woman's pancreas does not produce enough insulin. This is a hormone that helps her body convert blood glucose to energy. Recent research shows gestational diabetes occurs in up to seven percent of pregnancies.

During pregnancy, poorly controlled diabetes can result in a larger-than-usual baby. This may lead to surgical delivery of the baby. Stillbirth and PIH are other complications. Babies born to women with this disorder have a higher risk of obesity and diabetes as young adults.

Most women with gestational diabetes can control their blood glucose with diet and exercise. A careful balance of calories and nutrients helps women with this disorder to avoid other complications. Well-controlled blood glucose leads to good health for mother and baby, 8-11.

Rubella

Although it rarely occurs in the United States today, **rubella** (also called German measles) is a virus that can impact pregnancy. It may cause miscarriage, stillbirth, or serious congenital disorders. Rubella poses the greatest threat during the first trimester of pregnancy. Fortunately, most pregnant women are immune to this virus. They either had it as children or were immunized against it.

If a woman contracts the virus, the symptoms are quite mild. She will have a low-grade fever, a rash, and swollen lymph glands in the neck. For the fetus, the effects are much worse. If the baby survives, he

8-11 A nutritious diet and regular exercise can help a woman control gestational diabetes.

or she may have vision, hearing, or heart problems. Mental disability may also occur. A pregnant woman should inform her doctor if she thinks she has been exposed to rubella. Blood tests can determine if she is infected.

A vaccine can prevent rubella. Children in the United States usually receive the MMR (measles-mumps-rubella) vaccine twice before they go to school. Although all children should receive this vaccine, it is especially important for parents to make sure their female children receive it. The best time to receive the vaccination is in early childhood. How does a woman know if she is immune to rubella? If her medical records show she received the vaccine at the appropriate times or if she has a blood test that shows immunity, a woman needs no further vaccination.

If needed, adult women should receive the vaccine only if they are sure they are not pregnant. After receiving the vaccine, women should avoid becoming pregnant for at least a month. The MMR vaccine itself poses a risk to a fetus.

Rh Factor Disorder

Early in pregnancy, a doctor tests a woman's blood for a substance called Rh factor. Most people have the Rh factor in their blood. These people are Rh positive (Rh+). In most cases, both mother and baby are Rh+. Only about 15 percent of people do not have the Rh factor in their blood. They are Rh negative (Rh-).

Rh factor disorder occurs when a mother who is Rh- gives birth to a baby who is Rh+. During pregnancy, the mother and baby exchange substances through the placenta. The fetus produces substances that enter the pregnant woman's blood. Some of these substances contain Rh+ cells. These cells are incompatible with the mother's Rh- blood cells.

Once the Rh+ cells are in the woman's bloodstream, her body produces certain antibodies to fight them. These antibodies may cross the placenta and pass into the baby's bloodstream. In the baby's bloodstream, these antibodies will destroy red blood cells. This can cause anemia, brain damage, and even death of the fetus.

Rh factor disorder is not usually a problem in first pregnancies. It takes time for antibodies to develop. In second or future pregnancies, more antibodies are present and the risk to the fetus is much greater.

Doctors can easily treat Rh factor disorder with a vaccine called RhoGAM. This medicine destroys any antibodies the mother may have built up during pregnancy. An Rh- mother should receive this vaccine during the 28th week of pregnancy and again 72 hours after delivery. She should also receive it in every future pregnancy.

Sexually Transmitted Infections

Sexually transmitted infections (STIs) (also known as sexually transmitted diseases) are a number of infections and conditions that pass from one person to another through sexual contact. STIs have serious health consequences. A person can be infected even when he or she shows no sign of infection. They threaten a person's health, fertility, and in some cases, a person's life. Pregnant women with STIs endanger the health of their unborn children as well as their own health. A couple should keep themselves free of STIs for their own health and the health of their unborn children, 8-12.

HPV

HPV (human papillomavirus) is the most common STI in the United States, affecting between 75 and 80 percent of the

8-12 Avoiding STIs is essential for a healthy pregnancy. Waiting until marriage to begin a sexual relationship is the best way couples can protect themselves from STIs.

population. The virus is highly contagious with a 65 percent chance of infection each time a person has sex with an infected partner. Because symptoms are not always obvious, doctors rely on the results of regular PAP smears to detect abnormalities of cells. Some strains of the virus can lead to cervical cancer. Some women also develop genital warts. Although there is no known cure for HPV, treatments can lessen symptoms. A new vaccine for young women may prevent infection.

HPV does not pose a risk to fertility. However, because a woman's immune system is depressed during pregnancy, HPV can become more aggressive and lead to more problems with other infections. Genital warts can bleed and even grow large enough to block the vaginal canal, both of which complicate delivery. Bleeding warts puts babies at risk for infection. Within three years of birth, infected children may develop warts on their genitals or larynx.

Gonorrhea

Gonorrhea is a bacterial STI that affects more than 700,000 people each year. Women often show no symptoms. In men with symptoms, discharge from the penis and painful urination are common. Women who do show symptoms may have an abnormal vaginal discharge or uterine bleeding. Women may also have painful urination and infection of the vagina, urethra, and fallopian tubes.

A medical exam and culture can detect gonorrhea. Doctors can prescribe medicine to clear up the infection and cure gonorrhea. If left untreated, gonorrhea can cause arthritis, heart disease, and infertility.

Miscarriage and stillbirth are more common in pregnant women with gonorrhea. A woman can pass gonorrhea to her baby during delivery as the baby passes through the birth canal. Newborns who contract gonorrhea during delivery can develop an eye infection that leads to blindness. Since gonorrhea is so common, all newborns receive treatment with special eye drops just after birth. These medicated eye drops can prevent gonorrheal eye infection.

Syphilis

A bacterium carries the *syphilis* STI. The first symptom is a sore, or *chancre*, that appears 10 and 90 days after contact. The sore heals by itself four to six weeks later, but the disease does not go away.

Untreated syphilis passes through a second stage that includes a fever, rash, headaches, and sore throat. It may also cause wart like growths, fluid-filled sores, hair loss, and a loss of appetite. These symptoms may also disappear. If syphilis remains untreated, it will damage the person's internal organs. Years later, this damage may cause heart problems, insanity, blindness, paralysis, or even death.

Syphilis can cause serious damage to an unborn child. In early pregnancy, pregnant women usually receive a test for syphilis. Treatment during early pregnancy is possible. This prevents the disease from affecting the baby. Syphilis will pass through the placenta to the fetus if left untreated. Miscarriage or stillbirth may occur. Babies who survive will develop congenital syphilis, which can cause various physical disabilities.

Genital Herpes

Herpes occurs in different forms, and not every form is an STI. The form of herpes that is an STI has many different names. You may hear the names *herpes simplex virus type 2 (HSV-2)*, *herpes II*, or *genital herpes*. Genital herpes is a serious STI that has no cure, 8-13.

Most people with genital herpes experience symptoms of the virus within 2 to 20 days after contact. The most noticeable symptom is a blister or sore that appears on the genitals. Other symptoms may include headaches, fever, aching muscles, and swollen glands.

8-13 Genital herpes has no cure, but people can learn how to prevent flare-ups. As with other STIs, abstinence is the best protection.

These symptoms usually disappear in a week or two, but the virus is still present in the body. It may flare up at irregular intervals, causing the symptoms to reappear. Although there is no cure, persons with genital herpes should seek medical attention. They should learn how to prevent these flare-ups and spreading the disease.

Pregnant women with genital herpes may experience miscarriage or stillbirth. Genital herpes may infect a baby during pregnancy. Babies can also contract the virus by passing through the birth canal during delivery. For this reason, doctors often recommend surgical delivery for pregnant women with genital herpes. Newborns infected with the disease may develop a number of congenital disabilities.

Chlamydia

One of the most widespread STI is *chlamydia*. In many cases, women with chlamydia show no symptoms. When symptoms appear, they do so in one to five weeks. Men may notice a discharge from the penis, a burning or itching sensation, and painful urination. Women may notice abnormal discharge or bleeding from the vagina, abdominal or pelvic pain, and painful urination.

Chlamydia is a major cause of urinary tract infections in both men and women. Women may also develop *pelvic inflammatory disease (PID)*. PID is an infection of the female reproductive tract. It can lead to infertility. Medical tests can detect chlamydia, and antibiotics can cure it.

Pregnant women with chlamydia can pass it to their babies during delivery. Newborns with chlamydia may develop serious eye, ear, and lung infections. In severe cases, these infections may even lead to death of the newborn.

HIV/AIDS

AIDS is one of the biggest health risks of our time. Currently, there is no vaccine to prevent it and there is no cure. **AIDS (acquired immunodeficiency syndrome)** is a disease that breaks down a person's immune system. In healthy people, the immune system fights illness and heals the body. Someone with a weak immune system is more likely to become very sick and less likely to recover.

The virus that causes AIDS is **HIV (human immunodeficiency virus).** This virus enters a person's body and slowly begins to destroy the immune system. It puts the body at risk to diseases a healthy body could easily resist. When the immune system no longer protects a person from life-threatening illnesses, AIDS develops.

Early on, people with HIV usually show no symptoms. It can take as long as ten years for a person to notice symptoms of the virus. People usually acquire the virus during sexual contact with the blood, semen, or vaginal fluids of infected partners. Those with multiple sexual partners are at the greatest risk of acquiring HIV.

People can also contract the HIV virus by sharing intravenous needles. They may use these needles to inject drugs (usually illegal drugs) into their veins. If a person who has HIV shares a needle with another person, this person could contract HIV.

Before 1985, some people became HIV positive through blood transfusions. All blood now undergoes testing for the HIV virus. It is very unlikely people will contract virus in this way. There is no risk of contracting HIV by donating blood. HIV is also not spread through the air, by insects, or through casual contact such as hugging or a handshake.

The HIV virus can pass from mother to child during pregnancy, delivery, or breast-feeding. About one-fourth of babies born to HIV-infected mothers contract the virus. A pregnant woman may be unaware she has HIV until her infant shows symptoms of the virus. Most infected babies will eventually develop AIDS and die.

Reactions to Pregnancy

With the confirmation of pregnancy, couples are often in shock. They have likely been talking about and hoping for pregnancy, but the reality is somehow different. Once reality sets in, couples realize they have conceived a baby whose birth will forever change many lives. They are now parents-to-be with new responsibilities, 8-14.

Parents-to-be go through many emotional changes during pregnancy. These changes can be temporary or long-term. They also have effects on both marriage and parenting.

The Wife's Reactions

Emotional changes during pregnancy aren't as obvious as physical ones, but they are just as real. Like the physical changes, general descriptions are the norm. These changes vary widely from woman to woman

8-14 Couples go through many emotional changes during pregnancy.

and from pregnancy to pregnancy. As you read, hormones change during pregnancy. These physical changes result in emotional changes, or *mood swings*. Some mood changes are short-lived. A woman may become upset easily or cry for no reason. She may crave foods she has never liked before. A woman may become angry or frustrated more easily than before she was pregnant. She may worry about her emotional health and whether these mood changes are normal.

Other mood changes are more subtle, but long lasting. One woman may feel more self-assurance and confidence throughout pregnancy. She may overflow with hope and optimism. Another woman may feel more depression and worry throughout pregnancy.

Some women show concern due to changes in their body images. Changes in body proportions and stretch marks concern some women. Others enjoy their new look and the recognition of the pregnancy. Certainly today's clothing for pregnancy is much more stylish than clothing for women in past generations.

Some women may be afraid of miscarriage or having a baby with congenital disorders. Others fear having a difficult delivery. These concerns are most common in first pregnancies and for difficult conceptions.

The Husband's Reactions

A man's hormones do not change when his wife is pregnant, but he also experiences emotional changes. His wife's sudden mood changes may be upsetting. He may blame himself, thinking he has somehow made her angry. Other times, he may become angry with his wife for acting so strangely. He may worry she will never regain her pre-pregnancy behavior and personality.

A husband usually shares many of his wife's worries and doubts. He may worry the baby will not be healthy or his wife will have a difficult delivery. He may feel anxious about driving his wife to the hospital when she is in labor or participating during the delivery. He may wonder whether he will be a good father.

These feelings are normal. Despite any negative feelings, however, most husbands are truly excited about the upcoming birth of their children. A husband may think his wife has never looked so beautiful. He may be happy about becoming a father.

The Couple's Relationship

Pregnancy triggers dramatic changes in each spouse's life, as well as in the couple's married life. It is normal, even healthy, for a couple to wonder what their life will be like after the baby arrives. If this is their first child, the couple must adjust to the idea they are going to be parents. At first, this concept may seem a little hard for them to believe, 8-15. Their family structure will change, and they will enter a new stage of the family life cycle.

8-15 Couples may have many reactions to the news of a pregnancy. A combination of joy, pride, fear, concern, and confusion is normal.

Discussing Feelings as a Couple

Couples usually react favorably to pregnancy. This is especially true if they desire a baby and if this is the first pregnancy. Negative reactions most often occur if the couple didn't expect the pregnancy. Negative reactions may also occur if the marital relationship is unstable. The lack of a social network for emotional support can be a problem, too. How can couples be supportive of each other during the pregnancy? Think about this question as you read the following.

Talking About Emotions

Talking about the emotions they are experiencing can bring an expectant couple closer together. It is helpful for each spouse to share both positive and negative emotions. The more a husband and wife communicate, the more they learn about one another. By knowing each other better, they will find it easier to love, support, and understand each other.

When one spouse expresses negative feelings, the other can listen and offer reassurance. Sharing positive feelings with a spouse can lift his or her spirits. Each partner can remind the other they are a team. Together they will successfully adjust to becoming parents.

There may be times when one or both spouses wish the pregnancy had never happened. This is normal, even in a happy marriage where both spouses really want a child. They may fear the unknown. By talking about their feelings, spouses can help each other overcome these fears. Together, they will be able to look forward to the birth of their baby.

Creating Images

Parents often focus on new issues over the months of pregnancy. In doing this, they create images of what they think their baby and parenting might be like. According to Galinsky, this is the first stage of parenting, or image making.

Parents' images are an attempt to answer many questions dealing with the unknowns, 8-16. With image making, couples often base their answers to these questions on the their childhood experiences. They may also base their image making on other parent-child relationships and on ideas from books. Television and parent education programs may be other sources for image making.

Image making relates to early adjustments in the parenting role. Adjustments are easier when images are closer to reality and/or when parents can easily adjust their expectations. When couples make these changes, growth in parenting occurs.

Working as a Team

As a husband and wife share the emotions and experiences of pregnancy, they may feel closer to one another. The couple can

---

Parents' Image-Making Questions

What will our child be like?	What kind of parents will we be?
• Will our child be healthy and perfect?	• Will we be "good" parents?
• What will our child look like?	• What parenting activities will we each do alone? together?
• How bright will our child be?	• Will we be able to provide all we want for our child?
• What career might he or she enter?	
• How will our child interact with family members and others?	• Will our child love and respect us?
• What kind of person will our child become?	• Will we find parenting rewarding?

8-16 Images are based on parents' experiences. The focus is on what they want to maintain and what they want to change from these experiences in their own parenting.

work together as they prepare for the birth of their child. This spirit of teamwork draws the couple closer together. It also strengthens their relationship, 8-17.

The husband cannot physically experience pregnancy, but he can take an active role in his wife's pregnancy. There are many ways he can participate. Most importantly, the father-to-be can support and encourage his pregnant wife. He can encourage her to eat nutritious meals and get enough sleep. He can exercise with

Factors Affecting Emotional Response to Miscarriage and Stillbirth

- The couple's motivation to become parents
- The couple's difficulty involved in conceiving
- Whether this baby was the first or a later one for the couple
- Status given to the couple by family and friends due to conception
- The images the couple had of the baby, including attachment to the child
- The presence of guilt over some potential risk factor associated with complications in pregnancy
- The belief that the medical profession made a mistake in prenatal care
- The sensitivity of the medical professional in handling the trauma
- What the couple is told about the chances of a successful future pregnancy
- Support the couple receives from each other and from family and friends

8-17 Many factors affect the type of emotional response and its intensity following the loss of an unborn child.

her, which will put both of them in the best possible shape. The father-to-be can help his pregnant wife with some of the housecleaning tasks and child care tasks (if they have other children).

The expectant couple can work together to prepare for the baby's arrival. They can shop for the furniture, clothes, toys, and supplies the baby will need. The father may enjoy putting together the baby's crib or rearranging the house to make room for the baby. A father may want to help select possible names for the baby.

The husband can also go to prenatal medical checkups with his wife. He can listen to the baby's heartbeat and feel its movements. He can attend childbirth classes with his wife. The husband may choose to be with his wife during labor and delivery. His support and coaching during labor and delivery can make the experience easier and more enjoyable for his wife. This way, he can also participate in the birth of their baby.

A father who has been involved throughout the pregnancy is likely to stay involved after the baby is born. He and his wife will probably share the joys and burdens of caring for the newborn. As this sharing continues, it will enrich all aspects of their marriage and their life as a family.

Coping with Loss

As you read, miscarriage and stillbirth are complications of pregnancy. A portion of all pregnancies end this way. Most of the problems occur in the first trimester, so most are miscarriages. Many factors cause these tragic complications.

Emotional trauma generally follows the loss. The type and intensity of the feelings depends on several factors, 8-18. Because the woman carries the baby, trauma may be greatest for the woman. Both partners may feel intense sadness and grief over the loss of the child they were expecting.

Couples who have experienced a miscarriage or stillbirth may worry about their ability to have other children. Although these complications increase the risks of future problems, many couples have successful pregnancies in the future. This may, however, be of little consolation while the couple is grieving their loss.

8-18 Couples who experience the loss of a child through miscarriage or stillbirth grieve in many different ways.

Summing It Up

- Pregnancy begins after sperm and egg unite.

- Prenatal development occurs between conception and birth.

- Pregnancy is divided into three stages according to the baby's development. A month-by-month description of the unborn baby shows development in more detail.

- A woman may notice several signs that lead her to suspect she is pregnant. A pregnancy test can confirm whether she is pregnant.

- During the nine months of pregnancy, a woman's body grows and changes to accommodate the growing baby within her.

- Several complications may occur during pregnancy. A woman should be familiar with these complications so she can watch for warning signs during her pregnancy.

- Emotional changes may occur during pregnancy for both the wife and husband.

- Sharing emotions and experiencing pregnancy together usually strengthens the couple's relationship.

- The images the couple creates about their baby and about their parenting roles help them adjust to parenthood.

Recalling the Facts

1. How many trimesters occur during pregnancy?
2. Describe how a baby's gender is determined.
3. Contrast trimesters with the stages of pregnancy.
4. Identify when during pregnancy the developing baby is called each of the following: (A) zygote, (B) blastocyst, (C) embryo, and (D) fetus.
5. Describe the purposes of the placenta and the umbilical cord.
6. What three things does the amniotic fluid do?
7. Name the month in which each of the following occurs: (A) the baby's eyes open, (B) the baby's heart beats, (C) the baby's lungs are mature.
8. List three signs of pregnancy.
9. What hormone do pregnancy tests detect?
10. Differentiate between miscarriage and stillbirth.
11. Describe the symptoms of PIH.
12. What complications may result from uncontrolled gestational diabetes?
13. Compare and contrast the effects of rubella on a pregnant woman and the fetus she carries.
14. Which woman can experience Rh factor disorder, a woman who is Rh- or one who is Rh+?
15. Name three STIs and describe the possible effects of each on a newborn baby.
16. How can the couple work as a team during the pregnancy?

Applying New Skills

1. **Interview.** Interview a woman who has been pregnant about the physical changes she experienced during pregnancy. Which ones were the most uncomfortable? How did the woman adjust to these changes? Share your findings in an oral report.
2. **News review.** Read an Internet, magazine, or newspaper article about pregnancy. Discuss the key points of your article in a small group. Be sure to distinguish between relevant and irrelevant information.
3. **Research and report.** Investigate the resources for pregnancy counseling in your area through the telephone book, school nurse, health clinics, hospitals, etc. Use desktop publishing software to create a brochure that describes these counseling resources to share in your community.

Thinking Critically

1. Analyze the emotional changes that occur during pregnancy. Be sure to consider both the wife's and the husband's emotional changes. How are they similar? How are they different?

2. Compare and contrast the impact of discussing emotions during pregnancy with creating images about children and parenting? How does this impact a couple's relationship?

3. Evaluate how you think the complications described in the chapter might affect a couple's pregnancy experience. How might these complications make them feel? Which ones are especially threatening for the baby? How can couples prevent these complications?

Linking Academics

1. **Science.** Select one of the complications of pregnancy found in this chapter. Use Internet or print resources to research the topic further. Write a report to summarize your findings.

2. **Creative writing.** Write a creative story describing how a father should be involved during pregnancy. If you are female, write your story from the perspective of how you would like your husband to be involved in your pregnancy. If you are a male, write your story from the perspective of how you would like to be involved in your wife's pregnancy.

3. **Literature.** Read the passage about the image making parenting stage in Ellen Galinsky's book, *The Six Stages of Parenting*. Write a brief summary of your findings to share with the class.

4. **Literature.** Read a book about coping with loss after miscarriage or the loss of a child. Give an oral report to share your findings with the class.

Chapter 9

Prenatal Care

Key Terms

prenatal care
obstetrician
certified nurse-midwife
ultrasound test
chorionic villi sampling (CVS)
amniocentesis
MyPyramid
anemia
fetal alcohol syndrome (FAS)
sudden infant death syndrome (SIDS)

Objectives

After studying this chapter, you will be able to

- summarize the importance of quality prenatal care that begins early in pregnancy.
- describe medical care needed during pregnancy.
- compare and contrast the three types of prenatal tests.
- summarize nutritional needs before and during pregnancy and ways to meet those needs.
- explain why proper weight gain is important.
- summarize the importance of exercise.
- describe various factors that increase health risks to mother and baby.
- explain the role of the father-to-be as a member of the prenatal-care team.

Prenatal care is the name for the special care a woman and her developing baby need during pregnancy. When some people mention prenatal care, they may be talking only about the medical care a doctor provides during pregnancy. While medical care is very important, it is only one part of prenatal care. Good nutrition, proper weight gain, and exercise are also basic to a woman's prenatal care. Another aspect of prenatal care involves avoiding certain factors that increase health risks to the mother and baby. All the special considerations that are important during pregnancy are part of prenatal care.

Pregnancy is a special time in a woman's life. The way she cares for herself will greatly affect her baby's health. Babies are more likely to be born healthy if their mothers begin to follow good prenatal care practices early in pregnancy. In fact, if a woman is considering becoming pregnant, she should strive to be in the best health possible *before* her pregnancy, 9-1.

Medical Care During Pregnancy

As soon as a woman notices signs of pregnancy, she should see a doctor for a pregnancy test. The couple may meet with their family physician, an obstetrician, or a certified nurse-midwife. An **obstetrician** is a doctor who specializes in providing medical care for pregnant women and delivering babies. A **certified nurse-midwife** is a nurse practitioner who has extensive training and experience in providing prenatal care and delivering babies.

Friends or relatives often refer couples to an obstetrician or nurse-midwife. Other couples call a local hospital or their insurance provider for a list of obstetricians and nurse-midwives in the area. A couple should choose a doctor or nurse-midwife who helps them feel comfortable, confident, and secure.

9-1 Being physically fit is a good way for a woman to prepare her body for a healthy pregnancy.

If they have specific wishes concerning childbirth procedures, they should find a professional who will accept their wishes.

The First Medical Visit

The first medical visit is an important one. The doctor or nurse-midwife will review the couple's medical histories for possible congenital disorders. He or she will also ask the woman what signs of pregnancy she has noticed. The doctor will also want to know about any previous pregnancies and deliveries. A woman should tell her doctor or nurse-midwife if she drinks alcoholic beverages, smokes, or takes any drugs (legal or illegal). She should also tell her doctor if she has ever had any STIs.

A lab test will confirm her pregnancy. Next, the woman will have a thorough physical examination, including a pelvic exam. Her health care professional will also take her weight and blood pressure.

After confirming the pregnancy, the doctor will describe what changes the woman should expect. The doctor will also describe what health guidelines the woman will need to follow. He or she will schedule a series of checkups to monitor the health of both the pregnant woman and the developing fetus.

The doctor or nurse-midwife will also answer any questions the couple may have. One of the couple's first questions may be about when the baby will be born. To answer this, the doctor will need to know the date of the first day of the woman's last regular menstrual period. The doctor will then calculate the probable due date using the simple formula shown in 9-2. The average duration of pregnancy is 280 days, which is about 40 weeks or just over nine months. About midway through the pregnancy, the doctor may use the baby's image to determine fetal maturity and to adjust the delivery date. (Some women find it difficult to tell the difference between a menstrual period and the spotting that can occur when the zygote implants. This may cause the original due date to be incorrect.)

Another important question may concern the costs involved in prenatal care and delivery. Each doctor or nurse-midwife has different policies about fees. Fees may vary with a couple's specific needs, the location of the office, and other factors.

An expectant couple should review their insurance coverage and discuss fee payment with the insurance person at the medical office. If the couple has insurance, it will likely cover most of the pregnancy-related medical costs. In some cases, the couple may have to pay a deductible or co-pay for some services. In other cases, a single fee may cover all office visits.

If expectant parents do not have insurance, they should consider all options for paying the medical bills. Lack of money should not, however, cause a woman to delay her first medical visit. Receiving quality medical care early in pregnancy is very important to the mother's health and the baby's survival and health. If they cannot afford this care, expectant parents should contact their local social services agency or health department. These agencies can tell the couple for what affordable medical care, if any, the couple qualifies.

Medical Checkups During Pregnancy

About one month following an expectant mother's first medical visit, she should have another checkup with her doctor or nurse-midwife. For the first seven months of pregnancy, checkups usually occur once a month. During the eighth month, visits generally increase to twice a month. By the ninth month, a pregnant woman should have medical checkups once a week until the baby arrives.

During these visits, the doctor checks the woman's weight gain, blood pressure, and general health. The doctor will also check the size of the mother's uterus to be sure the pregnancy is proceeding normally. Near the end of pregnancy, the doctor or nurse-midwife will examine the cervix to see if it is preparing for labor and delivery.

The Centers for Disease Control recommends that women who are pregnant during the flu season receive an influenza vaccine (flu shot). Pregnant women should only receive the inactivated vaccine—not the

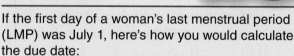

Calculating the Due Date

If the first day of a woman's last menstrual period (LMP) was July 1, here's how you would calculate the due date:

Formula:

(LMP − 3 calendar months) + 7 days = Due date

Examples:

- July 1 − 3 calendar months = April 1
- April 1 + 7 days = April 8 (of the next year)

9-2 Counting from the first day of the last regular menstrual period, pregnancy lasts an average of nine months.

live virus. A woman can receive this vaccine during a prenatal checkup.

Prenatal checkups give the doctor or nurse-midwife a chance to monitor any possible problems. He or she can also advise the expectant mother about her general health practices. This includes what she should or should not do in terms of exercise, nutrition, and weight gain.

Prenatal Tests

When the baby's heartbeat and movements become obvious, the doctor notes the baby's growth and activity at each visit on a woman's medical chart, 9-3. During these checkups, medical professionals may use special prenatal tests to determine the position, size, or development of the fetus. Prenatal tests can also reveal if the baby has a congenital disorder. If tests show a possible problem, the parents can prepare themselves to care for an infant with a disability. Three main prenatal tests are used. These are the ultrasound test, chorionic villi sampling, and amniocentesis.

Ultrasound Test

The **ultrasound test** provides a way to view the position and development of the fetus. This test can show if the mother is carrying more than one fetus. It can also reveal certain physical disabilities the baby might have.

The ultrasound can show how far into the pregnancy the woman is and the baby's probable due date. Later in pregnancy, an ultrasound test can reveal the gender of the baby. Some parents are eager to know whether their baby will be a boy or girl. Others want to be surprised when the baby arrives.

Ultrasound works by using a special machine to bounce high-frequency sound waves off the woman's internal structures. This creates a "map" of the fetus. Couples can view the outline of its skeletal growth on a TV monitor. A *sonogram* is a picture taken

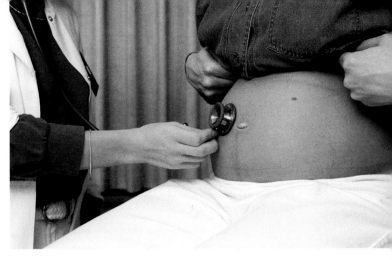

9-3 During later prenatal visits, the doctor uses a stethoscope to listen to the baby's heartbeat. The mother and father can usually listen to the heartbeat, too.

of the baby during the ultrasound test. The parents-to-be can keep this sonogram. Many enjoy putting this picture into their photo albums. It is the first picture of their new baby.

Most experts consider ultrasound safe for the mother and baby. Still, they advise its use only when valid medical reasons exist. Ultrasound should not be used unless medically necessary.

Chorionic Villi Sampling

A second prenatal test is **chorionic villi sampling (CVS)**. During this test, the doctor inserts a special instrument into the mother's vagina and cervix. With this instrument, he or she removes and examines a small amount of the tissue from the amnio-chorionic membrane. This examination can show problems with the developing baby's genes and chromosomes. It can also indicate the presence of any congenital disorders.

Doctors can perform CVS as early as the eighth week of pregnancy, but often wait until week 10. An advantage of this test is it provides results early in the pregnancy. Some risks to the baby are present with CVS, however. Not all expectant parents will want to have this procedure. Doctors may recommend that couples who meet certain conditions should have chorionic villi sampling done, 9-4.

- The woman is over 35.
- There is a family history of congenital disorders.
- One spouse is known to be a carrier of a congenital disorder.
- The mother has previously given birth to a baby with a congenital disorder.
- The mother has been exposed since conception to a substance or substances that might have harmed the developing baby.
- The mother has had previous miscarriages or stillbirths.
- One spouse has been exposed to an infection, such as rubella.

9-4 In some situations, prenatal tests may be recommended.

Amniocentesis

A third prenatal test is amniocentesis. During **amniocentesis**, the doctor inserts a hollow needle through the mother's abdomen and into the uterus. Amniotic fluid is drawn from the amniotic sac that surrounds the fetus. By examining cells in this amniotic fluid, lab technicians can detect chromosomal abnormalities or chemical problems in the genes. When problems are present, it usually means the baby has a congenital disorder.

A doctor can perform amniocentesis between weeks 14 and 16 of pregnancy. The procedure carries only a slight risk to mother and fetus—much less than CVS. Like CVS, doctors recommend amniocentesis for women who are at risk for giving birth to a baby with congenital disorders.

Nutrition During Pregnancy

Upon confirming pregnancy, many women wonder what they should eat (or not eat) to have a healthy pregnancy. Nutrition is an important concern. However, a woman's interest in eating healthfully should begin long before she becomes pregnant. Women who eat well are more likely to be healthy and continue good eating and health habits during pregnancy. These advantages can protect women from complications. Proper nutrition also improves their chances of having healthy babies.

A woman who is considering pregnancy can plan her meals using **MyPyramid**. This is a food guidance system developed by the U.S. Departments of Agriculture and Health and Human Services. National guidelines for healthy eating and physical activity form the basis of MyPyramid. This advice is helpful for healthy Americans who are striving to eat a balance of nutritious food and achieve good health.

MyPyramid is especially helpful for women before and during pregnancy. It can help women select the right foods, and the right amounts of food, for good health. See 9-5 for food amounts before pregnancy. MyPyramid groups foods based on their similarity in nutrient content.

When a woman is properly nourished, her body stores some nutrients. Early in pregnancy, the baby's development depends on these stored nutrients. Most women do not even know of their pregnancy for several weeks. During this time, all the baby's major organs and systems are forming. The baby's optimum growth depends on the nutrients the mother provides. If a woman waits until she knows she is pregnant to eat more healthfully, her baby may have already been deprived of needed nutrients.

The old saying "A pregnant woman should eat for two" is usually misunderstood. A pregnant woman should not eat twice as much food as she did before pregnancy, 9-6. During the first trimester of pregnancy, a woman does not need any additional calories. Instead, she must focus on eating nutrient-dense foods to meet the demands of both the fetus and her own body. In the second and third trimesters, a woman may need about 300 to 400 more calories per day to meet these needs. However, a woman's doctor and/or registered dietitian will guide her regarding her specific needs.

Basic Daily Diet Before Pregnancy
(Based on 2000 calories)

Food Group	Amount	Equivalents	Special Notes
Grains	6 ounce equivalents	*The following count as 1 ounce:* 1 slice bread 1 biscuit, muffin, or roll 1 cup ready-to-eat cereal ½ cup cooked cereal, grits, rice, or pasta	Look for whole-grain or enriched breads and cereals
Vegetables	2½ to 3 cups	*The following count as 1 cup:* 1 cup cooked or chopped raw vegetables 2 cups raw, leafy vegetables 1 cup vegetable juice	Eat at least one good source of vitamins A and C daily Good sources of vitamin A include dark green and deep yellow vegetables and fruits such as spinach, carrots, sweet potatoes, and cantaloupe
Fruits	2 cups	*The following count as 1 cup:* ½ cup dried fruit 1 cup juice ½ large grapefruit 1 medium fruit (apple, orange) ½ cup chopped, cooked or canned fruit	Good sources of vitamin C include citrus fruits, tomatoes, strawberries, broccoli, and brussels sprouts
Milk	3 cups	*To equal the calcium content of 1 cup milk, it would take:* 1 cup low-fat yogurt 1½ ounces Cheddar cheese 2 ounces processed cheese 2 cups cottage cheese	Remember to choose low-fat varieties
Meat and beans	5½ ounce equivalents	*The following count as 1 ounce:* 1 ounce cooked lean meat, fish, or poultry ¼ cup cooked dry beans 1 egg 2 tablespoons peanut butter ½ ounce of nuts or seeds	Eat a variety of protein foods from both animal and vegetable sources

9-5 As recommended by her health care professional, choosing a variety of foods from the five main food groups can help an expectant mother get all the nutrients she and her baby need.

9-6 Eating for two means eating foods that will meet the nutritional needs of both mother and baby. Pregnant women can meet these increased nutritional needs by selecting a variety of healthful foods.

If an expectant mother doesn't eat enough nutrients, she and her baby must compete for the nutrients she does consume. For some needed nutrients, the mother's body will first provide them to the fetus even if this means the mother's needs go unmet. Calcium, phosphorus, and vitamin D are such nutrients. They work in tandem to form strong teeth and bones. Thus, if a woman does not consume enough food from the milk group, she deprives her teeth and bones of these necessary nutrients.

For some other nutrients, the reverse happens. For example, the mother's body will have first call on the supply of folate she consumes through green, leafy vegetables. The remaining folate will go to the fetus. Because folate is essential to fetal health, a woman should be sure to eat enough green, leafy vegetables or take a prescribed supplement with folate.

Although a pregnant woman doesn't need to eat twice as much, her needs for certain nutrients increase dramatically. She must plan her meals carefully to include all the foods she and her baby need. Eating a variety of nutritious foods is essential to a healthy pregnancy.

A mother-to-be *must* work up an individualized eating plan with her health-care provider or registered dietitian. Her eating plan is part of her prenatal care. Then she can make food choices that are good for her health during pregnancy. Learning to choose nutrient-packed foods from all of the food groups can help a woman maintain her good health before, during, and after pregnancy.

Grains

The grains group includes bread, cereal, rice, and pasta. Foods in this group are made from grains, such as wheat, rye, and oats. Whole-grain breads and cereals are especially rich sources of the B vitamins. They are also good sources of fiber and *carbohydrates*—the body's main source of energy.

During pregnancy, a woman's overall need for energy increases. In the second and third trimesters, her body requires a few additional calories every day. Some of these extra calories should come from the grains group. The amount of food eaten from this group will depend upon a woman's body size, activity level, and her weight before and during pregnancy. A woman needs to rely on the advice of her doctor and/or registered dietitian regarding how much food to eat from this group.

Vegetables

Vegetables—especially those that are dark yellow, orange, or green—are an excellent source of vitamins and minerals. Eating vegetables can help meet a woman's increasing need for these nutrients. Vegetables also provide fiber and carbohydrates. During the second and third trimesters, some of a pregnant woman's extra calories should come from the vegetables group.

During pregnancy, demand grows for B vitamins and vitamins C, E, and K. Eating certain vegetables can help meet these increasing needs. Green, leafy vegetables are also a rich source of another vitamin, folate, which is essential for good health. Folate helps proper formation of the baby's *neural tube*. This is a tube that will develop into the brain and spinal column. Adequate amounts of folate are important before and during pregnancy.

One mineral that women need much more during pregnancy is iron. Iron is an important part of blood. A pregnant woman's body produces almost 50 percent more blood. This extra blood transports nutrients and oxygen to the fetus and carries away waste products from the fetus. The demands of the fetus are in addition to the woman's needs. Her blood must carry nutrients and oxygen to and wastes from all the cells in her own body, too.

As her blood supply increases, a pregnant woman needs extra iron. Iron also helps build the baby's blood and red blood cells. Additionally, the baby stores a supply of iron in its liver, upon which it will rely during the first few months after birth. To maintain her blood supply, a woman needs about twice as much iron during pregnancy as she did before she was pregnant. Women who lack enough iron in their blood have **anemia**, or iron deficiency. Green vegetables, such as spinach and kale, are a good source of iron.

A pregnant woman also needs increasing amounts of other minerals, such as magnesium, iodine, zinc, and selenium. The amount of other vitamins and minerals may not increase. However, it is very important for a pregnant woman to consume the amounts of these nutrients as directed in her individualized eating plan. Expectant mothers can get many of the vitamins and minerals they need from a variety of vegetables and vegetable juices.

Fruits

Fruits are another good source of vitamins and minerals women need during pregnancy, 9-7. Fruits also help provide the fiber and carbohydrates pregnant women need. Oranges, for instance, are a rich source of folate and vitamin C. They also provide some fiber. Apricots are a good source of vitamin A and carbohydrates. Raisins, dates, and prunes are a good source of carbohydrates, iron, and fiber. Including a variety of fresh fruits and fruit juices into her diet can help a pregnant woman meet her nutritional needs.

9-7 Snacking on fruits, such as apples, can help a pregnant woman meet her nutritional needs.

Milk

Foods in the milk group include milk, yogurt, and cheese. Foods in this group provide a variety of the nutrients a pregnant woman and her growing baby need. Milk and milk products are a rich source of several minerals, such as calcium and phosphorus. A woman does not usually need extra calcium or phosphorus during pregnancy. However, it is important she get the recommended daily amount of these minerals. They help build the baby's bones and teeth and help the woman maintain her bones and teeth.

Milk is also fortified with vitamin D. Like calcium and phosphorus, vitamin D promotes the development of strong bones and teeth. A woman does not usually need more vitamin D during pregnancy. However, she should consume the amount of vitamin D for women her health-care provider recommends.

Milk and milk products are also sources of protein and carbohydrate. Some of the extra calories a woman needs during the second and third trimesters of pregnancy can come from this group. Pregnant women should keep in mind, however, that many foods from this group are quite high in calories and fat. A woman may want to choose foods from this group with lower fat and fewer calories. For example, fat-free milk, reduced-fat cheese, and low-fat yogurt might be good choices.

Meat and Beans

The meat and beans group includes meat, poultry, fish, dry beans and peas, eggs, and nuts. Most of these foods are rich in *protein*. This nutrient helps build and repair body tissues.

Protein is vital for building the baby's cells, tissues, and organs. It also helps build the baby's blood. In addition, protein helps build the expectant mother's extra blood cells and repairs body tissues. For these reasons, a pregnant woman's need for protein increases.

However, most women already consume more protein than their bodies need. A pregnant woman may not need to consume any extra protein. Each woman should check with her doctor or registered dietitian about her protein needs.

As you recall, pregnant women need more iron than they did before pregnancy. Foods from the meat and beans group are the very best source of iron. Red meats and organ meats, such as liver, are the richest iron sources. Foods from this group also provide some of the B vitamins a woman needs during pregnancy. Cooked legumes, such as green peas, kidney beans, and lentils, are also good sources of protein and iron, 9-8.

A portion of a pregnant woman's extra calorie needs can come from this group. Pregnant women should keep in mind that many cuts of meat are quite high in calories and fat (such as organ meats). She may want to choose lean meats, beans, poultry, and some fish for most of her servings from this group.

9-8 A pregnant woman should pay close attention to her increased nutritional needs, especially for quality, low-fat protein.

Oils

Oils and fats are also part of a healthy diet. Foods such as butter, margarine, and salad dressings are part of this group. While fat is an essential nutrient, the body only needs a small amount of fat to function well. Oils and fats help the body use other nutrients, such as the fat-soluble vitamins A and D. Many people consume *much* more fat than they actually need. Some also eat foods high in oils and fat in place of more nutritious food choices. All people, including pregnant women, should limit foods that are high in fat and oil. Limiting these foods does not mean cutting them out completely. However, a woman should be sure the extra calories she needs do not come from oils and fats. These calories should come from other food groups.

Other Nutritional Concerns

Consuming the recommended amounts from each food group is important before and during pregnancy. Maintaining wise food choices help pregnant women maintain their health and the health of their babies. In addition, it is equally important for a pregnant woman to consume enough water. She should also watch her sodium intake and talk with her doctor or nurse-midwife before taking any dietary supplements. Following these guidelines will help a woman deliver a healthy baby.

Water

Water is an essential nutrient. During pregnancy, it can be even more important. The human body is over 70 percent water. Water supports fetal development. Drinking enough water will also help the pregnant woman rid her body of waste products, both hers and the baby's. A pregnant woman needs adequate amounts of water, juices, and other nonalcoholic, caffeine-free liquids each day. She should follow the guidelines established in her individualized eating plan.

Sodium

Sodium intake can be a concern during pregnancy. Salt used in cooking, at the table, and in processed foods is the main source of sodium in the diet. While sodium is important to good health, moderation is the key. Too much sodium might cause ankles, hands, or feet to swell during pregnancy. Higher blood pressure may also result from too much sodium. A woman should talk with her medical professional or a registered dietitian about whether she needs to reduce her sodium intake. If she needs to reduce the amount of sodium in her diet, she can cook foods without adding salt. Reading food labels carefully will help her select foods that are lower in sodium.

Dietary Supplements

During pregnancy, a woman's need for certain vitamins and minerals increases dramatically. Some women may have poor nutrition before pregnancy. Their body stores of certain vitamins and minerals may be quite low. Other pregnant women do not consume enough nutrients through the foods they eat. This can be especially true in the first trimester if a woman experiences continued nausea and vomiting.

Many doctors prescribe prenatal vitamin and mineral supplements, 9-9. A woman should only take supplements her doctor prescribes. Consuming larger amounts of certain vitamins and minerals (such as fat-soluble vitamins A, D, E and K) than recommended can be dangerous to both mother and baby.

Weight Gain During Pregnancy

For a woman of normal weight, the average weight gain during pregnancy is 25 to 35 pounds for a single-baby pregnancy. For twins, the normal weight gain is 40 to 45 pounds, and for triplets, the total gain is 50

9-9 A pregnant woman should take only the supplements her doctor prescribes.

to 60 pounds. Women who begin pregnancy underweight for their body type and size may need to gain more weight than this. Doctors may advise women who are over their ideal weight at the start of pregnancy to gain slightly less. A woman should consult her doctor or nurse-midwife about how much weight she should gain.

Women gain an average of 2 to 4 pounds during the first trimester. After the first trimester, a weight gain of 1 pound a week is normal. It is important a woman gain this weight in a slow, steady pattern. A quick gain or loss may signal a problem the doctor should monitor carefully. Because multiple-birth pregnancies are often of shorter duration, adequate weight gain in the first 5 or 6 months is critical.

If a woman gains too little weight, she is likely not getting enough nutrients. This can negatively affect her health and the baby's health. Medical research indicates babies born weighing at least 7 pounds have a better survival rate. Babies are more likely to be born at *low birthweights* (weighing less than 5 ½ pounds at birth) if their mothers do not gain enough weight. They are also at greater risk for congenital disorders and *neonatal* (soon after birth) death.

Gaining more than the recommended amount of weight can strain a woman's body.

It can also make labor and delivery more difficult. In addition, the woman will have even more weight to lose once the baby is born.

When a woman gains the recommended amount of weight, most of it relates to the baby growing inside her, 9-10. This weight gain includes the placenta and amniotic fluid. The mother's breasts and uterus also weigh more. Her body also produces extra blood and fluid. All these factors contribute to healthy weight gain during pregnancy.

Exercise During Pregnancy

Another common question pregnant women have concerns exercise. A woman might fear exercise will hurt her baby. Under normal circumstances, however, exercise is good for a pregnant woman. Physical activity helps keep her body strong. This can help her have an easier pregnancy and delivery.

A pregnant woman should check with her doctor or nurse-midwife regarding any exercise she plans to do. Generally, she should be able to continue most exercises

Sources of Weight Gain During Pregnancy

Baby	7–8 lbs.
Blood increase	3 lbs.
Placenta	1 lb.
Tissue fluid	2–6 lbs.
Uterus	2 lbs.
Fat deposits	5 lbs.
Breasts	1 lb.
Amniotic fluid	2–4 lbs.
Tissue fluid	2–6 lbs.
Total	25–35 lbs.

9-10 Gaining the recommended amount of weight during pregnancy is best for both mother and baby.

she was doing before pregnancy. During pregnancy, however, is not the time to begin new activities. A woman should not try a new sport or intense workout. If she did not exercise regularly before pregnancy, she may begin by taking a brisk walk every day.

Walking is the best exercise during pregnancy. Some women join special exercise classes offered by their hospitals. These classes are safe for pregnant women. They can also be a lot of fun!

Warming up and cooling down during each exercise session is especially important for a woman during pregnancy. Also, she should not exercise at intense levels for more than 15 minutes without cooling down. An expectant mother should stop exercising immediately and contact her doctor if she notices any of the following warning signs, 9-11:

- pain
- cramps in the uterus
- blood or fluid coming from the vagina
- dizziness
- shortness of breath
- fatigue

Late in pregnancy, a woman's doctor or nurse-midwife may recommend she stop exercising until after the baby is born. Until then, however, regular exercise can help a woman feel her best. It can also help her maintain a healthy weight.

Health Risks to Mother and Baby

In addition to getting the nutrients and exercise she needs, a pregnant woman must protect herself and her baby from harmful substances. Anything a pregnant woman puts into her body may pass through the placenta. Once through the placenta, it can reach the fetus and cause damage to the baby's developing body.

9-11 Certain medications can harm an unborn baby. A woman's doctor should approve all the medications she takes during pregnancy, whether they are prescriptions or over-the-counter medications.

Medications and OTC Drugs

An expectant mother should be sure to check with her doctor or nurse-midwife before taking any medications. Her doctor can advise her which medicines are safe and in what amounts. She should not take any medications that her doctor has not prescribed or approved.

A pregnant woman should consult her doctor about continuing to take prescription medicines. For instance, tetracycline—a common antibiotic, can affect the development of the baby's bones and teeth. A woman's doctor can help her weigh her need for a medicine against the potential harm to her unborn child.

Even common over-the-counter (OTC) remedies may harm a fetus. This includes heartburn medications, pain relievers, and laxatives. Aspirin, for instance, can cause the baby to bleed. Before taking any OTC medication, a woman should consult a doctor or pharmacist.

Illegal Drugs

No one should take illegal drugs, such as marijuana, heroin, cocaine, and hallucinogens. These drugs are dangerous for adults. They have even more deadly consequences for an unborn child.

Pregnant women who are heavy drug users often neglect their own health. This decreases their chances of having a healthy baby. Drug users are also more likely to have miscarriages or premature deliveries (delivering a baby earlier than week 37 of pregnancy), 9-12. Babies born to drug users may have low birthweights, physical disabilities, brain damage, or respiratory problems.

Another problem with drug use during pregnancy is that babies can be born addicted to the same drugs as their mothers. A pregnant heroin or cocaine user can also addict her baby. The baby will then go through withdrawal from the drug upon birth. Babies born addicted to drugs may not survive this withdrawal.

Infants who survive withdrawal from drugs may have emotional, visual, and hearing problems as well as mental disabilities. Babies born to mothers who use drugs may never have the chance to develop normally. Giving up drugs will also improve the mothers' health and increase their babies' chances for survival. Addicted women may

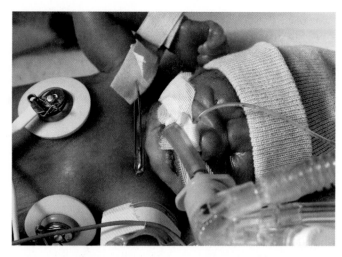

9-12 Avoiding illegal drugs can help mothers carry their pregnancies to term. Premature babies are often born with tremendous health problems and require special medical care.

need to seek help to stop using drugs. They should talk with their doctors or go to a drug counseling center to learn what help is available in their communities.

Alcohol

Alcohol passes through the placenta very quickly. An alcoholic beverage affects a fetus almost as quickly as his or her mother. Recent studies indicate even moderate drinking during pregnancy can affect the developing baby. The wisest choice is to avoid all alcoholic beverages (beer, wine, and liquor) during pregnancy. In fact, many doctors now recommend women avoid consuming alcohol if they are planning to become pregnant.

A strong link exists between alcohol use during pregnancy and miscarriage, stillbirth, and early infant death. A woman who drinks excessively or steadily also risks having a baby with fetal alcohol syndrome. **Fetal alcohol syndrome (FAS)** is a condition that includes physical and mental disabilities common among the babies of mothers who drink heavily during pregnancy, 9-13.

A major symptom of FAS is growth deficiency. An affected baby may be abnormally small at birth. He or she may never catch up to normal growth. This baby may have a heart problem severe enough to require surgery. A baby with FAS may also have a small head and brain, narrow eyes, a low nasal bridge, and a short upturned nose.

Babies with FAS often have moderate to severe mental disabilities. In later childhood, poor coordination, short attention spans, and behavioral problems are typical of children with this syndrome. A woman can protect her baby from FAS by not drinking alcohol during pregnancy.

Smoking

Smoking cigarettes is dangerous to any person's health. When a woman smokes during pregnancy, however, she risks severely harming her baby's health as well as her own. Medical research shows pregnant women who smoke are more likely to lose

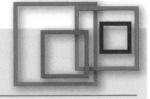

Effects of Fetal Alcohol Syndrome

- Prenatal growth deficiencies
- Growth deficiencies after birth
- Damage to brain and nervous system
- Small head and brain size
- Narrow eyes
- Low nasal bridge
- Short, upturned nose
- Heart problems
- Short attention span
- Poor coordination
- Irritability
- Mental disabilities
- Behavioral problems
- Academic problems

9-13 Mothers should not consume alcohol during pregnancy. Several serious problems can result from fetal alcohol syndrome.

their babies to miscarriage or stillbirth than nonsmokers. The infants of smoking mothers are also at greater risk for premature delivery and low birthweight. Premature birth or low birthweight puts babies at high risk for many other health problems.

Babies whose mothers smoke are also more likely to die in early infancy than babies of normal weight. Smoking increases the risk of death among the infants due to **sudden infant death syndrome (SIDS)**. In SIDS, a seemingly healthy infant dies without warning.

Babies of parents who smoke are more likely to develop respiratory infections and problems during their first year. As they get older, low-birthweight babies are more likely to develop learning or behavioral problems.

If a woman is considering pregnancy, it is best for her baby if she quits smoking before she conceives. Pregnant women who smoke should quit smoking for the health of their unborn babies. If a woman finds it impossible to quit smoking, she should at least cut back on the amount she smokes. Women who do not smoke have much healthier infants.

Caffeine

Caffeine is a substance found in coffee, tea, chocolate, and some soft drinks. Research is inconclusive about the danger of caffeine during pregnancy. According to the March of Dimes, however, caffeine easily passes from mother to baby through the placenta. Because the fetus is not fully developed, caffeine levels may remain higher for a longer time in the baby than the mother. If a mother experiences a faster heart rate and sleeplessness from high caffeine intake, it is likely her baby will, too. Many doctors still advise pregnant women to avoid or severely limit their caffeine intake. When a baby's organs are forming during the first trimester, the effects of caffeine may be especially dangerous. A pregnant woman should consult her doctor or a registered dietitian about consuming caffeine. Many coffees, teas, and soft drinks are available in caffeine-free form.

X-Rays

Radiation can be harmful to a pregnant woman. The most common source of radiation to which women might be exposed is X-rays. Exposure to X-rays can cause congenital disabilities in a developing baby. For this reason, dentists ask a woman to wear a lead apron that will protect her during an X-ray even if she does not think she is pregnant. An expectant mother should always tell her doctor or dentist she is pregnant before receiving any X-rays. If possible, a woman should postpone X-rays until after the baby is born. If a pregnant woman works at a hospital or in a doctor or dentist's office, she should inform her supervisor she is pregnant. She should not work near or operate any X-ray machines during her pregnancy.

Rest

During pregnancy, a woman may become tired much more easily. In the first trimester, her body requires a lot of energy because the baby's body is developing. Her body must adjust to being pregnant. Getting enough rest at night will help her feel her best. She may find she needs to take a short nap during the day as well.

During the second trimester, a woman may not feel as tired. By the third trimester, however, carrying the extra weight of the baby can tire the expectant mother. A woman should listen to the signals her body sends her. When she feels tired, she should rest, 9-14. Late in pregnancy, many women need daytime naps in addition to eight or more hours of sleep every night.

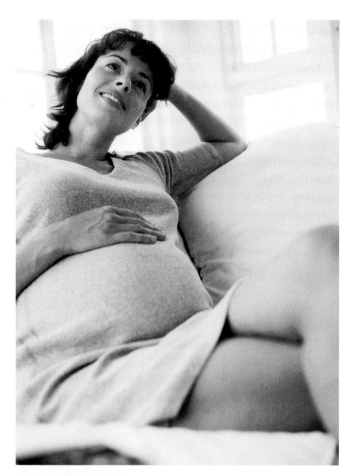

9-14 Late in pregnancy, a woman may have to stop and rest frequently. She should listen to her body's signals.

Maternity Clothes

As the expectant mother's abdomen and breasts grow, she will begin to notice her clothes fit differently. Tight or restrictive clothes will soon become uncomfortable. By the fourth month, she may need to start wearing different clothes.

Some women choose to wear maternity clothes, garments especially designed for pregnancy, during much of their pregnancies. A woman should select maternity clothing in her regular size. Other women wear regular clothing in larger sizes.

A pregnant woman should wear a well-fitting bra to support her fuller breasts. She may simply wear a larger-sized bra or choose a special maternity bra. Her growing abdomen should be free from tight waistbands and belts. Loose-fitting clothes are better because they do not restrict blood circulation.

Women who continue working during pregnancy may need to wear professional clothes to work. Maternity specialty stores often have business clothing that meets a pregnant woman's needs. These clothes may be quite expensive, however. If cost is a factor, borrowing maternity clothes from friends or family members may be an option. Garage sales and resale shops may be other alternatives.

A woman may find her feet are a size longer or wider during pregnancy. Fluid retention in her body tissues may cause this condition. During pregnancy, a woman should avoid wearing high heels. Shoes with low heels are better because they help the woman maintain good posture and balance. Good posture, in turn, helps her avoid backaches. Whatever a woman chooses to wear, she should remember that comfort is the key.

The Couple—A Parenting Team

Parenting begins when the baby is in the prenatal stage. As you will read in the next chapter, couples have many decisions to make during the prenatal period. The parents-to-be need to work as a team. How can the father-to-be play a supporting role on this new parenting team? He can support the mother-to-be by

- encouraging her to begin prenatal care early, keep all appointments, and take any recommended tests

- eating a well-balanced diet along with the mother-to-be and avoiding unhealthy eating habits

- exercising with her—walking together is a healthy habit and allows time for sharing as a couple

- encouraging her to avoid risky practices, such as smoking and drinking alcoholic beverages, that put her health and the baby's in jeopardy

- helping plan daily routines to allow time for proper rest

In addition to the above, fathers should be included during prenatal care visits if at all possible. Both parents can then ask any questions or share any concerns they might have with their medical professional. A couple's *good* relationship with their obstetrician or nurse-midwife promotes a healthy pregnancy and a healthy baby. A father who participates in prenatal care is generally more supportive of his wife and newborn, too. Fathers, as well as mothers, enjoy learning how their babies are growing and developing, 9-15.

9-15 Clothing especially designed for pregnancy gives comfort to the expectant mother.

Summing It Up

- If a woman is planning to become pregnant, it is a good idea for her to be in the best health possible beforehand.

- As soon as a woman notices symptoms of pregnancy, she should visit a doctor. Quality prenatal care early in pregnancy is important to the health of both mother and baby.

- Having regular medical checkups is important. During her first medical visit, the woman will have a complete physical exam and lab tests. The doctor or nurse-midwife will also calculate the baby's due date. Later medical checkups are also important.

- Three useful prenatal tests are the ultrasound test, chorionic villi sampling, and amniocentesis. Women who are over age 35, have family histories of congenital disorders, or have given birth to infants with congenital disorders may be advised to have prenatal tests done.

- A pregnant woman should eat a balanced diet that provides all the nutrients she and her baby need. This takes some planning, but it is very important.

- A pregnant woman should gain the recommended amount of weight during pregnancy to ensure her baby will be born at a healthy weight. Gaining much more or less than recommended can be harmful for both mother and baby.

- Factors that increase health risks to both mother and baby include medications and over-the-counter drugs (unless approved by her doctor), illegal drugs, alcohol, smoking, caffeine, and X-rays. A pregnant woman should avoid these substances.

- Getting enough rest is important during pregnancy. Wearing comfortable clothing can help a woman feel and look her best.

- As part of the parenting team, a father-to-be can support his pregnant wife in many ways.

Recalling the Facts

1. Describe what is included in prenatal care.

2. What kind of health care professional specializes in providing medical care for pregnant women?

3. Describe what occurs during the first medical visit.

4. What should a couple do if they do not have medical insurance to cover the costs of prenatal care and childbirth?

5. Contrast the ultrasound test with chorionic villi sampling and amniocentesis.

6. Identify two key nutrients that are provided by each of the following food groups: (A) grains, (B) vegetables, (C) fruits, (D) milk, and (E) meat and beans.

7. Why should a pregnant woman make sure she meets her daily need for water?

8. What complications may result from too much sodium during pregnancy?

9. Why might a doctor prescribe prenatal vitamins for a pregnant woman?

10. What average total weight-gain is recommended for pregnant women of normal weight?

11. Name two recommendations for exercise during pregnancy.

12. Identify four factors that increase health risks for mother and baby.

13. Describe the possible symptoms of fetal alcohol syndrome.

14. What health risks exist for infants of mothers who smoke?

15. How can caffeine affect a pregnant woman and her baby?

16. Why are X-rays dangerous for pregnant women?

17. What clothing is especially important for the expectant mother?

18. List two ways a father-to-be can support the mother-to-be during her prenatal care.

Applying New Skills

1. **Meal plans.** Plan a weekly menu for a woman who is considering pregnancy. Be sure to plan three meals and two snacks per day for seven days. While preparing the menus, consider a woman's food needs from the five main food groups of MyPyramid. After creating your menu, enter your food choices into the MyPyramid Tracker on the Internet to see how healthful your meals really are.

2. **Recipe roundup.** Using Internet or print resources, locate one or more healthful recipes for a food from each of the MyPyramid food groups. At the bottom of each recipe, identify why the recipe might be a good choice for a pregnant woman. Share your recipes with the class.

3. **Role-play.** In pairs, role-play a friend who is talking to a pregnant woman who has poor eating habits. The friend should try to convince the woman she should change her eating habits and suggest ways to do this. Have the class evaluate how successful the friend was at convincing the pregnant woman to make better food choices.

4. **Exercise plan.** In small groups, investigate exercise or fitness routines that are appropriate for pregnant women who were moderately active before pregnancy. Put together an exercise plan. You may want to consult a physical education teacher or someone who teaches fitness classes for pregnant women for ideas. Demonstrate your exercise plan to the class.

5. **Resource directory.** Working with a small group, create a directory that lists available sources of prenatal medical care in your community. Include Web addresses, street addresses, phone numbers, and a brief description of each source.

Thinking Critically

1. Assume you are an expectant parent in your late 30s. This will be the first child for you and your spouse. Analyze the criteria used to decide whether you should have certain prenatal tests. Use your text and reliable Internet or print resources to further investigate criteria. Would you choose to have prenatal tests recommended by your doctor? If so, which test(s) would you have done? If not, why not? Write a paragraph explaining your decision. Support your answer with evidence you analyzed about criteria.

2. Draw conclusions about the ethics and health risks of shopping mall ultrasound imaging. Why might parents-to-be like this option? What concerns might doctors and other health professionals have about these high-tech images?

3. Draw conclusions about what expectant fathers can do to make sure their babies are born as healthy as possible. In small groups, brainstorm a list of ways an expectant father can be actively involved in prenatal care and daily living routines.

Linking Academics

1. **Math.** Calculate the approximate due date for the following women given the first day of their last regular menstrual periods. Use the formula on page 206 of the text.
   A. Karen—July 5
   B. Natasha—November 17
   C. Sonia—February 12

2. **Writing.** Use reliable Internet or print resources to research one of the factors that increase health risks to mother and baby. Prepare a written report on your findings.

Chapter 10

Decisions Facing Parents-to-Be

Key Terms

prepared childbirth
birthing room
birth center
colostrum
job sharing
parental leave
Family and Medical Leave Act (FMLA)
primary caregiver
pediatrician
birth plan

Objectives

After studying this chapter, you will be able to

- summarize the benefits of preparing for childbirth.
- describe location options for the baby's birth.
- contrast essential and optional equipment and supplies for a newborn.
- compare breast-feeding and formula-feeding.
- explain the benefits of parental leave from employment.
- identify child care options for working parents.
- explain factors to consider when selecting a doctor for the baby.
- explain legal and business matters that need to be considered during pregnancy.
- summarize ways to get organized before childbirth, including creating a birth plan.

Expecting a baby is exciting. In the beginning, many couples may feel a variety of emotions. They may not believe they are really having a baby, especially if this is their first child. As the initial shock and excitement wear off, parents-to-be begin wondering how to prepare for the big event. This realization can be overwhelming.

The good news is expectant parents don't have to be ready in an instant. They have several months to prepare for their new arrival. Actually, the birth of a child is a process rather than a single event. A baby grows for nine months and is born through a series of events that last several hours, 10-1.

10-1 Parents have plenty of time to prepare for their new babies—it takes babies nine months to grow and develop before birth.

In this chapter, you will learn about the many decisions and preparations a couple will make. If this is their first child, the decisions may be more difficult. The pros and cons may seem less obvious since pregnancy, childbirth, and parenting are new experiences. People who are already parents will base many of these decisions on past experience.

Childbirth Preparation Decisions

One way to prepare for childbirth is to learn more about it. Parents-to-be should understand what happens during pregnancy, labor, and delivery. First-time parents may not know much about these processes. Parents who already have children may need to review what to expect.

Most parents learn about birth in a prepared childbirth class. **Prepared childbirth** is a birth method in which both parents learn about the birth process. Couples learn how to actively participate in their baby's birth.

Many couples take childbirth classes during the last six weeks of pregnancy. Counselors and trainers provide useful information for parents-to-be. Hospitals and birth centers usually hold childbirth classes. Some private and community agencies also offer classes. Often, a couple's doctor or nurse-midwife can make recommendations. Friends, family members, or neighbors might also know of classes in the area.

Taking a childbirth class has many benefits. Childbirth classes can do the following:

- foster a closer relationship between spouses

- promote the father's involvement in pregnancy, labor, and delivery

- allow the couple to meet other expectant parents

- answer expectant parents' questions
- build the confidence of the expectant parents by encouraging them to discuss their fears as well as expectations about the upcoming birth
- teach both partners how to control the woman's pain through breathing, relaxation, and coaching techniques
- provide a successful, pleasant, and less-stressful labor

Parents may also take infant-care classes. These classes will teach them basic parenting and child care techniques. Classes on parenting or child care are especially helpful for first-time parents. If they are not very familiar with infants, these classes can ease some parental concerns. They can also teach important daily care skills and help the parents-to-be form realistic expectations.

Where Will the Birth Take Place?

An important question parents answer during pregnancy is where their baby will be born. Several facility options are available. Couples can select the one that best suits them. Most parents-to-be choose to give birth at a hospital. Depending on where they live, there may be more than one hospital nearby. In many hospitals, couples may select either traditional delivery rooms or birthing rooms. Other couples choose to deliver at birth centers. A few couples deliver their babies at home by certified nurse-midwives.

A couple may have chosen an obstetrician or nurse-midwife to deliver their baby. If so, they may not have as many options about where the baby is born. Most medical professionals only deliver babies in the places they work, 10-2. For some couples, using a specific location matters more than having a certain doctor. These couples can choose a doctor who works in the location they desire.

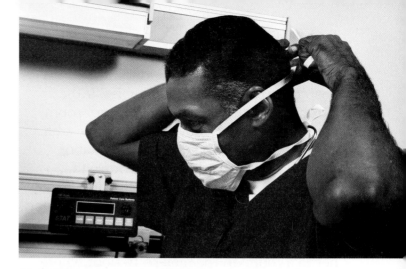

10-2 This doctor can only deliver babies in the hospital where he works. If a couple wants him to deliver their baby, they must deliver at his hospital.

Expectant parents may visit several hospitals and birth centers to find one that best meets their needs. It is important for them to find a place that feels comfortable. They will want to learn about any special policies and procedures each facility has regarding birth. Knowing these policies may help expectant parents make their selection. Couples will also need to make sure the hospital or birth center they choose is affordable.

At a Hospital

When the parents-to-be visit a hospital, someone from the medical staff will explain what they can expect during their stay. This can help them make a final decision about which hospital to use. It also helps couples know what to expect.

Hospitals often give expectant parents tours of the labor, delivery, and nursery areas. Introductions to the *obstetrics* staff are also common. These are the professionals who provide medical care for both mother and baby. Hospitals may offer a choice between a maternity room and delivery room or a birthing room.

Hospital Delivery Room

A delivery room is the traditional hospital area for delivering babies. If the parents-to-be use a hospital delivery room, they can expect to move around quite a bit. They will spend several hours in a labor room. Then hospital staff will move the couple to a delivery room just before the baby is born. After delivery, the mother will spend a short time in a special recovery room. When she's ready, hospital staff will transfer her to a room on the maternity floor where she will spend the rest of her hospital stay.

Hospitals use delivery rooms only during birth. These rooms contain all supplies and equipment health professionals need for safely delivering babies. A hospital delivery room is the best place for a mother to give birth if her pregnancy is *high-risk* (complications are thought likely to occur) or in an emergency.

Hospital Birthing Room

A popular delivery option in many hospitals is a birthing room. A **birthing room** is a special room in a hospital where a woman can labor, deliver, recover, and rest. The entire birth process occurs in just one room. A birthing room is a compromise between a delivery room and at-home delivery.

The room has all the necessary equipment for an uncomplicated delivery. If emergencies arise, obstetrics staff can transfer the woman to the delivery room. A certified nurse-midwife may stay with the couple during labor. When delivery nears, a doctor, nurses, and other medical staff may be present.

A birthing room is much more private and homelike than a delivery room, 10-3. In a birthing room, the furniture and decor are comfortable and calming. The room might even include a private bathroom, a radio or stereo, and television.

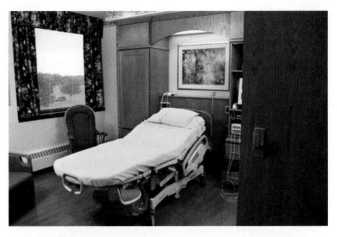

10-3 In this hospital birthing room, couples can enjoy a more homelike setting without sacrificing quality medical care.

Couples often enjoy this relaxed atmosphere. With such family-centered care, family members are often welcome, including siblings-to-be. Within hospital rules, expectant parents decide who may be in the room during labor and delivery. After delivery, both mother and baby rest quietly in this same room.

At a Birth Center

A couple may consider using a birth center. A **birth center** is a nonhospital facility that provides prenatal care and delivery services. These centers often employ certified nurse-midwives. The rooms are comfortable, much like a person's own bedroom.

Birth centers are not equipped to handle emergencies. If an emergency occurs, an ambulance must take the woman to a hospital. This can be dangerous, even if the hospital is close. For this reason, delivery may be less safe at a birth center than at a hospital.

At Home

Some parents wish to deliver their babies at home. They may want their newborn to arrive among family and friends in a warm and loving atmosphere. These couples feel all babies should be born at home, just as before hospital deliveries became the norm. However, maternal and infant death rates were also higher during these years.

Today, most health professionals do not commonly recommend home births. In fact, in some states they are illegal. Parents-to-be who wish to deliver at home should choose a qualified doctor or certified nurse-midwife to attend the delivery.

In the case of a high-risk pregnancy, home delivery is not an option. If something goes wrong, emergency services are not close at hand. A couple must be sure an ambulance can transport the mother and baby immediately to a nearby hospital if needed.

Preparing Baby's Living Space

During pregnancy, parents-to-be must prepare their home for the new baby. Babies need space for sleeping, bathing, and playing. Preparing the baby's living space is especially exciting. It can make the upcoming birth seem more real. If they have an extra bedroom, parents may wish to set up a nursery for their baby in this room. They can decorate, arrange the baby's furniture, and fill the nursery with the supplies the baby will need.

If there isn't an extra room, the baby may share a room with either the parents or an older child. When sharing a room, the baby will still need space of his or her own. Parents can divide a room into sections with a partition or room divider. They can then decorate and arrange the baby's furniture within the space available.

Furniture, Equipment, and Supplies

Babies need furniture, equipment, and clothes to wear. They also need various supplies for their daily care. Some items are essential, while others are not. Parents

should be sure to get all essential items before splurging on options.

When buying baby items, parents-to-be may want to prepare a budget. This will help them avoid overspending and ensure they get the most for their money. For instance, if they spend too much on an elaborate crib, they might not have enough for a stroller. Parents can reduce expenses in these ways

- *Comparison shop.* Rather than buying the first item they see, parents should shop around to get the best prices and values. To save time, some parents choose to use the Internet to comparison shop.

- *Buy gently used items.* Consider shopping for used items at garage sales or resale shops.

- *Borrow items.* Family, neighbors, and friends may be willing to lend baby items they are not using.

- *Make some items.* Check on making some of the items, such as furniture or baby clothes. Family members or friends often take pride in building treasures for the new baby.

- *Wait for gifts.* Many couples have one or more baby showers. Waiting to buy some items lessens the chance of having duplicate items, 10-4.

Baby Furniture

A baby's most essential piece of furniture is the bed. For the first few weeks, parents may prefer a cradle or small bassinet (basketlike bed). As the baby grows, he or she will need a crib. Be sure the crib meets the extra safety requirements found on those made after 1988. (See 10-5 for information on selecting a safe crib.)

Some parents opt for a three-sided crib they can pull up next to their mattress. This sleeping arrangement, or co-sleeping, allows parents to have their infant nearby for feedings and for times of comfort and bonding. The three-sided crib helps parents

10-4 Waiting to purchase some baby items until after a baby shower lessens the financial burden on new parents.

avoid the danger of infant suffocation. Note that the parent's bedding should meet the same safety criteria as the child's crib.

Babies may have other furniture needs besides their cribs. Many parents use a chest of drawers for the baby's clothes. This may be a chest they already have, or one bought especially for the baby. Some parents purchase a changing table. A changing table has a flat, padded top on which parents can dress and undress their babies. Many changing tables also have storage shelves or drawers. The two most important features of changing tables are sturdiness and a safety belt that prevents an infant or toddler from falling. Parents may also want a baby swing or an adult-sized rocking chair for rocking the baby.

Diapers

Diapers are a baby's most essential clothing need. Newborns use as many as 90 to 100 diapers a week. Parents can choose between disposable diapers and cloth for their babies. Each type has advantages and disadvantages, 10-6.

Disposable diapers are made of plastic and paper with an absorbent inner fiber. These diapers fit well and have elastic around the legs to protect against leaks. Two tabs of

tape, one on each side, help fasten diapers snuggly around the infant. Disposable diapers come in various sizes according to a baby's weight and age. Some companies offer different diapers for boys and girls. Parents

Guidelines for Cribs

All cribs made after 1988 must meet the following safety criteria:

- Finish on cribs should not use lead-based paint. Babies who ingest lead-based paint can develop lead poisoning. This can lead to severe physical and mental disabilities.
- Distance between the mattress top and the top rail should be 26 inches or more with the mattress set at the lowest level. This prevents older babies from climbing over the rail. Never leave a pillow or object in the bed that a baby can use as a step.
- Mattresses must be firm and fit snugly against the crib. The space between the crib and the mattress should be no wider than two adult finger-widths. This prevents possible suffocation and trapping of fingers, feet, arms, or legs. It also lessens the chance of a baby accidentally removing a fitted sheet and then suffocating in the sheet wrapped around the head.
- Distance between crib slats or bars must be 2⅜ inches or less. A baby's body can slip through wider spaces. This causes strangulation of the baby since the head, once through the slats, does not slip out.
- Drop sides, used to help adults lift babies out of cribs, must lock securely. If not locked securely, the drop side can give and the standing baby could easily fall.
- Top rails (also called teething rails) should have a plastic covering. Babies should not eat any furniture-finishing product.

10-5 Cribs made after 1988 should meet these standards. Parents-to-be must be extra careful about antique cribs although they may be special. Some of today's cribs fail, too, especially in the drop-side locking mechanism and in the mattress size that does not snugly fit the crib.

can choose among many available brands of disposable diapers.

Parents who don't want to use disposable diapers can choose cloth diapers. Cloth diapers are reusable and made of absorbent cotton. Some feel they are more environmentally friendly since you don't throw them away. However, parents must wash them after each use. Some parents choose to use a separate, disposable lining inside cloth diapers. This lining keeps the baby drier and more comfortable. It also prevents soiling and staining of cloth diapers, making it easier to keep them clean. To avoid hurting the baby when pinning on diapers, many parents use diaper wraps that secure diapers in place with hook-and-loop tape. This "no pins" approach to diapering is safer for the baby, too.

Diaper Choices

Diaper Type	Advantages	Disadvantages
Disposable Combination of plastic and paper with tape fasteners	• Convenient • Essential for use in child care centers and for some travel	• Expensive (costs may run $2,080.00 or more per year using an average of 70 diapers per week) • Not environmentally friendly (plastic coating does not decompose over time) • Can cause allergies due to plastic • Must purchase by size
Cloth— home launder Choices include flat diapers that caregiver must fold or prefolded diapers with or without elastic legs	• All cotton is comfortable and good for sensitive skin • Lower cost than disposables (usually under $100 for one baby) • Laundry adds to expense • Environmentally friendly because they are not thrown away (may be recycled for other purposes) • Seldom cause allergies	• Must launder daily • Increases time and energy parents spend on laundry • Not suitable for use in a child care center or for some travel • Baby must wear vinyl or plastic pants, or diaper covers to protect from leaks • Prefolded diapers must be bought by size • Some babies react to detergents, disposable linings, or coverings to protect from leaks
Cloth— diaper service Choices include flat diapers that caregiver must fold or prefolded diapers with or without elastic legs	• All cotton is comfortable and good for sensitive skin • Environmentally friendly (may be recycled for other purposes) • Service comes to the home each week to pick up soiled diapers and deliver clean ones • Saves laundry time and effort for parents	• Service may be expensive (about $1,110.00 per year using an average of 70 diapers per week) but well worth the money for parents who can afford it • Not suitable for use in a child care center • Baby must wear vinyl or plastic pants, or diaper covers to protect from leaks • Not available in all areas

10-6 The two basic types of diapers have their advantages and disadvantages.

For parents who want to use cloth diapers but do not want the inconvenience of laundering them, a diaper service may be the answer. For a set fee, these services pick up soiled diapers once per week and deliver a supply of clean, fresh diapers. During the week, parents store soiled diapers in a special hamper (that includes a freshening agent) supplied by the diaper service. Although diaper services generally cost more than laundering diapers at home, they may cost less than using disposable diapers.

Baby Clothes

Expectant parents often have fun buying clothes for their new babies. Parents should keep in mind, however, that newborns spend most of the time sleeping and eating. They don't need extensive wardrobes. Many baby clothes given at showers are in newborn sizes, too. Babies grow quickly, so garments that fit at birth will soon be too small. See Figure 10-7 for basic wardrobe items a newborn needs.

As parents shop for baby clothes, their main concern should be the baby's comfort. A second concern is ease of care, since parents must launder baby clothes often. Babies can get more wear from a few durable items than from many poorly made or hard-to-launder ones. Another important factor is how easy the garment is to put on and take off the baby. The climate, season, style, and price are other factors to consider.

Reading labels is important when shopping for infant clothes. Infant clothing is sized by age, weight, or both. Weight is generally a more accurate guide than age. Babies of the same age may be quite different in size. Labels also list the fiber content and care instructions.

The fabric in baby clothes is also important. It should be comfortable and washable. Cotton is an excellent fiber for baby clothes since it is soft and absorbent. Cotton is also durable and easy to launder. Acrylic is a fiber commonly used in baby

sweaters, booties, and blankets. It, too, is soft, comfortable, and washable.

Knitted fabrics are more comfortable than woven ones because they stretch with the baby's movements. Wraparound and snap-on styles are excellent for newborns. Pullover garments should have stretchable necklines. Baby garments should not have any drawstrings around the neck that could strangle the baby. Infant and children's sleepwear (size 9 months to size 14) must meet government standards for flame resistance.

Other Equipment and Supplies

When parents-to-be have obtained baby furniture, diapers, and baby clothes, they have accomplished a great deal. However, there are still many other items they will need for their new baby. Babies require special equipment and supplies for all their major activities, including eating, bathing, sleeping, and traveling.

Mealtime

Parents must decide whether they are breast-feeding or bottle-feeding their infants. Important considerations about that question are discussed later. No matter what they decide, parents of all newborns need some supplies and equipment for feeding. These include

- *Bibs for meals and burping.* Bibs help keep the baby clean and cut down on the number of clothing changes the baby will need.

- *Bottles for feeding.* Formula-fed infants need at least 8 traditional bottles or 2 or 3 bottles with packages of disposable liners and extra bottle nipples and caps. Parents will need bottle-cleaning brushes and sterilizing equipment to clean baby bottles thoroughly. Parents who formula-feed their infants can also buy disposable

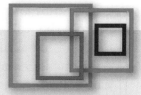

The Newborn's Wardrobe

Item	Quantity	Additional Notes
Diapers	Disposable diapers as needed 4 dozen cloth diapers if laundered at home	Keep 1 dozen disposable or cloth diapers for emergencies if using a diaper service
Diaper liners	As needed for use with cloth diapers	
Diaper pins	4 to 6 for use with cloth diapers	Be sure pins have safety heads Use overwraps or diaper covers for "pin-free" diapering
Vinyl pants, overwraps, or diaper covers	4 to 6 pairs for use with cloth diapers	They should not be tight around the waist and legs Replace pants when they become brittle
Cotton knit shirts	3 or more	Worn to protect the baby from drafts and to absorb perspiration
Cotton knit nightgowns	2 or more for both boys and girls	May have drawstring around the bottom to keep feet warm Long and loose so the baby can move freely Must meet federal standards for fire resistance
Stretch garments	3 or more one-piece or two-piece knit garments	May have built-in feet for day or night wear Should be comfortable and loose-fitting Lightweight, cool fabrics for warm weather; warm, cozy fabrics for cool weather
Special outfits	1 or 2	Cute outfits for special occasions
Sweaters	2 or more	Choose fabric according to climate Should fit comfortably without binding
Caps or hats	1 or more	Worn for warmth and protection from drafts Choose cotton or silk caps for warm weather; acrylic caps for cool weather
Mittens and booties	1 or 2 pairs of each	Allow plenty of room for the baby to move fingers and toes
Blanket sleeper or bunting	1 or more	Use for cold weather if needed
Cotton receiving blankets	3 to 6 or more	Use to wrap the baby after bath or when outdoors in warm weather Use to protect parent's lap during feeding Use as a lightweight crib blanket in warm weather or as a cozy sheet for the crib in cold weather
Acrylic or wool blankets	1 or 2	Use in cold weather as a crib blanket or to wrap the baby when outdoors

10-7 Comfort and ease of care are the major considerations when selecting a newborn's wardrobe.

bottles that are prefilled with formula. Infants that are either breast-fed or formula-fed will also need 2 or 3 bottles with packages of disposable liners for water. Equipment for cleaning will also be necessary.

- ***Breast pump and storage bottle.*** For times when she is unable to nurse her baby, breast-feeding mothers need a breast pump and bottle for milk storage.

Bath Time

Until the umbilical cord dries and falls off, parents should give their baby a sponge bath on a padded surface near a water source. After a few weeks, they can give the baby a "tub" bath in a small plastic tub, dishpan, or bathtub for infants, 10-8. When the baby can sit up on his or her own, parents can use a regular bathtub for bathing.

Parents will also need other items for bathing their infants. These items include a gentle soap, sterile cotton balls (for wiping around the eyes; use one for each eye), washcloths, and towels. If they choose, parents can buy special baby washcloths and hooded towels. They may also wish to use

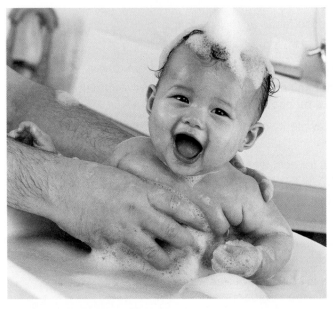

10-8 This baby is a few weeks old—ready for Dad to give him a tub bath.

baby lotion, oil, or cornstarch-based powder after the bath. Some parents buy toys for their babies to play with during bath time.

Bedtime

The goal of infant bedding is to provide a comfortable, safe sleeping area. In the crib, cover the baby's mattress with a waterproof pad or mattress cover. Use a fitted crib sheet over this pad or mattress cover. Parents should have more than one set of sheets. They will need to change sheets often, especially if the baby spits up or has a messy diaper. To cover the baby, parents can use one or more lightweight blankets in summer or a warm crib-sized blanket in winter. Blanket sleepers—special clothing items often made of lightweight, fleecelike fabric—are safer than blankets. Blankets can suffocate babies.

At one time, a set of crib bumpers was considered essential to keep the baby from getting hurt by rolling against the crib sides. Today, according to the American Academy of Pediatrics (AAP) and the Consumer Product Safety Commission (CPSC), a safer choice may be a breathable-mesh crib shield. This special mesh keeps the baby from poking his or her arms and legs through the crib slats and becoming stuck. At the same time, it allows a continuous flow of fresh air into the crib. Current research links the possibility of strangulation and SIDS to crib-bumper usage. Pillowlike crib bumpers restrict airflow into the crib, and may cause the babies to overheat or suffocate. Be sure to securely fasten the mesh crib shield to the crib and tuck it firmly under the mattress. If parents choose to use crib bumpers, the AAP and CPSC recommend that parents remove them once the infant reaches five months of age and becomes mobile.

Do not place pillows or stuffed animals in the crib until the baby is at least a year old. These items pose a risk of suffocation. Parents may also need to remove these items if the baby is a climber. A baby can easily fall out of a crib if he or she stands on them.

Travel Time

Among the most important items a baby requires is a car safety seat. Laws in every state require that parents secure their babies in an approved car safety seat when traveling in a vehicle. In fact, parents must take their infant home from the hospital in an approved car safety seat.

Until an infant weighs 20 pounds, parents should use a rear-facing car seat, 10-9. These infant seats must allow the baby to ride in a reclining position. Children who weigh over 20 pounds must use car seats that allow them to sit up and face forward. Infants and children should never ride in the front seat of a car. The force created when an air bag inflates during an accident can kill an infant or small child.

Parents must be sure their baby's car seat meets all current federal safety standards. For more information, they can contact their local highway safety department. They can also call the National Highway Traffic Safety Administration auto-safety hot line. As long as the car seat meets safety standards, parents can choose the car seat they like best. Ease of use is an important factor to consider.

In addition to a car seat, parents may need other traveling equipment. Items, such as baby carriages and strollers, must also meet current safety standards. Parents who travel often may choose a lightweight stroller that folds to transport easily. Other parents may choose a sturdier stroller that holds up well for a lot of walking. Some parents buy both types.

Feeding Choices

Another decision parents must make is how they will feed their babies. They may choose breast-feeding, formula-feeding, or a combination of both methods. Each method has advantages. Because parents must feed their baby soon after birth, they should make this decision during pregnancy. This way,

10-9 Infant car seats should be properly secured in the back seat. Infant seats should face the rear of the car.

they have time to learn about each method before deciding. They can also make any preparations necessary before the baby arrives.

Parents should talk to their doctor about the advantages and disadvantages of each method. However, their doctor should support whatever decision they make. Family and friends also offer advice to the expectant parents. At times, people may try to persuade the couple to choose one method of feeding over another. However, the parents are responsible for feeding the baby so they must make the final decision, 10-10.

Parents should feed their baby in the way they find most satisfying. If parents enjoy feeding times, they can relax and express their love, warmth, and tenderness to their infant. Feeding is one of the best times for parents and their newborns to be close and share quiet moments together.

Breast-Feeding

Many mothers choose to breast-feed their babies. Experts support breast-feeding as the preferred choice for newborns. The American Academy of Pediatrics (AAP) says breast milk is the best food for a baby's first year.

What makes breast milk such a good choice? Breast milk is nature's food for babies. In the mother's body, hormones naturally

Breast-Feeding or Formula-Feeding

Benefits of Breast-Feeding	Benefits of Formula-Feeding
• The newborn receives colostrum from the breasts for a few days before the milk "comes in."	• The nutritive value of formula never varies. What the mother eats or drinks, the medications she takes, or her state of mind does not affect the milk supply.
• The breasts adjust the quantity and rate of milk production to meet the baby's needs.	• Several types of formula are available and suitable for most babies. Some formulas require very little preparation.
• The baby is less likely to overeat, to have constipation or diarrhea, or to have allergic reactions.	• The quantity of food the baby eats can be measured.
• Breast milk is always available, sterile, and the right temperature. There is nothing to buy or prepare.	• Both father and mother can experience the emotional satisfaction of feeding their baby.
• Close physical contact is emotionally satisfying for both baby and mother.	• The mother is not tied down by the baby's feeding schedule. She can resume her career or other activities sooner.
• Nursing helps the mother's uterus return more rapidly to its normal size and position.	

10-10 Breast-feeding is a natural way to provide a baby with nutrients. Because it has so many benefits, many mothers today are choosing to breast-feed their infants.

produce this milk. It contains all the essential nutrients babies need, as well as extra antibodies to fight diseases and infections. Breast milk requires no preparation. It is always available and ready at the right temperature. In addition, breast milk is easy for babies to digest. Babies are not allergic to it as they might be with a formula based on cow's milk. The cost of breast-feeding is very low compared to formula-feeding. Additional costs may come from the small amount of extra food the mother needs and the possible cost of a breast pump.

Today, more women are choosing to breast-feed their babies, even if only for a short time, 10-11. Some research shows breast-fed babies develop cognitively at a faster rate than formula-fed babies. They also have fewer allergies and problems with obesity, and tend to be sick less often.

Breast milk is a thin, bluish liquid. It develops in the mother's breasts within a few days after the baby is born. Until that time, the baby gets a special substance called colostrum. **Colostrum** is a thick, yellowish liquid in the mother's breasts that nourishes the baby until the mother's milk supply is established. Colostrum contains special antibodies that protect the baby. When the mother's milk comes in, it replaces the colostrum.

Breast-feeding, which is also called *nursing*, provides a sense of closeness between mother and baby. The skin-to-skin contact promotes this feeling of connection. Holding a baby close makes the baby feel loved. It helps a baby trust that a parent will take care of his or her needs.

Nursing mothers also experience some benefits from breast-feeding. The baby's sucking action stimulates hormones that help the mother's uterus return to normal. The energy required to nurse and produce breast milk also speeds a mother's weight loss.

Mothers may worry about how they will feed their babies when they return to work. Some mothers, especially those whose babies

10-11 Breast-feeding is a natural way to provide a baby with nutrients. Because it has so many benefits, many mothers today are choosing to breast-feed their infants.

are cared for at the work site, may devise an alternate working arrangement that allows them to breast-feed during work hours. To continue giving the baby the benefits of breast milk, many employed mothers use a breast pump to collect the milk. The breast pump uses suctionlike pressure to "express" or remove the milk from the mother's breasts. The expressed milk is stored in a refrigerator or freezer. During work hours and possibly for at-home time, too, parents or caregivers can feed the baby the expressed milk from a bottle. If the mother cannot or does not want to breast-feed or use a breast pump during work, she can switch to formula-feeding while at work or for all feedings. Experts agree that even a short period of breast-feeding or some breast milk daily is helpful.

Nursing does have certain disadvantages. Unless a mother transfers breast milk to a bottle, she is the only person who can feed the baby. She is the one who gets up to feed the baby at night. Newborns may nurse as often as 8 to 12 times daily and spend 20 to 30 minutes at each feeding. This means the mother nurses every 2 to 4 hours. This may not give her as much flexibility for other activities.

Nursing does not allow the father to feed the baby. Fathers can develop close ties with their babies by being involved in other care activities. For instance, fathers can still dress, diaper, bathe, hold, and play with their infants. This can mean just as much to the baby.

Nursing in public can be inconvenient, and for some people, embarrassing. It does not offer as much modesty as feeding from a bottle. Some women simply do not feel comfortable with the idea of nursing. These women should not feel guilty about their choice.

Formula-Feeding

Despite its advantages, some parents choose not to feed their babies breast milk. Instead, they prefer formula-feeding from a bottle. Parents can purchase formula in liquid or powder forms. Most formulas are concentrated, which means parents must mix them with water before feeding. Formula uses a skim-milk base from cow's milk and is modified to provide babies with the nutrients they need. Babies who are allergic to cow's milk can drink a soy-based formula.

Many couples choose to feed formula if the mother plans to return to work soon after the baby is born. This allows the baby's caregiver to feed the baby. A few mothers use both breast milk and formula. However, using the combination may confuse the baby because both sucking and taste differ.

Some expectant parents prefer formula-feeding because they find nursing unappealing. Bottle-feeding offers more modesty for the mother, especially in public places, 10-12. If a mother does not want to nurse, it is better for her to formula-feed than for her to be unhappy. Babies can sense this unhappiness, making feeding times less pleasant for both mother and baby.

An advantage of formula-feeding is that both mother and father can feed the baby. This can help the father feel close to the baby and relieve some of the strain on the mother. Also, feeding from a bottle is easy and convenient. Parents can measure how much the baby eats, so they can feel reassured the baby is getting enough to eat.

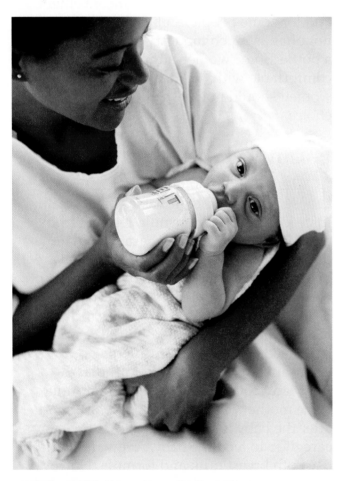

10-12 In public places such as restaurants, parents may find it much more convenient to bottle-feed their infants. Bottle-feeding also provides more modesty for the mother.

Parents who choose formula-feeding should not feel guilty. Formulas can provide needed nutrients. Holding the baby during feedings fosters closeness and nurturing similar to that of nursing.

Never feed a baby by propping the bottle on a pillow or other item. Newborns do not have the muscles necessary to drink from that position. They cannot stop the flow of milk from the bottle, which creates a potential choking hazard. Also, any stray milk that settles in the baby's ear can cause and ear infection. Holding babies during feeding gives them the closeness they need.

Who Will Share the Baby's Care?

Expectant parents are often very excited about having a baby. However, preparing for their new baby can also be stressful. Parents-to-be have many issues to settle before their baby arrives. Questions about who will be involved in caring for the baby can be especially difficult. Parents-to-be must determine what impact parenting will have on the jobs they do. They must decide who will provide the daily care for their newborn. Expectant parents must also choose a doctor to care for their baby. Making these decisions is best before the baby arrives.

Employment Decisions

When they marry, most couples discuss their goals regarding work. Whether one or both spouses work, the couple settles into a pattern. When pregnancy occurs, the couple's life changes. Now they have a child to consider. Both spouses must reevaluate their employment decisions.

When both parents work, the couple must talk about how they will divide household and parenting tasks. Work affects the family, and family life affects work. Some work-related factors that could affect the family include work schedule, number of hours worked, job location, job responsibilities, health and safety concerns, benefits, and income. Family-related factors that could affect work include child care issues, household tasks and responsibilities, family relationships, and available leisure time. Review "Parenting Factors to Consider Before Marriage" in Chapter 3. Couples should carefully think through the same factors, along with their advantages and disadvantages.

The success of dual-career families depends on how well spouses work together to achieve mutual goals. Parents in dual-career families need to revise their expectations, redefine their roles, and invent creative solutions for their problems, 10-13. For example, parents might consider the following options:

- *Plan other work options with their employers.* Some parents are able to arrange flexible work schedules. For instance, an employer may permit two employees to share a job, each working part-time. This is called **job sharing**. It allows each employee more time to be at home with family.

- *Make arrangements to work from home.* This may or may not be possible, depending on the type of work the parents do. Some companies allow an employee to work from home during certain hours or days. A little flexibility can greatly help parents juggle child care and work responsibilities.

Parental Leave

It takes time to adjust to new parenting roles. Taking parental leave from work after the baby is born may help parents concentrate on their new roles. **Parental leave** is paid or unpaid leave from work to tend to parenting duties. Parents most often take this leave when they give birth or adopt a child or if their child is seriously ill.

10-13 In dual-career families, it helps when Dad shares more of the household responsibilities, like taking the baby grocery shopping with him.

Two types of parental leave are *maternity leave* for mothers and *paternity leave* for fathers. Of the two, maternity leave is more common. Maternity leave allows the mother to develop a close and special relationship with the baby. Beyond the bonding benefits, maternity leave allows the mother's body time to rest and recover. This promotes her return to good health after the birth. For many mothers, even a short maternity leave is important.

As knowledge increases about the special role fathers play in their infant's development, paternity leave is becoming more common. Paternity leave allows a father to spend time with his new baby and help care for his recovering wife. Not all companies offer paid paternity leave, but some do. Some fathers start their paternity leave when the mother returns to work. This makes it possible for the baby to be home with at least one parent for a longer period of time.

Many experts advise three to four months of parental leave after the birth or adoption of a child. They believe having this time to concentrate solely on parenting is best for parents and child. By learning more about parenting, new parents may feel more confident in managing their multiple roles. If and when parents do return to work, they may feel a little less overwhelmed. Their parenting duties will have already begun to feel familiar.

To support this belief, many companies offer parental leave as part of their benefits packages. When a couple is expecting a baby, both spouses should check with their employers to know what options are available. Then they can decide what leave, if any, each parent will take. In the case of unpaid leave, parents must weigh how the benefits of being with their baby might offset the income they will lose. Companies have different policies for providing leave, such as

- *Length of leave time.* A company may grant a short period of leave (4 to 6 weeks) or extended leave (12 weeks or longer). A few companies have a *variable-leave policy.* With this type of leave, the length of leave time depends upon years of employment.

- *Paid or unpaid leave.* A company may have a paid leave policy in which the employee gets full or reduced salary while on leave. Salaried employees more often have paid leave than employees who are paid by the hour or paid by the assignment. The company might offer a period of unpaid leave. During unpaid leave, the person's job (or a similar job) is often held until he or she returns to work.

According to the **Family and Medical Leave Act (FMLA)**, employers with 50 or more eligible employees must give up to 12 weeks of unpaid leave in certain situations. FMLA helps balance workplace demands with needs of families. It also promotes the stability of families and the economic security of families. See Figure 10-14 for more information on FMLA.

In addition to paid and unpaid leave, some parents take vacation days and personal days owed to them by their employers. Many couples, however, use these days after they return to work for backup care for their infant. Parents often need extra days away from work if other caregivers are unable to care for the baby. They may also need

this time if the baby is ill or needs medical attention. Newborns and infants need frequent medical attention.

Choosing a Caregiver

The person who provides the most care for the baby is called the **primary caregiver**. This is the person who spends the most time with the baby. He or she answers the most cries, feeds the most meals, and changes the most diapers. This primary caregiver may be the father, a grandparent, an older sibling, or a babysitter, but it is often the mother.

Many experts believe a baby benefits from the consistent care given by a primary caregiver. This person is a constant in the

Family and Medical Leave Act

Who qualifies?
- Employees in companies with 50 or more employees. (Note: Employees who are in the highest paid 10 percent of a company's salaried workers may not qualify.)
- Workers in the following circumstances qualify:
  - Worker or worker's spouse has just given birth to or adopted a child.
  - Worker must provide care for a seriously ill family member.
  - Worker has a serious health condition of his or her own.

What is guaranteed under the law?
- Qualified employees have up to 12 weeks of parental leave.
- Leave is unpaid (although an employer can pay salary or wages during some or all of the leave time).
- Employer guarantees an employee can have his or her job (or an equal job) upon return to work.
- Employer guarantees that employee maintains all health care benefits during his or her leave.

10-14 About half of U.S. workers are covered by FMLA.

baby's life. The baby often forms a special attachment to this person. The primary caregiver helps the baby learn to respond to the rest of the world. The baby needs to know he or she can depend on this caregiver for love, comfort, help, food, and all other needs.

Parents will want to decide who will be this primary caregiver. In addition, they should decide who else would provide care for the baby. In many families, both parents plan to work outside the home after the baby is born. Finding quality child care is a top priority for these parents.

During pregnancy, parents may begin to investigate their child care options. They will likely want to decide before the baby arrives. Each family's situation and resources are unique. This makes each family's options slightly different. Some of the options include

- *Having a grandparent or other relative provide child care,* 10-15. If this person is willing and able to provide care, it is a good way for the baby to spend time with extended family members. Parents often trust their family members more than anyone else.

- *Asking a close friend or neighbor to provide care.* Parents may have to pay for this care, but they would still feel confident in the quality of care provided. They would feel comfortable knowing their baby was in the hands of a person they trust.

- *Hiring a caregiver.* Child care options include having a caregiver to come to the family's home, taking the baby to the caregiver's home, or using a child care center. Parents will want to carefully examine a situation before placing their child in someone's care. Local social service agencies can refer parents to reputable caregivers and child care centers.

10-15 If they're available, grandparents can make excellent caregivers for their grandchildren.

Choosing a Doctor

Choosing a baby's doctor is an important parental task. Parents want a capable, caring doctor to provide quality medical care for their baby. They must be able to rely on the doctor's knowledge, skills, and advice.

A few parents know exactly which doctor they want to care for their baby. Most others have to search for just the right doctor. Because this takes time, some experts believe parents should begin the search early in the pregnancy. The doctor will examine the baby just after birth, so parents should choose the doctor before the baby is born.

Parents must first decide which type of doctor they prefer. They may choose a **pediatrician**, a doctor who specializes in providing medical care for infants and children. These doctors receive special training in children's medical care. After passing certain exams, the American Board of Pediatrics (ABP) certifies them. A pediatrician only sees infants and children through the young-adult years, 10-16.

For some families, choosing a family-practice doctor can also be a good choice. In this case, the parents' family doctor provides care for the entire family. He or she already knows the parents fairly well. Parents may trust their family doctor more than someone new.

Parents will need to decide if they prefer a group practice or a doctor with a solo practice. In a *group practice,* several doctors work together and see each other's patients. A group practice often has longer hours and more availability of doctors. However, parents may not have a choice of doctors and may see different doctors on a regular basis. *Solo practice* means consistent care from the same doctor. However, the doctor may have limited hours. Solo-practice doctors may have special clinics or hospitals provide emergency care for them. Parents may not know the emergency backup doctors from the local emergency room.

Once parents make decisions about type of doctor and practice, they need to check in with their insurance provider. Insurance

companies list doctors and hospitals as health-care providers for whom they are willing to pay. Parents should make a list of doctors who are providers in their area. They should call the doctors' offices to determine which hospital each doctor uses for his or her patients. When choosing a doctor, parents are also choosing a hospital. Once they choose a doctor, parents should call the insurance company to confirm the listing is correct and up-to-date.

A couple may want to ask their obstetrician or nurse-midwife to refer them to a trusted doctor. Family and friends may also have suggestions. When couples interview a doctor, they should ask parents in the waiting room about the practice. They may ask questions, such as: "How long have you been coming here?" "Do you like the practice?" "Do you have any complaints?" "How long does it take to get an appointment?" "Is the waiting time at the office long?" Most patients have similar experiences.

Interviewing a doctor is an important step for parents in finalizing who will provide medical care for their child. Preparing a list of questions before the interview will help parents keep focused on things that are most important to them. Here are some factors for parents to consider:

- *Questions about the practice.* Parents will need general information about the practice including office hours, emergency and after-hours care, and office testing and the diagnostic labs the doctor uses. Answers to these questions tell the parents about the convenience of their child's care. During the baby's first year, they will make about 10 visits. Thus, convenience may be essential.

- *Questions about the doctor's beliefs.* Making sure that the doctor's beliefs and care practices are in line with the parent's desires is important. Parents

10-16 A pediatrician is specially trained in caring for children. This type of doctor knows how to put children at ease.

will need to find out about the doctor's views on second opinions and referrals to specialists, 10-17. They should also find out about doctor's opinion on other practices they are planning, such as breast-feeding (or bottle-feeding), working and having a care provider for the baby, and child-rearing practices. Parents should also ask about other child care topics important to them, such as using vitamins and giving vaccinations.

- *Questions about financial issues.*
  Because of the high cost of medical care, parents need advance information. What are the costs of services? What are the payment arrangements, such as when payments and co-payments (the part not covered by insurance) are due? Will the practice take the parent's insurance?

- *Impressions about the interview.*
  Parents should think about how easily they communicated with the doctor. Did they understand the doctor? Do they think their baby will like this doctor?

- *Impressions of waiting room and office.*
  Parental impressions are important because they will spend time there. Does it have two waiting rooms—one for well-child checkups and another for ill children? Is it clean? Is it bright and cheerful? Are the staff members friendly? Is it conveniently located even for peak traffic times?

Carefully choosing their child's doctor can reassure parents their baby will have quality medical care. The doctor is a valued member of the team who will share in the baby's care. Parents must have confidence in all members of their baby-care team.

Taking Care of Business

Babies not only change their parents' lives in terms of love and care, but also

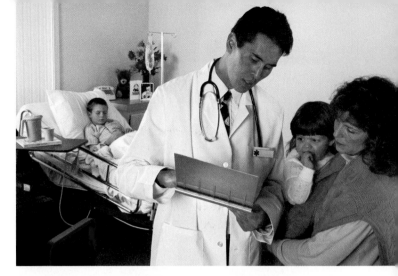

10-17 Interviewing potential doctors for their children is an important parenting task.

legally. Until they are adults, parents will manage their legal and business matters. Parents-to-be must take care of certain important matters prior to their baby's birth. However, some of the arrangements can take place after the birth.

Wills and Beneficiaries

First and foremost, parents need to prepare a will and name a guardian for their child. The unexpected can happen. Dying *intestate* (without a will) means the courts will make the decisions for the parents. The guardian may or may not be the same as the person in charge of the estate. In other words, the person who would be great with children may not be so good with money. Parents can appoint a guardian for the child and another person or bank-trust department to handle the financial matters of the estate. Think about what a prolonged court case could mean for a child, 10-18.

When planning their wills, parents also need to think about their life insurance and investments. They will need to add their child's name as a beneficiary to their life insurance policies. Parents should also list their child as a beneficiary of any investment or retirement accounts they may have through a "Transfer on Death" or a "Payable

10-18 A will makes sure your wishes for your child's care are followed. It should be kept safe with your other valuables.

on Death" form. Parents can get the forms in advance of the birth. They will need the baby's social security number to complete this task.

Birth Certificates and Social Security

Parents will need to apply for a birth certificate and a social security number for their baby. They will need the baby's social security number for claiming dependent exemptions and child-care tax credits on tax forms. In addition, parents will need this number to open a bank account, buy savings bonds, and obtain medical coverage for their child. When giving information for a baby's birth certificate, parents can apply for the social security number. Having both parents' social security numbers is required.

Health Insurance

To obtain health insurance coverage for their child, parents need to call their insurance provider about the process for enrolling their child. If each parent has a different policy, check the coverage and costs for including a child on each policy before making a decision. This decision needs to be made months before the birth so parents can choose the baby's doctor with insurance in mind. Parents will make the final call to the insurance company after the child's birth.

Getting Organized

For most parents, life will likely "turn upside down" for a few weeks before childbirth and after they bring their newborn home. Organization is the secret to preventing chaos. These suggestions may help parents get organized.

- *Prepare to leave work.* Whether taking a short or long parental leave, parents should be certain to meet work expectations before they leave. They should inform their supervisors about the status of their work so the supervisor can pass this information on to any substitute help. Workspaces should be left neat and orderly.

- *Begin cleaning the home before the last trimester.* Mothers have little energy during the last months of pregnancy. Starting to clean earlier makes the work easier. By putting away unneeded items, parents can make their homes easier to clean and childproof some areas at the same time.

- *Prepare and freeze foods for a few meals.* Meals are difficult to prepare with a newborn to care for. If possible, parents might double some recipes and freeze them for use after the baby comes.

- *Confirm child care plans.* If choosing a friend or other nonfamily child care option, parents should confirm they are on the acceptance list for a given date. The date should be about a week or more before the parental leave ends. This way parents have time to check out the new care arrangements for their baby.

- *Write "thank you" notes.* Write as many "thank you" notes as possible before the delivery date. Parents should have extra "thank you" cards, addresses, and stamps for writing notes to people who need thanks after the baby is born. Make a record of gifts brought after the baby's delivery. Remember, it is easy to misplace tags and small cards and some people who bring gifts do not insert cards.

- *Choose birth announcement cards.* Parents can address and stamp the cards before the due date.

- *Double-check on needed items for the baby.* Parents should set up and learn how to use all equipment before the baby's birth. Arrange items to easily find them. Organize and fill the diaper bag.

- *Make care arrangements for other children, pets, and home.* Lining up people to care for their other children, any pets, and their home can help relieve stress so parents can enjoy the birth experience.

- *Pack bags for the hospital or birthing center.* Mothers will need to pack personal items and the baby's items. The father needs to pack, too. See Chapter 11 for suggestions.

One of the most important tasks for parents-to-be is to write their **birth plan**. This plan combines all of their expectations about labor and delivery in one place. In this way, all members of their care team will know what the parents expect during labor and delivery, 10-19. Some doctors' offices have forms parents can use for the birth plan. This is best done as they make decisions. Parents

should review this plan in the last few weeks of pregnancy. They should make copies for their home medical file and for any labor/delivery partner(s).

Birth Plan

Labor and Delivery

- Where do you want to deliver?
- Who, if anyone, do you want present during labor and delivery? during a C-section?
- What method of childbirth have you chosen?
- What method of pain relief do you want?
- How do you want your baby monitored during labor and delivery?
- Do you want music in the labor room?
- Do you want a mirror positioned so you can see the birth?
- Who do you want to cut the umbilical cord?
- Do you want to bank the cord blood?

After Delivery

- Do you want to hold your baby immediately after birth? Would you rather hold the baby after cleaning, dressing, and finishing medical procedures?
- Will your baby stay in the nursery or room-in with you?
- How do you want to feed your baby?
- Do you want your son to be circumcised?
- Who do you want to visit your room? Or, *not* to visit?
- Assuming there are no complications, when do you want to return home? (An extra day or two may give you an opportunity to learn to breast-feed and to do other child care tasks plus give you a longer rest time before returning home.)

10-19 A birth plan makes your wishes known as to preferred medical procedures for labor, delivery, and for newborn care. Special situations may arise that will prevent health care personnel from carrying out every desire.

Summing It Up

- Prepared childbirth can make birth more pleasant for parents-to-be.

- Expectant parents should carefully review birth-location options. They should make this decision well before the actual delivery.

- Parents-to-be can use the time during pregnancy to gather supplies their new baby will need. Couples need to buy the essential items first and use any money left over for optional items.

- Babies need furniture, diapers, and clothes. They also need special equipment and supplies for meals, baths, bedtime, and travel. Parents should be aware of safety guidelines for all baby items and purchase those that meet current safety standards.

- Both breast-feeding and formula-feeding can provide the nutrients a newborn needs. After learning about each method, expectant parents should choose the one that is best for them.

- Making decisions about the baby's care may be challenging. Parents must decide about continuing their employment, taking parental leave, and choosing a care provider and doctor.

- Parents must make some decisions about legal matters before the baby's birth. They should plan ahead because they will need to address most of these matters shortly after the baby's birth.

- Parents-to-be need to be organized prior to the baby's birth. Caring for a newborn lessens energy and time for these activities once the "new" family returns home.

Recalling the Facts

1. Why should parents-to-be prepare for childbirth?

2. List four benefits of taking a class in prepared childbirth.

3. Briefly describe each of the location options expectant parents may choose for the delivery of their baby.

4. List four tips parents can use to reduce expenses when buying baby supplies.

5. Why should parents not use a crib that was made before 1988?

6. List two advantages and two disadvantages each for cloth diapers and disposable diapers.

7. List three factors to consider when buying baby clothes.

8. Describe one essential item for each of the following newborn activities:
   (A) eating, (B) bathing, (C) sleeping, and (D) traveling.

9. List two reasons mothers might breast-feed.

10. List two reasons parents might formula-feed.

11. Name two advantages and two disadvantages of employment for parents of a newborn.

12. Why do child development experts advise three to four months of parental leave after the birth or adoption of a child?

13. What is the purpose of the Family and Medical Leave Act (FMLA)?

14. List four child care options for a newborn.

15. What is the difference between a pediatrician and a family doctor?

16. Name three factors parents should consider when selecting a doctor for their baby.

17. Name two basic legal documents that parents must secure for their baby.

18. List five tips for getting organized before the baby is born.

Applying New Skills

1. **Observation.** Make arrangements to observe one or more sessions of a prepared childbirth class in your community. Note what parents-to-be are taught about the childbirth process, handling pain during childbirth, and preparations for the birth experience. If possible, talk with several prospective parents about the childbirth class. What do they feel is most helpful about the class? Write a summary about your findings to share with the class.

2. **Childbirth directory.** Create a directory of available birth locations in your area. Include contact information for every hospital and birth center in your community. For each location, describe available services. Use Internet and/or print resources to locate information on hospitals and birth centers.

3. **Parent interview.** Interview parents of an infant about the supplies they gathered before their baby's birth. Write a summary of your findings. Ask the following questions as well as any others you might have: Which items did you find essential? optional? Did baby supplies cost more than you expected? Which item was the most costly? What methods did you use to stretch your money?

4. **Infant care costs.** Individually or in small groups, investigate the cost of infant care in your area. Contrast in-home care with center-based care. For each type of care, ask whether the caregiver accepts infants. If so, what ages of infants are accepted? What is the infant to caregiver ratio? Does the infant/caregiver ratio impact the cost of care? What is the cost per month for full-time care (40 hours a week)? Share your findings with the class.

Thinking Critically

1. In small groups, debate the following statement: Childbirth is a natural event and should take place in the home. Use text and Internet or print resources for evidence to support your point of view.

2. Investigate the environmental impact of using disposable diapers versus cloth diapers to launder at home. Draw conclusions about which diapers are best for the environment and for babies.

3. Assume that you and your spouse are soon-to-be parents. Analyze the pros and cons about breast-feeding, formula-feeding, or a combination of the two. After completing your analysis, determine which feeding method you would choose. Write a paragraph on this topic, using information from the chapter to support your answer.

4. Compare and contrast the use of pediatricians or family doctors for a baby's medical care. Which do you feel is best and why? Use text or additional Internet or print resources to locate evidence to support your position.

5. Analyze the qualities of people who would make good guardians of an infant. Are these qualities the same for guardians of older children? Once a child reaches the middle school years, should parents consider changing their wills to name another person as a guardian? Why or why not?

Linking Academics

1. **Math.** Assume you are the parent of a newborn who uses 70 to 90 diapers per week. Would you use a diaper service, cloth diapers, or disposable diapers? Use Internet or print resources to investigate the weekly cost of diaper services in your area. In addition, gather the costs of both cloth diapers (to launder at home) and disposable diapers for a week. How do the costs compare? Which alternative would you choose? To extend this activity, calculate the percentage of monthly *net* income (take-home pay) it would take to pay for each diaper alternative for the following parental incomes: (A) $2,000 or (B) $3,600.

2. **History.** Research and report on the history of midwifery in the United States. When did midwifery as a profession begin? How is midwifery today different from early practices? What education and certification does a person need to become a midwife today? Write a brief summary of your findings to share with the class.

3. **Writing.** Assume that you and your spouse are soon-to-be parents. Use the questions in Figure 10-19 as a guide to writing a birth plan. Answer the questions completely, based on information you have learned in this text. Finalize your birth plan after reading Chapter 11. Save your birth plan for future reference.

Chapter 11

Childbirth

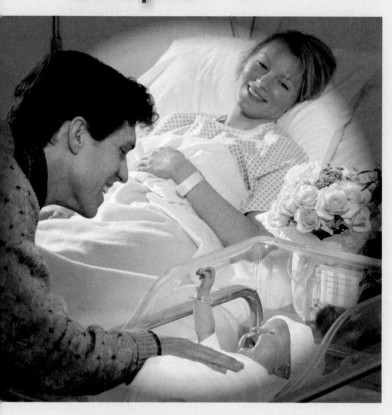

Objectives

After studying this chapter, you will be able to

- identify the signs of labor.
- explain common labor and childbirth procedures before, during, and after birth.
- compare different methods of childbirth.
- describe types of medications available during childbirth.
- identify key events in each stage of labor.
- describe neonatal care, including newborn screening tests and emergency medical care.
- summarize the effects of childbirth on the parents, including the importance of bonding and causes of negative feelings about childbirth.
- propose ways new parents can adjust during the postpartum period.

Key Terms

contractions
traditional childbirth
family-centered childbirth
Lamaze
Leboyer method
cesarean delivery
breech
epidural
dilation stage
delivery stage
episiotomy
afterbirth stage
Apgar test
neonate
Brazelton scale
Neonatal Intensive Care Unit (NICU)
circumcision
bonding
postpartum period
postpartum depression (PPD)

The last weeks of pregnancy may be a time of mixed emotions for parents-to-be. A woman may be eager for relief from the physical burdens of pregnancy. Both prospective parents may be eager for the birth so they can meet their new baby. At the same time, they may wish they could have a little more time for the final preparations.

In this chapter, you will learn to identify the signs of labor and describe the events of labor and delivery. You will be able to describe professional neonatal care. You will also learn why bonding is important and how new parents adjust after the baby's birth.

Final Preparations

As the due date approaches, the expectant mother will have weekly checkups. Her doctor or nurse-midwife will watch closely for signs the baby is ready to be born. The mother often has an additional ultrasound test to check the baby's maturity and its position in the uterus.

As you recall, parents need to pack their bags for the birth. It is best to pack several weeks before the due date because babies can arrive earlier than expected. Packing early reduces the chance parents will forget something important. Figure 11-1 shows a typical list of items to pack.

Signs of Labor

Like symptoms of pregnancy, signs of labor vary from woman to woman and from pregnancy to pregnancy. During the last few weeks before childbirth, mothers-to-be will note some of these signs. Other signs mean active labor is under way.

Approaching Labor

Prelabor contractions, or pains of muscle tension, can occur before labor. *False labor*, meaning not true labor, is another name for these prelabor contractions. For instance, *Braxton-Hicks contractions* may begin as early as 20 weeks of pregnancy. These muscle contractions happen infrequently. They last less than a minute and stop when the woman changes position.

Another sign labor is approaching is called *lightening*. This occurs as the baby's head descends into the mother's pelvis. When the baby moves down, it relieves pressure on the mother's abdomen. This can make breathing easier for her. In a woman's first pregnancy, lightening may occur anytime in the final month. In later pregnancies, it may not occur until the week or the day labor actually begins.

An additional sign that labor will soon occur is the passage of a blood-tinged mucus plug or *show*. The mucous plug is a gel-like substance that seals the cervix and protects the baby from infection during pregnancy. When it is passed, this generally means that the cervix is starting to thin out and dilate and the plug is no longer large enough to seal the uterus. Labor usually begins within 24 hours of the appearance of the show.

Labor Begins

Even when the signs of active labor are present, a woman who is about to have her first child may wonder if she is truly in labor. Questioning whether she is in labor is a normal reaction. It is never wrong for a woman to call her doctor or nurse-midwife to help confirm that she is in labor. When real labor begins, a woman will notice one or both of the following signs.

Passage of Fluid

Before or during labor, the amnio-chorionic membranes will rupture and release amniotic fluid through the vagina. You may also hear people refer to this as the "water breaking." If contractions have not begun when the membranes break, this generally will signal them to start. In a few

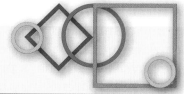

Packing for Birth

Person	Items Needed
Mother	• Two or three nightgowns and robe presentable for visitors and photos
	• Socks for cold feet during delivery; slippers for walking around
	• Undergarments, such as a nursing bra for breast-feeding and several pairs of panties
	• Outfit for trip home
	• Toiletries for self-care
	• Miscellaneous items, such as a clock with a sweep second hand for timing contraction; baby book for early entries; phone numbers of people to call after the birth; documents such as health insurance card, registration forms, and social security cards; notepaper and pen; camera and batteries; comfort items such as photos and pillows
Baby	• Installed car seat
	• Diapers (2 or 3 unless furnished at birth facility) and other diapering supplies
	• Baby clothes—one or two outfits for photos, coming home outfit, cap or bonnet, and sweater
	• Blankets—one or two receiving blankets and a coming home blanket, which is often warmer and larger than a receiving blanket
Father	• Two or three outfits and undergarments (depending on expected length of stay)
	• Comfortable shoes
	• Toiletries for self-care
	• Reading materials or something for entertainment while mother and baby sleep

11-1 In the last weeks before the baby is born, bags need to be packed for the mother, father, and baby.

cases, the membranes do not break naturally. The doctor may have to rupture them just before delivery.

Once the membranes have broken, delivery generally occurs within 24 hours. Amniotic fluid cushions the baby and regulates his or her body temperature. Without adequate fluid, the baby may be in danger. The mother or baby might also develop an infection if the baby is not born soon.

True Contractions

Contractions are pains felt during labor when the muscles of the uterus tense. The uterine muscles contract to open the cervix and push the baby out of the uterus. Contractions often begin as aches that occur infrequently in the small of the back. After a few hours, the pains move to the front. Some women also experience pain in their legs, especially the upper thighs. Each contraction begins as a slight twinge, builds in intensity, and reaches a peak. This peak is maintained for a few seconds, and then fades gradually.

Unlike prelabor contractions, true labor contractions last longer, increase in intensity, and are closer together. No matter what the woman does, these contractions will not stop. They become progressively more frequent, lengthy, and often evenly spaced. Between contractions, the woman is free from pain. Once contractions begin, couples should time the contractions. They should record when a contraction occurs and how long it lasts. This is important information to give the doctor or nurse-midwife.

Going to the Birth Facility

Once a woman notices signs of labor, she should make her final preparations before going to the birth facility. In the last weeks before delivery, a woman and her spouse (and possibly the health-care provider) will plan exactly what procedure to follow once labor begins. She should remain calm as she follows her preplanned procedures.

Before Leaving Home

A woman should ask her doctor or nurse-midwife what she can do after labor begins. Her health-care provider may allow her to take a shower (not a tub bath), eat a light meal, and rest. She will also want to be sure to let her spouse know if she thinks labor has begun, 11-2.

Medical professionals generally instruct soon-to-be-mothers to call them when labor begins. The doctor or nurse-midwife will review the signs of labor with the expectant parents. People who deliver babies assume patients will call anytime, night or day. The doctor or nurse-midwife can help the couple decide whether to go to the birth facility. If a woman is unsure whether she is in labor, she may want to call her doctor for instructions.

Generally couples go to the birth facility if the amniotic fluid is evident or if regular contractions occur five to ten minutes apart. The timing may also depend on the distance the couple must travel to get to the birth facility.

Many couples leave sooner than is really necessary. Labor may not have started or the contractions may be too far apart or too irregular. In this case, a woman and her partner will likely return home and wait. Having a false alarm is much safer than risking delivery at home or on the way to the birth facility.

11-2 Expectant fathers, hoping to hear that labor has begun, are eager to know when their babies will arrive.

At the Birth Facility

Most birth facilities use the same basic procedures. These procedures follow the natural sequence of labor and delivery. Each facility also has its own set of policies and restrictions patients must follow.

Many birth facilities allow expectant parents to fill out some of the necessary admittance forms early. If possible, couples should do this several weeks before the due date. Completing forms early makes it easier for the couple during labor. It can greatly speed up the admittance process. When they arrive at the birth facility, expectant parents simply check in at the appropriate desk and register.

After admittance, a nurse will take the couple to the appropriate room. If the woman delivers in the delivery room, labor takes place in a separate room. If the couple uses a birthing room, labor and delivery will occur there. The woman changes into a hospital gown. At this point, the woman undergoes an exam to see how she is progressing toward delivery. The doctor may check her occasionally, or the obstetrics staff only calls the doctor in for delivery. When nurse-midwives deliver babies, they usually stay with the parents throughout the entire process.

The obstetrics staff monitors a baby's heart rate during labor and delivery. To monitor the heart rate at intervals, the nurse or doctor uses a *fetoscope*, a special instrument to hear the baby's heart rate, 11-3. For continuous monitoring, an *electronic fetal monitor* is used. This device records the baby's heartbeat and the mother's contractions. The doctor or nurse-midwife can view this information on screen or on a printout. He or she will watch the baby's heartbeat and response to contractions to see how the baby is doing. Monitoring can also detect problems that need immediate attention.

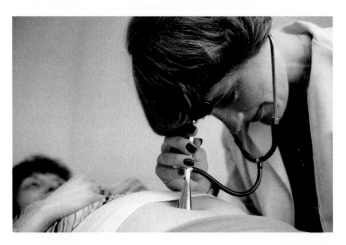

11-3 The doctor can use a fetoscope to monitor the baby's heart rate.

Methods of Childbirth

Childbirth is a natural human event. It is a set biological process. Opinions vary, however, about some of the details surrounding labor and delivery. What preparations should a couple make for labor and delivery? Who besides the mother should participate in the delivery?

Differing answers to these questions led to the development of various childbirth methods. Each method reflects a slightly different viewpoint or style. Couples have several options. Generally, they can choose the method they prefer. Sometimes the practices of the doctor or nurse-midwife limit their choice. A couple should decide which method they want to use long before the due date. The method they use, however, may change during labor or delivery. This happens when the health of the mother or baby is at risk.

The birth facility will often determine the method of childbirth, too. For example, hospitals usually have the most options. Birth centers and at-home deliveries often use family-centered childbirth combined with a prepared-childbirth method.

Traditional Childbirth

In **traditional childbirth**, attention focuses on the health of mother and baby. The woman's comfort is also important. As she needs it, a woman receives pain medication. A member of the medical team monitors the baby's health. Family members wait in a waiting room. Some birth facilities allow the father-to-be in the labor and delivery room(s) with his spouse. Traditionally, hospitals did not allow fathers in delivery rooms. Today, however, most hospitals and birth facilities allow them to be present for the birth of their children.

After a traditional delivery, a woman spends time in a recovery area and then spends the rest of her stay in a room. The baby generally stays in the hospital nursery. The rules about visitors may be strict. For instance, some hospitals may not allow young children to visit their mother or the new baby.

Family-Centered Childbirth

Some hospitals and all birth centers offer family-centered childbirth. **Family-centered childbirth** is based on the belief that childbirth affects the family as a unit and each family member as an individual. The birth of a new baby is important to each family member.

In family-centered childbirth, the father is encouraged to participate in labor and delivery. Other support people (in a few cases, even children) may also be present if the mother so desires and the doctor approves. Labor and delivery generally take place in a birthing room.

Anyone who will be present at the birth must first attend childbirth classes. These classes prepare them for what will take place in the delivery room. Some hospitals and birth centers also offer classes for children who are expecting a new brother or sister.

During labor and delivery, an obstetrical nurse or certified nurse-midwife is normally present throughout the labor and delivery. The doctor may attend the delivery or be on-call in case of complications. The medical personnel encourage and support the natural forces of labor, interfering as little as possible. They try to make sure everything goes right while respecting the family's desire to share this important experience.

After the birth, the family may spend as much time together as they wish. Rooming-in is common with family-centered childbirth. With rooming-in, the baby stays in the mother's room instead of a separate nursery, 11-4. Brothers and sisters can visit their mother and the new baby.

11-4 In hospitals where family-centered childbirth is practiced, rooming-in is common.

Lamaze Method

Lamaze is a philosophy of prepared childbirth. With Lamaze, parents-to-be prepare themselves for the childbirth experience. About two months before delivery, they start attending weekly classes. They learn what to expect in the final stages of pregnancy and during labor and delivery. When they know what to expect, parents are less afraid and more likely to enjoy the childbirth experience.

In Lamaze classes, mothers-to-be learn how to work actively with their labor. Fathers-to-be learn how to provide comfort through emotional and physical support. Delivery often takes place in a hospital birthing room, at a birth center, or at home. The parents choose.

Lamaze helps a woman maintain control of her body during childbirth. A normal response to contractions is to become tense. With Lamaze, women learn multiple ways to respond to their contractions without medication. Breathing and relaxation, massage, slow dancing, rocking, and walking are just a few of the ways women find comfort in working through labor. The father-to-be lends strength, comfort, and encouragement as the mother-to-be works through her labor. One-to-one nursing support is also a key component of Lamaze.

The goal of Lamaze is to make normal childbirth a safe, pleasant, and memorable experience for both parents. The knowledge gained through Lamaze helps build confidence in women and men as they prepare for the birth of their child. The woman does not fail if she needs some pain relief. Medical professionals view medication as a tool to help a woman relax during childbirth.

Leboyer Method

The **Leboyer method** focuses on the baby's birth experience. Its goal is to make birth less shocking and more comfortable for the baby. The medical staff tries to provide a quiet, cozy environment. Dim lights and soft background music add to the peaceful atmosphere. Immediately after birth, a doctor or nurse-midwife places the baby on the mother's warm, soft abdomen. When separated from contact with the mother's skin, health professionals place the baby in warm water.

Couples who use the Leboyer method often take childbirth classes to prepare for labor and delivery. Doctors and hospitals vary in the extent to which they accept the Leboyer method. Couples who want to use this method should talk to their doctor about their wishes early in pregnancy.

Cesarean Delivery

Cesarean delivery is major surgery in which doctors deliver a baby through incisions in the mother's abdomen and uterus. *Cesarean section*, or C-section, is another common name for cesarean delivery. Cesarean deliveries account for almost one third of births in the United States. Doctors use this method for a number of reasons, including the following:

- Labor has been too long, too difficult, or not productive (cervix does not open enough for vaginal delivery).

- The baby's health is in danger.

- The mother's health is in danger.

- There are multiple babies, especially preterm babies who come too quickly and in an uncontrolled way if vaginally delivered.

- There is a problem with the umbilical cord or placenta.

- The woman's pelvis is too small for the baby's head to pass through it.

- The mother has an active STI the baby might contract in the birth canal.

Doctors may also perform cesarean deliveries for other reasons. In some cases, a cesarean delivery might not actually be necessary. For instance, some doctors perform a cesarean delivery if the mother has had previous cesarean births. In reality, many women can have a vaginal birth after a previous cesarean delivery. The doctor may perform a cesarean for his or her convenience, or the mother's convenience. This alone is not a compelling reason to deliver by cesarean.

Often, cesarean delivery is used for babies in a breech position. **Breech** means the baby is in an abnormal position—either buttocks-first or feet-first—prior to labor. A breech delivery is much riskier than a normal, headfirst delivery. For more information on breech delivery, see 11-5.

Many reasons exist for having a cesarean delivery, but it is not the preferred method under normal conditions. Generally, a cesarean delivery is an emergency procedure. Although it can be lifesaving, it does carry some health risks. The recovery period is several days longer for cesarean births than for other births.

Breech Delivery

Doctors refer to how the baby is positioned in the uterus as *presentation*. Babies lie in the uterus in three basic ways:

- headfirst
- feet-first
- buttocks first

Under normal conditions, the baby's head settles into the mother's pelvic area during lightening. A baby's head is usually the first part to come down the birth canal and leave the mother's body. This is the safest way to be born and is called the *vertex presentation*.

A *breech presentation* is a feet-first or buttocks-first position. The cause for breeching is not always known. Sometimes it may be due to being premature, being one of multiples, or having a congenital defect.

By week 37, doctors may try to turn a breeched baby externally. If this does not work or if the baby rotates back, the doctor delivers by C-section before labor. Due to risks, breech vaginal deliveries rarely occur.

11-5 Breech deliveries carry more risk than normal, headfirst deliveries.

Childbirth Medications

The chosen childbirth method affects the type and amount of pain relief used. For example, the knowledge a woman gains from taking a class in prepared childbirth often lessens the amount of medication she needs giving birth. Some women do give birth with little or no medication, but many need at least some pain relief, 11-6. A woman and her doctor or nurse-midwife should decide together about what medications, if any, to use during childbirth. They should discuss the issue long before labor begins. This is true even if the woman thinks she will not want any medication. She should be aware of her options in case she changes her mind.

A woman should not feel guilty if she uses medication to ease the pain. No one knows ahead of time how much pain she will feel or how much relief she will want. She can discuss with her doctor any of her concerns and wishes. The final decision will not be made, however, until labor begins.

When deciding about pain relief during labor, safety is the most important point to keep in mind. The medication selected must be safe for the baby and for the mother. Any drugs used will cross the placenta and enter the baby's bloodstream. Some medications may make the baby sluggish or unresponsive soon after birth. Other drugs may have more dangerous effects. Two types of medications—anesthetics and analgesics—are commonly used.

Anesthetics block sensations in the nerves, including pain, another name for which is *anesthesia*. Anesthesia includes loss of pain in part of the body with or without loss of consciousness. Doctors may use three types of anesthetics during labor and delivery. They include

General Anesthetics. This type of drug puts a person to sleep for a short time. Patients under general anesthesia do not feel pain. Because it puts a woman to sleep, she misses out on the birth experience. She cannot help deliver the baby by pushing along with the contractions. General anesthesia also carries health risks for mother and baby.

Regional Anesthetics. This anesthetic reduces the discomfort of labor. An **epidural** is a regional anesthetic given by an *anesthetist*—a nurse or technician who specializes in anesthesia. He or she injects the drug into the epidural space during labor. The mother is alert and awake, but loses feeling in the lower half of her body. The anesthetist can adjust the amount of anesthetic to create a certain level of anesthesia. Regional anesthetics have side effects and risks. Mothers can have a drop in

History of Medicines and Childbirth

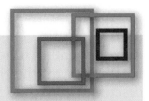

Today, doctors use general anesthesia only for some emergency deliveries. The use of other anesthetics and analgesics replace the use of general anesthesia during childbirth in most cases. Once a routine practice during childbirth, the use of general anesthesia became less common when understanding about the risks and side effects emerged.

- **Since the mid-1800s,** women have used pain medicine during childbirth. Doctors knew the pain women felt during childbirth could be almost overwhelming. A logical conclusion was to give medication to take away this pain. At that time, no one knew that substances in a woman's body could cross the placenta and harm the baby.

- **In the 1930s,** an English doctor, Dick-Read, began encouraging women to give birth without pain medication. This was known as *natural childbirth*.

- **In the 1960s,** doctors Lamaze and Bradley called for a method of *prepared childbirth*. Although their methods are different, both call for women to learn specific ways to relax during childbirth and then to decide on the use of medication.

- **Today,** many couples enroll in prepared childbirth classes. Due to increased safety of medications, most women will choose some type of medication. Thus, some instructors of childbirth classes include information on medications.

11-6 Using medications to relieve the pain of childbirth is not a new idea.

blood pressure. Because the anesthetic creates anesthesia in the lower body, women cannot walk or move much during labor. They are also not able to push during delivery.

Local Anesthetics. Usually given as an injection, this type of anesthetic takes away pain in a small area. Doctors often use local anesthetics to relieve pain in the vaginal area especially during an episiotomy. It causes few risks and side effects but doesn't reduce the pain of contractions.

Analgesics are another type of medicine doctors may use to reduce a woman's discomfort during childbirth. *Analgesics* reduce pain to a more tolerable level, but do not take it away entirely. Anesthetists can give analgesics intravenously, by injection, or by epidural. These drugs are short-lived and may have fewer side effects and risks than other drugs. However, they do not create a total loss of feeling as in anesthesia.

In recent years, doctors have been making changes to overcome the problems of both anesthetics and analgesics. They have been giving lower doses, combining both types of drugs, and changing how they are given. Some of these newer methods are taking the pain of labor out of childbirth. One such process is the *combined spinal-epidural anesthesia* (CSEA). A doctor injects a low dose of an analgesic below the spinal cord into the spinal fluid. The doctor then gives the laboring mother a diluted analgesic and an anesthetic as an epidural. Because of the low doses of combined drugs, the woman can still move and walk. This is called a *walking epidural.* A catheter (a small tube) is left in the epidural space in case larger doses of anesthetic need to be given, such as for surgical delivery. The main drawback of the CSEA is that an *anesthesiologist*, a doctor who specializes in anesthesia, must give it. These doctors work only in large hospitals.

A simpler method, *labor intrathecal analgesia* (LIA), can be done in rural hospitals. During active labor, either the hospital anesthetist or a family physician with LIA training injects an analgesic into a fluid-filled space (intrathecal space) of the spine. The one-time injection usually lasts through active labor and allows the woman to be both mobile and pain free.

Stages of Labor

Labor is a series of changes in the mother's body that enables the baby to be born vaginally. Delivering a baby is hard work for the mother's body. It requires strength, stamina, and muscle control. The three stages of labor focus on dilation, delivery, and afterbirth. Each part of this process takes longer for a mother's first baby than for later ones. Note that women having preplanned cesarean deliveries do not go through labor.

Dilation Stage

The first stage of labor is the **dilation stage**. The purpose of this stage is to dilate (stretch and expand) the cervix. It must open wide enough for the woman to push the baby out of the uterus and into the birth canal. Normally, the cervix is less than a centimeter wide. During labor, the cervix will dilate to ten centimeters.

Each contraction of the uterus causes the cervix to dilate a little more. During the first stage, contractions grow progressively longer, stronger, and closer together. The medical staff monitors the mother's blood pressure and other vital signs. The doctor or nurse will also exam her periodically for labor progress. He or she will measure the cervix for dilation.

When the woman's cervix dilates about 7 to 8 centimeters, she will enter a *transition* phase. Transition is often the most painful part of labor. This is the time when the cervix stretches the last little bit before delivery. The contractions are the most powerful during transition, and the time between them is very short. The mother-to-be will feel very tired, uncomfortable, and stressed. Her partner's support is very important at this time.

During transition, the medical staff may move the woman from the labor room to the delivery room. (If she is using a birthing room, she will remain there for the delivery.)

The nurses and doctor prepare the woman for delivery. Her husband will need to prepare by washing up and dressing in a sterile gown and mask, 11-7.

The amnio-chorionic membrane will likely have ruptured. If not, the doctor will rupture it when the cervix is fully dilated. At this time, the woman is ready to push the baby out of the uterus. This is the end of stage one.

The dilation stage is the longest stage of labor. It begins with the first true contraction and ends when the cervix has fully dilated. This may take anywhere from 8 to 20 hours for a first baby. For later babies, this stage is usually shorter.

Delivery Stage

The second stage of labor is the **delivery stage**. It begins when the cervix reaches full dilation and ends when the baby is born (free of the mother's body). The delivery stage doesn't last long—usually 30 minutes to two hours. The average length of time is 45 minutes.

During this stage, the mother is encouraged to begin pushing. The force of the mother's pushing will move the baby out of the uterus and through the birth canal. *Crowning* refers to the first view of the baby's head during childbirth. This is an exciting

11-7 A nurse can help the father-to-be dress for the delivery after he washes up. During delivery, everyone wears sterile clothing to prevent the spread of germs.

time for the couple—soon they will be able to see their new baby. The woman is also relieved because the end of her labor is near.

As crowning occurs, the doctor will decide whether to perform an episiotomy. An **episiotomy** is a small cut in the opening of the birth canal. This cut makes the vaginal opening wider so the baby has more room to be born. An episiotomy is not necessary in all deliveries. A local anesthetic may be given before making the cut or stitching the cut after delivery.

After the mother pushes the baby's head out of the birth canal, the doctor turns it gently. This allows the shoulders to slide out more easily. The rest of the body follows quickly. After delivery, the doctor or nurse-midwife suctions amniotic fluid from the baby's nose and mouth and cuts the umbilical cord. Then the baby is cleaned and examined. Unless the baby needs emergency medical care, a nurse generally hands him or her to the proud new parents, 11-8.

Some parents prefer holding their baby before he or she receives routine care. New research shows that when the mother holds her newborn against her bare chest or abdomen for an hour after delivery, babies sleep longer and fuss less in the coming weeks. The skin-to-skin contact especially

11-8 As soon as possible after birth, the new parents spend time getting to know their baby.

benefits premature babies. However, many premature babies cannot stay with the mother due to treatment needs.

Afterbirth Stage

The **afterbirth stage** is the third and final stage of labor. The afterbirth stage usually lasts 10 to 20 minutes. During this stage, the mother's body expels the afterbirth. The *afterbirth* is the name for the placenta and other tissues still inside the mother's body from the pregnancy. There is no longer a need for these tissues after the baby is born.

Mild contractions continue after the baby is born. These contractions cause the placenta to separate from the wall of the uterus and exit through the vagina. After the woman's body expels the placenta, the doctor examines it carefully. He or she wants to be sure the placenta has not torn, leaving excess tissue in the uterus. Tissues left in the uterus after birth might cause heavy and uncontrollable bleeding. A nurse may massage the woman's abdomen to help the uterus begin to shrink.

Immediately upon birth, the medical staff uses the **Apgar test** to evaluate a newborn's overall physical condition. It reveals the neonate's chance of survival on a scale of zero to ten. This allows the doctor to quickly evaluate the baby's condition. It can also call attention to the need for any emergency steps. See 11-9 for more information about the Apgar test.

Neonatal Care

After birth, the **neonate** (meaning *newborn*; a name for baby from birth to one month) requires medical attention. The doctor, nurse-midwife, or perhaps even the father will cut the umbilical cord that connects the baby to the mother as soon as it stops pulsating with oxygen and nutrients for the baby. As you recall, the doctor or nurse-midwife suctions the fluid from the nose and

Apgar Test

Vital Signs	Range from Good to Poor Condition
Coloring	From pink to blue in light-skinned babies or strong color to grayish color in dark-skinned babies (Color is best observed on the lips, palms, and soles of feet.)
Pulse rate	From above 100 beats per minute to below 100 beats per minute
Reflex irritability	From coughing or sneezing in response to a stimulus to making little or no response
Muscle tone	From active movements to little or no movement
Respiration	From healthy crying to slow or irregular breathing

Within one minute after birth, a baby is evaluated according to the Apgar test developed by Dr. Virginia Apgar. A score of 2, 1, or 0 is given for each of the five vital signs listed above. These scores together add up to indicate the baby's overall condition. A perfect Apgar score is 10. Scores ranging from 7 to 10 indicate the baby is in *good condition*. Scores of 4, 5, or 6 indicate *fair condition*. Scores of 3 or below indicate *poor condition* (the baby may need immediate resuscitation). The baby is evaluated again five minutes later. If the score is 6 or below, the baby may need special medical attention.

11-9 The Apgar test is used to determine a newborn's chance of survival.

mouth, allowing the baby to begin breathing. A member of the medical team bathes the baby. Particles of *vernix,* a white protective coating, may still be on the baby's skin. Vernix protects the skin before birth. After weighing and measuring, the staff member places an identification band on the neonate's wrist or ankle. He or she may also take the neonate's footprints.

Newborn Screening Tests

In addition to the Apgar test, another test is the Brazelton scale (actually called the *Neonatal Behavioral Assessment Scale*). The **Brazelton scale** does not check for diseases. It checks the baby's movement, reflexes, responses, and general state. This test is very thorough and focuses on the baby's abilities.

Other newborn screening tests require a small sample of blood that is generally taken from the neonate's heel. These screening tests can detect certain inherited disorders in newborns. Early detection can prevent serious problems, such as mental disabilities and even death.

Every state requires some newborn screening tests, but standards vary from state to state. All newborns receive tests for such conditions as anemia and PKU (phenylketonuria—an inherited condition in which an infant cannot properly digest protein; left untreated, PKU *will* cause mental disabilities). Neonates also receive eyedrops to prevent any STI-related eye infections. A physical exam checks for any obvious problems.

In states that do not require *extensive* newborn blood screening, parents can choose to order and pay for a supplemental newborn screening test. Many independent medical laboratories, including those at teaching hospitals, offer screening kits that test for more than 30 disorders including cystic fibrosis and sickle cell anemia. Parents preorder the screening packet from the medical laboratory of their choice. They take the screening packet with them to the hospital. A nurse obtains a small sample of blood from the routine "heel stick" (blood test) all babies receive for the state-required testing. The nurse puts the blood on a special material in the packet. The parents send the packet to the lab in the return envelope accompanying the kit. The results are sent to the parents. They can share these results with their baby's doctor.

Emergency Care

Sometimes a neonate might require emergency medical care. This might happen for one of several reasons including

- *Premature birth.* Premature babies, or babies born before week 35 of pregnancy, are at risk for numerous health problems. For example, 50 percent of twins and most other multiples are born preterm. The length of pregnancy decreases with each additional fetus, such as a 36-week average pregnancy for twins and a 30-week average pregnancy for quadruplets. Babies born too early require emergency care much more often than other babies. Commonly, the lungs of premature babies are not fully developed. This means they cannot breathe normally. Premature babies may need to use respiratory support systems until their lungs mature.

- *Low birthweight.* A low-birthweight baby is a full-term baby who weighs less than 5½ pounds at birth. Twins born at 36 weeks often weigh less than 5½ pounds. These babies are at risk for a great many medical problems. They are less likely to survive than normal-weight infants.

- *Drug addiction.* Often, babies whose mothers used drugs during pregnancy are born with a drug addiction. Their tiny bodies are not strong enough to fight this addiction. They experience withdrawal symptoms and other medical problems. Drug-addicted babies need the help of medical personnel to overcome their addiction and their other medical problems.

- *Low Apgar score.* This may mean the baby was not breathing, had a low heart rate, or both. A lack of reflex irritability and movement could mean the baby was unresponsive. Problems with coloring indicate the baby's body was not getting enough oxygen. One or more of these signals might indicate the baby was in immediate danger.

- *Serious health condition.* For instance, if the baby has a serious heart condition, he or she may need surgery immediately after birth. The medical staff might rush the baby from the delivery room to the operating room. After surgery, the baby might require an extended hospital stay to recover.

Newborns who require emergency care may receive this care in a **Neonatal Intensive Care Unit (NICU)**. These babies often need a variety of machines and monitors to help them survive, 11-10. For example, special incubators protect these babies from germs and air drafts. In the NICU, the medical staff continually watches and treats the neonate. Special tubes may allow feeding through the nose, mouth, or stomach, as needed. In the NICU, these babies receive whatever care they need to restore health.

When a baby needs emergency medical care, it can be very frightening for the parents. They may wonder if their baby will be okay. Normal emotions include fear, anger, sadness, and even guilt. Parents need reassurance the hospital staff is doing everything possible for their infant. The doctors and nurses who provide this care are experienced in working with newborns. They understand the seriousness of these situations and know how to help. Parents should also feel comfortable asking questions about their baby's care. They have a right to know what is wrong with their child and how the medical staff is working to correct the problem.

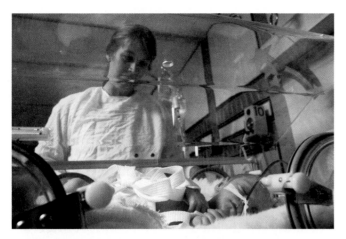

11-10 Parents may worry if their babies need emergency medical care. Visiting the baby in the intensive care unit can help ease their fears.

Many babies in the NICU stay at the hospital after the mother goes home. Generally, hospitals will not release babies until they reach 5½ pounds and are free from life-threatening problems. For example, the average hospital stay is nine to 25 days for twins, 11 to 90 days for triplets, and 120 days or longer for quadruplets. Life-threatening problems can add more months to the stay.

When the baby must stay at the hospital after the mother goes home, this can be difficult for parents. Hospitals generally allow parents to visit the baby whenever they like. Both mother and father can talk lovingly to their baby. If the baby's condition permits, they can touch and massage him or her. This is often possible even if the baby is in an incubator. Many times a mother can express milk from her breasts that the medical staff feeds her infant. This way her baby still gains the benefits breast milk offers. Parents can find ways to be close to their baby until the baby is well enough to come home.

Circumcision

Circumcision is the surgical removal of a male's foreskin. The *foreskin* is a flap of skin that covers the head of the penis. Many parents choose to have their newborn boys circumcised. Some do this for religious reasons. Their beliefs support circumcision of a male infant within a few days after birth. Other parents have their babies circumcised for health reasons. Removing the foreskin makes it easier to keep the genital area clean. In uncircumcised males, a substance called *smegma* can collect under the foreskin. Washing under the foreskin will remove the smegma and prevent irritation and infection. For circumcised males, cancer of the penis is also far less common.

At one time, circumcision was a very routine practice. Almost all newborn males had this procedure. Today, people disagree about the need for this procedure. A male with good hygiene habits can keep himself clean even if he has a foreskin. Some medical experts say there is no medical reason for circumcision. Others disagree. They believe benefits do exist.

Parents may want to ask their pediatrician and religious leader for advice, but the final decision should be theirs, 11-11. If they choose circumcision, the baby will have the procedure before he leaves the hospital. The doctor will tell them how to care for the area as it heals.

The Effects of Birth

Childbirth is an emotional as well as a physical event. Both parents feel strong emotions. These emotions may range from extremely positive (often described as ecstasy) to extremely negative.

Bonding—A Critical Experience

The first moments after birth are full of emotion. It is a time especially suited to **bonding**, the loving feeling parents have for their child. The most important aspect of the birth experience is to promote bonding which is critical to the parent-child relationship. Bonding is the "glue" that promotes later

11-11 When making a decision about circumcision for their newborn son, parents may seek advice from their doctor or religious leader.

long-term attachment between parent and child and child and parent.

Parents who experience early bonding often spend more time with their babies. They touch, cuddle, and soothe the babies more. They talk more and have more eye contact with their babies. This closer relationship between parents and their children seems to continue throughout infancy into childhood, and perhaps far beyond. In general, bonding seems to help parents be more patient and less demanding. It also helps children feel closer and more trusting of their parents.

What Promotes Bonding?

Most hospitals and doctors encourage bonding. The atmosphere in the delivery room or birthing room after the birth of a healthy baby is overflowing with relief and happiness. The parents claim the baby as their own with pride, happiness, and a sense of awe. Unless the baby is sleepy due to use of many childbirth medications, he or she is often alert after childbirth. The baby often looks toward the parent's faces, especially if they speak quietly. After all, their voices are already familiar to the newborn.

After the normal birth of a healthy baby, the mother and baby need to be together. The baby needs the mother's comfort after the difficult passage through the birth canal. The mother needs to relax after the physical strain of labor. She needs a moment to blend the mental picture of the baby she imagined with the reality of her new baby. The natural reaction of a new mother is to hold her new baby gently. She caresses the baby, touching the tiny facial features, noticing the hands and feet, and stroking the chest and abdomen.

As the mother learns about her baby, the baby responds to her touch and voice. These first interactions have a powerful effect on bonding, 11-12. If the father has been present throughout labor and delivery, he will bond with the baby, too. A common reaction of new fathers is to be somewhat protective and possessive. Birth transforms the fetus into a baby, and not just any baby. Suddenly, the baby has become his son or his daughter—a tiny, fragile being that needs his protection.

In birth facilities that encourage bonding, the new family is left alone together as soon as possible. In the next few days, the mother spends several hours each day holding, caressing, and feeding her baby. She assumes responsibility for the care of her baby. Depending upon the facility, the baby may even stay in her room. The nurses are there to care for her needs, answer her questions, and offer help when needed.

Delays in Bonding

Immediate bonding may not be possible in all circumstances. Birth by cesarean delivery is one example. If the mother remains conscious throughout delivery, she will see her new baby right away. She will be able to touch and maybe even hold the baby for a while. With general anesthesia, however, the mother may not be alert for several hours following the delivery. In these cases, the father may be able to hold the baby immediately after delivery.

Another example is premature birth. A premature baby's life may depend on immediate treatment. Once the baby is secure in an incubator, the medical staff encourages the parents to spend time with the baby. Touching and stroking help promote a baby's development. Gradually, parents get to know their baby. Both the baby and the parents benefit from the bonding.

If bonding cannot occur immediately after birth, it can still happen later. As soon as the parents and baby are reunited, bonding can occur. Bonding provides the basis for building a close parent-child relationship.

Handling Negative Feelings

Very few parents experience negative feelings when their babies are born. For those who do, these negative feelings are often mild. When negative feelings do occur, certain circumstances are often the source. These include circumstances, such as

- an unplanned pregnancy and an unwanted child
- many medical problems and treatments throughout the pregnancy and childbirth
- depression following childbirth
- stress resulting from the new responsibility (often expressed by first-time parents)

11-12 These new parents look at their baby with a mixture of love and curiosity. Having this time to bond will help them feel close.

- realistic or unrealistic appraisal of how the new baby will affect the family system, such as changing family life and routines or putting an added strain on family resources (often expressed by parents with other children)

Many negative feelings disappear quickly after childbirth. With the help of supportive family and friends, new parents can deal with negative feelings and move into a positive, loving relationship with their child. For those mothers with depression and for couples who have an unwanted child, negative feelings may linger. These couples should seek professional help because such feelings increase the risk of harming the baby.

Postpartum Period

The **postpartum period** is the time following the baby's delivery. It begins when the baby is born and lasts about six weeks. During this time, a woman recovers from the tiring experiences of pregnancy and childbirth. Her hormones and body return to their prepregnancy state.

Staying at the Birth Facility

Immediately after delivery, a new mother may be extremely tired. Her body has done an incredible amount of work. If she gave birth in a delivery room, the medical staff will soon move her to a recovery room. If she used a birthing room, she will likely recover in the same room. The new mother spends this time resting and getting to know her baby, 11-13.

For at least an hour after delivery, the medical staff will carefully monitor the new mother. They must be sure she is not experiencing complications. They will monitor her vital signs (breathing, heart rate, and blood pressure) to be sure her body is recovering well. Her body rids itself of any medications taken during labor. She will be encouraged to drink plenty of fluids and possibly eat a snack. Even if it is only as far as the restroom, the nurse will encourage the new mother to get up and walk unless medications used during delivery require a certain period of bed rest. Mothers who had cesarean delivery are also encouraged to get up and walk (with assistance) when medically permitted. Moving around helps speed recovery and prevents blood clots.

The nurses will continue to massage the mother's uterus. As the uterus shrinks, a woman may have pains similar to strong menstrual cramps. Heavy bleeding that is similar to a menstrual period will last for a week or more. The area surrounding her episiotomy may be tender and sore.

While staying at the birth facility, the new mother can ask the doctor and nurses any questions she might have. Obstetrics nurses are very familiar with the daily care skills new parents need. Some birth facilities offer classes for new parents. Others teach mainly one-on-one. Some of the daily care skills for newborns that parents learn at the birth facility include how to

- pick up and hold the baby

- diaper and dress the baby

- bathe the baby

- breast-feed if chosen (proper techniques for "teaching" a newborn to suck, how to relieve breast discomfort when the milk comes in two or three days after childbirth, and how to prevent and treat nipple soreness)

- bottle-feed if chosen (and how to handle discomforts felt as the breasts return to a prepregnancy state)

11-13 At the beginning of the postpartum period and before going home, a new mother can spend much time holding and talking to her baby. She should also spend time resting and recovering.

The father and the couple's other children may spend much time at the birth facility with mother and baby. Friends and family members may be eager to see the new baby, too. They may visit and bring gifts. The new mother may need to limit the number of visitors or the length of their stay so she can rest. Rest will help her rejuvenate her body. It will prepare her to handle all she must do when she goes home.

Going Home

Within a few days, the mother will leave the birth facility and go home. For mothers who have cesarean births, the hospital stay may be several days longer. Usually, the medical staff discharge the mother and baby at the same time. It is an especially joyous occasion. The father will likely take mother and baby home. They may take pictures or video clips of their journey home from the birth facility. Older brothers and sisters may come, too.

Once they return home, however, new parents face many challenges. They must fit their new roles and responsibilities into their old life, 11-14. Things will change. During this postpartum period, the mother adapts to the physical changes that continue as her body returns to normal. Both parents learn to manage emotional changes. The new mother must take care of her body.

Adapting to Physical Changes

Even after she returns home, the woman's body will continue to adjust. The uterus will keep shrinking until it returns to its normal size. Nursing the baby helps speed up this process and causes her abdomen to flatten. Her breasts will change, whether they are adjusting to breast-feeding or returning to normal if she bottle-feeds. The mother may continue to have a vaginal discharge, which

11-14 New parents face many challenges once they return home.

will slowly subside. If an episiotomy was necessary, she may have some discomfort as it heals.

The new mother will slowly lose the weight she gained during pregnancy. Immediately after birth, she will lose as much as ten pounds. This is the weight of the baby and the placenta. She will lose another five pounds within the first month. The other weight may be harder to lose. Exercise and healthful eating will help. Most women return to their prepregnancy weight within 6 to 12 months.

Handling Emotional Changes

Many mothers feel somewhat depressed shortly after childbirth. Mood disorders may range from mild (called baby blues) to serious (called **postpartum depression** or **PPD**). In a few cases, the mood disorder can be a mental illness, or postpartum psychosis. Family and friends need to be alert to these problems and seek medical help.

These feelings vary widely from woman to woman. Differing factors may be the cause. Hormonal changes in the woman's body, for example, may be one such factor. Another factor may be the sense of loss a woman feels when the baby leaves her body. She no longer feels the movements of the fetus inside her. No one can predict the emotional change in first-time mothers. When a first-time mother experiences postpartum depression, there is about a 50 percent chance it will occur again in later pregnancies. In the rare but most severe cases, doctors advise women not to become pregnant again.

Besides the maternal mood swings, both mothers and fathers can feel stress from the major change in their lives—a new baby! They may feel an emotional letdown after the excitement of delivery. They may worry about all their new responsibilities. New parents may doubt their ability to care for the baby. They may resent being tied down. The first days at home may be tiring and demanding.

During this time, the new parents need to be honest with one another about their feelings, 11-15. They need each other's understanding and support. Luckily, the feelings of stress usually do not last long. As the couple grows accustom to their new roles as parents, stress fades away.

Taking Care of Herself

Parenting a newborn takes much time and energy. New mothers must care for themselves in order to have energy and strength for parenting and other activities. Good nutrition, proper rest, and regular exercise are most important to the new mother.

Eating Right

During the last month of pregnancy, the mother-to-be should consult her doctor or registered dietitian about proper nutrition to fit her needs. After-delivery needs may include breast-feeding and losing pregnancy

11-15 New parents need to share their feelings honestly with loving understanding and support.

weight gain. Most breast-feeding women stay on their pregnancy diet for the first six weeks after delivery. After that, any extra calories must come from nutrient-rich foods to meet the growing baby's needs. Because the foods a mother eats affect breast milk, a doctor or dietitian may advise her not to eat certain foods that bother the baby. These are generally strong foods such as onions, cabbage, and brussels sprouts. Once breast milk is no longer the baby's source of nutrition, the mother can resume her regular healthy diet.

Getting Enough Rest

When the new mother returns home, she should continue to get plenty of rest. She should avoid lifting anything but the baby. Limiting visitors, except for relatives and close friends who are offering assistance, also allows the mother to rest. Helpful visitors can ease the burden of caring for the new baby.

When newborns are awake (even during the night) they require a parent's full attention. When they are sleeping, parents often try to clean house, wash laundry, or other tasks. If parents do this, however, they will not get enough sleep. The new mother should take advantage of the baby's sleeping schedule. When the baby is asleep, she can rest, too.

Starting to Exercise

Exercise will help a woman regain her prepregnancy weight and shape. A woman should consult her doctor before starting an exercise program. She should begin slowly, especially if she did not exercise much during pregnancy.

Walking is a safe and effective way to burn calories and rebuild strength. In a few weeks, the mother may decide to add other exercises, such as swimming, bicycling, aerobic dance, or jogging. She may do special toning exercises to flatten her abdomen. Strength training with weights can improve her muscle tone, which will help her burn fat more quickly. Exercise can be a good way to release tension and build self-confidence. It can also help a new mother feel more energetic.

Postpartum Checkup

The mother should be sure to attend her postpartum checkup. She generally schedules this medical checkup about six weeks after delivery. At this visit, the doctor will check her blood pressure and weight. A physical exam will reveal if the uterus and cervix are returning to normal. The doctor will check the episiotomy for proper healing. At this checkup, a woman can ask questions about any problems or discomforts she is having. She may also talk to the doctor about continued family planning, nutrition, and exercise.

Summing It Up

- Signs of labor vary somewhat from woman to woman and from pregnancy to pregnancy.

- Most birth facilities have the same basic procedures during childbirth. These procedures follow the natural sequence of labor and delivery.

- A couple may be able to choose the method of childbirth they will use. The choice may be limited by the practices of the doctor or hospital. A different method might be used if the health of the woman or baby is in danger.

- Several types of pain medication are available for use during childbirth. A woman and her doctor should decide what to use.

- Labor consists of three stages. Each stage plays a unique role in the childbirth process.

- All newborns must have routine neonatal care and screening, but some require emergency medical care.

- Circumcision is one decision parents must make for their newborn sons.

- Bonding often occurs during the first moments after birth. If parents and child must be separated right after birth, bonding can occur when they are reunited.

- In the postpartum period, a woman recovers from pregnancy and childbirth. Recovery occurs during her stay at the birth facility and after she goes home.

- The postpartum period is a critical time to adjust to the new baby, too. A new baby brings both joy and stress. New parents have many adjustments to make.

- About six weeks after delivery, the mother should have a postpartum medical checkup.

Recalling the Facts

1. Name three signs that might indicate labor is approaching.
2. Describe what a woman feels during a contraction.
3. How can a woman distinguish between true labor contractions with prelabor contractions?
4. Why might a couple want to fill out some of the birth-facility admittance forms before labor begins?
5. What is electronic fetal monitoring? Why is it used?
6. Name five methods of childbirth.
7. Give three reasons for using a cesarean delivery.
8. List the four types of medication that may be used during childbirth.
9. Name each stage of labor and identify the key event that happens in each stage.
10. Identify four procedures involved in routine neonatal care.
11. How does the Apgar test differ from the Brazelton scale?
12. Give two reasons a neonate might require emergency medical care.
13. What is bonding and why is it important?
14. What is the postpartum period and how long does it last?
15. Why is the postpartum checkup important?

Applying New Skills

1. **New-parent interview.** Interview new parents about their first birth. Ask them how they knew labor had begun, what they took with them to the hospital, what method of delivery they used, and what discomforts the mother had after delivery. Write a brief summary to share with the class.

2. **Birth facilities.** Gather information from local hospitals and birth centers about their policies concerning parent training for childbirth, methods of childbirth, the care of mother and baby during labor and delivery, and the father's involvement. Ask about the average costs related to the birth of a baby. Report your findings to the class.

3. **Birth plan.** Complete the "Birth Plan" you began in Chapter 10. Save your plan for future reference.

4. **New-parent adjustment.** In small groups, propose ten ways new parents can adjust during the postpartum period. What could they do to support the recovery process, adjust to a new baby, and cope with their emotions? How could friends and family help? List the group's suggestions on a sheet of paper to share with the class.

Thinking Critically

1. In small groups, compare and contrast the five methods of childbirth described in the text. Which method does your group think best benefits parents and their children? Why? Share your discussion conclusions with the class.

2. Analyze what you might say to a couple in which the father does not want to be present during labor and delivery.

3. Debate the use of medications during childbirth. If you think they should be used, which should be chosen and when? If you think they should not be used, explain why not. Use your text and Internet or print resources for evidence to back your reasoning.

Linking Academics

1. **Creative writing.** Research background information on postpartum depression (PPD). How common is it? How does it affect a woman's emotional well-being? What treatments help PPD? After locating background information, write a short story about a woman who experiences postpartum depression and tries to work through difficult feelings to regain emotional health. As an alternative, consider writing a story from the neonate's perspective. What might it be like to be a newborn whose mother is experiencing PPD?

2. **Science.** Using Internet or print resources, research supplemental neonatal test kits that parents can purchase from independent medical laboratories. When might parents choose to seek out this testing? What disorders can be detected using this screening process? What does the packet cost? Why would having this information be worth the cost of the packet? Share your findings in an oral report to the class.

3. **Health.** Investigate background information on the practice of circumcision in the United States. Use reliable Internet or print resources for your research. What are the pros and cons of circumcision for male health? Are all health-care professionals in agreement about this practice? Why or why not? Write a short report explaining reasons parents choose to circumcise their male infants.

Part Four

Understanding Children's Growth and Development

269

Your Potential Career

Is a Career in Education for You?

What do you remember most about your favorite teacher? Was it an ability to inspire and motivate you to learn? Did he or she understand your emotional needs? Do you share some of these same traits along with the desire to play a strong role in the development of children? If you do, a career in education and training may be for you.

With an emphasis on improving education for all children, highly qualified teachers are in *high demand*. The job opportunities in education and training continue to be excellent.

What can you do to prepare for an education and training career? First, determine your career plan and strengthen your academic foundation. Next, enroll in such courses as *child development*, *parenting*, or *psychology* to enhance your knowledge of child growth and development. After high school graduation, continue your education based on your career target. In general, teaching in the public schools (preschool through high school) requires a two-year or four-year college. Some jobs in child care and early childhood education require a two-year degree or a Child Development Associate (CDA) credential.

Wages in education and training are generally at a moderate level. In recent years, the average income for public school teachers was $43,500 to $48,600. Wages for child care workers and preschool teachers are much lower.

Up Close— Job Shadowing

Select an education- and training-related career from the chart on the next page that interests you. Then contact a person in your community that works in this career. Make arrangements for a job-shadowing experience. While job shadowing, note the knowledge and skills needed to perform on the job. What does this person like and dislike about this career? What education or training did he or she need?

Learn and Serve

Do you and your friends have strong reading, writing, and communication skills? If you do, consider creating or working with a literacy project in your school or town. Investigate the level of illiteracy in your area. What are the reasons for illiteracy despite the opportunity for education? With the assistance of your teacher, learn strategies that can help people learn to read. Then get involved. Many literacy programs have one-on-one tutoring programs matching high school students with younger children. Keep a journal about your experience. What have you learned from the experience? How have you helped someone learn to read?

FCCLA

If a career in education is for you, consider competing in an FCCLA STAR Event with an educational focus. As the foundation for your STAR Event, investigate using one of the FCCLA national programs, such as *STOP the Violence, Leaders at Work, Families First, Dynamic Leadership,* or *Career Connection.* Be sure to obtain competition forms and guidelines from your family and consumer sciences teacher.

You can read more about planning your career in Chapter 22.

Career Cluster—Education and Training

Cluster Pathways

Administration and Administrative Support	Professional Support Services	Teaching/Training
Sample Careers		
Superintendent	Clinical Psychologist	*Teachers:*
Principal	Developmental Psychologist	Preschool
Instructional Coordinator	Counselor	Kindergarten
Education Researcher	Social Worker	Elementary
Curriculum Developer	Parent Educator	Secondary
Instructional Media Developer	Speech-Language Pathologist	Special Education Teachers and Aides
	Speech-Language Audiologist	Physical Trainer
		Coach
		Child Care Director
		Child Care Worker
		Child Life Specialist
		Early Childhood Teachers Assistant
		Nanny

Chapter 12

New Parents, New Baby

Key Terms

fontanelles
reflexes
voluntary motor movements
self-demand feeding
cradle cap
diaper rash
sensorimotor stage
stressors
colic

Objectives

After studying this chapter, you will be able to

- explain changes that occur during the first days of parenthood.
- describe the appearance and abilities of a newborn.
- demonstrate proper techniques for holding, feeding, bathing, and dressing a newborn.
- describe what newborns learn in the first substage of the sensorimotor stage.
- compare and contrast three basic newborn cries.
- explain how parents can help their baby to become trusting.
- describe a newborn's sleeping habits.
- summarize adjustments families with newborns may need to make.

The baby has been developing for many months in a watery world within the mother's body. Now the newborn will continue his or her development in a new physical and social world. This is a big change as the baby begins living as a separate human being.

The baby's birth links to other changes, too. When parents have their first child, the family system begins a new phase of the family life cycle known as the *childbearing stage*. This stage, which lasts three years, is the building phase of the new family system. The family system has new roles. The woman begins her life as a mother. The man begins his life as a father. Parents of newborns are now in the *nurturing stage of parenting*. According to Galinsky, parents struggle to balance their baby's needs with their own needs during this time.

Existing relationships acquire new dimensions. For example, husband and wife must learn to relate to each other as parents as well as spouses. New relationships form with grandparents, aunts, uncles, and cousins. Household routines and schedules change. Beyond the family circle, other changes may occur, too, such as job schedules and friendships. That tiny bundle wrapped in a soft blanket creates many powerful changes!

In this chapter, you will learn about the development of newborns. As you read, check the "Newborn Developmental" chart at the end of this chapter. You will also learn how parents meet their baby's needs. Finally, you will learn about family stress and adjustments parents make during the first month of baby's life.

The First Days of Parenthood

The first days at home with their baby are exciting, but tiring, for new parents. Mom and Dad have to adjust to night feedings, diaper changes, and other needs of their baby. They are learning to enjoy their new little one. Their home may be overflowing with visits, gifts, and calls from friends and loved ones.

In addition, the mother's body is recovering from labor and delivery. Both she and the new father are catching up on their rest from the past few days of preparation and excitement. At the same time, parents are adjusting to their new baby and learning to care for him or her.

Newborns look fragile. They are totally dependent on parents to meet every need. This dependency can be overwhelming for new parents. New parents may wonder whether their baby is normal. Some things their baby does may seem a little strange, 12-1. Parents often worry about their ability to care for their new baby. Parents can enjoy this time more if they try not to worry too much.

How the Newborn Looks

At birth, the new mother and father see their baby for the first time. Naturally, they notice the obvious features first: boy or girl; lots of hair or none; flat, little nose; tiny fingers and toes. Emotion will sweep over them as they realize, "This is our baby!"

To parents, their newborn looks beautiful. Other people may not agree until a few weeks later. A newborn's physical appearance may not be quite what people expect. Several characteristics of a newborn disappear before long, 12-2.

At birth, a baby's skin is usually blotchy and has wrinkles. The newborn's ears are pressed to the head. Parents can barely see the eyebrows and eyelashes. The cheeks are fat. The nose is flat, and the chin is receding. These last two features are useful because they prevent the nose and chin from getting in the way when the baby sucks during feeding.

A newborn's head seems too large for the rest of its body. The head accounts for one-fourth of a baby's total length. (An adult's

Some Early Parent Concerns

Parents Are Concerned When...	Parents Must Understand...
Sniffles and sneezes occur during the first few days. Baby often snorts during sleep.	The amniotic fluid has not completely cleared. The breathing organs will soon clear. Babies do not have a cold.
The newborn seems to strain during bowel movements.	Newborns must learn to push waste products out of their bodies. Muscles strengthen with use and require less effort.
The fontanel looks fragile and may be seen moving with breathing.	Parents will not damage the fontanel with normal, gentle handling. It does not need to be protected.
Breathing and heart rates seem too fast.	Newborns breathe 46 times a minute and their heart rate is 120 to 150 beats per minute. Both of these rates are much faster than adult rates.

12-1 New parents may wonder whether their baby is normal. Most alert and active babies are healthy. If in doubt, call the baby's doctor or read from a reputable source.

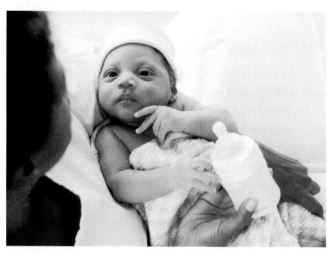

12-2 Newborns have their own distinct appearance. To a parent, the newborn looks beautiful.

head accounts for only one-seventh of his or her total height.) In order to make it easier for the baby's head to pass through the birth canal, the immature bones of the skull are not totally grown together at birth. There are two **fontanelles,** or soft spots on the top of the baby's head—a larger one toward the front and a smaller one toward the back. The scalp covers these openings and feels tight much like the skin of a drum. As a result of passing through the birth canal, the head of a newborn is often misshapen. Soon, however, it will regain its shape. Because the skin over the fontanelles is tough, parents should not be afraid of injuring the baby by gently touching them (although a severe bump to the head could cause injury). During infancy the skull bones will grow together. Then the fontanelles disappear.

A newborn's neck is short, with weak muscles, making the head unsteady. The newborn's shoulders slope, the chest is narrow, and the abdomen protrudes. The legs are usually bow-shaped because of the baby's position in the uterus.

The average newborn is 20 to 21 inches in length and weighs 7 to 7½ pounds. Boys are often longer and heavier than girls. Babies usually lose weight the first few days after birth. They quickly regain this loss, however, and then continue to grow.

What the Newborn Can Do

The newborn has remarkable abilities, including the use of all five senses: seeing, hearing, smelling, tasting, and feeling.

This new human being can breathe, suck, swallow, and get rid of wastes. He or she can also respond to various stimuli with reflex actions.

What the Newborn Can See

At birth, a newborn's eyes are almost always light in color. This is because the baby's eyes had no exposure to light before birth. If the baby inherits a darker eye color, this color will begin to show in the weeks to come.

The newborn's eyes function from birth, but both eyes don't always work together right away. This is because the muscles that keep both eyes pointing in the same direction are weak at first. As a result, the baby's eyes may cross. In a few weeks, this should correct itself as the baby's muscles develop. Parents should not worry if their newborn's eyes are crossed. If this problem persists for several months, however, parents may wish to consult an eye doctor.

Newborns' eyes are very sensitive to light. Their pupils adjust to both bright and dim lights. In fact, newborns squeeze their eyes closed when exposed to intense light.

In normal light, the newborn sees patterns of light and dark and can distinguish some shapes. The eyes focus best at a distance of 8 to 12 inches. When a parent places a brightly colored object within this range, the newborn becomes alert and tries to focus on it, 12-3. If the object does not move, the newborn will focus on it for only a short time. If the object moves back and forth, the baby will watch the movement. A little later, the baby will be able to follow an up-and-down movement if it is slow.

Newborns prefer patterns to plain colors. They prefer stripes and angles to curves and circles. They prefer moving objects to stationary ones. By the age of 3 weeks, the human face is what babies most like to see.

12-3 This newborn tries to focus on brightly colored, moving objects within his short range of vision.

What the Newborn Can Hear

Hearing develops even before birth. A fetus responds to loud noises while still inside the woman's uterus. At birth, the baby can distinguish between sounds, but does not yet know what these sounds mean.

Newborns will turn toward the source of a sound. If both a man and a woman speak at once, babies will turn toward the female voice. This is because a baby can hear its mother's voice during prenatal development.

Babies respond readily to the cries of other babies. When one newborn in a nursery cries, others are likely to start crying, too. Babies also respond well to higher-pitched sounds. This may be why parents tend to talk to their newborns in high-pitched voices rather than in low-pitched ones.

What the Newborn Can Smell and Taste

The senses of smell and taste are well developed at birth. Newborns can distinguish between two scents when both are presented at the same time. A baby soon learns to recognize its mother by her scent. By two to three days after birth, babies will cry and turn their heads away from strong, unpleasant odors.

Babies can tell the difference between flavors within two or three days of birth. They will reject a bitter flavor. Babies prefer sweet flavors. They will start sucking in response to a sweet flavor, such as breast milk or formula.

What the Newborn Can Feel

Newborns can sense changes in temperature at birth. Most babies dislike feeling cold. This is why many babies cry when parents dress or undress them. Newborns can also use their sense of touch to distinguish textures. In the first days after birth, they can feel pain.

From birth, newborns are extremely sensitive to touch. They respond quickly to a light touch on the skin. Newborns stop crying when parents rub them gently and hold them closely. Holding and cuddling enhance a baby's overall development, 12-4. This physical contact also tends to strengthen the emotional bond between parents and baby.

The Newborn's Reflexes

Nature provides babies with **reflexes**, or automatic reactions to certain stimuli. Some reflexes, such as rooting and sucking, relate

12-4 Both babies and parents enjoy time spent cuddling. Holding a baby stimulates all areas of the baby's growth and development.

to the baby's survival instinct. Other reflexes are clues to the health of the nervous system. (For this reason, the baby's doctor will check the newborn's reflexes during each well-baby checkup.) Some reflexes, such as grasping and stepping, lead to **voluntary motor movements**—those motions learned and done at will later in infancy.

Rooting Reflex

When a baby's cheek or mouth is touched, the baby turns toward the touch and begins rooting to find food. The mouth opens and the baby starts the sucking motion. The rooting reflex helps a newborn find the nipple of the bottle or breast. This reflex disappears after a few months when the baby learns to use his or her eyes to look for food.

Awareness of this rooting reflex can help a parent at feeding time. The parent should touch the cheek closest to the breast or bottle, causing the baby to turn toward the nipple. If a parent didn't know about this reflex, he or she might push the baby's head toward the nipple. That would mean touching the other side of the baby's head, causing the baby to turn away.

Grasping Reflex

Placing a finger or a long, thin object (such as the handle of a rattle) in the palm of a newborn's hand triggers the grasping reflex. The newborn will grasp the object and tighten the grasp if a parent pulls the object away. A newborn's grasp is very strong. The grasping reflex applies to toes, too. Placing a finger or object under a newborn's foot also causes the toes to curl in a grasping motion. The grasping reflex disappears in a few months when the baby learns to voluntarily reach for and hold objects.

Babinski Reflex

The Babinski reflex also involves the feet, but it has the opposite effect of the grasping reflex. When someone strokes the outside of the sole of a newborn's foot, the newborn's toes will extend upward and outward, 12-5.

Moro or Startle Reflex

When something startles the baby, the parents will likely observe the Moro or startle reflex. This reflex happens when the baby's position changes quickly or a loud noise occurs. The baby throws the arms apart, spreads the fingers, extends the legs, arches the back, and throws the head back. Then the baby brings the arms and legs back toward the body. To calm a startled baby, a parent can hold the baby or apply a light but steady pressure against the baby's body.

Stepping Reflex

When someone holds a baby in an upright position and the sole of a foot touches a surface, the baby raises a foot. When tilting the baby slightly from side to side (so alternate feet raise), the baby appears to be walking. Parents should realize this is the stepping reflex, not a signal their baby is learning to walk at an amazingly early age. Babies don't learn to walk until many months later. Then their stepping motion is voluntary, not a reflex action.

Caring for the Newborn

Parents may feel awkward as they begin caring for their new baby. Even with training, new parents are seldom fully prepared for the first days at home with their baby. By being patient, however, they can learn how to meet their baby's needs. If parents view changes in routines as positive, parenthood won't be just hectic and frustrating. It will also be fulfilling and rewarding.

Help from an experienced parent makes adjusting to life with a baby easier. Sometimes one of the new grandparents comes to stay with the family for a short time after the baby arrives. Even if a grandparent or other relative cannot stay, their trusted advice may be only a phone call away.

The new parents' friends and neighbors may also offer some help. In many

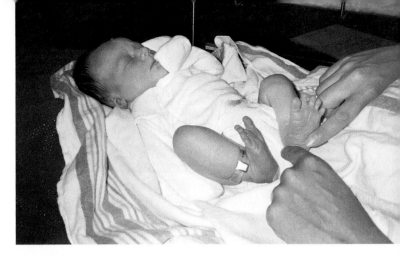

12-5 This baby's feet demonstrate the Babinski reflex. When the sole of the foot is stroked, the toes fan out.

communities, service agencies offer support groups and parenting classes for new parents. With friendly support and assurance, the couple will more quickly adapt to their new roles as parents.

Holding the Newborn

Newborns feel safe, secure, and loved when parents hold them close. Newborns also like it when people talk to them. In addition, this encourages the baby's intellectual and emotional development.

When holding newborns, parents should firmly support their newborn's back and head. The baby's neck muscles are weak at birth, so a newborn cannot hold the head steady. The neck, spinal cord, and brain are extremely sensitive to uncontrolled movements. If parents do not give adequate support to their baby's head, neck, and back, the baby will likely sustain injuries.

The Newborn's Sleeping Habits

Newborns spend most of their time sleeping—as much as 16 to 20 hours a day. Sleeping patterns vary from one newborn to another. How much sleep the baby needs and how often he or she is hungry influences the baby's sleep pattern. Some babies need more sleep than others. For example, premature babies sleep more than full-term infants.

Many newborns sleep about five hours during the night, but will not sleep through a seven- or eight-hour night until about 9 months of age. Because the newborn's sleeping pattern dictates the parental sleeping patterns, parents are usually exhausted and stressed.

As they sleep, newborns move their mouths to smile and make faces. They may make sucking motions in their sleep. They breathe irregularly and move their eyes beneath their closed eyelids. Newborns should be warm and dry as they sleep. They should be away from drafts, strong light, and loud noises. However, parents do not have to protect babies from common noises. Parents do not need to tiptoe and whisper while their babies are asleep. Babies are adaptable and will learn to sleep through ordinary noises, 12-6.

Lessening the Chance of SIDS

It can be heartbreaking to think about the death of an infant, but the fact is that some newborns or older infants die in their sleep of sudden infant death syndrome (SIDS). SIDS is a major cause of death among infants 2 weeks to 12 months old. Although its causes

12-6 Newborns need much rest. Their bodies are busy growing and developing, which takes a great deal of energy.

are unknown, there are risk factors associated with SIDS. These include low birthweight, premature birth, exposure to cigarette smoke before and after birth, little or no prenatal care, and having a sibling who died from SIDS.

Parents should talk with their doctors about trying to prevent SIDS in high-risk babies. They should also discuss ongoing research on this topic. SIDS is devastating to parents.

There are some simple things that parents can do that might prevent a SIDS death. According to the *National Institutes of Health*, practices for preventing SIDS include

- Place the infant on a firm mattress in his or her own crib in the parent's room. Avoid sleeping with the infant in an adult bed. If you breast-feed a baby at night in an adult bed, be sure to put the baby back in his or her own crib when finished.

- Place the baby on his or her back to sleep. Stomach and side sleeping can lead to suffocation. Save "tummy time" for baby's waking hours.

- Keep soft bed materials away from the baby's face. This includes comforters, pillows, and stuffed toys. Use a warm sleeper outfit instead of covers.

- Keep the infant warm, but not overheated. A room temperature comfortable for adults is appropriate. Becoming overheated or breathing too much stale air (air with low oxygen levels) has been linked to some SIDS deaths.

- Use a clean pacifier when placing an infant down to sleep.

- Keep the baby in a smoke-free environment.

- Breast-feed if possible. Breast-fed babies are less likely to die from SIDS.

Feeding the Newborn

Next to sleeping, the newborn's most time-consuming activity is eating. Feeding times provide both nourishment and nurturance. Feeding the baby is a perfect opportunity to enhance parent-child relationships. This is true whether parents feed the baby breast milk or formula.

Most doctors recommend parents use **self-demand feeding**. This means the parents feed the baby when he or she is hungry, 12-7. (Parents can tell the baby is hungry because the baby will cry.) Self-demand feeding differs from scheduled feedings, in which parents feed their baby on a set schedule, no matter when the baby is hungry. In the past, doctors more commonly recommended scheduled feedings.

If parents try to adhere to a rigid schedule, they may have trouble satisfying the baby's appetite and sleep needs. If they choose self-demand feedings, the baby decides when to eat and when to sleep based on natural needs. The baby soon sets his or her schedule, but this may not always be a convenient schedule for the parents.

Eventually, most babies develop fairly regular hunger patterns. Newborns need 8 to 12 feedings during a 24-hour period. When babies begin sleeping through the night, parents can eliminate night feedings. The babies will take larger quantities at the remaining feedings. Parents should not feed their babies solid foods for a few more months because their stomachs cannot yet digest them and they can choke when trying to swallow solids. Breast milk or formula is sufficient to meet a newborn's nutritional needs.

Breast-Feeding

If a mother breast-feeds her baby, she will have learned how to do so while at the birth facility. After she goes home, the mother can ask her doctor or pediatrician any questions she might have about nursing. A

12-7 Stronger parent-child relationships result from nurturing feeding times.

breast-feeding mother should remember the following:

- Every substance that enters her body will affect the breast milk she produces. Nursing mothers should check with their doctors before taking *any* medications. They should also avoid using illegal drugs, tobacco, or alcohol. These substances can enter breast milk and harm the baby.

- Nursing mothers generally need about 300 more calories a day than they did before pregnancy. This extra energy is required for producing breast milk. Adequate water intake is important, too. Women should talk to their doctors or dietitians about their increased nutrient and calorie needs. They can also use the interactive Web site MyPyramid.gov for breast-feeding moms to help choose healthful foods and track their food intake.

- Newborns generally nurse 8 to 12 times daily. The baby may nurse for 20 to 30 minutes at each feeding. The mother should have the baby begin with the right breast at one feeding and the left breast at the next feeding.

- The mother should position herself and the baby correctly during nursing for best results. A woman can ask her doctor, another nursing mother, or a representative from La Leche League about helpful hints for breast-feeding. La Leche League is an organization that supports breast-feeding mothers.

Formula-Feeding

If parents formula-feed their baby, they should use the formula their pediatrician recommends. If any problems occur using this formula, they should ask the doctor about switching to another one. Keeping the following suggestions in mind will help parents who formula-feed their infants

- Read the formula label carefully to properly mix the formula. This will ensure the baby's nutritional needs are met.

- Warm the baby's bottle if desired, but this is not necessary. When warming a bottle, parents should place it in a glass or pan of warm water. *Do not* warm bottles in microwave ovens. Microwaves heat unevenly, which can cause hot spots. This means some of the formula might be too hot, even if the bottle feels only slightly warm on the outside. Hot formula can burn the baby's mouth and tongue.

- Hold the baby in a semi-upright position. Hold the bottle so the nipple of the bottle is always filled, 12-8. This prevents the baby from swallowing too much air.

12-8 Like nursing, bottle-feeding can provide physical and emotional closeness between parent and child.

- Never prop the bottle or leave the baby alone to drink the formula. Babies need the nurturance and emotional closeness their parents provide by holding them during a feeding. Small babies can also choke if left alone with their bottles propped.

- Remove the bottle from the baby's mouth if he or she falls asleep during a feeding. Formula will drip from the bottle even if the baby is not sucking and possibly cause choking. This liquid pools in the mouth and can cause cavities and ear infections, too.

- Discard any formula left in the bottle. Bacteria could grow in leftover formula and make the baby sick.

Burping the Baby

Whether breast-feeding or formula-feeding, parents should burp the baby once during each feeding and again after each feeding. Parents burp the baby to bring up any air the baby swallows while eating. Sometimes the baby does not burp, and this is okay. He or she may not need to burp every time.

To burp a baby, the parent should hold the baby upright, either sitting on the parent's lap or lying up against his or her shoulder. (A parent may prefer to lay the baby, stomach down, across his or her lap.) The parent should place a towel or soft cloth under the baby's head while burping because air bubbles can push out some milk or formula. Then they should gently pat the baby on the back to release any air bubbles.

Bathing the Newborn

Birthing facility personnel usually show new parents how to bathe the baby safely before they go home. It takes practice, however, to feel comfortable bathing a newborn. Parents can bathe their baby at any time of day, whenever it is convenient. Bath time is a social time for the baby and parents. If the parents are relaxed and talk quietly in a soothing tone, the baby will learn to enjoy bath time.

The bathing area should be warm and free of drafts. Parents should gather all the bath items, clean diapers, and clean clothes beforehand. The most important rule to remember is: *never leave a baby alone on a table or in a tub, not even for a few seconds.* An unattended baby can roll off a table or drown in a few inches of water. Parents need to know how to handle these bathing techniques

- *Sponge baths.* Until the stub of the umbilical cord drops off and the navel heals, parents usually give their babies sponge baths. To prepare a baby for a bath, undress the baby except for the diaper. Wrap the baby in a blanket while washing the face and head. See 12-9 for further directions on sponge bathing.

- *Tub baths.* After a few weeks, a baby is ready to enjoy tub baths. The temperature of the water should feel warm to the skin.

A parent can test the temperature by dipping an elbow into the water. It should feel comfortably warm, not hot or cold. See 12-10 for directions on tub bathing.

- *Shampoos.* Newborns need shampoos two or three times a week. Parents should check with their pediatrician about a good, safe shampoo for their newborn. After gently soaping the scalp, rinse thoroughly. Be sure shampoo and water do not splash onto the baby's face, especially the eyes.

Some babies develop **cradle cap**, a condition in which a scaly crust appears on the scalp. Sometimes cradle cap develops on the fontanel, or soft spot. If cradle cap develops, gently rub mineral or baby oil into the crust. The oil will soften the crust so that the parent can easily remove it with a soft hairbrush. Parents should not be afraid of injuring the baby by gently brushing the hair over the fontanelles. Remember, the scalp over these areas is very tough. After brushing away the flaky crust, gently shampoo the infant's hair to remove the oil. A build-up of oil can actually make the condition worse. Parents should consult their pediatrician if the cradle cap becomes infected or more irritated. The best way to prevent cradle cap is through regular shampoos and air circulation to the scalp. Heat and head coverings worsen the condition.

Dressing the Newborn

Dressing a baby is another skill parents learn mostly by practice. While they are being dressed, babies enjoy hearing their parents talk and sing. Parents can turn this routine task into a fun time for themselves and their babies by following these important tips

- Be gentle.
- Guide the baby's clothes on as quickly as possible.

Sponge Bath for Baby

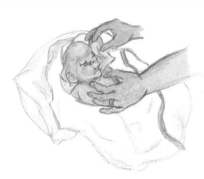

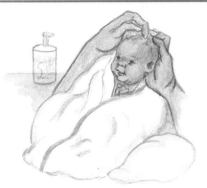

1—*Get ready.* You will need a basin of clean, warm water; mild soap or all-purpose, liquid baby wash; mild baby shampoo if not using baby wash; a soft washcloth; and a soft, large towel (a hooded towel if preferred). You will also need a clean receiving blanket, clean clothes, and a fresh diaper nearby. Except for the diaper, remove the baby's clothes and wrap the baby in the large towel for warmth. Place the baby on a padded flat surface for bathing, such as a counter, kitchen table, or a changing table. Make sure the room is a comfortable temperature to keep the baby warm.

2—*Wash eyes and face.* If there is a crusty residue around the baby's eyes (dried mucous), use a separate, water-moistened cotton pad to wipe each eye from the inside corner of the eye to the outside. Next, use a soft washcloth moistened with plain, warm water (no soap) to wash the baby's face. Begin at the center of the face and work outward. Be sure to wash around the nose, mouth, behind the ears, and creases in the neck. Pat the face and neck dry with a soft towel.

3—*Wash hair.* First place your arm under the baby's back and support the neck and head with your hand. (If you hold the baby's head back slightly, shampoo and water will run off at the back, not down the baby's face.) Next, wet the baby's hair with the moistened washcloth. In your free hand, place a small amount of baby shampoo or all-purpose body wash and gently massage it into the baby's hair. Use the washcloth and clear water to gently rinse the shampoo out of the hair away from baby's face and eyes. Finally, wrap the baby's head in the upper part of the towel and gently pat dry. Keep head wrapped in towel.

4—*Wash upper body.* Unwrap the baby's upper body. Using mild body wash and a washcloth, wash one area at a time and pat dry before moving to the next. Be sure to wash under the arms, arms and hands, chest, and back. When washing the baby's back, reverse your hold. Support the baby's chest and head with one arm. Rinse away body wash with the washcloth and clear water. (Note: Some body washes do not require rinsing.) Rewrap the baby's upper body in the towel to keep warm.

5—*Wash legs and diaper area.* Remove the baby's diaper. With the sudsy washcloth, wash the baby's waist, legs, and feet and toes. Wash around the umbilical area, but do not get it wet until it has healed. Rinse and pat dry. Wash the diaper area last. Be sure to carefully wash all creases and skin folds. Wash the diaper area from front to back for both girls and boys. Do not pull back on the foreskin of uncircumcised boys unless advised by your doctor. Rinse. Gently pat dry all areas, especially creases and skin folds. Moisture can irritate the skin once baby is diapered and dressed. Once dry, wrap the baby in a receiving blanket to keep warm before dressing. Use a gentle baby lotion if baby's skin seems dry. Simply massage the lotion into the skin on baby's back, abdomen, arms, and legs. If using powder, sprinkle a little on your hand away from baby's face. Then pat lightly over large areas of body.

12-9 Sponge baths are usually given until a baby is about two weeks old.

Tub Bath for Baby

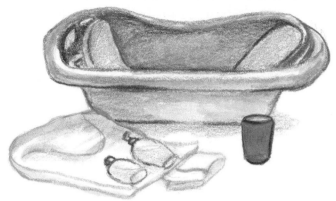

1—*Get ready.* For tub bathing, you can use a special plastic, baby-bath tub or the kitchen sink (with the faucet turned away). Be sure to line either the tub or sink with a thick, fluffy towel or a special foam bath insert. This helps keep the baby from slipping in the tub and provides a softer surface. You will need a plastic cup to pour water over the baby for rinsing and warmth. Use bath products as indicated for sponge bath. Add about two inches of warm, but not hot, water. Test the water temperature with your wrist or elbow before placing the baby in the tub. If using hot and cold tap water to fill the tub, swirl your hand in the water to ensure an even water temperature. Make sure the room temperature is comfortable to keep the baby warm. Quickly remove the baby's clothes and diaper.

2—*Place the baby in tub.* With one arm supporting the baby's head and back and the other supporting the buttocks, gently lower the baby into the tub feet first. Support the baby's head and back with one arm during the entire bath, keeping the head out of the water. Use the cup to pour water over the baby periodically during the bath to keep the baby warm.

3—*Wash face and head.* Use a soft washcloth with plain water to clean the baby's face and head as directed for sponge bath. If shampooing the baby's hair, proceed with shampooing as directed for sponge bath. To rinse shampoo during tub bathing, cup your free hand and gently pour water over the baby's head being sure to keep water and shampoo away from eyes, ears, and face.

4—*Wash the body.* Starting from the neck down, wash the baby's body. Wash the diaper area last. Be sure to wash baby's back, chest and abdomen, arm and hands, legs and feet, and all skin creases and folds. When washing the baby's back, reverse your hold. Support the baby's chest and head with one arm. To clean the diaper area, be sure to wash from front to back for both girls and boys. When cleansing a baby boy who has not been circumcised, do not pull back the foreskin on the penis unless your doctor advises you to do so. Use the cup to gently pour water over the baby's body for rinsing and to keep the baby warm.

5—*Dry the baby.* Place your hands under the baby's arms, supporting the head and neck. Quickly lift the baby out of the water and wrap him or her in a soft towel. Take time to cuddle as you dry off the baby. Once the baby is completely dry, diaper and dress the baby quickly to keep him or her warm. If desired, use baby lotion or powder as directed for sponge bathing. Once the baby is completely dry, diaper and dress the baby quickly to keep him or her warm.

12-10 During a tub bath, place a towel or special foam insert inside the tub to keep the baby from slipping.

- Minimize the need to move the baby's body position, arms, and legs. Imagine how you might feel if someone were jerking your body around, adjusting your arms and legs. This may explain why dressing and undressing is an unpleasant time for some babies.

- Keep the baby warm during dressing and undressing.

- Talk to the baby calmly and don't hurry. If you rush or seem anxious, it may upset the baby.

Dressing babies in layers of clothes makes sense. Babies are more sensitive to temperature changes than are adults. They can quickly become too hot or too cold. Parents can check whether their baby is comfortable by feeling the baby's hands and feet. If the hands and feet feel cold or hot, parents can add a sweater or remove a blanket accordingly.

A newborn's most important need is diapers. Parents may choose to use either disposable diapers or cloth diapers. As you know, each has advantages and disadvantages. In the beginning, newborns use as many as 12 to 15 diapers daily.

No matter which type of diapers parents use, they must be careful to prevent diaper rash. **Diaper rash** is a skin irritation caused by bacteria that build up on the warm, moist skin in a baby's diaper area. Diaper rash can make the skin rough, irritated, and even raw. Diaper rash is easier to prevent than it is to cure. The best defense against diaper rash is to regularly change the baby's diapers.

In mild cases, parents can treat the problem themselves. Parents should clean the diaper area carefully with warm water and a soft cloth. Baby wipes can further irritate the baby's tender skin. Before diapering, parents should make sure the baby's skin is thoroughly dry. They should change the baby's diaper more frequently, avoid using waterproof pants until the rash clears, and

allow air to circulate in the diaper area. Parents should be sure that diapers are not too tight around the legs and abdomen. Whenever possible, parents should expose the baby's bare bottom to air to help reduce moisture in the diaper area. (A few minutes of play on a waterproof pad gives the baby's diaper area the air needed for healing and helps prevent messes.) If needed, parents can apply a diaper-rash ointment to the affected areas. When diaper rash persists, parents should ask their pediatrician for advice.

How Newborns Learn

Newborns do not know about their new world. However, when they are awake and alert they are interested and curious about the world around them, 12-11. They come into the world ready to learn at an astounding rate that parallels their physical development. The rate of learning depends on brain growth and the experiences newborns have.

Experiences come from the sights, sounds, textures, odors, and tastes that surround newborns. Experiences also come from their own body movements. In addition, experiences come through the sounds they make—especially crying—and the responses of others to those cries.

The Sensorimotor Stage Begins

In Chapter 6 you read that Swiss psychologist, Jean Piaget, studied children's thinking. He began his studies by observing his own children and then observing and interviewing other children. From his studies, he believed that a child developmentally changes in four stages from birth through the teen years. He noted that children not only know more as they age, but also come to think in different ways. He saw four major stages—changes in thinking, 12-12. (See

12-11 Newborns have short periods in which they are quiet and alert. This is the time they learn the most.

Appendix B, "Piaget's Stages of Intellectual Development" for more information on the *sensorimotor* stage.) Newborn "thinking" is described as "exercising the reflexes."

From birth to age 2, children learn through their *perceptions* or their understandings of and reactions to what they see, hear, touch, taste, and smell. Infants also learn by doing things with their bodies (sucking, grasping) and by doing things to objects (dropping, hitting, shaking, rolling, pulling). Piaget called this first stage of development the **sensorimotor stage**, or learning through the senses and motor (movement) skills. This stage has six substages. In each substage, babies use their senses and motor skills in different ways.

Piaget's Stages of Intellectual Development

1. Sensorimotor
1A: *Exercising the Reflexes*
1B: *Primary Circular Reactions*
1C: *Secondary Circular Reactions*
1D: *Coordination of Secondary Circular Reactions*
1E: *Tertiary Circular Reactions*
1F: *Mental Representation*

2. Preoperational
2A: *Preconceptual Phase*
2B: *Intuitive Phase*

3. Concrete Operations

4. Formal Operations

12-12 According to Piaget, intellectual development begins with exercising the reflexes during the sensorimotor stage.

The first substage, "Exercising Reflexes," occurs during the first month after birth—the newborn stage. Newborns spend much of their waking time exercising their sucking, looking, grasping, hearing, and sound-making reflexes. These reflexes, unlike many other reflexes, do not disappear with time. Instead, they become voluntary motor actions.

By exercising their reflexes, newborns refine their skills. For example, with practice newborns learn to change the shape of their mouths to latch on to different objects. They also learn to suck with more vigor on some objects (the breast) than others (pacifier).

With practice, newborns learn to use their reflexes to control their world. For example, at birth a newborn will suck anything put in his or her mouth. At a later time, the same newborn will thrust a pacifier out of his or her mouth when hungry. The newborn will fret until receiving breast milk or formula through his or her sucking efforts.

Newborns enjoy sensory and motor activities during the newborn stage and in the months that follow. Activities, shown in 12-13, can become just a part of their normal

Sensory Learning for Newborns

Sensory Area	What Parents Can Do
Seeing	• Put bright objects of moderate complexity (patterns, not solids) within the newborn's 8- to 12-inch vision range. • Bring your face close to his or her face while talking. • Walk slowly around the house or yard and pause near interesting objects while carrying the alert baby. (If outside, stay in the shade and protect the baby's eyes with a head covering.) • Place a lighted fish tank in a dimly lit room for baby to enjoy.
Hearing	• Play soft music. • Hang wind chimes where the baby can hear them. • Sing lullabies and other songs. Babies love songs with a steady rhythm. • Talk to your baby as much as possible. • Play music boxes. • Move the baby close to a ticking clock.
Smelling	• Cuddle the baby close to you. • Walk near objects with good odors while carrying the baby. (Do not bring a baby into contact with the fragrances used in soaps, candles, and cosmetics because of possible allergic reactions.)
Feeling	• Rock and cuddle the baby. • Lightly rub cloths of different textures on the baby's skin—especially feet and hands. • Gently stroke the baby's abdomen or back.

12-13 Because newborns learn through sensory input, parents can make these activities part of their regular day. Parents should do only a few activities each day when their baby is alert. The activities should be repeated often.

daily routine. Newborns are not ready for any "lessons." Use of these simple ideas enriches the newborn's world.

Crying: The First Language

Crying is the only way newborns can communicate. They cry between 1 and 11 minutes per hour with an average daily total of 2 hours. No wonder parents think crying is all newborns do.

Why do newborns cry? They cry whenever they need something. Some experts think crying is a way for newborns to relieve tension, too.

Parents should not hesitate to respond to their baby's cries promptly and consistently. This doesn't mean parents must jump up and answer the first whimper right away if they are busy. However, parents should understand the importance of responding to their babies as soon as possible. Answering cries promptly and consistently does not spoil babies. Instead, it is a good way for parents to express their love and concern. This, in turn, helps babies learn to trust their parents to fulfill their needs.

In time, babies send clearer crying messages. Babies vary their cries according to their needs. Parents soon learn to interpret the various types of cries their baby uses

- *Hunger.* A hunger cry starts slowly and builds to a loud demand. It usually begins shortly before the baby's feeding time—which may be regular.

- *Attention.* A cry for attention is a fussy, whimpering cry. If parents ignore this cry, the baby becomes louder and more insistent. It sounds less natural than the hunger cry. The cry for attention may stop as soon as a parent appears, but often continues until the baby's needs are met.

- *Pain.* A cry of pain is an urgent cry that begins as a sudden, shrill scream. A brief silence and several short gasps generally follow. The baby repeats the scream-silence-gasps cycle until the pain is relieved and he or she is calmed. This cry can frighten parents, who need to assess the situation to determine the cause of the cry. Sometimes the baby is more surprised than hurt. In this case, parents can calm the baby by cuddling, rocking, and using soft, reassuring words or music. At other times, the baby may have a minor injury—such as a scratch—the parent can easily handle. In some cases, a baby may need medical attention. If the parents aren't sure whether the baby needs medical care, they should call their doctor for advice.

For the first two weeks after birth, newborns do not cry much. However, starting at two weeks the intensity and extent of newborn crying is often very stressful to parents, 12-14.

How Newborns Get to Know Their Parents

Although newborns spend most of their time eating and sleeping, they begin their emotional and social development right after birth. Emotionally, newborns come into

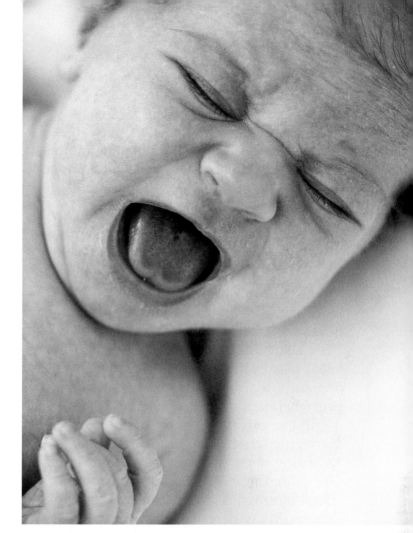

12-14 Hearing their baby cry can make parents uncomfortable. Soon, however, the baby will be sleeping peacefully again.

the world with their own temperaments. Parents can more easily see their baby's temperaments later in infancy. However, newborns do differ in their crying patterns and in their ability to soothe themselves or be soothed by parents.

Socially, newborns are more "takers than givers." Parents need to cuddle, rock, and talk to their newborns. However, it will be a few more weeks before newborns reach out to their parents. Yet, newborns are getting to know their parents and feel secure and loved in their new world.

As you recall, Erik Erikson, a psychologist, divided a person's life span into eight stages. The first stage—*trust versus mistrust*—begins at birth and lasts until age two. (See Appendix A, "Erikson's Theory of Personality Development," for detailed information on Stage 1.) In this stage, babies need to develop trust in their parents and in their world, 12-15. As you read the characteristics of this stage, note that infants need loving parents who consistently provide care.

New Baby, New Adjustments

Just as crying comes with a baby, so stress comes with the parenting role. Parents have new around-the-clock baby-care tasks. They also have routine family and household tasks. One or both parents may have career demands, too. No wonder new parents feel overwhelmed!

In the *nurturing stage* of parenting, managing stress is an important task according to parenting expert, Ellen Galinsky. Life changes can bring about tensions or stress. Hormones change to respond to this tension. Many people experience physical symptoms related to stress. Some people sleep too much, and others can't sleep enough; some become irritable, and others withdrawn. These reactions often create more stress. Over a period of time, stress can damage physical and emotional health.

Parenting Adjustments

Having a new baby is one of the happiest and most exciting times, yet one of the most stressful. Once home from the birth facility, maternal and baby care is no longer available by touching a call button. At this point, parents have truly entered the world of parenting.

Many **stressors**—anything that causes stress—seem to come with new babies. Although each baby and each parent differ, some stressors are common. Parents can often manage stress if they know what to do.

Learning Baby-Care Skills

Learning baby care takes practice. It is most helpful to study baby care before the baby arrives because these skills must be learned quickly. For example, new parents

Erikson's Theory of Personality Development

Stage	Approximate Age	Step Toward Stable Personality	Step Toward Unstable Personality
1	Birth to age 2	Trust	Mistrust
2	Ages 2 & 3	Autonomy	Shame and doubt
3	Ages 4 & 5	Initiative	Guilt
4	Ages 6 to 11	Industry	Inferiority
5	Ages 12 to 18	Identity	Role confusion
6	Early adulthood	Intimacy	Isolation
7	Middle age	Generativity	Stagnation
8	Late adulthood	Integrity	Despair

12-15 When a newborn is given loving and consistent care, he or she will learn to trust others and develop healthy self-esteem.

change over 100 diapers in the first week of a baby's life.

It's important for parents to find humor in those little mistakes all parents make. What parent hasn't had their baby's diaper fall off? What parent hasn't mismatched the snaps on a baby's outfit?

Handling Around-the-Clock Baby Needs

Newborns wake up every two to four hours with the need for diaper changes and feedings. Most newborns feed eight to 12 times per day. To ensure newborns get enough food, doctors will want parents to wake them every four hours if they do not awaken on their own. Parents should call the doctor if they must frequently wake their baby for feedings. They also should call if they must continually encourage the baby to suck. However, if the baby is gaining weight normally, the doctor may advise parents to let the baby dictate feeding times, or begin feeding on demand. How can parents function on such a varied schedule? These tips may help

- *Resist trying to put a newborn on a schedule.* A newborn's biological clock is not yet set and will not be set for several months. Trying to force a schedule usually causes more crying. Avoid the myth that feeding solid foods in addition to milk will help babies sleep through the night. Not only is this idea untrue, it is also dangerous. Solid food should not be given before 4 to 6 months of age.

- *Catch a nap when the baby is sleeping.* A 20-minute nap in the morning and afternoon can help. If parents cannot nap, they should stretch out and rest.

- *Try to get additional adult help.* For parents who work outside the home or who have more than one baby, extra adult help often becomes a necessity. Due to their small size, twins and other multiple babies usually require feeding every

two hours. Some parents ask relatives to help. Others hire home help. A new parent might schedule visitors to see the newborn so help is available during times of greatest need.

Soothing a Crying Baby

Nothing bothers parents as much as a crying newborn. Crying is a major stressor. As many as one-fourth of all baby cries are for no apparent reason. Perhaps you have heard of *colic*. **Colic** is inconsolable crying that cannot be comforted or soothed. It begins and ends for no known reason, lasts about three hours, occurs at least three days a week, and continues for at least three weeks. Colic often begins at two weeks of age, peaks at six weeks, and ends at about three months.

At one time, colic was thought to be severe abdominal pain caused by air or gas in the baby's digestive tract. Nationally known pediatrician T. Berry Brazelton found the so-called *colicky cry* is just the high-end of normal infant crying. Colicky babies do not have more digestive gas than other babies. They do not cry more often than other babies. They just cry longer and more intensely. What can parents do? See 12-16.

12-16 When newborns cry inconsolably, parents can try such soothers as singing or talking softly.

- ***Do not feel responsible for the crying.*** Realize that all babies cry, but this doesn't mean parents are doing anything wrong.

- ***Try some soothers.*** To soothe a crying newborn, parents can sing or talk slowly, gently stroke the baby's hand or face, or turn on an overhead fan for background noise. Parents should also correct any known causes of crying, such as a wet diaper or hunger.

- ***Get relief.*** Asking someone for help can give parents temporary relief. If need be, they may leave the baby crying in the crib for up to 10 minutes while listening to the wails from another room.

- ***Understand baby's adjustments.*** Parents need to remember that their baby is going through major adjustments, too. The baby is counting on the parent to help him or her through this stage.

- ***Focus on the joys of having a baby.*** When parents can focus on joyous times, coping with their baby's crying jags is easier, 12-17.

Family-Life Adjustments

A new baby means adjustments in family life. New parents are often amazed how much one tiny person can change an entire household. Adjustments are more positive when the couple has good health, open communication, and a high degree of commitment to parenting and each other.

Handling Household Tasks

Along with the important task of caring for their new infant, parents need to decide how to handle such tasks as laundry, cleaning the home, and making meals for other family members. They will likely have to reassign some tasks and chores. For example, couples will need to focus on tasks that are essential, such as meal planning and preparation and keeping the kitchen, bathroom, and baby's room clean.

Although women traditionally took the lead with household tasks, most couples today strive to delegate tasks or do them together to lessen the burden on everyone—especially the new mother. When older children are in the family, parents can recruit them to help with age-appropriate tasks. For example, a preschooler can help with setting the dinner table or matching and folding socks. Older children might help with washing dishes, dusting furniture, and taking out the trash.

Balancing Career and Family Life

The ability to balance family life and work is challenging for new parents. Setting priorities for family, work, and community involvement is important to maintaining balance. This is especially true in dual-career families.

Through government and corporate efforts, many programs and policies have been set in place to help families meet their needs. Both employees and employers

12-17 Focusing on the joys of having a baby helps parents get through the stressful times.

benefit from such family-friendly programs. Employees have higher morale and more motivation to work when they know they are able to meet responsibilities at home. Employers are more likely to retain current employees and recruit new ones.

Today many employers offer one or more family-friendly ways to work. These work arrangements often include

- *Job sharing.* With job sharing, two workers share the functions of one full-time job. They evenly share the wages and time at work. Job sharing is a mutual agreement between employers and employees. Successful job sharing requires both workers to frequently communicate with each other and their supervisor.

- *Flextime.* In contrast to working a nine-to-five shift for 40 hours per week, flextime schedules allow workers to vary their starting and departure times to fit family needs. Employers require that employees work a certain number of core hours per week and pay period.

- *Compressed work schedules.* As a variation of flextime, a compressed work schedule allows full-time employees to work more hours per day and fewer days per week. For example, a worker might work four, 10-hour days per week.

- *Telecommuting.* With increasing technology, many employees have an option to work from home for their employers, at least a few hours each week, 12-18. Employment from home generally requires communication with the workplace by phone, fax, computer, and the Internet. Telecommuting allows the worker to meet employer demands while caring for a child at home.

Couples find many other ways to balance work and home life. For example, some choose to start their workdays earlier or work longer on several days in order to

12-18 Telecommuting is one way that parents can meet both work and home demands.

get a half day or whole day off (a type of flextime). Others choose to take jobs with fewer demands, such as overtime, weekend work, or out-of-town duties. Yet, other men and women settle for making less money and pursuing a simpler lifestyle. They may also choose to live and work in a smaller community to avoid the time and expense of long commutes. What options might you consider?

Meeting Financial Needs

Juggling strained finances can also be stressful. Parents must refigure their budget to include the new child's needs. This can mean they have less money to spend on recreational items or activities. The problems are understandable considering that about 62 percent of women work prior to a baby's arrival and only about 12 percent quickly return to work. Here are some ways that parents can help reduce child-related costs

- Rethink the need for dual careers. Child care costs are high. Unless a parent makes $25,000 or more per year, child care costs may be more than income. It may cost less to have one parent stay home.

- Take advantage of all tax breaks for child care.
- Spend money wisely. Shop for bargains.
- Reduce recreational costs. Rent a movie instead of going to the movie theater. Get together with friends for a meal with each friend bringing food instead of eating out.
- Use good judgment when buying toys. Compare prices and buy toys, such as blocks, that children can use for a longer period of time. Rotate toys or periodically exchange toys with a friend for variety.

Helping Siblings Adjust

If they have other children, parents must help them adjust to having a new brother or sister. Rivalry tends to be greatest when children are closer than three years in age. When a child is at least three years older than a sibling, he or she holds the secure position of older brother or sister. The child may feel less threatened because the new baby is not robbing him or her of the family's "baby" position.

Even so, accepting a new brother or sister may be painful for a child. Parents need to be understanding. How they handle introducing the new baby will determine to a large extent whether serious rivalry develops. If possible, parents should make sure older siblings visit the mother and new baby at the birth facility. When taking pictures of the new baby, parents should take some of the older siblings, too. Each parent should also try to spend special time alone with each child daily— even if only for a few minutes. This makes each child feel important, and it may help the family maintain a feeling of harmony.

Using Grandparent Supports

Grandparents provide a major source of support for new parents. Grandparents also care for more than one-fifth of all children of mothers who work. Recent polls indicate that about 80 percent of new mothers talk to their own mothers at least once a week about baby and child care. Almost half of new mothers talk to their own mothers daily. Although the relationships between daughters and their mothers are very good, occasional areas of disagreement occur. New mothers don't always agree with their mothers on some baby-care tasks, such as feeding (new mothers tend to favor breast-feeding while grandmothers tend to favor formula-feeding) and sleeping arrangements.

What should new parents do when they have areas of disagreement with grandparents? Most experts agree that introducing outside sources about "best parenting practices" helps smooth over areas of disagreement. For example, recommendations on breast-feeding or sleeping arrangements from a nationally recognized pediatrician (or reading about these ideas in the latest baby magazines) can help bring grandparents around to new ways of thinking about rearing children.

Keeping the Couple's Relationship Strong

Caring for a newborn can be physically and emotionally tiring. Parents may not feel they have much energy left to share with each other. Even so, parents need to make an effort to keep their own relationship strong. They need to share their thoughts, concerns, dreams, and doubts. This will enable them to grow even closer together. A healthy spousal relationship builds a strong foundation for the entire family.

Spouses also need time together to nurture their relationship in the childbearing years, 12-19. Many experts believe that couples need a regular date night each week. Hiring a babysitter for a few hours every week may be well worth the money.

12-19 New parents need to spend time nurturing their marital relationship. This can keep their marriage strong and help them feel better able to handle the stresses of parenting.

Making Self a Priority

Parents need time alone, too. It is important to plan in advance how you want to use your personal time. Too often parents use this time for catch-up on career or household work. Instead parents need time for hobbies and friendships. Personal time used for sitting and eating, exercising, and napping is time well spent.

When Stress Is Too Severe

For some new parents, parenting stress becomes too intense or too long-term to manage. These parents may not have the personal coping skills or support of family and others to help them through daily parenting activities. Parents most at-risk include those who

- have negative views of the spouse or the marriage

- are most unrealistic about the changes the new baby brought

- have severe postpartum depression PPD (mothers)

- feel as though they might hurt their baby or themselves

- have multiple babies or babies with fragile health

Parents who experience severe stress should seek immediate help. Professionals can help most parents. Adjustments to parenting are easier when parents go to bed thinking of everything they did for their newborn and their family rather than thinking about everything they didn't do. Each parent should share the burdens and the joys of parenting with the spouse and with relatives and friends. Babies blossom in the love and shelter of these families who do their best.

1 Month*

Physical Development

Gross-Motor Skills

Does not control arm and leg movements—movements are still reflexive

Needs support for head. Without support, head will flop forward and backward

Lifts head briefly from surface in order to turn head from side to side when lying on tummy

Twitches whole body when crying

Moves body vigorously when startled

Fine-Motor Skills

Keeps hands fisted or slightly open

May grasp object if placed in open hand but drops it quickly

Intellectual Development

General

Uses all five senses

Prefers to look at patterned objects and human faces

Follows slow, up and down movements of objects with eyes

Listens attentively to sounds and voices

Is sensitive to touch

Distinguishes odors and flavors

Language

Cries to express needs

Turns toward source of sounds

Social and Emotional Development

Social

May seem to smile at faces or voices

May recognize parents' voices

Is comforted by human faces

Emotional

Responds positively to comfort and satisfaction, negatively to pain

Is comforted by cuddling and being swaddled in blanket

This chart is not an exact timetable. Individuals may perform certain activities earlier or later than indicated in the chart.

Summing It Up

- The baby's birth links to many family changes. New parents begin the childbearing stage of the family life cycle.

- The nurturing stage of parenting coexists with the childbearing stage. During this time, parents struggle to balance their baby's needs with their own needs.

- Newborns have a distinct appearance as a result of adjusting to life outside the mother's body.

- Newborns have remarkable abilities, including the use of all five senses.

- Newborns have reflexive actions or automatic reactions to stimuli.

- The newborn's care involves, holding the baby, helping the baby sleep, feeding, bathing, and dressing and diapering.

- According to Piaget, babies learn through their senses and motor skills. Newborns practice reflexes that will become voluntary actions and will aid future learning.

- Babies communicate by using different cries.

- Babies have their own temperaments.

- Socially, babies need loving parents who consistently provide care to learn trust.

- Parenting adjustments involve learning baby-care skills, meeting the baby's care needs, and soothing a crying baby.

- Family-life adjustments require changes for the whole family.

- Sharing the joys and responsibilities of child care strengthens the couple's marriage, and in turn, their family.

Recalling the Facts

1. Name two changes that parents experience in the first few days of parenthood.

2. Briefly describe three characteristics of a newborn's appearance.

3. What is the purpose of the fontanelles on the baby's head at birth?

4. Describe how a newborn is capable of using each of the five senses.

5. Name five newborn reflexes.

6. When holding a newborn, why is it important to firmly support the newborn's head, neck, and back?

7. Why should a baby be placed on his or her back to sleep?

8. How does *self-demand feeding* differ from scheduled feedings?

9. Why should a parent burp a baby during and after a feeding?

10. What is the most important rule to remember when bathing a baby?

11. What can parents do to protect their baby from *diaper rash*?

12. How do newborns learn?

13. Newborns are in what stage of intellectual development according to Piaget?

14. Contrast the three basic infant cries.

15. How does a colicky cry differ from other cries?

16. Summarize two adjustments families with newborns may need to make.

Applying New Skills

1. **Picture wall.** Create a picture wall filled with pictures of newborns. Label the physical characteristics described in the chapter.

2. **Observation.** Visit the nursery of a local hospital and observe newborns. Describe to the class your reaction to seeing real newborns.

3. **Demonstration.** Using a soft, limp, life-sized doll (or a computerized infant simulator), demonstrate skills needed to pick up, lay down, hold, feed, burp, bathe, and dress a baby.

4. **Research.** Use reliable Internet or print resources to research Sudden Infant Death Syndrome (SIDS). Reliable sites include the *American Academy of Pediatrics* and the *National SIDS Foundation*. What additional actions can parents take to help prevent SIDS? How can other people be of assistance to parents who have lost a child to SIDS? What is the purpose of the National SIDS Foundation? Summarize your findings and give a brief report to the class.

Thinking Critically

1. Debate whether self-demand feeding and sleeping or scheduled feeding and sleep are better for newborns. Use text or reliable Internet and print resources to give evidence to justify your opinion. Consider the advantages and disadvantages of each before reaching a conclusion.

2. Draw conclusions about ways that dual-career families can adjust to family life with a newborn. Share your conclusions with the class.

Linking Academics

1. **Writing.** Suppose that your aunt and uncle have just brought home a new baby. They already have two older children. You are the oldest in a family with two other siblings. Based on your personal experience, write a letter to your aunt and uncle offering suggestions about how they can help the older children develop relationships with the new baby.

2. **Reading.** Read a book about SIDS and grief, such as *Empty Cradle, Broken Heart* by Deborah L. Davis, Ph.D. Give a brief report to the class reviewing the key concepts outlined in the book.

Chapter 13

Parents and Their Infants

Objectives

After studying this chapter, you will be able to

- describe the physical, intellectual, social and emotional development of infants and practices that influence this development.
- differentiate between gross-motor skills and fine-motor skills.
- summarize how parents influence infant brain development.
- describe how different types of development relate to one another.
- explain how both stranger anxiety and separation anxiety relate to attachment.
- summarize why medical checkups are necessary during infancy.
- identify parenting concerns during the baby's first year of life.

Key Terms

infant
motor skills
gross-motor skills
crawling
creeping
fine-motor skills
mitten grasp
pincer grasp
eye-hand coordination
body image
finger foods
weaning
window of opportunity
object permanence
cooing
babbling
stranger anxiety
separation anxiety
immunizations

Most people separate the first two years of a baby's life into two stages—infant and toddler stages. An **infant** is a baby less than 1 year of age. Parents may think of their newborns as helpless. Twelve months later, *helpless* might be the last word they would use to describe their infants. Throughout the baby's first year, parents watch their infant grow in size and develop physical skills at amazing rates. It is important for parents to keep in mind that all babies go through the same series of developmental changes. Because babies are individuals, they go through these changes at their own pace.

Infants take giant leaps in developing their senses and intellect, too. They learn to understand many words and may even begin to say a few words. Their individual personalities also become more apparent, 13-1. During the *nurturing stage* of parenting, parents often struggle to keep up with their infant's needs. They provide many kinds of care and work to blend the new baby into their family.

In this chapter, you will study the infant's development in all areas—physical, intellectual, social, and emotional. After you study each section, check the "Infant Development" chart at the end of the chapter for month-by-month development. Along with medical care for infants, you will also study the major tasks of parenting infants.

Physical Development

In their first year, babies progress rapidly in their physical development. Only during the prenatal period, does physical growth occur faster. Although all children grow at their own rates, most infants add 6 inches to their birth length and double their birth weight in 6 months. By the end of the first year, they grow another 3 to 4 inches and triple their birth weight.

13-1 Each baby has a unique personality. Signs of this personality are evident from birth, but become much more obvious near a baby's first birthday.

As you read in Chapter 4, the *principles of growth and development* influence every child's maturation. These principles include

- *Development proceeds from head to foot.* At birth, a baby's head is more highly developed than his or her legs or feet. The upper body develops before the lower body. A child will hold up his or her head, learn to sit, and stand in that order.

- *Development proceeds from trunk outward.* Development begins near the spinal cord and moves outward toward the hands and feet. A child will roll over many months before he or she can pick up a small object. This is because the trunk muscles develop first enabling the child to roll.

- *Development follows a sequence.* A sequence of changes is part of the genetic blueprint. A child will sit before he or she can stand or walk. A child will coo and babble before saying words.

- *Rate of development varies.* The sequence of developmental events is the same from child to child. However, the timing of the sequence of changes *varies* with each child. Within one child, timing may be early for one aspect of development and late for another. One child may walk at 10 months and another child may walk at 14 months. Another child may be an early walker and a late talker. For these reasons, parents should not compare their children to other children of the same age. Children may have different abilities at a certain age and still be developing normally.

Understanding these principles can help parents better observe their infant's development. As you read this chapter, take note of the details regarding these essential principles.

Voluntary Body Control

Because newborns move by reflex, their movements may look disorganized. For example, the whole body twitches when the baby cries. With brain development during infancy, *voluntary movements*, or controlled movements, begin to replace reflexes.

With practice babies strengthen muscles and increase coordination. Babies work toward developing motor skills. **Motor skills are skills that require the movement and control of certain muscles.**

Babies enjoy being able to control their movements, and they practice endlessly. As their muscles develop, their arms and legs move more smoothly. With increased coordination, babies can move an arm and a leg on one side of the body in unison. They can also move both arms and legs at the same time with some control. Their kicking will become more vigorous. Parents often enjoy watching their infants practice and reach motor-skill milestones.

Baby care becomes more challenging as infants learn to control their movements. Wiggling babies are challenging to diaper and dress. Feeding is challenging and messy if babies grab for the spoon. As babies become more mobile, keeping them safe takes more effort.

Gross-Motor Skills

Gross-motor skills involve the use of the large muscles, such as the trunk, neck, arm, and leg muscles. Babies must master the initial steps of motor-skill development before beginning to learn more complicated skills.

Why are gross-motor skills important? Babies are physically more comfortable when they can move. They often become uncomfortable lying in one position and may cry. Mobility aids learning and socializing because children can get to objects and people of interest. Gross-motor skills are just fun, too. Babies often smile or laugh as they playfully show off.

Head-to-Foot Development

As you read earlier, physical development is directional. Control of voluntary muscles begins at the head and proceeds to the feet. There is an equally predictable sequence of gross-motor skills. Some of the major milestones include

- *Raising head and chest.* Babies can raise their heads and chests while on their stomachs when neck muscles strengthen. This occurs around 2 months of age. At 6 months, they can raise their heads while on their backs.

- *Rolling over.* The next new skill for babies is rolling over, 13-2. First, infants roll from side to side when on their stomachs. By the fifth month, they can

13-2 The floor or ground is the best place for babies to practice rolling over since they cannot fall.

roll over from their stomachs to their backs. The first time babies roll over they may look pleasantly surprised. Babies practice this skill repeatedly. About a month later, they learn to roll over the other way—from their backs to their stomachs.

- *Sitting.* Sitting requires strong neck and back muscles. Although babies can sit with support at 3 or 4 months of age, their bodies may slowly lean to one side as their trunk muscles tire. At about 9 months, babies can sit without support.

- *Crawling and creeping.* Soon after babies discover their feet, they begin **crawling** or pulling with the arms while the abdomen remains on the floor. Between 6 and 8 months, babies begin to creep. **Creeping** is moving on the hands and knees. On a flat surface, infants may get up on their hands and knees, only to lunge forward on their noses. Babies this age bounce back easily from tumbles instead of crying. Before long, babies learn to balance on their hands and knees. At first, they may just rock back and forth in this position.

- *Standing.* When held in a standing position on adults' laps, babies move their bodies up and down and stamp their feet. They work to pull themselves into an unsteady, half-standing position. Once standing, they discover a new problem—getting back down! At this point, some babies cry for help. Others simply let go and drop to a sitting position. In either case, babies try again and again. Slowly, they learn to sit from a standing position.

- *Taking steps.* Standing becomes a favorite activity for babies. As their leg muscles strengthen and their balance improves, babies become more daring. At first, they may practice stepping sideways. Usually, infants do this while facing and holding onto low furniture. This maneuver is called *cruising.* At first, they hold tightly; as their cruising skills improve, they lightly touch the furniture as they step around it. At this stage, parents can delight children by holding their hands and helping them take a few wobbly steps.

- *Walking.* Babies generally begin walking between 12 and 14 months. When a baby is ready to walk, he or she usually begins by taking a few steps, often toward a parent. The baby may totter forward on the toes, take a few steps, and fall into the parents' waiting arms. Learning to walk is a challenging task that demands total concentration. At first, babies extend their arms high as they walk in order to keep their balance themselves. Slowly, they develop the ability to keep their balance with arms down.

The Baby's Own Pace

As babies develop gross-motor skills, some move quickly and some linger in each stage, 13-3. Some babies get around by crawling rapidly. When placed in a play yard (or playpen), their desire to explore is so strong that some babies climb out and start roaming.

1—Newborns sleep on their backs with their legs curled up.

2—As infants gain more control of their neck muscles, they can hold up their heads.

3—Babies can keep their backs firm and heads steady when propped up in a sitting position for a short time.

4—With better muscle control and balance, babies can sit with slight support.

5—Soon babies can sit without support.

6—Once babies can creep, they are ready to explore.

(Continued on next page)

13-3 Crawling is a gross-motor skill. Each baby develops a unique crawling style.

7—Before long, babies stand whenever possible and cruise around furniture.

8—Stairs are challenging and fun. They can also be dangerous.

9—Babies like to walk holding onto a parent's hand.

10—A baby's first steps alone are wobbly, with hands held high for balance.

11—Eventually, babies learn to walk more steadily.

13-3 Continued.

Other babies have great fun standing. They may stand in high chairs, bathtubs, strollers, and grocery carts. Their parents must watch them closely to protect them from dangerous falls. With practice, babies add squatting and stooping to their standing skills.

Still other babies move more quickly through the crawling and standing stages. They seem to be in a great hurry to walk. They practice cruising around furniture for hours. They love to walk while holding their parents' hands. Then they advance to taking their first steps alone.

Fine-Motor Skills

Fine-motor skills involve the use of smaller body muscles, such as those in the hands, fingers, feet, and toes. Newborns have very little control over their small muscles. For the first few months, babies keep their hands fisted or slightly open. Parents may marvel at how a newborn's tiny fingers curl and grasp an adult's finger. The inborn grasping reflex causes this action, not the child. Babies do not begin to develop fine-motor skills until about 5 months of age.

Why are fine-motor skills important? When babies are able to grasp, they can begin the process of learning self-care skills, such as self-feeding. Fine-motor skills allow babies to learn about their world as they pick up objects, bring them close for inspection, and use their tiny fingers to turn objects and feel each part.

Trunk-Outward Development

Body control proceeds from the trunk outward. For example, infants can roll over before they can use their fingers. Trunk-outward development proceeds in a predictable sequence. Some of the major milestones include

- *Open-hand swiping.* By 3 months of age, reflexes fade and babies begin to practice voluntary movements. With their hands open, babies may try to reach or swipe at objects. Until eye development catches up, they may be far off target. For safety reasons, parents should remove from reach any object not intended for baby's hand or mouth. Babies need to practice grasping. They need the sensory experiences provided by reaching, touching, and mouthing objects. For example, a cradle gym and other lightweight handheld toys offer a chance for the baby to practice these skills.

- *Mitten grasp.* Infants continue developing better control of their hands. They practice grabbing and swiping at objects, gradually improving their aim. Babies often hold their feet with a **mitten grasp**, in which the palm and fingers oppose the thumb, 13-4. When infants learn to touch their mouths with their fingers, it triggers a whole new way of exploring. Babies stick every object they can grasp, including their fingers and toes, into their mouths at 6 or 7 months. As they refine their grasps, babies enjoy handling different objects. They can begin lifting pieces of food to their mouths. If their parents have introduced drinking from a cup, babies may try to grab it.

- *Pincer grasp.* With continuing practice, babies can grasp objects between their thumb and index finger. This is the **pincer grasp**. Around nine months, mastering this fine-motor skill is a great achievement. Although babies can pick up objects in a controlled way, they cannot release them with control. This skill develops later.

Babies use their grasping and holding skills to do many other activities. For example, when coordination develops, babies learn to drop things. This new ability is intriguing. Babies may pick up and drop

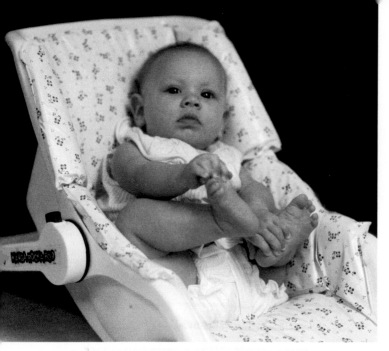

13-4 This baby uses a mitten grasp to grab her feet and toes. This grasp is an important fine-motor skill.

objects at will just to practice. They enjoy playing with any kind of container, putting objects in and taking them out. Dropping games may be frustrating for parents, but they help babies develop important skills.

Babies also quickly learn that hands can do more than grasp. They learn to stroke, pat, and feel different textures. By 9 months, babies have discovered their index fingers are useful for leading and pointing. They may poke their fingers into holes and even into parents' faces.

Most babies use both hands equally well throughout the first year. Another milestone occurs when babies begin using both hands in different ways on the same object. For instance, the baby might hold an object with one hand while manipulating it with the other.

Eye-Hand Coordination

Fine-motor skills are dependent on **eye-hand coordination** or the ability to move the hands in the direction that the eyes see. Until this develops, babies are off target in their open-hand swipes. Grasps at 4 months of age are simply accidental.

At first, babies look back and forth from the hand to the object. When 5 or 6 months old, babies know where their hands are and can keep their eyes on the target. Soon a visually guided reach develops, 13-5. When 9 or 10 months old, babies possess the skills necessary to capture moving objects.

The Baby's Own Pace

Because babies need many objects to grasp in order to develop fine-motor skills, they vary in how and when they learn these skills. Even preschool children vary a great deal in their skills. For example, some preschool children handle small blocks and beads in awkward ways and use a mitten grasp on pencils and crayons. Other preschool children can play a stringed music instrument, handle crayons correctly, and even weave.

Vision links strongly to grasping. Vision problems can slow infant development. For example, babies who have low vision or who are blind will not be able to grasp objects unless the environment changes, such as adding sound to objects.

Exploring Their Own Bodies

As babies grow and develop, they examine their bodies, 13-6. To the baby, body exploration does not differ from object exploration. Toward the end of the first year, babies view themselves as different from others.

Body image is how a person views his or her body and its functions. Body image develops long before other images emerge, such as intellectual or personality images. Before the ages of 5 or 6, body image almost wholly determines a child's self-concept and self-esteem.

Infants begin to develop positive or negative feelings toward their bodies and body functions based on their parents' reactions. Parents need to use a sensitive and matter-of-fact approach in handling all

1—As babies wave their arms, they begin to notice their hands.

2—As babies practice swiping and grabbing, their aim improves.

3—Babies playfully grab their feet with a crude mitten grasp.

4—Babies enjoy handling and mouthing anything they can grasp between the fingers and palms of their hands.

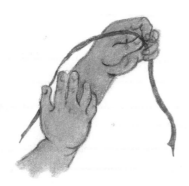

5—With a pincer grasp, babies can pick up a ribbon or string.

6—Improved grasping skills allow babies to feed themselves using their fingers.

13-5 Hand manipulation skills are dependent upon eye-hand coordination, an important fine-motor skill.

Body Discovery Timeline

Part of Body	Approximate Age of Discovery
Hands	3 months
Feet	5 months
Navel (belly button)	6 months
Ears and nose	6 to 9 months
Sex organs	8 to 12 months
Shoulders, elbows, and knees	12 months (and sometimes older)

13-6 Babies explore their body in a matter-of-fact way. Parents' reactions to these behaviors help determine body image, a major aspect of the self-concept and self-esteem.

baby explorations and in caring for their babies. For example, parents should not label touching any body parts as shameful. They should not use words, such as "nasty" or "dirty" to describe a bowel movement. Negative labels cause the baby to feel unacceptable.

Feeding

Infants need the right foods to assure growth and to lay the foundation for later healthy eating habits. Knowledge of the infant's developmental skills equips parents to provide the right foods in a positive and healthful feeding environment.

Feeding Breast Milk or Formula

The American Academy of Pediatrics (AAP) suggests exclusive breast- or formula-feeding for six months. At this time, parents may start to introduce solid foods to supplement breast milk or formula. When babies start eating solid foods, breast milk or formula still meets their major nutritional needs.

For parents who use formula, the formula should be iron-fortified. Pediatricians can find the right formula for babies who are sensitive to certain formulas. For example, there are lactose-free, soy, and hypoallergenic formulas. There are also formulas for older babies who are not getting enough calcium, protein, or iron from solid foods.

Introducing Solid Foods

Before they are ready, babies will spit back any solid foods that enter their mouths. This is because the sucking and tongue-protrusion reflexes are designed to bring milk from the breast or bottle to the back of the mouth for swallowing. These reflexes disappear around 4 months of age. Even then, eating is a messy process.

Although pediatricians say babies should never have solid foods before four months, some infants consume solids before then. Research shows that children will have fewer food allergies if parents wait until their infants are 6 months old to start solids. They will also be less prone to diabetes and obesity. Babies who start solids too soon tend to quit drinking milk too early and miss needed nutrients. Along with age, developmental signs showing infants' readiness for solids include

- ability to sit with minimal help or support
- doubled birthweight (a minimum of 13 pounds to start solids)
- signs of hunger after 8 to 10 feedings of breast milk or 32 ounces of formula
- interest in food on the parent's plate and grabbing for it
- ability to move food from the front of the mouth to the back and swallow

Once parents notice these signs, they should consult their pediatrician before giving solid foods. Following the doctor's advice is very important. He or she will indicate when to start solid foods, which foods to offer, how much to offer, and what to do if any food sensitivities appear. Parents generally give one new food at a time over a period of four to five days, and then add a new food.

As they introduce new foods, parents must watch for food sensitivities or allergies, such as breathing difficulties, rashes, or digestive upset. Food allergies to wheat, cow's milk, soy, egg whites, peanuts (and peanut butter), tree nuts, fish, and seafood are common. If there is a family history of food allergies, parents should not introduce these foods until after the child's first birthday. They should also consult their pediatrician before feeding infants any foods that may cause an allergic reaction. For some people, food allergies can be life threatening.

When babies are ready for solids, start by mixing 1 tablespoon of iron-fortified, single-grain baby cereal with about 4 tablespoons of breast milk or formula. Parents should mix the cereal to a smooth and creamy consistency, free of lumps. Next babies will advance to *single-ingredient* puréed foods. Introduce a variety of flavors and textures. When learning to eat solids, babies are not ready for food mixtures. Be sure to offer cooked and puréed fruits, vegetables, egg yolks, and meats as shown in 13-7. Parents may buy commercial baby foods or make their own.

When the baby is most hungry, feed solid foods first. Then feed the baby breast milk or formula. To feed solids, put a little food on the tip of a small, long-handled spoon. Put the spoon on the baby's lips and let the

Introducing Solid Foods

Approximate Age	Foods to Introduce, One at a Time*
4 to 6 months	Single-grain, iron-fortified baby cereal mixed with formula or breast milk
5 to 7 months	Strained or puréed vegetables, such as carrots, squash, sweet potatoes, green beans, peas, or broccoli Strained or puréed fruits, such as apples, pears, peaches, plums, or bananas **Note:** It doesn't matter what order you introduce fruits or vegetables, just introduce one at a time. Avoid feeding French fries to infants since they are high in fat and low in nutrients. Research shows French fries are often the only vegetable children eat.
6 to 8 months	Soft or strained cheese, yogurt, egg yolk, beans, meat, or poultry
8 to 10 months	Soft table foods, such as toast, cooked and mashed fruits and vegetables, and egg yolk, beans, meat, or poultry
10 to 12 months	Chopped foods, cooked fruits and vegetables, and finely chopped meats or poultry
12 months	Whole milk from cows along with a variety of whole grains, fruits, vegetables, and meats

*Introduce complementary solid foods in very small amounts, one at a time, and continue to feed breast milk or formula as the doctor advises. Be sure to pay attention to the infant's fullness cues. How much is one serving?

- Younger infants (4 to 7 months): 1 tablespoon or less (gradually increase amount to 2 to 4 tablespoons as baby becomes accustomed to new textures and flavors).
- Older infants (7 to 12 months): 3 to 4 tablespoons, two to three times daily.

13-7 Most doctors recommend a sequence like this one for introducing solid foods in baby's diet.

baby suck the food off the spoon. Food put on the front of the tongue will dribble out of the mouth. Food pushed to the back of the mouth may gag the child. Parents should not be concerned if their babies take in few solids during these initial feedings. Babies are learning a new skill. With patient practice, babies become skillful at getting the food back into their mouths.

When 8 or 9 months old, babies will grab for the feeding spoon. This is their desire for independence. Although babies cannot get much food into their mouths with a spoon until the toddler years, they can start feeding themselves with their hands. They may be a little awkward at first. Given the chance, infants usually do a good job of getting enough food into their mouths. Foods eaten with the fingers are called **finger foods**. Parents need to choose "safe" finger foods, such as cooked and diced fruits and vegetables and teething biscuits. Because babies can easily choke, parents should stay with them as they eat.

Parents will see their babies reject certain foods. To get babies to like variety, they should retry the rejected food every few days at least 15 or more times. Many parents give up too soon, usually after three to five tries. Mealtimes should be pleasant without forcing children to eat a given food. In addition, parents should *never* add sugar to a food in an effort to make the baby like it. Also, babies should be at least a year old before eating honey. Honey can be a serious source of foodborne illness for infants.

How can parents tell if their infants are full? Paying attention to fullness cues can help. When parents learn their infant's hunger and fullness cues, they are better prepared to help their infant understand when he or she is hungry or full. This is also a good way to avoid under- or over-feeding, which can lead to poor nutrition or childhood obesity. When infants are full, they often display the following behaviors:

- Younger babies may fall asleep, stop sucking, or spit out the nipple.
- Older babies often turn their heads away from the spoon, push foods away, spit out foods, or focus attention on their surroundings.

Parents might as well accept mealtimes at this stage will be messy, 13-8. They should stop an older baby from deliberately throwing food, but dropped food and spills are normal, especially in younger infants. Parents can cope with this stage by putting newspapers or sheets of plastic on their floors and large bibs on their babies.

Weaning

Weaning means phasing out the taking of milk from the breast or bottle. Weaning is a gradual process, just like the introduction of solid foods. Although the AAP recommends breast-feeding for a year, mothers can wean their babies from breast to a bottle with formula.

13-8 The parent's job is to clean up the mess baby makes trying to self-feed. Food may seem to go everywhere but in the baby's mouth.

After a year, most babies can be weaned from breast milk or formula. Parents should check with their pediatrician about when and how best to wean their baby. When toddlers are weaned, they drink whole cow's milk. Toddlers need the fat content of whole cow's milk for healthy brain development. Weaning is complete when drinking from a cup is more satisfying than the breast or bottle. Most babies are weaned by 13 to 15 months of age.

Teething

Tooth development begins during the prenatal period. The crowns (tops) of the baby teeth form in the gums before the baby is born. This is why the mother's diet during pregnancy is so important. The crowns of permanent teeth begin forming during infancy. Calcium, phosphorus, vitamin D, and fluoride are important nutrients that aid in tooth development.

Like other aspects of development, teething follows a predictable pattern, but the timing varies. The first two teeth to appear are the lower front teeth, 13-9. The average age for a first tooth is 5 to 9 months. However, some babies are born with a tooth, and others are still toothless on their first birthday. By age 2, most children have their full set of baby teeth.

Babies react differently to the process of teething. One baby will chew, fret, and drool before each tooth breaks through the gums. Another baby will produce new teeth without any fuss at all. In any case, teething does not cause serious health problems. If a baby has a high fever, diarrhea, or vomiting, parents should not assume that teething is the cause. Instead, they should consult a doctor. Parents can often ease minor teething discomfort. Helpful tips include distracting the baby with music, cuddling, or offering a teething ring or pacifier with bumps. (Do not freeze a teething ring or pacifier because this can injure a baby's gums.) You may also use a

13-9 Teething may mean a lot of drooling. Babies' lower front teeth break through the gums first.

teething gel, but do so sparingly and follow directions carefully. Dental care is important, even during infancy. Tooth care involves

- cleaning the first tooth twice a day by rubbing it with a piece of gauze or a clean washcloth.

- using a soft-bristled baby toothbrush after several teeth appear. Toothpaste is not needed.

- giving needed fluoride after baby is 6 months old. This need may be met through fluoridated tap water or a fluoride supplement. Parents should talk about this with their pediatrician.

- cleaning the teeth after the final feeding of the day and avoiding putting the baby to bed with a bottle.

- beginning dental checkups about 6 months after the first tooth erupts.

Sleeping Patterns and Problems

For the first few months, babies' bodies dictate their sleeping patterns—babies fall asleep when their bodies need rest. Newborns may sleep up to 20 hours daily. Only severe hunger or illness can keep them awake. Babies need between 14 and 15½ hours of daily sleep during the remainder of infancy. The National Sleep Foundation found most babies are sleep deprived— getting a daily total of less than 13 hours of sleep.

After the newborn stage, sleep patterns vary greatly from baby to baby. In middle to late infancy, babies learn to stay awake. As they become more active and more social, they may have trouble settling down to sleep. Babies may start refusing naps, especially the morning nap. They may also cry or call out for their parents.

Although one solution does not work for all sleep problems, some practices tend to work for most babies most of the time. For example, establishing sleep routines such as feeding, rocking, singing, or cuddling and darkening the room help babies settle down to sleep. Just like adults, babies can have restless nights. Parents need to make their own decision about handling sleep problems, and then be kind, but firm, with their baby.

Intellectual Development

As you recall, intellectual development refers to the development of a person's mental abilities. It includes thinking and language skills. Parents think of their baby as a physical being. However, when parents see their 1-year-old putting shapes into a sorting box and understanding many words (and even saying a few words), they know their baby has made great strides in intellectual development, 13-10.

13-10 This one-year-old is hardly helpless! He uses his fine-motor skills as well as his mind when playing with this telephone.

Connecting Physical and Intellectual Development

Intellectual and physical development are woven together. Physical development, such as brain growth, makes intellectual development possible. The child's intellectual activities such as exploring the world, in turn, helps brain development and motor skills.

The Brain Grows and Develops

The brain is a physical organ that processes all other aspects of development. Intellectual and physical development relate through brain development. At birth, the brain is one-fourth its adult weight. At 6 months, the brain has grown to half its adult weight. Three-fourths of a person's brain growth is complete by age 2.

Much of a person's intellectual ability depends on certain connections between *neurons* (nerve cells) in the brain. These connections activate the neurons. The number and kinds of connections between these neurons determines a person's capacity to learn. By age 10, the brain begins eliminating inactive connections. After this time, the potential to make new connections is severely limited, if not entirely gone. The first 10 years, then, are crucial to brain development.

In addition, brain research reveals that certain skills have a *window of opportunity.* This **window of opportunity** is a sensitive critical period in which a person's capacity to develop a certain skill peaks. Before this time, the person is not developmentally able to learn the skill. After this time, learning the skill is difficult, if not impossible. The window of opportunity for many skills begins and ends during early childhood. For instance, birth to 4 years is the window of opportunity for learning basic motor skills. It may be very difficult or even impossible to master these skills after age 4.

As a child's brain develops, the kind of care the child receives has a great impact. Cuddling and other emotional support stimulates brain development. Encouraging a child to develop skills and abilities during their specific windows of opportunity strengthens brain connections and the skills. For example, when parents spend as much time as possible interacting with their children (through reading, playing, listening to music, or making crafts and drawing) they enhance communication and relationship skills.

Just as positive experiences can promote brain growth, negative ones can hinder it. Infants who are malnourished, for instance, develop smaller brains than those who receive adequate food. Their bodies do not get the nutrients needed to build brain cells or make cell connections. A lack of nutrients during the first three to four years (when the most brain growth occurs) can cause permanent damage.

Without a nurturing environment, children's brains are not able to develop as many connections. Some parents do not or are not able to provide their children with experiences that stimulate brain growth. Repair to the brain may not be possible for the child who suffers from child abuse and neglect in the first three years. Young children who experience abuse or neglect develop smaller brains than children who have positive experiences. Chronic abuse can affect the balance of certain brain chemicals that further impact brain development.

Other Physical and Intellectual Ties

Physical development of the senses—seeing, hearing, touching, tasting, and smelling—relate to intellectual development. For example, by 2 months babies can see almost as well as their parents, 13-11. This enables them to see likenesses and differences in people's faces and objects. Once their eyes focus together, they can tell distance. When babies' sight improves, so does their intellectual development. In the same way, the development of other senses helps learning.

Babies also use their physical motor skills to learn about their world. For example, shaking a rattle helps them to hear how rattles sound. As they drop things, they learn

13-11 Infants spend hours staring at their surroundings. Providing a colorful mobile is one way parents can stimulate baby's mind.

what happens to the objects. Walking allows the baby to explore almost the entire home. Not only do motor skills help intellectual development, but intellectual development also enhances further physical development. For example, reaching a desired object may prompt the baby to walk for the first time.

Piaget and Intellectual Development

Piaget saw infants as curious about and active in their world. Babies are curious because they are not born with any knowledge of their world. Babies set out to learn about people and objects by using their senses and motor skills. As you recall, Piaget called this the *sensorimotor stage*. He found that development in a baby's first year went through three periods of change, 13-12 and Appendix B.

Primary Circular Reactions

Between 1 and 4 months, babies learn they can repeat reflexive actions. Now the actions are no longer reflexive, but voluntary. For example, they can suck and stop sucking at will, and they can open and close their hands at will. Because all these actions involve only the baby's body, Piaget called them *primary*.

Babies react to their new skills with pleasure. Because of the pleasure (*reaction*), they repeat the action (sucking or opening and closing their hands). They get the same reaction of pleasure. This causes another cycle of action and reaction (*circular*). Piaget called this second substage, *primary circular reactions*.

Although babies are not yet making contact with objects, this substage helps children gain control of basic motor actions. For example, babies learn to open and close their hands smoothly and quickly. This is needed to grasp a swinging object in a cradle or floor gym.

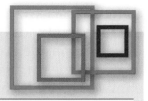

Piaget's Stages of Intellectual Development
1. Sensorimotor
1A: *Exercising the Reflexes*
1B: *Primary Circular Reactions*
1C: *Secondary Circular Reactions*
1D: *Coordination of Secondary Circular Reactions*
1E: *Tertiary Circular Reactions*
1F: *Mental Representation*
2. Preoperational
2A: *Preconceptual Phase*
2B: *Intuitive Phase*
3. Concrete Operations
4. Formal Operations

13-12 According to Piaget, one- to 12-month-old babies advance from controlling their own movements (substage 2), to creating simple effects on the environment (substage 3), and finally to achieving some of their own goals through motor actions (substage 4).

Around 4 months, babies combine some actions. For example, they can direct a hand toward their mouths and suck on their thumbs or fingers. Soon, babies will connect their actions with objects.

Secondary Circular Reactions

Babies 4 to 8 months old come to realize they cause things to happen with people and objects in their world (*secondary*). For example, a baby cries and mother comes. The baby kicks in the crib and the dangling objects move. These behaviors are not done on purpose at first. In fact, they may be done for some time before babies notice. When they first notice, babies often look puzzled. Then they again try their action (crying or kicking). It works! They find pleasure (*reaction*) from the response (mother comes or the dangling objects move). They repeat it many times (*circular*). Because of this, Piaget called this substage, *secondary circular reactions*.

Babies are now beginning to see *cause* and *effect*. If their world is consistent (mother comes most of the time or cradle gym objects move), they sense they have some control in their world. Babies begin to believe, "I can make this happen." Cause and effect is a complex concept that takes many years to fully understand.

Coordination of Secondary Circular Reactions

Babies who are 8 to 12 months old begin to have goals. To accomplish a goal, they have to solve a problem. Sometimes they problem solve by putting two actions together to achieve a goal. For example, a baby may want a ball in the corner of the room. To get the ball, he or she may push a footstool away (first action) and then grasp the ball (second action). Another way babies achieve goals is to use tools to help them. For example, a baby might get a ball that is out of reach by nudging it with a block. Thus, when babies coordinate two or more earlier-learned actions to reach a goal, Piaget called it *coordination* of secondary circular reactions.

At this substage, babies only try to problem solve one way. They do not change the way they attempt to do something. If certain actions do not work, they repeat actions the same way again or just fuss or cry. How they react to failure is often due to temperament differences.

Developing Key Intellectual Skills

Six major intellectual skills begin developing in infancy. The baby will use these skills over and over in life. The more they are used, the more skilled the baby becomes.

Developing Memory

Babies remember specific actions to use on an object to get a response. For example, the babies enjoy pressing a rubber duck to get a squeak. Babies remember and repeat the actions that bring them pleasure, 13-13.

13-13 Babies respond with pleasure to actions they remember.

Memory also develops through daily routines and predictability. Babies remember a sequence of steps leading to a reward. For instance, an infant may recognize a series of actions parents take to prepare for feeding times. If parents do these actions in the regular sequence, babies will wait, realizing they will soon eat. If the sequence of actions changes, they will become upset and cry.

Memory helps babies recognize family members and toys. Playing peek-a-boo and other hiding games helps babies retain those memories. They feel secure in the few seconds it takes to reveal the faces and toys again. Babies often laugh when they receive affirmation of these memories.

Memory, however, is short-term in babies. Some parents use photos to help their babies remember family members they rarely see. When parents get out a toy they have put away for a while, the baby thinks it is new. However, this does not work for a favorite toy, object, or blanket. Babies never seem to forget favorite items.

Seeing Similarities and Differences

Babies often see the similar features of different toys. For example, when given a new book, the baby turns the pages rather than shaking it as a rattle. Babies who can find their eyes or nose can touch the same body parts on a doll or on another person.

Babies note differences, too. If a favorite toy is lost or needs cleaning or repair, babies rarely accept a duplicate. They quickly see small differences and reject the new one. Babies also notice differences or changes, particularly in familiar environments. If parents move a chair or add a new decoration, a baby will spot the change immediately.

Making Associations

Almost from birth, babies learn to make simple associations. This skill develops with time. When they hear the refrigerator door open, they expect feeding time to follow soon. When they hear the front door open, they expect to see a family member enter the room. When looking at books with parents or siblings, they associate the words they hear with the pictures they see.

Babies can make associations between objects and animals and their location. For example, when an infant hears the sound of an airplane outside, the baby may learn to point to the sky. Later, a parent may ask, "Where is the airplane?" The baby will point to the sky even when there is no airplane sound. Older infants can identify a bird with a nest, a fish in a fish tank, and a dog in a doghouse if they see these pictures in books.

Parents can encourage these associations by allowing their babies to watch or participate in everyday activities. Babies soon learn sponges are used with water, spoons are for stirring, ovens are hot, and refrigerators are cold.

Understanding Object Permanence

Object permanence occurs when an infant understands that people and objects still exist even when they cannot see, hear, or touch them. Piaget studied object permanence by seeing what babies would do when familiar people and objects disappeared. If babies showed no response, Piaget assumed they did not understand object permanence. If they looked surprised or searched for the missing person or object, they had beginning ideas of object permanence.

This concept develops very slowly. It requires memory for what is "out of sight." At 6 months, babies stare in the direction where objects disappear, such as at the door through which mother leaves. They will also find a partially hidden object, such as a stuffed animal that is covered except for its feet. Between 8 and 12 months, infants will search for fully hidden people and objects.

Learning by Imitation

Imitation is one of the most important mental skills. Much of what a person can do is learned by imitation. For example, people learn language, for the most part, by imitation.

Between 4 and 8 months, babies imitate behaviors they already know how to do. For example, if you smile, they smile. If you clap your hands, they, too, can clap, 13-14. However, if you wink, they just watch with fascination.

Between 8 and 12 months, babies try to imitate less familiar behaviors. For example, now if you wink, they may try it by simply closing both eyes. They are better at imitating a new action if they can see

13-14 Babies learn by imitation, such as playing "peek-a-boo."

themselves do it. For example, if you touch your index fingers together, they may be successful in imitating you.

Engaging in Problem Solving

As babies make further advances in intellectual development, they learn to solve simple problems. They will pull a string to bring a toy closer or shake a bell to make it ring. Through trial and error, babies learn they can make more noise banging on certain objects than on others. As babies empty and fill containers, toy boxes, and drawers, they learn the concepts of in, out, one, more than one, and "all gone."

Babies may use trial and error to solve their own problems. Parents can almost see their little minds working as they try to open a container or push chairs to use for climbing. Babies work intently until they get nesting toys to fit together. Feeling good about their achievements and seeking their parents' approval, they repeat their successful actions, especially if parents seem delighted.

In later months of infancy, a baby will pick up a toy with the preferred hand, transfer it to the other, and reach for another with the first hand. If the baby wants a third toy, he or she may hesitate for a while before finding a solution. The baby may solve the problem by resting the second toy in the crook of one arm while reaching for the third toy with the free hand. Problem-solving skills are signs of advancing intellectual development.

Playtime Means Learning

Learning and playing go hand-in-hand for babies. Babies play during their alert periods. As babies grow, their alert periods lengthen. They use this quiet, alert time to learn more about themselves and their surroundings.

From the beginning, babies are social beings. Babies share their most valuable and fun playtimes with others, especially parents and siblings, 13-15. However, babies will and should play alone at times under the watchful eyes of parents. Playing alone fosters a baby's self-concept and sense of independence. Young infants will likely play alone for only 5 minutes. Gradually, older infants may increase that time to 30 minutes.

Observant parents pick up cues from their baby. They sense when their baby wants active, tumbling play versus quiet, cuddling play. This varies according to the baby's mood and overall temperament. What is right for one baby may be wrong for another. By observing their baby's reactions, parents will know how much stimulation the baby needs. A baby needs enough stimulation to stay interested and attentive. However, too much stimulation will overwhelm a baby and cause withdrawal.

Patient parents slow down their actions to match their baby's timing. When they smile at their baby, they should wait several seconds, giving their baby time to smile back. When a baby is learning new skills, such as reaching and grasping, parents need to wait patiently for them to respond. This gives the baby time to succeed in new and difficult tasks. When a baby crawls after them, patient parents walk slowly so the baby does not feel frustrated and left behind.

13-15 Infants learn from their play. They love it when their older sisters and brothers play with them.

The Play Environment

Because of the baby's intellectual stage, the right environment is one that provides a variety of sights, sounds, smells, textures, and tastes. Babies need sensory and motor experiences both inside the home and outdoors. They need safe places to play without too many "no's."

Toys that are inviting and sturdy encourage babies to act on objects with safety and delight. Some toys come from household items, but many are usually bought. Toy stores offer a variety of playthings. Good options for developmentally appropriate baby toys include the following:

- *Infants from birth to 6 months*—mobiles, crib or floor gyms, rattles and other handheld grasping toys, squeeze toys, wrist or ankle bells, texture balls, washable stuffed animals or dolls (small), unbreakable household mirrors, and fill-and-spill toys

- *Infants 7 to 12 months*—baby handheld mirrors, play animals (vinyl or rubber), pop beads, squeeze and squeak toys, floating bath toys, cloth or rubber blocks, two- and three-piece puzzles, nesting cups and stacking rings, containers to fill and empty, push-pull toys, and books (cloth, plastic, or cardboard)

Babies love to interact and play games with parents, too. Cuddling, "talking" with, and saying favorite rhymes with actions ("This Little Piggy" and "Patty-Cake") are among their favorites. Sometimes having parents sit nearby is all the interaction babies want.

The Need for Quiet Time

Some good-intentioned parents overstimulate their babies. For example, some believe that good parenting involves interacting with babies every minute they are awake. Working parents face challenges, too. They pick up their overstimulated baby from a child care setting and then want to pack in lots of interaction time before the baby's bedtime. Although these parents may have good motives, babies, like adults, need some quiet time.

Due to the immaturity of their nervous systems and the newness of their worlds, babies can easily become overstimulated. Beyond naptime, babies need a few minutes of quiet time several times a day. Parents must learn to read the baby's cues. Typical cues for needing quiet time include thumb sucking or hair twisting, going off alone, or looking away while the parent is trying to interact. During quiet time, babies may watch from a high chair, babble to themselves in a crib, crawl under a table, study a toy or look at a book alone, ride in a stroller, or just stare into space. Parents should not interrupt their baby. Babies will send very clear signals when quiet time is over.

Language

Babies are born into a social group—a family. Communication is basic to social relationships. Communication allows family members to express thoughts, feelings, and desires. Parents and their babies must develop a social dialogue.

Nonverbal Communication

Babies "talk" much more than you may think, but in nonverbal ways. Just as a baby's cries have different meanings, the baby's gaze communicates how he or she feels during a parent-child interaction, 13-16. Besides cries and gazes, facial expressions, which are like adult's expressions for similar feelings, send messages. Soon, babies learn to add appropriate gestures. They shake their heads when they say no. They wave their hands when they say bye-bye.

Babies become great imitators of gestures and sounds. They imitate coughs, tongue clicks, and kisses. They imitate tones of speech and inflections. They "sing" along with songs they hear, whether the parents are singing or a tune is playing on the radio or TV.

Verbal Communication

Babies make their first deliberate sounds at about 6 to 8 weeks. They begin cooing. **Cooing** is making one-syllable, vowel-like sounds, such as *ooh, ah,* and *aw.* Soon they practice talking. When they hear a voice, they respond by smiling and making sounds. They imitate the natural rhythm of conversations by pausing, waiting for the

The Baby's Gaze "Talks"

The Gaze	The Meaning
Face-to-face but sober	"I'm interested!"
Face-to-face with smile	"I'm pleased!"
Head is turned a little toward the side	"I'm interested, but you are playing too fast or too slow for me."
Head rapidly turns away	"I don't like this! Take it away!"
Head turned away, lowered, or tipped upward	"I'm not interested!"

13-16 Parents can understand their baby's gaze.

other person to speak. They listen until the person stops talking, and then make more sounds. Babies practice this kind of speech even when they are alone.

At 4 or 5 months, babies add their first consonant sounds to their speech (usually *p, b, m,* and *l*). These sounds are more like words. Something like *ma* may be heard, but at this point, the sound is not meant as a name. This repeated vocalizing is called **babbling**. Soon, it becomes a favorite activity. Babies babble a lot to themselves and even more in response to their parents' words.

At about 5 months, babies show intense interest in watching their parents' mouths move. It may seem they are studying the mechanics of talking. They can recognize people by their voices. By 6 months, they know their own names.

Generally, babies babble when they are happy. When they are upset, they are more likely to cry, wail, whimper, or fuss. Parents can reinforce conversation as a pleasant social exchange by responding happily to their babies' sounds. Conversations mean the most to babies when parents talk directly to them and make eye contact. Gradually, babies add more consonants to their vocabularies, such as *f, v, th, s, sh, z,* and *d*. They form two-syllable sounds by repeating their one-syllable words. They are excited about their new words and may make each one sound like an exclamation. Babies eventually make sounds like *mama* and *dada,* much to their parents' delight.

Next babies put together a long series of syllables such as: *ba-ba-ba-ba.* Before long, they will learn to string different syllables together such as: *ba-la-shoo-dee-sa.* This high-level babbling becomes so fluid it sounds like a new language. With different inflections, babies seem to ask questions, state facts, make exclamations, and tell funny stories.

Once babbling starts, parents encourage their babies to repeat sounds, such as mama and dada, and make associations with people or objects. In a month or so, babies make the association and start using those words as names. As early as 9 months, babies learn the meaning of a few specific words, such as *no*. They show their understanding by responding appropriately. They may repeat a word endlessly when they first learn it, making it a response to every question. Babies try to imitate any sound they hear, so parents will want to watch what they say. Babies repeat inappropriate words just as easily as other words.

Near the end of infancy, babies realize that particular sounds or words refer to certain people or objects. Parents can help them learn the meaning of words by using labeling words, as in this example: "Where did the ball go? Here is the ball. Here are Jimmy's socks. Let's put the socks on Jimmy's feet." Labeling words help babies learn to associate words with people or objects.

Social and Emotional Development

Social and emotional development relate closely. Social development is the process of learning to relate to people. Emotions reflect the outcomes of these social interactions and sometimes express a need. Through loving relationships with parents and others, infants develop a flexible personality and self-control.

Babies Interact Socially

The main social interactions of infants are with their parents and other caregivers, 13-17. Newborns interact with people by listening to their voices and trying to focus on their faces. They are especially sensitive to touch and will stop crying when they are held.

Soon babies become quiet when they see faces, and they try to make eye contact. By the time babies are 2 months of age, they can have give-and-take interactions with their parents. For example, when babies are

13-17 Infants mainly socialize with their parents and caregivers.

in distress, they cry. Parents respond to their needs, and babies are soothed. Babies' stares and smiles intrigue parents, who respond by giving them more time and attention.

Babies like this attention and become more responsive by 3 months of age. They smile spontaneously when someone plays with them. They experiment with different sounds and facial expressions. When they are pleased, they smile and chuckle with delight. When they are uncertain, infants look puzzled and make questioning sounds.

Between 3 and 4 months, babies have learned how to start social interactions with their parents. First, they look around the room to see if their parents are nearby. Then they make cooing sounds to capture the parents' attention. Next they fuss until the parents come. Finally they arch their backs and reach out their arms to be held. Even without words, their message is clear.

Babies often learn to play little games with their siblings. Babies soon start showing a sense of humor. They may giggle while playing with their siblings. They may repeat an action that causes their parents to laugh. They will wait for their parents to laugh and then start laughing themselves.

Toward the end of infancy, babies will imitate certain social behaviors, such as waving and blowing kisses. Until babies are preschoolers, they do not fully understand what these gestures mean. However, they are taking parents' cues on how to socialize.

Attachment in Parent-Child Relationships

All people are social beings who need and want some degree of closeness with others. As you recall, *attachment* is a relationship between two people who feel a strong emotional bond. This feeling causes attached people to form an emotional bond.

During infancy, social development becomes mature enough for babies to develop their first attachment. The attachment bond forms between babies and their parents and/or other main caregivers, 13-18. This bond often intensifies during the first year.

Parents' Role in Attachment

Attachment is not automatic. Parents have to pursue their baby for attachment to occur. How do they do this? They do this through unconditional love. Such love says to the baby, "I am valued." Babies, in turn, develop a sense of their own lovability—the beginning of self-esteem. Attachment also develops when parents are sensitive to the baby's needs and meet those needs appropriately. Babies come to see the dependability of their parents.

Attachment is key in developing a sense of basic trust. Trusting babies slowly, but surely, fall in love with their loving and responsive parents. This growing love is seen in the following ways during this first year:

- Around 4 or 5 months of age, babies prefer parents or other main caregivers. Babies smile at parents and act restless around others.

- By 7 months, babies want to have physical contact with parents. Babies are disturbed when parents are not nearby.

13-18 Attachment is important to early parent-child relationships.

Babies can develop attachment to both parents and even to another main caregiver. The relationship with each person determines the strength of the attachment. Babies have to sense love and caring before attachment takes place.

Signs of Attachment

Not all babies show the same degree of attachment because of different temperaments and needs. Parents, too, differ in how well they establish a loving and consistent world for their babies. Parents can observe signs of attachment in everyday life. Babies who securely attach to their parents

- are able to explore toys in a room when parent is present

- show concern or become upset when left with a stranger in a room

- do not go to a stranger for comfort and may show relief when the stranger departs

- return to play and are happy when the parent returns

Stranger Anxiety

Stranger anxiety, or fear of strangers, relates to attachment. For attachment to occur, babies must be able to tell the difference between parents and caregivers. Stranger anxiety begins around 5 to 6 months of age. Babies begin to realize they are separate individuals. With this new awareness, babies can now tell which people are not their parents. The result is they become more sensitive to strangers.

At this stage, babies who at first would smile at extended family members and at their parents' friends may turn away, fuss, and/or cry, 13-19. Interestingly, babies are only afraid of adults or older children, not other babies or young children. The fear grows throughout infancy, peaking in 8- to 12-month-olds.

As a kindness to babies at this stage, parents should try to prepare them for visits to strange places. Babies need time to adjust to a new setting. On arrival, parents should cuddle their babies and let them look at the people and surroundings. Parents may warn relatives not to approach or look at the babies right away. Eye contact with strangers can frighten babies. Gradually, the babies will relax. Their curiosity may overcome their anxiety.

Separation Anxiety

Babies who have a strong attachment to their parents become afraid of abandonment by 7 months. Infants try to stay with their parents at all times. **Separation anxiety** is a fear that occurs when babies can't see their parents. Babies may become uneasy or panic-stricken.

Separation anxiety can be frustrating for parents. At this stage, babies turn away from almost everyone except their parents. They will crawl wherever the parents go, if at all possible. They interrupt conversations, trying to demand parents' full attention. If parents hold another baby, their own baby will jealously try to push the other baby away and reclaim parental affection.

If parents temporarily disappear from sight, babies feel lost and helpless. They need the security their parents represent. If parents resist their attempts to stay nearby, babies will become more anxious and clingy. The best way to promote later independence is to let babies cling at this stage.

Because separation anxiety is so great at this time, parents should make preparations for emergencies. Babies should become familiar with at least one other caregiver. A close friend, relative, or neighbor is a good choice. In an emergency, babies are more comfortable with a familiar face than with a stranger.

Parents should not sneak away while babies are busy playing. Sneaking away just makes babies watch them even more closely. Instead, parents should warn the babies with a signal phrase such as, "Bye-bye for now." Then they should announce their return with another signal phrase such as, "I'm here

Importance of Attachment

Babies who develop a secure attachment have major benefits in all areas of development. Some of the long-term benefits of attachment include

- aiding the development of a sense of trust
- having a secure base for comfort in times of stress
- having a source of stimulation and joy
- fostering curiosity about the world and promoting confidence to deal with novel situations
- aiding the ability to cope with failure
- promoting the development of communication
- having a reliable model for other social relations

13-19 With stranger anxiety, babies may fuss and cry when confronted with unknown adults and older children.

again." If babies see their parents putting on their coats to leave, they may start fussing. Parents should cuddle their babies rather than scold them for such behavior.

Babies Express Emotions

Babies express emotions to communicate what they need. For example, crying might mean "feed me." Babies also express emotions to regulate social distance, such as a smile that means "come closer." Early emotions are often intense and seem to be tied to specific events. The following major emotions are expressed in the first year:

- *Happiness.* Babies begin smiling around 1 month of age and smile at almost anyone and anything, 13-20. When parents touch or tickle them in playful ways, 3- or 4-month-old babies laugh. By 5 or 6 months of age, babies smile at known people and laugh during social games. They can even screech in delight!

- *Anger.* As early as 2 months of age, babies cry angrily at being restrained or when hurt. By 7 months, babies show anger when left in the care of an adult other than the parent or the main caregiver. Some older babies show frustration and anger when unable to reach a goal, such as a toy that does not work for them.

- *Sadness.* Babies can show sadness in response to pain or separation. However, anger is a more common way for babies to react to these events.

- *Fear and anxiety.* Although newborns have a startle reflex, real fear begins to occur around 5 to 6 months of age. Babies become wary of unfamiliar people, but only show intense fear if alone when an adult stranger approaches. Attached babies show separation anxiety, too.

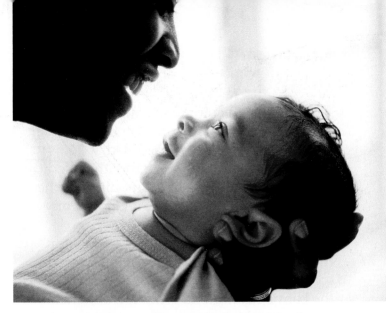

13-20 Babies begin smiling at about 1 month of age.

As infants become more mobile and aware of their surroundings, they may develop new fears. For example, they may be afraid to climb down from chairs in which they used to enjoy playing. Loud noises may frighten babies. Some infants, due to temperament, show stress to any novelty, including some toys.

Parents should enjoy their baby's positive emotions by joining in the baby's delight. For negative emotions, parents can increase their babies' emotional security by giving appropriate comfort and encouragement. Parents who are alert to their babies' cues know how to best respond and help their babies develop. When babies are startled, a hug may be all they need.

Parenting Concerns and Tasks

A baby's needs change rapidly during the first year. The first six months involve providing care and safety for the baby. In the later half of the year, parents add intellectual and social stimulation to their nurturing tasks.

Medical Checkups for Infants

The AAP recommends taking infants to their doctors five times during the first year. These visits should be scheduled at 2 to 4 weeks, and at 2, 4, 6, and 12 months. Medical checkups are important for monitoring the baby's health. The doctor can identify any problems and treat them early.

During medical checkups, the doctor thoroughly examines the baby's physical condition and recommends any tests to check the baby's health. The growth check includes measuring the baby's height, weight, and head size. The doctor also examines the eyes and ears. If there is cause for concern, vision and hearing screenings may be given. At this time, parents can also ask any questions they might have about the baby's health, nutrition, sleeping, and growth.

The doctor also gives parents an immunization schedule for their child's checkups. **Immunizations** are treatments that prevent people from developing certain diseases. A treatment may be given as an injection of a vaccine or an oral medicine. Children need various immunizations from infancy through the school-age years. These treatments protect them from serious illnesses. See Appendix C for a schedule of immunizations recommended by the Centers for Disease Control. Some require several doses over a period of time before a person is immune. Doctors record each vaccine and the date given. This is an important part of a person's medical records. Children cannot start school without the proper immunizations. Parents should keep a record, too.

Adjusting to Infants' Changing Needs

Infancy is a challenging period. Although babies are different, they are also alike. Typical infant behaviors cause common concerns among parents. Parents must cope with these concerns by making personal adjustments. Much of their focus is directly on the realities of parenthood. These new realities influence parenting now and in the future.

Scheduling

By 3 months, most babies establish a predictable daily pattern of eating, sleeping, and being alert. Now is the time to follow a baby's cues and schedule the family's day. Most babies like a routine because they know what will happen next. Parents also feel more in control of their days if they have a regular schedule.

To make a schedule work, it is important not to change a baby's eating and sleeping times. Except in emergencies, parents should schedule errands and other activities around the baby's needs. Parents should also put their schedules aside when the baby is overtired, cranky, or ill.

Soothing Baby's Emotions

The best way parents can soothe their baby is to respond to his or her needs. Parents cannot spoil their baby. During infancy, babies don't have wants—they mainly have needs. They need social contact to help them grow and develop. Because infants are not capable of using logic or reason to solve problems, they need help. Infants need attention, but they are not selfish or demanding. They simply are not capable of considering someone else's viewpoint.

When babies can trust their parents to answer their calls, they tend to be more flexible. Babies whose babbling, calls, and cries are ignored become anxious and demanding. They cannot build trust in their environment.

Babies begin self-soothing around 7 months old. Parents need to listen to their baby's cry. If the cry tapers off, parents should not respond immediately. If the cry intensifies, parents should respond. Babies can self-soothe by

- seeing the parent with a relaxed facial expression.

- playing with their hands or feet.

- playing with a crib toy as they fall asleep or first awaken.

- sucking on a pacifier. Most experts say to wean from the pacifier no later than 9 months of age.

- having a favorite toy nearby. When babies feel loved and secure, they can extend their interests beyond themselves. When they reach out to their special toy, they are taking their first steps away from depending on their parents for comfort. These are also their first steps toward independence, 13-21.

Setting Limits

With consistent and prompt care, babies attach to their parents. Attached children are willing to accept their parents' rules. However, during the first year, behavior limits mainly keep babies safe. "Baby proofing" the home and creating an engaging environment encourage positive behaviors.

By 12 months, babies may bite, hit, or poke people or animals, throw food, grab forbidden objects, or try unsafe activities. After seeing their parents' disapproval, babies know the difference between positive and negative behavior. When they know they have been good, babies seek their parents' approval. When they know a behavior is off-limits, babies may turn away from their parents.

At this time, babies also learn the meaning of *no*. They may shake their heads and say no to everything—even when they mean *yes*. Babies may try new tricks that get them into trouble, such as turning on the TV or radio. Babies often give themselves away by looking at their parents with guilty expressions before starting another off-limit behavior.

13-21 Babies form attachments to special objects and learn to play independently.

When parents face challenging infant behaviors, they should avoid overreacting. A better solution is to redirect their babies to a more acceptable activity. When parents offer alternatives, babies quickly abandon negative behaviors. If parents do not offer a different activity, babies often repeat the negative behavior. When parents reserve a sharp *no* for important times, such as a safety threat, babies will be more apt to listen. If parents overuse the word *no*, babies tune it out. Babies do test their parents, but need to learn that *no* means *no*.

Worrying About Slow Development

Parents often worry about whether their babies are developing normally. The normal range for reaching developmental milestones in infancy varies greatly. Why do babies reach developmental milestones at such different ages? Some of the reasons include

- *environmental differences.* Babies progress faster when the stimulation meets their needs—not too little or too much.

- *presence of siblings.* Babies often push themselves to keep up with slightly older siblings. Much older siblings may slow milestones if they help babies too much or too often.

- *amount of practice babies get.* For example, practice affects motor skills. Parents need to give young babies daily "tummy time" when awake or gross-motor skills will develop slowly.

- *temperament of babies.* High-energy babies and easily frustrated babies push themselves to achieve. More mellow babies sit back and watch; thus, their progress may be slower.

- *physical well-being and maturity of babies.* Babies with weaker muscle tone and overweight babies are slower to reach gross-motor milestones. During their first 30 months, premature babies often lag behind full-term babies. Vision, hearing, and intelligence problems can slow development, too.

- *dealing with too much at one time.* Family stress or their own illnesses can cause babies to regress or not move developmentally forward. Competing developmental skills cause delays, too. For example, walking may be more important to an infant than talking.

Developmental progress is more important than reaching milestones. Babies should be doing a little more each week. Parents should watch for possible signs of serious problems, 13-22. The earlier problems are found, the better the treatment results.

Making Family-Life Adjustments

Babies create major changes within their family system. Parents have to make adjustments to meet their baby's ever-changing needs. Because family life is unique, parents have to determine just what works for them.

Indicators of Developmental Problems

- Delay is noted in more than one area of development, such as motor and language.
- Delay is 2 or more months from the norm.
- Baby does not seem to respond to a hearing check (at 3 months), or a vision check (at 6 months).

13-22 Parents should consult their baby's doctor if they suspect a developmental problem.

Keeping Babies Safe

Parents must closely watch their infants and remove any potentially harmful objects from their reach. As their fine-motor skills improve, babies become better at such skills as uncovering containers and opening doors. Nothing is safe from a mobile baby.

By their first birthdays, babies can be very challenging. Parents can make this first year safe by recognizing dangers and following good safety practices. For example, they should make electrical cords inaccessible and insert outlet covers in unused outlets. In addition, parents should close doors or use child safety gates to protect children from danger, 13-23.

Returning to Work and Staying Organized

About 53 percent of mothers return to work when their babies are infants. When mothers work, more changes occur in the family system. All working parents have more daily responsibilities. Most will have to meet their tasks on a fixed schedule. Organization helps parents meet tasks more effectively and quickly. Some very basic ways to get organized include

- using a family calendar with all appointments and activities that affect the family

- keeping "to do" lists updated
- keeping a running list of purchase needs
- running errands during the work lunch-break if time permits (spouses should split errands when possible)
- keeping the home free of clutter
- getting things ready the night before, such as packing items going to child care, getting out clothes for each family member, making lunches for the next day, and setting the breakfast table
- preparing the work area for the next day's tasks before leaving the work site

Finding Quality Child Care

About 23 percent of all babies less than 1 year of age are in child care programs. Locating a quality program for their baby is a major problem for parents. Quality infant programs are difficult to find. Many people who work in child care programs have training and experience working with 3- to 5-year-olds. They may have little experience with infant care. Quality infant programs are much more expensive than programs for older children. One reason is a quality infant program requires a greater number of caregivers. The recommended infant/staff ratio is 3:1, with a maximum group size of six infants.

Before going back to work, parents should help their baby adjust to infant care. Because older babies experience stranger anxiety and separation anxiety, parents should consider enrolling babies earlier. Babies less than 6 months of age usually adjust easier. Attending a program for several weeks helps smooth the baby's transition when parents go back to work. Parents must also consider alternative care when their baby is ill or when a child care program is closed.

13-23 Safety must be a constant concern of parents.

Special Family Times

Each family has its own traditions. Many rituals begin during the infancy years. Some of these transitions come from the extended family, but others are unique to the new family. Babies enjoy little daily rituals. They make day-to-day life more consistent and delightful.

Rituals for babies might include special songs, rhymes, or games. Babies like rituals with each parent and both parents together. Some early rituals, such as reading bedtime stories, continue as children get older.

Parents often enjoy recording their babies' activities and milestones in words, photos, and audio/visual recordings. Busy parents can date and keep these treasures in a file until they can transfer them to a baby book and/or family album. When children are older, they can see how they looked and what they did as babies. These records show older children how much their parents love them. Each family member enjoys having memories to treasure.

2 Months*

Physical Development
Gross-Motor Skills

Can keep head in midposition of body when lying on tummy

Can hold head up for a few seconds when lying on tummy

Can turn head when lying on back

Cycles arms and legs smoothly

May roll from tummy to side

Fine-Motor Skills

Grasps objects in reflex movements

May hold object longer but still drops object after a few seconds

Uses improved vision to look at objects more closely and for a longer time

Intellectual Development
General

Coordinates eye movements

Is better able to follow moving objects with eyes

Shows obvious preference of faces to objects

Is clearly able to discriminate between voices

Associates certain behaviors with certain people (such as mother with feeding)

Language

Makes some sounds but most vocalizing is still crying

Shows interest in sounds and will stop sucking to listen

Social and Emotional Development
Social

Smiles spontaneously and fleetingly to sensory stimulation from parent

Looks at person alertly and directly

Quiets in response to being held, seeing human face, or hearing voice

Shows affection by looking at a person while kicking, waving arms, and smiling

Emotional

Is able to show distress, excitement, contentment, and delight

Can quiet self by sucking

3 Months

Physical Development
Gross-Motor Skills

Switches from reflexive to voluntary body movements

Keeps head in midposition so posture is symmetrical when lying on back

Moves arm and leg on one side of body in unison, then moves the other arm and leg in unison

Can move arms together or legs together

Turns head vigorously

Can hold chest up and keep head erect for a few seconds when lying on tummy

Can hold head erect for several minutes

Can sit briefly with support

Fine-Motor Skills

Keeps hands open most of the time. The grasp reflex is fading

Explores hands

Begins to control arm and hand movements

Begins to swipe at objects, such as a cradle gym. May accidentally hit object with fist

Intellectual Development
General

Is attentive for as long as 45 minutes at a time

Shows memory by waiting for anticipated feeding

Recognizes family members and familiar objects and sounds

Likes to look at a variety of objects since vision has improved

Is able to suck and look at the same time (thus doing two controlled actions at once)

Follows slow, side-to-side movements of objects with eyes

Language

Begins cooing one-syllable, vowel-like sounds—*ooh, ah, aw*

Practices talking by making sounds, pausing, and making more sounds in a conversational rhythm

Social and Emotional Development
Social

Uses sounds and facial expressions to communicate

Smiles spontaneously when parent plays with him or her

Recognizes all others as separate people

Responds with total body to familiar face

May stop or start crying if a certain person holds him or her

Tries to attract parents' attention

Emotional

Shows feelings of security when parent holds and talks to him or her

Whimpers when hungry, chortles when content

* These charts are not exact timetables. Individuals may perform certain activities earlier or later than indicated in the charts.

Infant Development

4 Months

Physical Development

Gross-Motor Skills

Can rock on tummy with arms and legs extended like an airplane with back arched

On tummy, can lift head and chest from surface using arms for support

On tummy, can roll from side to side and may accidentally roll to back

Can maintain a sitting position (with head erect and steady) for several minutes if given proper support

Fine-Motor Skills

Uses hands more skillfully

Begins to use mitten grasp for grabbing objects

Looks from object to hand to object in order to make contact

Swipes at objects, gradually improving aim

Intellectual Development

General

Is alert for as long as an hour at a time

Is aware of different distances of objects when grasping

Likes to repeat enjoyable acts, like shaking a rattle

Is able to discriminate among faces and may resent a strange face

Shows interest in details of objects, such as shape, size, and texture

Begins to imitate others, such as smile in response to a smile

Begins to see a connection between actions (shaking a rattle) and results (sound or movement)

Language

Makes first consonant sounds— *p, b, m, l*

Is able to babble strings of syllable-like sounds as if talking

Smiles and coos when parent talks to him or her

Prefers to babble when parent responds

Social and Emotional Development

Social

Recognizes others, especially mother, as separate from himself or herself

Shows increased pleasure in social interactions; may laugh

Responds to and enjoys being handled and cuddled

May babble and make sounds to imitate socializing.

Enjoys social aspect of feeding times

Becomes more sensitive to strangers

Becomes unresponsive if left alone most of waking hours

Emotional

Still depends on positive stimulation for feelings of security

Responds to continued warmth and affection

5 Months

Physical Development
Gross-Motor Skills

May roll from tummy to back accidentally

On tummy, lifts head and chest high off surface

Can rock, twist, roll, and kick to change position on surface while on tummy

Begins to use crawling (tummy on surface) movements and may move a couple of feet

When supported under arms, stands and moves body up and down, stamping feet alternately

Helps when being pulled to a sitting position

Can sit supported for 15 to 30 minutes with firm back

In sitting position, keeps head steady and erect

Explores feet

Fine-Motor Skills

Reaches for objects, such as the cradle gym, with good coordination and aim

Begins to grasp objects with thumb and fingers

Grasps objects with either hand

Transfers objects from one hand to the other, dropping objects often

Can grasp cover to pull it off when face is covered in peek-a-boo game

Intellectual Development
General

Is alert for as long as an hour and a half at a time

Can anticipate whole object when only part of object is visible

Explores objects intently, especially by mouthing

Knows how to repeat actions to get the same results; this leads to verification of how things work

Learns new actions almost daily

Language

Watches parents' mouths as they talk and experiments with own sounds

Understands own name

Can recognize people by their voices

Social and Emotional Development
Social

Smiles and babbles to initiate social contact

Shows anticipation when near people, especially parents

Emotional

Senses self as being separate from parent

Distinguishes between familiar and unfamiliar adults

Smiles at self in mirror (but doesn't see the baby as self)

Smiles at known people and stares solemnly at strangers

Builds trust when cries are answered; grows anxious and demanding when cries are unanswered

6 Months

Physical Development
Gross-Motor Skills

Rolls from back to tummy on purpose

Turns and twists in all directions when on back or tummy

Crawls with ease and covers lots of distance

Gets on hands and knees (creeping position); often rocks in this position; may fall forward

Is able to stand while supported

Sits with slight support and maintains balance

Is able to lean forward or to side while in sitting position

Is able to sit in high chair and use arms to reach for objects

If unsupported in sitting position, may slump forward on hands for balance

May be able to sit unsupported for short periods of time

Fine-Motor Skills

Is able to rotate wrist to turn and manipulate objects

Reaches with one arm and grasps object with hand; then transfers object to other hand; then reaches for another object

Holds an object in each hand

Learns to drop objects at will

Puts things in mouth

Intellectual Development
General

Is alert for as long as two hours at a time

Sees differences in shapes

Studies objects intently, turning them to see all sides

Learns that objects do not disappear when they are dropped; they simply fall to the floor

Develops preferences in toys, pictures, and activities

Language

Makes more consonant sound

Repeats sounds to make two-syllable "words"

Reacts appropriately to various tones of voice

Varies volume, pitch, and rate while babbling

Responds to name

Makes sounds when examining objects

Social and Emotional Development
Social

Laughs when socializing

Enjoys playing cooperative games with parents and siblings

Desires constant attention from parent

Prefers familiar adults and shows resistance toward unfamiliar adults

Emotional

Senses adults are different from children; enjoys playing with children

Responds to affection and may initiate signs of affection

Likes attention and may cry to get it

Prefers familiar adults and shows resistance toward unfamiliar adults

Calls parents for help and trusts them to respond

7 Months

Physical Development

Gross-Motor Skills

Creeps awkwardly; combines crawling and creeping when in a hurry

When pulled to a standing position, helps by keeping legs straight and supporting own weight

Likes to bounce when in standing position

May try to pull self to a standing position

Is able to sit alone for several minutes or with slight support for longer periods of time

Can lean over and reach while in sitting position

May be able to move from a lying position to a sitting position

Fine-Motor Skills

Has mastered grasping by using thumb in opposition to fingers

Holds an object in each hand

Brings objects together with banging noises

Keeps objects in hands much of the time

Fingers, manipulates, and rattles objects repeatedly

Intellectual Development

General

Begins making associations between an object and where it is located or the sound it makes

Begins seeing associations between objects and their uses, such as books are for turning pages and a pot or pan is for making a loud sound

Responds with expectation to repetition of an event

Sees differences in similar objects, such as a "lovey" bear and a new bear

May imitate a new action

Enjoys looking through books with familiar pictures

May be able to play "peek-a-boo"

May play "hide-and-seek" with a partially hidden object

Language

May have favorite, well-defined syllables

Imitates sounds, tones of speech, and inflections

"Sings" along with music

May say *mama* or *dada* but does not connect with parents

Social and Emotional Development

Social

Shows desire to be included in social interactions

May be responsive to other persons but is clearly attached to parent

Thoroughly enjoys company of siblings

Begins to develop sense of humor, teases

Emotional

May show more dependence on parents for security

Protests separation by crying or looking anxious

May show frustration when restrained, such as during dressing

May fear performing some familiar activities

8 Months

Physical Development

Gross-Motor Skills

Sits alone steadily for longer periods of time

Pushes easily into a creeping position from tummy

Often creeps with ease

May carry objects in one hand or both hands while creeping

Is able to pull self to a standing position by holding onto crib or furniture

May need help getting down from standing position

Achieves sitting position by pushing up with arms

Fine-Motor Skills

Learns pincer grasp, using just the thumb and forefinger

Is able to pick up small objects and string

Intellectual Development

General

Learns to solve simple problems

Likes to empty and fill containers, meanwhile learning concepts such as in, out, and "all gone"

Has short-term memory; remembers past events and past actions in his or her immediate world

Notices changes in the whole scene, such as a cup left on a table

Begins to understand cause and effect

Searches for a hidden object

Language

Begins putting together a long series of syllables

Uses different inflections when babbling

May label object in imitation of its sounds, such as *choo-choo* for train

Begins to recognize some words

Social and Emotional Development

Social

Definitely prefers parents to strangers

Is more aware of social approval and disapproval from family members

May cling to parent if taken to a strange place

Sustains interest in play, especially when playing with family member

Emotional

Exhibits fear of strangers

May develop separation anxiety and need constant reassurance of parent's presence

Wants to be held by parent when with strangers

May anticipate being left and become disturbed

Values quick display of support and love from parent

Likes to explore new spaces but wants to be able to return to parent

Enjoys playing with own image in mirror

9 Months

Physical Development
Gross-Motor Skills

Sits alone

Develops own locomotor style, such as, crawls, rolls, or creeps

May try to crawl up stairs

May be able to achieve a standing position without holding onto furniture

Is able to move from a standing position to a sitting position

May be able to move along furniture, touching it for support (cruising)

Fine-Motor Skills

Uses index finger to point, lead, and poke

May be able to build a tower of two blocks

Waves hands to say goodbye

Intellectual Development
General

Sees differences in size of objects; approaches small objects with hands open and large objects with arms spread

Sees depth—how far it is to the floor or ground

Tries more than one way to achieve a goal

Language

Responds appropriately to a few specific words

Says a few words and adds appropriate gestures

Says *mama* and *dada* as specific names

May follow simple directions

Social and Emotional Development
Social

Shows interest in play activities of others

Likes to play games like pat-a-cake with siblings

Recognizes the social nature of mealtimes

May be more sensitive to other children

Emotional

Shows new fears, such as fear of heights

Needs appropriate comfort and reinforcement during this stage

May begin to protect self and possessions

10 Months

Physical Development
Gross-Motor Skills

Achieves goals by using the appropriate skill, such as standing to reach a toy on the table

Steps sideways along furniture in cruising motion

Likes to walk holding onto parents' hands

Climbs on chairs and other furniture

Stands with little support

Fine-Motor Skills

Can hold an object in one hand and manipulate it with the other

Carries two small objects in one hand

Can release grasped object instead of just dropping it

Intellectual Development
General

Is able to play games involving object permanence

Will search to find hidden objects

Likes to open containers and look at their contents

Imitates behaviors in greater detail

Language

Learns more words and appropriate gestures

May repeat one word endlessly

Likes to listen to familiar words and songs

Understands and obeys simple words and commands

Social and Emotional Development
Social

Likes to play with siblings

Mimics others' play behaviors, such as hugging a "lovey" or moving to music

Likes to perform for family audiences; may repeat acts if applauded

Will not show off in unfamiliar surroundings

Emotional

Cries less often

Shows emotions other, more specific ways

Expresses delight, happiness, sadness, discomfort, and anger

11 Months

Physical Development
Gross-Motor Skills

Still creeps or cruises to reach parents fast

Stands alone

Uses support while standing and gesturing, leaning, or picking up an object

May push chair ahead of self for support while walking

Is able to squat and stoop

Likes to climb stairs

May be able to climb out of crib or playpen

Fine-Motor Skills

Uses hands together and separately

Likes to grab spoon and cup and bring to mouth in feeding attempt

Likes to squish foods in hands

Takes off shoes and socks

Intellectual Development
General

Shows increased individuality in interests and abilities

Likes to grab spoon and cup and bring to mouth in feeding attempt

Learns to make many kinds of associations

Becomes even more skilled in imitation

Knows the meaning of the word *no* but may disregard it

Likes to look at pictures in books

Language

Still uses babbling, but includes some meaningful words

Recognizes words as symbols for objects

Social and Emotional Development
Social

Seeks approval and tries to avoid disapproval

Imitates movements of other children and adults

Likes to say *no* and shake head to get a response from a parent

Tests parents to determine limits

Objects to having his or her enjoyable play stopped

Emotional

May not always want to be cooperative

Recognizes difference between being good and being naughty

May say *no* while shaking head, but will continue to do forbidden deed

12 Months

Physical Development
Gross-Motor Skills

May still prefer crawling to walking for speed but uses both

May back up or carry toys while cruising

May take steps to parent, falling into arms when reaching parent

Climbs in and out of playpen and crib

Climbs up and down stairs

In tub, makes swimming movements in water

Fine-Motor Skills

Masters pincer grasp

May show preference for one hand

May be able to pull off clothing

Can take lids off containers

Intellectual Development
General

Solves simple problems

Sets goal and takes action to achieve goal, as in pushing a chair in place to use for climbing

Puts nesting toys together correctly

May search for lost toys in more than one place

Can carry three objects

Language

Understands many words said by others

May have vocabulary of several words

Says words that imitate sounds of animal and objects, such as *bow-wow* for dog

Social and Emotional Development
Social

Enjoys playing, especially with siblings

Reacts to separation but may know it is temporary

Continues to test parental limits

Gives hugs and kisses to family and "lovey"

Emotional

Fears hurts from accidents

Begins to develop self-identity and independence

Shows increased negativism

Summing It Up

- During the first 12 months of life, physical development involves growing in height and weight and learning muscle control and coordination.

- Gross-motor skills require use of the body's large muscles. Fine-motor skills require the use of small muscles and eye-hand coordination.

- When introducing solid foods and weaning infants, parents should follow their doctor's recommendations and watch their baby's hunger and fullness cues.

- Teething follows a predictable pattern among babies, but the timing varies. Dental care is important, even in infancy.

- A baby's brain grows rapidly during the first year. Parents can do much to encourage or hinder brain development.

- Babies learn about the world through using all five senses: seeing, hearing, feeling, smelling, and tasting.

- According to Piaget, infants learn to repeat body actions that allow them to explore and act on objects.

- Many intellectual skills start developing in infancy.

- Babies learn through play. Parents can make the most of playtimes by being observant, patient, and creative.

- It takes babies a few years to learn to talk, but they can communicate nonverbally from birth.

- Attachment is essential in developing a parent-child relationship.

- Babies need regular medical checkups and immunizations.

- Parents have many concerns and adjustments during the baby's first year.

Recalling the Facts

1. How do infants change in weight and height at 6 months and at 12 months?

2. What are the principles of growth and development?

3. What is the difference between gross-motor skills and fine-motor skills? Give an example of each type of development during the first year.

4. Contrast a mitten grasp with a pincer grasp.

5. At about what age should parents introduce solid food into a baby's diet?

6. How can parents tell when weaning is complete?

7. Name two ways to relieve teething pain.

8. Name two ways parents can influence brain development.

9. What Piagetian substages relate to how babies learn?

10. What intellectual skill do infants need to play the peek-a-boo game?

11. What do babies learn by emptying and filling containers?

12. What is the major difference between *cooing* and *babbling*?

13. What is the difference between *stranger anxiety* and *separation anxiety*?

14. Why are immunizations important?

15. Name two ways that parents can set behavior limits for their babies.

Applying New Skills

1. **Interview.** Ask a parent to describe problems they had with their infant when establishing sleep patterns, teething, weaning, stranger anxiety, separation anxiety, or introducing solid foods. How did they solve these problems?

2. **Brain research.** In a small group, research brain development in infancy, especially *windows of opportunity*. Propose ways that parents can stimulate their baby's brain development. Create a PowerPoint® presentation on your research and share it with the rest of the class.

3. **Play environments.** Assume a couple you know has a 4-month-old infant. They want you to help choose toys for their baby's first year. They have a budget of $125.00. What toys would you choose? Use Internet or print resources to find examples and prices. Share your findings with the class.

4. **Analyzing infant care.** Visit a child care program for infants. Describe the program. Then answer the following: If you were the parent of an infant, would you want to enroll your baby? Why or why not?

Thinking Critically

1. In a small group, discuss how the types of development (physical, intellectual, emotional, and social) are interrelated. Draw conclusions about their implications for parents.

2. Propose ways parents can make the most of their infant's playtimes by being observant, patient, and creative.

3. Do you agree or disagree with the following statement: An infant's playtime should be devoted to learning. Give reasons supporting your position.

Linking Academics

1. **Quick write.** In 12 sentences or less, summarize when and how to introduce solid foods to infants.

2. **Writing.** Write a brief summary of how each of the following physical advances creates new safety and care concerns for parents: (A) rolling over, (B) sitting up, (C) crawling, (D) standing, and (E) walking.

3. **Science.** Use Internet or print resources to investigate the pros and cons of music CDs and videos or DVDs that claim to enhance infant learning and development. What scientific evidence exists showing the benefits of such activities? Are these "learning products" better than the intellectual stimulation infants receive from nurturing parents? Share your findings with the class.

Chapter 14

Objectives

After studying this chapter, you will be able to

- identify major steps in a toddler's physical, intellectual, social, and emotional development, and parenting practices that influence this development.
- summarize changes in the gross- and fine-motor skills of toddlers.
- summarize the importance of beginning to learn life skills in toddlerhood.
- describe the toddler's major intellectual development according to Piaget.
- explain the value of play for toddlers and the parents' role in play.
- summarize how language develops during the toddler years.
- identify changes in toddler social and emotional development, including the learning to make friends, struggling for autonomy, and understanding self.
- identify parenting concerns and tasks that occur during toddlerhood, such as scheduling medical checkups, guiding toddlers, and keeping toddlers safe.

Parents and Their Toddlers

Key Terms

toddler
gender identity
life skills
toilet learning
sphincter muscles
preoperational stage
preconcepts
prelogical
egocentric
open toys
closed toys
teachable moments
picture books
parallel play
autonomy
temper tantrums

As babies begin to walk and talk, they enter the toddler stage. The word *toddler* describes the way a young child walks in short, unsteady steps. **Toddlers** are children between 13 and 35 months of age.

Before 18 months, growth and development seem to be a smooth extension of the later months of infancy for the toddler. Between 18 and 24 months, development appears different. The toddler not only is more mobile, but also is talking and striving for independence and individuality or a sense of self.

Parents often wonder whether they have the energy to keep up with these active little children, 14-1. An even greater parent concern is how to positively handle a strong-willed toddler who constantly challenges parental authority.

In this chapter, you will study toddler development. After each section, review

14-1 Toddlers are bundles of energy. They love to run and jump, both inside and outside.

the "Toddler Development" chart at the end of the chapter for month-by-month development. You will also study the role of parents as they enter the *authoritative stage of parenting.* During this stage, parents define roles and rules for their toddler.

Physical Development

Toddlers grow and develop quickly, but not as rapidly as infants. The most noticeable physical changes in toddlers are the loss of "baby looks" and the appearance of childlike features. These changes in body characteristics help the development of gross- and fine-motor skills. Motor skills, in turn, assist playing, self-care, and socializing.

Toddlers' body proportions change. A toddler's head, about one-fourth of his or her total height, still seems large. The toddler's trunk grows rapidly. Early in the toddler years, the abdomen protrudes due to the size of internal organs. At about 30 months, when the toddler becomes taller and the chest becomes larger than the abdomen, the abdomen flattens.

The spine becomes S-shaped. This curve allows for an upright posture. The legs grow longer and stronger, too. These two changes result in better walking and the development of other gross-motor skills. A toddler's hands and feet are a little short and stubby, so fine-motor development still occurs slowly.

The "baby fat" of infancy begins to disappear, and gradually a leaner, more muscular shape forms. The decreased body fat and increased muscle mass allow better physical coordination. Body build becomes evident during the toddler years, 14-2.

Gross-Motor Skills

At age 1, children vary in their levels of gross-motor development. Some are walking alone. Others display prewalking skills. Parents are eager for their children to begin

Signs of Toddler Growth

Age (months)	Average Weight (in pounds)	Average Height (inches)
12	20–22	28–30
24	25–28	33–35
33	31–33	36–38

14-2 Toddler growth is steady, but is not as rapid as growth during infancy.

taking steps. As in other areas of development, however, timetables vary. Starting to walk early or late does not necessarily indicate a delay in another area of development. Healthy babies will walk when they are ready. Several gross-motor skills develop in the toddler years, including walking, sitting, climbing, jumping, and running.

Walking

When toddlers take their first steps, they walk with their feet flat and their toes turned inward. They walk with their legs spread apart and their arms held high at their sides for balance. Toddlers take many minor falls as they learn. Because of their fascination with walking and climbing, toddlers pay little attention to bumps and falls. Instead of crying, toddlers often jump up, scamper away, and try again.

At 18 months, toddlers are learning to walk sideways and backward. Eventually, they will be able to stand on either foot alone. They may even try walking on their tiptoes. By the time they are 2, toddlers are walking with more assurance. They can walk more quickly with ease. Toddlers walk fast, but this fast walking isn't true running.

Sitting

Once toddlers can walk well, sitting is the next skill to conquer. At first, the only way toddlers can sit is to fall into the sitting position. Within a few months, they manage to squat and sit down with control. Sitting in chairs is an accomplishment. It requires toddlers to judge distances, back up to chairs, and without looking, sit with controlled muscle movements.

Climbing, Jumping, and Running

Climbing begins when infants are able to creep. Babies and toddlers need parent-controlled chances to climb. Parents should block dangerous stairs, but allow toddlers to climb a few stairs safely with supervision. Generally, toddlers back down the stairs, but will sometimes turn around and descend by sitting and bumping on each step. Toddlers may begin walking up stairs by holding a parent's hand or stair railing. Coming down stairs is difficult for a long time.

For most toddlers, jumping involves stepping off a low object, such as a stair step or curb. At 24 months, toddlers may be able to make a small jump with both feet. Running begins at this age, too.

Other Movements

Toddlers move in rhythmic response to music. They enjoy bouncing and swaying in simple dancing movements by 1 year of age. With time, toddlers become more coordinated. They test their improved coordination and balance with all kinds of complex movements, 14-3. As they become more mobile, toddlers also become more curious about their world. They explore every corner of every room and every inch of the outdoors. Because everything is new and exciting, toddlers are almost always in motion.

Toddlers also use their improved mobility to socialize with parents. They want to go on walks with others, but do not learn to walk alongside an adult until age 3. Until then, toddlers walk toward whatever interests them—a bit of uneven ground, a puddle, or a low wall that looks good for climbing. As long as their parents are nearby, toddlers

14-3 This toddler shows off his improved balance and coordination as he plays.

are happy wandering in any direction. When parents move in a specific direction, toddlers want parents to carry them. They are not being lazy. Toddlers are following their natural instincts, knowing they cannot keep up with the parents. Holding toddlers' hands helps only for a few steps. They simply cannot match the pace and direction of an adult's walk. When a toddler is tired, allowing the child to ride in a stroller or on a parent's shoulders may help.

Fine-Motor Skills

Grasping and manipulating skills continue to improve in the toddler years. Toddlers practice these skills by picking up objects and lugging them from one place to another. Daddy's big shoes or Mommy's favorite doorstop may be found almost anyplace in the home.

Toddlers use the pincer grasp for stacking blocks, marking with crayons or pencils, handling puzzle pieces, and turning pages in a book, 14-4. Due to their fine-motor skills, toddlers can turn doorknobs with greater strength. Their scribbles now include circles and horizontal and vertical lines. Toddlers like to take apart simple objects and put them back together. They are also able to help with self-care activities, such as eating finger foods, brushing their teeth, and dressing. Toddlers also learn to add hand gestures to their new communication skills.

Although fine-motor skills and curiosity contribute to toddlers' learning, their explorations cause problems. For example, in a grocery store the toddler may fill a parent's cart with unwanted items. When they rummage through drawers and examine objects, toddlers see no limits to their explorations. Most of the lessons are fun, but some are not. For instance, toddlers quickly learn that closing drawers without first removing their fingers can be very painful. Because a toddler's world can be dangerous, adults must handle many things—especially removing objects a child could easily swallow.

Exploring Their Bodies

During the toddler years, children begin to understand **gender identity**—the concept that people are either male or female. Toddlers see differences in gender based on visual cues, such as clothing or hair length. Toddlers may have a puzzling look when visual cues do not match the label. For example, a man with long hair or a woman with a very deep voice may not fit a toddler's image of a man or woman. Because toddlers see other people more easily than they see themselves, they develop their own gender identity last. By age 3, most children label others and themselves as *boy*, *girl*, *he*, or *she*. They often call all women *mothers* and all men *daddies*. To toddlers, these are gender labels, not labels for parenthood.

Toddlers have not yet developed a sense of modesty. They are quite content to explore their world—home, yard, and community—without their clothes. Why do they lack modesty? Toddlers are not trying to embarrass their parents or attract attention. They would rather play than waste time dressing. If toddlers find a piece of clothing uncomfortable, they simply remove

14-4 This toddler shows her improving fine-motor skills by turning pages in a book.

it. Between 24 and 35 months is a peak time for exploring sex organs. Toddlers are unaware of reasons for keeping parts of their bodies covered. Parents should not shame or tease their toddlers. They can handle this by saying, "Now that you are 2, you need to keep your clothes on. There are special parts of your body that are not for everyone to see. You can take your clothes off for a bath."

Older toddlers may notice boys' and girls' bodies are different. They want to know why. Parents do not need to give detailed explanations. They should simply acknowledge the differences—little boys have penises while little girls have vaginas. When teaching children names for parts of the body, parents should use correct terms.

Learning Life Skills

Life skills are the routine eating, dressing, and grooming skills children must learn for self-care. Toddlers are eager to improve these skills to gain independence. They want to do many things for themselves, but get easily frustrated. Sometimes parents find it difficult to wait patiently while toddlers perform these skills. Toddlers learn these tasks more quickly with parental encouragement.

Eating

Toddlers can eat just about anything other family members eat. A parent's job is to provide nutritious meals, 14-5. Toddlers often have food preferences and may only eat a certain food for a period of time. Parents can allow toddlers to help choose some foods for daily meals, such as applesauce or peaches. Although toddlers may insist on eating certain foods, parents should not cook separate meals to please them.

Because toddlers grow at a slower rate than during infancy, they have smaller appetites. Many toddlers prefer to move around rather than sit and eat. This may lead parents to think their toddlers are

Improving Childhood Nutrition

With childhood obesity on the rise, recent research suggests the eating habits of many children need to improve. Here are some ways that can help:

- Serve nutrient-dense foods (those packed with nutrients). Avoid foods and beverages with little nutrient value, such as candy and soda.

- Serve a variety of dark green and yellow vegetables as a large part of the solid foods children eat. Avoid serving white potatoes as the *only* vegetable. Research shows that French fries are often the only vegetable young children eat.

- Encourage children to eat whole fruits prepared in an age-appropriate way.

- Serve only 100-percent fruit juice. Limit the amount of juice to 4 to 6 ounces per day. Do not give juice at bedtime.

- Avoid sugary foods and beverages since they supply little more than calories.

14-5 Improving their children's nutrition is an important parent responsibility.

picky eaters. If toddlers don't eat much at a meal, they probably are not hungry. Most toddlers meet or exceed their daily calorie requirements even if parents think they are picky eaters. Parents should not force toddlers to eat. Toddlers can judge when they are full.

Toddlers need small amounts of food every 3 to 4 hours. They should have three regular daily meals and small, nutritious snacks in the morning and afternoon. To prevent toddlers from overeating, parents should not fill the toddlers' plates. Food amounts should fit the child's size and energy needs.

Parents should not use food as a reward, bribe, or threat. Eating food is a means of satisfying hunger and providing nutrients for the body. A cookie has nothing to do with good behavior. Candy does not lessen

the pain of a skinned knee. Linking certain foods, especially sweets, to emotions may set the stage for a lifetime of poor eating habits.

Parents will need to feed most 12- to 18-month-old toddlers. Mealtime is a good time to encourage independence in older toddlers. Parents should cut food into small pieces so toddlers can feed themselves. If toddlers ask for help, parents should simply fill the spoon. The toddler may want to take over from there. If the toddler cannot handle the spoon, parents should be ready to help before the toddler becomes completely frustrated. Toddlers still find fingers more useful than spoons for self-feeding. Most toddlers quickly master drinking from a cup.

Mealtimes should be enjoyable. Using good table manners is not a reasonable goal for toddlers. Having such a goal makes mealtime unpleasant for everyone. Although toddlers are ready to share most mealtimes, they have trouble waiting for family members to finish eating. Parents may be able to prevent some battles by allowing toddlers to leave the table when they are full.

Dressing

Another life skill is dressing oneself. Toddlers make great progress in this area. Around 18 months, they may help by pushing their arms through sleeves. Gradually, they help more and more until they are able to take garments off. The last skill to develop is putting on garments. In the learning process, however, shoes may be on the wrong feet and clothes put on backwards, 14-6. Parents need patience to help their children with these learning goals. Children do not master dressing until the early school years.

Grooming

Toddlers are also eager to learn simple lessons in cleanliness and grooming. A step stool helps toddlers reach the sink and makes grooming tasks easier. Most toddlers like to wash their hands. When given a small soft

14-6 Self-dressing is one life skill toddlers enjoy.

toothbrush, they enjoy brushing their teeth. Toddlers are also helpful with their bathing and shampooing. When parents are ready to finish the task, they can say to the toddler, "I am just finishing up."

Caring for Teeth

Toddlers must learn that caring for teeth involves daily cleaning and regular checkups by the dentist. Parents should begin taking their children to the dentist before the first birthday. Most dentists suggest regular dental checkups every 6 months. A dentist usually cleans teeth and checks for problems, such as alignment and decay.

Between 18 and 24 months, toddlers can help with brushing. For toddler success with tooth brushing, parents should

- begin by having toddlers wash their hands.

- give their toddler a child-sized, soft-bristled toothbrush. Toothpaste isn't necessary. The American Dental Association says that parents should talk with their dentist before giving toothpaste to children under 2.

- show their toddler how to brush (a dental hygienist or dentist can help with this). Parents can show the toddler how to use short, gentle strokes or light-pressure circles on teeth and gums along both sides. Use back and forth strokes on the flat biting surfaces. When parents model what to do, their toddler can easily follow. Flossing is also needed.

- encourage the toddler by saying, "You did a good job! My turn!" Tooth brushing is a two-person job until age 6 or older. Parents should aim for a 60-second brushing time. If the toddler puts his or her head in the parent's lap, it is easier to see teeth, brush, and floss. Giving the toddler a separate brush to hold can keep the child from grabbing the toothbrush while the parents finish cleaning the child's teeth.

Eating nutritious foods has a major effect on health of teeth. For example, calcium helps build and maintain teeth and bones. Toddlers who eat breakfast tend to have less tooth decay or cavities. Breakfast skippers are more likely to develop tooth decay due to snacking and lack of tooth brushing.

As you read in Chapter 13, most babies begin teething before their first birthday. During the toddler years, teething continues. The sequence of teething is the same, but timing varies from child to child. The set of 20 baby teeth is usually complete by 30 months of age. See 14-7 for the sequence of teething.

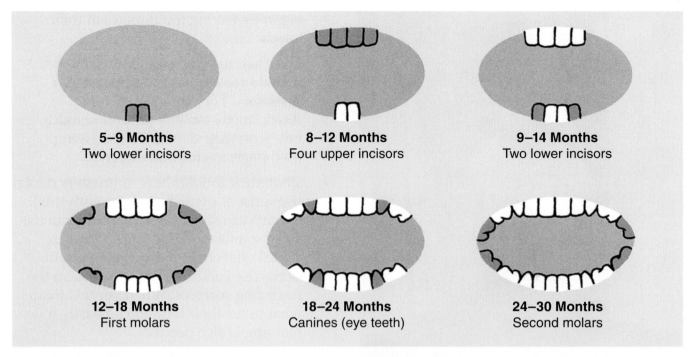

14-7 Teething follows a predictable sequence, but the timing is unpredictable.

5–9 Months
Two lower incisors

8–12 Months
Four upper incisors

9–14 Months
Two lower incisors

12–18 Months
First molars

18–24 Months
Canines (eye teeth)

24–30 Months
Second molars

Toilet Learning

During the toddler years, children become ready for toilet learning. **Toilet learning** is the process of children gaining control of bladder and bowel functions and successfully using the toilet. Toileting success is a major accomplishment for young children. The age at which children have consistent toileting success varies. Some children master this skill more quickly than others. It is a gradual process that takes about 8 to 10 months to learn. Most children achieve this milestone before age 4. Parents can feel confident in their child's success after age 3 when their child uses the toilet properly and doesn't have an elimination accident for 6 months.

The basic rule for parents is to provide an encouraging environment for toilet learning. If a toddler is resistant, parents should not push the child to learn this skill. Rushing may prolong the entire process and frustrate parents and toddler alike. Once a toddler is truly ready and shows interest, the toddler generally cooperates and toilet learning proceeds smoothly.

Signs of Readiness

How can parents know when their child is ready for toilet learning? Watching for certain patterns can help. Toddlers achieve bowel control first, daytime bladder control next, and then nighttime bladder control. Knowing this helps parents judge when the time is right. Parents should not necessarily expect toilet learning to begin before their child is about 30 months old. Boys often take a little longer to learn this skill than girls.

In addition to age, children generally show some other signs of readiness for toilet learning. Toddlers often desire clean diapers and may seek their parents when in need of a diaper change. Some toddlers may "help" by removing their diapers for the parent. This tells parents their toddler is recognizing the sensation of needing to empty the bladder or bowel. Showing interest in the toilet and how to use it is another cue. Parents may notice their toddler has dry diapers for longer periods during the day and after naps. This is a sign of developing **sphincter muscles**, the ringlike muscles that control the openings to the bladder and rectum. The ability to tighten these muscles to prevent immediate elimination is another clue to toddler readiness.

On the path to toileting success, children must be able to understand what parents want them to do. Talking with toddlers about the toilet and letting them observe a same-gender family member use the toilet, help increase toddler understanding. Children must be able to get to the bathroom, pull down their pants, and sit on a potty-chair. They must also be able to relax their sphincter muscles so they can empty the bladder or bowel.

Tips for Toileting Success

Although a toddler may show signs of readiness, parents should not begin toilet learning when changes are occurring in family life. For example, a new child care setting, new sibling, new home, or family crisis can interfere with toileting success. When the time is right, toilet learning may begin. The following tips will help:

- *Purchase the right equipment.* Equipment includes a separate potty-chair or potty-ring that fits on the toilet seat, disposable training diapers, and training pants (thick underpants with elastic bands at the legs for leak protection). If a potty-ring is used, place a step stool in front of the toilet. The child places his or her feet on the stool to keep the rectum muscles from tightening due to dangling feet.

- *Promote pretoilet learning.* Toddlers can practice sitting on the potty-chair with their clothes on. Once toddlers know the process and what to expect, they can teach a doll or stuffed animal.

- ***Take toddlers to the toilet at times they normally use their diaper.*** Remember, however, trying too frequently is disruptive to toddlers' activities and can cause a reverse in toilet learning.

- ***Make sitting on the potty fun.*** For example, toddlers may look at books or blow bubbles. Reading stories about toilet learning helps toddlers to know that all children learn to use the toilet.

- ***Do not react negatively to accidents or even total regression.*** Parents should simply clean up their toddlers and remind them what to do next time. They should not scold or punish them— accidents will happen. Most children feel upset about accidents. Parents should reassure them this happens to all children. They should also praise their toddlers for toileting success.

Sleeping

Toddlers younger than 18 to 24 months usually sleep as much as they did during infancy. Gradually toddler sleep needs begin to change. Most toddlers need 13 to 14 hours of sleep each night.

When sleep needs and patterns change, toddlers may become problem sleepers. What has happened? First, toddler negativity affects all routines, including sleep. Toddlers become less willing to take naps or go to bed at night. Instead, they fight sleepiness, 14-8. Second, although older toddlers generally need less total sleep, parents may not make needed changes. Most toddlers no longer need a morning nap, but do need a one- to two-hour afternoon nap. Sleeping too much during the day reduces the need for sleep at night. Moving toward a 1:00 to 2:00 p.m. nap and then putting their toddlers to bed a half hour earlier at night can help parents get their toddlers into a normal sleep routine.

Third, toddlers experience more fears that disrupt sleep. Fears now include the fear of the dark and being alone. Dreams and make-believe stories often fuel the toddlers' imaginations. They cannot tell the difference between real and make-believe. Toddlers need reassurance when feeling fearful. However, parents must be firm about bedtime rules.

Piaget and Younger Toddlers

By age 2, toddlers complete the last two substages of Piaget's *sensorimotor* stage. See the substages in 14-9 and the description shown in Appendix B. Young toddlers still use their senses and motor activities to explore the world. Their explorations become more varied, more intense, and much more skilled. Around 18 months, they gradually move beyond sensory and motor learning and begin mental ways of thinking.

Tertiary Circular Reactions

Toddlers between 12 and 18 months try new ideas by planning changes in their actions on objects to meet a goal. For example, the toddler might see a toy stuck in a small area. If the toddler cannot free the toy at first, he or she will rotate the toy to free it. At other times, the toddler plans action changes just to see what happens. For example, toddlers may throw a toy with varying force to watch the

Piaget's Stages of Intellectual Development

1. Sensorimotor
1A: *Exercising the Reflexes*
1B: *Primary Circular Reactions*
1C: *Secondary Circular Reactions*
1D: *Coordination of Secondary Circular Reactions*
1E: *Tertiary Circular Reactions*
1F: *Mental Representation*

2. Preoperational
2A: *Preconceptual Phase*
2B: *Intuitive Phase*

3. Concrete Operations

4. Formal Operations

14-9 Younger toddlers still use their senses and motor activities to explore their world. At about 18 months, they begin to think in mental ways about how actions cause certain results. Older toddlers' ability to think allows them to represent their images through language, art, and make-believe play. However, their thinking is not always logical.

14-8 Fighting sleepiness is one aspect of toddler negativity.

Intellectual Development

On-the-go toddlers are curious about everything, but unlikely to sit still for more than a few minutes. Anything and everything is a plaything. Whether pushing shapes into a sorter or screeching into a sand pail, they do the same activities countless times a day and for many days. It's their way of checking to see whether their actions always get the same results.

Parents play an important role in this phase of toddlers' intellectual development. Parents' enthusiasm can be contagious. Toddlers who see the world as an exciting place full of things to do are more likely to explore.

different results. They may also tear, pinch, and mash a piece of Play-Doh® to see what happens.

In the stage of secondary circular reactions, the baby did not vary the actions. The toddler, however, plans varying actions. Because this is the third change in the child's behavior toward objects, Piaget called this substage *tertiary circular reactions*. In this stage the child repeats different actions over and over (creating a *circular response*).

Piaget considered toddlers in this stage to be "little scientists." They use trial and error to solve problems. Their goal is to see what else they can do with a particular object. Piaget said this is the starting point for human curiosity of the new or different.

Mental Representation

Around 18 months, toddlers begin to have mental images. This helps in problem solving. Toddlers can then think about actions and their results without performing the actions. For example, the young toddler can mentally "turn" an object to put it through the shaped hole in a sorting box.

Toddlers express their mental "pictures" through words, artwork, and make-believe play. Thus, Piaget called the last sensorimotor substage *mental representation*. This substage is the bridge to the next stage in which mental thinking replaces motor actions.

Two intellectual skills develop during the mental representation substage. First, the idea of *object permanence* is, for the most part, complete. For example, toddlers hunt for a completely hidden object and even look in places in which they have never seen the object, 14-10.

Second, the ability to imitate takes a major leap. One-year-olds, for example, can imitate others when they are present and model their action. With increasing memory and the ability to have mental images around 18 months, toddlers can imitate what they saw someone do at an earlier time.

14-10 Toddlers may look for unseen objects in hidden places.

Piaget and Older Toddlers

As their new skills continue to flourish, older toddlers are not yet able to do advanced forms of reasoning or logical thought called *operations*. Piaget said older toddlers are in the **preoperational stage**—the period before logical thought. This stage is divided into two substages.

According to Piaget, 2- to 4-year-old children are in the first substage of preoperational thinking, called the *preconceptual phase*. Although toddlers make major advances in intellectual ability, their concepts and reasoning are often illogical and confused. To show the difference between logical concepts and confused concepts, Piaget referred to the toddlers' concepts as **preconcepts**. For example, have you noticed how toddlers get facts and the sequence of events mixed up when they try to retell a favorite story? Older toddlers and preschool children who have preconcepts are in the *preconceptual phase*. Piaget indicates these children use symbols and think prelogically.

Use of Symbols

As you know, 18-month- to 2-year-old toddlers develop the ability to see images in their minds. These images represent objects, people, and events in their real world. Although these images are picturelike symbols in their minds, parents will soon see toddlers express them in words, art, and pretend play.

Symbols represent objects (and eventually ideas) that are not present at the time. Each symbol brings together many ideas and emotions. For example, the word *dog* is a symbol. When you hear this word, you can mentally picture a dog, hear its sounds, and even have positive or negative feelings about the animal. Because of symbols, humans are able to think very quickly and solve problems mentally.

Symbols express what a person knows about people, objects, and events, not necessarily reality. The use of symbols follows a developmental sequence that blossoms later in the preschool years. Older toddlers are able to create the following kinds of symbols:

Words. Toddlers who use multiple-word sentences can describe what they know about their world. For example, they may excitedly tell you about an elephant at the zoo. Parents should not be surprised if the elephant roars like a lion or flies. The toddler may mix animal characteristics or merge the real elephant into a favorite story. Parents should listen attentively and not correct or add to the story.

Art. Infants who scribble are simply enjoying the motor action. Toddlers, however, are expressing what they know. For example,

a red line may represent the color of a ball, its texture, or the path it rolls, 14-11. By age 2, toddlers may make realistic pictures, such as circles for heads with randomly placed marks inside to represent eyes, nose, and mouth.

Pretend Play. Toddlers begin pretend play by doing a single act in the same setting in which the real act takes place. They may "drink" from an empty cup in the high chair or in the kitchen. Between ages 2 and 3, toddlers may pretend using very realistic objects, such as a doll for a baby or a toy telephone for a real one. The make-believe action is one-way at this time. The toddler feeds the doll, but the doll does not respond. The setting remains realistic, too, such as feeding the doll in the chair mother uses for nursing a new baby.

Prelogical Thinking

Piaget also focused on what older toddlers do not yet understand. Because toddler thinking is often illogical and irrational, Piaget called this thinking **prelogical**. Here are some examples.

- *Confusion of cause and effect.* Toddlers may have problems with cause and effect, especially when they are not causing the results. For example, toddlers may say, "Because I put on my raincoat, it is raining."

14-11 A toddler enjoys using watercolors just to see the colors on the paper.

- *Egocentrism.* Piaget called children this age **egocentric** because they cannot see things from the perspective of others. In fact, children do not even realize that two or more perspectives exist. Toddlers display egocentric behavior when they cover their eyes and believe others cannot see them.

- *Animism.* Piaget noted that young children believe everything has life, just as they do. To toddlers, all objects are lifelike and capable of actions. This is called *animism.* For example, the toddler thinks a "tree" can make a naughty child fall or "thunder" wants to scare bad children. Animism helps toddlers accept the mythical "sandman" and later the "tooth fairy."

- *Focus on the "bits and pieces."* According to Piaget, toddlers and young children notice only some aspects of an object or an event. For example, after asking what they did in child care, toddlers may only tell you about the teacher's smock with many pockets.

Playtime Means Learning

During toddlerhood, much intellectual development occurs through play. Play is fun, too! In their first year, babies mainly explore—they try to find out what objects do. In contrast, toddlers try to find out what they can do with objects.

Physical Play

With active physical play, toddlers develop their muscles and refine their balance and coordination. They use energy and build stamina. Toddlers are more likely to maintain proper body weight if they are active. This sets a pattern for exercise that will help maintain good health as they grow. Toddlers enjoy running, jumping, and climbing, 14-12. They learn to push themselves on riding toys, which gives them a new way of traveling.

14-12 Physical play, such as climbing, helps toddlers develop their gross-motor skills.

Object Play

Young toddlers are more interested in an activity itself than in any outcome of the activity. They love to empty and fill containers just for the fun of it. Older toddlers refine this skill and become more concerned with all they can do to control the objects. Older toddlers typically play with two or more items at the same time.

Play is a method of trying out ideas. Toddlers soon learn the results of their actions when they push the radio buttons—loud noise! Children can use different objects to do many things. They learn simple math and science lessons as they stack blocks and pour sand from a large pail into a small one. Toddlers begin learning the meaning of *more* and *less*, *tall* and *short*, and *big* and *little*. They also begin learning numbers, colors, shapes, and names for objects.

Playing with objects develops fine-motor skills, too. Toddlers use eye-hand coordination as they string beads, work with puzzles, use art materials, stack blocks, and turn pages in a book. The eye-hand coordination will lead to success in life skills and other fine-motor activities used throughout life (handwriting, keyboarding, or playing a musical instrument).

Pretend Play

Toddlers' mental images allow them to begin pretend play. Between 2 and 3 years, pretend play becomes based on imitation of others' experiences. For example, the older toddler may pretend to read a book, sweep the floor, or talk on the phone. Many of these imitations are short in duration. For example, the toddler may only say "hi" and "bye" on the phone. In the preschool period, imitation becomes much closer to reality, such as make-believe "conversations" on the phone.

The Play Environment

Toddlers need open spaces to use their large muscles. For object play and pretend play, toddlers seem to enjoy cozy areas. For example, the spaces under tables or between pieces of furniture are toddler favorites. Most of all, toddlers need *safe* places because they focus on the play, not on the dangers.

Play materials need to be attractive and durable. Toddlers can be very rough on toys. Toys are needed for gross-motor play, fine-motor play, and pretend play, 14-13. Most toys should be open in nature. **Open toys**—such as blocks, art materials, and dress-up clothes—allow children to use their imaginations and creative-thinking skills to devise new play activities. **Closed toys**, such as electronic toys that work one way, are not usually good toys for toddlers because they limit creativity. In addition to purchased toys, common household objects (plastic containers and spoons, or pots and pans) can inspire toddlers to use their imaginations.

The Parents' Role in Play

Parents are responsible for creating a safe environment and for choosing toys and household objects that encourage their toddler's play. As they observe their toddler, they may think of new toys or objects that challenge their toddler. Likewise, parents often need to remove some toys until their child develops further. Parents must judge the fit between their toddler and the play environment.

14-13 Toddlers need a variety of play materials to encourage gross- and fine-motor development.

Play is most valuable if toddlers are allowed to try out their own ideas. Parents need to allow their toddlers to take the lead in play. When parents insist on their way of building a house with blocks or making a sand castle at the beach, children feel defeat. Parents can interact in ways toddlers enjoy, however. For example, if there are enough blocks, parents can make a low tower alongside their toddler's higher tower. In pretend play, parents can interact by taking the "sip" their toddler offers and then commenting on how good the drink tastes. Engaging in interaction games, such as hide-and-seek, is fun for toddlers and parents alike.

Considering their toddlers' needs, parents should decide how their toddlers should play: inside or outdoors? Using gross-muscle or fine-muscle toys? With others or alone? Toddlers also need balance between new and familiar experiences. Parents should make sure toddlers have a balance of among playtime, quiet time, and other activities. Each day has many **teachable moments**, or spontaneous learning experiences parents can use to introduce new ideas to toddlers. These experiences expand on children's natural curiosity. Parents must manage learning environments to keep them stimulating, but not overwhelming.

Language Development

In toddlerhood language begins slowly, but develops quickly in the second year. One aspect of language development involves *vocabulary*, or knowing what others say, speaking the words, and linking them to the right person, object, or action. Infants begin to know what others are saying after six months. This aspect of vocabulary remains stronger throughout life than spoken vocabulary.

A child's first spoken word is often said in infancy—typically by 11 or 12 months of age. Some children do not talk until 18 months or later. Using words to name objects or people usually begins at 13 months. On the average, toddlers say about 50 words at 18 months and 200 words at age 2. By the end of toddlerhood, their vocabularies may contain more than 500 words.

Words always reflect the toddlers' world. Common words are *mama* and *dada*. Toddlers also know names of objects in their world, such as *doggie* or *cookie*. Some toddlers use phrases to express demands, such as *gimme dat*.

Toddlers often use a known word to describe anything that is similar. For instance, the word *dog* may be used to refer to all animals until the child learns differences between animals. The name *daddy* may be used for the child's father, but it might mean all other men, too. *No* is the most commonly used word for several months. Toddlers often say *no* to everything, even when they mean *yes*. Some words the toddler uses are distantly related to real words. For example, "bankie" may mean *blanket* and "coocoo" may mean *cookie*.

Along with developing a vocabulary, toddlers begin to use groups of words to express themselves. Before 18 months, most toddlers say a single word with expression and gestures to convey meaning. Parents often know the meaning by the way the child says it and by the context (what is happening). For example, as the father walks through the door, a toddler might excitedly say "daddy!" The toddler means "Hi, Daddy! I'm glad you are here."

Once toddlers are comfortable using many single words, between 18 and 22 months they start combining them in two-word sentences to express ideas. Toddlers add the second word to make their meaning clearer. For example, "my baby" means "this is my baby doll." "See doggie" means "look at what the dog is doing" or "here comes our dog." Toddlers do not just mimic sentences they have heard. They invent sentences to convey their thoughts to others.

The Importance of Books

Books are vital to a child's intellectual development and enjoyment of learning. By introducing books at early ages, parents can help their children develop language skills, enjoy and value books, and develop a lifelong fondness for reading, 14-14.

A child's first books are often *picture books*. **Picture books** can be books that contain only pictures, have pictures that dominate the text (such as counting and alphabet books), or have words and pictures that are equally important (picture storybooks). In contrast, books for children in the middle grades and older have occasional illustrations or pictures within the text.

14-14 Parents and siblings play a vital role in introducing books to toddlers.

Many parents begin by reading books to their infants when they are about 6 months old. Reading books together should continue well into the school years. Literacy experts suggest reading together at least 20 minutes a day. For active toddlers, parents can spread the reading into three sessions.

Special family times and routines often involve books. In many homes, reading a book is part of the naptime and bedtime routine for toddlers. Children look forward to picking out a special book they want to read. When reading books to toddlers, parents should find a quiet, comfortable place. Small children may prefer to sit on the parent's lap. The floor can be a good place for reading a large book, but bedtime stories are usually read in a child's bed.

Books can also provide a restful quiet period in a child's busy day. Toddlers do not sit still for long periods of time, but they can learn to enjoy a little quiet time with a book. Books can help parents occupy children when traveling, when they are ill, or when waiting in the doctor's office for an appointment. Parents often say reading together is a time to get to know each other better and build family ties.

The Parents' Role in Language Learning

Parent-child interactions are important for language development. Because of the rate of language development, the parents' role is most important during the toddler years. Parents can help their toddlers learn language by

- *matching their interaction style to toddlers' skills.* For example, parents talk for infants and young toddlers. This talk is not one-sided because parents ask a question, then pause (as though the child is answering), and then respond to "answer."

- *reducing the language difficulty during the early stages of development.* For example, "r" is difficult to pronounce. So parents can substitute daddy or papa for father, and bunny for rabbit. They can reduce the number of new words for a while by referring to lions and tigers as big kitties.

- *expanding the language after 18 months or 2 years.* Parents can use many labeling words—especially those for common objects, for shape, size, and color, and for movement (roll, bounce, fly, run). Describing both toddler and parent actions help expand language.

- *responding to toddlers' attempts to start a conversation.* When toddlers show or hand parents their toys, they want to talk about them.

- *trying to understand what toddlers want or need as they use their limited vocabularies.* Much the same as trying to understand nonverbal cues, this helps lay the foundation for open communication.

- *reading books, saying rhymes, and singing songs daily with toddlers.* These actions help provide a solid foundation for building vocabulary.

- *using puppets, dolls, and stuffed animals to encourage talking.* Parents can "bring them to life" by having them "talk" to toddlers in pretend play. Shy toddlers may respond to these toys more often than to people, 14-15.

- *playing "I spy."* Parents call out words and toddlers show them the object, part of the body, or a picture. For older toddlers, parents can reverse the game.

- *using positive, approving words with toddlers.* Orders and demeaning words decrease language-learning attempts and damage self-esteem. Never tease a child about pronunciation or grammar.

14-15 Shy toddlers often respond when parents make their toys "talk."

- *respecting times when toddlers do not want to talk.* Too much talk can decrease toddlers' efforts.

Recognizing Language Delay

The rate of language development varies as much, if not more than, any other aspect of development. Many parents are concerned about the number of words their toddlers say. However, the toddlers' desire to understand others and to make their needs and wants known is more important than the number of words they say. Parents should seek professional help if their toddlers

- do not babble with expression by 1 year.

- show little understanding of words.

- do not say a few understandable words by 18 months.

- communicate with only gestures at 2 years.

- cannot speak in short sentences after age 2.

Up to 10 percent of toddlers have delays in language. Language delay may be a sign of a hearing loss or developmental delay. Multiple-birth children and bilingual children often have language delays, but do catch up in a few years.

Social and Emotional Development

The toddler years reveal many changes in social and emotional development. Once toddlers can walk and talk, social development occurs rapidly. Their new skills allow them to take a more active role in interactions with others. Toddlers behave inconsistently as they struggle for independence. They show their desire for independence by trying to do more for themselves. They also seek hugs of security and reassurance. Toddlers are more self-aware and determined. They know what they want and are set on getting it. Toddlers also have quite fragile emotions. They may laugh one minute and cry the next. They have little patience and are easily frustrated.

Friendships Begin

Infants and young toddlers like others their age. Upon seeing age-mates they wiggle and raise their arms. Young toddlers often approach other children playing with like toys. To toddlers, having the same toys means, "we like each other." Toddlers who have the same toys sit near each other, but each plays and talks to himself or herself. For example, several toddlers might sit alongside each other, each playing with blocks. They may watch each other, grab blocks from one another, or completely ignore each other. This type of play is called **parallel play**. Although the children's primary interest is in their own play, they are also learning about specific children in the parallel-play group and play activities of other children, 14-16.

By age 2, toddlers have clear preferences for certain age-mates, especially those who like doing the same activities or who have similar temperaments. Toddlers may show affection with hugs, but more often through imitation of each other. They may fight, too, because they feel safe in acting out around people they trust. These fights are often over "my toys" which are broadly defined as anything I have now, had in the past, or might want in the future. Hitting is often their only way of talking about ownership. In this instance, parents must intervene to keep toddlers safe and introduce positive behaviors. Older toddlers also like smaller preschool children. Preschool children are often good teachers if gentle with toddlers.

Toddlers play best with only one other child at a time. Parents cannot make friends for their toddlers, but they can help interactions by

14-16 In parallel play, toddlers play near each other but have little interaction.

- talking and playing with their toddlers, which prepares them for friendship. (This begins during infancy.)

- having enough similar toys to reduce disputes.

- planning good play activities both can enjoy.

- joining in the play as a guide.

- intervening in disputes to keep toddlers safe and to help solve disputes.

- making positive remarks about sharing behaviors.

- working on turn-taking, if this seems to be a problem.

Autonomy Relates to Independence

The first few months of toddlerhood are an extension of Erikson's stage of *trust versus mistrust*. Young toddlers, who are securely attached, see their parents as trustworthy and themselves as competent and worthy of care. Attachment sets the stage for developing empathy and willingness to comply with the requests or "rules" of caring parents.

Attached infants and young toddlers think they are extensions of their parents. Between 18 and 24 months, toddlers begin to recognize boundaries between themselves and others. This new knowledge comes about due to physical development (especially walking, talking, and learning life skills) and to a growing sense of self. At this time, toddlers develop other attachments, such as those with grandparents and child care teachers.

According to Erikson, once toddlers recognize their growing skills and see boundaries between themselves and others, they begin to struggle for **autonomy** or independence. He called the stage of personality development, which occurs between 2 and 3 years of age, *autonomy versus shame and doubt*. Toddlers want to play the dominant role in almost every situation. Even a little taste of freedom leads to going overboard. In effect, toddlers are saying, "I will tell you what I want, what I will and will not do, and when I might do it." The sweet child becomes a stubborn child who gets into mischief, refuses to obey, and uses one word, *no*. Autonomous toddlers want to conquer the world once they realize they can control their actions and make things happen. They have an overwhelming urge to try everything just to see what happens.

During the toddler years, children have many successful explorations, but they also run into obstacles and frustrations. For example, young toddlers get frustrated when they cannot snap their jeans. When parents refuse to buy a desired toy, toddlers learn they cannot control the adult world. In situations such as these, toddlers become frustrated and defiant with adults.

Toddlers quickly forget frustrations and become sweet and loving again. They also quickly forget lessons about power struggles, too. Toddlers' drive for independence repeats many times daily and for many months.

Erikson points out that toddlers must have some independence for healthy personality development, 14-17. (See Appendix A, "Erikson's Theory of Personality Development" for detailed information on Stage 2.) Gaining some autonomy in the toddler years is critical for teen identity and independence. When parents control with severe punishment and rigid rules, or do everything for their toddlers, shame and doubt develop.

The Growing Sense of Self

By 15 months, children begin to sense a separate existence from others. Toddlers develop the "me self" attitude. They recognize themselves in mirrors and in photos. They also note how others respond to them. By 18 months, they gain a better sense of separation between self and others. They know which of their actions please and displease others, and they seek approval and feel distress when they fail to get it.

Intense Emotions Continue

Positive and negative emotions are a normal part of toddlerhood. Parents need to understand it is natural for toddlers to be changeable and intense in expressing all kinds of emotions. The right side of the brain, responsible for intense emotions, dominates brain functioning for the first three years. Toward the end of toddlerhood, children begin to show more control over their behavior. As toddlers learn to express

Erikson's Theory of Personality Development

Stage	Approximate Age	Step Toward Stable Personality	Step Toward Unstable Personality
1	Birth to age 2	Trust	Mistrust
2	Ages 2 & 3	Autonomy	Shame and doubt
3	Ages 4 & 5	Initiative	Guilt
4	Ages 6 to 11	Industry	Inferiority
5	Ages 12 to 18	Identity	Role confusion
6	Early adulthood	Intimacy	Isolation
7	Middle age	Generativity	Stagnation
8	Late adulthood	Integrity	Despair

14-17 Parents need to give toddlers as much independence as possible, but within safe and acceptable boundaries.

feelings, they learn what it means to have them, too. Toddlers commonly express the following emotions:

- *Happiness.* Many toddlers are happy and pleasant most of the time. Happiness often comes from achieving goals of their choice and meeting adult expectations.

- *Anger.* The expression of anger peaks at age 2. Outbursts usually last about 5 minutes and "grudges" are rarely seen. Some causes of anger include being tired, hungry, or ill. Conflicts with parents over established life skills result in many outbursts. Older toddlers show anger toward friends especially in a dispute about toy ownership.

- *Fear and anxiety.* Older toddlers struggle to tell the difference between reality and make-believe. Thus, a character on TV may not frighten toddlers. However, a life-size character at a birthday party may confuse toddlers and make them fearful. Because the real and make-believe worlds are hard to separate, toddlers are more aware of what they see as fearful possibilities. For example,

they may become afraid of the bathtub drain and the toilet flushing. Separation anxiety often continues well into the toddler years but gradually diminishes. As toddlers' understanding matures, they realize parents do not disappear forever when they are out of sight. As memory improves, toddlers can remember other times their parents went away and returned. Advances in language skills help, too. Older toddlers understand when parents explain they must leave for a little while, but will return later.

- *Pride or shame.* Around 2 years of age, toddlers express pride and shame. They look for approval when they have achieved. When they feel shame due to the lack of achievement, they look or turn away or show distress.

- *Empathy.* As toddlers develop empathy, they may imitate the emotions of an injured person. For example, they may rub their own knees if a friend scraped a knee. Toddlers may direct empathy toward a family member by sharing a favorite toy with an upset parent or a sibling who is hurt.

Parenting Concerns and Tasks

Toddlerhood is a challenging period. It is a fast-paced change for toddlers who go from infancy to early childhood. Parents struggle to meet these changing needs. In a way, toddlerhood proves that children bring up their families as much as families bring up their children.

Medical Checkups for Toddlers

The American Academy of Pediatrics (AAP) recommends toddlers see their doctors at 1 year, 15 months, 18 months, and 2 years. These medical checkups are important for monitoring a toddler's health, 14-18. The doctor can note any problems and treat them as early as possible. Routine medical checkups are in addition to any visits due to illness or injury.

The doctor thoroughly examines the toddler's physical condition—checking growth by measuring height, weight, and head size—and ordering any tests necessary to check the toddler's health. In addition, the doctor examines the toddler's eyes and ears and makes referrals for vision and hearing screenings if necessary. During the exam, toddlers also get any appropriate immunizations. During medical checkups, parents can ask any questions they might have about their toddler's health, growth, and development. Parents may also want to share concerns and ask advice about their toddler.

14-18 Regular medical checkups are important for toddler health.

Adjusting to Toddlers' Needs

Toddlers are busy explorers. Although their understandings of the world and of themselves grow rapidly, their exuberance and misunderstandings can cause major family upsets. Parents often wonder how they can merge their toddlers into the family system with all its roles and rules. When they have to say *no* so often, parents may wonder whether they can positively guide their toddlers.

Providing Structure and Setting Limits

Toddlers need to learn and follow some family routines. Structure helps young children feel secure. With structure, toddlers learn certain things happen at specific times and in a certain order. For instance, they may be able to predict a specific bedtime routine consisting of bath time, toothbrushing, bedtime story, and goodnight kiss. Toddlers are less likely to resist bedtime if their routine is consistent. It doesn't take long for children to learn routines, and they often are the first to remind parents if a routine changes.

Toddlers must also learn there are limits. After love, limits are the most important gift parents give to their children. Parents enforce limits to prevent accidents and chaos, and build character.

Parents must tailor limits to the ages and stages of their children. Before 18 months, children are not capable of regulating their own behavior. Toddlerhood is an important stage for establishing parental control and initiating self-discipline. If children do not learn behavioral boundaries, limits will be harder for them to accept later in their lives.

The first limits pertain to child safety, protection of property, and respect for others (not grabbing another child's toy). Then parents add life-skill routines and insistence on waiting for short periods of time. Finally, parents add such rules as putting away toys and using a few manners, such as saying "please" and "thank you."

Parents must be careful not to overwhelm their children with limits. Too many limits are also hard on parents who must consistently enforce them. Toddlers understand discipline better when it is consistent. This does not mean limits cannot be flexible in some situations. For example, there may be times when an extra bedtime story is more important than watching the clock.

Coping With Sibling Jealousy

Toddlers who are firstborns often have major difficulty accepting a new brother or sister (sibling). They may show jealously of the new sibling. Some toddlers revert to outgrown behaviors, such as wanting to nurse again, for a month or so. Many toddlers refuse to follow family rules and routines and become more demanding. These behaviors may continue for eight or nine months. Parents can do several things to help. See 14-19.

Soothing Intense Toddler Emotions

Although the toddler emotions are not fully understood, parenting experts believe the tone of the parent-child relationship is set at this time. Knowing how to handle toddler behaviors becomes most important. Meeting the emotional needs of toddlers tends to result in happier children. Here are some ways to soothe common toddler problems.

Separation Anxiety. Parents provide a security base for toddlers. Without this base, toddlers feel lost, alone, uneasy, and helpless. To help, parents might give older toddlers a small, family photo album to carry along. Parents can also encourage toddler attachments to their caregivers and friendships with other children. Sharing warm moments when parents and toddlers are reunited can also help ease separation difficulties.

Fearfulness. Some toddlers are more sensitive and fearful than others. Parents should not pressure toddlers to be "brave." Verbally comparing their toddlers to other less-fearful children can negatively impact self-esteem. Because the imagined seems so real, the fears are difficult to dispel. Parents might arrange stuffed "guard" animals on the bedroom windowsill to keep the toddler safe at night. They might also decorate a spray bottle of water to "spray" away monsters.

Hurting Others. Parents should focus on their toddlers' positive behaviors, such as saying, "I like the way you are sharing," before any aggression starts. Parents should quickly stop toddlers who hit or bite and then comfort the victim. They should tell the aggressive toddler, "Children are not for biting! Stop! Biting hurts!" Parents should not punish by hitting or biting the toddler in return.

Throwing Objects and Food. Throwing is a natural way toddlers explore objects. Providing "throw objects" and "throw places" help curb undesirable throwing. Toddlers especially need to learn food is not for throwing. To stop food throwing, put only a small amount of food on the plate. If food is thrown (not dropped), parents should remove the plate and say, "You must be done eating." Parents should not give additional food until the next snack or meal.

Taking Another Child's Toy. Toddlers often feel every toy belongs to them. Parents should consistently say, "No, this is not yours." Parents should return the toy to the owner and redirect their toddler to what he or she owns.

Experiencing Negative Outbursts. **Temper tantrums** are violent outbursts of negative behavior. Almost all children between the ages of 1 and 3 have them. Toddlers experience two types of tantrums. The very intense *temperamental tantrum,* in

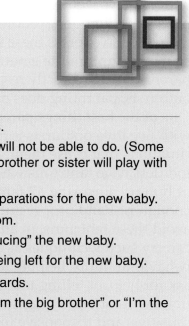

Avoiding Sibling Jealousy

What Parents Can Do	Helpful Tips
Prepare the toddler in the last trimester of pregnancy.	• Show the toddler his or her newborn photos. • Tell the toddler what the new baby will and will not be able to do. (Some parents make a mistake by saying the new brother or sister will play with the toddler.) • Ask the toddler to help with some of the preparations for the new baby.
Welcome toddler soon after the new baby's birth.	• Put photos of the toddler in the mother's room. • Hug and talk with the toddler before "introducing" the new baby. • Have a few gifts for the toddler if gifts are being left for the new baby.
Ask the toddler to help announce the new baby's birth.	• Have the toddler help mail announcement cards. • Have the toddler wear a T-shirt that says, "I'm the big brother" or "I'm the big sister." • Ask the toddler to tell the grandparents about the new baby.
Give toddler needed attention.	• Enlist Dad's help. This helps a toddler miss Mom less. • Tell toddler you'll spend time with him or her after you help (feed, bathe, diaper-change) the baby. A specific promise is better than a vague "in a minute." • Set aside time just for the toddler.
Be positive about the toddler's regressive behaviors.	• Avoid saying, "Act like a big boy," or "Act more grown up." • Talk about activities big children can do that babies cannot, such as listen to stories, work puzzles, play ball, or eat an apple.
Show the toddler how important he or she is to the new baby.	• Make the toddler your baby-care assistant. • Show the toddler how the baby looks or smiles at him or her.

14-19 With a little creatively, parents can help their toddler overcome jealousy of a new brother or sister.

which toddlers are out of control, is most common. Something unimportant to parents sets these off, such as a quick change in activities. With a *manipulative tantrum,* toddlers try to get their way with their parents. Parents are usually aware of what sets this type of tantrum off, such as a refusal to buy a toy. With manipulative tantrums, toddlers often stop their outbursts long enough to check on their parents' reaction.

Dawdling. Toddlers have almost no sense of time. Because they are egocentric, they also believe the world revolves around

their wants and desires. Parental frustration increases when children "play" during daily routines that cause delays for parents. Some parents find timers helpful because the timer, not the parent, tells the toddler it's time to leave the house or to eat. Parents should put away items that distract toddlers. For example, if the toddler's bedtime book is in sight, the toddler will likely "read" it instead of dressing in the morning. Parents should also give toddlers an appropriate amount of time for each activity. Rushing toddlers often results in temper tantrums.

Negative feelings and tantrums are a big part of toddlerhood. Toddlers do not have the words to express these intense feelings, so they communicate emotionally. Although parents are not directly responsible for these outbursts, parenting does make a difference. One of the best things parents can do to deal with negative outbursts is to try to avoid the situations that cause them. For example, some toddlers have tantrums when they are tired or hungry. Ensuring all family members get enough rest and proper nutrition can help avoid these tantrums. In addition, parents can try such techniques as avoiding too many behavioral limits, helping toddlers when they ask for help, or telling toddlers what to expect in new situations. Parents who are nurturing, sensitive, and responsive in meeting their toddlers' needs minimize tantrums.

Making Family-Life Adjustments

Family life is busy when parents have toddlers. Along with meeting toddlers' constant needs, families, too, must make adjustments. Keeping mobile and curious toddlers safe requires adjustments. Finding child care and communicating with teachers are also major parenting tasks.

Keeping Toddlers Safe

Toddlerhood is a time for parents to make regular safety checks of their homes. Viewing each room (including the basement, garage, and yard) from a toddler's point of view is helpful. Parents should keep in mind toddlers like to climb onto and crawl under things. They like to empty and fill containers. Toddlers like to put things in their mouths. Toddlers may swallow or choke on coins, buttons, safety pins, small pieces of jewelry, and paper clips. Parents should store all poisons, cleaning agents, and medicines out of reach. Using locks provides the most protection. See 14-20 for other safety tips.

Finding Quality Toddler Care

Parents must carefully choose the right child care program for their toddlers. What type of program is best? The program should understand brain development in children and support their developmental needs. The program should also respect the cultures and unique characteristics of the children and their families. Other qualities of good programs include

- meeting state standards
- having low staff turnover (the same teacher provides care from infancy through the toddler years)
- maintaining small groups to help toddlers feel they belong
- having teachers who nurture, encourage toddler initiative, and interpret reasonable boundaries through structure and rules
- communicating with families frequently about the child's progress

Parenting in the Authority Stage

Parents enter the *authority stage* of parenting when toddlers reach age 2. During this stage, parents' images of their always-sweet children change. Accepting their toddlers' angry and unpleasant feelings and actions is part of parenting. Loving their children by setting clear limits and enforcing them, and dealing with angry outbursts, requires open communication between parents. As parents recognize their parenting strengths and weaknesses, they must also learn from and repair their mistakes, seeking help when necessary.

Special Family Times

Toddlers are family people. They like to imitate. Toddlers want to try on their parents' hats, gloves, jackets, and shoes. They think the things their parents do look like fun. Parents need to include them in family tasks,

Keeping Toddlers Safe

Window hazards—Close and lock all windows or use childproof window guards. Toddlers have enough strength to open a window and crawl through it or slam a window shut on their fingers.

Door hazards—Lock or barricade doors to prevent toddlers from gaining access to potentially dangerous areas.

Toy safety—Examine all toys to make sure they are safe. The eyes on dolls and stuffed animals should be securely fastened so a toddler cannot pull them off and swallow them. No toys should have sharp edges. Painted toys should be free of lead paint.

Car safety—Use safety seats in cars. Toddlers should be put in safety seats in the middle of the backseat whenever they ride in cars. Make sure the seat is fastened securely in the car, according to manufacturer's directions.

Fire hazards—Store matches or cigarette lighters out of children's reach.

Falling obstacles—Keep low shelves free of dangerous items. Toddlers like to reach for things on shelves. By grabbing the bottom can on a kitchen shelf, they could cause a dangerous avalanche.

(Continued on next page)

14-20 These tips can help parents keep adventurous toddlers safe.

Kitchen range hazards—Keep toddlers away from the kitchen range. With their fascination with knobs, toddlers may turn on burners or elements. Keep handles of all pots and pans toward the back of the range away from the heat source to prevent spills and burns.

Climbing dangers—Watch toddlers at all times. As toddlers' physical skills improve, they may try to climb anything in sight and end up in danger.

Traffic dangers—Keep toddlers away from the street. They are not sufficiently aware of traffic dangers and may run after a rolling ball or a pet without thinking about oncoming traffic.

Pet dangers—Warn toddlers about pets. Toddlers think all pets are friendly. Parents should teach toddlers that a friendly pat or squeeze might cause an animal to scratch or bite.

14-20 Continued.

such as gardening, baking, and doing dishes. Many toddlers want to help with cleaning, but most appliances are unsafe for them to use. A good option is to find toy versions so they can "help."

Toddlers like parents to play with them. Parents can make hideouts from cardboard boxes and sheets draped over tables. If toddlers hide, parents can have a fun time "finding" them. Toddlers really enjoy excursions to local parks, playgrounds, beaches, and zoos—or a wagon ride around the block.

Because older toddlers are learning how the world works, they enjoy funny changes. Parents can make laughter part of every day. When parents mix up the details of a funny story or wear a hat in silly ways, toddlers giggle with delight. Comic relief is good for all family members. Laughter can be part of the special times in any family.

13 to 15 Months*

Physical Development
Gross-Motor Skills

Creeps forward and backward with varying speed

Creeps over small barriers

May creep like a bear, with hands and feet in contact with floor

May stand erect with only slight support

Takes steps while holding onto parents' hands

Takes a few steps alone with feet spread and arms held high

Sits by collapsing when first taking steps

Climbs stairs on hands and knees and backs down stairs

May climb out of crib, high chair, or stroller

Climbs on chairs, sofas, and tables

Sits in a small chair but kneels and turns to get into the seat

Fine-Motor Skills

Grasps objects easily, but finds it difficult to turn objects in hands (manipulation)

Turns cardboard or cloth pages of picture books

Enjoys filling and emptying containers with small objects

Can open small, hinged box

Builds small towers of blocks

May try to turn doorknobs

Uses spoon, spilling little

Intellectual Development
General

Explores different features of objects as if studying them

Discovers ability to make things happen by own actions

Tries different actions on an object, such as dropping, pounding, pinching, and tearing Play-Doh®

Tries the same action on different objects, such as throwing different objects from a high chair

Experiments with actions never tried before

Notices actions of other children and adults. Loves to mimic all actions

Likes to look at picture books and pats recognized pictures

Can push a sphere through a round hole in a sorting box; can place a circle in the correct inset on a form board

Language

Babbles with expression. Amuses self with vocal play

May use sounds to indicate specific objects

May attempt to imitate words others say

May repeat sounds without understanding the meaning of sounds

Increases vocabulary slowly to 4 to 6 words

Points to familiar body parts, toys, or persons on request

Follows simple commands, such as *give*, *come*, *stop*, and *show me*

Social and Emotional Development
Social

Enjoys solitary play

Prefers play with older siblings or familiar adults

Shows off for an audience

Is easily diverted and entertained

Likes to go for stroller or car rides

Recognizes self in mirror and may communicate with sounds

Emotional

Likes to exhibit affection to humans and objects

Shows pride in personal accomplishments

Often becomes attached to a special toy or object

Prefers to keep parent or caregiver in sight while exploring environment

Is more demanding and self-assertive

Shows increased negativism

Demands personal attention

* These charts are not exact timetables. Individuals may perform certain activities earlier or later than indicated in the charts.

16 to 18 Months

Physical Development

Gross-Motor Skills

Walks without support but falls over toys or objects on the floor

May take a step or two sideways

Squats down smoothly from standing position

Pushes and pulls large toys around the floor

Walks into ball; is unable to kick the ball

Fine-Motor Skills

Enjoys grabbing anything and everything

Adds hand gestures to spoken language

Begins to scribble

Continues to enjoy filling and emptying containers

May turn knobs of radio and TV

Builds tower of three cubes

Places round pegs in a pegboard

Clumsily works wooden puzzles with three or less "whole" (not divided) pieces

Clumsily tries to make marks on taped-down paper with a crayon or pencil

Intellectual Development

General

Is the inquisitive *scientist* who gets into everything

Remembers where objects belong

Uses senses and motor skills in constant experimentation

Discovers new uses for familiar objects, such as toilet paper can be spread over a floor or milk can be spilled on the floor

Achieves goals by trial-and-error

Knows lost objects exist; looks in place where last seen

Has short attention span so goes from one activity to another

Language

Imitates simple sounds on request

Says 6 to 10 words

Replaces some gestures (holding arms up) with words (*up*)

Says "no" more often than any other word

Refers to self by name when asked

Understands more words than is capable of saying

Identifies objects by pointing when requested

Obeys command, "Give it to me"

Responds to increasing number of verbal directions if combined with actions

Social and Emotional Development

Social

Is very socially responsive to parents and caregivers

Realizes different people react in different ways

Demands personal attention from family members

Shows or hands objects to parents and expectantly awaits their reaction

Responds to simple requests

Enjoys sociable play before bedtime

Will perform for an audience

Is unable to share

Plays with others as though they were objects (punches and pokes)

Emotional

Is emotionally unpredictable and may respond differently at different times

Hugs favorite toys and may carry them all the time

May hug pets too hard when wanting to show affection

Shows or hands objects to parents and expectantly awaits their reaction

Is unable to tolerate frustration

May exhibit fears of such things as thunder, lightning, or large animals

May be less afraid of strangers

May reveal negativism and stubbornness

Enjoys ability to do things independently

Responds to parents' emotional expressions by imitating them

19 to 21 Months

Physical Development

Gross-Motor Skills

Walks sideways and backward

Walks hurriedly; this resembles, but is not, running

Walks up stairs without alternating feet if supported by an adult or rail

Clumsily walks down stairs without alternating feet if supported by adult

Steps off low objects, such as a curb, without support by an adult

Backs up and sits in a chair

Squats easily in play

Sits on floor from standing position quite easily

Fine-Motor Skills

Helps with dressing by pushing arms through sleeves and by removing some clothes

Builds stable tower of three blocks

Holds container in one hand, puts small objects into it with other hand, then dumps the objects out

Puts pegs in pegboard

Strings large beads on cord

Turns several book pages at a time

Covers paper with marks; pinches and pats clay

Intellectual Development

General

Pauses in mid-action to "figure things out"

Looks for a *lost* object in many places

Imitates actions of a model after model is finished

Imitates simple actions on request

Can remember familiar objects without seeing them

Can obtain familiar objects from different room when asked

Inserts circles, squares, and triangles into form board

Studies pictures in picture books

Completes simple wooden puzzles

Associates tool with function it performs, such as hammer for banging

Learns to distinguish different sounds and smells

Language

Has a vocabulary of about 20 words

Enjoys labeling objects and parts of body

Responds to speech with speech

Uses speech to get desired results

Combines two different words

Constantly asks, "What's that?"

Likes to respond to directions

Understands some personal pronouns such as *me*

Matches sounds to the animals that make them

Social and Emotional Development

Social

Continues to desire personal attention

Indicates awareness of absence of person by saying "bye-bye"

May enjoy removing clothing and is not embarrassed about being naked

Plays contentedly alone if near adults

Likes to play next to other children but does not interact with them

Shows some signs of resistance to adult requests

Emotional

Shows affection to family members, children, and pets

Often needs a toy or blanket for security

May direct anger at person responsible for frustration

Likes to claim things as "mine"

Gives up items that belong to others upon request

Detects fear in adults

Shows empathy for a crying child or adult

22 to 24 Months

Physical Development

Gross-Motor Skills

Walks with more coordination, but still falls often

Walks sideways and backward with ease

Bounces and sways in simple dancing movements

Alternates between standing and sitting positions easily

Can seat self in small chair with ease

Jumps by stepping off low objects with both feet in the air for a second

Throws small objects with a rigid underhand throw

Throws large balls by holding ball overhead; ball drops behind child or is released near toes as the child bends

Catches balls by squatting and picking them up

Fine-Motor Skills

Shows increased coordination and smoother hand and finger movements

Puts several blocks together to make a train or stack them to build a tower

Scribbles vertical and horizontal lines and loops that may resemble a circle

Folds a piece of paper if shown how

Likes to play with modeling clay

Opens screw-type closures

Intellectual Development

General

Shows more and more curiosity about the environment

Becomes interested in the outcome of activities rather than just the activities themselves

Is able to match familiar objects

Identifies familiar objects on a TV or computer screen

Recognizes when picture in book is upside down

May distinguish between *one* and *many*

Becomes interested in the precise placement of objects; enjoys form boards and simple puzzles

Language

Has vocabulary of 50 or more words

Can ask for things, such as food, water, and toys

Understands and asks for *another* and *more*

Is interested in sound repetition

Understands more words than is able to use

Substitutes some words for some physical acts

Answers simple questions such as "Where is the doggie?" and "What does kitty say?"

Listens to and enjoys simple stories

Imitates parents' words and inflections

Social and Emotional Development

Social

Is more responsive to and more demanding of adults

Likes playing near siblings and other children

Continually tests the limits set by parents and caregivers

Desires approval in social situations

Sometimes becomes aggressive with others if frustrated

Refers to self by name or with the word *me*

Helps put toys away

Likes to control others and give them orders

Emotional

Displays strong positive or negative reactions

Recognizes own power to be effective

Displays signs of love for parents and other favorite people

Expresses possessive attitude by using *me*, *my*, or *mine* to indicate possession

Wants own way in everything

Becomes frustrated easily

May show some aggression by biting or hitting

Fears rejection and is hurt by criticism

May dawdle, but desires to please parents

24 to 30 Months

Physical Development

Gross-Motor Skills

Improves motor skills as torso lengthens and baby fat begins to disappear

Walks with a stabilized rhythm due to better balance; monitors foot placement to prevent falls

Begins true running with arms held outward

Jumps off low objects with both feet; arms retract rather than go forward

Throws objects in many ways, but without aiming

Climbs everywhere indoors, even in forbidden places

Fine-Motor Skills

Tries to open doors by turning knobs

Shows improvement in turning book pages

Tears paper; manipulates clay

Scribbles with vertical and horizontal lines crossing (× and +)

Helps with grooming (brushing teeth and hair, washing and drying hands)

Intellectual Development

General

Combines two or more objects in play, such as hits a pan with a wooden spoon or fills pan with small blocks

Notices simple cause and effect in terms of own behaviors, such as playing with art materials, water, sand, or blocks

Thinks in terms of actions; thus, might define a cookie as "to eat"

Pretends by doing an act on himself/herself, such as closing eyes to pretend sleep

Knows how to use some objects, such as a spoon is for eating (functional associations)

Becomes increasingly interested in children's TV shows

Likes to listen to CDs of stories and songs

Language

Vocabulary starts at 200 words and increases to 500 or more words

Uses two-word sentences

Enjoys learning names for new objects

Uses words to make requests

Understands a few prepositions such as *out*, *in*, *on*

Follows two-step commands

Social and Emotional Development

Social

Likes to give affection to parents

Prefers certain age-mates instead of others

Likes to play near other children and will often imitate their actions

Does not like to share toys

May grab desired toys away from other children

Emotional

Continues to be self-centered

May exhibit increasing independence one minute and then run back to security of parents the next

Likes immediate gratification and finds it difficult to wait

Angry outbursts peak

Has trouble sharing, but may give back a toy that belongs to someone else

Continues to seek parental approval for behaviors and accomplishments

Displays jealousy

May develop fear of dark; needs reassurance

30 to 36 Months

Physical Development
Gross-Motor Skills

Likes to be in constant motion, walking, running, or jumping

Walks on tiptoes

Enjoys running but cannot start or stop quickly; may collide with people or obstacles

Can run up to a ball and kick it; often stops before kicking

Climbs everywhere indoors, even in forbidden places

Climbs on play structures designed for toddlers

Likes chair or sling-seat swings; cannot swing self

Throws small objects four to five feet

Tries to "catch" large balls with arms outstretched or in a hoop position

Sits in adult chairs and may prefer these to smaller chairs

Fine-Motor Skills

Turns book pages one at a time

Cuts with scissors if an adult holds the paper

Clumsily holds crayons with thumb and fingers

Paints with some wrist action along with whole-arm action

Turns doorknobs with greater strength

Strings large beads

Builds towers of six or more blocks

Takes objects apart and puts them back together

Intellectual Development
General

Begins to classify objects into general categories

Pretends with objects, such as a doll for a baby; pretend actions are based on others' experiences such as rocking a baby (doll)

Pretend is an abbreviated action, such as picking up a phone and saying, "Bye"

Drawing now represents something to the child (not to others); for example a red line might be the color of a ball or the path of a rolled ball.

Knows use of almost all house and yard tools (functional associations)

Begins to make part-whole associations, such as *cup and saucer* and *wheel and car*

Knows who uses certain objects, such as child's toys, dog's toys, and mother's or dad's tools and appliances

Stacks rings on peg in order of size

Tries new play activities to discover more about how things work

Language

Vocabulary starts at about 500 words and increases to 900 or 1000 words

Begins to categorize in language, but overextends terms, such as calling all men a daddy

Creates two- to three-word sentences, including verbs

Asks names of objects and repeats them

Connects names and uses of objects

Understands relative size (big and small)

Starts to use past tense and plurals

Understands question forms *what* and *where* and negatives

Enjoys stories and tries to sequence a few events

Says first and last name

Social and Emotional Development
Social

Likes to be accepted by others

Briefly joins in other children's play

Defends own possessions

May continue to show aggressive actions to get own way while playing with others

Sings, claps, or dances with other children if encouraged

Distinguishes between boys and girls

Likes to play with adults on one-to-one basis

Enjoys tumbling play with older siblings and parents

Emotional

May dawdle but insists on doing things for self

Likes to dress self and needs praise and encouragement when correct

Desires parental approval

Wants independence but shows fear of new experiences

May reveal need for clinging to security object

May have trouble sleeping if day's events have been emotional

Displays negative feelings; has fewer temper tantrums

Feels bad when reprimanded for mistakes

Summing It Up

- Body proportions are the most noticeable physical changes in toddlers.

- Gross- and fine-motor skill help develop stamina and coordination, learning, socialization, and play.

- Exploration of their bodies is normal as toddlers develop gender identity.

- Toddlers are eager to learn life skills, but parents must let them practice.

- The rate of teething varies from child to child, but the sequence is always the same.

- Children cooperate with toilet learning when they are ready. Parents should not push their children, but should wait until the child shows signs of readiness.

- According to Piaget, intellectual development takes a major leap as toddlers develop the ability to think with mental images.

- Many toddlers can say more than 500 words and use two-word "sentences."

- Friendships begin in the toddler years.

- Although toddlers show their desire for independence by trying to do more things for themselves, they need security and reassurance.

- Toddler experience intense emotions. Overcoming separation anxiety is a significant developmental milestone.

- Routine medical checkups are an important part of toddler health.

- Parenting concerns and tasks involve such things as setting limits, soothing toddlers' emotions, coping with temper tantrums, and keeping toddlers safe.

Recalling the Facts

1. Describe how a toddler's body proportions change.

2. Name five tasks toddlers can do with their improved fine-motor skills as they approach age 3.

3. Name three life skills toddlers must learn.

4. How can parents promote good eating habits with their toddlers?

5. What developmental characteristics indicate a toddler is ready for toilet learning?

6. Name five tips parents can use to help their toddlers achieve toileting success.

7. List two major intellectual skills that develop during Piaget's substage of mental representation.

8. Name three types of play important to toddlers.

9. Contrast open and closed toys.

10. What are four ways parents can help their toddlers learn language?

11. How is toddlers' behavior inconsistent as they struggle for independence?

12. Name three ways parents can help their toddlers interact with other children.

13. Why do toddlers struggle with fear and anxiety?

14. Name three common parenting concerns and tasks during the toddler years.

Applying New Skills

1. **Observation.** Make arrangements to observe a group of toddlers for 30 minutes. Be sure to obtain permission to observe. As you observe, write down all gross- and fine-motor skills you see the toddlers using. What differences did you see? What does this tell you about toddler development? Share your findings with the class.

2. **Life-skill demonstration.** Talk with a toddler parent or a child care teacher who works with toddlers about simple practices to teach toddlers life skills. Choose one life skill. Then prepare a way to teach this skill to a toddler. For example, you might learn an easy way to help a toddler put on a shirt, prepare a food that encourages self-feeding, or create a fun way to promote tooth brushing. Demonstrate your life skill to the class. What challenges might parents face in teaching toddlers this skill?

3. **Reading with toddlers.** Talk with a children's librarian about books that encourage language development in toddlers. Choose one book to read to a toddler at a child care center or another toddler you know. Write a summary about your reading interactions with the toddler.

4. **Teachable moments.** As a class, brainstorm a list of potential teachable moments for parents and their toddlers. Then identify ways parents can make the best use of these teachable moments. Discuss your ideas in class.

5. **Safety investigation.** With improved walking and grasping skills, toddlers become great explorers. Use Internet or print resources to find practical ways parents can "toddler-proof" their homes to keep toddlers safe. Share your findings with the class and parents you know.

Thinking Critically

1. Watch older toddlers engaging in pretend play at a child care center (with permission). Draw conclusions about the mental images these toddlers express. What might these expressions mean? What does this tell you about social/emotional development of toddlers? Discuss your observations in class.

2. Identify the false thinking in the following statement: Making a toddler repeat a word over and over until the pronunciation is correct is a good way to help the child build vocabulary skills. Rewrite the statement to reflect correct thinking in helping a toddler build vocabulary skills.

3. Compare and contrast ways that providing structure and setting limits for toddlers may help parents deal with such common toddler problems as separation anxiety, fearfulness, throwing objects, dawdling, and tantrums.

4. Analyze whether quality toddler care is more dependent on the program (daily activities) or teacher characteristics. Give evidence to support your answer.

5. How can including toddlers in routine and fun family activities promote all aspects of toddler development?

Linking Academics

1. **Reading.** Read one or more picture books for toddlers, such as *Peter's Chair* by Jack Ezra Keats or *A Baby Sister for Francis* by Russell Hoban. Write a summary of the book explaining how it might help parents and their toddlers with the struggle for autonomy. Write your summary on a note card for future reference. Continue by creating a card file of favorite books to use when caring for children or your own future family.

2. **Writing.** In 12 sentences or less, write a summary of the key toddler struggles during Erikson's *shame versus doubt* stage of personality development.

Chapter 15

Parents and Their Preschoolers

Objectives

After studying this chapter, you will be able to

- identify characteristics of physical development, including advances in gross- and fine-motor skills, gender understandings, and life skills.

- explain why enuresis occurs and how parents can help children overcome it.

- summarize characteristics of preschoolers' intellectual development, including the process of learning, the role of play in learning, and key aspects of language development.

- list three major intellectual learnings of preschoolers according to Piaget.

- describe characteristics of preschoolers' social and emotional development, including friendship development, sibling relationships, and parental influence.

- describe how preschoolers express initiative according to Erikson.

- summarize key parenting concerns and tasks during the preschool years, including medical checkups and family-life adjustments for preschooler safety, care, and special family times.

Key Terms

preschooler
locomotor skills
gender stability
gender constancy
enuresis
perceptual thinking
associative play
cooperative play
stuttering
lisping
toilet talk
baby talk
bilingualism
sibling rivalry
developmental screening

Parents can't help describing their preschoolers as charmers. A **preschooler** is a child 3 through 5 years of age. Preschoolers' advances in motor skills allow them to observe what is happening in their world in contrast to the toddlers' focus on walking and carrying things. Children take part in many physical activities. They also learn from their physical and social worlds. The social world of preschoolers, which may include preschool programs and kindergarten, is rapidly expanding, too. Outgoing and full of questions, preschoolers are interested in everything.

These years can be great fun for parents because preschoolers are less moody and more willing to comply with parental rules than toddlers. Parents watch with joy as their preschoolers delight in discovering their ever-expanding worlds, 15-1.

In this chapter you will study preschoolers' development. Certain patterns of development are common among preschoolers although each child's development is unique. After each section, review the "Preschooler Development" charts at the end of the chapter for month-by-month development. You will also study the role of parents as they attempt to make their rules clear and develop their parenting style.

Physical Development

Although preschoolers don't grow as fast as infants and toddlers, they take big steps in physical development. During the preschool period, children grow out of babyhood. Physical changes lead to advancing motor skills.

Physical Growth

The rate of growth for preschoolers is much slower than for toddlers. During the preschool period, children grow about 2½ to 3 inches and gain about 5 to 6 pounds yearly.

15-1 Preschoolers are fascinated with everything.

On the average, a 3-year-old will be about 38 inches tall and weigh about 32 pounds. By age 6, the child will be about 48 inches tall and weigh 46 to 48 pounds.

Body proportion and shape continue to change during the preschool years. The child loses more baby fat. At age 5½, body fat is about half as thick as it was during infancy. Muscle and bone growth account for most weight gain. Preschoolers' bones and joints are still somewhat soft and flexible. Because of this, parents need to monitor children's activities to avoid harm from strenuous pulling and pushing.

As you recall, the head makes up one-fourth of the height of a 2-year-old. In contrast, the head of a 6-year-old is one-sixth of preschooler height. The stomach flattens as the torso becomes longer. A rather squat-looking 3-year-old will look much taller and leaner by age 6.

In general, internal organs are more mature and stable. However, the digestive tract remains immature. Preschoolers may have more digestive upsets than older children. The brain is maturing and beginning to *specialize* (different areas of the brain process different types of environmental input, such as visual, motor, and language). For example, the frontal lobes of the brain process reasoning. The right side of the brain controls spatial information and visual imagery, which the left side of the brain receives, processes, and produces language.

Gross-Motor Skills

Preschoolers are just starting to hop, skip, climb, and ride tricycles and bicycles, 15-2. They enjoy the challenge of practicing these new skills. As they practice, they take great strides in gross-motor development. Preschoolers also thrive on repeating new, playful acts. When one playmate tries something new, all the children soon follow suit, repeating the stunt over and over. Through this practice, preschoolers learn new skills and refine and improve their body control.

Locomotor Skills

Locomotor skills involve moving from place to place through use of the gross-motor skills of the legs. These skills also involve balance. Locomotor skills include walking, running, climbing, hopping, galloping, skipping, and pedaling.

During the third year, children can walk with their arms at their sides and maintain balance. Their arms swing with each step in

15-2 Safety is important, especially when children are playing on climbing equipment.

an adultlike walking pattern. Preschoolers can adjust their walk to different terrains, such as up and down hills. They can even do a heel-toe walk by age 4.

Early in the preschool years, "running" is fast, flat-footed walking. At age 3, their favorite trick is swerving from side-to-side. Preschoolers cannot completely change running direction without stopping until they are almost 5 years old. True running, in which one is very briefly airborne, does not occur until 4 to 6 years.

Three-year-olds climb stairs by stepping up on one foot, pulling the other foot up to the new level, and balancing briefly on both feet. When preschoolers are almost 4, they can alternate feet going up steps. A year later, they can alternate feet going down.

Becoming airborne is critical not only for running, but also for jumping, hopping, galloping, and skipping. Although toddlers do small vertical jumps, forward jumps do not occur until the preschool years. Between

4 and 5 years, preschoolers use their arms and body correctly and have a balanced landing on a forward jump. Hopping, galloping, and skipping require even more balance and coordination than jumping because preschoolers use one foot at a time. Hopping becomes much better by age 4. Galloping and skipping occur a year or so later.

Most 5-year-olds are ready to ride bicycles with training wheels. Learning this new skill is exciting for parents and children alike. Once children take off and feel comfortable with this new kind of balance, they enjoy praise for their accomplishment.

Preschoolers are adventuresome, adding their own new challenges to activities. They test their improved balance by whirling around, turning somersaults, and hanging upside-down. Preschoolers love to climb up slides instead of using the ladders. They race to scramble to the top of the jungle gym. They may jump off the porch instead of walking down the steps. Bumps and tumbles occur, but preschoolers are usually too busy to stop for sympathy.

Toward the end of the preschool years, children are more graceful in their motions. They run, swerve, and turn corners with greater speed and smoothness. Running turns to racing anytime someone accepts the challenge. They enjoy active games of all kinds.

Upper Body and Arm Skills

Gross-motor skills of the arms lag somewhat behind locomotor skills. Preschoolers need arm skills for throwing and catching. These skills improve during the preschool years.

Preschoolers go through a sequence of skills in ball throwing and catching. At age 3, they throw balls with one hand, but the body remains stiff while throwing. Within a year, preschoolers throw with a slight twist of the shoulder as their arms move forward.

By age 5, children show a weight shift as they step forward on the throwing-arm side and release the ball.

Three-year-olds catch balls by trying to trap them with their arms, hands, and body. By age 4, children open their hands, but their elbows are still straight when they catch. Five-year-olds assume an adultlike catching posture. They close their fingers around the ball, but their reaction time is slow. Because preschoolers cannot judge the speed of airborne balls, they rarely catch them.

Structured Activities for Preschoolers

Preschoolers need several hours of active play daily to exercise their growing muscles, 15-3. Some parents want to start their preschoolers in structured physical activities, such as gymnastics, dance, or team sports. Most experts say that starting these activities early does not give children an advantage and likely results in burnout by age 12. Some programs are too stressful for preschoolers who would rather just play. The American Academy of Pediatrics (AAP) recommends parents wait until the school years to enroll their children in such programs.

Fine-Motor Skills

When people envision active preschoolers, they think about their gross-motor skills. These skills are most visible. Yet, preschoolers' fine-motor development is also impressive. Picture a 3-year-old trying to draw, cut with scissors, or button a jacket. Then imagine an almost 6-year-old doing the same skills with ease and confidence.

Artwork

Preschoolers use fine-motor skills involving the arm and wrist more easily than the fingers. For example, young preschoolers can handle a paintbrush with more ease than a pencil. Drawing something large on a big piece of paper is easier than drawing a figure on a small piece of paper. Artwork

15-3 Active play is good for preschoolers, and it paves the way for future healthy exercise habits. However, most preschoolers are not yet ready for structured physical activities and competitive sports.

requires fine-muscle control and eye-hand coordination. Children's artwork generally progresses through four stages during the preschool years. These stages include the following:

- *Scribble stage.* In the scribble stage, children use fine-motor skills of the arms and wrist to make random scribbles on paper for the pure joy of scribbling. Before age 3, children may not be able to keep their scribbles on the paper.
- *Shape stage.* During the shape stage, 3-year-olds begin to draw distinct shapes, such as circles, ovals, and crossed lines.
- *Design stage.* By the end of their third year, preschoolers make designs by putting shapes together. By age 4, children can subdivide shapes, such as drawing lines through circles and squares. They can also make stick figures. Children often attach the arms and legs of these figures directly to the head.
- *Pictorial stage.* Near the end of the preschool period, children's artwork becomes more realistic as they enter the pictorial stage. They draw people, animals, houses, trees, flowers, and vehicles. However, they have not yet developed the eye-hand coordination for artistic detail. A 5-year-old can tell you more about a person or an object than he or she can draw.

Construction and Other Activities

In addition to artwork, preschoolers use fine-motor skills for handling pegs, puzzle pieces, and small blocks. They also use these skills for stringing beads, using tools (hammers and scissors), and doing many life skills. All of these skills develop if preschoolers have the opportunity. Parents need to provide the materials and give a little help with some skills, such as using scissors, 15-4. Most of all, they need to show patience and encourage their preschoolers.

Role of Hand Preference

Most fine-motor skills require the use of both hands. Can you cut, write, button, snap, or tie shoelaces easily with one hand? Although a person uses both hands, a preferred hand takes the lead. Genetics and experiences determine hand preference. Once a person begins to use a preferred hand, the eye-hand coordination becomes brain-wired.

Scissors Skills for Preschoolers

Parent Role	Tips for Teaching
Purchase good materials.	• Choose scissors made for children with a straight edge and blunt tips. Make sure they cut easily. • Choose scissors for right-hand or left-hand preference. Child must have an established hand preference. • Use stiff paper, such as construction paper or paper bags.
Model use of scissors.	• Hold blades of scissors closed with non-preferred hand in cutting position. • Put thumb in top hole ("Thumbs up!") and put second and third fingers in lower hole. • Keep elbows close to the body and hold scissors perpendicular (to paper). Parent can call the perpendicular position "a frog or alligator mouth." • Cut the air holding scissors vertically.
Show what to cut.	• Start by cutting a one-snip fringe around the paper edges. • Then cut short straight lines that have been drawn. • Finally, cut slightly curved lines. Curved lines require holding paper taut and turning paper at the same time.
Provide more help if needed.	• Hold paper for child. • Select a pair of teaching scissors for adult-child co-cutting.* These scissors have a double set of holes—one for the child and one for the teacher. Some have handles and not holes so the entire hand is used. Some also have a spring that opens the scissors after each snip.*

Note: These are sold in teacher supply stores.

15-4 One-on-one help is the best way for a preschooler to learn how to use scissors. Using scissors is a difficult skill, so parents must be patient.

Hand preference is usually definite by age 3. Most children are right-handed, but parents should allow children who prefer to use their left hands to do so. Trying to force children to use their right hands will only frustrate them.

Although left-handed children may have some problems fitting into a right-handed world, they can adapt. They may have to think ahead to take a left-handed desk or use left-handed scissors. Parents can help by showing a left-handed child how to do various tasks in the most comfortable way. For instance, writing is more comfortable when the lower right-hand corner of the paper is nearest the body.

Healthy Sexuality Development

In the infant and early toddler years, children primarily explore their bodies and learn some physical concepts about gender. Toward the later part of the toddler years, sexuality begins to develop. *Sexuality,* or everything associated with maleness and femaleness, develops gradually throughout a person's lifetime. It involves all four major areas of development. Children not only learn physical facts about gender, but also begin to sense how they feel about themselves as boys and girls. They sense how their parents act toward each other and toward others. From this foundation, children learn to function as complete, unique human beings.

Teaching children about sexuality is not easy. It is a responsibility that evolves out of love for children and the honest desire for them to live abundant and happy lives. Parents should consider a child's age and needs when offering information about sexuality. Learning about masculinity or femininity is a lifelong process that begins almost from birth.

Gender-role development continues in the preschool years. Around age 6, children develop the gender-role concept of **gender stability**, the understanding that boys become men and that girls become women. During the same time, preschoolers begin to learn about the concept of **gender constancy**, the understanding that despite outward changes or desire, gender does not change. Preschoolers often show confusion about how a change in hairstyle or clothing affects gender although they know sex organs are different for males and females. Instead of dealing with this difficult concept, they engage in very stereotypical behaviors. They believe boys and girls should differ in how they look and in their play activities.

Preschoolers often ask questions about sex, too. A common question is "Where do babies come from?" Children are not ready for a full lesson in reproduction, but the best answer is the truth. "Babies grow inside their mothers" is usually all children really want to know, 15-5. Parents should not put the explanation off by saying "we can't talk about that now." It is important for parents not to suppress their children's curiosity about sexuality or respond in a negative way. This is a time to be open and truthful in communication.

Sometime around age 4, children may want to know more. If parents have openly answered previous questions, children feel free to ask more questions. They may ask, "How does the baby get out?" Again, a

15-5 When children ask where babies come from, they should be told the truth, but in very simple terms. They are not ready for a full lesson in reproduction.

simple answer, "There is a special opening for the baby to come through," will satisfy them for the time. They think a lot about all these things, and they may ask for more details about birth. Preschoolers make little connection between the size of a pregnant woman and the presence of a baby.

By this age, preschoolers have been exposed to other sources of sex information—TV and stories from their friends. Parents who have open, truthful communication with their children have less anxiety about their children receiving incorrect information from others about sex. If children know they can ask their parents about sex, they are less likely to ask others. Five-year-olds are generally more interested in the baby itself than in the baby's origin.

Preschool children observe gender roles. They notice how their parents act. They may act out roles they see their parents perform. Today, adults have many different roles than in years past. Both men and women work outside the home, and many parents share household tasks. Consider this preschool example. A little girl is busy at the play sink "washing dishes." A little boy comes in, puts his arm around her shoulders and says, "I know you are tired, so you sit down. I'll wash the dishes tonight." Evidently, he saw his father act this way. It is natural to him to adopt this role.

Learning Life Skills

Parents find it encouraging to see their preschoolers learn to handle most of their eating, dressing, and grooming tasks. These life-skill achievements please both preschoolers and their parents, but result from great effort. Children need lots of practice, and parents need lots of patience.

Eating

Before the end of the preschool period, children can handle all pieces of flatware if parents help them learn these skills. Early childhood teachers report many young children come to school unable to use forks and knives. Eating fast foods regularly may keep children from having the experiences needed to learn these skills.

By the preschool stage, children are ready to begin learning table manners. Parents can teach manners in pleasant ways. Preschoolers follow the examples set by parents and siblings.

Preschoolers can generally eat the same food as the rest of the family. Parents should not prepare special foods for them, but should accept the fact preschoolers have strong food preferences. One day they may like a food,

and the next day they may not. They may ask for a certain food, such as breakfast cereal, for both breakfast and lunch several days in a row. Parents should ignore these eating desires and continue providing healthy foods. They might also add some "extras" to make them even more nutritious, 15-6.

When parents involve them in shopping and cooking food, preschoolers often have fewer problems at mealtimes. Those who learn how food looks, smells, and is cooked have fewer food dislikes. Preschoolers can also help with table setting. With parent assistance, children can prepare and serve a nutritious dish for a family meal or snack. Food preparation provides practice using fine-motor skills, too.

Dressing

Preschool children learn dressing skills at different rates. Although some children insist on independence more than others, parents should encourage these skills in the preschool years. Watching for teachable moments helps. When children show an interest in dressing skills, parents can be ready to help them learn those skills. Trying to hurry children only leads to discouragement and frustration. Laughing at their efforts hurts tender feelings. Making negative comments lessens their desire to learn. How can parents help? Some ways to help include the following:

- *Choose outfits that are easy to manage.* For example, larger buttons with well-sewn buttonholes are easier to manage than smaller buttons and buttonholes. At the same time, children need challenges to learn. For example, children cannot always wear clothes and shoes with hook-and-loop tape fasteners.

- *Mark clothing to identify front from back and left from right.* For example, place a mark on the inside edge of shoe soles to help children put them on the floor with the marks together. They can then slip their feet into the correct shoes.

Make Healthful Eating the Rule

Rules	Healthful Eating Tips
Add "extras" to make healthy foods even healthier.	• Add steamed and puréed carrots, peas, and peppers to tomato sauce. • Add steamed and puréed cauliflower to mashed potatoes. • Add shredded slaw to tuna salad. • Add steamed and puréed cabbage to soups. • Add grated tofu to cheese on lasagna. • Add cooked and puréed beans to meat loaf.
Try new ways to serve foods.	• Cut fruit to dip in yogurt. • Make deli-turkey roll ups. • Thread fruit bites onto wooden skewers. • Put rainbow sprinkles on top of cooked cereals and yogurt.
Avoid obesity traps.	• Do not require a "clean plate." • Give a nutritious snack between meals to avoid overeating at mealtimes. • Do not buy sugary or high-fat snack foods. • Eat only in the kitchen or dining room. Avoid eating in front of the TV. • Make good restaurant choices, such as those offering child-sized portions and vegetables, salads, and fruits. Avoid sodas, double sizes, and deep-fried entrées. • Encourage children to drink water and eat whole fruits.
Make family meals extra fun once a week or more often.	• Choose a meal theme. Preschoolers who are learning alphabet letters might enjoy a meal in which all foods begin with the same letter. • Discuss a favorite picture storybook. • Cover the table with a paper tablecloth. Have mugs of crayons on the table so everyone can draw or write. • Try a candlelight dinner with floating votive candles. • Have a brunch, picnic, barbecue, or holiday meal complete with decorations.

15-6 Involving children in food preparation helps lead to healthful eating habits for a lifetime.

- *Plan ways to explain how to put on clothing with the front and back in the correct position.* Some preschool teachers have children lay clothing on the floor with the front side up. Then the child gets on the floor to slip head and arms through the holes of a top or feet and legs through the pants. By age 5, most children can dress without using the floor.

- *Help the child only as much as needed.* For example, the parent helps get the jeans started on the correct legs, and the child completes the job. The child buttons the two top buttons while the parent works from the bottom button up.

- *Break difficult tasks into simple steps.* As children master simple steps, such as tying shoelaces, they gain confidence, 15-7.

15-7 Five-year-olds may be able to tie their shoelaces if they have been shown how to do it in a step-by-step process.

By the end of the preschool years, most children can dress themselves. They are ready to go to school and need little, if any, teacher help in dressing.

Grooming

Parents may still need to assist and guide their preschoolers with some grooming tasks. For example, preschoolers need help with thorough tooth brushing, shampooing hair, and cutting fingernails and toenails. They can handle most other tasks, such as washing their faces and hands. If they have simple hairstyles, preschoolers enjoy combing their own hair.

At the beginning of the preschool years, children often need some help using the toilet. If they can recognize the need to use the toilet, they have taken a big step. Clothes that are easy to remove help preschoolers become more independent. By the time they are 5, most children can use the toilet and get dressed again on their own. These skills are necessary for children to begin kindergarten.

Toilet Learning

During the preschool years, two toilet-learning problems may occur. First, some children regress in their learning. This may be due to stress or just forgetting to urinate when busy at play. Parents can try to reduce stressors and remind children to use the toilet.

A second problem is **enuresis,** or bedwetting, in children over age 3. Because boys mature more slowly than girls, enuresis is a more common problem for boys. Almost every child has an occasional nighttime accident. Some children experience enuresis frequently in the preschool and early school years. A few children have problems beyond these years.

Incomplete toilet learning may be the cause of enuresis in a young child. If the problem disappears gradually, parents may just need to be patient and reassuring. If it continues, parents should consult their pediatrician. Physical causes include improper functioning of the bladder, sphincter muscles, or urinary tract. Treatments are available. If the cause is psychological, such as stress or even fear of getting up in the dark, parents can best treat the problem with additional emotional support. Parents should never punish or belittle a child for wetting the bed, since this may make the problem worse.

Sleeping

Preschool children need a total of 11 to 12½ hours of sleep daily. If a child has difficulty waking up in the morning, sleep deprivation is likely the cause. Recent research shows that preschoolers who sleep less than 10 hours per night are more likely to have accidents, such as falls. These same children are also listless, cranky, and prone to headaches in the afternoon.

Many preschoolers develop bedtime problems, too, such as crying, resistance to going to bed, and getting out of bed. Why do preschoolers have sleep problems? Some preschoolers

- never learn to fall asleep on their own
- have too little "wind down" time or inconsistent bedtime routine
- have fears about sleep and/or have bad dreams

Nightmares are dreams from which the child fully awakens and can describe in detail. Some young children also experience *night terrors*—a dreamlike state in which they seem to be awake, are confused, and have a look of panic or fear. Children with night terrors are inconsolable and often push away the comforting parent.

Parents need to help preschoolers' develop good sleep habits. Maintaining a regular sleep schedule and bedtime routine are a priority. Making sure that preschoolers have enough down time is important, too. For example, parents should turn off the TV and stop rough and tumble games at least an hour before bedtime. Playing quiet games and having the parents' full attention helps preschoolers settle down for sleep, 15-8. If children get up during the night, parents should return them to their own beds. Eliminating stressors or frightening stories can help prevent nightmares or night terrors. If these ideas do not work, parents should consult their child's pediatrician.

Intellectual Development

During the preschool years, intellectual development progresses in an orderly manner. Motor coordination enables children to interact with objects in complex ways. A greater attention span allows them to pursue activities for a longer time. Better memory skills enable preschoolers to recall more detailed sequences.

15-8 Maintaining a regular bedtime routine and sleep schedule are important aspects to healthy sleep.

Preschoolers are most interested in their immediate surroundings and what is happening at the moment. They are keenly aware of the environment and study it with all their senses. Preschool children construct their own concepts. They do not simply accept ready-made concepts and principles. Their favorite question is "Why?" They need to understand before they are ready to believe. Because of their efforts to understand everything, their thinking becomes more complex.

Piaget and Preschoolers' Development

Preschoolers are in Piaget's *preoperational stage*, which means they are still not logical thinkers, 15-9. Younger preschoolers complete the *preconceptual phase* of the stage. They have many mental images and express these images through language, art, and play symbols.

As they turn 4, preschoolers enter Piaget's *intuitive phase*. In this phase, preschoolers use intuitive or **perceptual thinking**—thinking based on how things appear—to solve problems. Because perceptions may provide correct information, their knowledge may be correct. For example, preschoolers may correctly notice that the weight of a bucket depends on how much water or sand is in it. Many times, however, appearance and reality are not the same. For example, a very loud sound may appear softer than it really is due to distance. Because preschoolers' thinking remains *prelogical*, they cannot understand this.

Piaget's Stages of Intellectual Development

1. Sensorimotor
1A: Exercising the Reflexes
1B: Primary Circular Reactions
1C: Secondary Circular Reactions
1D: Coordination of Secondary Circular Reactions
1E: Tertiary Circular Reactions
1F: Mental Representation

2. Preoperational
2A: Preconceptual Phase
2B: Intuitive Phase

3. Concrete Operations

4. Formal Operations

15-9 Using perceptions help preschoolers solve problems. However, their thinking is limited by their inability to use logic.

As preschoolers approach the school years, they begin to use logic. For example, they may see that the same amount of water poured into various-sized containers comes to different heights. When asked *why* this happens, they may guess the right answer but cannot explain why it is true. This is because preschoolers do not yet understand that quantities remain the same despite changes in appearance, such as changes in diameter and height of containers. Although their thinking is changing, it is still intuitive. Older preschoolers are still basing their answers on what they see.

Preschoolers' Learning Abounds

The preschool period is an interesting time of intellectual development. It is the prime time for fantasy. Children express fantasy thoughts through language, art, and pretend play. These thoughts are more than childish thinking; they are the beginnings of creative thought. Beyond fantasy, children's intense quest for knowledge results in some basic concepts and the budding of logical thought.

Asking "Why?"

Preschoolers ask an abundance of questions. Because they are trying to figure things out, many of their questions are "why" questions. Often one question leads to another, sometimes over months. For example, while taking a bath, a child may ask where the water comes from. If the parent says "the faucets," the child may ask at a later time, "How do faucets get water?" The parent then replies, "from pipes under the house." Still later, the child may ask, "How do pipes get water?"

Because preschoolers believe everything exists for a purpose, they like answers in terms of purpose, such as "Rain falls to make flowers grow." Preschoolers give a purpose to things they notice even when others have not stated a purpose. For example, a preschooler might say, "we have clouds to make the sky pretty." The purposes preschoolers give most often are for their direct benefit, too. For example, snow is for play purposes rather than for moisture.

Learning Physical Attributes

Preschoolers study their world through their senses. This makes them delightful companions on family outings and vacations. They smell odors and hear sounds adults rarely notice. Preschoolers also notice the physical attributes, or traits, (color, shape, size, texture, sound, odor, and taste) of things they see, hear, touch, smell, and taste, 15-10. They spend much time sorting and classifying objects by observable traits. However, preschoolers seldom classify by basic categories. For example, they may put "blue" things in a group, but rarely put tools, furniture, or fruits in a group.

Preschoolers realize that attributes have labels and want to know the labels or words. For example, the main attribute may be the name of an object, such as a shape. In another case, an attribute describes an object, such as a blue crayon.

Separating Fantasy from Reality

Due to dreams and the lack of certain types of knowledge and experiences, reality and fantasy blend in the preschool years. Although these years are prime for fantasy, 3-year-olds are not always sure where reality ends and fantasy begins. They have vivid imaginations. By the time they are 4, the line between reality and fantasy is still hazy. Children this age have great imaginations and love to tell tall tales. At the same time, their memories and language skills are improving. They can repeat factual stories with accurate details. Most 5-year-olds can separate reality from fantasy, but may want some clarification. Pretend play reaches its peak in 5-year-old children.

15-10 Preschoolers spend a great deal of time noting the attributes of things in their world.

In years past, childhood fantasy was thought to indicate a lack of contact with reality. For example, Freud thought children used fantasy play to make up for an unhappy childhood. Child development experts now believe fantasy is important to development. According to Piaget, pretend play with its use of symbols, such as make-believe props and characters, helps children progress in all developmental areas. Adult creative abilities seem to stem from childhood imaginations. This is why some people call fantasy the "genius of childhood."

Puzzling over Time

Time is a difficult concept for preschoolers to understand. Full understanding may not come until children are about 11 or 12 years of age. Most preschoolers relate the word "yesterday" with anytime in the past, from several hours ago to several days ago. They recognize "tomorrow" as a time to come, but they do not know how far away that time is.

Time concepts are also made more difficult because preschool children do not realize the passage of time. Life is static to them. When shown a photo of their parents as children, they cannot understand that their parents were once young. For example, a child will think "dad is not a child; he's my dad."

Developing Preliteracy Skills

During the preschool years, most children become aware of counting and writing numerals and letters. Parents and preschool teachers primarily introduce preliteracy skills to preschoolers. Media influences such as *Sesame Street*, however, also affect preliteracy skills. Preschoolers vary in how far they progress in these skills, although the sequence of learning is similar for most children, 15-11.

Developing Preliteracy Skills

Type of Skill	Sequence of Learning
Counting and comparing numbers	• Saying number names in a stable, repeatable order. • Assigning a single, number name to each item. • Including every item in the count without skipping items or doing repeat counting. • Knowing that the final number name in a counting sequence tells "how many" items are in the group. • Realizing the order in which a person counts items does not affect "how many." • Comparing two numbers with *more* or *less,* such as 6 is *more than* 3 or 3 is *less than* 6.
Being aware of print	• Pretending to read by looking at pictures. • Realizing adults read print and recognizing print in books and in the environment. • Noticing print characteristics. For example, children will notice that print is arranged in lines that may be straight or curved. They may also note that letters are different. Some may find it difficult to see differences between "E" and "F" and between "D" and "O." Preschoolers rarely master letters that differ only by spatial position, such as "b," "d," and "p." • Realizing letters have names and saying some letter names, such as the letters in the child's name. • "Reading" by pairing each letter with a said word or syllable while moving finger from left to right. • Realizing letters "make" sounds in pairing some letters with their sounds.
Writing letters and numerals	• Writing by scribbling. • Making marks that somewhat resemble letters and numerals, called *mock writing.* • Writing some letters, numerals, and words, such as own name from left to right.

15-11 Toward the end of the preschool period, most children have developed some preliteracy skills. A few preschool children have advanced skills by age 6.

Playtime Means Learning and Fun

Play has many benefits. As children learn to use their bodies, play has physical benefits. For example, preschoolers love to twirl around in circles. This stimulates the inner ear that governs balance. Vigorous play strengthens muscles and helps prevent obesity, too.

Play also helps intellectual development. Piaget said children practice their intellectual skills through play. Children learn as they play, and they play as they learn. They do not think of learning and play as separate activities. For example, imagine children playing in the kindergarten housekeeping center. They scribble a grocery list (a preliteracy skill). Then they shop, cook dinner, eat, and wash dishes (sequence events—a time concept). Finally, they return dishes to the cabinets (sorting flatware, cups, and saucers by using the physical attributes of each item). Other play activities develop intellectual skills, too. Toys that children can push, pull, roll, or throw help them learn basic scientific concepts. Household objects can help them learn some of the basic concepts of arithmetic—*more, less, empty, full, bigger, and smaller.* Play also promotes planning, problem-solving, and creativity skills.

Play enhances social development of preschoolers. Young preschoolers move beyond parallel play and want to associate or be with other children, but they do not develop group goals for play. This stage of play is **associative play**. Although they share toys and talk with each other while playing, their play remains independent of each other. For example, several children may play firefighters. However, they do not work as a firefighting team as is typical with adult firefighters. During this time, preschoolers also learn how to get along with others, express their feelings, take turns, and share.

Toward the end of the preschool years, children begin to organize and plan their play. Parents and preschool teachers may observe children join forces and work together toward a play goal. For example, with this type of cooperation, older preschoolers may actually work together as a firefighting team. This is the beginning of **cooperative play.**

Finally, play has emotional benefits. As children relax and laugh, play helps relieve tensions. Children may even overcome some of their fears through play. For example, a common preschool make-believe game involves scaring off monsters.

Types of Play

Preschoolers' play can be grouped into five types of play. Each type has its own benefits. The types include the following:

- *Rough-and-tumble play.* More common among boys than girls, this play involves "play" fighting, wrestling, scaring another person, dragging, and other rough activities. Children use exaggerated movements, laugh, and rotate roles, such as the chaser becoming the one chased. If the play becomes aggressive, parents must stop it.

- *Physical games.* Running, jumping, climbing, and playing with balls need to be part of daily play.

- *Constructive play.* Using building materials or blocks, art materials, making up a story, and playing electronic games help develop fine-motor skills and creativity.

- *Pretend play.* Also called *fantasy play,* this play involves the creation of symbols, 15-12. Symbols include props (seashells for cups), roles (child talks and acts like mother), and/or plots (mother cares for her baby). Pretend play often involves other types of play, such as riding a tricycle and calling it a truck.

15-12 Preschoolers use imagination as they dress up and experiment with different roles and behaviors.

Due to gender-role development, gender stereotypes are common (such as daddies go to work and mothers take care of babies). Pretend play often involves every day situations and favorite stories—plots that help children distinguish reality and fantasy.

- *Games.* Preschoolers enjoy simple physical games, such as "hide and seek," and board games if parents and older children play with them.

The Parents' Role in Play

Parents are responsible for creating a safe environment. During the preschool years, accidents are a major cause of injury and death. The outdoor area is often very dangerous. Because children forget hazards during play, parents may need to fence play areas. They also need to childproof outdoor areas, such as garages and storage sheds. Supervision is still the best way to keep young children safe.

Parents must also choose play materials for all types of play. For example, parents might provide a wagon, tricycle, and an assortment of balls for outdoor play. Assortments of blocks, puzzles, art materials, and musical instruments are essential for constructive play. Dress-up clothes, puppets, play scenes, and transportation toys encourage pretend play. Shape sorters, number and letter puzzles, and printmaking materials help develop preliteracy skills. Before buying play materials, parents need to consider the play situation at home. Some questions parents consider include

- *How many hours will my child play at home?* Many children attend daily preschools. Good programs have a variety of play materials. Some preschoolers also participate in special activities, such as dance, music, and art. Toy needs may differ depending on hours of at-home play and other out-of-the-home activities.

- *What does the community offer for child's play?* Some families live near parks with gym equipment designed for children of all ages. Some communities have discovery centers, museums, and libraries with programs for children. Parents need to consider community resources when deciding on play materials for the home.

- *Is my home suitable for certain play materials?* For example, can a child safely pedal a tricycle outside or is the terrain too rough or unsafe? Is there room in the home for floor blocks?

- *Will my child be playing alone or with others most of the time?* A seesaw (teeter-totter) takes two children. Usually one or two children use small play scenes for pretend play. When pretend play involves several children, they need child-sized role-playing equipment, as seen in preschool programs.

- *Could I use household or natural materials instead of buying some play materials?* For example, what household items could be used for pretend play?

- *Can I find play materials my child will not quickly outgrow?* Preschoolers can use open toys, such as blocks, art materials, and balls, in a number of ways and over a long period of time.

- *What really interests my child?* If children do not use play equipment, it is worthless. Preschool children develop many kinds of preferences. Parents should try to match play equipment with their child's interests, 15-13.

Guiding play is an important parenting task. Providing experiences, reading books, and making suggestions enhances children's play ideas. Parents can help their children make games out of everyday experiences,

15-13 Finding age-appropriate toys and playthings is an important action for parents.

too! For example, drawing on a chalkboard in the corner of the kitchen while parents are making dinner may be a lot of fun. Stacking plastic bowls and sorting canned goods are other types of play. Children may enjoy fluffing pillows and helping make beds. Parents, however, should not tell their child what to play or how to play.

Parents can also play *with* their preschoolers, but children should take the lead. Many preschoolers spend quite a bit of time playing alone. When alone, they use their imaginations to think of play activities. Preschoolers are very social by nature, so they often prefer to play where they can interact with their parents. Serving a cup of tea to their parents while playing house delights children. Children also see their parents' interest in their activities.

Playing with siblings or peers is fun and educational for preschoolers, but disagreements will happen. Most of the time, children can settle their disputes. Adults should watch the situation and step in, if needed, to mediate serious disputes or to stop hostile actions.

Peer reactions strongly influence children's self-esteem. If playmates accept them, preschoolers tend to be pleasant and cooperative. If their playmates reject them, they are more likely to be disruptive and uncooperative. Parents should try to avoid reprimanding a preschooler in the presence of his or her friends. Later, the friends might make fun of the child for getting into trouble. This can hurt a child's self-esteem.

Preschoolers are competitive in their play activities. Each tries to outdo the others. In their games, they like to win prizes. This competitive spirit may be encouraging for some. The child who never wins, however, may feel hurt and develop a poor self-image. Parents need to be aware of competitive games that create damaging images. Games in which everyone has a chance to succeed are better in most situations.

Language Development

The language children use reflects their level of intellectual development, 15-14. Vocabulary grows very rapidly in the preschool period. Toddlers learn words because parents label objects for them. Preschoolers learn most of their words by deriving them from situations. For example, the parent may say, "I think the penguin is such a cute bird." Because the child is in front of the penguin cage, he or she learns the name *penguin* and the classification word *bird*. Preschoolers add about 50 words per month to their vocabularies if their environment is language-rich. During the preschool years, the child's speaking vocabulary grows from about 900 to almost 3000 words. By age 6, children understand about 14,000 words—many more than they use in conversation.

Preschoolers think all words stand for objects, but by age 6, they may know a few abstract words, such as *love* and *wish*. Because of the concrete way in which they view words, preschoolers take idioms, exaggerations, and slang expressions very literally. They may reject idioms, such as "clocks tell time" because only people tell time. Children may worry when they overhear adult conversations with such phrases as "I almost died when..." and "I thought he'd never come home."

If preschoolers do not know a word or cannot remember it, they will invent words to explain things. For example, a child may say, "She's a lady grandpa" (meaning "grandma") or "a man with feathers on his face (meaning a man with a beard)." Preschoolers may even substitute a word they know for a word they don't know, such as Rudolph's nose *blows* instead of *glows*.

As vocabulary grows, sentence-length increases. The average sentence length for 3-year-olds is three words, and for 6-year-olds, eight words. Sentence structure becomes more complex, too. By age 4, children use and

15-14 "Reading" to his father helps this preschooler feel he has an important role in his family. It also gives him a chance to show off his growing vocabulary.

make compound verbs and sentences. Long sentences are common with *and* inserted between four and five simple sentences. As children learn locator words, prepositional phrases become part of sentences. Children use *in*, *on*, and *under* at age 3 and *beside*, *between*, *in front of*, and *behind* by age 5.

Preschoolers learn grammar by listening to others. To learn grammar, children must hear separate words in speech. Children hear tense in verbs and plurals in nouns. As children learn grammar, they hear the general rules, such as the "ed" sound makes verbs past tense, and the "s" and "es" sounds make nouns plural. They also learn word order in sentences. As children learn these rules, they apply them to every situation. English has many irregular verbs, however. It is common for a preschooler who once said "went" to say "goed." What has happened? The child has applied the "ed" rule to an irregular verb. If he or she continues to hear the irregular form "went" often, the preschooler recalls it from memory and uses it correctly. Relearning irregular verb forms is not a fast process.

Other grammar problems also occur. Preschoolers learn the negative contractions, such as *don't* and *won't*. However, they fail to drop the "no" they used during the toddler or early preschool period. Preschooler sentences often have double negatives, such as "I don't want no broccoli."

Questions are also difficult due to different subject and verb order compared to statements. Usually, the grammar develops in this sequence: "Where you go?" "Where you are going?" "Where are you going?" Children ask questions with *what, who,* and *where* (concerning objects, people, and locations) before *when* and *why* (concerning time and cause and effect).

The Importance of Books

Story and concept picture books are pleasant tools for developing concepts, expanding vocabulary, and exploring social behaviors. Books are the main source from which children learn the rules for how language works. Children's authors allow the sounds, patterns, and moods of language to shine through their short prose and poetry lines. Reading to children gives parents opportunities to expand their children's curiosity and awareness. Story time is the basis for many happy memories for parents and children. Sharing books also increases children's desire to learn to read on their own, 15-15.

15-15 Parents can inspire their children to read on their own.

Concerns About Language Development

As with other areas of development, parents may worry about some apparent language problems of their preschoolers. Language experts believe many of these concerns really are not problems because they are common. These speech issues may cause parental concern.

Stuttering. An involuntary disruption in speech, **stuttering** tends to run in families. With stuttering, parts of words are hard to say, prolonged, or repeated. It is more common in boys and identical twins. Some preschoolers stutter because their thoughts are more advanced than their vocabularies and speaking skills. Others may stutter to get attention or to imitate a playmate who stutters. Stuttering is usually temporary and soon stops when parents pay less attention to it. Parents should not try to push or speed the flow of speech of their preschoolers because this may create more serious stuttering problems. If stuttering begins after age 4, becomes more frequent, or causes a child stress, parents should seek medical attention.

Lisping. The mispronunciation of words by dropping or distorting letter sounds, usually consonants, is called **lisping**. For example, the child may pronounce *smell* as "mell," *frog* as "wog," or *rabbit* as "wabbit." Most lisping problems are not serious and quickly resolve. Experts do not expect preschool children to master the letters L, R, and S. Lisping, however, may be caused by a hearing loss, weak muscles, or immature speech. The earlier a problem is detected and treated, the easier it is to correct.

Toilet talk. Talking about bodily functions in a playful way is called **toilet talk**. Using toilet talk is a way preschoolers get laughs from their peers. They sense it is forbidden and are thrilled by the reactions of others. Parents cannot stop all toilet talk, but do not have to allow it in their presence. If they explain those words are not to be used around them or other people, children will get the message. Parents should try to be calm and firm about this, not outraged and emotional.

Baby Talk. Regressing to expressions used as an older infant or young toddler, such as "me want cookie" or "Bobby up," is **baby talk.** Preschoolers may use it to imitate a media character, to get attention, or indicate they are tired or feeling bad. Parents should not encourage these baby expressions because children may have trouble making themselves understood by others.

Bilingualism. Knowing and speaking two languages is **bilingualism.** This may positively or negatively affect preschoolers. On the positive side, children learn a second language more easily when they are young. On the negative side, some children in bilingual homes may have trouble learning the fine points of either language. Parents need to consider all the pros and cons of making their child bilingual.

Social and Emotional Development

Preschoolers' advances in physical and intellectual development directly impact social and emotional development. They use their new physical skills to play and interact with others. They feel more confident of their hand movements and coordination. Improving language skills allow preschoolers to express their thoughts and feelings. They develop an awareness of social roles with parents, siblings, extended family, and friends.

If parents surround their children with love and understanding, self-esteem grows stronger. Children become more self-reliant and responsible for their own behaviors. They begin to sense other people as individuals with needs and feelings of their own. Preschoolers can also predict parenting behaviors and are very sensitive to the way parents respond to them.

Friendships: The Goal Is Play

Preschoolers are more social than toddlers. At age 3, children play mainly with parents, but by age 5 they play mainly with friends. Preschoolers often play in groups of four or five children, and most friends are the same gender, 15-16. Although preschoolers form some temporary friendships around shared play interests, they tend to have stable friendships, too. In preschool programs, best friends share about 30 percent of their free time. Best friends are the most common partners in fantasy play.

The goal of preschool friendships is play. When asked why they like certain children, preschoolers may describe their friends' willingness to play. Aggression is the main reason preschoolers give for not liking some children.

Sibling Relationships: Forming a Bond

About 80 percent of children have siblings. Because siblings generally outlive parents and have steady relationships with

15-16 Good times with same-gender friends are a major part of preschool social interactions.

each other, the bond between them is the most enduring of all family relationships. By the end of the preschool years, children have spent twice as much time with siblings as with their parents.

Children learn many positive things through sibling relationships. For example, they learn how to provide companionship and social support for each other. They also learn how to interact with others and provide care especially to younger siblings. Some siblings, however, compete for parental attention and are jealous of each other. This is called **sibling rivalry.**

Handling Sibling Rivalry

Conflicts and jealousy between siblings have existed as long as there have been families with children. Although some sibling rivalry is a natural part of childhood, it can be upsetting and frustrating to other family members. What can parents do to reduce the squabbling and bickering between sisters and brothers? Here are some guidelines to follow:

- *Avoid comparing children.* Parents should make positive statements to all their children about their strengths. Children need to know their parents love and accept them as individuals.

- *Set limits for acceptable behavior.* Preschoolers must learn that name-calling, yelling, and hitting are not appropriate behaviors.

- *Listen to arguments before taking action.* Ignoring trivial arguments allows siblings to work out solutions to their problems. If arguments escalate to hurtful aggression, parents need to separate the children. After a cool-down period, parents can help mediate the conflict.

- *Reduce sibling stress.* Parents should try to provide a private space for each child because toddlers can be a nuisance to

preschoolers' play. Helping preschoolers learn about younger siblings' feelings can help, too. For example, a parent might say, "Your brother wants to play with you because he likes you, but he's too young to know that he shouldn't knock over your blocks." Stress-reducing activities, such as bubble blowing, are relaxing and can help reduce rivalry due to fatigue. Nutritious snacks can eliminate irritable feelings due to hunger.

- *Provide time for children to be apart.* Time for individual, quiet activities is important for all children. Parents might also consider arranging separate play dates or special activities for their children. This allows parents to spend some one-on-one time with each of their children.

Erikson and the Sense of Accomplishment

If preschoolers have successfully completed Erikson's last stage, their feelings of autonomy prepare them to develop initiative ("I can feelings"). Initiative reflects the confidence preschoolers feel in mastering objects, activities, and relationships, 15-17. (See Appendix A, "Erikson's Theory of Personality Development" for more detailed information on Stage 3.)

Preschoolers' sense of initiative is due to their curiosity and unlimited energy. They do things and ask questions with the intent of learning. Through this effort, preschoolers discover personal limits by failing to achieve goals and having conflicts with others.

Healthy development blossoms with the support of parents and others in their social world. Through others, children feel good about their successes and learn it is human to make mistakes. When they are punished too severely, or too often, for their initiative,

Erikson's Theory of Personality Development

Stage	Approximate Age	Step Toward Stable Personality	Step Toward Unstable Personality
1	Birth to age 2	Trust	Mistrust
2	Ages 2 & 3	Autonomy	Shame and doubt
3	Ages 4 & 5	Initiative	Guilt
4	Ages 6 to 11	Industry	Inferiority
5	Ages 12 to 18	Identity	Role confusion
6	Early adulthood	Intimacy	Isolation
7	Middle age	Generativity	Stagnation
8	Late adulthood	Integrity	Despair

15-17 Preschool children need support and assistance in their efforts to express initiative and to avoid guilt.

children feel guilt. Feelings of guilt inhibit positive behavior and lower self-esteem. These negative feelings keep preschoolers from exploring and learning.

The Self: A Big Ego

Preschoolers define themselves in terms of their physical characteristics and behaviors, such as "I can run fast." They are beginning to evaluate themselves and their achievements. They tend to view themselves as either "all good" or "all bad." Most see their own positive qualities. They tend to ignore failures and believe they can achieve. Children who experience abuse, however, often see themselves negatively. Abusers make them feel they deserved the abuse.

Preschoolers can compare themselves with others. In these comparisons, they are egocentric. They see their own importance. Preschoolers' talk is filled with personal pronouns. They want—and may demand—others notice them. Because their homes and families are important, they may boast about who has the biggest house, the strongest dad, or the smartest mom.

Emotions: Quick Mood Swings

Preschoolers display changing emotions from happy to moody and back again. Three-year-olds usually have cooperative personalities. Their frustrations lessen as their physical skills improve. They tend to be agreeable with parental requests. Preschoolers are also learning to take turns and practice give-and-take with friends.

Four-year-olds experience many emotional changes. Although they are learning how to express their emotions verbally, they may seem to have less control over them. Four-year-olds are often moody, or feel upset longer, as they try to deal with their feelings, 15-18.

Around age 5, children seem more peaceful and cooperative. At this age, preschoolers' emotions are more settled. They are better at handling their feelings. Five-year-olds are often more patient, generous, and conscientious. Due to their sense of fairness, they are more reasonable in a quarrel. They have become more realistic and practical, too.

15-18 Four-year-olds work at expressing their emotions verbally and in appropriate ways. They enjoy jokes and funny stories.

During the preschool years, children become more and more capable of expressing a variety of emotions, such as

Happiness. Preschoolers are generally happy children. They particularly enjoy slapstick humor and funny jokes and stories. They tell many jokes that do not make sense because they often cannot recall the punch lines. They laugh anyway and recover quickly from various upsets.

Anger. Preschoolers show anger when they cannot achieve a goal without help, when parents instill boundaries (such as bedtime), or when frustrated with peers who take toys or do not share. When angry, preschoolers may sulk, cry, yell, or show aggression.

Fear and Anxiety. Fear and anxiety occupy a major part of preschoolers' emotional life. Vivid imaginations and awareness that they cannot control all events lead to some of their fears. Typical fears include darkness, storms, unfriendly animals and insects, ghosts, monsters, and events in nightmares. Separation anxiety occurs when preschoolers are left in new settings, such as preschool and kindergarten. New anxieties emerge as children feel the stress of not knowing others while facing new learning and social challenges. Anxiety about abandonment often surfaces after a death in the family or parental divorce or separation.

Empathy. Compared to toddlers, preschoolers are more sensitive to the needs of others. They target helpful reactions directly to a problem. For example, preschoolers may comfort a hurt child or return grabbed toys if the toy owner shows distress. Preschoolers learn empathy from parents' actions and books with themes about kind caring behaviors. Some TV shows also teach empathy.

During the preschool years, children begin to learn social and cultural rules about when a person should, or should not, display true emotions. As they learn emotional-display rules, children may begin to mask emotions to protect the feelings of others or to protect themselves. For example, to protect another's feelings, preschoolers may smile and say "thank you" although they do not like a certain gift. After taking a hard fall on the playground, preschoolers may get up and act as though nothing happened (even when hurting). This is a self-protective action to avoid ridicule from playmates. Preschool girls mask emotions better than boys.

Parenting Concerns and Tasks

Keeping children healthy remains a top parenting goal. As preschoolers develop, parents must give preschoolers chances to discover their personal abilities and test their limits. During this stage of parenting, parents meet preschoolers' needs through communication more than physical assistance. Accepting children's emerging traits and goals while helping them conform to society's rules and family expectations require careful balance and adjustments by parents.

Medical Checkups for Preschoolers

Preschoolers need fewer routine medical checkups than infants or toddlers. The American Academy of Pediatrics (AAP) recommends yearly checkups at ages 3, 4, and 5 years. These medical checkups are important for monitoring children's health, such as measuring height and weight and noting physical condition, 15-19. Checkups allow the doctor to detect any problems and treat them as early as possible. Routine medical checkups are in addition to any doctor visits for illness or injury. During medical checkups, parents can ask any questions about their preschooler's health, growth, and development. Parents may also want to discuss any childrearing challenges.

During the preschool years, children should also have regular dental visits. Dentists recommend cleaning and examination of teeth every 6 months. Vision and hearing exams are also necessary during the preschool years especially if children display vision or hearing problems.

Developmental Screenings

Children may also need a **developmental screening**, a test that can identify possible developmental delay or below-level skills. Tests such as the Denver Developmental Screening Test examine skills in social, language, gross-motor, and fine-motor areas. Many doctors, early childhood educators, and other child-development specialists give such tests. If diagnosed with developmental

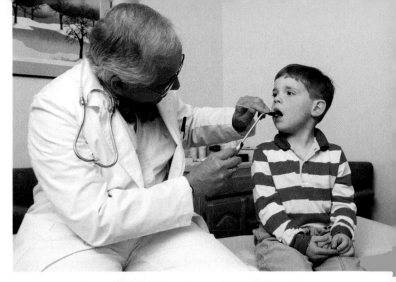

15-19 Routine medical checkups help ensure preschoolers are healthy and growing as they should.

delay, children receive other diagnostic tests to pinpoint the problem.

Adjusting to Preschoolers' Needs

Preschoolers direct their energy toward many different goals, but their enthusiasm and egocentrism may cause them to resist parental explanations. For example, preschoolers may ignore parents when they explain that a bossy attitude will damage friendships. Some disobey family rules, such as no hitting or tattling. When sensitive and responsive, parents help their preschoolers learn to be more realistic about themselves. They also teach preschoolers to show empathy toward others and display self-control as they approach school age.

Encouraging Positive Interactions

Conflicts with siblings and peers are behavioral and social problems for preschoolers, but a normal part of growing up. Socially competent preschoolers are outgoing and use self-control in their interactions with others. Peers generally dislike those who interact negatively. For the most part, preschoolers engage in friendly play with siblings and peers.

Due to better verbal skills, aggressive physical behaviors lessen after age 4. Some preschoolers, however, do act aggressively and display other negative behaviors, such as whining, tattling, crying, and possibly hitting, 15-20. What causes some preschoolers to have difficulty with give-and-take interactions? Some major reasons include the following:

- **Problems due to temperament.** Temperament problems link to lack of self-control. Until age 5, temperament is the major factor affecting how easily a preschooler gets mad.

- **Lack of needed social skills.** Some parents mistakenly believe social skills are inborn so they do not teach them.

- **Excess stress due to parental conflicts, depression, or substance abuse.** When events such as these occur, children fail to learn how to positively interact with others.

- **Insecure attachment to a parent or another adult.** By the preschool years, children with insecure attachments may display impulsive, hostile, or withdrawn behavior. These children may have mental-health problems.

Preschoolers generally respond positively to parental strategies to control aggression. When aggressive behaviors persist, however, parents should talk with their pediatrician. In some cases, doctors may make referrals to social-service agencies that offer counseling and other mental-health services for children and parents. Some preschooler behaviors that are warning signs of possible mental health problems appear in 15-21.

Accepting Heroes and Fantasy Friends

Role models have great influence on preschoolers. Family members and teachers, with whom children interact most, are often influential role models. Children may also look up to people they have never met, such as heroes from a book or a revered family member. As children begin to play career roles, they may admire groups of people, such as doctors or firefighters.

Positive Parenting Strategies for Handling Aggression

- **Model calmness, problem solving, and making compromises.** For example, walk away from the child and use the "win/win" method.

- **Reinforce the preschooler's positive behaviors.** When children share toys with playmates, for example, parents should praise them for being kind and generous.

- **Reduce frustration in children's daily lives.** Have a regular routine. Tell children when there will be changes in the routine and give them choices. Control noise levels and make sure children have appropriate toys for play.

- **Set clear limits and consistently reinforce them.** Connect the rules to the consequences.

- **Use time-out to help children calm down.** Explain to children why time-out is necessary. Limit time-out to 5 minutes or less or until children are calm.

- **Mediate conflicts.** Help children state their view using "I" messages. Help them use the decision-making process to solve conflicts.

- **Avoid using physical punishment.** If children see the parent modeling aggression, they feel the punishment is retaliation for misbehavior. Children do not learn alternative actions.

- **Avoid ignoring aggressive behavior.** Children feel rewarded and get the idea that parents approve of their aggressive acts.

15-20 Parents can do much to prevent and control their preschoolers' aggression.

15-21 Defiant and hostile symptoms are serious. Children showing these symptoms need early treatment by mental-health specialists.

Why do preschoolers look to others as role models in addition to their parents? Other role models broaden children's understandings about how people should interact and can affirm parental rules for positive behavior. Preschoolers like to hear how their heroes make decisions and deal with mistakes. Heroes and role models can reinforce family values, too. When the same expectations come from several sources, such as parents and teachers, children take them to heart.

Some preschoolers have crushes on cartoon characters, such as Barney™ or Scooby-Doo™. These characters possess or do something children desire. Because these crushes come when preschoolers are giving up comfort items (such as favorite toys or blankets), these characters serve as security for the transition. Parents should accept their preschooler's fascination with these cartoon characters unless they display objectionable values.

Almost half of all preschoolers have imaginary friends. Some are giants, heroes, animals, and even "siblings." Having make-believe buddies is associated with a creative, healthy personality. These companions help preschoolers face the real world. Parents should humor their children about their "best friend," unless the pretense goes too far. For example, parents do not have to cook special meals for imaginary playmates. Also, parents can let their children know that they, not the imaginary friend, are responsible for their own actions. Most children give up make-believe friends by age 7.

Making Family-Life Adjustments

Do you think parenting becomes easier when preschoolers can do more for themselves? Most parents will tell you the challenges just change. Parents continue to feel much stress during the preschool years. This is due to the fact that they have less parenting support than they did when children were younger. As you have read, parents must balance acceptance of their child's traits while helping him or her become more competent in social relationships and self-control. Families also have to keep their preschooler safe and provide stimulating experiences, often through group programs.

Keeping Preschoolers Safe

Preschoolers are prone to accidents. They play with tools in the home, garden, and workshop. They may also open and try household cleaning products and medicines. Their toys and games become more dangerous, too. Parents have to be concerned about dangers not only in and around the home, but also in the neighborhood and at playmates' homes. See 15-22 for some safety tips.

Power-tool safety—Preschoolers may want to use power tools just as their parents do. When not in use, unplug and store power tools well out of children's reach. For cordless models, store batteries separately from tools.

Water-play safety—When playing near any body of water, children should wear safety-approved life jackets or vests. Small wading pools are fun, too, but preschoolers may slip, fall, or even drown in a small amount of water. Parents should closely watch their children during all water play.

Playground safety—Supervision is necessary when preschoolers play in public playground areas. High slides, swinging swings, and other playground equipment may cause injury to a child who is too excited to be cautious.

Indoor safety—Preschoolers like to run fast. They do not think about rugs that slip or items to trip over. Some parents rearrange furniture and remove rugs during this period. Others make certain areas of the home "off limits."

Medicine safety—Preschoolers may mistake vitamins, aspirins, cough syrup, or other medications for candy and eat them. All bottles should have safety caps, but more importantly, none should be within the reach of children. Parents should store all medicines in a locked cabinet, or if necessary, in a locked box in the refrigerator.

15-22 Preschoolers have the curiosity and motor skills to get themselves into trouble. Parents should try to constantly be aware of where their preschoolers are and what they are doing.

As preschoolers better understand what they see and hear, media content poses more dangers. Parents should support and manage their children's experiences with TV programs and Internet sites. Limiting the time children watch TV or use the Internet is an important parenting task. Parents can also make use of the V-chip technology on their TV sets. This technology allows parents to review and block undesirable programming. Filters to block Internet sites are also available. Most importantly, parents need to communicate with their children about media dangers and monitor use of various media technologies.

Finding a Quality Preschool Program

About 50 percent of 3-year-olds and 70 percent of 4-year-olds participate in preschool programs. Working outside the home is only one reason parents give for enrolling children in such programs. Most parents want their preschoolers to have a strong foundation in learning and building the positive social experiences needed for kindergarten.

Parents often choose preschool programs based on cost, hours of operation, and location. Over one-third of preschoolers change programs during the year. Some of these changes are due to family mobility or to a change in a parent's job location. Others are due to disappointment in the quality of the program.

Parents need to find a quality program that fits their child's needs. In addition to meeting state standards, quality programs have teachers who are sensitive and responsive to children and their families. These programs provide experiences that teach children to relate positively with others and encourage parental involvement. For example, parents may be asked to do daily learning activities with their children at home or at the center. Quality programs also include a learning curriculum that

- has clear and challenging goals for children
- provides a wide range of firsthand experiences
- uses learning methods that involve fine- and gross-motor play, movement, and exploration
- allows for children's special interests and skills

Overcoming Kindergarten Jitters

Toward the end of the preschool years, most children enter kindergarten. In recent years, kindergarten has become more like first grade. Although the shift in the kindergarten curriculum has not been good for all children, states mandate children meet certain expectations before they enter first grade, 15-23. What can parents do to prepare their children for school success? Helpful guidelines include the following:

- ***Enroll the child in a preschool that appropriately teaches skills necessary for kindergarten entry.*** Kindergarten entry requires such skills as taking turns, sitting still, knowing colors and shapes, and recognizing letters in names. Parents who teach their children at home should use a good preschool curriculum guide.

15-23 Kindergartens today have higher expectations for children as they prepare for first grade.

- *Consult with preschool teachers about the child's kindergarten readiness.* If developmental lags are noted—such as speaking little, using toddlerlike sentences, or playing alone or in parallel play—ask for developmental screening and further advice.

- *Call the school.* Parents should ask about enrollment procedures, documents needed for enrollment, and other necessary requirements.

- *Prepare the child for transition to kindergarten.* Parents can help their children with this transition by inviting them to tour the bigger school building, ride a bus, or eat in a cafeteria.

- *Attend meetings.* Parents should attend orientation meetings and read materials provided for parents of new students.

Parenting in the Preschool Years

Families with 3-year-olds leave the childbearing stage and enter the *parenting preschoolers stage* of the family life cycle. Families continue in this stage until first-born children enter school. Family interactions involve the preschooler more and more.

Parents realize that how they guide their child greatly influences his or her values and behaviors in later life. During this stage, parents redefine their roles, rules, and boundaries that emerged in the childbearing stage. Parents decide how they will parent, what specific behavior rules they have for their child, and how they will use discipline. Although parents tend to make parenting decisions on a case-by-case basis, one of the three parenting styles (authoritarian, democratic, or permissive) emerges.

Parents of preschoolers remain in the *authoritative stage of parenting* according to parenting expert Ellen Galinsky. Parents focus on helping their child learn the rules and boundaries for family living. They also help their children learn social rules for interactions outside the family. Getting children to comply with these expectations is a major parenting task. Parents may adapt their parenting style in response to "what works" with their child.

Because preschoolers are more self-sufficient, parents have more time for fulfilling personal interests. At this stage, parents often pursue their careers more intensely, engage in community activities, further their friendships, and enjoy individual interests. Parents must also work at balancing their own personal needs with their "parent" and "couple" needs.

Special Family Times

Because they are so social, preschoolers often form close attachments to extended family members, especially grandparents, 15-24. The relationship between grandparents and their grandchildren is very special. Their time together often includes such memorable experiences as baking cookies, feeding pets, and playing in the park. Grandparents often have the time and patience to read a story over and over again or mend broken toys. They also enjoy helping their grandchildren make new discoveries.

Grandparents have another important role in families. They serve as the focal point of the wider family of aunts, uncles, and cousins. When families gather for holidays and special events, they often do so at the grandparents' home. Even when families live apart, grandparents bind them together emotionally. They help family members remember all they have in common.

Grandparenting is one of the most fulfilling parts of the *middle-age years* and *aging family stages* of the family life cycle. When people become grandparents, they accept a new role. Some people think grandparenting is a fringe benefit of parenting. People can enjoy their grandchildren without having total responsibility for raising them. Grandparenting is a rich and rewarding experience for many people.

A challenge for grandparents is knowing the difference between indulging their grandchildren and spoiling them. If they truly love their grandchildren and want what is best for them, grandparents will respect the parents' wishes and authority. Grandparents can offer love and attention while still enforcing parental rules and limits. They can enjoy their grandchildren without upsetting the family order.

Grandparenting allows mature adults to continue growing and expanding their lives. Erikson called this last stage of personality development, the stage of *integrity versus despair*, Appendix A. The stage also helps the family recognize the continuity of life. The family's past links with the future as grandparents pass their heritage on to their grandchildren.

Preschoolers also enjoy sharing special times, such as birthdays, with friends. Because preschoolers can be easily overwhelmed, parties should be kept simple with only a few guests. Parents should also plan noncompetitive activities preschoolers enjoy.

Preschoolers enjoy seeing their accomplishments displayed. Not only can parents attach the child's drawings and other

15-24 Grandparents play a special role in the lives of preschoolers.

paperwork to the refrigerator, they can also photograph and make audio recordings of their accomplishments. Parents often make scrapbooks of their children's work. Studies show children have higher levels of achievement when parents treasure and preserve some of their work. To the child it says, "I am loved, and what I do is worthwhile."

3 Years*

Physical Development

Gross-Motor Skills

Walks with arms swinging in an adultlike manner

Does a heel-toe walk (forward)

Walks on tiptoes

Runs with arms alternating

Adds swerving to running style while maintaining balance

Jumps from height of 18 inches (46 cm) without assistance

Alternates feet in climbing up stairs (ascending)

Climbs low slide and slides down

Balances on one foot for a few seconds

Hops one or two times but has shaky landings

Throws ball underhanded with only slight twist of the body; aim is wild

Catches by trapping the ball in arms or with body

Uses pedal toys

Fine-Motor Skills

Draws straight lines, circles, crosses, rectangles, and triangles

Draws "potato-man" faces

Rolls balls, snakes, and "cookies" with Play-Doh®

Begins to handle a fork

Can pour liquid from small pitcher with little spilling

Builds a tower of 9 or 10 blocks

Easily handles smaller objects, such as Lego® blocks

Pounds on a "carpenters' pounding board" toy

Hand preference is definite

Unbuttons buttons and pull up large zippers

Intellectual Development

Expresses thoughts through language, art, and play

Confuses appearance and reality, such as a ball of clay gets "bigger" if you roll it into a snake or two one-half cup servings are more than one one-cup serving.

Asks many "why" questions; tries to understand cause and effect

Knows the attributes of objects, such as color and size; colors and sizes can be matched

Wants to find out about size and shape of everything

Asks questions about how things work

Begins to understand when parents try to reason with him or her

Has vocabulary of 900 to 1000 words

Speaks in 2 to 5 word sentences

Tells tall tales

Connects adventures with self and may inject self into adventure stories

May understand more of adult conversation than adults realize

Can enjoy humorous situations

Counts two or more objects; counts numbers to 10

Can hold up fingers to indicate age

Social and Emotional Development

Personality

Is usually cooperative, happy, and agreeable

Feels less frustration because of improving motor skills

Substitutes language for primitive displays of feelings

Follows directions and takes pride in doing things for others

Is learning to share and take turns

May feel jealous

May show fear of dark, animals, stories, and monsters

Family

Seeks praise and affection from parents

May still seek comfort from parents when tired or hungry

May act in a certain way to please parents

Friends

Seeks friends on own initiative

Makes friends easily

Begins to be choosy about companions, preferring one over another

Seeks status among peers

Uses language to make friends and alienate others

May attempt to comfort and remove cause of distress of playmates or siblings

Plays by sharing toys but not goals (firefighters do not work as a team)

* These charts are not exact timetables. Individuals may perform certain activities earlier or later than indicated in the charts.

4 Years

Physical Development

Gross-Motor Skills

Does a heel-toe walk on a circular line

Walks a few steps forward on a balance beam

Jumps vertically and horizontally with arms going forward and with a balanced landing

Can hop several times in a row

Alternates feet in going downstairs (descending)

Rides pedal toys, gaining speed with increased strength

Plays on playground equipment such as slide and seesaw

Throws balls with somewhat more pronounced weight shift

Catches balls with open, but rather stiff, hands

Fine-Motor Skills

Draws or paints by subdividing shapes

When drawing, adds lines next to face to represent arms and legs

Enjoys finger painting

Copies a few capital letters in manuscript style, such as E and T

Cuts on line with round-end scissors

Builds straight towers of blocks with steady hands, but may knock down existing tower

Laces shoes and wants to learn to make knots

Intellectual Development

Is aware of intellectual advances and may remind parents "I'm not a baby anymore"

Continues to ask "Why?" and "How?"

Confuses fact and fantasy; loves to tell tall tale

Likes to try new games and test ability to play them

Has only a vague concept of time; relates the word yesterday with the past and tomorrow with the future

Solves problems based on how things appear; when appearance and reality are not the same, concepts are incorrect

Believes everything has a purpose often for his or her benefit

Can begin to identify opposites

Identifies most of the basic colors by name

Sorts objects by some category, such as size

Uses spatial concepts to play hide-and-seek

Counts objects to 10 or more

Knows letters in name.

Has vocabulary of 1500 words

Realizes power of words and often begins statements with "You know what?"

Uses *and* to make compound sentences and "run-on" sentences

Knows many rules of grammar but has problems with irregular verbs, question form, and negatives

Social and Emotional Development

Personality

May seem less pleasant than at age three

May be more moody, tries to express emotions verbally

Strives for independent; resents being treated as a baby

May be stubborn and quarrelsome

Resents directions; may think he or she knows it all and can do it all

Learns to ask for things instead of snatching things from others

Is increasingly aware of attitudes and asks for approval

Family

Needs and seeks parental approval often

Has strong sense of family and home

May quote parents and boast about parents to friends

Friends

Friendships are for play purposes

Becomes more interested in friends than in adults

Share possessions and toys, especially with special friends

Suggests taking turns but may be unable to wait for his or her own turn

5 Years

Physical Development

Gross-Motor Skills

Performs physical activities more gracefully and with less wasted motion

Runs lightly on toes with more speed, turning corners with ease and stopping suddenly

Balances on one foot longer

Hops on alternate feet in skipping motion

Skip and may be able to jump rope

Descends ladder, alternating feet easily

Enjoys obstacle courses and play structures that require use of all gross-motor skills

Rides bicycle with training wheels

Throws ball by stepping forward on throwing-arm side as ball is released

Catches ball by moving body and using arms and hands to cradle the ball

Fine-Motor Skills

Shows improved eye-hand coordination

Builds buildings and bridges in addition to towers

Places small toys, such as animals in position with precision

Draws human figures with a neck and torso; begins to include more body details, such as eyebrows

Colors within the lines

Cuts simple shapes

Makes little figures with Play-Doh®

Folds paper diagonally

Copies shapes and letters; writes first name in manuscript

May tie shoes

May enjoy playing with child-sized tools

Intellectual Development

Uses more concepts that will lead to logical thinking, such as classifying, arranging by size, understanding spatial concepts, and understanding time concepts

Shows more understanding of cause and effect

Understands number concepts; can follow instructions involving numbers

Understands quantitative thinking in terms of "more than"

Begins to separate fantasy from reality

Enjoys using many props in pretend play

Begins to see written words and numerals as symbols; sees the connection among talking, writing, and reading

Seeks information and serious answers to questions

Accepts that there are rules, even though unable to understand reasoning behind rules

Has vocabulary of 2000 to 2200 words

May not know the meaning of all words used

Speaks with grammatical construction comparable with adults in the home

Likes humor including silly names and words

Social and Emotional Development

Personality

Shows increased willingness to cooperate

Is more patient, generous, and conscientious

Expresses anger verbally rather than physically

Is more reasonable when in a quarrel

Develops a sense of fairness

Becomes more practical

Family

Likes supervision, accepts instructions, and asks permission

Has strong desire to please parents and other adults

Still depends on parents for emotional support and approval

Is proud of mother and father

Delights in helping parents

May act protective of younger siblings

Shapes ideas of gender roles by watching parents' behavior

Friends

Is increasingly social and talkative. Is eager to make friends and may develop strong friendships

Prefers friends of same age and gender

May pick a best friend

Stays with play groups as long as interest holds

Learns to respect the property of others

Summing It Up

- During the preschool years, children grow taller, leaner, and better coordinated. Preschoolers practice *locomotor skills*. Their fine-motor skills also become much more precise, especially when hand preference is definite.

- Preschoolers develop two gender-role concepts—*gender stability* and *gender constancy*.

- Preschoolers handle most life skills by themselves.

- Some preschoolers experience problems with *enuresis* and sleep deprivation.

- According to Piaget, preschoolers do not think logically, but do use perceptions (how things appear) to solve problems.

- Preschoolers ask many "why" questions to learn about their world.

- Fantasy play is a sign of creative thinking.

- Play enhances all aspects of preschoolers' development. Parents have an important role in making play safe, challenging, and suitable for their child.

- Language skills advance greatly during the preschool years, helping children clearly express their feelings and thoughts.

- Advances in physical and intellectual development are the most important factors in preschoolers' social and emotional development. Preschoolers spend more time playing with friends and siblings.

- Some preschoolers have serious mental health problems that need early treatment.

- During the preschool years, parenting style emerges as parents make adjustments for their preschoolers' needs.

Recalling the Facts

1. What changes occur in the proportion and shape of a child's body during the preschool years?

2. List three locomotor skills children typically learn in the preschool years.

3. List the stages of art development for preschoolers.

4. How should parents handle preschoolers' questions about sex? Give an example.

5. What can parents do to reduce mealtime problems and food dislikes with their preschoolers?

6. What is a common psychological cause of *enuresis*?

7. Name two things parents can do to help preschoolers develop good sleep habits.

8. Why do some people call fantasy the "genius of childhood"?

9. Name five types of play typical during the preschool years.

10. What are five language concerns of parents with preschoolers?

11. How can parents lessen rivalry between siblings?

12. What does the Denver Developmental Screening Test examine?

13. How should parents react to their preschoolers' heroes and fantasy friends?

14. Name three parenting tasks for parents with preschoolers during the authoritative stage of parenting?

15. What is a key challenge for grandparents as they build relationships with grandchildren?

Applying New Skills

1. **Preschooler observation.** Visit a preschool and note signs of progress in gross- and fine-motor skills as the children run, jump, skip, climb, ride pedal toys, throw and catch a ball, build towers of blocks, draw, and use scissors. What differences do you see between 3-year-olds and 5-year-olds? Share your observations in class.

2. **Cooking with preschoolers.** Collect some recipe books written for young children. Name four nutritious recipes that preschoolers could help prepare. If possible, prepare one of the recipes with a small group of preschoolers. Write a summary about your experience.

3. **Reliable resources.** Use reliable Internet and print resources to make a list of Web sites and books that help parents answer children's "why" questions. In addition, you may want to talk with the children's librarian at your local library for ideas.

4. **Play activities.** List two play activities that support each of the following areas of preschool development: physical, intellectual, social, and emotional. Select one activity. Use Internet or print resources to develop the activity for parents to use with their preschoolers. For example, you might create a simple "shape" matching game using a file folder and construction paper.

Thinking Critically

1. Draw conclusions about why gender constancy would be a difficult concept for preschoolers in Piaget's *intuitive phase*.

2. Debate the following statement: A child who shows a preference for the left hand should be encouraged to change and use the right hand.

3. Give two reasons to justify fantasy play as beneficial to preschoolers' intellectual development.

4. Select four or five heroes of today's preschoolers. In small groups, analyze the attributes of each hero. What attributes make these heroes desirable to preschoolers? Do these heroes display any objectionable values? How might parents handle their preschooler's admiration of such heroes?

5. Because of changing standards for kindergarten readiness and completion, some children who do not meet these state mandates remain in kindergarten and do not advance to first grade. Brainstorm a list of pros and cons in regard to retaining or advancing children who do not meet kindergarten completion requirements.

Linking Academics

1. **Reading.** Read a children's book about sibling relationships. Consider such books as, *Sheila Rae's Peppermint Stick* by Kevin Henkes or *Do You Know What I'll Do?* by Charlotte Zolotow. Write a short review explaining how the book promotes good sibling relationships.

2. **Writing.** Write a creative story about three 4-year-olds involved in a pretend or fantasy play activity. What is the plot? How do the children use symbols?

3. **Technology.** Investigate the use of computer software and other types of technology that can assist preschool children with readiness skills for kindergarten. How do child development experts view such software to encourage learning? How can parents make the best use of such technology products with their children? Write a summary of your findings to share with the class.

Chapter 16

Parents and Their School-Age Children

Objectives

After studying this chapter, you will be able to

- identify changes in the physical development of school-age children and factors that impact development.
- summarize characteristics of school-age children's intellectual development.
- list major intellectual learnings of school-age children according to Piaget.
- describe changes in school-age children's social and emotional development, including the role of the peers, sibling relationships, finding a balanced self-view, and coping with emotions.
- describe how school-age children express industry according to Erikson.
- summarize key parenting concerns and tasks during the school-age years.

Key Terms

gender-role identification
puberty
classification
seriation
conservation
reversibility
creativity
work ethic
phobias
self-care children
conformity

Parents may be surprised to realize their children are now grown up enough to start school. For children, going to school opens up a new world outside the family, 16-1. Their world expands throughout the *school-age years*, the time when children are between ages 6 and 12. The school and peers take on increasing importance in children's socialization although parents remain important. Toward the end of this stage, children spend more time away from the family than with them.

In this chapter you will study the development of school-age children. You will learn about new developmental skills that emerge and help children take steps toward fitting into society. After each section, check the "School-Age Development" charts at the end of the chapter for year-by-year development. You will also study the role of parents as they maintain a balance between parental control and allowing their children to act more independently. Parents must also adjust to the presence of others in their children's lives.

Physical Development

Children in the school-age years develop a more adultlike body structure. Physical development is relatively smooth. During these years, children mainly refine their gross- and fine-motor skills.

Physical Growth

For most of the school-age years, boys and girls develop physically at much the same rate. They grow about 2 to 3 inches taller and 5 to 7 pounds heavier each year. By the time they are 12, children are about 5 feet tall and weigh about 80 pounds.

Toward the end of the school-age years, children show a wide variation in maturity. This is especially true for girls and boys who begin to show major differences in their

16-1 When children go to school, they learn about the world around them.

physical development. At an average age of 10½, girls begin a major growth spurt. They may actually grow taller than the boys in their classes. Boys begin their growth spurt at about age 12½. These growth spurts start a child's transition into adulthood.

Children begin to look more like adults in their body proportions. Facial features become more mature, too, with the loss of baby teeth and the growth of the larger, permanent teeth. Skin becomes less delicate and lighter hair often darkens.

Gross-Motor Skills

During the school years, children become stronger and their coordination improves. Many children under 9 years are often awkward because their motor skills have not kept pace with their growth. With time, their coordination improves and their movements become smoother.

For younger school-age children, bicycling, skipping, and jumping rope are popular activities. Children also like other sports and activities. By ages 9 and 10, children may begin narrowing their interests. If they enjoy sports, they are now ready to learn the proper techniques for organized games. They can run, kick, throw, catch, and hit better because of improved coordination, timing, and balance, 16-2.

16-2 By age 9, many children are ready for organized team sports.

Children may begin to approach physical activity in different ways in the school-age years. Many boys and girls are keenly interested in their physical strength and increasing motor abilities. Some children are very active, and they like competitive team sports. Some boys and girls may be less competitive and prefer to engage in noncompetitive physical activities, such as bicycling, skiing, or dance. Still other children are not really interested in sports. They may prefer less-active interests.

Some schools do not provide a physical fitness program for all children. The daily school environment often involves sedentary tasks. Children spend more after-school time on homework with each advancing grade.

Team Sports

By the fourth grade, physical education classes emphasize skills for team sports. Only 20 percent of children participate in competitive school sports. About 50 percent of children engage in moderate to vigorous physical activity, usually for less than an hour daily.

Many children enjoy the competition and friendship that exist in team sports. Children play team sports in physical education classes, during recesses, and in community programs. Combining physical play with healthy competition can help children's development in all areas. Through athletics, children can learn to appreciate physical fitness, respect authority, develop leadership skills, and cooperate with others.

Before participating in competitive team sports, children should have a doctor's exam. Parents should talk with the doctor about the nature of specific sports and follow the doctor's recommendations. Participation in sports may have negative physical effects for some children. For example, some inborn conditions make children especially susceptible to injury. Even healthy children may risk injury to developing bones and muscles. In a few cases, prolonged exertion may cause heart damage. Some children, if pressured to win, may develop high blood pressure.

Participation can also have some negative psychological effects. Children who are pushed into sports against their wishes may develop a negative attitude toward exercise and physical fitness. Children who see their parents and coaches argue with game officials may fail to learn respect for authority. Children who try to impress others with their individual achievements may develop conceit rather than a spirit of cooperation. Some children may feel unworthy if they cannot match the athletic success of a parent or older sibling. Children who seldom or never win may suffer a loss of self-esteem. They may feel humiliation and think of themselves as failures. After a while, they lose interest in playing.

Parents should allow children to decide whether they want to play competitive sports. Children who are physically and psychologically ready are usually eager to begin. Parents should

- encourage children to consider the time they need to fulfill all school and home responsibilities along with playing competitive sports.

- allow children to quit competitive sports if they feel no joy or find their daily load too stressful. (Before they quit, children should think through their choices and avoid a spur-of-the-moment decision.)

Children should not specialize in a sport during the school years. Playing the same sport throughout the year puts extra strain on the same body parts. Children can profit from learning and enjoying several sports, including team and individual sports.

With all the risks, parents may wonder if and when their children should play competitive sports. While children do not have a definite need to play sports, they do need physical exercise. Parents should encourage their children to get plenty of exercise. Some children need little encouragement; others need a lot. It may help if parents exercise with their child, 16-3.

Fine-Motor Skills

Fine-motor skills greatly improve in the school years. This is evident in handwriting. Boys' fine-motor skills often lag behind those of same-age girls because of differences in brain maturity. If children have a good supply of small construction toys, art and craft materials, and writing materials, their fine-motor skills will continue to improve.

Healthy Sexuality Development

Gender-role development continues in the school-age years. Once school-age children understand gender constancy, they begin developing *gender-role identification*. **Gender-role identification** means behaving in ways consistent with gender and cultural rules. Because male and female roles are continually changing, children may experience some confusion.

Gender-role identification is a slow process. People must feel their own

16-3 When parents take time for physical activity with their children, they help their children develop healthy habits for a lifetime.

he or she adopts gender roles. Male roles include being a boy, brother, man, husband, and father. Female roles include being a girl, sister, woman, wife, and mother.

Children usually begin this process by imitating same-gendered adults, especially parents. The gender roles parents portray in their homes greatly influence school-age children. Children also imitate same-gender peers. By the school years, boys and girls often stop playing together in mixed-gender activities. Instead, they form same-gender play groups. Gender stereotypes are common during this age. Children describe their own gender more positively than the opposite-gender. The school environment, where roles are less stereotypical, also influences children.

The school years are critical for teaching children about sexuality. Although some schools and religious groups assist parents by providing sex education, parents still have the major responsibility. Children need honest answers.

In the early school years, children begin to think about how a baby comes through the special opening at birth. They may also ask how a baby starts to grow inside the mother. A parent can use a simple answer such as, "When a father and mother want to have a baby, a cell from the father meets with another cell inside the mother. This is how a baby begins."

During the later school years, children want to know more specifics about sex. Parents can tie sex information with what children need to know about *puberty*. **Puberty** is the process through which the body becomes capable of reproduction. Many guides are available for parents, who can choose one that reflects their attitudes and values about sex. Parents must interpret family values and model them.

Eating

Although physical growth is slower during the school-age years, children continue to need a nutritious balance of foods for growth and energy. Age, height, gender, and activity level are important factors for determining children's food needs. When the growth spurt occurs near the teen years, children often need healthful foods that provide more energy, 16-4. As parents plan family meals, they should consider that school breakfast and lunch programs meet up to one-half of children's daily food needs.

Learning to make healthful food choices is the main concern during this age. Peers and media advertisements have great influence on children's food choices, and not always to the benefit of children's health. Children often choose foods that are too high

16-4 To encourage healthy growth and avoid obesity, parents should provide an array of healthful foods for their children.

in sugar and fat. Poor food choices combined with large portions can lead to obesity. School-age children are generally considered overweight when they weigh 15 percent more than their ideal weight as shown on medical charts. About 17 percent of school-age children are obese, and the numbers are increasing. This greatly concerns parents, teachers, and medical professionals alike. In addition, the following factors contribute to childhood obesity:

- *Family lifestyles that promote poor exercise habits.* Some families lead sedentary lifestyles. Children who spend two or more hours per day watching TV or using a computer are more likely to be overweight.

- *Stress.* Stress often causes behavior problems for children. Those with such problems have a greater risk for becoming obese. Children with low self-esteem may turn to overeating for comfort.

- *Frequent restaurant meals.* Children who eat restaurant meals four or more times per week (excluding school lunches) are at greater risk for obesity and the accompanying health problems.

- *Too many "treats."* Foods high in fat or sugar that once were occasional treats have become daily food choices for many children. These include pizza, snacks, desserts, carbonated soft drinks, and fruit drinks.

Overweight or obese children risk having other health problems, including Type 2 diabetes, high blood pressure, heart problems, dental problems, and bone loss. These children suffer in other ways, too. Peers often tease or reject them, which tends to lower self-esteem. Such children may perform poorly on tests and have lower grades.

Weight-loss diets are often ineffective and dangerous for children. When dieting, for example, children do not get the nutrients they need for growth and good health—especially protein and calcium. Overweight children often become concerned about their body images, too. This can lead to life-threatening eating disorders. If parents suspect their children are overweight, they should consult their pediatrician. Most doctors recommend school-age children stabilize their weight rather than lose excess pounds. As children grow taller, they outgrow their weight problems.

What else can parents do? See 16-5 for more ideas on helping children make good food choices. Using learning tools, such as those found on MyPyramid can also help parents and children learn more about healthful food choices.

Sleeping

School-age children need 9½ to 11 hours of sleep nightly. Research from the National Center on Sleep Disorders shows that one-third of all school-age children do not get the sleep they need. Sleep deprivation is primarily due to the attraction of media, homework demands, and social activities.

School-age children pay a price for sleep deprivation. It makes children in this age

Helping Children Make Good Food Choices

When children see their parents making good choices, they are likely to follow the example. Here are some other actions parents can take to encourage healthful eating:

- **Involve children in meal planning and food shopping.** These activities increase interest in healthful eating. Offering a variety of foods also interests children in making good food choices.

- **Choose cooking methods that benefit health.** Try baking, grilling, or steaming instead of frying.

- **Use a variety of herbs and spices to flavor foods.** This is a healthful alternative to salt.

- **Try new recipes.** Involve children in choosing new recipes that offer a variety of nutrients and flavors.

- **Limit certain foods.** Keep pizzas, hot dogs, and hamburgers as occasional foods, not part of the weekly family meal plan.

- **Purchase and prepare healthful snacks.** Teach children to ask "Am I really hungry?" before snacking. Keep a variety of low-fat protein foods (yogurt, cheese, or peanut butter), fresh fruits and vegetables, and whole-grain crackers and breads.

- **Offer water and low-fat milk for beverages.** Many children consume too many sugary beverages. This contributes to obesity and dental problems.

- **Make breakfast an important daily meal.** Children who skip breakfast tend to have lower test scores, slower thinking, greater fatigue and irritability, and poorer memories.

- **Demonstrate healthful portions.** Children need to recognize healthful serving sizes of a variety of foods. Parents should discourage them from "super size" portions.

- **Encourage mealtime conversation.** Keeping the TV turned off limits distractions during mealtime. This helps children focus on eating healthful foods.

16-5 Parents need to help their children avoid the serious problems of obesity.

group overactive—unable to relax. They become accident-prone. They do poorly on tests measuring memory and attention span, both of which are essential for best school performance. How can parents help their school-age children get enough sleep? Parents should

- help their children plan a daily schedule around a regular bedtime
- encourage a relaxing, 30-minute bedtime routine, without media
- discourage caffeine use especially within six hours of sleep
- plan to exercise with their children before the evening meal or several hours before bedtime
- keep the bedroom dark for sleep and light when awakening
- prevent their children from sleeping more than two extra hours per night on weekends

Intellectual Development

Major changes occur in children's thinking skills during the school years. The inconsistencies in thinking during younger years very slowly give way to logical thinking by age 8. School-age children face a variety of challenges in school. During these years, they develop basic literacy skills in reading, writing, arithmetic, and computers. Creativity is also part of the school experience for most children. As school-age children learn these basic skills, they also "learn how to learn," a skill needed for academic progress.

Piaget and School-Age Intellectual Development

As children enter school, Piaget's preoperational stage draws slowly to a close. At this time, children enter the *concrete operational stage*, 16-6 and Appendix B. In this

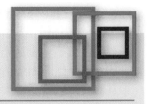

Piaget's Stages of Intellectual Development

1. Sensorimotor
1A: Exercising the Reflexes
1B: Primary Circular Reactions
1C: Secondary Circular Reactions
1D: Coordination of Secondary Circular Reactions
1E: Tertiary Circular Reactions
1F: Mental Representation

2. Preoperational
2A: Preconceptual Phase
2B: Intuitive Phase

3. Concrete Operations

4. Formal Operations

16-6 As they get older, children no longer rely on their perceptions to reason. They can think logically about objects or events in their real or imagined worlds.

stage, which lasts until the early teen years, appearances no longer mislead children. They can perform logical-thinking actions (operations) on information about real things in their world or what they can imagine (concrete). Children make several significant intellectual gains during the school-age years. These are signs that the children's thinking is going through fundamental changes. The concepts children learn include

- *Classification.* The process of putting a person, object, or event in a group or category according to one or more common characteristics is **classification**. For example, a child knows he or she can be a son or daughter, a brother or sister, a student, a team member, a Scout, and a friend all at the same time.

- *Seriation.* The ability to arrange items in a logical order—such as short to long, long to short, light to dark colors, or more to less—is **seriation**. School-age children must develop this concept to understand the number line.

- *Conservation.* The understanding that certain properties (number, substance, weight, and volume) remain the same (are conserved) even if they change in appearance is **conservation,** 16-7. For example, school-age children understand 10 pennies are 10 pennies whether they are stacked, spread out, placed in a circle, or dropped in a piggy bank.

- *Reversibility.* The principle that any process done on an object can be undone—in actuality or through mental thought—to restore it to its original form is **reversibility.** For example, in math a child learns that adding and subtracting are reverse operations; thus $6 + 2 = 8$ and $8 - 2 = 6$. In like manner, multiplication and division are reverse operations. As another example, a school-age child mentally knows that if you take a ball of dough and divide it into twelve rolls there is still the same amount of dough. If you combined all the rolls back into a ball, it would appear the same as it did when you began.

- *Various perspectives exist.* School-age children can understand another person's physical and social positions. For example, they know why seating arrangements affect what a person sees and hears (physical position). They also know others may not hold the same views they do (social position). Because school-age children are less egocentric, they are willing to listen and consider others' ideas.

16-7 Children understand conservation when they realize pouring water from a tall, narrow container to a small, wide container does not change the amount of the water.

Learning How to Learn

As school-age children become more logical, they "learn how to learn" or process information. Schoolwork requires attending to the important aspects of a lesson. It also requires remembering what is taught and awareness of what a person knows and does not know. All these tasks involve developing information-processing skills. During the school-age years, children develop these skills almost totally through teacher instruction.

Learning how to learn involves forming a knowledge base or long-term memory (all that people know about the world, about themselves, and about knowing). A person's *short-term* or *working memory* is not usually part of the knowledge base. This memory is less important because it only lasts a few seconds. People use it to accomplish something immediate. For example, with short-term memory you remember the first words of a sentence as you read the last words. You remember a telephone number as you place a call.

In contrast, you want to remember some items of knowledge much longer. These items build on prior learning and make up your *long-term memory* or *knowledge base*. In building a knowledge base, a person uses various methods to store knowledge in long-term memory. For example, methods for building a knowledge base can include

- rehearsing or repeating information by saying or writing it.

- organizing information, such as putting a list of words to be learned into groups (fruits, tools, pets).

- elaborating by connecting to existing knowledge. For example, a person can remember cardinal directions (north, east, west, south) by thinking of the letters in the word *news*.

- creating scripts by repeating sequenced tasks. Through each repetition, a person remembers more details and steps. For example, repeating a recipe several times creates a script and helps a person cook the dish without the written recipe.

Learning how to learn also involves knowledge of thought processes. Through self-appraisal a person knows what he or she knows and does not know. Then through self-management, a person sets up the learning environment (finds a place to work; gets needed tools), decides what information has to be learned, chooses and uses learning strategies, and confirms learning.

Parents need to help their school-age children, especially those in the early elementary grades, learn how to learn, 16-8. Parents can talk with teachers and look at textbook formats to help determine methods to help their children learn. Parents can point out how effective learning methods save time and energy. Parents can also encourage their children's self-appraisal and self-management.

16-8 As children learn self-management, they are able to set up their learning environments.

The School Experience

Because the school experience is so important in these years, it becomes the major force in the lives of children and their parents. New developmental tasks occur yearly as children progress through the school years. Parents realize their children's challenges, along with their successes and disappointments, often lie beyond parental control.

Mastering Basic Skills

Although children face many challenges during their school experience, the major academic challenge is learning basic literacy skills. These skills are necessary for future academic learning and career success. The level of children's success influences feelings of self-esteem.

Reading is the most basic literacy skill, and it requires much mental effort. Children use visual-sensory memory to compare letters in print with letters stored in memory. To figure out words, children must pair the letter or letters with the sounds they make using the *phonics approach*. With the *whole-word approach*, children simply recognize what the "letters say," such as the word "stop." Although each approach has its weaknesses, when they are used together children learn to read effectively. Most school reading programs use a combination of both approaches.

Children learn to read most words with phonics skills, but also learn some words—sight words—using the whole-word approach. Once they know the words, children bring meaning to them from their knowledge base (comprehension). Because meaning is so important, teaching reading involves discussing vocabulary, predicting the content from titles and pictures, and discussing each segment.

Writing is another basic skill. Children learn to form letters first, which requires visual memory of the letters and fine-motor skills, 16-9. Children usually begin learning to write using *manuscript writing* (sometimes called *printing*). Around age 8, children learn *cursive* writing (rounded letters that join to the next letters in a word). Besides learning how to make the letters, children must learn to make letters the correct size, put space between words and sentences, and keep everything in alignment. This calls for much eye-hand coordination, which children do not fully develop by the early school years. Writing eventually involves putting thoughts on paper. Good writing involves

- collecting information
- deciding what to say
- writing the ideas with correct spelling, grammar, and punctuation
- revising the material one or more times
- correcting errors

Arithmetic—the understanding of numbers and the operations of addition, subtraction, multiplication, and division—develops best in Piaget's concrete operational stage. In many schools, children learn these arithmetic skills through real-life, concrete ideas rather than through memorization without understanding. Teaching helps

16-9 Writing is a skill that must be learned. Teachers guide children as they learn to write letters and numbers.

children grasp concepts, such as conservation and reversibility. Then children practice these skills.

Computer literacy involves knowing how to use computers well. In classrooms today, children learn about more than just how the computer works. They learn how to use computers to solve problems and how technology affects society. They also learn about ethics of computer use.

Creativity

Creativity means producing a new or original idea, product, or process. You may have heard others refer to creativity as "thinking outside the box." Creativity involves every human field of work. To be creative, a person must know subject matter (science, art, math, business) and be able to communicate ideas to others. Learning to be creative is part of the school experience. Teachers can encourage creativity in children by the questions they ask and by the assignments they give. For example, teachers help stimulate curiosity and build creativity skills through such activities as brainstorming, imagining, and making associations. They also encourage children to be creative through trial and error experimentation, viewing a problem or idea in multiple ways, or thinking about future possibilities.

The Role of the Parent

How children learn the basic literacy skills and creativity can predict academic achievement in the teen years. Parents need to encourage children's learning activities in the home. They can also work with the school to support their children's progress.

Encouraging Learning

The school experience gives children an opportunity to increase their competence in many ways. Although parenting becomes more indirect, parents can help make their child's school experience a good one. Parents need to help their children discover the fun and excitement of learning. Children who have helpful, non-pressuring parents are most prepared for school. Parents encourage and help their children in many ways. These include the following:

- sharing children's excitement about learning

- taking children to the library, museums, and other places for enrichment activities

- buying and making good learning materials, such as puzzles, art and music materials (16-10), games that involve strategy, and hobby materials

- reading books aloud as a daily family activity

- getting involved with the children's home projects

- having parent-child discussions to expand vocabulary, and clarify meanings

- making reading, writing, arithmetic, and computers part of everyday life

- following through on general enrichment activities suggested by teachers

- enrolling children in groups that promote learning, such as youth programs

- playing games that teach skills, such as "concentration" for memory skills

16-10 Encouraging children to pursue music activities adds to a well-rounded education.

- carefully monitoring their children's school performance and watching for any slips in achievement levels

- keeping positive expectations for school success—the most important factor for a child's success

Helping Children Adjust to School

The school years bring adjustments for the entire family. Adjustment, including some separation anxiety, is most difficult the first year and often takes several weeks. Parents should talk with their children about what changes will occur, what to expect, and what feelings are normal during this time. Children may face similar but shorter transition periods at the beginning of each school year.

The second major transition occurs in the upper-elementary years. Adjusting to upper-elementary grades may be even harder for many school-age children. In lower-elementary grades, most children have one teacher and stay in the same classroom throughout the day. In upper-elementary grades, students often have several teachers in different classrooms. Students also have additional responsibilities, such as keeping their books in a locker, finding their classes, and arriving on time.

As was true of kindergarten or first grade, children enter once again as the youngest at their new school. A parent's understanding and encouragement are necessary at this time. Taking children to visit the new school can be very helpful. Although parents cannot make adjustments for their child, they can make home life less stressful to ease adjustments. For example, packing backpacks the night before and laying out clothing for school help eliminate stress during the morning rush. Talking with children about their day and checking on homework assignments right after school shows children their parents are interested in them.

Children take home-stress to school, causing home-stress to compound school-stress. If children have significant problems adjusting to school, parents will want to seek counseling for them.

Supporting Homework Assignments

When the school day ends, children's learning tasks are not complete. Homework is high on the list of students' responsibilities. It gives students a chance to polish skills they learn earlier in the day. It also helps them learn to think critically and solve problems away from the school setting. Both parents and children have responsibilities concerning homework. Parents are responsible for locating resources and encouraging, supporting, and helping during practice. Children are responsible for doing the assignments and returning them to school in a timely way, 16-11.

Parents should talk with the classroom teacher to be sure their children are doing satisfactory work on homework assignments. Children should not spend all their time studying, however. Having a balance between work, rest, exercise, and recreation is important.

Becoming a School Partner

In past years, parents did not play much of a role in their children's school experience. Now schools want to partner with parents who are the first and most important nurturers and educators of their children. How can parents partner with a school? Some basic ways include the following:

- providing a home environment that supports learning
- communicating with school personnel about educational decisions made on behalf of their children
- volunteering their services at school
- joining school organizations or boards to help identify school needs and find solutions

Language Development

Language development parallels the dramatic changes in school-age children's intellectual development. Language improves profoundly because children are less egocentric. They also profit from having better learning skills.

School-age children add 20 or more words a day to their vocabulary. Vocabulary refers to all the words people must know to communicate well. Vocabulary has two components—*oral vocabulary* and *reading vocabulary*. Oral vocabulary involves the words people use when speaking or recall when listening. Reading vocabulary involves the words people use or recognize in print. Both are important in learning to read. Recent studies show that by age 12, most children have about 40,000 words in their oral vocabularies. Oral vocabulary plays an important role in reading for two reasons. First, oral vocabulary allows a person to recall an exact pronunciation. Sounding out a word does not always give the exact pronunciation. Second, oral vocabulary helps

Responsibilities for Homework

Child's Responsibilities	Parent's Responsibilities
Recording assignments properly and bringing them home along with materials to do work.	Going through all homework with their children. Helping children plan a prioritized "to do" list. Encouraging children to tackle more difficult assignments first.
Setting up to work.	Providing a quiet place to work.
Eating a snack if hungry.	Providing a nutritious snack with protein.
Avoiding distractions.	Setting limits about media and telephone calls.
Gathering home and school materials.	Purchasing home supplies.
Working on assignments.	Monitoring the work. Helping the child with materials needing practice, such as calling out spelling words or review items.
Asking for help when he or she needs it.	Explaining or providing strategies and resources. Some good online sites include: • www.homeworkspot.com • www.zen.org/~brendan/kids-homework.html • www.mathforum.org/dr.math/ • www.mathnerds.com • www.factmonster.com • http://school.discoveryeducation.com/ • http://kids.yahoo.com/learn
Putting completed assignments and materials in backpack.	Checking to see whether assignments are completed and packed.

16-11 If parents help their younger school-age children develop the skills and responsibility for doing homework, their children can handle most, if not all, their homework assignments without parental help when they are older.

students give meaning to words they read once they figure out the right pronunciation. This helps children comprehend what they read.

Once school-age children enter Piaget's *concrete operational stage*, the way they define words changes. Preschoolers define words by physical attributes (orange is round), by actions (ball is for rolling or bouncing), or by examples (dogs sleep under...). School-age children define words by class (orange is a fruit or a color) or by a synonym (*under* means *below*). School-age children understand abstract words, such as mammals. They also can describe differences in similar terms, such as *big* and *gigantic*.

By age 9, most children have almost complete knowledge of the grammar they hear. They understand and use the passive voice, comparatives, and the subjunctive mood. They know correct from incorrect grammar for the most part, but most often use the grammar they hear.

Once school-age children realize other people have viewpoints that differ from their own, they master persuasive communication in their attempt to win others over. They also like to play with language. School-age children like to ask riddles and tell jokes. These often focus on playing with words. For example, "Where do sheep get their hair cut? At the baa-baa shop." Some school-age children develop secret languages so they can communicate privately with friends.

In addition to oral language, school-age children develop literacy skills that deal with written symbols. To a great extent, children learn these skills through direct teaching before grade 4. In later school years, children refine and use these skills to learn other subject matter, such as science and social studies.

Social and Emotional Development

Although parents are still the most important people in the lives of their children, the school-age years are a time of expanding friendships and interactions with others, 16-12. The social world is full of challenges for children. At this age, society expects children to refine their awareness and understanding of others. Other people also expect children to interact positively and control their negative feelings. Parents expect their children to stay close to the family's values.

School-age children know the difference between inner feelings and outward expressions of emotions. Regulating emotions is still difficult. These years are important for learning how to handle frustration, anger, disappointment, and stress more easily. Because they must maintain composure during school and other settings away from home, children often vent their frustrations the minute they get home.

Children's Friendships

During the early school years, peers have limited influence on each other. The peer

16-12 During the school-age years, friendships with peers expand.

group becomes most important by the upper-elementary school grades. Peer relations fulfill the need of older children to belong to a group beyond the family. At this age, peer groups often require members to follow similar actions and have some independence from adult authority.

Changes in Peer Interactions

Exclusive relationships begin to emerge in the late preschool and early school-age years. The groups are usually small and loosely organized. Group membership changes often. Children choose friends on the basis of self-serving needs, such as "someone who plays with me and gets along with me." Girls tend to choose friends in terms of friendliness and kindness. They engage in quiet activities in small groups or with a single best friend. Boys tend to choose friends in terms of same interests. They play noisy, rough-and-tumble games often in rather large groups.

During the upper-elementary school years, peer groups unify and become more selective. They also become more organized and structured. Throughout these years, children meet their desire for group activities in part by organizations, such as scouting groups and 4-H clubs. These groups provide learning experiences and fill some of children's needs. Children select friends who fulfill their emotional needs and share common interests. Some choose friends who complement rather than match skills. For example, a shy child may have an outgoing best friend.

Roles of Peer Groups

Healthy, positive friendships can enrich children's lives. Peers provide a network that offers stability, trust, cooperation, and a capacity for growth that children cannot find in other ways. Peer groups serve many roles, such as

- *Providing friendships.* Friendships help children learn to establish and maintain relationships with people of both genders. Children learn give-and-take through friends. The friendships children have during the school years influence the relationships they establish later in life, 16-13.

- *Identifying gender roles.* Choosing same-gender friends becomes most noticeable around ages 7 or 8 and continues until the teen years. The peer group sets gender standards that help children complete the process of gender-role identification.

16-13 Friendships teach children important lessons about relationships that will influence them throughout their lives.

- *Allowing independence from adult authority.* Because they must obey adults, but desire peer acceptance, children learn to make compromises between two patterns of behavior. For example, they may dress neat enough and within dress codes to pass adult inspection, but daring enough to gain peer acceptance.

- *Transmitting knowledge.* Peers often compare family values and may take on values different from their own. Children also learn which friends are good students in certain school subjects. They often rely on them for informal tutoring.

- *Learning to follow rules.* By school age, children conform to rules and roles in their family system and in school. Similarly, the peer group teaches rules through games and activities. The idea of rules spills over to the strict code of acceptable behaviors and control by the peer group. Peers may ignore or reject children who do not follow peer rules.

Siblings and Verbal Conflicts

School-age children can better view the needs and wants of siblings because they are less egocentric. However, they also learn siblings will react to what they do or say. Their verbal development allows siblings to express rivalry through teasing and long arguments.

Conflict among siblings relates to how well parents get along with each other. School-age children imitate what they see and hear. Sibling conflict also relates to competition among brothers and sisters. Rarely, school-age children have conflicts with their much younger siblings; rather, they often help care for them. Opposite-gender siblings compete less with each other and often get along better.

Conflict often increases throughout the school-age years. With time, status and power equalize and competition weakens. For most siblings, there is a positive, growing relationship under the conflict.

Erikson's View: Moving from Play to Work

According to Erikson, school-age children face the challenge of developing a healthy sense of *industry* as opposed to *inferiority*, 16-14. (See Appendix A, "Erikson's Theory of Personality Development," for detailed information on the characteristics of Stage 4.) Industry involves learning cultural skills in order to become productive members of society. Industry also means developing a positive attitude toward work.

The term *industry* and the preschool term *initiative* sound much alike. The theme of industry, according to Erikson, is "making things together." Children work at mastering skills in the family system, the school, youth programs, and the peer group. Teachers and peers evaluate school-age children's performance more objectively than parents. Also, school-age children begin developing notions of *work ethic*. **Work ethic** involves standards for work conduct that guide responsibilities and careers.

Inferiority is a sense of worthlessness, especially in comparison to others. This feeling negatively impacts peer interaction. This in turn, makes children feel even more worthless. Inferiority can also result when children value work more than social relationships. Eventually, peers ignore or neglect them without acknowledging their work.

Finding a Balanced View of Self

School-age children tend to have a balanced self-view. By age 8, they can evaluate their physical skills, intellectual abilities, and social skills with peers. They can also blend positive and negative qualities and rate their overall feelings of self-worth. Some children, however, focus more on their negative traits. Focusing on the negative may color their overall feelings of self-worth. Having a positive self-view helps children make the most of their abilities. The only time it is better to minimize abilities is in unsafe situations. For example, misjudging your ability to swim a given distance is dangerous.

Erikson's Theory of Personality Development

Stage	Approximate Age	Step Toward Stable Personality	Step Toward Unstable Personality
1	Birth to age 2	Trust	Mistrust
2	Ages 2 & 3	Autonomy	Shame and doubt
3	Ages 4 & 5	Initiative	Guilt
4	Ages 6 to 11	Industry	Inferiority
5	Ages 12 to 18	Identity	Role confusion
6	Early adulthood	Intimacy	Isolation
7	Middle age	Generativity	Stagnation
8	Late adulthood	Integrity	Despair

16-14 School-age children need to develop a sense of pride in accomplishing a variety of skills and in being dependable in performing assigned tasks.

Emotions: Anxiety and Frustration

School-age children are eager to grow up and meet new life challenges. However, trying to meet the expectations of parents, teachers, and peers leaves them ripe for anxiety and frustration. These children often feel much stress because they do not openly talk about their feelings unless alone with a supportive person. Here are some common feelings of school-age children.

Happiness. Younger school-age children are often happier than older children, 16-15. Younger ones believe they can master anything in time. They are optimistic that negative traits in themselves and others will change for the better. Older children think their traits and those of others are fixed; thus, they are unhappy about negative traits. Preteens are often moody when comparing themselves to peers. Some unhappiness even from self-assured children is normal. Some children are unhappy due to unhappy family situations, school achievements, or peer reputations.

Fear and Anxiety. Many fears of earlier years decrease because school-age children can separate reality from fantasy. Other fears replace earlier ones and are more common in girls than in boys. Major fears include snakes, storms, wars, and terrorism. **Phobias**, extreme fears out of proportion to the threat, also surface in the school years. Some phobias interfere with normal functioning. About five percent of school-age children experience school phobias. These children often feel sick or become sick each school day. School phobias relate to school failures, rejection or criticism by teachers, school activities (oral reports), or fear something could happen to parents while children are at school. Children may also have anxiety over future threats. Anxieties about families and peer relationships are common. For example, children may have concern about family finances, rejection by friends, or attacks by bullies.

Loneliness. Young school-age children describe feelings of being sad and alone. These children often do not have friends due to shyness or other social weaknesses. Loneliness can keep children from interacting with others, which only intensifies the feeling.

Anger and Aggression. Anger is common in children who are frustrated or who have parental models of anger. Often the source of the anger lies below the surface. An outburst from time to time is normal. However, continual angry outbursts require children to learn other ways of venting their feelings. Aggression is common in the school years. It is most evident in children who do poorly in school, who have poor peer relations, and who view violence in life or in the media. Children do not outgrow aggression. Aggressive punishment does them harm. Mental-health treatment is often needed for aggressive children.

Empathy. Because school-age children can understand the viewpoints of others, they can offer helpful ideas to relieve stress. In a gesture to offer comfort to friends with

16-15 Some older school-age children and preteens are often moody when comparing themselves to peers.

problems, school-age children may invite friends to their homes for social activities. They may also offer to attend parties or school functions with friends in need of companionship.

Parenting Concerns and Tasks

During the school-age years, parents have new concerns for their children's ability to succeed in meeting the demands of society. Societal expectations focus on children's achievement of intellectual and social skills. Parents share the responsibility for their children's socialization with peers and the school. This requires parents to let go of some family control. At the same time, parents must closely watch their child's progress and respond with encouragement and needed help.

Medical Checkups for School-Age Children

During the school-age years, routine medical visits are less frequent. The American Academy of Pediatrics (AAP) recommends school-age children have medical checkups at ages 6, 8, 10, and 12. They allow the doctor to monitor children's health and treat problems early. Routine medical checkups are in addition to doctor visits for illness or injury. During medical checkups, parents can ask questions about their children's growth, health, and development. Parents may also want to discuss any childrearing concerns.

Some schools require complete health exams before children can enroll in school. Nearly all school districts require children to have certain immunizations before starting school. Parents should contact their local school district to find out the immunization and health-record requirements. If their children lack necessary immunizations, parents should consult the children's doctor about getting them.

Participation in sports is another reason children might need a physical exam. Most teams require a physical checkup before each sports season begins. Even if a checkup is not required, parents may want their child to have an exam before entering school or starting a sport.

Regular dental visits remain important during the school-age years. Vision and hearing exams can identify problems that may exist. Correcting these problems early may keep them from getting worse and prevent learning problems.

Adjusting to School-Age Children's Needs

Until the school years, the family remains the center of the children's world. When children begin school, their world greatly expands. Children learn demanding intellectual tasks and interact with new people. Due to these new adjustments, children often experience stress. A challenge for parents is to help their children cope with experiences that lie beyond direct parental control.

Setting High Expectations

Most school-age children start school with confidence in their abilities to learn school skills. Within a year or two, children mirror their parents' positive or negative expectations for school success. Parental expectations are more important than test scores for mental ability in predicting school success for children.

Most parents have high expectations and are warm and nurturing toward their children. They view their children as competent and promote learning age-appropriate skills. These securely attached children want to please their parents and their teachers. They have strong feelings of self-worth, show self-control, are persistent in working on skills, and respond positively to school challenges. Parents support their children as they adjust to school, 16-16.

Encouraging Friendships

As parents begin to loosen their control on family ties, they encourage their children to form friendships and strive for greater independence. Although good friendships are part of growing up socially healthy, parents will have concerns about their children and certain peer behaviors involving conformity and acceptance among peers.

Conformity. Peer groups generally require conformity for acceptance. **Conformity** means to be similar in manner, character, and conduct. Some conformity, such as wearing the same clothing brands, liking the same music groups, movies, and computer and video games, usually does not upset parents. However, parents may object to some popular ways of dressing, behaving, or speaking. What should parents do? Understanding that children need to feel separate from their parents as they grow toward adulthood helps. Eventually, children

sort out what is right for them and establish their individuality. Parents should realize this is a normal part of human development that will eventually pass. Until then, parents are probably wise to express mild disapproval of questionable behavior rather than scorn, disgust, and ridicule. Children are most likely to choose values and lifestyles similar to those from their own backgrounds.

Acceptance by Peers. Children who are accepted by peers are friendly, outgoing, and low in anxiety. They interact comfortably with age-mates. Lack of children's acceptance by peers is a problem that parents should not take lightly. It can lead to depression, delinquency, dropping out of school, and mental-health problems. About 10 percent of these children not only lack acceptance, but are also abused by their peers. Children who experience rejection, especially those who are aggressive, need mental health assistance early in the school years.

Handling Uncooperative Behavior

School-age children often test family values against peer values. To test values, children may not cooperate with parental expectations, such as doing tasks and obeying family rules. High on the parental list of concerns is having their children maintain family values about sexuality and moral issues. Parents cannot stop school-age children from considering and perhaps trying alternative behaviors approved by peers. Parents can encourage the adoption of family values and limit uncooperative behaviors in the following ways:

- Explain the pros and cons of a given value and the reasons for the family choice.

- Encourage participation in healthy activities with approved peers and adults, such as in youth programs.

16-16 Children whose parents have high expectations for school success tend to have high self-worth and persistence in working on skills.

- Let children know parents' primary concerns are their safety and long-term happiness.
- Use fair discipline.
- Have family decision-making sessions.
- Help children feel competent in countering arguments against their values.

Teaching Children to Deal with Stress

Most parents cling to the idea that childhood is a time of constant happiness. Parents want to protect their children from discomfort and worry. They don't want their children to be unhappy or anxious. This is impossible and generally not in their children's best interests.

Stress can be both positive and negative. Positive stress can be a reaction to an exciting event, such as winning a contest or scoring high on a test. Positive stress offers children the challenge to do their best. It also teaches them how to deal with change and adapt to stressful situations. Learning to deal with stress in the school-age years sets the stage for how children will handle stress as adults.

Negative stress, or distress, can include feelings of fear, hopelessness, worry, anxiety, and doubt. These emotions can be overpowering. They require a person to change or adapt his or her method of coping. Mild to moderate feelings of distress once in a while are healthy and normal. Intense or lasting feelings of distress can be more problematic. These feelings can interfere with a person's ability to function normally. Children may need professional help to deal with this kind of stress.

Many situations and events can cause stress in a child's life. Stressors include conflicts with others, poor health and unhealthy habits, having an overly full or empty schedule of activities and major life changes. Major life changes, such as parental divorce, death or illness of a family member, and moving, are the most serious stressors. You can read more about these stressors in Chapters 18 and 19.

Parents should watch for signs of serious stress in their children, 16-17. Children commonly exhibit one or more of these signs of stress. When stress interferes with a child's normal functioning, parents need to step in and offer help. Children need to be taken seriously. They need their parents to assure them their feelings are valid. Parents also need to teach their children to deal with stress effectively. Effective coping skills help children as they become adults.

Signs of Serious Stress in Children

- Loss of interest in previously enjoyed activities
- Explosive crying or screaming
- Cruelty to pets and playmates
- Complaints about not feeling well due to unusual physical symptoms, such as rapid heartbeat, headaches, fatigue, restlessness, upset stomach, and neck pain
- Loss of humor or sense of joy
- Nightmares, sleepwalking, or teeth-grinding during sleep
- Hair-twisting, nail-biting, stuttering, and excessive fidgeting
- Threats of harming someone or destroying property
- Behaviors of escape—immersion in the computer, e-mail, or TV
- Display of temper over prolonged periods
- Increased behaviors of acting out

16-17 Children may display one or more of these signs when feeling serious stress.

Making Family-Life Adjustments

The challenges of school-age children and their families are more complex than those of previous developmental stages. Adjustments in family life are profound as children progress through the elementary school years. Children leave the parents' direct control when they begin school and spend more time with peers. This requires parents to monitor and guide their children from a distance.

Keeping School-Age Children Safe

School-age children have many new opportunities to explore and become more self-reliant. They also face new dangers. Parents can improve their children's awareness of potential dangers and options for safety. See 16-18 for several safety tips for parents of school-age children.

Because children do more activities on their own or with peers, both accidents and becoming victims of predator abuse increase. Warnings are not enough. Parent teaching is required in all areas, such as

Transportation. Accidents often occur on the way to or from school, regardless of the means of transportation. If children walk to school, parents should instruct them to use intersections where crossing guards can help them. If no crossing guard is available, children should use marked crosswalks and corners with pedestrian signals. Parents should watch children from a distance to see whether they are following safety rules. If children ride bicycles, they should know and follow all traffic rules. Children who ride in cars should sit in the back seat and wear proper restraints. Children also need to learn to watch for traffic as they step out of a bus or car.

Household Accidents. School-age children who take on household tasks do not always get proper instructions for using home appliances or proper supervision. As a result, children are injured and even killed. Parents have the responsibility to share safety information with their children. They also need to supervise appliance use many times before allowing children to operate appliances.

Kidnapping and Predator Abuse. School-age children are vulnerable to becoming victims of a predator. Parents should warn children about talking to strangers and acquaintances that make them feel uneasy, 16-19. Children should never go anywhere with *any* adult without parental permission. Many schools and community organizations have programs to discuss such situations with children.

Parents must also inform their children about the dangers of sexual abuse. They should talk to their children about "good touches" and "bad touches." Parents should tell their children to talk to them if the children don't like how someone touches them. Children should also be told they have the right to determine who can and cannot touch their bodies. Children need to know they have permission to say "no." Parents need to talk openly with children about the dangers of sexual abuse, including behaviors that seem harmless but can lead to sexual abuse.

Adjusting to Maternal Employment

Most mothers of school-age children work outside the home causing both positive and negative outcomes for the family. On the positive side, the family has more income and mothers' skills and self-esteem increase. On the negative side, mothers can experience work overload and often have concerns about possible negative effects on their children.

Children also experience both positive and negative effects when their mothers work outside the home. On the positive side, girls have higher levels of achievement. Boys develop more respect for women's expanding gender roles. Both girls and boys are more self-sufficient and often willing to help their mothers with household chores. On the negative side, the lack of proper supervision can pose problems when children are left on their own.

Supporting Self-Care Children

Today, more and more children come home after school to empty homes because parents are at work. These **self-care children** must meet their own needs until a parent returns home. Parents should be cautious when deciding if their children can care for themselves. Self-care is not an appropriate arrangement for all, or even most, school-age

Safety During the School-Age Years

Traffic safety—School-age children enjoy riding bicycles. Parents need to be sure their children are aware of bicycle safety rules and traffic laws.

Medicine safety—Medicines still fascinate children in the school-age period. These should be stored where children cannot reach them, preferable in a locked cabinet.

Kitchen and appliance safety—More and more children are using household appliances without knowing the possible dangers. This child has not learned the hazards of electric shock. Parents need to teach children how to use household appliances safely.

Safety from predators—School-age children are generally friendly and may be easily influenced by strangers or adults they know. Parents should teach children to recognize potentially dangerous situations. Predators use common tricks, such as showing children a puppy, to lure children within grabbing distance.

16-18 School-age children are sometimes too eager, active, and curious for their own good. Parents need to alert them to possible dangers and inform them of safety procedures.

Keeping Children Safe from Predators

Parents can teach their children to lessen their chances of becoming victims of predators by doing the following:

- Tell parents where they are going and for how long.
- Check in by phone after arriving and before leaving anyplace and when going from place to place.
- Stay with at least one friend, or better yet, a group of friends.
- Avoid unfamiliar, dim, untraveled, and hidden areas.
- Know safe places to go in an emergency, such as a trusted neighbor's home, a restaurant, or store.
- Say "no" to rides from anyone.
- Stay close to parents or friends in malls.
- Take safety measures if someone might be watching or following.
- Make a scene by screaming and retreating if someone gets too near or tries to grab them.

16-19 Because they are vulnerable to abduction and predator abuse, parents must talk with their children about these issues.

children. Many state laws declare that children under a certain age may not be home alone. Parents must check to be sure their children are legally old enough to care for themselves.

Most importantly, parents must assess whether their children are mature enough in all developmental areas to be left alone, even for a short time. Parents should talk with their children and assess whether they would be comfortable at home alone. If children are not up to this responsibility, it is the parent's obligation to make other arrangements. Many schools, religious groups, community groups, and child care centers offer after-school programs. Some programs may be low-cost or free of charge. Parents can also ask for referrals for child care providers.

If parents and their children decide to try the self-care arrangement, parents must make sure their children have certain skills. Training in self-sufficiency skills includes

- keeping track of house keys while at school and handling a house alarm and lock system, 16-20
- coming straight home from school and calling the parent upon arrival at home
- following guidelines for use of telephone, computer, appliances, and other equipment
- knowing and practicing safety precautions and emergency procedures
- following the approved schedule of activities at home as planned together by children and parents

16-20 Self-care children come home after school to an empty house or apartment. They may feel frightened and lonely until their parents return from work.

- avoiding items that are strictly off-limits, such as weapons, alcohol, power tools, and adult medications

Parents should post hot line numbers next to the telephone. Telephone hot lines provide sources of reassurance for children who are home alone. Children can call for help in emergencies, to report problems, or just to talk.

Special Family Times

Family vacations are special times for school-age children. A recent poll found that children often say they "need a vacation." When on vacations away from home, children indicate they talk and eat with their families more and argue less.

For a successful family vacation, parents should plan ahead to obtain medicine from the pediatrician for motion sickness and insect bites. Maintaining typical sleep/wake cycles and eating healthful foods are also important. When children help choose vacation destinations, they build literacy skills and are more likely to have fun. Children often prefer theme parks and beach or lake vacations. Parents should also make sure that the lodging offers amenities that suit children.

Once home, families enjoy reliving the vacation through photos and souvenirs. School-age children often enjoy sharing special vacation details at school and with their friends, too.

Parenting in the School-Age Years

Families with school-age children leave the preschool children stage and enter the *parenting school-agers stage* of the family life cycle. This stage continues until first-born children reach age 13. Parents continue to focus on encouraging their children's achievements at school and with peers. While families focus on more structure, they also expect children to follow the rules and values of home and school and become more responsible.

Parents of school-age children enter the *interpretive stage of parenting* according to Ellen Galinsky. As school-age children grow and mature, major changes take place in parent-child interactions. Parents share more information about the world and interpret other authority figures, such as teachers and youth leaders. Parents also teach values and morals. Because parents have less direct control over their child's behavior, they often join other authorities in their child's life. Parents may also seek out support groups on behalf of their child.

During the school-age years, parents guide their children in learning to make decisions. As children consider and make many decisions, parents monitor them and give feedback, 16-21. This process is an evolving experience for parents and children and a healthy bridge to the teen years. It helps children learn social realities and responsibilities.

16-21 As children learn to make decisions, parents must monitor and give them feedback.

Physical Development

Body becomes more slender with longer arms and legs; babyhood physique continues to disappear

Loses baby teeth, which are replaced by the first permanent teeth

Needs proper rest and nutrition to fuel busy mind and body

Is better at gross-motor than fine-motor coordination

Is constantly active; prefers running over walking and fidgets when asked to sit still

May have frequent minor tumbles and scrapes

Dances to music

Ties own shoelaces

Intellectual Development

Concentrates on doing one activity for a longer period of time

Has improved memory

Has better understanding of the concept of time

Begins to conserve, puts objects in a series, and reverses actions but only explains correct answers with the word because; fails to arrive at correct answers in many other cases—thus not fully logical

Is inquisitive and eager to learn in school

Asks more complex questions than just "Why?"; wants detailed answers

Begins reading, writing, and arithmetic at school, which requires symbolic thinking skills

Learns vocabulary words introduced at school

Has mastered articulation (making the sounds of a language)

Begins to know left from right

Often confuses letters that look much alike, such as *b*, *p*, *d*, and *q*

Copies more difficult shapes, such as a diamond but may turn paper 180º to make this shape; copying shapes prepares the child for manuscript writing

Social and Emotional Development

Becomes more socially independent; chooses own friends

May feel less jealous of siblings as outside interests become more important

Is still egocentric, but is becoming interested in group activities

May still have a hard time waiting and taking turns

Wants desperately to be right and to win

Tattles often to check sense of right and wrong

Is full of energy and ready for new challenges

Wants all of everything; making choices is difficult

May have nightmares

May need reassurance as adjusts to new demands of school

* These charts are not exact timetables. Individuals may perform certain activities earlier or later than indicated in the charts.

Physical Development

Proper rest, nutrition, and exercise are important

May look lanky due to thin body and long arms and legs

Becomes better coordinated; movements become more fluid and graceful

Develops improved sense of balance and timing

Shows greater upper body strength (boys) and more accuracy of aim (girls)

Enjoys skating, skipping, and jumping rope

Enjoys sports, especially boisterous games

Shows improved reaction time, but is still rather slow

Intellectual Development

Has longer attention span

Uses more logic about how events and objects can be changed and often gives correct reasons for answers; cannot solve problems that he or she has not experienced or imagined

Begins to understand multiple classifications of objects (a pencil may be wood, yellow, a cylinder, and a writing tool all at the same time)

Resolves problems with letters that look much alike

Reads more fluently and writes with more and more correct spellings

Enjoys realistic books; shows some preferences for subject matter of books

Uses arithmetic skills in functional ways, such as counting money or trying a simple recipe

Understands some concepts of time, such as clock time and calendars; does not understand birthdates and age or historical periods

Accepts idea of rules and knows harm might result if rules are not followed

Begins to show interest in collecting certain objects

Social and Emotional Development

7 Years

May seem withdrawn and moody

Likes to spend time alone or in the background

May feel everyone is against him or her

Wants and needs approval of adults and peers

Is very conscientious; strives hard to please

Is sensitive and hurt by criticism

Likes to help the teacher

8 Years

Shows more spirit; is willing to try just about anything

May turn to tears and self-criticism upon failure, but recovers quickly

Is able to get along well with others

Chooses companions of same gender and age

Is very sensitive to what others think

Shows intense interest in groups

Wants to look like and act like peers

Enjoys group activities in organization and in own secret clubs

Chooses a best friend but may change best friends often

Physical Development

Proper rest, nutrition, and exercise are important

Continues to improve coordination

Improves sense of balance and timing

Can run, kick, throw, catch, and hit; catching flying balls can be a problem due to inaccurate perception of a ball's trajectory

May develop particular physical skills

Enjoys organized games

Further refines fine-motor skills

Is able to use hands skillfully in building models, learning handcrafts, or using tools

Enjoys drawing

Intellectual Development

Is able to consider more than one conclusion to problems and choices

Understands more about truth and honesty

Is still enthusiastic about learning

Likes games that involve mental competition

Enjoys quizzing parents and impressing them with new facts

Determines others left and right

Draws 3-D geometric figures

May continue to show interest in collecting certain objects

Has vocabulary of about 5400 words

Has better use of language and is able to converse well with adults

Social and Emotional Development

9 Years

Is relatively quiet

Worries about everything

Complains a lot

Has definite likes and dislikes

Begins a new drive for independence; resents being "bossed" by parents

Knows right from wrong; will accept blame when necessary, but offers excuses

Shows increased interest in friends and decreased interest in family

Is interested in group's activities and concerns

10 Years

Is happy with life in general

Likes to act in a more adult manner

Shows increasing capacity for self-evaluation

Likes people and is liked by others

Is dependable and cooperative

Shows increasing capacity for self-evaluation

Obeys adults easily and naturally

Likes to accept responsibility and tries to do things well

Likes praise and encouragement

Still has strong group spirit, but it may be diminishing

May begin to show more loyalty to a best friend than to the group, especially girls

May enjoy being part of a team

11 to 12 Years

Physical Development

Proper rest, nutrition, and exercise are important

May grow little in height (male)

May experience growth spurt (female)

Body may begin changing into adultlike form

Becomes very conscious of clothes and overall appearance

May like to test strength and be daring

Enjoys engaging in sports and games with friends of the same gender

Shows more precision, greater strength, and flexibility in all physical activities

Intellectual Development

Shows improved attention span (if interested); enjoys long periods of time to think and work on projects

Is becoming very logical but is not an abstract thinker

Likes active learning—reading aloud, reciting, science projects, and working on the computer

May like group projects and classes based on the cooperative effort

Is able to detect problems in daily situations and work out solutions

Uses science and math concepts and applies them to daily activities

May allow peer relationships to affect schoolwork

Has vocabulary of about 7200 words

May enjoy lengthy conversations with grandparents or teachers

May show interest in reading; mysteries, adventure stories, and biographies are favorites

Likes to recite in front of class if self-esteem is secure

Social and Emotional Development

Is less self-centered

May express great enthusiasm

Likes to plan and execute plans for the group

Is willing to reach out to others for friendship

Has improved social skills

May show more tact, especially with friends

Is patient and friendly with younger children

May become moody about body changes

May show signs of emotional turmoil as body changes

Has strong desire to conform to peers' ways of dressing and behaving

Enjoys youth organizations, such as scouts or 4-H

Summing It Up

- Physical development is slow and smooth during the school-age years. Children refine gross- and fine-motor skills.

- Children who are generally healthy and fit are physically active, eat healthful foods, and get plenty of sleep.

- *Gender-role identification* begins in the school-age years, but is a slow and sometimes confusing process.

- To prevent childhood obesity, parents should provide a variety of healthful foods and encourage their children to be active.

- According to Piaget, the school-age child learns to think logically.

- Children "learn how to learn" mainly through school instruction. Schools require children to learn and then use basic literacy skills. *Creativity* is also important.

- Parents encourage learning, help their child adjust to school, support homework assignments, and become a school partner.

- Language development reflects the child's logic, learning skills, and growing literacy skills.

- For children, peer group membership demands conformity and some independence from adult authority.

- Children's emotions of most concern to parents are phobias, anxieties, anger, and loneliness.

- Parents must closely watch their child's school achievement and peer acceptance.

- Parents must be alert to children's distress and help them learn to cope with it.

- With more independence, children must learn new safety rules.

- Parents interpret others' views, reaffirm family values, and guide their children in making decisions.

Recalling the Facts

1. Describe the physical characteristics of a typical 12-year-old child.

2. Identify three ways children develop gender-role identification.

3. Name two ways parents can prevent or combat obesity in school-age children.

4. How can parents make sure their children get enough sleep?

5. What are three major intellectual gains in the school years?

6. Contrast short-term and long-term memory as they relate to learning.

7. Name four basic literacy skill areas.

8. List three ways parents can encourage learning.

9. Name three advances in language skills that occur during the school-age years.

10. What are four roles of peer groups?

11. Why do verbal conflicts with siblings often increase in the school-age years?

12. According to Erikson, what are two ways that industry differs from inferiority?

13. What are three causes of anxiety in school-age children?

14. Name three characteristics of children whose parents have high expectations for school success.

15. List five ways school-age children can lessen their chances of becoming victims of kidnapping or predator abuse.

16. How do parents guide their children in making decisions?

Applying New Skills

1. **Research and report.** Use Internet or print resources to further investigate the growing problem of childhood obesity. What are the issues related to this problem? What can parents, schools, and health professionals do to fight this problem? Write a brief report to share with the class.

2. **Interview.** Interview a school principal or a teacher concerning the specific ways the school encourages a parent-school partnership. Report your findings to the class.

3. **Observing social patterns.** Obtain school permission to observe the social patterns of a class of school-age children. As you observe the children, pay close attention to same-gender group interest, secret clubs, best friends, interest in a group's activities, and conformity. Report your findings to the class.

4. **Teaching self-sufficiency.** In small groups, brainstorm a list of self-sufficiency skills about which parents must teach their self-care children. For example, one task may be to teach children how to prepare a healthful snack using the microwave. After brainstorming a list, choose one task. As a group, devise a method by which parents can teach the task to their children. Then demonstrate your method to the class.

5. **Family activities.** In small groups, brainstorm a list of activities that parents can do with their school-age children at home and in the community. Then sort through the list and determine which activities have low or no cost. Share your group's list with the class.

Thinking Critically

1. Attend a sporting event involving school-age children, such as a Little League game. Take notes about the children's ages, coaches' attitudes, parents' involvement, condition of the facilities, and the use of protective equipment. Draw conclusions about how you think these factors affect children's attitudes toward competitive sports. Share your conclusions with the class.

2. Draw conclusions about what parents might do if they are concerned about the friends their children choose. How can they encourage their children to choose friends with values similar to their own?

3. Analyze ways that school-age students might help peers who feel neglect or rejection.

4. Propose five or more strategies for parents to use when helping their school-age children deal with stress, other than those listed in the text. Share your strategies with the class.

Linking Academics

1. **Writing.** In 15 sentences or less, summarize the physical changes that occur during the school-age years. Include key changes in gross- and fine-motor skills.

2. **Math.** Develop an original approach to demonstrate the concepts of classification, seriation, conservation, and reversibility. Demonstrate your approach to someone who understands these concepts and someone who does not. Compare the reactions and discuss your findings with the class.

Chapter 17

Parents and Their Teens

Objectives

After studying this chapter, you will be able to

- describe the characteristics of physical growth and development during adolescence.
- summarize reasons why teens are preoccupied with body image and how it impacts such problems as acne, eating disorders, and use of anabolic steroids.
- identify changes in the way teens think during Piaget's formal operational stage.
- describe characteristics of intellectual development during the teen years.
- summarize key changes in adolescent social and emotional development, including issues with friends, dating partners, and siblings, and emotional disturbances teens may experience.
- describe factors for forming an identity according to Erikson.
- identify key parenting tasks and concerns during the teen years, including factors related to self-discipline (self-regulation), high-risk behaviors, violence, and teen employment.

Key Terms

adolescence
sexual maturity
menarche
spermarche
acne
eating disorders
anabolic steroids
cliques
high-risk behaviors
abstinence
homicide

Many parents are satisfied with how they guided and protected their young children. These same parents anticipate some challenges during the teen years, but generally approach this time with confidence. As children move into the teen years, most will slowly and steadily gain their independence in ways that are socially acceptable. Some parents anticipate battles with their teens during these years. Unfortunately, society tends to focus on the rebellious aspect of teen behavior. Conflicts and problems that were already present at younger ages may escalate in the teen years.

Adolescence is a time of change in which people move from the dependency of childhood to the independence of adulthood. It includes changes in every area of development. Adolescence has no specific beginning or end, nor do all characteristics apply to every teen. Some experts think of adolescence as the teen years—ages 13 through 18. Others divide this time into two periods. *Early adolescence* (ages 11 through 15) is the first period when most physical changes occur. *Late adolescence* (ages 16 through 18 or later) is when psychological changes dominate development.

The teen years are full of change. Teens are striving for maturity and self-sufficiency, 17-1. Along with physical changes, teens face many intellectual, social, and emotional challenges. They strive for more independence from their families and a sense of belonging with peers. They also want stronger emotional connections in close friendships and a better self-understanding.

The quality of family relationships greatly influences how teens meet these changes. Teens still need the love and support of their parents. If family relationships are strong, teens adjust more easily. Teens with less-positive family relationships may have a more difficult transition.

In this chapter you will study teen development. You will learn that

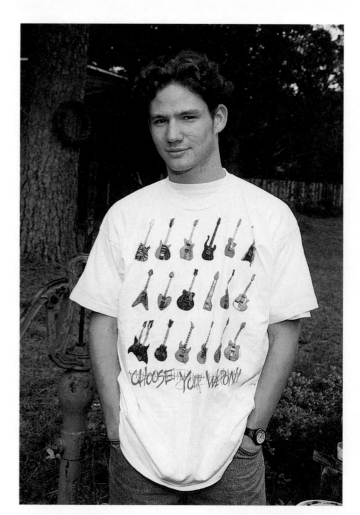

17-1 During the teen years, people grow and develop in many ways. After the teen years, most will become mature and self-sufficient adults.

developmental changes occur and often confuse both teens and their parents. After each section, check the "Adolescent Development" charts for a summary of development. You will also study the role of parents as they promote their teen's achievement of an adult status.

Physical Development

Puberty begins with a surge of hormones starting at about age 8 for girls and age 11 for boys. Although there are no physical changes initially, these hormones first affect growth and then physical sexual development. People often view the dramatic and fast changes, which affect every aspect of development, as the rite of passage between childhood and adolescence.

Adolescent Growth Spurt

The growth spurt usually begins at age 10½ for girls and 12½ for boys and lasts about two years. The growth spurt begins with weight gain due to an increase in fat. As height increases, teens slim down. Muscle gain comes later in puberty for both boys and girls.

The peak growth spurt occurs around age 12 years for girls and age 14 years for boys. Girls reach 98 percent of their adult height at 16 years. Boys reach 98 percent of their adult height just before 18 years. The rapid bone growth causes joint pains, or "growing pains" in some adolescents. Eventually bones completely harden as teens achieve their full height.

Body proportions change during the growth spurt, too. The growth spurt begins with the hands and feet, progresses through the arms and legs, and finally the body trunk (torso). This growth may not occur at the same rate on both sides of the body, but eventually evens out. After adolescents reach their complete height, the males' chests and shoulders broaden and the females' hips broaden.

Facial features, especially the chin and nose, grow rapidly. Brain development in the teen years does not increase brain weight, which reaches its peak at age 6. During adolescence, the head does not grow much.

Internal organs also rapidly change. For example, the lungs triple in weight and the heart doubles in size. Even the eyeballs elongate causing some teens to need corrective lens. Only the tonsils and adenoids decrease in size, resulting in fewer respiratory problems for teens. Because internal organ development lags behind the height and weight changes, teens can be hurt if the physical demands of work or sports are too great.

Motor Skills

Physical skills for athletics reach their peak during the teen and early-adult years. Strength, stamina, coordination, and reaction time are highly developed in teens. Most teens, even those who will not be athletes, know the importance of physical activity. Physical activity is good for the body and the mind. It increases the self-confidence and self-esteem and relieves stress. For example, teen girls who play sports are three times more likely to graduate from high school than other teen girls. They are also less likely to have unwanted pregnancies or take illegal drugs as compared with their peers not in sports.

Unfortunately, the level of physical activity among many teens is low. Many avoid physical activities due to difficulty in adjusting to their growth spurt. They often feel clumsy due to uneven growth of their bodies. The increasing time demands of school, studying, and part-time work reduce teens' participation in motor activities. Computer and TV time also account for sedentary lifestyles of many teens.

Parents and teachers alike should encourage teen involvement in physical activity. Many teens prefer informal physical activities rather than organized sports. In these settings, they can easily match their changing skills to the activities. Informal activities often lead to lifetime physical activities.

Physical Sexual Maturation

Just as hormones stimulate the growth spurt, they also stimulate the teen's process of becoming sexually mature. Hormones control both primary and secondary sex characteristics. *Primary sex characteristics* are biological features that directly involve reproduction. These features are present at birth but grow larger and mature during puberty. *Secondary sex characteristics* are visible body changes that occur in puberty that distinguish males from females, but are not related to reproduction. These include breast development, facial and/or body hair, and lowering of the voice (especially in males), 17-2.

Sexual maturity occurs with ovulation in females and sufficient numbers of sperm for fertility in males. In females, the first menstrual period, or **menarche**, signals the arrival of sexual maturity. Menarche generally occurs at about 12½ years, however, it normally begins between ages 10 and 16. In the same way, **spermarche**, or first ejaculation, marks the arrival of sexual maturity for males. Because spermarche can occur during sleep, it is also called *nocturnal emission* or *wet dreams*. Spermarche occurs at an average age of 13½ but varies between ages 11 and 15.

After menarche or spermarche, teens require more sexual maturing before they can reproduce. The period of maturing, or *adolescent sterility*, lasts about 12 to 18 months. Because teens can reach this maturity at any time, pregnancy is possible.

17-2 During the teen years, males and females develop secondary sex characteristics not related to reproduction.

Teens have many different feelings and reactions to puberty. Over 50 percent of teens say their parents or sex education classes do not provide the sex information they need. Some common feelings and reactions include the following:

- concern about skin condition (acne), oily hair, weight gain, and body odor
- frustration and confusion about menarche and spermarche
- belief that maturity entitles them to more freedom from parents
- longing for peer acceptance
- desire to be alone and enjoy daydreaming
- moodiness and tension
- loss of some self-confidence

Because the timing of puberty varies a great deal, some teens complete puberty before others begin. For very early and late-maturing teens, psychological effects are common. These effects are individual and do not affect all teens in the same way. For example, early maturing girls react positively to changes of puberty and are readily accepted by older peers. Late-maturing girls may envy peers and feel left out of the peer group before they complete puberty. Early maturing boys are confident in boy-girl relationships, but may engage in risk-taking behaviors if they spend time with older teens. Late-maturing boys may have less self-confidence and feel some rejection by peers. With either early or late maturation, parents should intervene and get help for their children if they notice any problem behaviors.

Healthy Sexuality Development

Hormonal and bodily changes create new sexual feelings. During this stage of development, a teen's personality may be at its shakiest. Although each teen must find his or her own way through this transition, parents can help by providing a base of security, 17-3.

Gender-Role Identity

As teens make the transition from childhood to adulthood, they must finalize their gender-role identification—their male or female role within adult society. As you know, gender-role development begins at birth. Parents and later peers socialize the child. They do this through gender-role modeling. They also give direct advice and provide or encourage certain experiences. For example, parents may give advice about certain school courses, assign household tasks, or approve certain part-time jobs.

In the teen years, hormones and all the changes they produce affect gender-role development. Puberty signals adulthood is approaching. Teen boys begin to think in terms of their masculinity. Teen girls begin to think in terms of their nurturing roles. For both males and females, these feelings are in keeping with traditional gender roles.

Gender roles are more complex in today's society. Although some adults adopt traditional roles, many others embrace roles that include desirable masculine and feminine behaviors in both genders. For example, many fathers take on a more-nurturing role in caring for their infants than fathers of previous generations. Some mothers take on the financial responsibility for meeting family needs—a challenge once reserved for males. Gender-role development may be confusing for both parents and their teens.

When today's young men become fathers, the expectation exists for them to achieve at work and take on a supportive role as husband and father. The expectation exists for young women to provide the nurturing and supportive roles of wife and mother while contributing to the family's financial security.

17-3 Parents provide a solid foundation for teens in healthy sexuality development.

Responsible Decision Making

Parents are the first sex educators of their children. Teens should feel free to discuss their attitudes, opinions, and questions with their parents. Parents who have spoken openly about sex with their children have established frank and honest communication. As their teens mature, parents should continue communicating in ways that are relevant to teen intellectual, emotional, and physical maturity, 17-4.

Providing accurate information about human sexuality and reproduction is an important role for parents. Teens with accurate knowledge about sex are likely to demonstrate responsible sexual behavior and postpone sexual activity.

Because the mass media exploits sexuality, many teens receive the wrong messages about the role of sexual expressions in their lives. Parents can help their teens by talking with them about these mixed messages. They can also set a positive example in their own lives. Most teens can learn from their parents what the proper

17-4 Although he feels a little reluctant, this teen knows he can ask his dad questions because they have established open communication.

role of sexuality is in a loving, lasting relationship. A good example helps teens realize both the positive and negative aspects of sexual behavior.

Parents need to help their teens realize that involvement in sexual relationships requires acceptance of adult responsibilities. Every teen must understand that each act of sexual intercourse can result in pregnancy, an STI, or other negative consequences.

Parents may feel uneasy about discussing sexuality with their teens. If so, they may want to seek help from professional resources or training groups. Many groups offer courses shared by parents and their teens. Many schools also encourage parents to participate in family-life education classes.

Teens do not want parents to make decisions for them. However, they do value their parents' loving concern and guidance. Teens' relationships with their parents help determine how they make the transition into responsible sexual adulthood.

Sleeping

Teens generally need nine hours of daily sleep, but sometimes get as little as six. Sleep deprivation occurs more frequently in the teen years than at any other time in life. Teens today are trying to do everything and be successful. For many teens, sleep is at the bottom of their "to do lists." The consequences of sleep deprivation for teens include the following:

- greater risk of accidents, including car accidents
- greater irritability, anxiety, and depression and risk of suicide
- lower grades in school due to problems in paying attention, concentrating, and learning
- more likelihood of stimulant use, such as coffee, caffeinated soft drinks, and energy drinks

Eating

Although adequate nutrition is important throughout life, it is extremely important in the teen years. Due to the growth spurt and other physical changes of puberty, active teens need more food energy than at any other time in life, 17-5. The greatest need for food energy occurs for girls around age 14 and for boys around age 17. Food needs vary greatly due to the individual growth rate, body composition, and activity levels of teens.

17-5 Healthful food choices help teens meet their energy needs.

Most teens eat enough calories, but many do not get the nutrients they need for good health. For example, about 14 percent eat the recommended number of servings of fruits and vegetables. Most teens consume only half of the calcium, iron, zinc, and vitamin D they need. Over 66 percent of teens eat foods that are too high in fat and sugar, and weight becomes a problem for many. Body image suffers when teens are overweight. Teens can use the tools in "MyPyramid Tracker" on the MyPyramid Web site to help build and monitor a healthful eating plan.

Body Image

Because of body changes that occur during puberty, teens often change how they think about their body image. They may become preoccupied with physical appearance and spend hours grooming and looking in the mirror. They do not always like what they see. Worries about new skin blemishes, hairstyles, weight and body shape, and about whether their clothes fit the trend occupy much time for many teens. Why are teens so preoccupied with body image? Some reasons include

- negative or insensitive comments about their appearance during the growth spurt or puberty
- knowing peer acceptance is heavily influenced by attractiveness
- idealizing media images of beautiful bodies
- assuming everyone is looking at them and is concerned about what they do as individuals

Parents cannot prevent their teen from developing problems associated with body image, but they can reduce the likelihood. From the time a child is very young, parents can promote healthful eating and exercise habits, 17-6. Parents should also be

17-6 Exercise is a healthy way to maintain a proper body weight. Parents can help their teens develop good exercise habits.

supportive. Boosting a child's self-esteem can make a child more resistant to body-image problems.

Erikson believed that a healthy body image is a necessary aspect of becoming an adult. However, many teens tend to think their bodies are far from ideal. Their quest for an ideal body becomes physically and psychologically unhealthy and even deadly. Many teens struggle with such body image issues as acne. Others face serious consequences from eating disorders and the use of illegal body-enhancing drugs.

Acne

Acne is a skin disorder involving inflammation of skin glands and is characterized by blackheads and pimples. For some people, it also includes inflamed sores and cysts. Acne can affect the face, chest, upper back, and shoulders of teens and young adults. Many teens experience some acne.

Although there is no exact cause of acne, hormone changes during puberty likely contribute to the condition. These hormones may cause excess oil to collect in skin pores. When skin pores clog, inflammation occurs, causing pimples to form. Squeezing pimples then causes scarring.

Teens with acne often feel embarrassment, anxiety, or self-consciousness. Some believe the myth that poor diet and poor hygiene cause the problem. Parents need to reassure teens that eating greasy foods or chocolate will not cause acne. Excessive face washing will not prevent acne. Although some over-the-counter medications may help mild acne, some cases require treatment by a doctor. Parents should encourage teens to develop good skin-care habits, such as regular face washing with products that clean the pores.

Eating Disorders

Eating disorders are real medical illnesses with complex emotions and behaviors that involve abnormal eating patterns and concerns with weight and body image. People with eating disorders can be adults or teens, males or females. Because of the many physical, social, and emotional changes occurring in their lives, as compared with other age groups of children, teens are more likely to develop eating disorders. These teens often have low self-esteem and feel rejection from peers. Radical attempts to reduce food intake or extreme overeating result from distress about body image or weight. An explanation of the basic types of eating disorders follows.

Anorexia Nervosa. Severe fasting and extreme weight loss characterize anorexia. According to the American Psychiatric Association, people with anorexia relentlessly pursue thinness. They fail to maintain a normal body weight for their height, age, and activity level, 17-7. Anorexics are seriously afraid of gaining weight. Physical problems may include malnutrition, continual weight loss, loss of menstrual periods for females, imbalance in body chemicals necessary for life, or death due to heart failure. Anorexics are often insecure and display unusual food behaviors, such as hiding food or showing extreme interest in recipes and cooking.

Bulimia Nervosa. Frequent, secretive episodes of binge eating followed by purging characterize bulimia nervosa. People with bulimia have an uncontrollable urge to

17-7 People who suffer from anorexia are obsessed with their weight and fail to maintain a normal body weight for their height, age, and activity level.

eat large amounts of food quickly. After bingeing, bulimics get rid of the food by self-induced vomiting, using diet pills or laxatives, fasting, or excessive exercising. Bulimics are often perfectionists who rely on family and peer approval for self-worth. Depression and feelings of guilt (because they know their eating behavior is inappropriate) are common.

Binge-Eating Disorder. People with this disorder have impulsive and uncontrolled episodes of continuous overeating beyond the point of feeling full. Unlike bulimics, binge eaters do not purge after eating. As a result, they are often overweight. Binge eaters have low feelings of self-worth and often feel guilt and shame after eating large amounts of food. These feelings often lead to more binge eating.

Combination Eating Disorders. These disorders may include any combination of symptoms of anorexia, bulimia, or binge-eating disorder.

Although eating disorders involve serious threats to health and life, recovery is possible with medical and psychological treatments. Awareness of the signs and symptoms of eating disorders can help parents identify when their teens need help. If parents suspect a problem, they should seek help immediately. Waiting to get help only makes the problem worse.

Anabolic Steroids

A growing concern among parents, teachers, and doctors is the increased use of performance-enhancing drugs by teens. Social pressures about body image (for males to look more masculine and for females to look thinner and muscle-toned) and pressures to succeed in competitive sports may cause teens to use *anabolic steroids.* **Anabolic steroids** are synthetic hormone drugs that mimic the action of the natural male sex hormone, testosterone. These drugs cause the body to grow larger and stronger and can increase athletic performance. However, the health risks are devastating, and possibly deadly, to developing teen bodies.

How do anabolic steroids hurt teens? In both teen males and females, anabolic steroids can cause acne, stunted growth, liver tumors, high blood pressure, clogged arteries, impaired immune systems, an enlarged heart muscle, gallstones, and kidney disease. Teen males may also experience irreversible breast growth, testicle shrinkage, or reduced sperm count. Teen females may have breast shrinkage, increased body and facial hair, menstrual problems, or fetal damage if pregnant.

Along with the devastating health effects, anabolic steroids can also cause behavioral problems. These drugs can cause users to commit violent acts against people and property. They also impact mood changes and increase the likelihood of other illegal drug use and depression.

Physical problems that result from using anabolic steroids require medical treatment. Some problems may never get better. Body image and behavioral problems require intensive psychological therapy.

How can parents prevent anabolic steroid use by their teens? The best defense is to keep the lines of communication open. Parents need to talk openly with their teens about the serious health risks related to performance-enhancing drugs. Use of anabolic steroids is illegal without a doctor's prescription.

Intellectual Development

Combining physical development and education can result in an intellectual growth spurt. With the right education, teens can develop a new and mature way of thinking. Parents can observe this more imaginative but rational thinking in how their teens handle school assignments and use language. Increasing intellectual skills help teens add many concepts to their knowledge base.

School experiences in classes and extracurricular activities help teens prepare for adult life. Choices teens make about experiences during these years will impact the rest of their lives. Parents not only need to allow their teens to make decisions, but must also encourage and teach good decision-making skills.

Piaget: Intellectual Development of Teens

As the teen years begin, Piaget's *concrete operational stage* draws to a close. At this time, teens enter the last stage of intellectual development, the *formal operational stage*, 17-8. In the formal operational stage, teens are no longer tied to the real world of experiences. They can perform logical thinking actions (operations) on possibilities beyond reality (formal).

During this stage, teens learn to reason about *phenomena*, or events that do not or could not exist. In math, for example, formal-operational thinkers solve problems with unknowns (Xs and Ys) and with imaginary numbers (3i + 4i). When they encounter problems in science, they think in terms of the factors involved and how these factors help determine the solution. Formal-operational thinkers can also think in abstract terms about concepts, thoughts, and rules—matters that are not tangible.

Teens generally learn such thinking skills in higher-level math and science classes. However, some students may simply memorize solutions, but appear to be applying concepts to new problems. Recent research shows that formal-operational thinking may apply only to areas in which a person has a great deal of knowledge. He or she then uses that knowledge to reason in logical ways.

Using Information-Processing Skills

In the school-age years, children develop information-processing skills (learn how to learn). During adolescence, teens use information-processing skills to achieve school tasks. Their knowledge base grows from a *novice* in many areas to an *expert* in some areas. What school subject, hobby, or game do you completely understand? Attention spans increase and memory expands during the teen years. Teens can easily monitor and assess what they learn.

The School Experience

As teens enter high school, they must adjust to different schedules, new teachers, and possibly more classmates. These changes may be unsettling for teens, but parents can help teens adjust. They can attend orientation programs with their teens. They can express interest in their teen's school experiences, classes, and extracurricular activities. Although teens are maturing, parents must still monitor their school progress.

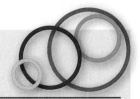

Piaget's Stages of Intellectual Development

1. Sensorimotor
1A: Exercising the Reflexes
1B: Primary Circular Reactions
1C: Secondary Circular Reactions
1D: Coordination of Secondary Circular Reactions
1E: Tertiary Circular Reactions
1F: Mental Representation

2. Preoperational
2A: Preconceptual Phase
2B: Intuitive Phase

3. Concrete Operations

4. Formal Operations

17-8 Teens are capable of, but may not achieve, the stage of formal operational thinking.

Academic achievement in high school is important to future career plans. Learning about possible careers and making course decisions that relate to their career goals helps lead to career success. High school counselors can advise teens about courses that prepare them for college, trade school, technical school, or other career-related learning experiences.

The most powerful influence on school achievement is the family. When parents are enthusiastic about education, teens are more likely to have positive attitudes about school, 17-9. They are more likely to enjoy their classes, develop good study habits, and do well in school. When teens have school success, it encourages them to learn more, study harder, achieve more, and have self-discipline (self-regulation)—an essential skill for adulthood.

Extracurricular activities can promote teens' physical skills and extend their academic learnings. These activities foster creativity or enrich special hobby interests. All activities offer chances for teens to socialize with peers, learn leadership skills, cope with frustrations, and feel the joys of success. As parents support their teens' interests, they also provide guidance if academic and other goals conflict.

Language Development

Teens' language development reflects their abstract-thinking skills. The teens' vocabulary grows, especially in technical and other specialized areas. For example, the key terms listed at the start of each chapter of this text are technical vocabulary. Teens often know several meanings of various words instead of a single meaning.

As teens speak and write, they know which thoughts are most important and which are not as important. They use clauses in complex sentences to express thoughts in logical order. In complex sentences, the main ideas

17-9 When parents are supportive of their schoolwork, teens develop positive attitudes about school.

comprise the independent clauses and less important ideas are in subordinate clauses.

Teens' language development also reflects their understandings of abstractions. Teens enjoy the abstract (not literal) meanings of political cartoons, poetry, and fables. They also use similes, metaphors, satire, and irony.

Social and Emotional Development

With the physical and intellectual changes of teens, are quests for independence from the family and for belonging with peers. Through these quests, teens begin to search for an integrated self; that is, they become a mature adult.

Teens often feel insecure as they face the future's many options. Insecurity may grow as teens desire more independence and pull away from the security of their families. At the same time, teens may feel even more pressure to perform well socially among their peers and adults. In facing these challenges, teens may have many emotional ups and downs. Some teens find adolescence overwhelming. These teens and their families need professional help. In contrast, most teens have a positive outlook throughout this stage and into the adult years.

Friendships and Belonging

Peers are very important in the teen years. Due to the long school day and extracurricular activities, teens spend twice as much time with peers as with their parents. Peers become dependent on each other for companionship, which offers opportunities for self-exploration, learning, achieving, and developing self-esteem.

Teens' attitudes, values, and behaviors influence their acceptance by certain groups of peers. In high schools, especially large ones, teens associate with certain *crowds*. High schools often have four or five crowds that differ by reputation, values, and behaviors. These groups often carry stereotypical labels, such as *jocks* or *nerds*. From within the larger crowds, teens form *cliques*. **Cliques** are smaller, exclusive groups of closer friends (often 5 to 9) of the same or mixed genders.

Teens in cliques feel great peer pressure to conform their behavior to fit the values and behaviors of the group. These friendships influence teen behaviors in surface areas, such as language, fashion, and music. Peers also influence more profound areas of life, such as friendship choices and decisions about dating and sexuality. These decisions also influence adult choices, 17-10.

17-10 Teens' friendships serve a very important role. They set the stage for future adult relationships.

Conformity peeks during the early teen years, but it gradually declines as older teens realize they can be their own person. A few teens remain rather free from peer influence throughout the school years. Some teens feel rejection from peers. This leads to serious problems, such as delinquency, aggressive behaviors, or withdrawal.

Parents often have concerns about their children's selection of friends. They do not want their children with a "bad" crowd. Parents hope their teens will find friends who encourage and uplift them. Parents cannot pick their teens' friends, but they can voice their fears. If parents have genuine concerns about one or more friends, teens are more likely to choose different ones.

Parents can also teach their children to resist peer pressure. They can help their teens plan what to say in difficult situations. For example, when teens feel pressure to do something wrong, they can avoid the situation by falling back on their parents' rules. They can say, "I'd be grounded for the rest of the year if my parents caught me. I guess I'd better not."

Teens have many conflicts and disagreements with friends. Parents need to be sensitive to a teen's friendships. If their teen seems distressed over a problem with friends, parents should not ignore these signs. Instead, they can help by offering love, support, and understanding. Often through active listening, parents can guide their teen to decide what to do.

Although friendships are very important in the teen years, parental influence often remains strong, too. Parental influence is important in areas of social and moral values and in career decisions. When parents show little attention, teens turn more often to peers for advice and approval. Compared with other peers, these teens show less interest in school, engage in high-risk behaviors, and hold a negative self-view.

Dating: A Closer Relationship

Dating usually begins in the teen years. In many high school crowds and cliques, the peer pressure to date is strong. Some teens feel their social success depends on their dating relationships. These teens might accept or request dates just to conform to peer expectations. Other teens do not waver from their values under this pressure. They may postpone exclusive couple dating while pursuing other activities. Dating, like other peer relations, helps teens learn about themselves while preparing for later relationships.

Cultural standards usually define dating practices. In addition, parents may set their own rules and standards regarding dating. For example, some parents allow group dating at age 14 and individual dating at age 16.

In many cases, school functions offer the first opportunities for dating, 17-11. Teens may come and leave in groups, pairing off occasionally during the evening. After a while, one girl and boy may start developing a closer friendship. They may begin to go on individual dates.

As is true of other friendships, dating requires the support of parents. Parents need to show understanding and support as their teens experience their first feelings of romantic love. Parents may worry about couples that seem too serious too soon. They voice their concerns, such as the need to date others before making a commitment to one person. Parents also need to discuss their teen's career preparation and readiness for the responsibilities of adulthood and marriage. It is important for parents to talk with their teens about dating relationships in a trusting and caring way.

17-11 Dating often begins during the teen years at school events.

When their teens' relationships break up, parents should be understanding and supportive. During these times, parents may need to comfort, advise, caution, or encourage their teens. Teens may even ask their parents to reminisce about their own teen years.

Sibling Interactions

Sibling conflicts are less intense in the teen years. Many teens say they really enjoy their siblings, and their siblings understand them better than their parents. Teens and their siblings often unite in asking their parents for new privileges and for family rule changes.

Younger siblings, however, often tease teens and invade their privacy. Teens may resent younger siblings who get privileges they didn't get at a similar age or who find the parents' favor in an argument. Although teens do not dominate their younger siblings as much as they once did, they may fight with their siblings when in a bad mood.

A Quest for Self-Identity

From birth, a child begins to look for answers to these questions: Who am I? What can I become? In an effort to find answers, Erikson says that people meet specific challenges in eight stages of life. The challenges of childhood—trust, autonomy, initiative, and industry—prepare teens for a sense of *identity* in Stage 5, 17-12. (Appendix A "Erikson's Theory of Personality Development" for detailed information on the characteristics for Stage 5.)

As teens search for identity, they merge their childhood challenges. They consider what values are important and which they should keep. These values and attitudes provide the foundation upon which teens build the rest of their lives. This foundation broadens self-understanding as the adult develops and refines other roles, such as spouse, parent, and worker.

Forming a sense of identity involves exploring values and beliefs, trying different roles, and sometimes experimenting with

Erikson's Theory of Personality Development

Stage	Approximate Age	Step Toward Stable Personality	Step Toward Unstable Personality
1	Birth to age 2	Trust	Mistrust
2	Ages 2 & 3	Autonomy	Shame and doubt
3	Ages 4 & 5	Initiative	Guilt
4	Ages 6 to 11	Industry	Inferiority
5	Ages 12 to 18	Identity	Role confusion
6	Early adulthood	Intimacy	Isolation
7	Middle age	Generativity	Stagnation
8	Late adulthood	Integrity	Despair

17-12 When teens have a healthy sense of self, the process of forming a personal identity is easier.

other ways of life. These changes may come and go quickly and bewilder parents. For the teen, the peer group is the major source for exploration. A sense of identity also requires a commitment to chosen values. Some teens do not reach a personal sense of identity. This may occur for many reasons including

- *Identity foreclosure.* In this situation, a teen makes commitments, but not on his or her own. He or she adopts parental or peer values without rejecting alternatives.

- *Identity moratorium (delay).* Some teens are bewildered and confused in trying to make a commitment. They need more time to seek answers and make decisions. These teens may achieve a sense of identity as young adults, but some never make a commitment.

- *Identity diffusion.* Some teens have trouble taking risks and are therefore unable to make decisions or commitments. These teens may profess a commitment, but never really make a choice. Erikson believed the majority of teens and adults experience identify diffusion.

If a teen forms a true sense of identity, he or she can set boundaries between self and others. This teen has truly become autonomous—or is his or her own person. A teen with a true sense of identity has a chosen direction in life, 17-13.

Emotional Stress and Disturbances

Most teens rate their overall moods as positive. However, many report high levels of stress at times. Why is there so much stress even for those who were relatively stress-free before the teen years? Hormones responsible for rapid growth and puberty can cause mood swings. The changes in the body itself can be confusing and often result in negative

17-13 Teens spend a lot of time thinking about themselves and their futures.

images. The intellect allows teens to brood about the past and be concerned about the future. Teens are also sharply aware of and sensitive to stares and comments directed at them. They even react to their imagined opinions of others. All of these stressors are in addition to the concerns and crises in their family's life. With support of family and close friends, most teens are *resilient*. They bounce back in the face of stress.

A small percentage of teens experience emotional disturbances. Disturbances are much more serious than stress. Troubled teens must have professional help because waiting makes their problems more resistant to treatment. Some disturbances include

- *Anxiety.* Anxiety is often a result of poor relations with family or peers, fear of failure, or poor physical health. Strong and chronic anxiety can be debilitating to a person's life.

- *Rage.* Rage often comes from past angers. These hostile feelings can explode into violence against the family, school, peers, work associates, or society in general.

- *Depression.* Depression has many causes. It may involve a short-term sense of emptiness or a feeling of total defeat. Severely depressed teens may be suicidal.

Parenting Concerns and Tasks

Although many parents say they enjoy this stage, some find the teen years almost overwhelming. What makes the teen years so challenging to parents? All teens must make profound adjustments in every area of development as they change from children to young adults. Parents, too, have to make adjustments as they let go of their role after 18 years. Even as the parenting role comes to a close, parents must be as deeply committed as they were in earlier stages. Parental love and support help teens develop and emerge as confident, responsible young adults.

Medical Checkups for Teens

The American Academy of Pediatrics (AAP) recommends checkups for teens at ages 14, 16, and 18. If teens are sick or injured, they may need more doctor visits. Next to toddlers, teens have the highest rates of acute illnesses. Teens are often required to have a physical exam before participating in sports. Teens should also visit their eye doctors and dentists regularly.

Regular checkups are a good time for teens to talk to their doctors about the changes that occur during puberty. The doctor can explain what the teen should expect and reassure that he or she is developing normally. Teens need to know the importance of good health habits and how to adopt them while avoiding unhealthy ones.

Teens should also talk to their doctors about reproductive health care. Beginning at age 18, females need an annual checkup of their reproductive organs. Young men can ask their doctors what reproductive health checkups they may need. Both women and men should learn about examining themselves (breasts for women and testes for men) for cancer.

Adjusting to Teens' Needs

The teens' world is almost totally outside the family system. Teens spend only about 15 percent of their time with their parents. Much of this time is with friends or other family members. Most of a teen's waking hours are school-absorbed, friend-absorbed, and self-absorbed.

With each passing year, parents have less control over their teens. Because their bodies are almost mature, many teens think they are fully grown. However, teens still want parental love and consultation. They want to become more self-governing and independent without giving up warm family relations. Parents have to find just the right balance between support and control in order for their teen to become self-disciplined.

Nurturing and Supporting

Teens are often confused by the many changes that occur during these years. More than anything else, teens need their parents' unconditional love, 17-14. Parents can provide support by

- expressing optimism about their teen's developmental progress and reassurance that it is normal

- accepting of their teen's feelings

17-14 Parents show support for their teens by offering reassurances.

- understanding their teen's need for growing independence
- sharing their past experiences
- accepting their teen as a separate person

Parents must realize their teen is always different, and many times much better, than the child of their dreams. Most importantly, a teen needs to know how proud he or she has made his or her parents.

Encouraging Self-Discipline

Teens do not need parents as buddies. Friends are teens' buddies. Parents are teens' loving and available teachers, consultants, and supervisors. By law, parents are responsible for their teens until they reach the age of majority.

As you read in earlier chapters, the major goal of parenting is to raise children to become adults who are self-disciplined (also called *self-regulated*). Parents' firm, but always appropriate and fair, standards and limits promote self-discipline. Standards teach and limits protect teens until they are ready to take the responsibility for and accept the consequences of their own actions.

How do parents best teach self-discipline? Teens learn self-discipline from parents who gradually lessen their power over their teen's actions while giving more freedom with responsibility. These parents use behavioral control; they calmly explain reasons for behavior expectations and monitor and supervise the teen's actions. They avoid using psychological control, which makes teens feel guilty, or threatening them with the loss of parental love.

Effective parents also use open communication and active listening while discussing any conflicting standards or limits with their teen. Some parents find movie or television scenes help open communication with their teens. Also, effective parents model their values and expectations. While making sure their teens do not compromise certain basic standards and limits, parents need to give their teens a decision-making voice. When teens make poor choices, parents must make tough decisions regarding how they respond to their teens. They build their teen's self-esteem by celebrating his or her advances in independence, such as doing homework well and making good grades.

Making Family-Life Adjustments

Some people consider adolescence a troublesome time in parent-child relations. Although some teens have serious behavioral problems, many teens do not. Although some parents are unresponsive to their children, many have been nurturing and supportive since their child's birth.

Why do some people think adolescence is a troublesome time? As a whole, teens love their parents and say their greatest fear is losing a parent. However, family relationships are changing during the teen years. Adolescents focus on establishing freedom from the controls of parents and other adults. For parents, this results in rewriting the roles, rules, and boundaries that direct their parent-child relationship. Stressors affecting the teen, the parents, and the parent-child relationship result in making many family-life adjustments.

Teen Safety from High-Risk Behaviors

According to the Centers for Disease Control and Prevention, nearly 75 percent of deaths among teens are due to unintentional injuries and violence. This is more than the deaths from all diseases combined. The main threat to teen safety is participating in risky behavior.

Teens engage in many **high-risk behaviors**, or risky actions in which teens often know the dangers, but believe they are exempt from the risks. As you read earlier, dangerous behaviors of teens often relate to body image and low self-worth. These behaviors include risky ways of losing weight (eating disorders) and becoming more muscular (taking anabolic steroids and performance-enhancing drugs). Other high-risk behaviors include using tobacco in any form, taking illegal drugs, drinking alcohol, driving recklessly, and having unmarried sexual relations, 17-15.

Why do many teens take dangerous risks? Some of the most common reasons for high-risk behaviors include the following:

- *Belief that "it won't happen to me."* "I will not get addicted to drugs" or "I will not get pregnant." Teen denial of addiction, pregnancy, or STIs may delay treatment and cause more risks.

- *Desire to impress others.* Teens overestimate the extent to which their peers engage in the same risky behaviors. Trying to impress others is often due to low self-esteem and lack of personal confidence.

- *Immature view of real-life consequences.* Teens may think that coping with a pregnancy wouldn't be so bad, but fail to look at the responsibilities involved in parenting for the next 18 years.

- *Ignorance of the full effect of possible actions on others.* For example, teens often do not consider how drinking and driving (DWI) can affect others, such as their passengers and people in other vehicles or on the street.

- *Inability to recognize the long-term consequences of risky actions.* For example, some illnesses caused by tobacco use may not completely develop into cancer and other major illnesses for 20 or more years.

Although teens are curious and like to experiment, parents can lessen the chance of high-risk behaviors. The first step parents can take is to provide information. They can obtain written information from Web sites of national organizations that deal with the consequences of high-risk behaviors. Some examples are the National Center on Addiction and Substance Abuse, the National Highway Traffic Safety Administration, or the National Eating Disorders Association. Parents should provide this information in the middle school-age years.

In addition, parents should try to reduce situations linked to high-risk behaviors. One situation is too much commitment to moneymaking opportunities rather than to school courses and activities. Other situations involve having too much spending money or recreational time, especially on weekends and school breaks.

Talking openly about issues and providing honest answers is another important parenting task. For example, a parent can say, "The only sure way to prevent pregnancy and STIs is abstinence." **Abstinence** means refraining from sexual intercourse. Then parents must back up their statements with facts.

Risky Teen Behaviors

Reasons for teen behavior	Dangers of behavior
Using Tobacco	
• Think smoking makes them look attractive and grown up • See smoking as a social benefit • Have parents or friends who smoke • See tobacco ads with "sexy" women and men • Find tobacco easy to get	• Causes nicotine dependence • Causes gum disease, tooth abrasion and loss, cancer, heart disease, and respiratory disease with such complications as asthma and bronchitis • Causes health risks to unborn babies and nonsmokers
Taking Illegal Drugs	
• See drugs as a fun, recreational activity with peers • Desire pleasant sensations • Like the thrill of breaking the law • Find escape through drugs • Find drug use reinforces fantasies of success • Live in homes in which parents use drugs, little or no parental supervision occurs, abuse occurs, or life is stressful	• Taking drugs is illegal and addictive and may lead to use of other more dangerous drugs • Causes lethargy, changes in blood pressure and heart rate, sleeplessness, nausea, or convulsions • Adds to teen problems instead of solving them • Slows reaction time • Increases risk of HIV/AIDS from injected drugs
Drinking Alcohol	
• Think alcohol is more socially acceptable • Think they look older; believe drinking alcohol makes them "cool" • Believe drinking reduces anxiety • Have peers who drink • Live in homes where alcohol use is heavy or parent is alcoholic • Find alcohol easily available	• Leads to adult use of alcohol and can lead to dependency • Causes more motor vehicle accidents for teens • Can cause liver damage, harm to fetus for pregnant females, and death • Impairs perception, coordination, and thinking speed • Impairs judgment and may lead to sexual relations while intoxicated
Driving Recklessly	
• Inexperience, immaturity • Distractions from other passengers or talking on cell phone • Feeling a strong need to keep up with traffic or for drag racing • Driving while intoxicated • Exposure to unsafe driving from friends, parents, and media	• Cause injury or death of teen or others • Damage to vehicles or property • Cause other drivers to be involved in accidents • Arrest for moving violations • Loss of license • Pay increased insurance rates

(Continued on next page)

17-15 There are many causes of high-risk behaviors in teens. The dangers are very high, even fatal in many cases, for far too many teens.

Risky Teen Behaviors

Reasons for teen behavior	Dangers of behavior
Having Unmarried Sexual Relations	
• See sex as their reward (boys); see sex as a way to keep a boyfriend • Think sex shows maturity • See unmarried couples living openly together, more flaunting of sex in the media, unwed pregnancy no longer a stigma • Realize birth control is readily available • Feel pressure from peers • May be a victim of sexual abuse	• May become a single parent and experience problems associated with teen pregnancy and parenting • Potentially getting or spreading STIs • Regret in not waiting to have sex • Negative outcomes for others besides the involved teens, such as grandparents raising teens' children or children of teens living in poverty

17-15 Continued.

As good role models, parents encourage their teens to choose friends with positive values. They help their children develop decision-making skills from the earliest years through the teen years. They also show their teens how to decline invitations to high-risk behaviors, explain family values, 17-16, and set limits, such as curfews.

If their teens do participate in high-risk behaviors, it is best for parents not to overreact. Instead, they should express concern by focusing on immediate dangers of behaviors. When high-risk behaviors are a concern, parents should seek immediate help from medical professionals and counselors.

Taking Action on Teen Violence

Violence is a growing problem among teens. Sometimes the violence is physical, involving hitting, biting, choking, sexual abuse, or use of a weapon. Violence can also be nonphysical involving verbal bullying, a menacing posture that blocks someone from entering or leaving an area, or cyberspace bullying. Violence involves teens as victims and as *perpetrators*. Violence also involves teens' families, teachers, school administrators, and others. Violence may occur in the home, on the street, in school buildings or on school grounds, at the workplace, at a party, or on a date. **Homicide**, or the intentional taking of another's life, ranks second to accidental deaths (in vehicles) as a cause of teen deaths. Besides deaths, violence often leads to serious injuries and emotional scars. What causes teens to become violent? There are many causes, but the most common ones include

- *Violence in the home or community.* Children learn patterns of violence and repeat these patterns throughout their lives. Family violence is common with 25 percent of families exhibiting some form of violence in their homes. Many families live in high crime areas, too, with daily violence on the streets.

- *Media violence.* Research shows that the best predictor of teen aggression is the amount of TV violence the child watched at age 8. Violent video games in the hands of children or teens also stimulate violence, including homicide.

- *Drugs.* Buying and using drugs places teens in situations in which violence is more likely to occur.

- *Physical or sexual abuse.* Besides the physical harm caused by such abuse, which can be substantial, these forms of abuse lead to long-terms mental-health problems and feelings of low self-worth.

- *Mental-health problems.* Teens prone to violence have problems coping with stress, angry feelings, feelings of wanting revenge, and have low self-esteem. Some teens are willing to do violent acts to be members of gangs, Chapter 19.

- *Firearms.* About 70 percent of violent acts involve firearms. Teen actions are often impulsive, so preventing firearms from easy accessibility may provide for much-needed "calming time."

How can parents take action on other-directed violence? Parents can work to prevent the causes in their families. If their teen (or younger child) is showing warning signs, 17-17, they need to get help quickly from a qualified mental-health professional. Parents can also work to make the culture less violent.

17-16 Parents need to talk to their teens about the facts related to alcohol use. They should also explain their feelings and beliefs about alcohol use.

Overseeing Teens' Work

In any given school year, about 75 percent of teens have jobs. Most teens have worked before high school graduation. The typical high school senior works 16 to 20 hours a week. Today, even younger teens are working more hours than they did in the past.

Teens commonly work in retail stores, in restaurants, or as clerical assistants. Summer jobs offer more employment opportunities because of special summer needs of employers. Some teens may work at summer recreation sites and camps. Others serve as substitutes for regular vacationing employees in a variety of jobs.

Teens use their income for many purposes, including entertainment, clothing, car and its operation, saving for college, investing, or school supplies. Some teens work to help support the family income.

Although income is often helpful, parents and their teens need to weigh all the pros and cons of teen work, 17-18. For some teens, employment may not be in their best interest. If employment seems suitable, parents and their teen should discuss the types of jobs, locations, and maximum number of working hours before the teen begins a job search. Once a teen receives a job offer, parents and their teen should review the job details. They should also negotiate the ground rules about working, such as keeping up with schoolwork or how income should be saved and spent.

After the teen is employed, parents need to carefully oversee their employment. For example, does the actual work match the offer? Does the teen work the agreed-upon hours? Are the conditions safe and appropriate for teens under age 18? Parents should also note how well their teen manages work with other life demands. For example, is he or she fulfilling the agreed-upon ground rules for working? Is he or she overwhelmed by too many demands? If so, parents should help their teen make another plan.

Warning Signs of Potential Violence

General Violence	Date Violence*
• Threatens violence	• Expects dating partner to spend all time with him or her
• Blames others for problems and/or believes he or she should be treated in special ways	• Acts extremely possessive or jealous of dating partner
• Expresses themes of violence in essays, reading selections, artwork, or conversations	• Controls where dating partner goes and with whom he or she talks; keeps track of dating partner by insisting he or she check in regularly
• Preoccupation with themes and acts of violence in the media	• Treats dating partner and his or her friends and family with disrespect
• Uses drugs or is socially isolated	
• Has a dating partner "stolen"	• Belittles dating partner's ideas and goals
• Has humiliating (shameful) experiences or disciplinary problems at school	• Loses temper frequently over even minor things
• Displays history of violent or aggressive behaviors including bullying, cruelty to animals, vandalism, and arson	• Takes no responsibility for his or her actions
	• Makes threats to harm or leave dating partner if he or she refuses to do as told
• Involvement in cults or gangs	• Makes dating partner feel guilty by insisting the relationship would improve if the dating partner just changed as a way to show his or her love
• Shows signs of mental illness, such as anxiety or depression	

Warning signs of date violence closely resemble warning signs for spousal abuse.

17-17 Many acts of violence can be prevented if warning signs are noticed.

Encouraging Teens to Stay in School

Some teens drop out of school before they graduate. More than half of these teens are average to above average in intelligence. Most often, teens who never complete their education will lack essential skills that lead to earning a good income. School problems are the responsibility of teens, but parents should provide guidance as needed. Parents should

- communicate their concerns about how decisions will affect their teen now and in the future.

- question the source of school problems for the teen. Typical reasons include disliking school, expulsion or suspension from school, wanting to work, poor peer relations, low grades, or failing state-required tests for graduation, and pregnancy.

- seek remedies, such as tutoring or alternative school programs for pregnant or working teens.

- support their teen by encouraging school-grade improvements, lessening other home or work demands if the teen stays in school, or finding other means of completing his or her education.

Monitoring Teens

During adolescence, teens often adopt a more active lifestyle. They may participate in several extracurricular activities. Some teens have jobs; others spend more time with their friends. The changes in a teen's lifestyle also impact the family's lifestyle. Teens may come home later at night. Some activities might interfere with normal family mealtimes. Busy teens may not have enough time to

Pros and Cons About Teen Employment

Pros	Cons
Has income to meet more needs and wants	Limited on-the-job training
Learns how to manage income	Difficulty balancing the demands of work, school, peers, and family
Learns how to budget time	Drop in grade-point averages with more hours of work
	More absences from school
	Less enjoyment of school compared to before working
	Feels loss over extracurricular activities
Understands how the business world works	Spends less time with families
Learns how to get a job; develop a work ethic	Shows an increase in substance abuse, especially for teens who work 30 or more hours per week
Better evaluates goals, such as staying in school, getting more education, and perhaps finding a career of interest	Are subject to accidents or violence on the job or while going to or from work

17-18 Working may be rewarding, but it also places special demands on teens. Parents need to weigh the pros and cons with their teens and oversee their work.

do their share of household tasks. Parents and younger siblings may become upset. Family members will need to settle these conflicts in ways that seem fair to everyone. These are times that call for calm discussion, understanding, and cooperation.

Special Family Times

Teens spend much of their time away from their families. Yet, they still want a warm family life. Doing things together maintains and strengthens family ties. Special family times are often shared with grandparents, cousins, or other family members.

What can parents do with their teen? Family fun can be as simple as playing a game when everyone is home. It can be as involved as a vacation that includes the teen's best friend. Some families regularly enjoy sports activities together, such as camping, bicycling, hiking, fishing, boating, or swimming, 17-19.

Many families find ways to make household and outdoor cleanup fun. Most teens are willing to help when tasks are divided among the entire family. Don't be surprised if your teen's friends want to help, too. Special foods and music can make the work more enjoyable.

Special family times can take place with others. Family members can take an aerobics, self-defense, social dance, or hobby class. Family members can team up for a special party or a sports event. Many parents and their teens benefit greatly from working together in volunteer efforts.

Parenting in the Teen Years

Families with teen children leave the *families with school-age children* and enter a new stage in the family life cycle, the *parenting adolescents stage*. This stage continues until firstborn children reach age 18. Families must now aid teens to become more independent

17-19 A family vacation, such as camping, can be enjoyable for teens and their parents.

of the family system. Families gradually loosen their structure as teens become more responsible for making decisions within and outside the family setting.

Parents of teens enter the *interdependent stage of parenting* according to the parenting expert, Ellen Galinsky. This stages focuses on the greater freedom and control teens have over their decisions. Although parents remain more separate from their teens, they must be available to them. Teens often seek out their parents for advice and at other times need loving parents to set boundaries.

Parents must help their teens learn how to make decisions that minimize potential harm to themselves or others. Parents also have to let go of much control over their teens' lives. Parents sometimes fear their teens will not maintain the family system, although they most often do.

This stage signals the coming end of the parents' childrearing influence. Most teens seem to do just fine as they approach the young adult years. The stage is often more overwhelming for parents than for their teens.

Summing It Up

- Adolescence is a transitional time during which people graduate from the dependency of childhood to the independence of adulthood.
- Both a physical growth spurt and physical sexual maturation occur during the teen years.
- The teen years are important for finalizing gender-role identification.
- When body image suffers, teens are apt to develop eating disorders or use anabolic steroids or performance-enhancing drugs.
- About one-third of teens use abstract reasoning skills in areas in which they have a strong knowledge base. Teens' language development reflects their abstract thinking skills.
- The roles of peers take on even greater significance in the teen years.

- Forming a sense of identity is difficult for many teens.
- Although almost all teens are moody at times, most are resilient. Some teens suffer emotional disturbances of anxiety, rage, or depression.
- To parent teens effectively, parents must find the right balance between support and control.
- Parents need to help protect their teens from engaging in high-risk behaviors.
- Parents must take action on their teen's violence toward others.
- Parents also need to oversee their teen's job and school progress.
- The interdependent stage of parenting is often more overwhelming for parents than for their teen.

13 to 18 Years*

Physical Development

General

Period of little growth is followed by growth spurt; at first, teens may look awkward and lanky, but as growth continues, body proportions equalize

Skull grows larger

Jaw lengthens

Chin becomes more pointed

Nose increases in size

Facial profile becomes more adultlike

Acne may develop

Females

Ovaries increase production of sex hormones

Hormones add a layer of fat on buttocks, thighs, and arms

Breasts become fuller

Hips widen

Pubic hair appears

Ovulation begins

Menstruation begins

Males

Testes increase production of sex hormones

Reproductive organs mature

Muscles develop rapidly and double in strength

Shoulders widen

Waist narrows

Neck thickens

Voice drops to a lower pitch

Hair appears on face, under arms, and in pubic area

Sperm production begins

Ejaculations may occur

Intellectual Development

Learns many new concepts; begins to show strength and interest in one or more academic areas

Learns to use the decision-making process

May solve problems mentally without reference to experiences (abstract thinking)

Considers several ideas and concepts at one time

Achieves a new awareness of people and issues

May think more often about the future

May speculate about what might be instead of what actually is

Learns to weigh the relative consequences of an action for the individual and for society

Can evaluate self and make necessary correction to get back on the right track

May think about and compare moral values

May insist upon fairness

May believe individuals are justified in breaking an unjust rule

Uses strategies when playing games or engaging in sports activities

Social and Emotional Development

Strives to establish a sense of personal identity

May experience role confusion (feelings of not knowing who he or she is and where he or she is headed)

May feel lonely and isolated

May have dramatic mood swings

Asserts independence but feels insecure

May wonder about the future, which is both exciting and frightening

May judge self according to perceived opinions of others

May be preoccupied with own thoughts and forget reality

Feelings of autonomy may result in conflict with parents

Has an overall positive relationship with parents—sees them as humans who may make mistakes

Seeks emotional support from parents or peers

Is generally influenced by both parents and peers

May show tendency to conform to peers in early teen years, but later may resist peer pressure

Tries out different social roles

Learns to interact with an increasing number of people from home, school, and community

Is capable of forming close relationships with peers of the opposite sex; may begin dating

* These charts are not exact timetables. Individuals may perform certain activities earlier or later than indicated in the charts.

Recalling the Facts

1. List four physical changes that occur during the adolescent growth spurt.

2. What characteristics signal sexual maturity in males and females?

3. Explain why gender-role identification is more complex in today's society.

4. How can parents counteract the mixed messages teens receive from the media about the role of sexual expression in their lives?

5. Name three reasons why teens are often preoccupied with body image.

6. Contrast eating patterns associated with each of the following eating disorders: anorexia nervosa, bulimia nervosa, binge-eating disorder, and combination eating disorder.

7. How do anabolic steroids impact developing teen bodies?

8. Explain how a person's thinking changes in Piaget's *formal operational stage*.

9. How does parental enthusiasm about education impact teen achievement?

10. Describe how *cliques* influence teen values and behaviors.

11. How can parents be supportive of dating?

12. What challenges do teens face as they search for identity?

13. Name three major emotional disturbances that may occur during the teen years.

14. List three ways parents can best teach their teen self-discipline (self-regulation).

15. What are three reasons why some teens engage in high-risk behaviors?

16. How does parenting change during the *interdependent stage of parenting*?

Applying New Skills

1. **Making decisions.** Select a typical decision that teens face. Apply the decision-making process to this decision. Write out the steps as you work through them. Share your decision-making process with the class.

2. **Research and report.** Use Internet or print resources to research the intellectual changes that occur during the teen years. Write a paper explaining what you have learned. Share your findings with the class.

3. **Community resources.** Investigate resources in your community that offer help to teens with any two of the following problems: eating disorders, anabolic steroid use, tobacco use, substance abuse, reckless driving, sexual health problems, teen pregnancy, and violence toward others. Create a PowerPoint® presentation to share your findings to the class.

4. **Role-play.** Role-play a parent talking to a teen about problems the teen has with a friend. Show how the parent can help the teen reach his or her own solution.

Thinking Critically

1. Gather evidence to support or refute the following statement: "Parents must find the right balance between support and control in order for their teen to develop self-discipline."

2. Draw a cause and effect chain to show the relationship between one or more risky teen behaviors and the consequences of those behaviors. What can parents do to prevent risky teen behaviors?

3. As a class, devise a code of conduct that seems workable for teens today. Analyze the role parents should play in setting limits. How can a positive or negative parental attitude affect a teen's attitude toward the parental limits?

4. Draw conclusions about why you think parents of teens often feel overwhelmed.

Linking Academics

1. **Writing.** In one page or less, summarize the physical changes in primary and secondary sex characteristics during the teen years.

2. **Reading.** Read a fiction or nonfiction book about teens that are struggling in some area of physical, social, or emotional development. Briefly summarize the book and indicate how the teen(s) worked through the challenge.

Part Five
The Challenges of Parenting

467

Your Potential Career

A Desire to Serve and Protect

What thoughts run through your mind when you watch a news report about a tragic accident, devastating weather event, or perhaps a missing child? Does a desire to serve and protect others drive your enthusiasm for a career related to law, public safety, corrections, and security?

- **Job outlook.** Many careers in this cluster will continue to see increasing *demand* in coming years.

- **Education or training.** A written exam and certification or licensing is required for many of these careers. Some entry-level jobs require a high school diploma and on-the-job training. A degree from a two-year or four-year college is required for many *higher wage* jobs.

- **Skills and personal qualities.** An ability to act quickly and make accurate decisions is a must. People's lives depend on it. Can you remain calm in dire emergencies? Are you physically strong, agile, and coordinated? Which skills and personal qualities are most important for your career choice?

- **Wages or salary.** As with most careers, education and training go hand-in-hand with income. For example, a *First Responder EMT* will make lower wages than someone with a degree in fire science. A lawyer will make higher wages than a court clerk.

Build Your Portfolio

Evaluate the materials you have been collecting for your portfolio. Do all items represent your best and most relevant career-related qualities? Write your résumé and get your references in order. Put your portfolio items together neatly in a binder or small file box.

FCCLA

If public safety and providing security for parents, children, and families is the career for you, participate in an FCCLA STAR Event to share your passion. FCCLA National Programs such as *STOP the Violence, Dynamic Leadership,* and *Power of One.* These programs can provide the foundation for such STAR Events as *Illustrated Talk, Parliamentary Procedure, Interpersonal Communications,* or *Job Interview.* Obtain all necessary forms and guidelines from your family and consumer sciences teacher.

Up Close—Job Shadowing

Choose a career of interest in law or public safety and security from the chart on the following page. Locate one or more individuals who work in this career. If possible, follow each person on the job for several hours. Take notes on the types of knowledge and skills each person uses, the types of workplace-related skills needed, and the education and training each person has acquired. Be sure to ask each person what he or she likes best and least about this career. Write a brief summary of each job-shadowing experience to share with the class.

You can read more about planning your career in Chapter 22.

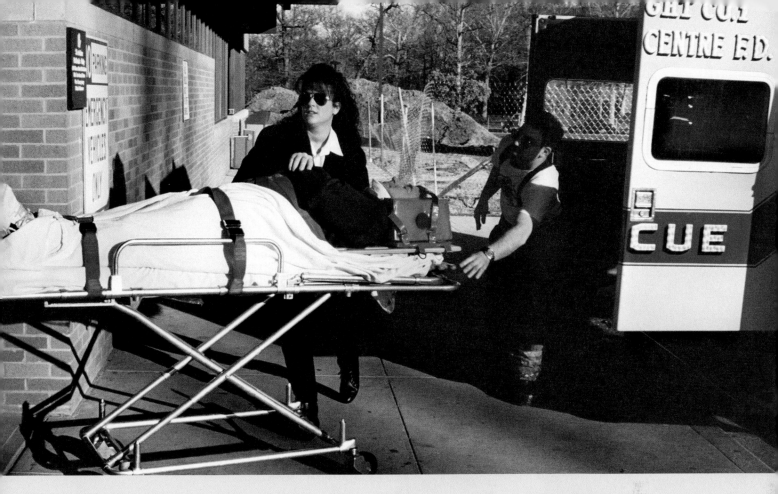

Career Cluster—Law, Public Safety, Corrections, and Security

Cluster Pathways

Correction Services	Emergency and Fire Management Services	Security and Protective Services	Law Enforcement Services
Sample Careers			
Youth Services Worker	Emergency Management Response Coordinator	Loss Prevention or Security Manager	Missing Persons Investigator
Program Coordinator	EMT	Security Systems Technician	Criminal Investigator
Public Information Officer	Firefighter	Loss Prevention Assistant	Highway Patrol
Program Coordinator or Counselor	Hazardous Materials Responder	Life Guard	Police, Fire, and Ambulance Dispatchers
Warden	Rescue Worker	Ski Patrol	Sheriff
Foodservice Staff		Physical Property Security	Deputy Sheriff
Dietitian			Park Ranger
Support Staff			

Chapter 18

Family Concerns

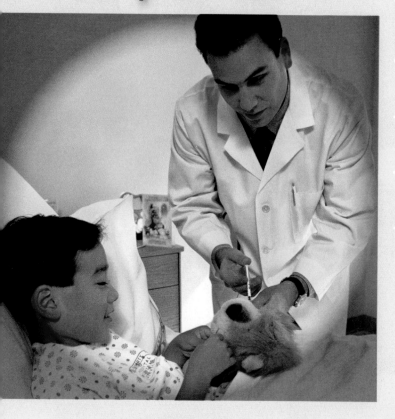

Objectives

After studying this chapter, you will be able to

- summarize issues related to balancing work and family roles.
- identify ways that divorce impacts children and parents, and actions parents can take to help their children cope with divorce.
- describe the challenges that single-parent families face and helpful supportive strategies.
- explain the difficulties associated with stepfamily formation and strategies parents can use to overcome these challenges.
- summarize the challenges associated with parenting in special family compositions.
- describe the challenges families face when a family member has a serious health concern or disability.
- list strategies parents can use to help support children who are grieving.
- identify ways parents can make a move easier for their children.

Parenting brings many joys, but it also brings challenges. Along the way, parents may have concerns about their family life. At times, difficult situations may arise. Because parents, children, and certain events are never exactly the same from family to family, the effects on the parent-child relationship differ, too. However, all families must make some adjustments when facing challenges.

A sign of successful parenting is the ability to cope with both the predictable and unpredictable family-life events. Parents must help their children adjust to these events. At the same time, they must also take care of their own needs. In this chapter, you will read about several common family concerns and how parents can help their children through these difficult situations.

Balancing Family and Work Roles

In today's society, most mothers and fathers combine working outside the home with parenting. When the single parent or dual-career couple works, parents must find ways to balance family and work roles. This requires dedication and some creativity on the part of parents.

Reasons Parents Work

Most people work to financially support themselves and their families. They use their income and benefits (health insurance, life insurance) to meet their family's basic needs, such as food, clothing, housing, health care, and transportation. This is true in single-parent families and in nuclear families, 18-1. Some families use income for other long-term goals, such as purchasing a home, saving for children's education, saving for a special vacation, or investing for retirement income. The additional income makes it possible to meet these goals.

18-1 Even in two-parent families, it is often necessary for both parents to work.

Parents work for other reasons, too. Some mothers work for a sense of fulfillment in their careers more than for income. This is especially true for highly educated women. For many adults, work roles can be important for both financial and personal reasons.

Managing Multiple Roles

Managing the responsibilities of family and career can be challenging. The challenges are greater in most single-parent families. Often one parent provides the family's income and has the responsibility to care for the home and children. Most single parents find all this responsibility stressful. They do the best they can to balance their roles of parent and worker. Single parents may have to ask for help from family members or friends. When they work, they hire a caregiver for their children. At home, they may have to ask older children to take on more of the household tasks.

In many nuclear families, both parents work to meet the family's income needs. In some nuclear families, however, one parent provides the family income. Parents must consider many factors before deciding whether one parent, most often the mother, will stay home or whether both parents work. Questions parents may think about include

- *How will a parent feel about becoming a stay-at-home parent?* Parents must think about the benefits and possible consequences of having one parent stay at home with the children. Some may have concerns about career plans and the impact of reentry into the workforce.

- *How will a parent feel about working outside the home?* Marriage morale is higher when both partners support the decision about working. They need to think about whether one or both partners will feel guilt if both work or only one works.

- *Is the work situation family-friendly?* Considering whether the employer offers programs and policies that help parenting is important to deciding whether a parent works or stays home with the children.

- *How does working versus not working impact family finances?* Parents must think about the costs involved with working or not working. For example, taxes, child care costs, and other typical costs such as, work wardrobe and transportation, can easily consume a large percentage of a parent's income. Parents also need to think about what expenses they can eliminate when one parent stays home.

- *Is quality child care available and affordable if both parents decide to work?* Finding state-licensed child care that effectively serves their children's needs is important to parents, 18-2. Child care often becomes unaffordable for families if it costs more than 10 percent of the family income.

- *How will household tasks be completed if both parents work?* Determining how to fairly divide household tasks can be a challenge for dual-career families. It is possible for parents to spend almost as much time on home tasks as they do at work.

Dual-career families, like single-parent families, often report multiple stressors. Parents often feel pulled in many directions when they have multiple roles and responsibilities and feel unable to do them all well. In most dual-career families, men and women generally divide the household and parenting tasks. Regardless of how spouses share home tasks, it is not easy to balance these multiple roles.

Many couples find ways to balance their multiple roles. How they manage their many responsibilities varies from one household

18-2 Family-friendly work policies, such as on-site child care, are important for dual-career families.

to the next. How well they succeed often depends on the attitude of both partners toward the dual-career arrangement. Stress lessens when couples are happy about their work situations and divide household and child care tasks. It also helps parents to know that their children have quality care while parents are working. Taking time for rest, relaxation, and personal interests also relieves the tension of multiple stressors.

The Effects of Work on Parents and Children

Parental work status and workplace experiences affect parent-child relationships. Parents, children, and work situations are never the same from family to family. Most studies identify few harmful effects for children in dual-career families. In fact, there are even some benefits for children who have working parents. Research indicates the following:

- Dual-career and single-earner parents monitor children's behaviors equally well.

- Compared with other children, children in dual-career families have less traditional views about the roles for men and women.

- In dual-career families, fathers spend time with children individually as well as in whole-family activities. In father-earner families, fathers spend most of their family time with children in whole-family activities.

- Children of dual-career families tend to be very independent and achievement oriented.

- Children of dual-career families are often more outgoing than other children.

- Children in dual-career families more often share in household tasks, 18-3. By sharing tasks that help the family, children learn concern for others.

18-3 Husbands and wives often share child care responsibilities in a dual-career family.

Successful Working Families

Tensions between personal life and career will likely occur no matter how dedicated parents are toward making it work. The most successful working parents are those who can manage their time, tasks, and finances. Without these management skills, daily life is stressful for all family members.

Almost all parents feel there is not enough time within a 24-hour day. In order to manage time well, parents must establish priorities and make choices. Because some relaxation is important, leisure activities can be more important than "need-to-do activities."

Many parents plan time in advance for the family to be together. They find this makes them more likely to fulfill their plans. These parents also make the most of family time when they are not working and work hard when they are on the job.

Working parents must also manage tasks, such as laundry, house cleaning, shopping, and driving children to various places. Careful task planning helps parents get everything done. For example, a parent may shop while his or her child takes a music lesson. Family members may need to talk about reassigning tasks so everything gets done. They may need to alter housekeeping standards or miss some activities. At times, some things may be left undone.

In order to manage their finances well, working parents need to have a spending plan. Single parents may have to budget most carefully. Without a spending plan, dual-career couples may have financial problems. They may find themselves short of cash with no idea where their money went. If parents need help creating a budget, they may want to consult a financial adviser.

Working parents have many pressures, but also many rewards. Job success benefits family members emotionally and financially. In addition, a supportive and happy family can boost energy for meeting job demands.

Coping with Divorce

When a husband and wife decide to divorce, it is never easy. If they have children, the decision is even more difficult. Marital happiness contributes to parents' self-confidence and their skills as parents. Parental divorce affects children in negative ways. Parents' concern about their own problems leaves little energy for parenting. Divorcing couples often have unresolved conflicts. The level of the conflict is a powerful predictor of children's adjustment. The stress of unresolved marital conflicts affects parents' skills and behaviors with children. Young children who witness severe family conflict are at risk for harmful changes in brain development. Exposure to this conflict causes release of a stress hormone, which is damaging to the brain.

Couples often view divorce as the only way to resolve their unsatisfying marriage. Children are more likely to view divorce as the breakup of their family. In a child's eyes, divorce may seem like the end of the world.

What Is Divorce?

Divorce is the legal dissolution of a marriage. For a legal divorce, one or both spouses must file a divorce petition in their county's civil court. A court date will be set for the divorce hearing. At the divorce hearing, one or both spouses explain to the judge why they want to divorce. The judge must make a decree on the property settlement, (an agreed upon split of the couple's property—such as the home, bank accounts, or furnishings) within the requirements of state law.

In addition to these issues, the couple must resolve custody of their children. **Custody** means the right and responsibility to raise a child and make decisions about the child's care, upbringing, and overall welfare, 18-4. Sometimes the court awards **joint custody**, which means both parents keep their parenting rights and responsibilities. Joint custody works best when the couple demonstrates ability to work together in making decisions regarding their children.

In joint custody cases, the parents and the court determine with which parent the children will live. In many cases, the children live permanently with one parent. The other parent will have **visitation rights**, or the right to visit the children during certain specified times and under certain conditions. In other joint custody situations, the children may live with each parent for a specific amount of

18-4 Divorce is painful for children. Parents should assure their children that both parents will continue to love and care for them.

time each year. Living arrangements should be set up in the best interest of the children. For example, in most cases children should be in one school for one term. Changes in living arrangements result in visitation rights shifting back and forth between the parents. Joint custody allows parents to better share parenting responsibilities.

In other cases, only one parent receives custody, or **sole custody**. Generally, a judge grants sole custody after determining that joint custody will likely produce further conflict. A judge may also grant sole custody if one parent is unfit to raise the child. In sole custody cases, the custodial parent lives with the child and makes all the decisions about the child's care. The other parent may or may not have visitation rights as the court determines.

Even after a divorce, both parents have an obligation to financially support their children. This is true no matter who has custody. In almost all custody cases, the judge will decide about *child support payments*. **Child-support payments** are payments one parent makes to the other parent to help meet the children's financial needs. The parent with whom the children live is the one who receives child support payments. However, this parent must also help support the children with his or her income.

When parents agree on custody, visitation, and child support, the divorce proceedings run smoothly. The judge may be able to finalize the divorce at the initial hearing. In fact, parents should try to reach an agreement on these issues before going to court. This will make the entire legal process quicker and more agreeable for everyone.

When the parents cannot agree on the terms for custody, visitation, and child support, the judge must decide these issues for them. In this case, each person tells his or her side of the story. Each person states what terms he or she would like and support these with valid reasons. The judge then decides what is in the child's best interest. These cases can be the most upsetting for divorcing couples. They may drag out indefinitely, requiring several court appearances. This type of divorce can also be upsetting for the children. Parents should not use their children as weapons in their divorce battle.

Throughout the legal proceedings, parents should be truthful and treat each other with respect. They should not magnify each other's faults or tell lies about one another. Appearing in court is not easy for either of the adults. They should try not to focus on themselves, however. Their goal should be to work together with the judge to decide what will be best for the children. Unless the judge requests to talk with the children, parents should not involve their children in the divorce hearing or custody settlement.

Beyond the legal proceedings, divorce is a series of stressful events for a family. Divorce results in two new family units. Following their parents' divorce, families often move. Children may experience the stress of a new neighborhood, school, and friends. Parental roles change. Generally, one parent assumes most, if not all, authority for the children. Family income and spending patterns change with divorce. If mothers receive child custody, family income is often lower.

Explaining Divorce to Children

Once parents make a final decision to divorce, they should tell their children right away. This protects children from hearing this news from someone else. Children do not need to hear all the details of their parents' failed relationship. They do deserve a brief explanation of why the divorce is happening. The explanation should be age-appropriate and sensitive to each child's feelings.

Parents need to carefully consider how and what they will tell the children about their divorce. It is less confusing for children if the parents tell them about the divorce together. If this is not possible, parents should talk with each other and agree upon what each will say to the children. Parents should choose their words carefully and remember that the *truth* is always best. They might say, "We made a mistake. We could not repair the mistake, so we are seeking the legal way to correct the mistake—a divorce. We are sorry; a divorce makes us all sad. We love you and will always take care of you."

Parents need to listen and respond to their children's questions and feelings. Children need to hear that difficulties between their parents, not the children's behavior, caused the divorce. Parents should explain the reason for each change as it occurs during and after the divorce. For example, children need to know about custody arrangements and where they will live once the divorce is final.

Effects of Divorce on Children

Some parents feel complete devastation by divorce; others simply feel relief. Children often feel a constant threat to their security—their way of life. Parents, situations, and children are unique. This explains why children have different reactions when their parent's divorce. For each developmental stage, certain reactions are common, 18-5.

A Supportive Environment for Children

Next to death, parental divorce is the second most stressful event in a child's life. Because of the stress, divorce is one of the top five reasons children go through counseling. However, children tend to get the least amount of support during this difficult family time.

Children need as much love and support as possible from each parent during and after a divorce. Parents should try to be sensitive to their children's feelings and make special efforts to keep lines of communication open. Even when they are no longer married, the mother and father are still parents. Ideally, they should work together as a team to continue parenting their children. Parents need to create a supportive environment in which their children adjust to a new way of life. Parents should do the following:

- make flexible "tradeoffs" to accommodate the other's needs
- tell each other in advance about necessary changes in plans
- encourage their children to work out parent-child problems directly with the parent involved
- find a safe transfer for beginning and ending visitation—such as a police station or YMCA—if there is too much animosity between them

- decide how to share the children during holidays

As parents create a supportive environment, they should continue to do good parenting. They need to tell their children that they love them. They also need to provide structure and organization for daily life. For example, maintaining firm household rules and using firm, but fair discipline help children adjust to new

Children's Reactions to Divorce

Age	Reactions
Infants and toddlers	• Adjust well if they have consistent care and nurturing
	• May show regression behaviors (child reverts to past behaviors he or she has since outgrown)
	• May be insecurely attached
	• May idealize missing parent and not accept a stepparent if the noncustodial parent remarries (older toddlers only)
Preschool children	• May feel abandoned and overwhelmed and react with fear; may grieve for absent parent
	• May show regression behaviors
	• Often become less obedient and have temper tantrums
	• May be less affectionate and more dependent and whiny
	• Often believe they may have caused the divorce; may bargain with parents to stay together or reunite
School-age children	• May fear no one will love or care for them
	• Usually understand parents' explanations of divorce, but are sad or angry
	• May deny the divorce is real (denial relieves grief and avoids embarrassment with friends)
	• May express feelings through physical ailments, such as headaches and stomachaches; often cannot focus on school tasks
	• May think good behavior will reunite parents, or may set one parent against the other
Teens	• May resent divorce and any family changes
	• May rethink their previous positive ideas about love, marriage, and family
	• May experience low self-esteem if they feel their parents no longer love them
	• May take the side of one parent against the other parent or may try to get parents to reconcile
	• May withdraw or rebel with drugs, alcohol, shoplifting, or other illegal activities
Older teens and young adults	• Have lower educational attainment and often earn less money
	• Are more likely to be alienated from parents
	• Are more likely to be an unmarried parent
	• Have higher divorce rate

18-5 Experts believe children's reactions to divorce vary with age. While each child is unique, many children in the same age group try to handle their parents' divorce in somewhat similar ways.

routines. Encouraging children to seek support from their siblings and other family members, such as grandparents, can help adjustments go more smoothly. Positive friendships and teachers who are aware of the situation can also offer support to children. In addition, parents can use age-appropriate children's books to help explain divorce and the following adjustments. If necessary, they should seek counseling help for their children and the family.

Adapting to Single Parenthood

At its best, being a parent or a child in a single-parent family is difficult at times. Separation, divorce, the death of a spouse, or an unplanned pregnancy can be traumatic. Single parents may not have expected or wanted to raise children alone, 18-6. However, single parents may carry the burden of providing all the child care and guidance. Many single parents also have total responsibility for earning the family's living and running the household. Finding affordable child care, making enough money, and having only 24 hours a day to meet life's demands can be overwhelming. Time for leisure is almost nonexistent for single parents.

Life for children in a single-parent family is challenging, too. If their parents were once married, children may find it difficult to adjust to living with just one parent. They may have intense feelings about the separation, divorce, or death of their other parent. Children usually love their other parent and may feel sad about the changes in the family. Hardworking parents often have little time for family pleasures. So children may feel their needs are neglected. The specific problems depend upon how the single-parent family was formed and the characteristics of its members.

18-6 Many single-parent families function successfully, although life can be challenging at times.

Support Environments for Single-Parent Families

Despite the many challenges, single-parent families can be happy and successful. The following strategies can help all members of single-parent families:

- *Develop a support network.* Enlist the help of people who will be supportive, such as the other parent, grandparents, and friends. Join local support groups for single parents. Some national organizations, such as "Parents Without Partners" may have a local group.

- *Ask for help before becoming overwhelmed.* Parents should be specific about the type of help they need, such as advice on a discipline problem, a babysitter for a night out, transportation for a child, or sick child care while at work.

- *Get help in selecting quality, affordable child care that meets the family's needs.* Generally speaking, family child care homes are less expensive than center care. Single-parent families often qualify for lower-cost care at not-for-profit centers. The additional child care fees are subsidized by an organization, an agency, or through government funding.

- *Create some sanity-saving times each day.* Exercising, listening to music, reading, or keeping in touch with others can be rejuvenating for single parents, 18-7.

- *Develop some long-range goals.* With increasing financial needs, some single parents set such goals as getting a college degree, working toward a promotion, taking a trip, or buying a house. Creating a chart to track progress toward these goals is a good reminder and helps single parents stay positive.

- *Focus on the good.* Rather than getting trapped in despair about problems and challenges, focus on what is good about single-family life.

Although living in a single-parent family may be challenging, this structure may have certain advantages for children. For example, children of single parents are likely to have many opportunities to become self-reliant. Having a well-adjusted single parent may be better for children than growing up in an unhappy two-parent home. One happy parent may be able to give children more love, guidance, and attention than two conflicting parents. Children in single-parent families can feel just as much love and security as those living with two parents. They can grow up to be just as intelligent, cooperative, friendly, mature, and responsible as other children. A single-parent family can provide stable, close parent-child relationships.

Remarriage and Stepfamilies

Following divorce or the death of a spouse, adults are single once again. As their lives continue, they may begin new relationships. In time, the majority will

18-7 Time for relaxation is especially important for single parents.

remarry. People who remarry are usually excited about finding new life partners. They look forward to building a permanent relationship together.

Quite often, however, these couples have children from their previous relationships. When they remarry, it means two families merge and form a stepfamily. At first, adjusting to the new family structure may be hard for everyone. Before marriage, each family operated on its own with its own way of doing things and in its own space. When two families merge, they blend their way of life.

Stepfamilies face unique challenges, but many are successful. Becoming a stepfamily can take some getting used to, especially for the children. Challenges are greatest in stepfamilies in which children are between 9 and 15 years old at the time of the remarriage. Young children find it easier to adapt to the new family. Older teens are not as involved within their new family, preferring to spend time with the families of friends. Additional challenges many stepfamilies face include the following:

- *Larger family size.* Children in stepfamilies may have four parent figures, eight grandparents, and a variety of siblings, half-siblings, and stepsiblings. Parents must spread attention, money, and living space among more people. At times, this leads to stress and conflict.

- *Additional roles.* With remarriage, parents must take on more roles. For example, they must build ties with a new marriage partner, sustain ties with their biological children, and develop ties with stepchildren. They also work to develop a new family system and promote harmony within the family, 18-8.

- *Relationship changes with children.* Parents are naturally closer to their biological children than to their stepchildren. Although they may be tempted to favor their biological children, stepparents need to work at bonding with their stepchildren. The relationships between stepparents and stepchildren are different before and after marriage. Before marriage, stepparents do not play a parenting role with their stepchildren. Children must view their stepparent as fair over a long period of time in order for bonding to occur.

- *Conflicts with noncustodial parents.* Noncustodial biological parents may become negative after their former spouse remarries. They may fear losing their children's love. Children may not adapt to the new relationships when their parents and their new spouses have conflict.

18-8 Cooperation and respect for one another can bring members of stepfamilies closer together.

- *Negative behaviors of children.* Severe family problems can occur when stepchildren display negative behaviors. During the single-parenting period, older children may relate to their custodial parent more as peers rather than as children. They often see the new stepparent as a threat to this relationship.

Members of a stepfamily must work together to overcome these challenges. A positive attitude and willingness to make the most of the situation are a good start. Family members must learn patience, cooperation, and good communication skills. Life runs more smoothly if they can show understanding toward one another. Children seem to adjust well to their new family structure over four or five years. Parents can help facilitate this adjustment.

Developing a stepfamily can be a positive experience for everyone involved. As husband and wife form a team, the entire family is strengthened. Spouses can share parenting tasks and responsibilities. Each family member can develop several new relationships, which can be very rewarding. With humor, cooperation, empathy, and creativity, stepfamilies can be happy and strong. Focusing on the family's strengths can bring the family closer together.

Special Family Compositions

Just as family structures often present certain parenting challenges so do special family compositions. These special family compositions include families with multiple-birth children, families with foster children, and families with adopted children. Family compositions affect parenting concerns and methods. Parents in these families not only deal with the typical developmental challenges of their children, but also with unique parenting concerns.

Parenting Multiple-Birth Children

About 3 percent of all babies born in the United States are multiples. Of these, 95 percent are twins. Families with multiples are often larger than the typical family size of two children per household. Parents of multiples have some special challenges. For example, parents of multiples may need to purchase duplicates of some items, such as cribs, car seats, carriers, and feeding chairs. They will also need a stroller for multiple children.

In addition to extra equipment, parents of multiples will likely need help with physical-care tasks. Because multiple babies are often born prematurely, they require more frequent feedings. Mothers may need to learn special breast-feeding techniques for multiple children. They also need to learn how to supplement breast-feeding. Time parents need for diapering, dressing, and bathing increases with the addition of each child. Assistance from family, friends, or hired help becomes a necessity in families with multiple-birth children.

Most parents of multiples say they enjoy seeing the similarity and uniqueness of their children's development, 18-9. These parents notice how their children interact with each other in rich and interesting play and how they can almost read each other's minds. They see them intensify and expand their behaviors in reaction to each other. For example, as babies, if twin A cries, twin B cries louder, and then twin A cries even louder in response. The same thing happens with giggles. In the preschool years, multiples intensify and expand their behaviors by engaging in rounds of clowning one-upmanship. Most parents speak of their children's closeness as built-in buddies, especially as they enter new situations.

18-9 Parents of multiple children enjoy the similarities and differences in their children's development.

Parenting Foster Children

Over a half-million children currently live in foster-care families. Within two years of placement, about 66 percent of these children will once again live with one or both birth parents. Others wait a long time before the courts return them to their birthparents or place them with a relative. Others are on long waiting lists for adoption or are waiting for some other permanent arrangement.

The greatest challenges of parenting foster children come from the reasons the state child-protection agency removes children from their parents' home. The most common reasons include such parental problems as abandonment, neglect, abuse, and physical or emotional illnesses. Parental incarceration, substance abuse, and death are other reasons why children are in foster care. Sometimes children are in foster care due to their own severe problems. For example, when children run away from home, abuse substances, threaten parents, or perform violent or illegal acts, parents may feel they cannot handle their children. The fact that foster care in a certain family is usually temporary offers other parenting challenges. Many foster children will struggle with the following feelings:

- *Guilt.* They may blame themselves for their parents' problems and wish to return home even if suffering from neglect or abuse.

- *Feeling unwanted.* Planning for a foster child's future, or **permanency planning,** and other legal decisions often result in children waiting a long time for parents. Many foster children say, "All I want is someone to love me." A few never have a permanent home.

- *Insecurity.* Most foster children cope with many life changes. After they enter foster care, they may move from one foster home to another. Sometimes they are returned to their birthparents only to be removed again. These children often have insecure attachments to parenting adults. Friendships with peers are often short-term due to their changes in homes and living in different communities and attending different schools.

Foster parents face many challenges, too. About 30 percent of foster children have severe problems and complex needs. Most of the problems come from their backgrounds. Support services for these children often require a team approach involving foster parents, child-protection agency social workers, health-care professionals, and teachers, 18-10.

Because foster care is temporary, foster parents must prepare to release foster children to their biological or adoptive parents. It can be difficult for them to let go, especially when they care for a foster child for a long time. Foster parents and their foster children may develop a special relationship that continues for life. A few foster parents adopt some of their foster children.

No matter how long foster care lasts, it can be rewarding for both foster parents and foster children. To be successful, foster parents must not only open their homes but also their hearts to children in need of loving

18-10 Foster parents often work with others to best meet children's needs.

care. Foster parents have the satisfaction of helping children grow and develop. They can experience parenting and contribute to a foster child's life in positive ways. Foster children gain a loving home and quality care until a permanent arrangement comes along.

Parenting Adopted Children

About 2 percent of all children in the United States are adopted. The numbers of adopted children remain constant, but the sources of adoptions are changing. Private adoption agencies and kinship adoptions, such as stepparents, were at one time the major sources of adoptions. In current times, public agencies account for over 40 percent of adoptions. International adoptions account for 15 percent of adoptions.

For acceptance by an adoption agency, adoptive parents must meet the agency's criteria and standards. Adoptive parents must then go through an extensive screening process. This process usually includes interviews, criminal background checks, and a home study interview. In a home study, the agency visits the adoptive parents' home.

After acceptance as adoptive parents, people may wait a long time for a match with an available child. People who desire to adopt infants may wait longer. Many adoptive parents prefer to adopt an infant so they can be parents from the start of their child's life.

Because they are choosing to become parents, adoptive parents are usually very dedicated to parenting. Parents who adopt infants have fewer parenting challenges due to adoption. Adoptive parents of older children may face more challenges mainly due to a child's background. All adoptive parents face some parenting issues. These issues include

- *Knowing health status of children.* Health information is vital to the well-being of all children. Adoption agencies usually provide this information at the time of placement. In cases of abandonment or international adoptions, health information may be scarce. Before the adoption, parents should have a doctor examine the child and review his or her health records.

- *Transitioning to new home.* For infants and younger children, parents should learn the caregiving and comforting methods to which children are accustomed and continue using them, 18-11. With older children, parents should visit the place they live before the adoption. Adoptive parents should be warm, but give the child time to adjust. As with stepfamilies, full adjustment may take several years.

18-11 Adoptive parents should continue caregiving methods and routines to which their children are accustomed.

- *Telling children about the adoption.* Adoptive parents should always tell their children about the adoption. They should explain it in a sensitive way the children understand. Some experts say that parents should tell children about the adoption at about age 3. Others say it is best to tell children when they are old enough to understand the difference between birthparents and adoptive parents.

- *Handling children's feelings.* Adoptive children may display a variety of troubling feelings. Younger children may deny the adoption (adoption photos can help here). Children from a race, country, or culture different from the adoptive family may struggle with identity issues. Joining support groups with parents and children from the same race or culture helps. Adoptive children may also be curious about their birthparents. Adoptive parents should support their children's interest and understand this is part of developing self-identity.

Although they may face a few special challenges, adoptive families function in the same way as other families. Adoptive families are just like other families, except they are formed differently. Members of an adoptive family also form lasting and loving bonds and create special family memories.

Serious Health Concerns

The serious illness or disability of any family member places a heavy burden on the family. These health concerns affect parenting in many ways. The physical demands of caring for a person who is ill or disabled or taking over his or her tasks can easily drain the caregiver's personal energy. The emotional impact of having an ill or disabled loved one causes additional stress. The financial hardships due to high medical costs and potential loss of a parent's income may be totally overwhelming for the caregiving parent.

Parenting is made challenging because of the stress of dealing with the burdens of an illness or disability. At the same time, children also need special attention. Parents and caregivers should encourage children to share their fears and ask questions. Parents should answer these questions simply and truthfully, 18-12. When a parent is ill, children should keep in contact with the parent as much as possible. If hospital visits are not possible, even a short phone call can reassure children the parent still loves them. When children are ill, parents can

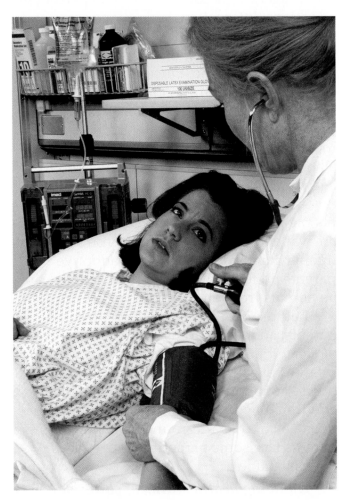

18-12 When a parent is seriously ill, it can cause financial and emotional concerns in the family. Telling the children the truth about their mother's condition will help them understand the situation.

reassure them by answering their questions. By finding out about hospital procedures in advance, parents can prepare their children for what may happen.

There is no way, however, to anticipate the emotional or physical burdens a serious health concern can place on a family. Some family members may feel cheated because of the burden. Other family members make the best of an undesirable situation and grow closer together. Families can better manage serious health concerns if they look ahead and provide financial security through insurance or savings for emergencies. Many social services are also available to help families in times of need. Relatives, friends, and neighbors can often lessen the pressure a health concern creates in a family.

Explaining Death to Children

Most children are far more aware of death than their parents realize. About 4 percent of children experience the death of a parent by age 15. A few more children experience the loss of a sibling. Through time, children experience other significant deaths, such as a death of a grandparent or other relative, friend, classmate, or pet.

Death is a painful reality that touches young and old alike. It is a part of life. Children must learn to cope with the reality of death. Children form concepts about death at their developmental level, 18-13. Even if a family death occurs during a child's infant or toddler years, eventually he or she must address the reality.

Helping Children Grieve

Death is a traumatic experience. Most children are **resilient** or able to recover, but recovery cannot happen alone. Children need support from a loving parent or another caring adult.

To be supportive, the parenting adult must understand childhood grief differs from adult grief. Children tend to express grief through emotional reactions, such as sadness, anger, or withdrawal. They may also express grief through their actions, such as dramatizing or drawing. Children may grieve a "piece at a time." For example, they may miss the deceased parent. Later they may fear losing the other parent. Still later they may feel a special day, such as their birthday, is "just not the same."

There are many things that parents can do to help their children through the grieving process. Helpful support strategies include the following:

- *Avoid euphemisms and statements that are not true.* The substitution of an unpleasant word, such as *death*, for one that sounds more pleasant is a **euphemism**. Euphemisms, such as "lost," "passed away," or "went to sleep," convey confusing images to children. Parents should always tell children the truth instead of saying, "Grandma went on a long trip." Parents must also avoid using phrases for death that may cause fear, such as "Grandpa died because he was sick." It would be better to say, "Grandpa died because he was very old and had a special disease."

- *Provide answers.* Children need their parents to provide answers to their questions about the death and grieving rituals. Answers should be simple, truthful, and at the child's level of understanding, 18-14.

- *Quiet children's fears about the future.* The number one fear of children is the death of a parent. Parents should never assure their child that they will not die. Instead say, "Grandpa was very old and had this special disease. I am not old and do not have this disease." An even better answer is "I'll always make sure you are taken care of and will not be alone."

Children's Developmental Concepts of Death

Child's Age	Understanding About Death
Infancy through 3 years	• Have little to no understanding of death.
4 years	• Are familiar with the word *death*, but not its meaning.
5 years	• Believe death is temporary and reversible. • Associate death with "not moving" due to TV cartoons. Cartoon characters are often run over or blown up one minute and spring back to life the next. Children may play death scenes in the same way.
6 years	• Have more realistic concepts of death. • Think death occurs to older and other people. • Associates unrelated events to death, such as a child's "bad" behavior could cause a parent's death.
7 Years	• Talk about grieving rituals, such as funerals, visitations or wakes, and cemeteries. • Realize even children could die.
8 years	• Accept the reality of each person's eventual death. • Talk about death as "not breathing."
9 years and older	• See death as a natural biological process. • May ask religious questions about death.
Teen years	• Consider the impact of death on others, such as what will happen if their parents die or if they themselves die. • Compare what their current lives are like to what death might be like. Suicide rates are high for teens that feel life is too stressful and death is peaceful.

18-13 Parents must address the reality of death on a child's mental developmental level.

• *Attend grieving rituals.* Parents should carefully consider taking their children to grieving rituals, such as funerals and visitations (wakes). The loving support and concern that family members share could be helpful for the children to see. Experts advise that parents should consider the child's age, personality, and maturity level when deciding about taking children to grieving rituals. Generally, children age 7 and older can handle these events. Parents should ask their children if they want to attend and accept their decision about attending. The parent should explain what will happen and what everything means.

• *Share memories.* Teaching children how to remember people warmly is part of helping them grieve. This may include telling stories about loved ones who have died or looking at photos.

• *Allow children to express feelings of grief without guilt.* Parents should never say, "You have to be strong," "Don't cry," or "Get over it." Instead parents might say, "It's a hard time—we all loved grandpa" or "it's very sad for all of us."

• *Accept stress reactions.* Typical stress reactions, such as lack of concentration, sleep disturbances, regression behaviors, having aches and pains, and believing

18-14 When a death occurs in the family, children should be allowed to grieve. Their questions should be answered simply and honestly.

no one understands are common among children. Although they should accept these behaviors, parents should work toward helping their children feel less stress.

- *Ask for help.* Enlisting the support of teachers, youth workers, and others can help prepare a child's peers for his or her return to the group.

- *Read books.* Many books are available for parents and for children and teens on the topic of death. Talk with your local librarian or consult such Web sites as Compassion Books.

- *Offer affection and maintain routines.* It is important for parents to provide children with extra hugs and maintain family routines as much as possible. As time passes, life should return to a normal pattern.

As children work through their grief, parents need to watch for signs of severe stress. For example, severe stress includes guilt (children blame themselves for the death) or panic (children wonder who will love them). If severe stress lasts longer than a month, parents should seek professional help. Parents should also carefully monitor children following the suicide of a friend because other suicides of close friends sometimes follow.

Suppressing grief over the death of a loved one may have a devastating effect on anyone, especially children. Parents need to allow children to complete the task of grieving over the death of a loved one. Otherwise, children may have overwhelming feelings of unresolved grief at a later time.

Managing Family Moves

Although some people live in one home all of their lives, many live in several locations. About 20 percent of all families move each year. The reasons families move vary. Sometimes a move is necessary due to a job transfer, death in the family, divorce, or unemployment. Parents may look forward to a move if it means advancing in their careers and beginning a new life. Children, however, may have quite a different view.

Studies show children are vulnerable to family moves. The effects depend upon the children's ages. Infants pick up on the parental stress and are sensitive to changes in routines, especially sleep schedules. Toddlers may miss their former home, play space, or room. Kindergartners often regress in their ability to separate from their parents and adjust to other authority figures, such as teachers. Moves interrupt friendships for older children and teens, and may cause school problems.

As parents and children anticipate a move, it may be a good idea to gather information about the new community, schools, and activities together. Viewing a community Web site allows parents and children to take a "virtual tour" of their new community. Learning about the community together helps build excitement and can make the transition smoother.

To make moving easier on their children, parents can prepare them in several ways. The first priority is for parents to explain to their children why the family is moving. They need to answer their children's questions and be sensitive to their reactions. Keeping regular family routines not only helps the children, but also helps relieve parental stress. Involving children in the tasks of moving, such as planning and helping to pack their possessions, can help build excitement for the new location, 18-15. If a garage sale is part of the moving plan, parents should not include the children's belongings. Keeping all toys the last few weeks before a move helps children feel secure. It's important for parents to remain positive throughout the moving experience.

Before arriving at the new location, parents should ensure that transfers to new child care centers or schools are as easy as possible. Obtaining information before the move helps with this transition. It is best to move when children do not have to be uprooted during the school year. As soon as possible after the move, get children involved in local activities. Meeting new friends can help children settle into their new lives. It is also helpful for parents to assist their children in keeping in touch with their old friends by telephone, letters, or e-mail.

18-15 Having children help pack their possessions can help build enthusiasm for the move.

Summing It Up

- A sign of successful parenting is the ability to cope with predictable and unpredictable events of family life.

- Balancing family and work roles can be challenging, but with determination and planning of time, tasks, and finances, it is possible.

- When parents divorce, they should reassure their children they will still receive loving care and attention and their daily needs will be met.

- Finding affordable child care, making enough money, and having the needed time to meet all their tasks are common challenges for single parents.

- Children in stepfamilies often find adjustments to family life difficult.

- Physical care tasks of multiple-birth infants and toddlers can be overwhelming.

- The greatest challenge of parenting foster children comes from the reasons children are removed from their birth parents' home.

- Adopting older children and those from backgrounds different from their adoptive parents presents parenting challenges.

- The serious health concern of a family member can devastate a family physically, emotionally, and financially.

- Parents find explaining death and supporting children's grief difficult.

- A positive parental attitude can make a family move easier.

Recalling the Facts

1. List two reasons parents work.

2. What are two benefits of dual-career families for children?

3. Who should tell the children about the divorce? Why?

4. Name two ways parents can create a supportive environment for their children after divorce.

5. What are three strategies that can help all single-parent families?

6. True or false. Good relationships between children and stepparents often take time to develop.

7. List three challenges parents of multiple-birth children often face.

8. What feelings are often struggles for foster children?

9. List four parenting issues all adoptive parents face.

10. How should parents answer children's questions about a family member's illness or disability?

11. How does a 5-year-old's view of death differ from that of an 8-year-old?

12. List three ways parents can support their children in the grieving process.

13. What effects does moving have on children of various ages?

14. Name two ways that parents can help make the moving process easier for their children.

Applying New Skills

1. **Role-play.** Select a problem, such as conflicting work and family schedules, a dual-career family might face. Role-play a conversation in which the family discusses ways to resolve problems with their multiple roles.

2. **Interview.** Interview three to five working parents and ask how they divide the tasks in their household. Who is primarily responsible for child care? Who takes off work when a child is ill? How are the couples similar and different?

3. **Research.** Use Internet or print resources to research your state's requirements for becoming foster parents. What resources are available to foster parents who care for children with special needs? Write a summary of your findings to share with the class.

4. **Community resources.** Working with a small group, select one of the family concerns described in the chapter. Investigate resources in your community that could help families in this situation. Use page layout software to create a brochure listing resource agencies that may be most helpful to parents in this situation.

Thinking Critically

1. Debate the pros and cons of dual-career families versus single-earner families with two parents.

2. Propose ways for single parents to build stress-reducing time into their daily lives. What types of activities might be most beneficial? As a friend of a single parent, what might you do to help him or her on a daily or weekly basis?

3. Analyze the issues surrounding when to tell children they are adopted. Why do some experts have opposing views? Use Internet or print resources for more background information if necessary.

4. Draw conclusions about why parents are sometimes not sensitive to problems moving creates for their children.

Linking Academics

1. **Writing.** In your own words, write a paragraph explaining the meanings of the terms *custody, visitation rights,* and *child support payments* as they relate to children and divorce.

2. **Reading.** Read a book about explaining death to children. Some examples include *The Fall of Freddie the Leaf* by Leo Buscaglia or *Nana Upstairs and Nana Downstairs* by Tomie dePaola. Write a summary explaining how the book is helpful in discussing death with children. Share your thoughts with the class.

Chapter 19

Family Crises

Objectives

After studying this chapter, you will be able to

- explain why a healthy family system can weather a crisis but a dysfunctional family cannot.
- identify the effects of unemployment on a family system.
- summarize how parental substance abuse interferes with good parenting.
- explain the impact of partner abuse on families, mothers, and children, and ways the cycle of abuse can be broken.
- summarize the characteristics of various forms of neglect and abuse, and how parents and family members can protect children.
- distinguish between the types of peer violence and ways children and teens can protect themselves from such violence.
- examine issues related to missing children, including family and nonfamily abductions and runaway children.
- summarize the impact of suicide on families and children.

Key Terms

dysfunctional family
substance abuse
codependency
partner abuse
child neglect
child abuse
physical neglect
failure to thrive
emotional neglect
Shaken Baby Syndrome (SBS)
incest
peer violence
bullying
cyberbullying

You might think good marriages and happy families have no problems or conflict. In reality, problems and conflict occur in every relationship and family. The most important factor is how the family handles the problems, whether they recognize conflict, and how they manage it.

Most problems and conflicts within a family are minor. A family's normal method of coping with everyday problems is important. With good coping skills, a strong family can easily overcome small problems. This is good practice for handling larger problems, such as a family crisis.

In this chapter, you will learn about the risk factors for several types of family crises. You will learn how family members adjust during crises. You will also learn about community resources available to assist families in times of crisis.

What Is a Crisis?

A **crisis** is an unforeseen situation that demands adjustment by all members of a family. A crisis might be short-lived or long-term. For example, job loss might last a few weeks or perhaps years. Crises are more severe than family concerns. Some crises may even link together. For example, substance abuse can lead to violence even within the family. Crises occur at one time or another in most families.

Crises affect family systems, impacting each member either in direct or indirect ways. Strong, healthy families can weather a crisis, 19-1. Members pull together to help each other meet their needs and cope with change. These families often become stronger and closer after helping one another deal with a crisis.

Some families do not adapt well to crisis. In response to a crisis, these families might become dysfunctional. A **dysfunctional family** is one that cannot function properly

19-1 In strong families, members support and help one another through good times and bad.

because of certain overwhelming problems. In a dysfunctional family, the needs of all family members are not met. Interactions between the members are not healthy. The problems of a dysfunctional family prevent parents from caring for and nurturing their children.

Financial Crises

Parents have the responsibility to provide financially for themselves and for their children. As a family, they can set financial goals—such as buying a house, paying for the children's education, or saving for retirement—and work to meet them. Parents may plan and budget carefully to get the most from their money.

To help prevent a financial crisis, families must be careful not to let their spending get out of balance with their income. Families who increase their standard of living beyond their income will not be financially secure. Families who live within their means, who spend wisely, and who save for the future will be better able to weather emergencies.

Causes of Financial Crises

Unemployment causes a family's financial situation to change rapidly. A person may lose a job due to their personal characteristics or behaviors. Sometimes employers close the business or downsize. Changes in the economy affect employment. Sometimes economic changes, such as the Great Depression, affect nearly everyone. At other times, economic changes affect certain jobs. For example, many people experience job loss due to *outsourcing*—a practice of sending work to other companies with lower labor costs.

Besides unemployment, families may also go through financial crises due to natural disasters, such as fires, floods, tornadoes, or hurricanes. During these disasters, families may lose major investments, such as their homes and cars. Business losses may result in long layoffs or job loss. A financial crisis often occurs if any family member has a serious accident or has a severe or long-term illness.

Some families gradually sink into a financial crisis. These families often go further into debt month after month to live a lifestyle beyond their current income. Soon they are not able to meet their obligations. Other families may sink into a financial crisis due to other crises, such as drug or gambling addiction.

Homelessness

Homelessness is a lack of permanent housing. It has a strong link to financial crises. Homelessness includes people and families who live in shelters, motels, abandoned buildings, parks, and cars. It also includes those who live with extended family members or friends. Homelessness also impacts older children and teens who run away from home and live in nonpermanent housing.

Homelessness most often results from extreme poverty and lack of affordable housing. Another common cause of homelessness is the lack of a stable living environment. For example, mothers and children may flee their homes due to family violence. Children and teens often leave home to avoid conflict or abuse.

Families are the fastest growing segment of the homeless population. A young single-mother with two children under age 6 is a typical homeless family. About 40 percent of the children living in homeless shelters are under age 5.

Children are especially likely to be harmed by homelessness. Without a home, parents face many obstacles in their abilities to support their child's development. All areas of development are at risk, 19-2.

Local communities often have several resources that serve the homeless. Every state must have a coordinator for the education of homeless children. Every school district has a person who plans services for homeless students. These individuals can help parents with other contacts, too.

Effects of Unemployment on the Family

Unemployment is the most studied financial crisis. This type of crisis directly affects family members' personal well-being. Unemployment indirectly affects children due to parental stress and poor

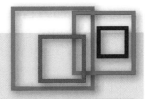

Developmental Risks of Homeless Children

Type of Risk	Risks to Development
Health	• Have poor nutrition and are frequently hungry; express anxiety about not having enough to eat. • Lack immunizations. • Have high lead levels in blood. • Are prone to health problems due to lack of health care and crowded living conditions. • More likely to have low birthweight and asthma.
Social and emotional	• May have parents with depression who do not provide positive parenting. • Often suffer from abuse or neglect. • Suffer effects of trauma, such as anxiety or depression, mental disorders, or aggressive and delinquent behaviors. • Often stigmatized by peers and even some teachers.
Intellectual and educational	• Possible brain damage due to lack of proper nutrition and family stress during infancy and toddler years. • Possible learning problems associated with low birthweight. • Have barriers to attending school (school enrollment difficult with lack of a permanent address; transportation problems getting to school). • Do poorly in school due to inconsistent attendance, lack of a time and place to do homework, and lack of parental involvement at school.

19-2 Homeless children are at-risk for an almost unlimited number of problems.

parenting practices. Younger children tend to do more poorly in school and often repeat grades. School suspensions or expulsions are common. Studies show that unemployment can have the following negative effects:

- harm to physical health if family members go without food, shelter, or health care

- harm to mental health due to loss of self-esteem as a good provider, to loss of worker identity, and to stress within the family

- increased divorce rate

- hampered school progress, especially when parents cannot afford school resources such as supplies and books

- loss of self-esteem in older children's and poorer adjustment to school

- decreased work ethic in children when parents have pessimistic views about their unemployment

Family Adjustments to Unemployment

During a financial crisis, a family must assess their obligations and assets, and set up a budget to balance them. One or both parents may temporarily take a second job to earn more money. Teens may be able to find part-time work to help ease the financial burden. Extended family members may help out, too.

Sometimes parents try to shield their children from knowing about a financial crisis. They may worry it will upset the children. However, even younger children need to be aware of the financial changes in their families, 19-3. Children feel better when parents treat them as part of the team. This way they can better understand why their parents are upset and concerned. It will also help them understand why they have to "do without" certain wants. Parents can instill in their children the values of wise spending, budgeting, and saving.

Family members need to be supportive as the unemployed person seeks new work. In some cases, a person may seek a job in a different field. A new job may require concentrated training or study that uses time normally devoted to the family.

19-3 Parents can include their children in talks about finances. They can teach children to budget, set financial goals, and save.

Families can lessen the potential impact of unemployment. When workers face unemployment due to situations beyond their control, they are often eligible for unemployment compensation. This is an insurance program run by the federal and state governments to help replace some lost income. It does not replace the full income. Savings also help during emergencies.

During unemployment and other financial crises, community resources can be most helpful. These can include social-service programs that provide food, shelter, and other necessities. Families may also wish to seek financial-planning services. Telephone directories often list such services under *Financial Planning Consultants, Debt Counseling Services,* or *Credit Counseling Services.*

Financial crises are often temporary. They require the adjustment and cooperation of all family members. With careful planning, the family can often manage until the unemployed parent is working again.

Substance Abuse

When a family member abuses substances, it can devastate the entire family. The term **substance abuse** means the use of any substance that can cause addiction. Substance abuse includes alcohol, illicit (not legal) drugs, misused or over-prescribed prescription drugs, inhalants, and even some herbal substances with druglike effects.

At first, a substance abuser develops psychological dependence, the feeling that he or she needs the substance to feel good. The abuser also develops physical dependence, a tolerance for the substance requiring larger amounts of it to achieve the desirable effect. When a person stops using an addictive substance, he or she often has withdrawal symptoms. These symptoms include vomiting, muscle cramps, convulsions, flashbacks, or delirium.

The United States has the highest substance abuse rate of any industrialized nation. Many Americans over the age of 12 abuse substances. The majority abuse alcohol only, but others abuse illicit drugs or a combination of alcohol and drugs, 19-4. Why do people abuse substances? What are the consequences of substance abuse? How can people find help for substance abuse? Read the following for answers to these questions.

Reasons for Substance Abuse

People abuse substances for many reasons. Many people feel substances are a cure for their negative feelings and problems, especially a low self-esteem. Some want to escape reality altogether. Others feel peer pressure to use substances. Soon they use substances for recreation. They particularly like any "pleasurable" feelings that come from the substance.

Still others use substances for more specific reasons, such as increasing muscle mass. People may use substances to feel energized, relax, or relieve physical pain. People in this group can unknowingly become dependent on substances, especially prescription drugs.

Consequences of Substance Abuse

Substance abuse interferes with a person's ability to function in a normal way. The chemicals in alcohol and other drugs alter the mind's ability to work properly. A person's addiction invades every aspect of his or her life, including work and family life. Parenting roles suffer. Children of substance abusers pay high prices that will likely affect them for life. An individual's substance abuse creates problems for society, too.

When a family member abuses substances, it can be devastating for the whole family. The abuser may experience

19-4 Instead of solving problems, substance abuse can cause even more. People who abuse substances need help to put their lives back in order.

health problems due to poor nutrition, lack of sleep, or sexually transmitted infections. Accidents from driving under the influence can destroy property and lives. Substance abusers often leave their families without money to meet daily living needs. Children of substance abusers are more likely to suffer from abuse than other children.

Dealing with Substance Abuse

When one family member has a substance abuse problem, it affects the entire family. Often nonabusing family members must take the first steps to seek help. First, family members must recognize and get help for unhealthy *codependent* behaviors. **Codependency** is a psychological condition in which a person is controlled or manipulated by another with an addiction. Codependency may involve enabling the abuser to continue using substances by supplying money, covering up the problem, or denying it exists. Out of love or fear of the consequences, family members tend to become codependent. These problems will not go away. Instead, problems often worsen when people ignore them. Individual and family therapy can help codependent family members learn healthy ways to respond to an addicted family member.

A nonabusing parent or extended family member can help children with stable parenting and support. Age-appropriate counseling can also help children learn healthy behaviors. In addition, school-age children can distance themselves from the situation. Instead of focusing on family problems, these children follow their own pursuits and obtain happiness from school, peers, and hobbies or other activities.

In addition to family members seeking help, the substance abuser will need help, too. He or she must decide to stop using the substance and seek appropriate help. Medical treatments in the form of drug and behavioral therapies help abusers free their bodies of addicting substances. Individual and group counseling along with support groups help the recovery process. Often the family is involved in counseling, too. The abuser must learn that addictions do not have a cure; he or she must work daily to avoid using the substance.

Many organizations provide services for substance abusers and their families. For example, *Alcoholics Anonymous, Al-Anon, Alateen,* and *Narcotics Anonymous* sponsor support groups that meet in most communities throughout the country. Other resources can be found in a phone or Internet directory under *Alcoholism Information and Treatment, Drug Abuse Information and Treatment,* or *Drug Addiction Information and Treatment.*

Partner Abuse

Partner abuse is any physical, emotional, sexual, stalking, or economic abuse of a partner, 19-5. The partner may be a current spouse, or non-married partner, or a former one. Other names for this form of abuse include *spousal abuse* (which only covers married partners) and *domestic violence* (which includes partner abuse and child, elder, and sibling abuse).

Both men and women can be abusers. However, in most cases, women are victims of male abusers. Most women who suffer abuse are young—between the ages of 19 and 29. Physical abuse is the type most often reported because it is a crime and easy to prove in court. Abuse is the single largest cause of injury to women between the ages of 15 and 44. About four million women are victims of physical abuse each year. Some die from their injuries.

Risks Factors for Abuse

Every family has stress that can lead to conflict. Some families are not able to calmly work through problems in a constructive manner. When conflicts arise, an abuser chooses violent forms of behavior to seek compliance.

Abuse occurs in all types of families. Abusers are found in all ages, racial/ethnic groups, socioeconomic levels, educational levels, and occupational groups. The partners may be living together, separated, or divorced. Abusers may even have restraining orders from the court prohibiting contact with their family members and victims.

Although abuse is widespread, certain people are more likely to become partner abusers. Usually these other abusers are 18- to 30-year-old males lacking a high school diploma. Other high-risk factors include the following:

- witnessing domestic violence as a child
- using aggression to solve problems with peers
- committing child abuse
- having economic hardships
- having a jealous and controlling personality

Partner Abuse

Forms of Abuse	Examples of Abuse
Physical abuse: Use of physical force against another person that causes injury or puts a person at risk	• Slapping or hitting • Choking, burning, or confining • Killing
Emotional abuse: Using words or actions to hurt a person's self-esteem	• Name-calling, threatening, or criticizing • Destroying a person's property; killing pets • Embarrassing or blaming the victim for the abuse • Forbidding the victim from communicating with family or friends
Sexual abuse: Using force to get a person to witness or participate in unwanted, unsafe, or degrading sexual activity	• Forcing any sexual act • Forcing a person to witness sexual activity or pornography
Stalking: Searching for and following a person in a secretive or threatening way over time	• Repeated phone calls (sometimes with hang-ups) • Tracking a person—suddenly showing up where the victim works or lives • Watching or threatening the victim
Cyberstalking: Using the Internet or other technologies to stalk	• Sending disturbing messages to the victim
Economic abuse: Using finances and physical resources, such as food, clothes, shelter, and medications to hurt a person	• Withholding money or credit cards; stealing victim's money • Withholding physical resources • Refusing to let the victim work

19-5 All forms of abuse hurt and humiliate the victims.

In over 50 percent of abuse cases, the abuser was using alcohol or other substances before the assault. Substance abuse increases the rate and severity of domestic violence. Substance abuse, however, does not directly cause the violence. Successfully treating substance abuse does not stop the violence. Substance use by abusers reduces any controls they may have to prevent violence. Abusers sometimes use substance abuse as an excuse for "being out of control."

The Cycle of Partner Violence

Abusive people seek power. Abuse is not the result of losing control. Rather partner abuse is intentionally trying to control another person. The abuser's angry actions instill fear in and exert power over their victims.

Because the abuser shifts responsibility for the abuse to the victim, the victim begins to feel guilty due to self-blame for the incident. The victim often believes the abuse will not happen again, especially if he or she "just becomes a better person." Because the abuser is to blame, abuse repeats and escalates in severity. For example, the abuser begins with verbal abuse, then violence, and finally murder.

Why do victims stay with their partner-abusers? Abuse usually follows a predictable three-phase cycle, 19-6. During this cycle,

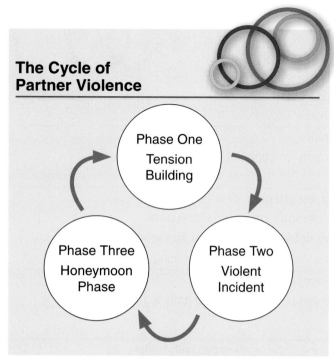

The Cycle of Partner Violence

Phase One
Tension
Building

Phase Three
Honeymoon
Phase

Phase Two
Violent
Incident

19-6 The cycle of partner abuse continues until one partner seeks help to stop it.

abusers can be pleasant part of the time. The cycle of violence includes

- *Phase 1.* Tension builds in the relationship. The couple may have increasing arguments. The victim generally knows a violent incident is coming. He or she may be very careful not to arouse the abuser's anger.

- *Phase 2.* Eventually a violent incident occurs. This phase can play out any place, such as the home, the workplace, in a car, or on the street. The incident may occur in private, but often occurs in front of others, including children.

- *Phase 3.* Immediately after the violent incident is the honeymoon phase. During this phase, the abuser excuses his or her actions by blaming them on stress, substances, or having a "bad day." The abuser often expresses remorse for the damage to the victim and promises it will never happen again. Gifts, romantic dates, and other signs of seeking forgiveness are evident.

Over time, the remorse fades. The cycle happens over and over. Typically, these cycles shorten in time, and the abuse becomes worse. The cycle of violence continues until either the abuser or the victim seeks help or until it is too late for help.

Effects of Partner Abuse

Because the family operates as a family system, what affects one member affects all members. Thus, partner abuse has devastating effects on the whole family, especially mothers and children.

Effects on Mothers

The partner conflicts prior to the abuse, the abuse itself, and the secrecy or disclosure of the abuse affect women in different ways. However, there are common symptoms among women who are victims of abuse. Physical symptoms are present in physical abuse and in some cases of sexual abuse. The psychological symptoms are always present. Because partner abuse tends to escalate, these symptoms worsen over time. Some common symptoms include the following:

- bone fractures, head injuries, cuts, and bruises

- fear of partner

- anxiety as reflected in sleeping problems, "jumpiness," inability to focus on tasks, and full-blown anxiety attacks

- low self-esteem as seen in self-hate, self-blame, and sensitivity to rejection

- lack of trust in others and, hence, poor relationships

- workplace problems, such as frequent and sudden absences, harassing phone calls or e-mails, isolation from others, and bouts of depression and crying

Effects on Children

Over three million children witness parent violence each year. Exposure to parent violence affects children and teens as they develop and the effects may last a lifetime. Children from these violent homes also experience neglect and abuse at a rate 15 times greater than the national average. Children who live with the effects of partner abuse are more likely to

- become abusers, more likely to and commit sexual assault
- resort to substance abuse and other risky behaviors to cope with abuse
- run away from home or attempt suicide to escape abuse
- have academic problems, usually an inability to focus on school due to sleepiness or agitation
- have no real friendships and a home unsafe for entertaining friends
- become the protector of the mother and siblings
- display anxiety and depression due to blaming themselves or staying afraid

Some children who witness partner abuse in their families are resilient and become healthy adults. They generally have healthy self-esteem and have good interpersonal skills with peers and adults. Because of the support they receive from extended family members or other trusted adults, these children have a chance for fulfilling lives, 19-7.

Breaking the Cycle

Generally, abusers do not admit they have a problem. For this reason, only the victims break the cycle. They can do this by seeking help and refusing to continue being victims. Often this means the victims must leave their abusive relationships.

The National Domestic Violence Hotline (1-800-799-SAFE) offers advice on making a plan of escape from an abusive home life. In

19-7 With the support of extended family members, children who witness or experience abuse can become healthy, well-adjusted adults.

addition to this hotline, victims can turn to social workers and medical professionals for help. Police intervention may be necessary in coping with some partner-abuse situations. They may arrest the abuser. A victim's plan for leaving usually involves the following:

- *Planning ahead for a safe place.* The home of a friend or relative or a shelter are often the safest places to go. Victims must be careful when discussing their plans with anyone. For example, they should send e-mail messages from a friend's house or library.
- *Packing an emergency bag and hiding it.* This bag should have house keys, money, important papers, medications, and some clothing. Pack a bag for each child, too.

- *Taking children along.* The top priority for abuse victims is keeping their children safe.

Once in a safe place, victims should seek help by filing for a court order of protection. If children are in school, notify school officials about custody, restraining orders, and threats.

Both the abuser and the abused family members should seek counseling. Communication, decision-making, and conflict-resolution skills are important for families to develop. These families almost always need professional help to attain such skills.

Child Neglect and Abuse

Children must depend on adults for physical care and nurturing. **Child neglect** is failing to provide for a child's basic needs. In addition to neglect, children are also prone to be victims of violence because they are defenseless. The National Committee for Prevention of Child Abuse (NCPCA) uses the following definition of *child abuse.* "**Child abuse** is a nonaccidental injury or pattern of injuries to a child. It is damage to a child for which there is no reasonable explanation. It includes nonaccidental physical, sexual, and emotional abuse."

More than three million children in the United States suffer neglect and abuse by parents, guardians, and others each year. The rate of neglect and abuse is likely three times greater than is reported. Of the known cases, about 1,500 children die from their injuries. Many of these are deaths of very young children. In fact, about 80 percent of children who die of abuse are under age 4.

Forms of Neglect and Abuse

Much is known about the different forms of neglect and abuse, their risk factors and their effects. However, about 90 percent of neglected or abused children experience more than one kind of maltreatment. Think about this as you read to more clearly see the true risks for children.

Physical Neglect

Physical neglect is the failure to provide sufficient food, clothing, shelter, medical care, education, and supervision for a child. Physical neglect can also mean failure to protect a child from abuse. The risks and effects of neglect are often easy to see. For example, children who experience neglect may display

- disinterest in objects and people
- irritability
- lack of clothing appropriate for weather
- poor hygiene, a soiled appearance, or strong body odor
- hunger and efforts to steal food

Because these effects are visible, physical neglect is the most-reported form of child neglect and abuse. Doctors can diagnose *failure to thrive* in infants and toddlers. **Failure to thrive** describes children who significantly miss the normal milestones in weight gain, height increase, or brain development. Other developmental lags soon follow these symptoms. Although failure to thrive may result from several causes, it is mainly due to the lack of proper feeding or due to medical neglect.

Emotional Neglect

Emotional neglect is the failure to provide children with love and affection. Children may receive good physical care and still experience emotional neglect. For example, if a parent never holds his or her newborn, it can be a sign of emotional neglect. Children need to be loved and held, 19-8. Emotional neglect is often difficult to prove.

Often a parent who neglects a child is young, does not want to be a parent, and does not understand how children grow and

19-8 Children need to be held and cuddled. Nurturing a child stimulates growth and development.

develop. A neglectful parent may also have a substance abuse problem or depression.

Children may show symptoms of neglect including slow brain development, an insecure attachment to parents, and frequent crying. Some children become overly dependent and clingy, while others feel unloved and look to people other than the parent for attention. In older children, a lack of self-discipline may be a sign of emotional neglect.

Physical Abuse

Physical abuse as it relates to children is the intentional infliction of physical injury upon a child. The adult uses physical force, such as hitting, slapping, biting, burning, beating, shaking, pushing, or kicking to punish or hurt the child. Children who suffer from physical abuse often have repeated injuries, such as broken bones, burns, and severe bruising or bleeding. When these children get older, they often engage in high-risk behaviors or commit violent acts.

Children under age 3 experience the most abuse. They also suffer the most deaths from this physical abuse. A common form of physical abuse of young children is *shaken baby syndrome*. When a caregiver violently shakes an infant or small child, the child has symptoms of **Shaken Baby Syndrome** (SBS). SBS is a form of physical abuse. The abusers in SBS cases are almost always parents or other caregivers and most are male. These abusers shake the baby out of frustration when he or she is crying inconsolably. See 19-9 for several ways to cope with infant crying.

Because an infant's neck muscles cannot support the head, the infant's head whips back causing the brain to move within the skull. This tears blood vessels, nerves, and brain tissue, causing swelling. If the shaking ends with a shove and the baby's head hits a hard object, more swelling occurs.

Within a few days of shaking, one in five babies die. Those who survive often have severe, and permanent brain damage. This damage can cause paralysis, seizures, cerebral palsy, hearing loss, speech difficulties, and mental disabilities. Damage to the retina of the eye is one of the most common injuries. This can cause blindness or vision problems. Even in the mildest SBS cases, irritability, lethargy, tremors, vomiting, and learning and behavioral disorders can occur.

No one knows how much force creates SBS or how many instances of shaking can happen before damage occurs. For these reasons, doctors and parenting experts strongly caution parents to never shake their babies. Many tell parents to never play roughly with their infants because rough play might lead to an accidental brain injury.

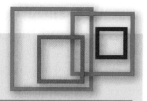

Ways to Cope with Crying

- Make sure the baby's needs are met (the baby in not hungry, thirsty, wet, dirty, cold, hot, ill, or in pain).
- Offer a pacifier, toy, or other distraction.
- Rock the baby gently or walk with the baby in your arms or an infant carrier.
- Take the baby for a walk or a car ride.
- Play soft music, sing, or speak soft and comforting words to the baby.
- Ask someone to relieve you for a few minutes or hours.
- Take time to relax if you are tense. Don't hold the baby until you can relieve tension. The baby will sense the tension in your body and cry harder.
- Put the baby in bed for a few minutes, go to another room, and take a short break if all else fails. Relax. Continue to check on the baby every few minutes.
- Call a trusted friend or a crisis hot line to talk about your frustration.
- Remember an infant's crying is not a sign of bad parenting. Crying is the only way babies can communicate.

19-9 Every year babies die from Shaken Baby Syndrome. Parents must find nonabusive ways to deal with their frustration when their babies won't stop crying.

Sexual Abuse

Sexual abuse as it relates to children means having a child engage in or witness sexual activities. By law, children cannot consent to sexual activities. Sexual offenders include not only adults but also juveniles who are five or more years older than the victim or who have power or control over the victim. "Sex offender" is another name for a person who sexually abuses. *Pedophiles* are adult sex offenders who prefer sexual activity with children rather than with other adults.

About one-third of all sex offenders are relatives of the victim. **Incest** refers to sexual activity between people who are closely related. Incest is forbidden by law. It occurs most often between fathers and daughters. Other relative offenders are often uncles, male first cousins, and grandfathers. Incest often begins when a child is very young. The child regards the acts as a sign of affection. He or she does not know that what is happening is wrong. When incest leads to greater sexual involvement, the child may become confused. The majority of sexual abusers are acquaintances of the child, such as family friends, neighbors, child care and school staff members, coaches, youth leaders, music and dance teachers, and even religious leaders. The remaining offenders are strangers.

In most cases, sex offenders are male. The majority of these men are under age 35. Teens commit about 40 percent of sexual abuse against children under age 12. Many sex offenders were abused as children. They are also likely to abuse alcohol and display other forms of violence.

Both girls and boys are victims of sexual abuse. About one in three girls and one in seven boys under age 18 experience this form of abuse. Children are most vulnerable to sexual abuse between ages 7 and 13. About 75 percent of these children experience abuse multiple times, and often over years.

Like other forms of abuse, the effects of sexual abuse can be devastating to children. Signs that children are experiencing abuse include unusual sexual knowledge or behavior for their age, trouble walking or sitting, pregnancy, or symptoms of sexually transmitted disease. These children may also display fear, aggressive behavior, and poor self-esteem. Many have nightmares. Some attempt suicide or run away from home to escape the abuse.

The effects can differ in their severity depending on the abuser, the frequency and duration of the abuse, and the type of sexual activity. Whether children have maternal support when they report the abuse also contributes to long-term effects. For example, children expect their parents to love and protect them. If incest occurs between a father and a daughter over many years and the mother blames the daughter or refuses to protect her, the effects on the daughter are severe.

Emotional Abuse

Emotional abuse is the use of words to reject, belittle, threaten, or exert control over a child or other person. This may include humiliation, name-calling, and other belittling remarks. These remarks are intentional and hurt the victim's self-esteem. Children who suffer emotional abuse may display aggressive or withdrawn behaviors. Many times, however, abusers do not use hurtful words in front of potential witnesses. Often this form of abuse overlaps other abusive actions. For example, name-calling may occur during physical abuse. Even when this is the only form of abuse, the mental-health scars often last a lifetime.

Why do some people emotionally abuse children? In many cases, such people find childrearing a burden. They lack knowledge about how children grow and develop. Because of this, they also lack knowledge in how to guide and discipline children appropriately.

Protecting Children from Abuse

As you know, violence is prevalent in current society. Children and teens not only see violence in movies, television programs, and computer games, but also see it in their families, child care programs, schools, and neighborhoods. Sadly, they also are the victims of these violent acts.

Children and teens experience family abuse and nonfamily assaults. Because this violence mainly involves family members and others close to the family, children experience intense trauma. Neglect and abuse of children is a growing public-health concern.

To protect children and teens and stop abusers, caring people must do three things. First, they must know the overall risk factors for becoming an abuser. Second, they must know specific ways to protect children and teens. Third, they must insist that victims and offenders receive the treatment they need.

Knowing the Risk Factors

You may wonder how to spot a child abuser. You cannot distinguish a child abuser from other people. You may ask what kind of people abuse children. The answers are not simple. Reports of child abuse cross all economic, social, and ethnic boundaries. Most child abusers are ordinary adults caught up in situations they do not know how to handle. Because of this, the person most likely to abuse a child is his or her own parent. Others are substitute caregivers who abuse children in their care, and more rarely, strangers.

Some abusers prey on children and teens to satisfy their own desires. These are mainly sexual abusers. Some see children as easy to lure, and others are pedophiles. Why would a person abuse a child? Some common factors are explained here.

Lack of Knowledge of Child Development or Parenting. Some parents and a few caregivers do not know what they can realistically expect of children. They may feel a child is purposely misbehaving, when in fact the child is acting appropriately for his or her development. For example, suppose a toddler has a toileting accident. People who understand child development do not expect children to master toilet learning before age 3. This parent would be understanding and comfort the child, 19-10. A parent without this knowledge

19-10 Parents who understand child development have appropriate expectations for their children.

is likely to be angry at the accident. Parents who do not understand the developmental stages and needs of their children cannot feel empathy. They can only feel frustration.

Stress. Parental stress is another risk factor for child abuse. In families where the stress level is high, abuse is much more common. These parents may love their children, but in times of stress, respond abusively to them. Parents may have family problems, financial stresses, or addictions to alcohol or drugs. In addition, stay-at-home parents may feel isolation from other adults. They begin to feel trapped, unable to get away. The day-to-day pressures of parenting may build up and lead to abusive behavior. Caregivers and teachers working long hours and coping with too many children and other problems sometimes vent their frustrations through an abusive act.

Experiencing Abuse as a Child or Teen. For many parents who abuse their children, abuse is a learned behavior. They repeat abusive behaviors their own parents used. They grew up with abuse. Parents who were abused as children think their actions are appropriate parenting techniques. They may not know their behavior is wrong. Abusive parents often do not know more acceptable parenting behaviors.

Depression and Mental-Health Problems. Some parents and other abusers have mental-health problems that result in abuse.

Feeling Helpless. Sometimes a nonabuser will not attempt to stop his or her partner or another member of the family. He or she may fear the abuser. Often, he or she is being abused, too. A parent may know that speaking out about the abuse will break up his or her family. A parent may also doubt his or her ability to provide financially for the children alone.

No risk factors are reasons to excuse abusers. The reasons simply explain possible factors behind the actions. More needs to be learned about risk factors in terms of the culture, the family system, and individual traits.

Protecting Children, Stopping Abusers

Children and teens need the protection of caring, healthy adults. The following suggestions help minimize the likelihood of child and teen abuse:

- *Learn how to be a loving and caring parent.* By reading books, taking child development and parenting classes, and caring for other people's children, you can gain insight into your possible future role as a parent, 19-11. Also, understanding child development makes you less likely to have unrealistic expectations of children.

- *Work to prevent cultural violence.* Violence against others is "contagious." When less violence appears in the media and community, there are fewer incidents of all forms of family violence, including child abuse.

- *Check out all people who care for or work with children and teens.* Parents should get references and screen any babysitter. From time to time, they should make "surprise" checks on their children under a babysitter's care. Parents should

19-11 Taking child development and parenting classes can help people understand child development and may even prevent some instances of child abuse.

use only licensed or accredited child care that welcomes parents to check in unannounced. Parents should insist that child care workers, teachers, or coaches have yearly criminal background checks.

- *Check the community's registry of sex offenders.* Parents should caution their child to stay away from these houses and not to talk with people who live there. Parents must realize that others in the neighborhood who are not on the list may be offenders, too.

- *Teach children safety measures.* Many parents, who teach equipment, pet, and car safety, fail to teach abuse prevention. Figure 19-12 gives some basic safety concepts. Some communities have programs that help children learn these lessons. Police departments, schools, and various agencies, such as children's protective services, escape centers, family outreach centers, and *Parents Anonymous,* educate parents and/or children.

- *Watch friendships.* Parents should observe their children's friendships involving people four or more years older. Danger signals include the older friend's excessive attention, gift giving, and lack of friends his or her own age.

Teaching Children Safety Concepts

Advice for Younger Children
- Say "no" to anyone who tells you to do something that doesn't seem right.
- Reveal secrets to a trusted adult about frightening or hurtful experiences.
- Keep your body safe by covering private parts—the parts hidden by a swimsuit—except when bathing or during a doctor's exam. Report anyone who shows pictures of private parts or uncovers private body areas.
- Never follow someone away from the place where your parents told you to be.
- Look for a family member or store employee if separated from a parent in a store or other place.

Advice for Older Children and Teens
- Stay with friends when traveling, playing, or waiting for a school bus or other transportation.
- Get parental permission before going anywhere without parents.
- Follow parental rules when staying home alone.
- Stay away from alcohol or drug use and known users.
- Follow dating rules and remember parental advice on how to prevent violence and date rape.
- Use the Internet wisely to avoid the attention of sexual abusers. Never provide personal information or meet a stranger alone. If an Internet "friend" mentions sex or shows pornography, report this to a parent and call the police.

19-12 Parents should reinforce safety advice so their children will not become victims of abuse.

- *Supervise children's use of technology.* Protecting children from Internet pedophiles or pornographers is a parenting challenge. Parents should learn how to check for safe sites and supervise their children online.

- *Supervise children responsibly.* Parents must supervise their children at all times. For example, parents should stay with their child during special lessons, sport's practices and competitions, and school or club activities. Parents should make sure their children or teens never go inside any home that does not have parent approval.

Reporting Child Neglect and Abuse

Any person who knows about or observes child neglect or abuse should report it. Every state has laws that require certain persons to report suspected cases of child abuse. These persons are called *mandated reporters*. In every state, physicians are legally bound to report child abuse to the authorities. Other groups of mandated reporters vary from state to state. Teachers, nurses, and counselors are often mandated reporters. Although the law only requires certain persons to report suspected cases of child abuse, any citizen may file a report. A person who reports a suspected case of child abuse in good faith receives immunity from civil and criminal liability.

A person who suspects child neglect or abuse can call the Child Help Hotline (800-4-A-CHILD). Hotline staff members refer the reporter to local authorities. Each state has an agency that receives and investigates reports of suspected child abuse. In addition, many states maintain a central registry of known and suspected child neglect or abuse cases. In these states, any new report is cross-checked against the central registry for previous incidents. Reporter's names are always kept confidential.

Reporting suspected cases of child neglect and abuse is a step in the right direction, but reports alone will not end abuse. If children, families, and society are to benefit, supportive programs are needed. People must educate themselves about

child abuse. Abusers need rehabilitation programs to help them choose new and healthier behaviors. Abusers can attend these programs voluntarily or by court order. Potential abusers need to know programs exist for the prevention of child abuse.

Responding to Abused Children

Although parents may try hard to protect their child from abuse, some children experience abuse. To a great extent, how parents respond makes a difference in how the child is affected. Parents or other adults should respond to claims of abuse in the following ways:

- Let the child tell his or her story. Listen carefully. Do not assume anything.

- Be very calm. If parents react with anger or fear, the child will be more fearful or confused.

- Believe the child's story. Parents should tell the child they are glad he or she told about the abuse. Explain to the child he or she is not to blame for what happened, 19-13.

- Confirm the child's feelings and assure him or her that these feelings are all right.

- Tell the child what actions will be taken to keep him or her safe and get him or her some help.

The impact on a child is worse when a close family member is the abuser. The child finds it difficult to trust again. Some parents find it difficult to support their children, especially if they experienced abuse themselves. They may have blocked the abuse from their thinking, and may want to deny their child's claim of abuse because it churns up painful memories. Other parents may find support of their child difficult because of their love for the abuser. In time, many parents resolve these issues. Fortunately, many spouses of child abusers do speak out and take their children out of abusive situations.

19-13 Parents should listen calmly to their child when he or she tells about an incident of abuse.

Peer Violence

Peer violence is violence directed at a person by someone in the same peer group. Peer violence has become a major public-safety concern because this violence is escalating and increasingly deadly. Peer violence among children and teens is a major concern of parents and the entire community.

Peer violence includes bullying, gang violence, and school violence. These forms of violence are interrelated. For example, a bully could enter a gang, or his or her victim might become violent at school.

Bullying

Bullying occurs when one or more people inflict physical, verbal, or emotional abuse on another person. *Physical bullying* means attacking a person in a physical way, such as hitting. *Verbal bullying* means name-calling or threatening. *Emotional bullying*

means spreading rumors. **Cyberbullying** involves verbal and emotional bullying through online e-mail or chat rooms. In cyberbullying, the bully hides under the cover of a screen name but can be caught. Bullying often involves "bystanders" who laugh and taunt the victim and thus are bullies, too.

Bullying involves an imbalance of power. The more powerful person or group attacks the less powerful one, such as those who are younger, smaller, or more fearful. Bullying occurs repeatedly over time. In general, bullying becomes more severe as the bully watches his or her victim's reactions, 19-14.

Bullying begins as early as kindergarten. Patterns of aggression start to become stable by age 8. Bullying peaks in grades 6 to 8, but persists into high school. About 25 percent of students admit to being a bully. Over three-fourths of all students have been victims of bullies. About 14 percent of victims call their bullying experience *severe*.

Bullies and their victims have behavioral problems that require counseling help. Bullies often have difficulty making friends. Many have academic problems, abuse substances, or are angry and depressed. Victims of bullies often have few friends and are easily

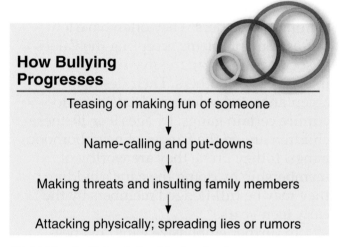

How Bullying Progresses

Teasing or making fun of someone

↓

Name-calling and put-downs

↓

Making threats and insulting family members

↓

Attacking physically; spreading lies or rumors

19-14 The bully's violent behavior becomes more hurtful with time.

intimidated. Many have low self-esteem. Without counseling, the problems worsen for bullies and their victims. Bullying can lead to homicides and suicides.

Gang Violence

Gangs are groups of bullies who seek to inflict power through physical means. They set up territorial restrictions and codes often identified by graffiti. They often wear identifiable clothing to designate membership in a certain gang. Violence is the mainstay of the gang culture.

Why do older children and teens join gangs? As you read earlier, bonds to parents and teachers weaken in school-age children. Around age 9 or 10, they begin spending more time with peers. This further weakens the bonds to adults. This is normal development and a needed step toward becoming an independent person. Some groups of children form positive networks and even join adult-sponsored youth groups, such as Scouts or 4-H. Others join negative networks, or gangs, which engage in violence and illegal activities. Both positive and negative networks channel the behaviors of members toward their group goals.

The lure of gangs is powerful for older children and teens who are almost totally disconnected from parents, teachers, and community leaders. They often have low self-esteem, problems accepting the values of society, and an aggressive response in dealing with others. Their desire for acceptance and belonging leads them to admire certain gangs. By ages 9 or 10, these children are on the fringes of neighborhood gangs. If they prove they are worthy of membership by doing the gang's bidding, they may be full-fledged members by the early teen years.

To further emphasize gang "oneness," gangs often target violence against rival gang members. Violence is also a part of many illegal gang activities. This violence leads to injury and death of gang members and innocent people, too.

School Violence

In recent years, peer violence has tragically spread into school violence. Certain groups of students and school staff members have been targets of this violence, but random people are also victims. School violence occurs at all school levels.

School violence is a very high-profile form of violence because schools are supposed to be safe places. About one-third of parents say they fear for their children's safety at school. Although almost 300,000 students are physically attacked in high schools each year, schools are still safer than most other places. Less than one percent of all homicide deaths among school-age children and teens are violent deaths at school.

Because one death is too many, experts are studying the causes of school violence. Teens say that revenge is the main reason for school shootings. Because these children and teens have been bullied, they kill to get back at those who hurt them. Teens also report that violent students often suffer abuse at home or witness violence in their homes. Experts agree that almost every teen goes to school with a peer troubled enough to kill. Those wanting to kill will get access to weapons, and some will get them past security. Many school tragedies are averted, however, due to students who listen to their peer's threats, take them seriously, and report them to adults.

Protecting Children and Teens from Violence

Anyone can be a victim of violence. Parents and other adults can help prevent children from being victims. Adults can

- communicate openly about all forms of peer violence.

- know what their children are doing, where they are, and who their friends are.
- listen to their children's feelings and concerns about themselves and peers.
- be aware of signs (changes in behavior) that may indicate their children are victims of peer aggression, 19-15.
- tell their children what to do when confronted with a bully or gang (such as do not fight back or be assertive by saying, "Stop it now—I don't want to fight you.")

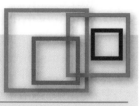

Signs of Peer Violence

Parents should watch for signs their children are possible victims of peer violence.

Victims of bullying or gangs usually...
- act moody, sullen, or quiet; or withdraw from family interaction.
- become depressed.
- lack self-esteem.
- lose interest in schoolwork and activities (grades usually drop).
- become loners; possibly shy away from friends.
- experience change in normal appetite.
- wait to use the restroom until they arrive home.
- arrive home with torn clothes and unexplained bruises.
- display anxiety about going to school, taking school trips, or participating in extracurricular activities.
- ask for extra money for school lunch or supplies, and extra allowance.
- refuse to go to school.
- avoid going to certain areas in school and in town.
- have trouble sleeping.
- begin to carry self-protection weapons, such as a pocketknife.

19-15 These signs may indicate to parents their child is a victim of peer violence.

- insist their children stay away from areas frequented by gangs.
- keep their children from wearing clothing items that resemble known gang symbols or colors.
- have children avoid clothing or jewelry items that attract attention.

In many communities, parents and children are creating youth forums to rid their communities of gang activity. Schools and communities are establishing clear, strict codes of behavior that prohibit bullying and gang activity. They are developing programs to educate teachers, parents, and community leaders about managing behavior. Communities are taking a stand and sending the message to gangs and bullies that they will not tolerate peer violence.

Missing Children

One of the worst fears parents have is their child will disappear. Often parents and others who hear these words have mental images of the high-profile cases of abductions. Although these cases have made everyone more aware of the problem, these cases are only one piece of a much larger picture.

The term *missing children* is not easy to define. For example, a child might be abducted or unlawfully taken. The abducted child may or may not be "missing." For example, the child is not "missing" if the caretaker knows who has the child and where the child is. "Missing" does not apply to an abducted child or teen who escapes or is released relatively soon. If a child's body is found before a parent files a missing person report, the child is not considered missing.

Caretaker missing is the term that experts use to refer to a case in which a caretaker does not know the whereabouts of a child or teen. With caretaker missing, the parent or caretaker is alarmed for at least one hour and makes an attempt to find the child or teen. *Reported missing* is the term experts use for a case in which parents or caretakers report a missing child or teen to law enforcement agents.

Abducted Children and Teens

An abduction of a child or teen can be a family or nonfamily abduction. There are many more family than nonfamily abductions each year. For the most part, the cases are very different.

Family Abductions

Legally, a *family abduction* is the taking or keeping of a child by a family member in violation of a court custody order. This type of abduction involves hiding, fleeing, or the attempting to remove the child from the lawful caregiver. For a teen age 15 or older, there has to be threat or force used, except in cases in which the teen has a mental disability. Over 200,000 children and teens are victims of family abductions. In a little over half of the abductions, children are listed as caretaker missing. About 57,000 cases are listed as reported missing.

The main goal of family abductions is to regain custody of a child. The primary abductors are birth fathers, birth mothers, and grandparents. Most cases of abduction involve children under age 6. Equal numbers of boys and girls are abducted. Most abducted children live in single-parent homes. Others live with one parent and the parent's partner, or they live with relatives or in foster homes.

Nonfamily Abductions

Nonfamily abductions include all abductions by nonfamily members, including friends, acquaintances, and strangers. Stereotypical kidnappings are part of this group of abductions. The U.S. Department of Justice defines these as "abductions by a stranger or slight acquaintance and involving a child who was transported 50 or more miles, detained overnight, held for ransom or with the intent to keep the child permanently, or killed." About 58,000 children and teens are victims of nonfamily abductions, including 115 stereotypical kidnappings. High-profile stereotypical kidnappings make up a very small percentage of nonfamily abductions.

Unlike family abductions, a large percentage of nonfamily abductions and stereotypical kidnappings involve victims 12 years and older. A few cases involve young children. Two-thirds or more of these cases involve girls. The abductors often use force with weapons. Sexual assault and robbery are often motives for these abductions.

Parents often think that most nonfamily abductors involve strangers; this is not true. In most nonfamily abduction cases, the child knows the abductor. Abductors may be a family friend, a neighbor, a person in authority, or a babysitter. Strangers are the perpetrators in about one-third of all nonfamily abductions.

Most of these children and teens are taken from public places, such as the street, parks, wooded areas, or other public areas, 19-16. Family abductions most frequently occur in a home or yard. Many of the victims of nonfamily abductions are kept in isolated locations.

Protecting Children from Abductions

Parents and other caregivers must be alert to the dangers of abduction. They should do what they can to prevent their children from being abducted. The following tips are important:

- Fingerprint your child. Keep a copy of the prints on hand for identification purposes.

- Know your child's current height and weight. Keep a record of any distinguishing marks. Take a color photo

19-16 To prevent nonfamily abductions, parents should carefully watch their children on the street and in parks and other public places.

four times a year for younger children, twice a year for school-age children, and three or four times a year for teens.

- Choose babysitters with good references. Enroll children in licensed child care programs.
- Check sex-offender registries for neighborhood sex offenders.
- Watch for any signs of discomfort in your child or sudden changes in behavior. Encourage your child to talk as much as he or she will.

Parents also need to work with community leaders on public awareness about abductions. This includes developing educational programs for children, teens, and parents. It also means fighting for aggressive prosecution of abductors.

Runaway Children and Teens

Runaways are children under age 18 who have left the homes of their parents or legal guardians without permission. No one often knows the whereabouts of these children. This group includes "throwaway" children. These youths leave because they are abandoned, asked to leave, or subjected to severe neglect or abuse. Many of these children have been in foster care and returned to birthparents who are still unable to provide a secure and loving home life.

Statistics on runaways are not clear because in some cases neither parents nor police know whether the youth has been abducted or is a runaway. Also, runaway youth, especially throwaways, are not always reported missing. The National Runaway Switchboard estimates there are between 1.3 and 2.8 million runaways who live on the streets or in shelters. One out of seven children will run away at least once. Over three-fourths of runaways are situational runaways who run away after a disagreement with their parents and return home in a few days. Some youth, however, are chronic runaways. They repeat running away, go further each time, and remain away longer. Eventually most chronic runaways do not return home.

Why Do Youth Run Away?

Reasons for running away may vary. In most families, teens feel unhappy at times and parents are sometimes disappointed. These teens are often situational runaways.

In most cases, chronic runaways come from more troubled backgrounds than do other children. The primary causes include parental neglect or abuse or family violence. For example, 87 percent of girls who run away experience sexual abuse before age 10. Other youth simply have serious conflicts with their parents due to a change in family, such as a divorce or remarriage, or due to the teen's high-risk behaviors. Still other youth have severe school and peer problems.

Youth who run away believe this is the most acceptable way to solve their problems. They are looking for a "way out" instead of a way to cope with their problems.

Risks for Runaways

Runaways soon find their actions create many other problems. This is especially true for those who do not return home within a week and who are homeless. They often do not find the independence they seek. Some risks that runaways face include

- malnutrition
- prostitution and pornography (about 70 percent engage in prostitution in order to meet their daily needs)
- sexual and physical assault
- medical problems, such as STIs and unwanted pregnancies
- substance abuse problems
- becoming a school dropout
- becoming a victim of theft or stealing for daily survival
- unsafe housing

Effects of Runaways on Parents

The families of runaways live in constant fear. They have no way of knowing what happened to their children. Reports of other runaways who have been molested or killed add to their fears. Parents feel so helpless. They should not give up hope. Instead they should work closely with the police and other organizations in looking for their children.

Parents often feel they are failures as parents. Out of guilt, they blame themselves, the other parent, the teen, or others. The home situation often worsens. If parents get professional help for home conflicts and other problems, they will be better able to provide the support their child needs if he or she returns home.

Runaway Prevention and Reconciliation

Children and teens often make the decision to run away over a period of weeks. In most cases, children and teens show signs they are thinking about or preparing to run away. For example, potential runaways often have changes in eating or sleeping patterns. They may isolate themselves from friends and have conflicts at home and school. Some threaten to run away, and often keep their belongings in a packed bag or backpack in a closet. Some may join cults or remove money from their savings accounts.

If parents notice a number of these signs, they should confront the child with their suspicions. If parents confront the child out of concern, rather than out of fear or anger, the child may decide to stay home for a while. It is important for parents to actively listen to their child's views. Counseling for the child and the family may help. Teen runaways who return home and go back to school have a good chance of preparing to live on their own as adults.

Several local and national agencies are available to help runaways, 19-17. Runaways and their families can find these agencies in telephone directories. They include *Covenant House*, *"Home Free" Bus Service*, *National Runaway Switchboard*, and the *National Youth Crisis Hotline*.

19-17 Teens who run away from home can call a toll-free hot line to ask for help with returning home.

Many runaways return home. How should parents reconcile or restore good feelings with their runaway child or teen? They should welcome the child with love. After meeting the child's basic needs, the family should address the root causes of the problem. The worst actions parents can take are to bribe the child to stay or threaten and punish the child. Children who suffer from neglect or abuse in their own families should receive help through social-service agencies rather than return home.

Suicide

Dealing with the death of a loved one can be overwhelming for any family. However, when a family member voluntarily or intentionally takes his or her own life, committing suicide, the effects on children and families can be even more devastating. According to the Centers for Disease Control, suicide is the eleventh leading cause of death for all ages in the United States. It is the second leading cause of death for people ages 25 to 34, and the third leading cause of death for youth ages 15 to 24. The number of children and teens affected by the loss of a parent or sibling to suicide is not known. Experts believe at least 30 to 50 percent of suicidal deaths affect at least one child or teen.

Suicide: A Complex Problem

Experts have long sought answers to this question: Why do people take their own lives? The factors seem to vary and include current stress or long-term problems, such as childhood abuse, chronic pain, or a physical disability. The most common symptom of suicide is depression. Other mental illnesses and severe personality problems are also involved. These various factors are true for children, teens, or adults who take their own lives.

When a person takes his or her life, the person leaves behind the family and friends who love him or her. The suicide of a friend or family member is a crisis, 19-18. It is a sudden and unexpected event that requires huge adjustments by those involved.

Family members have many "if only" thoughts. Although there are some common signals that indicate a possible suicide, these signals may be quite subtle and indirect. Even experts on suicide find such deaths difficult to predict. Criticizing what was or was not done after a death may be easy but not always helpful. Survivors should not blame themselves or each other for the victim's death. Even when someone specific is blamed in a suicide note, survivors must remember someone with severe mental and emotional problems wrote the note.

Anger is another common reaction of survivors. Survivors often feel anger due to underlying feelings of being deserted or rejected by the suicide victim. Survivors should remember the victim probably felt isolated and hopeless. Thus, the victim's

19-18 When a friend or family member dies of suicide, it can be hard to understand. Feelings of sadness, grief, and anger are common but will fade in time.

intense emotional pain likely clouded any rational judgment about how his or her survivors would feel.

Teen Suicide

Suicide also occurs in the teen years. Thinking about suicide occurs in almost half of teen girls and one-fourth of teen boys. Although a small percentage of teens actually attempt suicide, the rate of teen suicides has tripled in the last 30 years. Just like violence toward others, suicide is a teen epidemic.

A teen's movement toward suicide often follows four stages. First, there is a long history of problems beginning in early childhood. Second, as children progress to the teen years, problems escalate beyond the normal stress of adolescence. By the third stage, teens show more failure to cope with both old and new problems. They may have more social isolation. In the last stage, teens cut off ties in all meaningful relationships. Because these stages occur over many years, thinking about suicide has many warning signs, 19-19.

Preventing Suicide

What can parents and other caring people do to prevent suicides? Children who have problems in early childhood need professional mental-health care. Parents

Warning Signs of Suicidal Thinking

Warning Sign	Symptoms
Severe home problems	• Receives excessive criticism and little positive feedback; has little parental affection
	• Feels too much pressure to be successful and to set a good example
	• Is a victim of abuse
	• Has family members with mental-health problems
Overwhelming, stressful life events	• Experiences losses, such as death of a parent, breakup with a boyfriend or girlfriend
	• Feels pressure to achieve in school; has school problems
	• Develops health problems
	• Has peer pressure to engage in behaviors that conflict with home values
Depression	• Feels empty and lonely; has low self-esteem
	• Lacks concentration on schoolwork
	• Engages in deliberate acts of self-injury, such as burning or cutting the body
	• Abuses substances; often drinks heavily alone
Display of specific symptoms before an attempt	• Sends a verbal message of suicidal thoughts to others
	• Changes sleeping and eating habits; neglects appearance; quits trying to achieve in school
	• Gives away prized possessions and breaks off social relations
	• Complains about nonexistent physical problems
	• Believes life will never get better; wants to do something to relieve psychological pain
	• Knows someone who has committed suicide

19-19 Often teens cry for help through their many warning signs. Parents and peers need to be alert to this growing problem and know ways to get help for these teens.

need to seek immediate help if teens show warning signs. Because depression is a common symptom of suicidal tendencies, children teens may be prescribed drugs for this condition. Parents should carefully watch how their children respond to any antidepressant drug and report their concerns to the doctor.

If a teen or other family member exhibits signs of suicide, friends and family members should encourage the person to talk about his or her feelings. Knowing that others care may make the person feel life is less hopeless. Friends and family members should also seek intervention with medical professionals and counselors. With counseling, a person has the best chance possible to break away from self-destruction thinking.

Across the country, private and group-counseling services can help people cope with suicidal thoughts. These services are often listed in phone and Internet directories under *Crisis Hot Line, Crisis Intervention, Suicide,* or *Suicide Prevention.* In an emergency, friends and family members can call the police or the emergency room of a local hospital.

The Needs of Survivors

All survivors must work through these negative feelings and resolve the grief of losing a loved one. Adults are working to deal with their own grief. Sadly, children's and teen's feelings are often forgotten by bereaving adult family members.

Parents and caregivers should not forget children and teen survivors. Studies show the loss of important people, especially a parent, a sibling, or a friend during one's childhood or teen years, may make the survivor more prone to depression and other mental-health problems. More than half of children ages 6 to 12 are grieving the suicidal death of a close family member who suffered significant problems. Compared with children who lost parents to cancer, children whose parents died of suicide suffer even more emotional and behavioral problems. The greatest trauma occurred for children who witnessed the family member's suicide or found the deceased. Emotional reactions include profound sadness, anxiety, guilt, shame, and lack of pleasure in daily activities. Thinking about suicide is also common.

Family members need to help each other. Some ways they can help include

- knowing how children grieve
- finding the right words and talking about the death
- talking about the good and bad times shared with the deceased
- getting involved with support groups and seeking professional help, 19-20

In time, family members learn to come to terms with the suicide of one they love. They must work through their grief and resume living their own lives.

19-20 Children and teens greatly benefit from talking to their family members. This can make them feel loved and secure.

Summing It Up

- A dysfunctional family is one that cannot function properly due to overwhelming problems.

- Unemployment is a major cause of a financial crisis in a family. Often families can adjust to short-term unemployment and manage until the unemployed parent is working again.

- Homelessness has developmental risks for children.

- Substance abuse has devastating consequences for the family system.

- Partner abuse endangers the spouse and the children. The effects of family violence on children may last a lifetime and make them much more apt to be neglected or abused as a child and to become an abuser as an adult.

- Children and teens suffer both physical and mental health insults as a result of child neglect and abuse. Most child abusers are ordinary adults and parents caught up in situations they do not know how to handle.

- Parents play an important role in protecting their children from peer violence, such as bullying, gang membership, and school violence.

- Parents and caregivers must be alert and do what they can to prevent family and nonfamily abductions. They must also help older children and teens realize running away is not an option to solving their problems.

- Children and teens bereaved by the suicide of a parent, a sibling, or a friend need special support.

Recalling the Facts

1. Contrast the ways healthy families and dysfunctional families respond to a crisis.

2. List effects of unemployment on family members.

3. List five developmental risks for homeless children.

4. How does substance abuse devastate the whole family?

5. Briefly describe each phase of the cycle of partner violence.

6. What effects can partner abuse have upon children who live with it?

7. Contrast child neglect and child abuse.

8. List three forms of child abuse.

9. List four possible effects of *Shaken Baby Syndrome* (SBS).

10. Name three risk factors associated with child abuse.

11. List four ways parents can help prevent their children from becoming victims of peer violence.

12. What is the difference between *caretaker missing* and *reported missing* in cases of missing children?

13. What is the main misconception about nonfamily abductions?

14. List three tips parents can use to prevent their children from being abducted.

15. What risks do runaways face?

16. What are three ways surviving family members can help each other after the suicide of a loved one?

Applying New Skills

1. **Role play.** Working in a small group, choose one of the crises described in this chapter. Create one role-play in which a dysfunctional family tries to cope with the chosen crisis. Create a second role-play in which the family successfully copes. Show the family researching and using community resources.

2. **Public service announcement.** Create a public service announcement for radio or television warning parents about the dangers of shaking a baby. Give tips to help parents cope with an infant's crying.

3. **Research.** Research laws in your state about mandated reporters of child abuse. Who does the law require to report suspected cases of child abuse? How do they make such a report? Share your findings with the class.

Thinking Critically

1. Debate the following: What should the punishment be for causing SBS? Should child care providers suffer stiffer penalties than parents and relatives?

2. Analyze the skills parents need to deal with each of the crises discussed in this chapter. How are the skills similar and different?

3. Draw conclusions about steps students in your high school can take to prevent peer violence.

4. Analyze resources available in your community to help families experiencing various crises. What are the best ways to access these resources?

Linking Academics

1. **Writing.** Write a paragraph explaining what a person could do if a friend or a family member were ever a victim of partner abuse.

2. **Social studies.** Investigate opportunities for volunteering at a family shelter, crisis hot line, or other local agency that assists families and children in times of need. Find out ways that you can help others and take action on at least one opportunity. Share your experience with the class.

3. **Technology.** Research ways that parents can use various forms of technology to protect their children from harm. Make a list of recommendations you think are the best options. Share your findings with the class.

Chapter 20

Objectives

After studying this chapter, you will be able to

- explain criteria families use in deciding whether to use child care.

- analyze the different types of child care, including factors to consider when selecting child care and the advantages and disadvantages of each type.

- identify ways that parents can recognize quality standards of child care programs and ways they should monitor their child's care.

- identify child care concerns of parents.

- summarize suggestions for managing the child care experience.

Child Care Options

Key Terms

in-home care

babysitting

nanny

au pair

play groups

not-for-profit centers

for-profit centers

cooperative child care

Child care resource and referral agencies (CCR&Rs)

developmentally appropriate practice (DAP)

registration

licensing

accreditation

quality rating systems (QRSs)

During the first few years of life, children need constant supervision and care. Infants are helpless—they depend on adults to meet all their needs. Toddlers need guidance, discipline, and support as they learn to perform life skills and interact with others. Preschoolers can meet more of their own needs. However, they still are not mature enough to provide total care for themselves. School-age children attend school during the day, but they need supervision and care when they are not in school.

Parents are responsible for making sure their children receive the care they need. In fact, many experts believe the ideal care for a young child is provided in the home by a loving and caring parent. These experts recommend having one parent be the child's primary caregiver for at least the first three years of life. They say the other parent should also be closely involved in the child's care. Other family members and friends can help by caring for the child occasionally to give the parents some time to themselves. This is the type of care most parents would like to provide for their children, 20-1.

Not all parents can care for their young children 24 hours a day, however. Many parents must work outside the home. If this is the case, parents must make alternate arrangements for the child's care when they work. Care that is provided by a caregiver other than parents is called *child care*. This type of care has become increasingly common as more parents enter the workforce.

Decisions About Child Care

As you read early in this text, couples should discuss their attitudes about child care when they discuss family-planning issues. Ideally, couples should talk about this topic before they marry. Both prospective parents should agree on whether they want to use child care. This way, they will discover any differences in opinion before they marry and have children. After a couple marries and once they plan to have a child, they should look realistically at their child care options. Each situation is different.

Pros and Cons of Child Care. Parents need to review their parenting and career goals and investigate alternatives that will help them meet their goals. Choosing an option that is consistent with their values, attitudes, and beliefs helps parents select care that is best for their children and family.

Some recent studies of children in child care have caused concern. For example, one study found that infants who spent more than 20 hours a week in nonparental care were at risk of developing insecure attachments. Another study showed that preschool children who spent more than 30 hours a week in nonparental care were more likely to be aggressive and defiant in kindergarten than their age mates who spent less time in child care. These studies, however, do not prove that being in child care causes behavioral problems. Perhaps some child care programs do not appropriately respond to children's needs. Some parents may not provide a nonstressful home

20-1 Most parents want to stay home with their young children. They would prefer to be the ones to provide the care their children need.

environment during at-home hours. Thus, parents cannot just look at what can happen. They must judge how their child reacts to child care. If their child has behavioral problems, parents must seek causes and solutions.

Availability of Quality Programs. If parents choose child care, the most important factor is the quality of care. Most studies show no major differences between children who receive child care and those who do not. Either option is viable, as long as a child receives the care he or she needs at all times.

Availability of quality care depends on different factors. For example, parents of infants, toddlers, and children with special needs may have more problems in locating quality programs for their children than parents of preschool children without special needs. Generally speaking, larger cities have more program options than rural areas, but quality programs in large cities may be far from a parent's home or place of work. The cost of child care links to quality. Thus, some parents find it difficult or impossible to afford available quality programs. Parents should always search for quality programs. All or some of the costs may be met through other sources of funding for families in financial need.

Determining the Costs. Child care is a major family expense. Families may spend between 10 and 25 percent of their income on child care. When comparing costs, parents need to consider transportation, hours of operation, and program services, such as education and special activities.

Having highly qualified caregivers increases quality, but also increases care costs. This is because labor is the most expensive aspect of child care. In the same way, the increased number of adults needed to care for younger children and those with special needs makes this care more expensive than care for preschool children. The hourly cost of part-time care is often greater than the hourly cost of full-time care.

Some child care programs are more affordable because the government, religious groups, and businesses pick up some of the costs. Parents may receive discounts based on income, enrolling more than one child, and service the parent gives to the program. Parents need to inquire about ways to reduce child care costs.

Types of Child Care

Child care programs can be grouped in many ways. For example, they can be grouped as in-home, family, or center care. They can be grouped as part-time or full-time care. Several types of programs will be described in this section.

Choosing child care requires careful consideration. Parents should keep in mind that no one type is all good or bad. Each type should be evaluated by how well it meets the family's needs. Many families use two or more types of care. For example, a family might use center care for working hours and babysitting for an occasional night out. Another family might use preschool center care for the preschool child and after-school care for the school-age child on a daily basis.

In-Home Care

Many consider the most desirable type of child care to be care given in the child's own home, 20-2. During **in-home care**, the caregiver comes to the home and the children remain in their familiar surroundings. The caregiver can promote the family's values and give the children one-on-one attention. For parents who have jobs with unpredictable schedules, this arrangement may be the best match. Some in-home caregivers may do some household tasks for an additional fee. Parents may also pay extra for caregiver transportation. There are three types of in-home care.

Babysitting. Occasional in-home care, or **babysitting,** is the most common type of in-home care. Most parents, at one time or

20-2 Having a caregiver come to the family's home is convenient for parents and comfortable for the children.

Au Pair Care. An **au pair** is a young person who comes from another country to live with a family to provide child care and do housework for them. The family provides room and board, as well as transportation. Similar to some nannies, they are on-call 24 hours a day but have scheduled days off. An au pair may not have as much education and training as a nanny. He or she may not be fluent in the family's language. If parents plan to employ someone who is not a United States citizen, they should be sure the person has the correct documents needed to work in this country.

Although in-home care has many advantages, there are some disadvantages, too. This type of care is usually expensive for families with one or two children. Parents pay the total cost for this type of care, including transportation, meals, and possibly a room. Because the parents are the employer, they must do a background check before hiring any caregiver. They also are responsible for FICA taxes and may possibly pay for liability insurance. Parents must also plan for back-up child care to cover the caregiver's scheduled time off.

Family Child Care Homes

Another common type of child care includes *family child care homes*. With this type of care, the caregivers provide child care in their homes. It is often available in the child's own neighborhood. In most cases, caregivers own their own businesses. Only a few of these caregivers are associated with businesses, charities, or government agencies that pick up some or the entire child care cost.

Often these caregivers begin their businesses while staying at home with their own children. Those who enjoy taking care of their own children often feel comfortable in caring for a few other children—usually no more than five or six children, including their own, 20-3. Family child care homes closely resemble care in the child's own home

another, hire someone to care for their children in their home. Parents might need this type of care for special events or to have some adult time. Babysitting generally lasts a few hours at most. Parents often have one or more persons they call for this type of child care.

Nanny Care. A **nanny** is a specially trained child care provider who may or may not live in the family's home. Nannies provide child care for the family. When nannies are on-call 24 hours a day, the family pays the nanny a salary and provides him or her with room and board. If nannies travel with the family, their expenses are paid. Nannies, like all employees, have scheduled days off and vacations.

20-3 Parents can learn a lot about a child care situation by making impromptu visits. This way they can see what the situation is really like.

by either a parent or caregiver. Children benefit from having the same care provider for several years, which is very important for infants and toddlers. Because they truly enjoy children, they often continue their businesses after their own children are in school. The cost for this type of child care is often less.

Most of these caregivers follow a flexible daily schedule. They seldom have special equipment and supplies. Activities are, for the most part, more homelike rather than specially planned. In many states, family child care homes are not highly regulated. Some require these homes to have a state license and meet minimum requirements for this type of care. However, these homes do not have routine inspections. Parents are responsible for judging the care their children receive. If parents are uncomfortable with any caregiver actions, they should remove their children from this type of care.

Child Care Centers

Facilities that provide care and education to children on a daily basis away from home are *child care centers*. These centers generally provide full-day care, often from early morning hours to early evening. Some centers provide care 24 hours per day to meet the needs of parents who work varying hours. Quality centers provide learning activities along with meeting children's nutrition, health, and safety needs. Some centers care for infants, toddlers, and preschoolers. Others may limit their care to preschool children. Some offer before- and after-school care for school-age children and drop-in child care.

School-age child care. Many working parents seek before- and after-school child care programs for their children. Schools (both public and private), family day care homes, houses of worship, community centers, and some child care centers offer this type of care for school-age children. School-age child care offers children chances for activities, rest, and snacks. Activities may involve tutoring on school subjects and/or recreational activities. These programs may vary from one community to another. Parents can ask their child's teacher or other parents to recommend an area program.

Drop-In Child Care. Many stores and shopping malls have drop-in child care centers that provide occasional part-time care. This type of care may also be available in community centers, houses of worship, or schools. Drop-in centers are often the first step toward entering children in a full-time child care program.

Play Groups

Parents of small children may organize **play groups** to provide social activities for their children, 20-4. These play groups give parents the chance to exchange part-time child care services without cost. Play groups are generally informal in nature. Although children have chances to interact, parents also have opportunities to socialize and learn from one another.

Play groups must be small in size, not only because of space, but for manageability. Parents who join with one or two other parents in play-group care are often nonworking mothers who need some

20-4 This mother takes her children's play group for an afternoon swim. It's a fun time for the children, and the other mothers get to take a break.

babysitting services. Most groups use a system of tokens or a time-exchange record to make sure the sharing of babysitting services is fair. Play groups are not suitable for working parents.

Child Care Ownership and Sponsorship

There are many types of ownership and sponsorship for child care centers and education programs. For example, **not-for-profit** programs operate as a service to parents and use the profits to run the program. Because they are service oriented, not-for-profit programs are often less expensive. **For-profit** programs operate as a business with owners using the profits as they see fit. Some for-profit centers have private ownership and some have national franchises similar to many fast-food restaurants. Sponsorship is another way to group child care programs. For example, houses of worship or religious-linked organizations, employers, or the government may sponsor child care programs. Within each type, there is also a great deal of variation.

Cooperative Child Care

Groups of parents who want low-cost, high-quality child care often join together to form a cooperative child care center. With **cooperative child care**, parents provide many of the services needed to operate the facility. For example, parents usually hire one preschool teacher. Then the parents take turns assisting the teacher. This gives them an opportunity to be part of their child's care experience and get to know other parents in the community. Because cooperative child care programs do not operate as money-making businesses, the fees for care are low. The success of such programs depends on the services of the parents.

Parents may work at the center one day a week for each child they have in the center. Parents with special skills or talents share them with the children. In most cooperatives, parents handle the business operations of the center. For example, they may set the budget and determine the program goals and policies. Parents may also provide building maintenance at "work parties" or on an assigned basis.

Religious-Linked Child Care

Some parents rely on religious-linked programs or programs run through charity donations, (such as United Way or other private organizations) for child care. Many religious-linked child care programs operate centers on a part-time basis and may only be available to members of the religious group. In other programs, a member of the religious group provides part-time in-home child care for another member family who needs it, 20-5. Programs run by charities or groups such as the YMCA, may also offer full-time child care for children of all ages.

Child care centers with religious or charity links may operate in much the same way as privately owned centers with a hired director and staff. Others may operate more like cooperative child care programs with a hired director and with parents or members of the religious group or charity volunteering services or donating goods. These centers often have a board of advisors composed of several people from the religious-group membership or charity organization. These centers may or may not offer religious teaching as part of their child care services.

Most of these programs have very high standards and have staff members with high qualifications. Their goal is to serve families rather than to make a profit. Fees are often kept low due to volunteer services and supply donations.

Individually Owned Child Care

Individually owned child care centers are as different as the people who own them. Some are simply "play schools" where caregivers are little more than babysitters. Other centers have excellent educational programs run by well-qualified staff members. Good centers have plenty of safe toys and play equipment and a variety of supervised activities.

Individually owned child care centers operate as businesses. Like other businesses, they come in all sizes. Some are small centers with one group of children while others are similar to elementary schools with many groups. Costs vary with the quantity and

20-5 This woman provides child care for children who go to her place of worship. The family knows her, and she shares their religious beliefs.

quality of services offered. For example, programs that provide an educational program in preparation for school are often more expensive than those that offer only the most basic child care. In addition to education, some high-cost centers provide special programs, such as music, gymnastics, dance, and foreign languages for children.

Individually owned centers can have many advantages for children and their parents. For example, every state requires that centers meet certain minimum standards in order to operate. A person from the state licensing bureau regularly checks on these centers to ensure health and safety standards are met. These centers also hire substitute teachers when regular teachers are not working. They may also lower the cost if a family enrolls more than one child.

On the downside, some centers may try to operate without a license. Parents should always check a center's license before enrolling their children. Other centers may not provide infant, toddler, or school-age child care. If they do provide this care, the fees may be higher. Large centers may be overwhelming for timid children, and parents may need other sources of care when their children are sick. When a child is absent from the center, parents are still responsible for paying for the day of care because the center "holds" the child's place.

National Child Care Chains

National child care chains are centers that are *for-profit* businesses. They are like any other chains. Thus, they offer uniformity in child care. Some larger businesses include KinderCare® and Bright Horizons®. The equipment and overall programming are much the same from center to center, 20-6. There are, of course, some differences from one center to the next. Similar to other chains that operate throughout a state, region, or nation, the management studies parent needs and wants for child care and attempts to meet them.

20-6 National child care center chains usually offer well-developed programs, lots of safe play equipment, and trained personnel.

Child care centers that are part of national chains offer many advantages to families with children. These centers are often well-located in communities, operate for extended hours, and have programs for children of all ages. They generally have good, safe equipment for the number of children in their care. They have well-developed programs and highly qualified personnel. Families who move frequently find comfort in the familiarity from center to center within a chain. The fees are often moderate compared to other centers.

As a disadvantage, the uniformity in programming may not meet the needs of all children. The center quality may vary due to the skill of local personnel. Parents pay the entire cost of the children's care.

Government-Sponsored Child Care

State and federal governments also sponsor child care programs. Head Start, Early Head Start, state university laboratory schools, state prekindergarten programs, and programs for government employees receive part of their funding from the government. Some of these programs, such as Head Start, were created to help children from families in financial need. They offer child care, educational activities, meals, health care, and social services. The services are paid for by a combination of government and local monies. For example, funds for Head Start are 80 percent federal and 20 percent local. A few states have preschool programs available for all children.

Government-sponsored programs must comply with the guidelines set up by the funding agency and with the state's licensing agency. Children receive good care, education, and social services in these programs. These programs strongly emphasize parent education and involvement. In some cases, parents can be trained to work in these centers. The main disadvantage is that program quality may vary due to training and staff experience. Some programs do not operate during the summer, leaving children without quality care.

Employer-Sponsored Child Care

Business managers and professional leaders know many of their employees are parents. They understand that these employees are concerned about their children's welfare. As a result, many businesses are taking an active role in child care.

Some businesses and professional groups provide on-site child care for employees' children. As an employer, the United States military has the largest on-site employer-sponsored child care program. Businesses that specialize in children's products or who employ many women, such as hospitals, often have on-site child care centers.

In addition, many colleges and universities have campus child care programs for children of faculty and students. These centers may also offer educational opportunities for university students studying child development. Because the caregivers are university students and teachers, the children receive excellent care and guidance. The children in these centers are exposed to all kinds of educational equipment and techniques. These programs often have long waiting lists because they are quite popular among parents.

The main advantage of on-site child care is that it allows parents to be close at hand if their children need them. Employees are able to spend additional time with their children while traveling to the job site and perhaps during the lunch hour. Fees for employer-sponsored care are generally low. When employers meet family needs, they benefit by retaining employees with more experience.

Not all employers can offer on-site child care. Some offer a "voucher system" instead. In this system, parents receive coupons or vouchers to redeem at whatever child care facility the parent chooses. With the voucher system, the employer pays for a portion of the employee's child care costs.

Other employers offer a "cafeteria style" package of benefits. Employees may choose any of several different kinds of benefits. For example, parents may choose company-paid child care. Adults without children may choose dental insurance. Older employees may prefer a pension plan. The options from which employees choose vary from one employer to another.

Laboratory Schools

Laboratory schools are unique among child care and early education programs. They often are employer-sponsored and receive some government funding for research. These centers are located on college and university campuses that offer studies in child development, parenting, and/or early childhood education. Some laboratory programs enroll children from many backgrounds for research and training, 20-7. Other centers focus on children who "fit" the need of the researcher, such as children who live in poverty. These programs are expensive, may operate only half-days, and often have long waiting lists for enrolling children. Although these centers receive partial government funding, parents often

20-7 Campus child care programs offer educational opportunities for the children who attend, as well as for the university students who work there.

pay high fees for the quality. However, scholarships may be awarded to some families to cover part or all of the parent fees.

Selecting Child Care Options

If parents choose child care for their children, they need to put some time and effort into their selections. People shop long and hard for clothes, furniture, houses, and cars. Because caregivers and the environment greatly influence children's development, it makes sense that parents should put even more effort into choosing care for their children. Parents need to consider both their own needs and their children's needs when selecting care.

Parents who are thinking about child care may want to contact local child-related organizations for information, especially **Child care resource and referral agencies (CCR&Rs)**. CCR&Rs are service agencies that provide information to parents who are looking for any type of child care. These services help parents weigh options as they look for quality care. Parents may also contact city and state licensing agencies, elementary school teachers, friends, neighbors, and coworkers about child care. They need accurate information about the types of child care available in order to make wise decisions.

When selecting child care, parents should have realistic expectations. They should expect good care for their children. They should not expect caregivers to fulfill their roles as parents. For example, parents are responsible for helping their child make the daily transitions between home and child care. Parents are responsible for having back-up care plans when their child is ill. Parents must do their part in communicating with caregivers. They must also meet all parent policies as set up by the child care provider, such as picking up their child on time and paying fees.

As parents study their child care options, they need to consider many factors. Five major factors include the physical setting, program, adult-child ratios and group size, caregiver characteristics, and consistency of care.

The Physical Setting

A desirable child care setting is one with a welcoming, homelike atmosphere. An inviting entryway, gives parents space to interact with their children as they drop them off and pick them up. Because parents or parents and staff members often need to talk, two or three chairs and a coffee table add to the homelike setting. Parenting materials, such as magazines or a bulletin board, can be available in this area, too.

The room design should consider the needs of the children and adults who will spend many hours in it. The decor should be colorful and interesting. Nonglare indoor lighting gives a warm appearance, while light from the outdoors flows into the room through child-height windows. Pleasing sounds, such as a bubbling fish tank or a wind chime, and aromas, such as flowers and foods make the rooms even more appealing.

The rooms should have an overall soft appearance with cushions and pillows, some carpeting, and some toys with a soft texture. Cozy furniture groupings provide comfort in areas for looking at books and less-active play, 20-8. An abundance of toys and books need to be attractive, clean, and in good condition. Caregivers should display them on shelves throughout the room. Low shelves allow children to get toys and books and to return them. Open areas in the rooms provide space for active play. Washable floors and table surfaces are essential for art areas and eating places. Restrooms should be clean and have child-size fixtures.

Because outdoor play is important to children, the outdoor space requires careful planning, too. Outdoor space should be pleasing to all the senses, similar to a well-designed park. The space and equipment must meet safety standards. The design should fit the needs of children. For example, toddlers need places to walk and explore. At the same time, preschool and school-age children need action-oriented space, such as

20-8 Comfortable furnishings and interesting décor help create a welcoming, homelike atmosphere in a child care facility.

places to climb, slide, run, dig, and engage in fantasy play.

The Program

The program refers to what children do during the child care day. No single type of program can meet the needs of all children. Parents must look for the type of program that best fits the needs of their children.

One term parents may commonly hear is *developmentally appropriate practice (DAP)*. **Developmentally appropriate practice (DAP)** involves attempting to make all aspects of a program "a fit" for each child's development. DAP in child care and early education programs should be

- *Age appropriate.* Activities should be provided for all areas of development (physical, intellectual, social, and emotional) and should fit the child's age.

- *Individually appropriate.* Because children are unique, teachers should consider each child's personality, way of learning, and family background when deciding on possible activities.

- *Culturally and socially appropriate.* Teachers should consider how each child's family, ethnicity, neighborhood, and community affect the child.

DAP programs for infants and toddlers follow each child's own developmental agenda. A positive relationship with the caregiver is the most critical aspect of these programs. Three popular DAP programs for preschool children are *High Scope®*, *Reggio Emilia*, and *Montessori*, 20-9. Recently High Scope and Reggio Emilia have expanded their programs to include infants and toddlers.

Adult-Child Ratios and Group Size

Children need personalized care. One adult can provide adequate care for only a few children. State standards may vary slightly in their ratios for the maximum number of children for which one adult can provide care. Generally, one caregiver is needed for every three to four infants. For young toddlers, the common ratio is one caregiver to every four toddlers. For older toddlers, one caregiver may serve five toddlers. One caregiver can provide care for about eight to 10 preschoolers. For mixed-age groups, which happen often in family child care homes, the ratio is calculated based on the age of the youngest child. Thus, if a caregiver provides care for an infant, the maximum number of children would likely be three regardless of the age of the other children.

Group size refers to the number of children cared for in one room. Although there may be slight variations from state to state, group size is determined by square footage per child. For example, some states require 35 square feet of space per child. Most standards set the maximum of two groups in one room. For example, two adults could provide care for six infants in one room. Experts feel each child should have a primary caregiver, so one adult provides the daily care for a group of three children. The other adult provides daily care for the other group of children.

Caregiver Characteristics

Caregivers with excellent training and experience are the keys to good child care. Effective caregivers have many positive traits. Parents should evaluate the characteristics of prospective caregivers. A good caregiver

- transmits positive feelings about himself or herself and the job

- spends most of his or her time interacting with or observing the children

- knows the various stages of child development and helps children realize their potential

DAP Programs

Programs for Infants and Toddlers

Program Features	Program Characteristics
Reinforce home values	• To prevent confusion, teachers and parents work for continuity between home and child care program. Uniform care methods, ways of interacting, and use of home language help provide continuity. • Teachers and parents keep the lines of communication open.
Strive for secure teacher/child relationships	• Teachers express warmth and joy in the relationship, and they respond quickly and lovingly to children's needs. They develop play interaction, such as "peek-a-boo," to help reduce separation anxiety and other stresses. • Teachers reinforce children's attempts to gain independence.
Allow children to take the lead in learning	• Teachers know everyday life, rather than a formal program, is the best way for infants and toddlers to learn. • As the child develops, teachers encourage sensory activities, pretend play, art, music, listening to stories and rhymes, building with blocks, interacting with the natural world, and engaging in motor activities.
Emphasize language	• Teachers talk with (not to or at) children, read stories, and help children learn to share and control conflict expression.

Preschool Programs

Program Name	Program Characteristics
High Scope®	• Children choose activities, help plan goals for learning, carry out activities using objects, and reflect on activities. • Teachers plan some activities and ask questions that require creative thought. • Children use problem solving to resolve conflicts.
Reggio Emilia	• Teachers observe children's interests. Then teachers and children decide on projects, such as how to build an aquarium, for the classroom. Older children may assist younger ones, and teachers provide assistance as needed. Community members may also help with children's learning projects. • Teachers and children document their work using such items as photos and labels.
Montessori	• Children work with materials for sensory, language, math, motor, and life skills. • Teachers recognize when children are ready to learn a skill. They demonstrate the skill using the appropriate materials. Then the child uses the materials for his or her learning. • Children work alone more often than in groups, so learning is self-paced.

20-9 Many programs meet the developmentally appropriate practice (DAP) principles. Where DAP programs are available, parents can feel confident in their choices.

- attends promptly to children's physical, intellectual, social, and emotional needs
- exhibits a calm and gentle demeanor
- demonstrates flexibility and a sense of humor
- encourages healthy curiosity
- uses fairness to settle disputes
- tells children what they can do and sets limits on what they cannot do in a positive manner
- believes in discipline but not in harsh punishment

Parents should also look at how well a caregiver handles a group, 20-10. Making impromptu visits allows parents to notice how caregivers interact with their children. Just before lunch is a good time to see group management. This is a time when children tend to be the most restless. If the children seem to be fairly content at this time, they probably are happy most of the time. Parents should pay attention to the noise level, too. A pleasant hum of activity is a good sign. Loud noises and reckless running may be warning signs of ineffective care.

The Consistency of Care

Consistency of care is one of the most important qualities in child care. Having the same caregiver is important for young children. Ideally, infants and toddlers should have the same caregiver until they reach preschool. Most infants and toddlers adjust poorly when caregivers change frequently. When parents consider all the pros and cons when first selecting care, they increase their chances of choosing the best situation the first time.

Consistency within a child care program is also important. Children need to depend upon their child care routine. They should be able to expect a similar schedule from day to day. The rules should remain the same with

20-10 Effective caregivers handle a group of children well, especially before mealtimes.

consistent reinforcement. This gives children a sense of security. Parents can watch for consistency within the program when they visit the child care center.

Evaluating Program Quality

Careful program selection is key to finding appropriate child care. After enrolling their children, parents must continually evaluate the care their children receive. How do parents know the quality of a child care program? Here are some items to consider to make good choices and monitor care.

Making a Good Choice

Selecting the right child care situation for children can be challenging even when parents examine all important factors. Experts measure child care quality standards in these three ways:

Meeting Government Standards. Parents should only use child care programs that meet appropriate government requirements. Most programs, but not all, must meet state regulations. For family child care homes, most states require *registration*. **Registration** means the caregiver has informed the state about the program and is receiving state information on good practices, but has not gone through an inspection. To operate legally, states require *licensing* for child care centers. **Licensing** ensures that a child care facility has been inspected and meets basic standards. Parents should always ask to see the caregiver's registration or licensure document.

Accreditation. Some child care programs voluntarily meet even higher standards than those required by state licensing. These programs also seek **accreditation**—a credential ensuring the program meets the highest standards as set by the professional group offering accreditation. The major groups offering child care accreditation are the *National Association for the Education of Young Children* (NAEYC) (for college training programs only), NAEYC *Academy for Early Childhood Program Accreditation*, the *National Association for Family Child Care*, the *Ecumenical Child Care Network*, the *National Child Care Association*, and the *National School Age Child Care Alliance*. If program directors advertise their programs as accredited, parents should ask to see this certificate. Similar to accreditation, all centers operated by the United States military must meet very high standards set by Congress.

Ratings for Quality. More and more states are creating parent-friendly **quality rating systems (QRSs).** These systems use various standards of quality—such as licensing, accreditation, financing, and parent education—to give each child care program a rating. As an example, a five-star center might be accredited whereas a three-star center might only be licensed.

Once parents locate quality programs, they should do some comparison shopping. Program staff members always do their best when under inspection. Parents should visit programs unannounced and rely heavily on their instincts. See the factors in 20-11.

Monitoring Child Care

Once parents enroll their children, they must also continually evaluate the care their children receive. After a period of adjustment, parents must monitor how well their choice is working for the entire family, especially their children. Parents can tell a great deal about the care their children receive by watching the children's reactions. If children complain daily about going to child care and they seem tense and unhappy when parents return, parents should find out why. If parents have uneasy feelings, they should trust their instincts and take action. However, if parents have positive feelings, they will know their choice meets their children's needs. Instinct and common sense can tell parents a lot about the well-being of their children.

Acknowledging Concerns of Parents

Parents using child care may have a number of concerns, especially about medical or emergency events. They want to know program procedures for children who need immediate medical or other special care. Many hospitals will not administer care without the consent of a parent or legal guardian. These hospitals make exceptions only for life-threatening emergencies. A hospital may spend hours searching for parents before treating a child whose life is not in danger. What can parents do? They can take the following actions:

- Check whether caregivers have certification in first aid and CPR (cardiopulmonary resuscitation) procedures. Regulations require staff certification in CPR.

- Follow the plan of action for emergency events as outlined by caregivers or the program director.

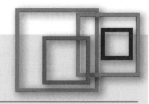

A Checklist for Choosing Child Care

Regulations
- Does the child care program meet city, county, state and/or federal requirements?
- Is the program accredited?
- Does the program have a good reputation?

Program
- Do the caregivers encourage the physical, intellectual, social, and emotional development of children?
- Do the caregivers use developmentally appropriate practices (DAP)? Is each child respected as an individual?
- Is the routine consistent from day to day? Does the routine allow for active and quiet times?
- Are children taught how to share and to resolve conflicts without resorting to aggressive means?

Discipline
- Do the caregivers spend more time on guiding or on punishing children? Do they avoid harsh punishment?
- Do the children seem happy?

Health
- Is the facility clean?
- Do children have a comfortable, quiet place for naps?
- Is there an isolation place for a child who becomes ill? Can the caregiver easily supervise the area?
- Is the food nutritious, well prepared, and suited to the age and culture of the children? Is the kitchen and serving area clean?
- Is good emergency care available for the children if the need arises?

Physical Setting
- Does the setting have a warm, homelike atmosphere?
- Are the inside and the outside areas planned with children in mind?
- Is there an abundance of learning and play materials?

Teachers and Staff
- What is the adult-child ratio? Is it maintained throughout the day? What is the indoor and outdoor group size?
- Are the caregivers well trained and experienced?
- Do the caregivers attend promptly to children's needs?
- Are the caregivers calm, gentle, and fair to children? Do they have a good sense of humor? Do they express joy in children's accomplishments?

Parents
- Are parents who visit unannounced welcomed?
- Do caregivers recognize the needs of parents and have open communication with them?
- Is there a policy handbook for parents?

Family Needs
- Is the child care facility in a convenient location?
- What is the cost per child? Does tuition cover the entire cost, or are there more fees for other activities, such as field trips?
- Are alternative schedules available to meet various needs for hours per day and days per week?
- Is care available for an ill child, or do parents need to make back-up care plans?
- What are the expectations for parental participation?

Safety
- Is the facility equipped with a variety of safe play equipment? Is it arranged with safety in mind? Are there protective materials in the fall zone under equipment?
- What precautions are taken to prevent children from wandering away? What precautions are taken to prevent abduction?
- Is an evacuation plan in place and practiced?
- Are all areas of the facility supervised at all times? Are risky behaviors prevented or stopped?

20-11 Parents should consider these factors in choosing a child care program.

- Complete a medical consent form to give the care provider permission to make decisions regarding the child's medical care in the event of an emergency.

Parents are often taken aback when caregivers describe their children differently than they do. This is natural. Children may react differently in different situations, just as adults do. Children may behave quite differently in the presence of their parents than when their parents are out of sight. Parents may have other concerns they cannot easily express.

Guilt About the Use of Child Care. Some parents struggle with feelings of guilt despite their good reasons for using child care. There are days when their children cling to them and beg them not to leave. These times are just as difficult for parents as they are for children. Parents can make parting easier by reassuring their children they will return. Parents should try to be on time so their children do not become anxious watching other parents greet their children.

Jealousy Over Children's Relationships with Caregivers. From the first day of care, parents learn to share their children with their new caregivers. Mothers and fathers have to accept they are no longer the only special people in their children's lives. This may be an unsettling realization. Parents may have fears about what will happen to their parent-child relationships because caregivers spend more time with children than the parents. Some children may develop closer attachments to their caregivers than to their parents, 20-12.

Negative Feelings About Caregiver Methods. Parents may ask themselves "Are other people really caring for our children the way we would?" Caregivers' ideas may differ from those of parents on simple things, such as asking children to eat everything on their plates. If parents have special concerns, they should talk with the caregivers to ease their minds.

20-12 This mother may feel jealous when her child reaches out to a caregiver. She should take this as a sign her daughter is receiving good care.

These feelings are normal, and parents can learn to handle them. Instead of feeling guilt, jealousy, or other negative feelings, parents can feel assurance in the good care and emotional support their children receive. They should take pleasure in knowing their child is happy and well-cared for in the child care arrangement. Unlike child care, parenting lasts a lifetime. Over the years, parents remain the most special people to their children.

Managing the Child Care Experience

Using child care services can be stressful or fulfilling for parents. In order to learn how to manage the child care experience and reduce parent-child stress, parents should do the following:

- Read and follow the written policies for their child care programs. If the program does not have written policies, discuss procedures with the director or caregiver.

- Complete all forms before leaving a child at the facility the first day. Request a copy of the completed forms and review them regularly, making changes as needed.

- Keep a list of supplies the child needs and pack them, if possible, the evening before they are needed.
- Label all supplies and toys with their child's name.
- Carry a suitable bag for staff members to place things that go home each day. In some centers, caregivers place this bag in the child's "cubbie" and fill it throughout the day. A folder for carrying older children's work and written communication between the home and the program is also a good idea.
- Put the exact amount of money for special events or projects, along with a note about what the money is for, in a sealed envelope with the child's name on the front.
- Write any messages for the caregivers before arrival at the facility each day. Caregivers need to be aware of any family situation that may affect the child's health or behavior. Professional caregivers keep this information confidential.
- Keep a folder for program-related materials, such as a log on medications given, accident/illness reports, behavioral problems, and periodic developmental progress reports.
- Set specific times for conferences with caregivers. Generally speaking, do not hold conferences in front of children or other adults. Share concerns before they become major problems.
- Read all individual and group messages daily. Individual messages are often put with the child's supplies, but group messages may be posted on the center bulletin board or put on a Web site.
- Attend parent meetings.

The most important aspect of managing child care is to keep the lines of communication open between the family and the caregiver. Parents must also watch for signs of stress in their children and act quickly if something seems wrong.

Summing It Up

- Parents may choose child care for a variety of reasons. Other parents may decide against using child care. Either option is viable as long as the child receives the care he or she needs at all times.
- Choosing child care requires careful consideration. Children's total development is influenced by the care and attention they receive.
- Each type of child care has advantages and disadvantages. Parents should consider how well each locally available type meets the family's needs.
- In looking at child care options, parents should consider the physical setting, program, adult-child ratio and group size, caregiver characteristics, and consistency of care.
- Before making a final decision, parents should check quality standards for a given child care program.
- After enrolling their children in child care, parents must monitor how well their choice is working for the family, especially the child.
- Parents using child care often have various concerns, especially care during medical or event emergencies.
- Parents often feel guilt about using child care and jealousy regarding their children's positive relationships with their caregivers.
- To reduce stress, parents need to learn how to manage the child care experience.

Recalling the Facts

1. What are three general factors parents should consider when making decisions about child care?

2. Contrast *nanny* and *au pair* care.

3. List two reasons child care in a family child care home might be desirable.

4. What is the difference between school-age child care and drop-in child care?

5. Identify two advantages of cooperative child care programs.

6. Name two reasons why parents might choose an individually owned child care center.

7. What are two advantages of national child care center chains?

8. How do children of families with financial needs benefit from government-sponsored child care?

9. Name three ways employers can help parents acquire child care.

10. What services do *child care resource and referral agencies* (CCR&Rs) provide for parents?

11. Name five major factors parents need to consider when selecting child care.

12. What qualities should parents expect from a child care program described as using *developmentally appropriate practices* (DAP)?

13. List the adult-child ratios parents can expect for each of the following:
    (A) infants; (B) toddlers; and
    (C) preschoolers.

14. List five characteristics of good caregivers.

15. What are three ways experts identify quality child care programs?

Applying New Skills

1. **Research.** Use Internet or print resources to research child care programs available in your community for infants and toddlers, preschoolers, and school-age children. Give a brief description of each. Explain the services provided, hours available, location, transportation, and cost.

2. **Presentation.** Create a PowerPoint® presentation to show the various types of child care options available in your community. Identify addresses, photos of the facilities, descriptions of the programs, and fees. If possible, use your presentation for an FCCLA *Illustrated Talk* STAR Event.

3. **Parent interview.** Interview parents who use child care. Ask them about what concerns they have for their children and themselves. Ask them how they deal with these concerns. Report the results of your interview to the class.

Thinking Critically

1. Debate this statement: For the first three years, the ideal child care situation for a child is in the home with one parent as a primary caregiver.

2. Assume a friend of yours is the parent of a young child. Your friend has asked for some advice about choosing child care. Draw conclusions about which standards of quality you might suggest your friend use to select child care. Summarize how your friend might apply such criteria in selecting care and services for his or her child.

3. Analyze reasons why parents might feel guilty about using child care services or experience jealousy over their child's relationship with a caregiver. Brainstorm some effective ways parents can deal with these negative feelings.

Linking Academics

1. **Writing.** In 12 sentences or less, summarize strategies parents can use to effectively manage their child care experiences.

2. **Technology.** Use the Internet to further research qualities of *developmentally appropriate practice* (DAP). For instance, you might check out the Web site for the National Association for the Education of Young Children (NAEYC) to identify their views on this topic. Write a summary of your findings.

Chapter 21

Children's Health, Safety, and Special Needs

Objectives

After studying this chapter, you will be able to

- describe parents' roles in their children's health care, including keeping disease resistance high, controlling infections, and caring for sick children.

- summarize common safety risks for young children and how parents can help protect them from each risk.

- describe the characteristics of children with physical disabilities, mental disabilities, learning disabilities, attention deficit disorders, autism spectrum disorders, behavior disorders, and gifts and talents.

- identify the challenges facing families who have children with special needs.

- summarize ways that parents can support their children with special needs.

Key Terms

infections
communicable
unintentional injuries
emergency care
first aid
physical disability
mental disability
learning disability
attention deficit disorder (ADD)
attention deficit hyperactivity disorder
   (ADHD)
autism spectrum disorder (ASD)
behavior disorders
gifted and talented
inclusion
Individualized Family Service Plan (IFSP)
Individualized Education Plan (IEP)

Parents have a most demanding job that includes a broad range of tasks. For example, parents may take children to many activities, help them with homework, and also teach the difficult lessons of a self-disciplined life. However, one of the most important parenting tasks is helping children lead healthy lives. Health and safety go hand in hand. To ensure good health and safety, care must cover all aspects of development. Care also involves taking actions that help prevent illness and injury.

In this chapter, you will read about the active roles parents should take in caring for their children's health and safety. Some of these roles are preventive and others involve caring for children who are ill. You will also learn how parents can prevent injury. Finally, you will see how parents who have children with special needs experience additional care responsibilities.

Children's Health Care

Because children and teens are growing and developing, their health care needs differ from those of adults. In fact, their unique needs change with each developmental stage. All children and teens depend on others, especially their parents, for health care including access to professional health care.

Promoting Good Health

Promoting children's good health is a major parenting responsibility. What are the features of a healthy child? Signs of physical, mental, social, and emotional health in children include

- growing at the proper rate
- developing firm muscles
- having good posture
- having straight, clean, cavity-free teeth with gums that are pink and firm

- playing vigorously
- resting well to maintain alertness
- developing gross-motor control and eye-hand coordination
- increasing attention span
- maintaining cheerfulness and tolerating some stress
- enjoying other children and adults
- becoming more and more cooperative with others
- showing more and more self-control
- adapting to new situations and people

In assessing the signs of health, parents and other adults should note the age/stage aspects of growth and development. They should also assess children's nutrition, freedom from diseases and accidents, and stress level.

All children become ill many times during their childhood years. Parents can keep a children's disease resistance high by helping their children learn and use good health practices, 21-1. These practices include providing adequate nutrition, rest, and activity; stopping germs; and having necessary immunizations.

Providing Adequate Nutrition, Rest, and Activity

Except for breast milk or formula during infancy, no one food contains all the nutrients the body needs to be healthy. Children and adults need to eat healthful foods. Parents can take several actions to promote healthy eating with their children. The most important action is to model healthy eating. Making healthful meals and snacks, talking with children about food choices, and limiting foods and beverages with few nutrients are also important.

Children who have long-lasting or recurring health problems or disabilities often need a special diet. Some children have

21-1 Proper nutrition, rest, and activity are practices that contribute to the good health of children.

nutritional problems, too. For example, some may be unable to chew or swallow normally. Others struggle with obesity, dietary deficiencies, or eating disorders. Parents can meet their children's nutritional needs with the help of a doctor or dietitian.

Sleep and rest are also essential to good health. The lack of sleep makes children more susceptible to illness or injury and slower to recover. Sleep also affects other aspects of development, too. For example, children who lack sleep are less alert for learning and less likely to have positive relations with family members and peers.

Depending on their age, children need 9 to 15 hours of daily sleep. Children who are ill or who have stress need even more sleep. Parents can play a positive role by scheduling adequate rest and sleep times. Removing such distractions as a television or computer from their children's bedrooms encourages better rest. Developing a relaxing bedtime routine is important, too. If sleep problems persist, parents should talk with their children's doctor.

Daily exercise is also a key to children's health. Exercise stimulates the appetite. It also uses calories, helps coordination and motor skills, and keeps the body healthy. Parents

can help their children to be more active by planning indoor and outdoor places to play. Playing with their children and planning fun, physical activities for the whole family lay the foundation for lifetime fitness. Enrolling children in exercise, dance, or sports programs can help, too.

Controlling Infections

Infections are illnesses from *pathogens*, such as viruses, bacteria, or parasites. The nose, throat, lungs, digestive tract, blood, urine, or other body fluids are places pathogens live in a sick person. Many diseases are **communicable** (transmittable). They spread through coughs, sneezes, and contact with bodily fluids. Contact with objects, food, and water that can absorb, retain, or transport pathogens, also spreads disease. The one exception is tetanus that lives in soil or dust.

The pathogen enters a person who becomes infected. The disease grows in the favorable, warm body conditions. The *incubation period*—the time between exposure and appearance of symptoms—depends on the disease. Symptoms may appear days or years after exposure. Nonspecific symptoms, such as a headache or a low-grade fever, will eventually occur. When symptoms become specific to a certain disease, the person is in the *acute* cycle of the illness. With treatment or time, the symptoms lessen and the person recovers.

Parents can limit illness by promoting certain hygiene habits that support good health. These include the following:

- *Handwashing.* Handwashing is the single most effective way to control infection. Parents should wash infants' hands frequently because they put their hands on the floor and eat with their hands. When toilet learning begins, toddlers need to learn how to wash their own hands, 21-2.

Washing Hands—Dodging Germs

1. Place a towel for drying near the sink.
2. Wet hands with warm, running water.
3. Apply soap and lather.
4. Rub hands vigorously for 20 to 30 seconds—between fingers, too. (Young children can "count time" by saying a rhyme.)
5. Rinse hands with fingers pointing down.
6. Dry hands with a towel.
7. Turn water off with a towel.
8. Open the door with towel.

21-2 Effective hand washing and disinfecting are two ways to control infections.

- *Covering coughs.* Parents should teach children to cough into the crooks of their elbows. Coughing into the hands spreads illness.

- *Rubbing eyes or nose with knuckles.* Parents should teach children not to scratch an itchy eye or nose. If an itch persists, teach children how to rub with the knuckles.

- *Using separate personal items.* Children need to learn not to share cups, combs, toothbrushes, pillows, towels, or cosmetics for the lips or eyes.

- *Protecting babies.* Unless there is an emergency, do not touch baby's face, hands, bottle, or pacifier without first washing. When away from home, keep a baby's hands tucked under a blanket to keep others from kissing them. Kissing the feet is less likely to cause illness than kissing the hands. When handling a baby, adults should frequently change their clothing tops, too.

Regular household cleaning can help keep the family home a healthy environment. Medical science today believes everyday household dirt is not harmful. It actually helps build children's immunity to pathogens. In families with infants and toddlers, however, certain areas need regular disinfecting. These include a changing table, car seat, crib, play yards and safety-gate rails, strollers, and high-chair feeding trays. A mild solution of one tablespoon of chlorine bleach to one quart of water is helpful for these surfaces. Parents can put the solution in a spray bottle. They should wash surfaces with soap and hot water and allow them to air dry. Then spray them with the chlorine mixture and air dry again.

Objects children mouth, such as pacifiers, teething objects, and rattles also need regular disinfection. Wash these items with hot, soapy water, rinse, and air dry. Washable items can also be disinfected in a dishwasher. Parents should disinfect all nonshared toys weekly and more often during an illness.

Getting Immunizations

Immunity is the body's defense against infectious diseases. A person needs a specific immunity to defend against a certain disease. Vaccines are substances made in laboratories from the bacteria and viruses that cause the diseases. They are much weaker than the diseases themselves. A doctor injects vaccines into the body. These *immunizations* build up antibodies, which protect a person against the disease for several years, or perhaps a lifetime. Immunizations are available for many diseases, such as diphtheria, tetanus, whooping cough, polio, measles, mumps, rubella, Haemophilus influenza (flu), and chicken pox. The *Centers for Disease Control* (CDC) recommends that children receive certain immunizations by age 2. See Appendix C. Schools generally require children to have certain immunizations before enrollment.

Some parents do not want their children to have immunizations. Why? A few parents do not accept immunizations for religious reasons. Some parents do not realize the diseases can be life threatening. Others believe these diseases no longer exist. A few more parents have concerns about side effects of immunizations, although these rarely occur.

Many children do not get the recommended sequence of immunizations by age 2. Some get them later due to child care and school requirements. As more families refuse this preventive measure, more disease outbreaks are likely. This endangers children too young for certain vaccines and other children and adults who cannot have immunizations because of health problems.

Having Routine Medical Checkups

Routine medical checkups give doctors a chance to detect health problems early, 21-3. They also help the doctor to follow a child's growth and development. The *American Academy of Pediatrics* (AAP) recommends eight well-child visits by age 2. Less than half of all children see their doctors that often. Due to lack of health insurance, older children and teens are less likely to have adequate health care.

Recognizing Childhood Illnesses

Even with routine preventive health care, children still become ill at times. Those who attend group child care encounter many

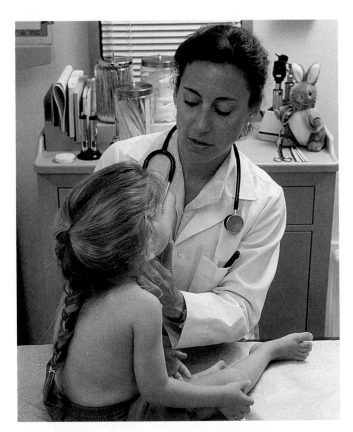

21-3 Children should see a doctor on a regular basis to identify illnesses that might cause serious health problems.

other children and become ill more often. Children who are ill may have some of the following nonspecific symptoms:

- behavior changes (for example, a normally active child is very quiet)
- frequent sleepiness
- irritability and easy upsets
- refusing to eat
- chills (often a sign of fever)
- vomiting or have *diarrhea* (watery stools)
- aching muscles, ears, head, or stomach
- difficulty breathing, standing, or seeing

These symptoms may indicate the onset of a cold, other respiratory infection, or digestive tract infection. They may also signal the beginning of a childhood disease. As you read, vaccines can prevent many diseases. For some infectious diseases, 21-4, vaccines are not yet available. Parents must watch for symptoms.

Childhood Diseases

Diseases	Symptoms	Care
Common cold	Coughing, sneezing, nasal discharge, headache, ear infection, upper respiratory problems	Rest, drink fluids, eat chicken soup, reduce aches and fever* Give doctor-prescribed antiviral drugs in some cases
Ear infection	Ear pain; pain felt when sucking, swallowing, or moving ear lobe; fever; drainage from ear	Drink fluids; reduce fever Use doctor-prescribed eardrops and sometimes antibiotics
Head lice	Itching scalp or neck, nits glued to hair, open sores and crusting from infection	Remove lice and nits by using prescription shampoo; use a fine-toothed metal comb to remove nits from sectioned hair Wash all clothing and bedding in very hot water (over 120°F); dry in a hot dryer each day for a week or longer Consult doctor for resistant cases
Impetigo	Small pimples or blisters with crusted scabs found on face and sometimes body	Wash crust with warm water or with an antiseptic wash Apply topical antibiotic creams as advised by doctor Give doctor-prescribed oral antibiotics for severe cases
Influenza (flu)	Fever, chills, headache, sore throat, coughing, muscle aches and pains, less energy	Rest, drink fluids, reduce fever* Elevate head to ease coughing Give doctor-prescribed antiviral drugs and decongestants
Mononucleosis (Mono)	Low-grade fever, sore throat, swollen lymph nodes, fatigue	Rest, drink fluids, avoid strenuous exercise and sports, reduce fever*
Conjunctivitis (Pink eye)	Red or pink eye, pain in eye, discharge—if caused by bacteria, virus, or allergy	Use warm compresses on eye Use doctor-prescribed eyedrops depending on cause
Respiratory Syncytial Virus (RSV)	Cold-like symptoms, briefly turn blue or stop breathing for a time (young infants), bronchitis or possible pneumonia	Treat the same as common cold Contact the doctor for severe cases
Roseola	High fever (over 103°F) lasting 3 to 7 days, red raised rash appearing after fever breaks	Reduce fever* Give doctor-prescribed antiviral drugs in some cases
Streptococcal Infections (Strep Throat and Scarlet Fever)	Sore throat, fever, headache, decreased appetite and stomachache Rash prominent in armpits and groin area, area around mouth appears pale	Use over-the-counter throat lozenges to ease throat pain for older children only Give doctor-prescribed antibiotics (untreated cases often lead to serious health problems)

*To reduce children's fever, doctors often recommend acetaminophen (Tylenol®, others) or ibuprofen (Advil®, Motrin®, others). For anyone under age 20, aspirin given during a viral illness has been associated with the development of Reye's syndrome, which can be serious and even deadly.

21-4 Parents should watch for symptoms of illness, consult with their child's doctor, and follow the doctor's treatment plan.

Calling the Doctor

Children's illness and injury symptoms can make most parents fearful. When parents note symptoms, they often wonder whether they should call their child's doctor. A few parents call needlessly, but most parents are good judges of their child's need for medical help.

Doctors who care for children expect and want parents to call. They know that children are vulnerable to disease. Of course, no one doctor is available day and night for seven days a week. Parents must inquire about medical backup plans when choosing a doctor. When calling the doctor, parents should have the following information ready:

- A list of symptoms and a timeline indicating when the symptoms appeared, worsened, or improved.

- The child's current temperature and where the parent took the measurement (such as the ear, mouth, armpit, or rectum).

- Any medications or other treatments given in the last 24 hours.

- The child's current weight.

- Any recent visits to doctor's office or hospital. Without a medical record, doctors will not remember these details.

- The name and phone number of a nearby 24-hour pharmacy.

Parents know how their children act when free of illness or injury. See 21-5 for symptoms that merit a call to the doctor. Most parents know when symptoms are severe enough for a doctor's attention. Doctors want parents to trust their instincts about medical needs.

Caring for Ill or Injured Children

When children are ill or injured, they need extra attention. Most illnesses no longer require exclusion from child care

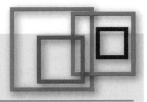

When to Call the Doctor

Parents should call the doctor when their children display any of the following symptoms:

- Fever of 100.3°F and higher in babies 3 months and younger and of 101°F and higher in older infants; fever of 103°F and higher in older children

- Fever lasting more than 3 days or accompanied by a skin rash or neck stiffness/pain

- Cold symptoms lasting longer than a week; coughing for more than two weeks

- Difficulty in breathing (noisy, labored); paleness or blueness

- Sudden limpness or collapse; lethargy (will not wake up or respond well)

- Vomiting (not "spitting up") for more than 6 hours if age 6 months or younger or for more than 24 hours if older

- Difficulty swallowing and noninfant drooling

- Blood in stool or urine; persistent diarrhea

- Blood-red rash that doesn't fade when pressed

- Severe abdominal pain

- Burns (including sunburn) that are red and cover more than 10 percent of body or any electrical burn

- Abnormal, inconsolable crying

- Severe headache that doesn't respond to pain relief medication

- Signs of dehydration—sunken eyes, dry mouth, no tears, and scant urine

- Head bump followed by loss of consciousness, confusion, difficulty with movements, watery discharge from ears or nose, and/or repeated vomiting

- Bleeding that cannot be stopped

- Serious injuries

21-5 Severe symptoms of illness require a call to the doctor.

programs or schools. However, when a child is contagious to others or does not feel well enough to participate in the activities, he or she should not attend child care or school.

Children who are sick need special care so they can restore their health quickly. Parents may have to take time off work or make other special arrangements to care for a sick child.

Parents should not fear spoiling an ill or injured child. The extra attention makes children feel nurtured. They recuperate much faster if they sense someone cares about their condition. Most babies and young children want parents to hold and rock them constantly when they are sick. Older children enjoy quiet games, books, television, CDs, and coloring to pass the time.

Parents quickly learn how to manage illness symptoms, such as diarrhea, earaches, fever, headaches, sore throats, and vomiting. Rashes sometimes need treatment, too. The child's doctor or nurse can explain best practices for managing symptoms based on the child's age and any other health concerns.

If the doctor orders a medicine or gives directions for an over-the-counter medicine (OTC), parents should be sure to give it to the child. Young children should not take their own medicine. With detailed instructions, older children may be capable of this. See the suggestions in 21-6 for giving medications. If children resist taking medicine, parents should not coax them. Stopping everything—such as TV watching or reading books together—often gets quick results. Parents can also ask a pharmacist about flavorings for various medicines. Mixing medicine with fruit may also help.

Some children have chronic conditions, such as allergies, asthma, diabetes, seizures, HIV/AIDS, or sickle-cell anemia. Parents and teachers must learn to manage these conditions on a daily basis. They also need to recognize when the child needs prompt medical help. By age 13, teens can care for their own conditions with parent support and supervision.

Many schools do not allow medicating on school grounds even if a teen is responsible. Parents and children must follow this policy for everyone's protection. Although children may have frequent illnesses, they tend to recover quickly. Alert and caring parents recognize the symptoms of illness. They also provide the proper care for their children. Parents need patience and understanding as children regain their health.

Children's Safety

Unintentional injuries are accidental and are preventable. They may include hazards, such as faulty equipment and toys or the lack

Giving Medications

- Keep over-the-counter (OTC) and prescription medicines in a locked area.
- Read instructions three times before giving medications. Ask the pharmacist about what "on an empty stomach" or "with food" means.
- Give medications on time. Keep a written log of when medications are given. Logging is really important if two or more people are giving medications, when medications are given during the night, or if two or more children are ill.
- Give only the amount prescribed even if symptoms persist, but call the child's doctor. For liquid medicines use an accurate measuring device which can be purchased from a pharmacy.
- Ask the pharmacist about potential interactions with other drugs or food.
- Ask the pharmacist or doctor about any medication side effects.
- Finish the full course of medications as the doctor prescribes.
- Throw away any outdated medications.
- Never tell children that medicine is candy. Explain that flavors make medicines easier to take.

21-6 Adults must carefully administer medications. If child is attending child care or school, read and follow all policies about administering medication by caregivers.

of children's car seats. Parents may also fail to plan the right type of activities or supervise their children.

Unintentional injuries are the leading cause of disabilities and death among children before the teen years. About half of these deaths occur in children under age 4. Deaths occur due to children's fragile bodies, poor impulse control, and lack of mature reasoning.

Reducing Safety Hazards

Caring for children is an all-consuming task. It's easy to make safety mistakes. Sometimes parents have momentary distractions. These times often occur when parents come home carrying groceries, when the phone rings, or when they forget a needed item. At these times, the child may do something he or she has never done before, such as crawl up the stairs behind the parent. In other cases a child willfully disobeys parent safety rules, such as not wearing a safety helmet when riding a bicycle. Many times these unsafe acts do not result in tragedy. However, good fortune does not always protect children.

How can parents avoid mishaps? Knowledge of child growth and development plays a key role in parental abilities to protect their children. As children grow and develop, the dangers change. Parenting strategies must change, too. The most common dangers during the first four years are

- falls from changing tables and front carriers (birth to 6 months)

- falls from furniture and tub drownings (6 to 11 months)

- suffocations from swallowing or choking on small objects (8 to 11 months)

- burns from hot liquids and tub drownings (12 to 19 months)

- poisonings from medication (18 to 36 months)

- accidents, both in and around motor vehicles (36 to 48 months)

Parents need to be aware of many specific risks, 21-7, and constantly assess their child's interests and skills. Parents need to know their children can get into safety trouble very quickly. "Thinking ahead" of their children is critical.

Although older children and teens can judge risks, they believe these risks do not apply to them. Parents must explain the right behaviors and enforce limits with consequences. Older children and teens need safety education before parents allow certain activities. For example, driving and sports participation require special training and practice. Parents need to supervise their children and teens throughout the growing years.

Teaching Safety

Teaching safety can begin as soon as children understand the words. Early lessons often lead to lifelong safety habits. Here are some basic principles for parents to follow:

- *Use safety lessons as incidental learnings.* For example, teach slide safety when your child is playing on a slide or pedestrian safety on a shopping trip, 21-8. Make rules about risks your child is taking or talking about taking, such as sliding down head first. However, rules should not suggest risks.

- *Use "teachable moments" to talk about safety.* For example, when a minor bump occurs, talk about ways to prevent it next time.

- *Make safety rules clear.* Parents should state rules in the positive rather than the negative. For example, say, "Hold the bar with both hands."

- *Teach self-protection skills.* Parents should show children how to properly

Preventing Common Injuries

Injury Type	Prevention Factors
Motor vehicle	• Use rear-facing infant carriers for babies up to 20-22 lbs. and younger than one year; use forward-facing car seats for children 20-40 lbs. and able to sit up without support. • Use booster seats with lap belts and shoulder harnesses for children over 40 lbs. but less than 54 inches tall. Use lap belts and shoulder harnesses for children between 55 -58 inches tall. • Store items on the floorboard, under the seats, or in built-in car containers, or in the trunk of the car. • Handle problems with children only when the car is safely stopped. • Check for fingers and feet before closing car doors and windows.
Drowning	• Never leave children alone in a tub or wading pool. • Never leave children around open or frozen water or a bucket with water. • Install domed drains with small openings in pools or hot tubs. Place the filter shutoff valve near the pool or tub.
Burns	• Set water heater temperature to a maximum of 120°F. • Install baby guards around heat registers, floor furnaces, and wall heaters. • Keep children away from grills, kerosene lamps, trash burning containers, and space heaters. • Keep electrical items away from water. Leave unplugged when not in use. • Buy flame-retardant children's clothing.
Suffocation	• Safely dispose of filmy plastics, such as dry-cleaner bags. Static electricity or inhalation can prevent a baby or toddler from removing the plastic from his or her face. • Check outside play areas for old refrigerators and cars and remove them or disable all latches. • Avoid latex balloons. Mylar balloons with 6-inch strings are safe. • Keep strings on crib gyms, pacifiers, drapes, and blinds to 6 inches or less to avoid strangulation.
Falls	• Never set an infant seat or car seat any place other than the floor. A baby's movements can cause a seat to fall. • Help children get in and out of tubs. Use rubber mats or appliqués in bathtubs. • Keep chairs and tables away from the outside edges of decks or balconies. • Install child-height handrails on stairs. Cover stairs with nonslip surfaces.
Poisons	• Store *all* poisonous substances in locked cabinets. Choose nontoxic children's art materials. • Keep live plants out of children's reach. Many are poisonous. • Keep alcoholic beverages out of children's reach. • Prevent lead poisoning. Do not allow children to chew on windowsills or other painted surfaces. • Keep purses out of children's reach because they often contain cosmetics, medicines, and small or sharp items.

21-7 All children face many dangers. Parents must see the risks and make their child's world safer.

wear a helmet, how to avoid giving personal information on a computer, or how to get away from anyone who seems threatening.

- ***Enroll children in programs that teach safety.*** Activities—such as swimming, a team sport, bicycling, and driver's education—emphasize safety as part of the skill building.

- ***Supervise children's activities.*** Compliment your child for doing things safely, and apply logical consequences if he or she takes forbidden risks.

- ***Avoid stating the dire consequences for taking certain risks.*** Young children can become too fearful. Older children may not believe what you say when certain consequences do not happen. Studies of children and teen's beliefs indicate they believe bad consequences only happen to others.

- ***Be a role model for safety.*** For example, children notice parents' driving attitudes and practices years before they drive. Parents are profound role models for their children.

Knowing Emergency Procedures

No matter how safety-conscious parents are, accidents do occur. Parents need to have basic skills in **emergency care**—the treatment of life-threatening injuries. Learning how to properly dislodge objects or food in the airway is also essential. Parents should also know how to handle profuse bleeding, head injuries, and poisoning, too. Many groups, such as the *American Red Cross*, offer training in emergency care.

Knowing **first aid** helps parents treat injuries that are not life threatening. Parents need to have a first-aid kit on hand to best treat these injuries. Common injuries include minor burns, cuts, nosebleeds, seizures, sprains and fractures, or bites. First aid may be all the care a child needs, or it may be the first step parents take before seeking professional medical help.

Along with knowing how to call for more help, parents should also teach their children how and when to place a 911 call, 21-9. Practicing emergency plans for house fires, storms, and other life-threatening events is key for family safety. Regularly practicing safety routines helps children remain calm and make good decisions in actual emergencies.

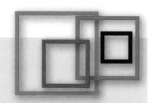

Playground Safety

- Make sure openings in equipment are smaller than 3½ inches or larger than 9 inches.
- Avoid excessive height on playground equipment. It increases danger. Maximum equipment height for older children is about 6 feet off the ground.
- Make sure all equipment is anchored with bolts in concrete that is recessed 4 to 6 inches below ground.
- Make sure acceptable "fall surfaces" are under and around all equipment.
- Ensure equipment does not have protruding bolts or S-hooks that can entangle clothing or jewelry and cause strangling.
- Use swings that have lightweight seats.
- Make sure slides and climbing structures have slip-resistant decks.
- Ensure all equipment is in good repair before allowing children to play on it.
- Make sure pools of water are inaccessible to children and ropes are not near playground equipment.

21-8 Parents need to be aware of safety features for playground equipment. They also should teach their children how to play safely on such equipment.

21-9 Learning when and how to make a 911 call is important for all children.

Meeting Children's Special Needs

Each child has unique needs. Most children display typical growth and development for their ages. Some children with special needs, however, are significantly behind or ahead in one or more areas of growth and development. Children with disabilities have conditions that may hinder growth or development. Those who are gifted and talented are often ahead developmentally. They show evidence of being highly capable in one or more areas, such as academics, creativity, music, or art. Although they are more alike than different from others, children with special needs require extra care and guidance from parents and families. Today, families have rights to resources to assist them in their parenting efforts.

Describing Children with Special Needs

Children with special needs may have a variety of conditions. The following passages describe only some of these special needs. When two people have the same disability, each may experience it differently. One factor may be the severity of the disability. For example, children with low vision may not experience their disability in the same way as children who are blind. Another factor may be that children often respond differently to medications and other treatments.

Children with Physical Disabilities

A **physical disability** refers to a limitation of a person's body or its function. Many types of physical disabilities exist. Each is unique in terms of the needs it requires. For example, some people with physical disabilities have limited mobility. They may use crutches, braces, artificial limbs, walkers, or wheelchairs to assist movement. Other people have limited vision, hearing, or speech abilities. They may wear glasses or hearing aids, and use braille or sign language. Other children may have chronic health problems. These include asthma, cystic fibrosis, hemophilia, sickle-cell anemia, heart problems, diabetes, or seizure disorders.

Children with Mental Disabilities

A **mental disability** begins before age 18. The characteristics of mental disability include significant limitations in cognitive functioning (the way the brain works). Mental disability may also include limitations in two or more adaptive skills. These are daily living skills people need for self-care and independence. Adaptive skills include communication, self-care, social skills, leisure, self-direction, and basic academic skills. Some children have both types of limitations, 21-10.

Mental disabilities range from mild to severe. This means that *mental retardation* does not refer to all people with mental disabilities. Many children with mild mental disabilities do not have mental retardation. They have higher IQ scores and function at higher levels in adaptive skills. Learning may take more effort from both teacher and student. However, children with mild mental disabilities can learn both academic and daily living skills. These children can learn to live on their own as adults.

21-10 Children with cognitive or mental disabilities may require one-on-one attention.

According to the *American Association on Mental Retardation*, people with mental retardation have profound mental disabilities. Their IQ scores are well below normal, and they show serious problems in two or more adaptive skills. Most of these children attend public schools. As adults, they often work in supervised settings, such as work centers for people with developmental disabilities. They may assemble products or do other tasks. People with moderate disabilities can live full lives, but are less able to live on their own.

Children with severe mental disabilities usually have very limited abilities. They may require almost total care and supervision. They may not be able to feed, dress, or groom themselves. These children may not be able to make decisions or keep themselves safe.

Parents of children with severe mental disabilities may not be able to provide all the care their children need. Many of these children live in care centers for children with disabilities. Some families care for their children with severe mental disabilities at home.

Children with Learning Disabilities

According to the *Individuals with Disabilities Education Act* (IDEA)— a federal law governing the education of children with disabilities—a **learning disability** is a "disorder in one or more psychological processes involving the use of spoken and written language." Children with learning disabilities have problems with such skills as listening, thinking, speaking, reading, writing, and doing math, 21-11. A learning disability is not a mental disability but is a learning problem. In fact, children with learning disabilities often have average or better intelligence. Children cannot have other problems that limit achievement, such as a hearing or vision loss, in order to be defined as having a learning disability.

What causes learning disabilities? Learning disabilities seem to be due to a different brain structure or functioning. The problem may be genetic in some cases. About 40 percent of children with these disabilities have one or more family members who have the problem. Physical damage to the brain can cause a learning disability, too.

A learning disability affects a person in all facets of life. As a student, the child struggles with academic work. Social relations are hurt because others see a bright student or friend as simply "not achieving." As an adult, the person may often lack basic academic skills. Low self-esteem is the most severe lifelong effect of a learning disability.

Children with Attention Deficit Disorders

Attention deficit disorders are not learning disabilities. Each has a separate diagnosis and treatment. In some cases, the same child may have both problems.

Common Learning Disabilities

- Dyslexia—a reading disability
- Dyscalculla—a math disability
- Dysgraphia—a writing disability

21-11 Children with learning disabilities have academic learning problems.

Attention deficit disorder (ADD) includes symptoms of distraction and inattention that are more frequent and severe than those of others at a similar developmental level. ADD causes children to have shorter-than-average attention spans. They are less able to focus on an activity for a long period of time. Other people and activities easily distract them. They often fail to finish tasks at home and school.

Some children with ADD are also hyperactive. A diagnosis of **attention deficit hyperactivity disorder (ADHD)** means a child is overly and uncontrollably active. A child with ADHD, for example, might be unable to sit still and be calm. Instead, the child might fidget constantly. He or she might get up often and run around. This happens even if a teacher tells the child to remain seated and work on an assignment. Because healthy children are active and may seem too active at times, only a doctor can diagnose this condition.

Unlike learning disabilities, which deal with brain functioning, ADD and ADHD may have underlying causes. For example, these children may have problems with how the body handles certain substances or brain chemicals. They may also have vision or sensory problems, or allergies to foods, molds, dust, or other environmental factors. Drug treatment is sometimes a successful therapy for ADD and ADHD. These drugs require a doctor's prescription. Some drugs have negative side effects that may lead to poor appetite, sleepiness, and growth problems. Behavior training is successful for some children. Other children receive special vision therapy to learn how to better pay attention. Treating allergies can diminish ADD and ADHD symptoms for other children. Although children with ADD and ADHD have problems learning because they cannot focus on tasks, once attentive they learn as others do, 21-12.

21-12 Once children with ADD or ADHD receive treatment and become attentive, they learn as others do.

Children with Autism Spectrum Disorder (ASD)

Autism spectrum disorder (ASD) is the name of a group of complex developmental disorders that becomes apparent before age 3. ASD affects verbal and nonverbal communication. It also affects social relationships and the ways children explore their environment. Many children with ASD also have sensory problems, mental disabilities, and seizures. Some children display symptoms from birth. Others do not show visible symptoms until 18 to 36 months. At this time, they begin losing many of their acquired milestones, such as speech and social skills.

Children with ASD display a very wide range of symptoms that differ in severity. For example, children with classic *autism* have the most severe ASD symptoms. In comparison, those with *Asperger's syndrome* have more mild symptoms. Children with ASD do not follow the same developmental patterns as children without the disorder. Early symptoms of ASD may include

- lack of babbling or making meaningful gestures by age 1
- inability to speak at least one word by 16 months of age
- lack of response to own name
- inability to combine two or more words by age 2
- repetitive behaviors, such as lining up objects over and over or continually repeating the same word
- poor eye contact or lack of eye contact
- lack of smiling

ASD seems to be on the rise. Although exact numbers are not available, recent studies by the *Centers for Disease Control* indicate a range of one in 500 to one in 150 people may be affected. ASD is four times more common in boys than in girls, but girls more often have the more severe symptoms.

The exact cause of autism is unknown, but something interferes with normal brain development before and/or after birth, 21-13. Genes are likely involved. For example, because their genes are the same, identical twins are more likely than fraternal twins to both have autism. One study also showed that parents and siblings of a child with ASD often display some minor symptoms. Because of this link, some experts think environmental problems, such as viruses, may cause susceptible genes to produce the full-blown disorder. Early diagnosis and treatment help children with ASD. However, there is no cure for ASD. The majority of adults with autism or ASD need training and supervision throughout life.

Children with Behavior Disorders

Behavior disorders include a wide variety of social and emotional problems ranging from mild to severe. A behavior disorder may be present at birth or develop later. Some disorders are hereditary. Life events, such as a crisis, may trigger others. A behavior disorder may be temporary or lifelong. If it impairs a person's ability to function normally, it is a disability.

One behavior disorder is *oppositional defiant disorder (ODD)*. These children break rules, destroy property, and through aggressive behavior violate the rights of others. Children with this conduct disorder and ADHD are most apt to get in trouble with the law.

Anxiety disorders are also behavior disorders. Anxiety disorders include separation problems in which the child fears strangers and clings to known caregivers. The reactions can be long lasting and severe. Over dependency is also an anxiety disorder. Over-dependent children may whine or tattle to get adult attention. Withdrawal from social play is another symptom of an anxiety disorder. A few children also have panic attacks. These are short episodes of dread along with intense and unpleasant physical symptoms, such as chest pain and nausea.

Mood disorders are disturbances in emotions. They are more likely to occur in the teen years, but they do occur in younger children, too. Depression—a feeling of hopelessness—is the most common mood disorder. *Bipolar disorder* is another. Once uncommon and difficult to diagnose in children, doctors often see evidence of early onset of bipolar disorder in children. Symptoms include mood swings ranging from fidgety, giddy, and sleep problems (the *manic* cycle) to despair (the *depressive* cycle). Unlike adults with bipolar disorder, children may go through these cycles many times a day.

Characteristics of Autism Spectrum Disorder (ASD)

Type of Problem	Characteristics
Language problems	• Have little or no speech throughout life. Some children coo, babble, and say a few words that appear to be typical development, but stop before age 3. • Use repetitive phrases for many situations. May also mimic what they hear from others. • Do not convey emotions when they talk or recognize body language in others.
Social problems	• Appear indifferent about and remote from others. They do not make eye contact. They show no distress when a parent leaves them with others or steps out of sight and show no pleasure when a parent returns. • Resist attention and affection. Prefer being alone and do not form emotional bonds with others. Cannot predict others' responses to their actions. • Readily lose control—they may break objects, attack others, and/or harm themselves.
Problems exploring the environment	• Repeat the same behavior for hours, such as spinning wheels or lining up toys. • Move bodies in "odd ways," such as self-rocking (no chair), flailing arms, walking on tiptoes, and freezing in certain positions. • Demand consistency in the environment. Children with ASD may become almost hysterical at small changes in location of objects or in routines. • Do not engage in pretend play.
Sensory problems	• Painfully sensitive to sensations. For example, a moderately loud sound may cause a child with ASD to scream. • Senses seem out-of-balance. For example, head banging may never cause child to wince or cry. In contrast, a gentle touch may cause the child to scream.
Mental disabilities and seizure problems	• About 80 percent of children with ASD have a mental disability; about 15 percent are severely retarded (IQ below 35); few have very high IQs. • About one third of children with ASD experience seizures, which usually start in the early childhood or teen years.

21-13 Autism spectrum disorder (ASD) leads to multiple and profound developmental disabilities.

An untreated behavior disorder can affect all areas of a person's life. These disorders do not go away or improve without treatment. Actually, they often get much worse. Treatment involves a team of medical professionals, counselors, teachers, and parents. Medications, counseling, and behavioral training are all useful in helping these children lead active, full lives.

Children with Gifts and Talents

According to federal definition, children who are **gifted and talented** show outward signs of high achievement or potential for high achievement in such areas as intellectual, creative, artistic, or leadership ability. About 16 percent of all children fit this definition. Some of these children have intellectual skills that are well above average. Other children have extraordinary gifts and talents in areas such as art, music, or athletics. These children may require services beyond those the school supplies.

Children with gifts and talents may also have some disabilities, including physical or learning disabilities. Children with gifts and talents who also have a disability may be eligible for special education services to reach their full potential. No single description fits every child with gifts and talents. Most do share common characteristics, 21-14.

Because general intelligence is often genetic, some signs of giftedness may be evident from birth. As infants, children who are gifted may be more alert and require less sleep. From an early age, they may be more independent and show amazing perseverance. Children with gifts may also possess more originality, logic skills, common sense, ambition, and talent than their peers. Children with gifts are often very curious.

Talents are often nurtured through exposure and training. However, some aspects of the talent may come from genes, such as good motor coordination for dance or sports or a good ear for musical tones and rhythms. Thus, talents may show a little later than giftedness. However, when they think about it, parents can often recall their child's early display of talent. For example, a parent of a talented athlete may tell stories about her child's strong arm, speed, or ability to jump as a toddler.

Children with gifts and talents have special needs, too. Developing their special gifts and talents requires vigorous challenges. Changes in curriculum and special instruction help children develop their gifts

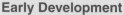

Characteristics of Gifted and Talented Children

Early Development
Most gifted children talk early. Their vocabularies are more advanced and descriptive than those of their peers. About half learn to read before they start school, usually teaching themselves.

Long Attention Span
The child's concentration may be so intense that it resists interruption, or the child may appear to daydream. Gifted children tend to be persistent, know what they want, and refuse to be distracted from reaching their goals.

Superb Observational Skills
An alert toddler might remember which of ten blocks is missing. A creative child might observe the fried egg on his or her plate looks like Alaska.

Advanced Reasoning Skills
The gifted child understands complex concepts and relationships. For example, a disagreement about simple household chores may drag on as the child gives logical explanations of why he or she did not do the assigned chores.

Questioning Mind
A gifted child usually asks penetrating questions and demands responses. Many questions reflect an intense curiosity: If you can feel the wind, why can't you see it? Why do people have to grow old?

Interest in Structure and Order
Gifted children may like objects or ideas that are consistent like number systems, clocks, and calendars. Gifted children may be highly skilled at taking things apart and putting them together.

Imagination
A gifted child may be the leader in pretend games. He or she is likely to have an imaginary playmate and see toy cars alternately as football players, mountain climbers, or superheroes.

High Energy and Restlessness
The child's mind will not stop, even when the body needs to sleep.

Unusual Talents
Children gifted in specific areas generally display their talents and interests early.

21-14 Parents are usually the first people to notice many of these characteristics in their children with gifts.

and talents. They must learn to accept peers or adults who do not possess their abilities. Like all others, they have to measure their own strengths and weaknesses and accept who they are.

Understanding Family Challenges

When parents first learn their child has a serious disability, they often grieve. In the process of grieving, parents' reactions vary. A few parents deny anything is wrong regardless of the child's appearance or behaviors or of the doctor's explanations. Other parents acutely feel the wide gap between their dreams and reality. In the *image-making stage of parenting*, they imagined their child engaging in many home and school activities and attaining life's milestones. The plans and dreams that they made for their child are not the reality they face. Some blame themselves—their genes, their actions before and during pregnancy, and even what happened after pregnancy—for their child's disability. The unknown causes of many disabilities often add a sense of self-blame. These reactions are normal as parents learn to face their new reality.

Some families also face many urgent decisions. In some cases, they must make decisions immediately for the sake of the child. Parents make other decisions over the years. These challenges come in addition to other concerns and tasks with which all families deal. Special problems parents might face include the following:

- *Painful or life-threatening medical treatments.* In many cases, such treatments happen again and again.
- *Heavy costs of medical treatment and of other special needs.* A child may need special equipment, home adaptations, and travel costs for care.

- *Employment problems.* Some parents have work-related problems due to taking off work for medical care, consultations, and other needs of the child.
- *Greater care taking demands than usual.* Routine care is often much more involved and time-consuming for children with special needs compared with other children.
- *Child care issues.* Many parents find it challenging to locate child care and special programs that "fit" the child's needs.
- *Resentment of other family members.* Siblings may feel resentful when so much focus is on the brother or sister with special needs. All children deserve to have their needs met. Thus, parents have to work for a fair balance.
- *Discomfort when "strangers" ask about their child.* Most people show genuine interest in and often admire the coping skills of parents who have children with disabilities. It takes parents some time to feel less discomfort with questions that may seem rudely personal.
- *Making the marriage work.* All the various challenges put serious stress on the best of marriages. A couple needs to find ways to keep their marriage strong.

Supporting Children with Special Needs

Most parents accept the reality of their child's disability and deal with their feelings of disappointment. As grief subsides, parents start on the challenging path of helping their child achieve all he or she can. Each challenge parents and children overcome is a victory. Most importantly, they begin to find joy in their child, and like all parents, celebrate the achievement they see.

Getting a Diagnosis; Becoming Informed

For some children, doctors can diagnose a disability before or at the time of birth.

Usually, however, accurate diagnoses require many more tests and consultations before doctors and parents know the extent of any problem. This can take years because some tests are not possible in the very early years of life.

Some disabilities are not obvious because they are mild or borderline. For example, parents and caregivers rarely notice learning disabilities before the preschool or school years. In a few cases, a special need may mask a coexisting one. For example, giftedness may mask *dyslexia*—a reading disorder. Because the gifted child may easily memorize passages in a beginning reader, it appears that he or she is reading. In all of these cases, parents or the child's doctor or teacher may eventually suspect something is not "right," 21-15. Testing and diagnosis usually follow.

Diagnosis, as soon as the symptoms are apparent, is to the child's advantage. Waiting and just hoping for the best does not make a disability go away. Early treatments are the most successful. Early treatments can also prevent the spread of disabilities, such as a hearing problem that can lead to a speech problem if untreated.

21-15 Parents should request an academic evaluation if they suspect their child might have a learning disability.

Once they receive a disability diagnosis, parents need to research their child's disability and learn what treatments, if any, exist. This way, they know whether their children are getting the care they need. Parents are their child's best *advocates*—those who plead in favor of their child's needs.

Learning about their child's disabilities also prepares parents to give the child the proper care at home. Parents must know how to help their child reach his or her potential. For example, if a child cannot speak or hear, parents may learn sign language and teach it to the child. This will help the child communicate with his or her family members, 21-16. If the child uses a hearing aid, parents should know how it functions.

Parents must share information about their child's disability with the child's other caregivers and teachers. This will help them understand the child's special needs. It will also allow others to provide proper care and assistance for the child.

Developing a Support Network

Parents of children with special needs, like all parents, need support for their parenting role. For most special needs, there are national organizations that work on behalf of the children and their families. They raise funds for research and education for the disability. On behalf of those who have the disability and of those who care for them, these groups propose laws and work to get them passed. In many cases, local chapters of these organizations help parents meet their challenges through expert help and support groups.

Local human-service agencies and other community resources, such as schools, can provide support, too. Caseworkers often make referrals for treatment. They can also help parents find financial help.

Parents may also need the help of extended family and friends. Family members and friends are often willing to

21-16 Sign language can help people without hearing communicate with others.

provide support when a parent needs rest, babysitting services, or just a listening ear. The loving care of family and friends is the best kind of support for all families.

Planning for a Child's Primary Residence

Most children with disabilities live with their families. Parents of children with profound disabilities may feel full-time care outside the home is best for the child and family. For example, parents may not be able to meet the care needs of their child with severe mental disabilities. These parents choose centers designed for children with disabilities. If their child lives in such a center, parents can still be very active in the child's life. They visit the center regularly and make decisions about the child's care.

Some children with disabilities live with their families until their later school age or teen years. Then, the parents choose other living arrangements. For example, older children and teens with moderate mental disabilities can live in assisted-living centers or group homes. These centers provide care and supervised living for people with disabilities. The staff members receive training to work with persons with mental disabilities.

Those parents who plan to keep their children with moderate and profound disabilities at home permanently must have back-up plans. If parents become unable to care for their children or die, they must make provisions for their child's care. Some parents make plans with other family members. Others make a contract with a professional guardian who arranges care.

Learning About Laws and Services

As you read earlier in this chapter, the *Individuals with Disabilities Education Act* (IDEA) is a federal law that governs the education of children with disabilities. This law guarantees the rights of children with disabilities to receive a free and appropriate public education. IDEA, in combination with the *No Child Left Behind Act* and the *Americans with Disabilities Act*, outlines ways to meet the special educational needs of children with disabilities. With a goal of helping children with disabilities develop independent living skills and work-related skills, IDEA indicates that learning should take place in the least restrictive environment.

Much research today reveals that most children with special needs reach their potential in an inclusive classroom. **Inclusion** means that children with disabilities learn in the same classroom as those children without disabilities, 21-17. Inclusive environments are often the least restrictive for learning and achievement. Children with special needs may be in inclusive classrooms for all or part of the school day. Inclusion helps children with disabilities prepare for life in society at large.

IDEA identifies two written documents that make provisions for children with disabilities and their families—the *Individualized Family Service Plan* (IFSP) and the *Individualized Education Plan* (IEP). These

21-17 Inclusion means students of all abilities share a classroom. The children in this class may have physical disabilities, mental disabilities, learning disabilities, and behavior disorders. Other children may be gifted or average in learning.

documents outline services for families who have a child with disabilities and educational goals for a child with special needs.

Receiving Assistance from the Start—the IFSP

Families can receive help from the **Individualized Family Service Plan (IFSP)** as soon as their child with special needs is born. Services under the IFSP focus on the unique needs of the family until the child with disabilities reaches age 3. The child and family receive services through a team approach. The team consists of the parents and others who have knowledge and expertise regarding the child's disability or disabilities. Team members may be from multiple agencies, including schools and social-service agencies. One of the experts serves as a case manager. He or she makes sure the child and parents get all the services they need. The delivery of services takes place in natural environments that the family typically uses. The child's home, parks, shopping centers, or museums are a few examples. The IFSP encourages families to learn the information and skills they need to meet the challenges of parenting their child.

Working with Public Schools—the IEP

The IDEA law states all children with disabilities between the ages of 3 and 21 are eligible to receive appropriate educational services. A team consisting of the child's parents, special education experts, evaluators, counselors, and teachers, draw up an **Individualized Education Plan (IEP).** The IEP outlines educational goals for a child with disabilities. It describes the child's current developmental level along with annual and short-term goals for the child. The plan outlines special services the child needs, and the placement of the child for his or her education, and the dates of the services. Assessment to determine the child's achievement of goals is a key part of the IEP.

As you read, IDEA requires that all children with special needs be in class settings in which they best learn, or the least restrictive environment. Separate classrooms for children are restrictive if students do not need the level of services they provide. Special education and regular classroom teachers develop plans about how to adjust lessons to fit the abilities and needs of all students.

Some children with disabilities benefit more from one-on-one teaching in a special education classroom. If a child cannot get this help in an inclusive classroom, he or she receives services in a separate special education classroom. As the child progresses in skills, his or her IEP may then call for inclusion placement.

The IEP team discusses the benefits and drawbacks of inclusion for each child. The team also looks at the regular classroom teacher's training and experience in working with various disabilities. The team also evaluates whether a special education aide can help the child achieve in an inclusive classroom. The team notes all decisions in the IEP document. After the annual IEP meeting, no one can make changes to a child's IEP without another team meeting.

Meeting Education Needs of Children with Gifts and Talents

Unless children with gifts and talents also have disabilities, they do not qualify for special-education services under IDEA. However, there are several ways schools can meet the needs of children with gifts and talents. These include

- *Acceleration.* Acceleration often occurs in the lower or middle grades. School officials may allow some gifted and talented students to skip a grade level in school. Before placing a child with older peers, parents and school officials need to look at the degree of giftedness and the general maturity of the child.

- *Enrollment in schools for the gifted and talented.* Many of these schools are for secondary school students who have gifts and talents in the fine and performing arts, music, or academics, 21-18.

- *Placement in enrichment programs.* These programs vary from one school to the next. One school may offer honors classes in which students study subjects at a more advanced level. Another school

21-18 Parents may enroll children with gifts and talents in special schools to increase achievement.

may integrate students into classrooms with enrichment opportunities. In these classes, teachers might assign special projects for students with gifts.

- *Early school entrance or quicker school completion.* Some gifted and talented children enter school a year earlier than other students. This is a type of acceleration but does not involve grade skipping. Gifted and talented high school students may also take additional classes each year beyond the typical load. These students graduate a year or more before their peers and often enter college at younger ages.

Summing It Up

- Parents need to recognize the signs of good health and the symptoms of common childhood illnesses.

- Parents have a major role in keeping their child's disease resistance high and controlling infections in the family.

- Parents need to protect against unintentional injuries, teach safety, and supervise their child.

- Parents must have basic knowledge of emergency care and first aid. They need to make plans for and teach their children how to handle emergency events.

- Children who are significantly behind or ahead in one or more areas of growth and development have special needs.

- The family system is disrupted when a child has a serious disability. With various supports, families can meet their challenges and become stronger.

- Once diagnosis of a disability or gift or talent is made, parents can become informed which is necessary as they seek needed support.

- Parents of a child with special needs can receive support for their child and themselves through national support groups, community resources, federal programs, the schools, and their family and friends.

Recalling the Facts

1. What are three good health practices children need for a lifetime?

2. Name the single most effective method to control infection.

3. Why do children need immunizations?

4. Name five symptoms that merit a call to a child's doctor.

5. List four common safety risks of young children.

6. Compare and contrast *emergency care* with *first aid* treatment.

7. Name three types of physical disabilities.

8. What is the difference between *mental retardation* and a *mental disability*?

9. What skills might be problems for children with learning disabilities?

10. Describe how *attention deficit hyperactivity disorder* (ADHD) can interfere with a person's ability to learn.

11. Name three early symptoms of *autism spectrum disorder*.

12. List three behavior disorders.

13. What are two characteristics of children who are *gifted and talented*?

14. How does *inclusion* benefit children with special needs?

15. Explain the differences between an *IFSP* and an *IEP*.

Applying New Skills

1. **Research.** Use reliable Internet or print resources to research one of the childhood illnesses from Figure 21-5, or ways to treat minor injuries such as insect stings, animal bites, cuts, scrapes, minor burns, or nosebleed. Prepare a PowerPoint® presentation and share your findings with the class. Ask your teacher how to cite your references.

2. **Safety demonstration.** Select a home safety practice to demonstrate to the class. For example, you might demonstrate how to use a fire extinguisher or how to "stop, drop, and roll" in case clothing catches on fire.

3. **Resource directory.** Work in a small group. Select one of the groups of children with disabilities described in the chapter. Use desktop publishing software to create a directory of community services, agencies, or support groups available to help parents and children in this group. Provide the following information for each service: name of service or agency, address and telephone number, Web site URL, e-mail address, contact person, services, and fees.

Thinking Critically

1. Brainstorm a list of suggestions about how to soothe a child during a medical checkup. Also make a list of some things you think parents should never say or do.

2. Identify six minor injuries that may impact children. Draw a cause and effect chain to show the consequences of failing to protect children from such injuries. Then identify preventive actions parents can take to avoid these injuries.

3. Analyze the pros and cons of *inclusion*. If necessary, interview a special education teacher and a regular classroom teacher to obtain additional background for your analysis.

Linking Academics

1. **Reading.** Collect and read children's books about disabilities. Write a brief synopsis of these books for members of your class. Explain how parents or teachers might use these books to help children understand their own disabilities or those of their peers.

2. **Social Studies.** Investigate ways that parents can become the best possible advocates for their children with special needs. What organizations exist to support parents in their endeavors? How does the *IDEA* law help parents acquire services for their children?

3. **Science.** Use Internet resources to research the latest information on developmental disorders, such as *autistic spectrum disorder (ASD)*. How do immunizations impact ASD? What environmental factors may impact ASD? Check out information sources, such as the *National Institutes of Health* (www.nichd. nih.gov) or the *Centers for Disease Control* (www.cdc.gov).

Chapter 22

Careers Related to Children, Parenting, and Families

Objectives

After studying this chapter, you will be able to

- identify career opportunities for working with children, parents, and families.
- describe the key trends and job outlook for careers related to children, parents, and families.
- analyze the personal traits needed for careers serving children, parents, and families.
- identify ways to assess your interests, aptitudes, and abilities.
- identify ways to build and strengthen your workplace knowledge, skills, and attitudes.
- summarize how to develop a career plan, including the use of career clusters and setting short-term and long-term career goals.
- describe work-based learning programs.
- identify skills that can be developed through a student organization, such as FCCLA.
- summarize how to find and secure employment.

Key Terms

job
career
teacher
parent educators
entrepreneur
interests
aptitudes
abilities
teamwork
leadership
career plan
career clusters
job shadowing
work-based learning programs
cooperative education
apprenticeships
internships
parliamentary procedure
Family, Career and Community Leaders of
    America, Inc. (FCCLA)
portfolio
résumé

Many people besides parents interact with children on a daily basis. These people include child care providers, school personnel, children's librarians, youth and recreational leaders, social workers, and health care professionals. Often children benefit from the work of people who do not actually interact with them. For example, creators of children's books, television shows, computer software, and toys have careers that support children and families without daily interaction.

In this chapter, you will learn about ways to prepare for a career. You will learn about some requirements, challenges, and rewards of careers in working with children and families. In addition, you will learn ways to match your own interests, aptitudes, and abilities with those necessary for various careers related to parenting, children, and families, 22-1. Most importantly, you can learn the steps needed to find a career in many fields.

Working with Children and Families

As a parent, you will apply your learnings to your child. As a person in the workplace, however, you may apply them to other children, parents, and families. A wide array of jobs focusing on children and families are available. People who are drawn to these jobs may even want to plan a career serving the needs of children, parents, and families.

A difference exists between a *job* and a *career*. A **job** is work a person does to earn money. A job is one work experience. A **career** is a series of related jobs and work experiences. Developing a career is a lifelong process that includes many small goals. To have a career, a person might first need to learn several related jobs. The person might also need specific types of education and

22-1 A career as a child care worker can be rewarding.

training in his or her chosen field—all of which are discussed later in the chapter. What types of careers are available working with children and families? Read on to discover the range of possible options for your future career.

Working Directly with Children and Families

Many people enjoy interacting with children. These people might want to be actively involved in the care, education, and training of children. If you are one of these people, you might want to choose a career working directly with children.

Child Care Providers

Child care providers work very closely with children every day in many places of employment. These include private homes, caregiver's homes, and child care centers operated by individuals, parent groups, religious groups, colleges, business corporations, youth organizations, and government agencies. The size of the child care setting may vary from serving a single family to serving several hundred families. Titles and responsibilities of child care personnel may vary with the setting. The most common titles *nannies, assistant teachers* or *teacher aides, teachers,* and *directors.*

Nannies. As you read earlier, nannies provide families with quality care for young children in their homes. This meets the need of growing numbers of working parents for consistent child care. Live-in nannies receive room and board plus a salary.

Training programs for nannies vary in length from four hours to one year. An accredited program of study in a nanny school must include 200 classroom hours and 50 hours of on-the-job training. Most schools require students to complete an internship with a family. Students receive certification only after successfully completing the program.

Assistant Teachers* or *Teacher Aides. In some programs, the term *assistant teacher* or *teacher aide* is another name for *child care aide.* Professional experts prefer the use of the term *teacher* in their title. These assistants or aides work under the direct supervision of a teacher.

Because an aide is an entry-level child care position, this job requires little education and training beyond high school. People in these positions may have spent time babysitting or volunteering with children. Once hired in a quality child care program, they are expected to begin training to become a child care teacher.

Teachers. The *National Association for the Education of Young Children* (NAEYC) defines a **teacher** as an adult whose primary responsibility is for a group of children. Teachers in accredited child care programs must have a Child Development

Associate (CDA) credential or its equivalent in order to meet the demand for highly qualified teachers, 22-2. Teachers design the indoor and outdoor areas for children, plan the daily activities, and develop the schedule. They provide physical care and protection for children. They broaden children's interests and support their developing skills and knowledge. Teachers guide children toward ever-increasing levels of autonomy, dependability, and respect for others. Teachers also work with other adults, often as part of a team. Most importantly, teachers communicate with parents on a daily basis.

Directors. Directors in child care are responsible for personnel leadership and for management of all aspects of the program. In

Child Development Associate (CDA) Credential

What Is the CDA?

The CDA is a national credential for those working with children in child care programs. The center-based credential is available with either an Infant/Toddler or Preschool endorsement. The credential is also available with a Spanish-language endorsement.

To receive a CDA, the person must complete the following:

- 480 hours of work experience with children in a center within the past five years
- 120 clock-hours of training in specific areas of center work, such as health and safety, child growth and development; and working with parents
- a work portfolio
- an assessment to show competence

CDA Equivalent

The CDA equivalent is 12 semester hours of course work in child development, early childhood education, or early childhood special education.

22-2 Teachers and directors in accredited child care programs must have a CDA credential or its equivalent.

very small programs, the owner is both the director and the teacher. In larger programs, the director does not teach. Large centers often have a local director or manager and other administrators who work out of the main office in another location. However, in most child care programs, the director is solely responsible for reaching the program goals and managing the day-to-day tasks.

In child care programs, most directors come from the teaching ranks. Teaching gives them a good understanding of the needs of children and their parents and experiences in working with others. In addition, a director should have a four-year degree in child development, early childhood education, family studies, early childhood special education, or elementary education. He or she should also have special training in leadership and management.

School Personnel

Schools employ professionals who work directly with children and families. Positions are similar to those in child care except they work with children who range from preschoolers to high school teens. The schools may be public or private. Some schools operate government-sponsored programs, such as Head Start. A few schools also have a child care program for school-age children or for laboratory use with high school students studying occupational courses in child care. The most common titles for school personnel include *teacher's aide, teaching assistant, teacher,* and *principal.*

Teacher's Aide. A teacher's aide primarily helps with the care of children during snack and mealtimes or when they enter or leave the classroom. Aides also prepare materials for teaching and provide cleanup after an activity. Many aides serve more than one teacher each day. For this entry-level position job, a high school education is the minimum requirement. Aides receive much on-the-job training.

Teaching Assistant. Teaching assistants often tutor one-on-one or work with small groups of children using the teachers' instructional plans. In schools without aides, teaching assistants may also provide care during meals and cleanup after activities.

In most states, teaching assistants must have two years of college, a two-year degree, or a passing score on a state test. Like an aide, a teaching assistant receives additional on-the-job training.

Teachers. Because schools must meet certain academic standards, teachers spend much of their time in instruction in the required areas. To be a teacher, a person must have a *license* or *certification,* which requires at least a four-year degree, 22-3. Different degree requirements are set for teaching children of different ages, children with special needs, and different subject matter areas. Most states require teacher applicants to pass a national test. Any teacher who moves to a different state must meet certification requirements

22-3 Teachers have an important influence on children's lives. To be an elementary school teacher, you would need at least a four-year degree in education and meet other state requirements.

in the new state. If a teacher decides to teach a different age group or different subject matter, he or she must meet additional requirements.

Most school systems encourage their teachers to work for graduate degrees. Teachers who do may receive leadership roles among teachers. They are often called *lead teachers* or *master teachers*. More education and experience also lead to a better salary.

Principals. Principals are responsible for both leadership and management roles in a school. Principals work directly with children, their parents, teachers, and other staff members on a day-to-day basis. Most principals begin their careers as teachers. Before becoming principals, they must meet their state's licensing or certification requirements for principals, which generally require an advanced degree in school administration. In addition to course work, prospective principals may complete an internship as an assistant principal. This provides necessary on-the-job training.

Children's Librarians

If you enjoy books and want to share the joy of reading with children, you might consider a career as a children's librarian. Librarians may work in a school library or in the children's section of a public or private library. They design programs to stimulate reading and improve reading skills. Librarians teach children how to use the library. They may initiate story hours and read to groups of children. Children's librarians also evaluate new books to add to the library.

In most cases, a librarian must have a four-year degree in library science. A position as a children's library assistant may not require a degree. Someone who has taken college courses in children's literature may have an advantage when applying for an assistant's position.

Youth and Recreation Leaders

Youth and recreation leaders combine their enjoyment of recreational activities with the challenge of working with children. They involve children in sports, recreation, fitness, arts, crafts, and new hobbies, 22-4. Some job examples include recreation leaders and counselors for youth in civic, religious, and camp programs.

Work settings include city parks and recreation departments, theme parks, tourist attractions, campgrounds, and recreation areas. High school graduates fill some recreation positions. Other positions require a two-year degree in parks and recreation or social work. A recreation supervisor must have a four-year degree in an area, such as parks and recreation management, leisure studies, physical education, or other related fields.

Social Workers

Social workers help children in need. Many social workers are involved in child welfare and family services. Their role is to ensure the well-being of children. They may counsel parents who need help guiding

22-4 As a recreation leader, this man combines his love of children with his love of sports.

their children or youth. They may find homes for children who experience neglect or abandonment. Social workers may also work in child protective services. They may investigate reported cases of child abuse and neglect. These workers decide what steps are necessary to protect the children.

Government agencies, community and religious organizations, hospitals, and other social-service agencies employ social workers. A four-year degree in social work is the minimum requirement for most positions in social work, but an advanced degree is often preferred for social workers.

Health Services Personnel

The demand for health-care specialists who focus on children continues to grow. Some of the professionals who provide health care for children include pediatricians, pediatric dentists, pediatric nurses and school nurses, dietitians, child psychologists and psychiatrists, and physical therapists.

Health-care specialists must have at least a four-year degree. Most require advanced degrees and internships. Passing a state exam in their field is also part of licensure to practice in the health services. Positions requiring less education include dental hygienists, nurses' aides, and physician's assistants all of whom work under the supervision of the specialist.

Working on Behalf of Children and Families

Many people work in careers that do not have direct contact with children, but children benefit them indirectly. These various professions require four-year degrees at minimum.

Family Life Educators

Family life educators teach teens and adults about effective family living, which thereby benefit the children. They might lead parent seminars and training sessions sponsored by businesses, civic groups, or religious organizations. Family life educators might also teach in high schools, community colleges, and universities.

Parent Educators

Parent educators are people who teach parenting or child development. They may teach parents, parents-to-be, and adults who are training to become parent educators. Some parent educators teach in group settings, while others work one-on-one with a parent, often in the parent's home. Early childhood teachers and other professionals in child development, family life, or education also serve as parent educators. Most parent educators have a four-year degree.

Child Development Teachers

Child development teachers teach child development and parenting classes to students from junior high to college level. These teachers may supervise child development laboratory classes. They may also teach students to work with children in child care settings. A four-year degree is the minimum, however, college-level teachers are required to have advanced degrees.

Teacher Educators

Teacher educators work with college students to prepare family life educators and child development and early childhood teachers for their positions. They often do in-service training in their work settings and at professional conferences. Teacher educators must have an advanced degree at minimum.

Researchers

Researchers work in hospitals or laboratories studying childhood diseases, 22-5. At universities, researchers may study aspects of child development such as learning or the effects of violence. Researchers have advanced degrees and many years of experience in their fields of expertise.

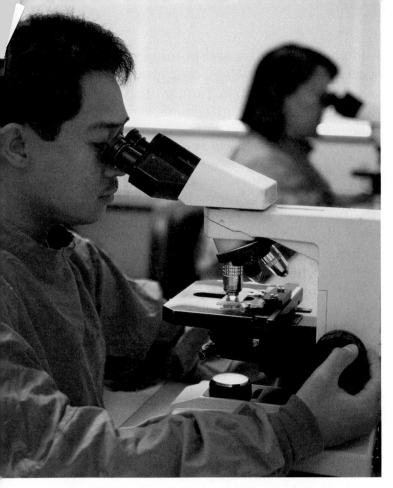

22-5 This researcher is studying a disease in children. Preventive health care and treatments for illnesses require years of research.

Consultants

Consultants take research data and share it with those in other child and family services careers. For example, a legislative aide may work for a government agency, specific program, or elected official. These consultants locate research studies, summarize them, and report findings that help with handling issues concerning children and families.

Creating and Selling Products and Services for Children

Perhaps you might like to create or sell a child-related product, such as children's clothes, toys, or books. You might enjoy a career in the children's entertainment field. Because these careers are so diverse, training and education requirements greatly vary. For example, creators of textiles have degrees in chemistry. Marketers of children's products have business degrees, but people who pack and ship products work in entry-level positions. Designers, writers, or entertainers are creative, but may not have college degrees.

Designing and Selling Children's Products

Creative designers, educational experts, and safety specialists often join forces to design children's furniture, toys, and games. A child's basic needs are kept in mind, especially learning and safety needs. The most successful products undergo careful research and design.

Although products may exist for many years, creative designers always look for ways to improve them. For example, baby-bottle design has changed several times over the years. Manufacturers make continuous improvements in materials and design of diapers. Advances in textile products often make children's clothing safer, more comfortable, and easier to maintain.

Writers, Artists, and Entertainers

Do you like to work with words? Do you find writing a good way to express your ideas? Do you enjoy drawing to express your thoughts? Perhaps a career in writing or illustrating children's books is for you. Many children's books become classics as thousands of new books are published yearly. A career as a writer or illustrator of children's books can be very rewarding.

Children's writers must be able to capture children's interest. They must be able to visualize stories through the eyes of children. An illustrator must have the ability to interpret a writer's stories using appealing artwork, 22-6.

Books are one form of communication used to entertain children, and television is another. The average child watches 21 to 23 hours of TV weekly. Writers, entertainers, directors, and producers create special programming for children. Many of their creations include movies and live shows that entertain and educate children.

Entrepreneurs

An **entrepreneur** is a person who owns and operates his or her business. Many opportunities exist for entrepreneurs in child-related areas. For example, a hobby or special talent may form the basis for self-employment. A part-time or full-time job may give you an idea and the experience necessary to start your own business.

Many entrepreneurs work in the child care field. They often own in-home child care businesses or small center programs. Perhaps they work as a director or director/teacher of their own businesses or employ others to staff their programs.

Other entrepreneurs form businesses that provide children's products or services. For example, a person might design and sell a line of children's clothes or a new toy or game. Some entrepreneurs plan and carry out children's parties or provide entertainment at special children's events. Such entertainers include clowns, magicians, and artists.

Before investing your time and money in starting a business, it is wise to consider both the pros and cons of business ownership. Many people like the idea of being their own bosses. It is possible to make a good income, but it is also possible to lose a great deal of money. You might have the freedom to set your own hours, but you may have to work long hours to stay in business. There are no company benefits except those you provide for yourself.

If self-employment appeals to you, be sure you are prepared to handle all aspects of the business. You will need training in child development. In addition, you will need to take courses in marketing, accounting, business management, and business law. With the proper training and a willingness to work hard, the rewards of a profitable business can be yours, 22-7.

Key Trends and Job Outlook

Careers take investments in both time and money, so you will want to evaluate job trends and future prospects for a particular career. By studying trends, you learn what employment opportunities exist when you complete the education and/or training for your child and family related career. Trends can also tell you about future opportunities in a particular field. Knowing which careers will be in high demand and offer good wages is necessary for your future employment and success.

As careers continue to change, workers must change along with them. Because many families need help from professionals, the job outlook for many careers related to parenting, children, and families is expanding. Here are a few opportunities to think about.

22-6 An artist illustrates children's books with vivid and realistic drawings.

22-7 This entrepreneur is a music teacher. People hire him to teach their children to play the piano.

More Entry-Level Child Care Careers

The child care field is growing rapidly. As more parents enter the workforce, the demand for child care providers is increasing faster than average. This has many implications for careers in the child care field.

Because child care providers are in high demand, there are many entry-level openings in the child care field. Some people may be able to work as a part-time teacher assistant while in high school or college. After high school graduation, some find full-time employment in child care. However, quality programs require them to continue their education as they work.

As the field grows, the number of people interested in child care careers grows, causing more competition among applicants. Employers will more likely hire applicants who are better qualified to provide care. This means a person's skills, knowledge, and experiences become more and more important even at entry-level positions.

The demand for highly qualified employees stimulates the need for more training programs. Today, more colleges offer education and training programs for future child care workers. This also opens up more

career opportunities for those working on behalf of children and families, such as child development teachers, teacher educators, and parent educators.

Increasing Need for Quality Child Care Programs

Another trend is the growing emphasis parents place on the quality of care their children receive. This emphasis has led both child care centers and family child care homes to seek accreditation. Because staff training is the most important aspect of quality, accreditation agencies advocate higher professional qualifications. In the future, more child care careers will require a four-year degree for employment. This will raise many child care careers to a professional status. Higher status usually leads to better salaries and fringe benefits.

Expanding Early Childhood Education Programs

Today, parents want their preschool children to spend most of their time learning concepts and skills. In response, educational centers for young children are emerging and hiring early childhood education teachers. These teachers work with children from preschool through grade 3. Many school districts have more job openings for early childhood teachers with specialized training than they can fill. Schools especially need highly qualified teachers to work with the following children:

- *Preschoolers at risk for school failure.* These children do not necessarily have disabilities. They have developmental lags due to poverty, lack of good parental care and education, or stress. With quality programs, these children often overcome their developmental lags before entering kindergarten or first grade, 22-8.

- *Young children with special needs.* As you read earlier, federal law mandates public special education for children with disabilities who are ages 3 to 5. This has increased the demand for early childhood special education teachers.

- *Children who are English Language Learners (ELL).* Young children whose primary language is not English can be at a disadvantage when they enter school. Teachers who are bilingual and who can train children in English as a second language are in high demand.

New Settings for Child Care

With so many types of child care programs available, child care workers can find more jobs in less-conventional settings. New settings for child care operations include programs at private employer sites, malls, hospitals, and military facilities. These settings may result in some special needs for children and their parents. For example, at military facilities teachers may need to help children deal with excess fear due to a parent sent to another country thousands of miles from home. Also within this child care setting, teachers must plan for children and parents who come from diverse cultures and who speak many languages. In like manner, each child care setting is unique with its own rewards and challenges.

Growing Needs for Family Services

More parents are working long hours outside the home. Extended families and nuclear families are decreasing, while single-parent families are increasing. Economic problems and lack of education leave many families in poverty. With all of these trends comes the increasing need for a variety of family services.

22-8 Schools need highly qualified teachers to work with young children who must overcome developmental lags before entering kindergarten.

More than ever, families need support, prevention, intervention, and treatment services. As a result, careers related to parenting, children, and families are expanding and becoming more specialized. Thus, careers in social work, family life education, and parent education are growing.

Are You Suited to Working with Children and Families?

Perhaps you see several positions related to children and families that interest you. Maybe you learned that job trends indicate increasing opportunities for these positions and you want to begin making career plans. Before moving to that step, you need to consider whether your personal qualities are right for this type of work.

Important Personal Traits

Personal traits include your personality and attitudes that you do not learn through career-specific training. These traits are highly important for careers that involve working with people. Often these traits can make a difference between success or failure even for a well-trained professional.

Traits for Working with Children

Personal traits, such as a positive personality and attitude, are essential for working with children. Young children in child care need to form attachments to their teachers. Bonds between teachers and children, even teens, are often strong. Certain personal traits are necessary to succeed in a job working closely with children. These traits include

- *Liking children.* Do you like children? If you can answer yes to this question with no reservations, then you possess the most important trait, 22-9. You must enjoy being with children no matter what the circumstances might be.

- *Concern for children.* Liking children means you have concern about their welfare. A recreation leader, for example, should remain positive even if one child doesn't contribute to a winning team. Children need recognition for their efforts as well as their successes.

22-9 Liking children is an essential quality for those who work directly with children. Coaches enjoy teaching children the skills they need in order to play sports.

- *Sense of humor.* You must be able to laugh with children. Humor often helps children achieve.

- *Comfort with closeness.* Children like to be physically close to adults and feel loved. Comfort with physical closeness is an important care provider trait. Listening to and communicating openly with children are also necessary.

- *Adaptability.* Children can be unpredictable. You must be able to adapt to changing circumstances. Adults need to define limits to provide guidance, but children need to know they can make choices within those limits.

- *Patience.* Working with children requires patience. For example, children are usually very eager to learn anything new, yet they often move slowly and deliberately. Because their gross- and fine-motor skills are developing, children need more time to accomplish tasks. Lack of patience with children and taking over tasks for them might interfere with growth and development. The bright smile that crosses a child's face when he or she finally completes a task will more than repay you for any lost time.

Traits for Working with Adult Family Members

Professionals who provide family services to adults share a concern for people's problems and a desire to help. Leadership and organizational duties are also primary tasks of men and women who choose to work directly with families. Some specific personal traits needed to work with adults include sensitivity to others' needs, patience, and trustworthiness. Maintaining composure during a crisis, thinking creatively, and using effective communication skills are also necessary traits. Working with the staff of agencies and organizations that provide family services also requires such personal traits.

Your Self-Assessment

Finding a career that brings happiness and a sense of fulfillment requires knowledge of yourself—especially your interests, aptitudes, and abilities. It may also mean looking at your personality and your values as motivating factors.

The ideal career combines your interests, aptitudes, and abilities. When planning your career, taking a careful inventory of your unique assets—or a *self-assessment*— is important. Your high school counselor is your best guide to tools you can use to assess your interests, aptitudes, and abilities, 22-10.

Some assessment tools are self-directed, meaning that you can take the assessment and review the results yourself. Some of these are available online. Other assessments require the help of a person who is licensed or trained to interpret the results. To make sure any assessment tool you use provides accurate results, check with your school counselor.

Interests

What are your *interests*? **Interests** are activities that appeal to a person over a period of time. One way to determine your interests is to review the way you use your time. You likely give more time to things you find engaging. Some interests are mainly age or stage related. These interests often disappear in time. Other interests are more individual, and some of these grow with time.

You may want to think about family interests in connection with your own. Family life influences the formation and development of interests. Some of your interests may become hobbies and simply bring you pleasure and relaxation. Others may provide a foundation for your career. Interests have a great deal to do with your motivation to achieve.

Career learning and job satisfaction highly connect to interests. For this reason,

22-10 Meeting with your high school counselor is the first step in assessing your interests, aptitudes, and abilities.

people sometimes use *interest inventories*—measures of preferences, often in a multiple-choice style—as a guide in planning their careers. These inventories help you see what interests you most and ways to link your interests to possible careers. One such inventory is the *O*Net® Interest Profiler*. You can take this assessment on your own and interpret the results yourself. You can directly link the results to many occupations through *O*Net® OnLine*.

Aptitudes

What are your aptitudes? **Aptitudes** are your natural talents. A person's best chance to achieve without too much stress comes in areas in which he or she has natural ability. Furthermore, people feel a sense of fulfillment when they work in careers for which they have aptitudes.

Going into a career for which you have an aptitude is simply putting your inborn talents to work. For example, a person may have aptitudes in areas, such as motor performance, music, art, verbal, mathematics, or interpersonal (people-oriented) relations, 22-11. Aptitudes come in various degrees, too.

Because employers invest time, money, and other resources in their employees,

22-11 People may have aptitudes in various areas, such as working with people.

they need to know about their employee's aptitudes. When employees find their work too hard or unchallenging, both the employer and the employee lose. Employers may assess employee aptitude by using an aptitude test. Aptitude tests are not new, but employers are using them now more than ever. Today, companies spend over $400 million annually on employment tests of all kinds, including aptitude tests.

How can you discover your aptitudes? Sometimes you recognize your aptitudes as something you can do easily. Other times, someone else recognizes your aptitudes and tells you about them. Testing is generally the best way to learn about your aptitudes. To learn more about your aptitudes, talk with

your guidance counselor. Many guidance counselors receive training to give such aptitude assessments as the *O*Net® Ability Profiler.* This assessment looks at skills such as verbal ability, arithmetic reasoning, computation, spatial ability, form perception, clerical perception, manual dexterity, and finger dexterity.

Abilities

What are your present abilities and what abilities can you develop? Skills that you learn and develop are your **abilities.** Some abilities are important for many careers, such as communication skills. To a great extent, you learn these general abilities before graduating from high school. You learn career-specific skills through specialized training and experiences. Both types of abilities should continue to develop throughout your working years. You might also check out reliable career Web sites, such as *O*Net®, CareerOneStop,* or the *Occupational Outlook Handbook.*

Building Workplace Knowledge, Skills, and Attitudes

As you think about your future, you may want to pursue a career working with parents, children, and families. If so, you may wonder how to start preparing for this career while you are still in high school. The first step to building your career foundation is strengthening the knowledge, skills, and attitudes needed for a successful career.

Strengthening Academic Skills

Throughout your school years, you have worked at acquiring skills needed to live and work in the adult world. By now, you probably have a good idea about the strengths and weaknesses in your skills. This is the time to improve weak skills and strengthen those you already do well. What academic skills do all employers look for in employees? They include communication, speaking, listening, writing, reading, and math and science skills, 22-12.

Communication Skills

Communicating—such as speaking, listening, and writing—is central to your success in working with parents, children, and families. Employers need employees who express themselves clearly on the job.

When speaking with another person, you should always try to be positive. Watch for clues that the listener understands what you said. Use words that match the ability level of the listener, keeping messages to children very simple.

22-12 Developing strong academic skills will benefit you in the workplace.

When listening, it is important to pay close attention to what the person is saying. Encourage that person, whether a child or an adult, to take the time needed to express his or her thoughts. Respond to the speaker so he or she knows what you understand the message to be.

Verbal communication uses words, but *nonverbal* communication sends messages without using words. Messages are sent through facial expressions, posture, and bodily gestures. Folding your arms, avoiding eye contact, or turning away from a speaker says you are not open to his or her ideas. A relaxed posture and comfortable distance (not too close or too far) help show the speaker you are interested in the communication. This is true in the workplace as well as in your personal life.

Writing Skills

Written communication must be especially accurate and clear because it is not a two-way communication. Employers expect clarity of ideas and accuracy in written reports and correspondence. Avoid grammar, punctuation, or spelling errors. As a writer, you must imagine your reader. Ask yourself questions, such as: Does this make sense? Have I written too much or too little? Then revise your written communication accordingly.

Reading Skills

Reading is a necessary skill for all careers. You should be able to easily understand materials written for your grade level. Do you turn to the dictionary or other resources to find meanings of words you do not know? Can you read a graph or understand the details of a budget? People who work with children and families often need to read reports, interpret data, or research background information.

Math and Science Skills

Few careers related to parenting, children, or families require advanced math or science skills. Generally, you should be able to use basic math skills, such as operations (adding, subtracting, multiplying, and dividing), fractions, and percentages. You should also be able to construct and read graphs and charts that show relationships among numbers. As an early childhood teacher, you will teach children how to sort by size and shape and how to use numbers in counting. In tracking income and expenses in a child care business, you will use math and basic accounting principles.

In contrast, advanced math and science skills may be used in careers that benefit children and families. For example, a pediatric medical researcher might use complex statistical analysis when developing a cure for disease. A registered dietitian uses knowledge of human physiology and chemistry in developing meal plans for people with special dietary needs, such as children with juvenile diabetes.

Strengthening Thinking Skills

In addition to having a strong academic foundation, employers also expect employees to have strong critical-thinking, decision-making, and problem-solving skills. Especially in careers involving children, parents, and families, the ability to think critically and creatively can have a lifelong effect. Can you analyze and evaluate a problem or situation? Can you take your knowledge, expand on it, and use it to make decisions and solve problems effectively? The ability to make well-reasoned, ethical decisions that consider the best interests of all people involved is of great value to employers.

What can you do to strengthen your thinking skills? One thing you can do is to look for opportunities to use these skills in daily life. Be intentional about thinking critically and making wise decisions to solve problems. Another option for improving your skills is to seek out volunteer or service-learning opportunities that relate to your career choice. These activities offer you real-world experiences for using your thinking skills.

Strengthening Employability Skills

All workers need the academic and thinking skills described earlier. They also need a basic understanding of how to operate computers needed for their work. In addition, they need important personal skills that will help them interact well with others in the workplace.

Computer Skills

In today's workplace, many jobs require the use of a computer to get work done. As a result, employers expect job applicants to have basic computer skills. These skills include word processing, sending e-mail, accessing the Internet, managing data, and creating slide presentations. Your computer skills will impact your ability to find and keep a job, 22-13.

An employer will expect you to know how to write business letters, office memos, and e-mail messages. Some people write more easily with a computer than with a pen and paper. This requires basic keystroking skills that you can perfect with practice. Do not get into the habit of using shorthand or abbreviations common in instant and text messaging. Electronic communications should always use proper grammar, capitalization, and punctuation. Write them with the same care and courtesy as other more formal types of business communications.

22-13 The strength of your computer skills will impact your ability to find and keep a job.

Teamwork Skills

Teamwork involves working with other people to achieve common goals. Teamwork is essential to careers involving parenting, children, and families. For example, in most child care programs and many schools, teams rather than individuals do the teaching. Teachers and assistant teachers are the key members, but parents and students in child development classes also participate. When working with children, employees must work directly with parents to create a partnership focused on the children's best interests. Teamwork is also required among child care program administrators, their boards, funding agencies, and others at the organization's highest levels.

Good teams allow each person to use his or her own talents to enhance the group's effort. Teamwork always begins with a full review of all needs and ideas. It involves using problem-solving and decision-making skills.

Teamwork has advantages over individual work. Decisions are often better or more creative due to combining of ideas. Because all members are responsible for a decision, much effort goes into making a correct one. People tend to support a group decision that involved their help over a decision made by some other person. Morale, or group enthusiasm, is important for teamwork. Morale is higher when each person contributes to the team instead of competing with others.

Perhaps the best way to learn teamwork skills is to engage in these tasks in the classroom. Another way is to join and participate in school or community organizations. Through teamwork, you can learn to clarify goals, manage conflicts, find group solutions, and put ideas into action with others. You can develop many communication skills through teamwork, too.

Leadership Skills

Leadership is the ability to direct and influence others to achieve goals. Leadership skills can help you succeed in school and on the job. They help build your confidence. Effective leadership skills make you feel good about yourself and your accomplishments, and encourage you to set and achieve goals.

No matter what their position, good leaders share similar characteristics. These characteristics include the following:

- *Display consideration.* Leaders recognize the needs of all group members and strive to meet them.

- *Use effective communication.* Good leaders express ideas clearly, effectively, and in a way that generates enthusiasm.

- *Provide structure to team efforts.* Effective leaders share their expectations of team members with the group and report what others can expect from their leader.

- ***Show flexibility.*** Leaders are open to fresh ideas and are good problem-solvers, but they know when to seek outside help.

- ***Demonstrate integrity.*** Effective leaders are honest. They firmly adhere to workplace ethics and expect the same of those with whom they work.

- ***Display accountability.*** Leaders are accountable for group results. If problems occur, they take responsibility and find solutions.

- ***Build trust.*** Strong leaders consistently follow through in meeting commitments.

Leadership skills are well worth developing. Groups, employers, and communities need good leaders to help them achieve their goals. What are some ways that you can enhance your leadership abilities?

Strengthening Workplace Attitudes

Success on the job requires as much or more effort than your job search. Read the characteristics of a good employee listed in 22-14. People with these qualities most often find their careers a rewarding part of life. All qualities of a good employee connect to attitude.

A positive attitude is probably one of the most important qualities for employability. Attitude is a state of mind. People may have positive or negative attitudes about specific situations. More importantly, people have overall positive or negative ways of viewing life, including work. Employers know that employees with positive attitudes are more pleasant to work with, and they are also more productive. How can employers tell about employees' attitudes? Employees with positive attitudes

- get along with other people by being warm, friendly, polite, and respectful.

Qualities of a Good Employee

- Positive attitude
- Courteous and friendly
- Respectful to others
- Patient
- Dependable
- Honest
- Loyal
- Enthusiastic
- Shows initiative
- Follows rules and regulations
- Follows directions
- Accepts criticism
- Willing to help others
- Clean, neat appearance
- Cooperative
- Adaptable
- Invests in career

22-14 A good employee will try to develop these qualities.

- do not complain about work assignments and look for excuses about not meeting deadlines. They do not blame others when things go wrong.

- accept change although it requires new learnings and new tasks.

- put the employer's goals above their own. Thus, they are willing to assist when others need help or when extra effort is needed to meet goals in a timely way.

Courtesy, respect for others, and patience describe some of the most important qualities people need for all aspects of their life including their work. Manners affect your relationships with your employer, coworkers, and clients or customers.

Dependability, honesty, and loyalty are desirable workplace qualities. *Dependability* means being at work when you are scheduled to be there. It means giving your best for the entire work time. It includes arriving on time, working except for normal breaks, and staying through your scheduled time.

Honesty is more than not lying or not stealing. Honest people give their best skills or abilities to their job tasks. They separate their personal lives from their business tasks. They do not take care of personal matters during work hours or use work property for personal business.

An employee who shows *loyalty* is faithful to and supportive of the ethical goals of the business. Sometimes this means keeping certain matters private. Even when problems arise, the loyal employee works to resolve them without undue hurt or stress.

A good employee is enthusiastic and shows *initiative*. Enthusiastic people are eager to learn, and others are eager to teach them, 22-15. A person who shows initiative can work without being told to do each task and without constant supervision. Most

importantly, initiative makes a difference between average and high performance. Even people with gifts and talents can and do fail in careers unless they work hard.

When you accept a job, you are agreeing to follow present and future workplace rules and regulations. By following directions, you avoid confusing others and wasting time and resources. It also means that you will do your best to keep yourself and others safe. Accepting criticism is a way of learning and growing. A mature person can accept criticism without becoming angry or defensive.

Your interpersonal skills with your coworkers and clients or customers will help you succeed. Your willingness to help others and be cooperative will make you a true member of your workplace family.

Careers are ever changing. By adapting and changing to new conditions, you further your career opportunities and your own development. Invest in your career by trying new experiences and getting additional training and education. Each position you successfully fill will bring you one step closer to reaching your career goals.

Personal Appearance for the Workplace

Personal appearance not only influences your chances of getting a job, but it also influences your workplace success. Your grooming and what you wear says a great deal about you; that is, whether you take pride in yourself. Of most importance, is a clean, neat appearance. For example, a neat hairstyle, clean and trimmed fingernails, and subtle makeup help you look your best.

The choice of clothing depends on where you work and what you do. In other words, the way you dress shows pride for your employer and for your responsibilities. Because there are many types of careers related to children and families, the exact clothing requirements cannot be spelled out. Those working directly with young children

22-15 Employees who are enthusiastic and show initiative on the job are more likely to perform tasks well.

often wear casual, washable clothing. For example, a child care worker might wear well-pressed cotton slacks with a casual shirt, blouse, or sweater. Employees in some of these settings also wear uniforms. Professionals who work in administration or some human-services careers may wear dressier attire.

Generally speaking, a simple, classic style that makes the employee look confident and comfortable is preferable for all of these careers. Some fashion choices are inappropriate for the workplace, 22-16. You should avoid them regardless of career choice. All clothing should be clean, neat, and in good repair, too.

Developing a Career Plan

A **career plan** is a program of study to reach a desired career goal. Career plans involve short- and long-term goals. *Short-term*

goals are goals you can achieve in the near future, usually within a year. Entering an essay competition next month and joining a student organization are examples. *Long-term goals* take longer than a year to achieve. Examples are graduating from high school and finishing a two-year program to become a child care assistant.

A career plan is basically a guide to the specific education and training needed for a chosen career, 22-17. It is a roadmap that shows what steps to take to prepare for your career goals and desires. A personal career plan identifies the specific courses, learning experiences, and co-curricular activities to pursue year-by-year while in school.

You should review your career plan at least annually to make sure it still reflects your goals. If your interests change, so may your goals.

Using the Career Clusters

What is the best way to study careers? One important way to start is by checking the *career clusters*. **Career clusters** are 16 broad groupings of occupational and career specialties, 22-18. The clusters link school-based learning to the knowledge and skills students will need for success in the workplace. States, schools, educators, employers, industry groups, and professional organizations worked together to set the guidelines and standards on which the career clusters are based.

Within each career cluster are *career pathways*, or subgroups of occupations that require a certain set of common knowledge and skills for career success. Each career pathway includes several related occupations, ranging from entry-level positions to those more challenging. Your teachers and guidance counselors can help you investigate the career pathways that lead to occupations focused on your career goal.

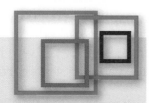

Inappropriate Workplace Attire

- Gaudy jewelry
- Clothing that is too big or too small
- Frayed belts
- Unpolished shoes
- Low-cut blouses; skirts with high slits
- Halter and strapless tops
- Underwear tank tops
- Belly shirts
- Many types of sleeveless shirts
- Shirts with inappropriate images or sayings
- Ultra-short skirts
- Jeans
- Workout attire, capri pants, and low-waist slacks
- Clunky shoes, flip-flops, and sandals
- Lack of socks, hosiery, or appropriate undergarments
- Overdone makeup and heavy fragrance

22-16 What message would these inappropriate clothing items send to your employer?

One Career Plan for a Future Child Care Worker

Short-Term Goals	
Education and training	• Take courses in child development, parenting, psychology, health, and child care • Select topic in parenting for senior paper
Extracurricular activities	• Join FCCLA • Serve on an FCCLA committee focused on children
Work and volunteer experiences	• Volunteer to help with child care for parents attending school and community meetings • Babysit on weekends
Long-Term Goals	
Education and training	• Get an associate's degree at the local community college in child development or early childhood education • Work on Child Development Associate (CDA) competencies after employed
Extracurricular activities	• Join the college chapters of AAFCS and NAEYC • Join professional chapters of AAFCS and NAEYC after graduation
Work and volunteer experiences	• Volunteer for 10 hours a week at the Head Start center • Work 30 to 40 hours per week at a child care center or preschool during summer breaks

22-17 A career plan helps people stay focused on the steps toward their career goals.

By using the career cluster approach to prepare for a career, students will have the core requirements for several related occupations. This will allow more career flexibility. Tomorrow's workers must be prepared to keep their knowledge and skills updated so they can change jobs easily if needed.

Checking Education and Training Options

Checking education and training options is an important part of building your career plan. For many entry-level jobs, a high school diploma and on-the-job training may be all you need. If your goals are leading you to higher education, the following options are available:

Vocational-Technical Schools. Institutions such as these offer hands-on, occupation-specific education and training in many areas, such as health services. Vocational-technical schools focus on providing students with the skills needed to move directly into the workforce. Many offer certificate programs and associate's and bachelor's degrees.

Two-Year or Community Colleges. These colleges generally offer certificate programs or associate's degrees you can earn in two years or less. For example, you could earn EMT First Responder certification or an associate's degree as a paralegal. Because costs are generally lower than at four-year colleges, many students obtain an associate's degree on the path to obtaining a bachelor's degree.

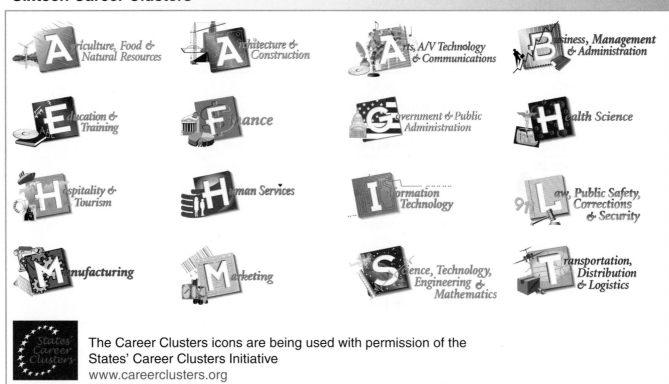

The Career Clusters icons are being used with permission of the States' Career Clusters Initiative
www.careerclusters.org

22-18 The career clusters help you identify various careers and the knowledge and skills needed for employment.

Four-Year Colleges and Universities. Many higher-level careers serving children and families require a *bachelor's* degree from a four-year college or university. For example, many careers in education, human services, health sciences, and protective services require a bachelor's degree. Some require advanced degrees.

Distance learning. In recent years, distance learning—off-site learning or off-campus education—has been gaining momentum. This form of learning allows students and teachers to communicate via print or electronic media, or through technology that offers real-time communication. Many private and public institutions offer certification courses and degree programs in this format. Make sure that any distance-learning institution is fully accredited.

Military Service and Training. While on active duty or after an honorable discharge, military personnel have many options for education and training. Some options involve learning trades in such areas as electronics, auto mechanics, or clerical jobs. With educational funds available through the *Montgomery GI Bill* (during active duty) or the *Veterans Educational Program* (after honorable discharge), military personnel can also earn an associate's or bachelor's degree.

Work-Based Learning

Many high schools have career days or weeklong programs in which students learn about a career through job shadowing. **Job shadowing** is simply learning about the job by following an employee as he or she works. If you think about it, children job shadow their parents for years. Thus, they understand many aspects of their parents' work.

Work-based learning programs are school programs that help students get firsthand experiences in the world of work. Work-based programs involve the student, a *program coordinator* (a school faculty member), and one or more people at the work-site, 22-19. A student often works with a work-site mentor who teaches him or her how to do a job well. The school's *program coordinator* consults with the work-site supervisor and others who need to know about the student's work performance. The program coordinator also works with the student, providing support and guidance with workplace issues. Work-based programs in high schools often take on one of these three forms.

- *Cooperative education.* To help students make a transition to the world of work, **cooperative education** combines classroom training with paid, on-the-job training in a certain occupation. Generally offered to seniors, students take required and elective courses in the morning or afternoon. They also enroll in a cooperative education class to learn more about careers and to develop employability skills. For the remainder of the day, the student works at the job. Students earn credit for the class and receive pay for the part-time work.

- *Apprenticeships.* Specialized job-training programs in a craft, trade, or any career (such as child care) are **apprenticeships.** The student takes a class in the career area at school and then applies this knowledge on the job under the supervision of a *master.* (Student apprenticeships are not *registered apprenticeships,* which require several years of training after graduation.)

- *Internships.* School programs that offer paid or unpaid supervised work experience to learn about specific jobs or careers are **internships.** Students often continue their studies while taking part in these experiences. They enroll in school internship programs like other classes and receive credit toward graduation. Students meet internship work requirements during or after school hours.

Regardless of the form of work-based learning programs, all help students develop their career goals. They also help students gain valuable work experience in a career area and possibly earn part-time pay. Upon graduation, some students find full-time employment with the employer who provided their work-based learning.

Joining Student and Professional Organizations

Most teens enjoy being part of a student group and high schools usually offer several options. Communicating in a group can give you chances for individual expression and group sharing. You will develop interpersonal skills as you learn to work for mutual goals. You will also learn to work with a variety of people in different settings. Learning to work effectively in a group will help you in your future roles. Make the most of the chances for group participation while you are in high school, both as a member and as a leader.

22-19 Work-based learning programs in the high school offer students the opportunity to develop real-world workplace skills.

Joining a student organization lets you participate in group activities. Most groups conduct their meetings using *parliamentary procedure*. **Parliamentary procedure** is a set of rules for making decisions and conducting business in an orderly manner. *Robert's Rules of Order* is the most commonly used method among adult civic groups and many professional organizations. This method helps meetings proceed in a timely manner. It ensures members appropriately handle important business during the meeting. Learning this process during high school will help you feel more comfortable in meetings you attend as an adult.

Family, Career and Community Leaders of America, Inc. (FCCLA) is the only national career and technical high school student organization with the family as its focus, 22-20. Local chapters are active in high schools that offer family and consumer sciences education. Because FCCLA provides many opportunities for growth, the organization is an excellent choice for students taking parenting education courses. Through the FCCLA, you can apply your parenting knowledge to numerous projects and competitions. You can also develop critical skills needed in any career—leadership, teamwork, and communication.

Family, Career and Community Leaders of America, Inc. (FCCLA)

Purposes
- Provide opportunities for personal growth through family and consumer sciences education, such as making decisions and accepting responsibilities
- Strengthen the functions of the family as a basic social unit of society
- Advance democracy in the home and community
- Help achieve global harmony and cooperation
- Prepare for multiple adult roles
- Promote family and consumer sciences and related occupations

Program
- Functions as part of family and consumer sciences curriculum
- Focuses on family
- Teaches leadership and teamwork skills through participation at local, state, and national levels (students can work on individual, cooperative, and competitive projects in different aspects of family, career, and community life)
- Offers team and individual competitive events, such as STAR Events (Students Taking Action with Recognition), *Career Investigation, Early Childhood,* and *Focus on Children*
- Has competitively awarded scholarships

Permission to use granted by FCCLA.

For more information, check the FCCLA Web site at www.fcclainc.org.

22-20 The FCCLA provides students with opportunities to apply their family and consumer sciences education and to prepare for possible careers.

Membership in professional organizations is usually available to high school students in their last semester. Membership is a good way to keep current with information in your career field, which enhances your employability skills. It also offers many chances for leadership while serving on committees or serving as an officer of the organization. Professional organizations focused on working with parents, children, and families include the following:

- American Association of Family and Consumer Sciences (AAFCS)
- American Psychological Association (APA)
- National Association for the Education of Young Children (NAEYC)
- National Association of Social Workers (NASW)

Building a Portfolio

As you prepare for a career, think about ways that you can showcase your achievements. A useful tool for many people who work with parents, children, and families is a *portfolio*. A **portfolio** is a collection of materials that you can use to document your achievements over time. When building your portfolio, preserve items that show evidence of your career skills and academic skills. See 22-21 for items to include in your portfolio.

Your Job Search

You, like many students, may want to prepare for a future career by working part-time. Gaining valuable work experience while still in high school can help you set goals for your career. In many situations, you will able to obtain an entry-level job in a career field of choice. Unlike work-based learning programs, high schools do not

Building a Portfolio

Building a portfolio takes time, thought, and careful planning. Items that you might put in your portfolio include the following:

- Written summary of career skills and goals
- Work samples that show mastery of certain skills, including photographs or videos of projects
- Writing samples that demonstrate communication skills
- Letters of recommendation from employers or teachers that document specific career-related skills
- Achievement awards and special honors
- Certificates of completion
- Transcripts, licenses, or certifications
- Summary of any volunteer or service-learning project participation
- Copy of résumé
- List of references (if references have given permission to use their names and contact information in your portfolio and when applying for work)

22-21 An effective portfolio shows evidence of your career skills to potential employers.

sponsor or supervise part-time employment. As you think about looking for a job, you might wonder where to begin. The first step is to use as many sources of information as possible to locate possible jobs.

Sources for Job Leads

As you begin your job search, learning how and where to locate job leads is a valuable skill. If you are interested in a career related to parenting, children, and families, and have your career plan ready to go, you can narrow your search to employers in these areas. There are several resources you can use to find job leads. These resources include the following:

- *Networking.* Talking about your interest in finding a job with friends, family, neighbors, teachers, school counselors, and others you know can be an effective way to find work.

- *Want ads and community bulletin boards.* Some job leads are found in the "want ads," or classified section of the newspaper. These ads may give you specific or general information about various jobs and who to contact for application. Community bulletin boards often post jobs available within your local area. These bulletin boards may be located in supermarkets, shopping centers, or community recreation centers. You might also check out the "help wanted" signs in the windows of many businesses.

- *Employment agencies.* These agencies help people find jobs. Private agencies generally charge a fee for their services to either the employer or applicant. Public employment agencies are government-sponsored and charge no fees. To find local employment agencies, look for listings such as *Job Service* or *Employment* in your telephone directory.

- *Internet.* The Internet is a good way to find job leads, 22-22. When you search using such key words as *career, job opportunities,* or *employment opportunities,* many sources of career options appear. You can search for jobs in your local community or across the country. You can search the Internet for specific jobs or post an electronic résumé on a job-search bulletin board.

Writing a Résumé

You can do several things to prepare for a job interview. First, you can create a *résumé.* A **résumé** is a document that contains detailed information about your education, work experience, and qualifications for

Career Information Web Sites

Web Site	Type of Information
The Occupational Outlook Handbook (OOH) www.bls.gov/oco/	• Describes education and training, expected earnings, working conditions, job outlook, and related occupations • Updated every two years
The Occupational Information Network (O*NET®) www.doleta.gov/programs/onet/	• Offers the latest information on education and training, counseling, and employment of workers • Includes Web-based career-exploration tools along with ability and interests assessments
CareerOneStop www.careeronestop.org	• Offers job outlook and trends for all types of careers • Includes information on education and training and earnings potential for every state
Career Voyages www.careervoyages.gov/	• Contains information for students, parents, job seekers, and career changers • Offers information on career clusters, emerging industries, and education and training needed for *in demand* careers

22-22 Internet Web sites can be a good source of career information when exploring careers.

employment. See 22-23 for a description of what to include on your résumé. You can use your résumé as a guide when filling out a job application. You can also leave it with the potential employer if appropriate. By keeping your résumé on your computer or saving it to a CD-ROM, you can update it on a regular basis.

When sending a paper copy of your résumé to a potential employer, you should send it with a cover letter. Your cover letter should capture the reader's interest and explain why you are sending your résumé. Be sure to explain how you learned about the job. Briefly call attention to your important qualifications that relate to the position. Write a positive letter that clearly reflects your motivation and attitude for the job. A well-written letter also shows your written communication skills.

Electronic Résumés. Many employers and Internet job boards require the use of an electronic résumé. In contrast to a printed résumé, an electronic résumé has no formatting (no columns, indents, bullets, and bold or italic type). Along with a brief cover letter, electronic résumés are inserted directly into an e-mail message and then sent to the employer. If using an electronic résumé for an Internet job board, be sure to remove all personal information to prevent identity theft and Internet stalking.

Completing an Application

Most employers will ask you to fill out a job application form. This may occur at the time of an interview or beforehand. Employers often use these forms to compare the qualifications of job applicants. Complete the form accurately. Look over the entire form before you begin. Follow all instructions and place the requested information in the correct spaces. Try not to leave blank spaces. If a question does not apply to you, draw a line through the space or write "does not apply."

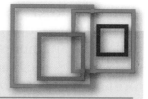

Résumé Information

Include the following information in your résumé:

- Contact information—name, address, telephone number, cell phone number, and e-mail address
- Employment objective
- Current employer; date of employment
- Previous employer(s); date(s) of employment
- Education and training—schools and dates attended; general course of study
- Honors and achievements—school and community
- Special interests and abilities
- Availability of references—most often on request, separate from the résumé

22-23 A well-written résumé offers information about your employment qualifications will capture the interest of potential employers.

Print neatly and legibly. Use correct spelling, punctuation, and grammar. Some employers may ask you to complete an electronic application on the computer.

Interviewing for a Job

You can do several things to prepare for a job interview. When you learn of a position that interests you, contact the employer. You may do so by telephone, by letter, or in person. Express your interest in the position and ask whether the job is still open. If it is, ask for an interview. Be positive, confident, and polite. Your initial contact must make a good impression. This is true whether that contact be by phone, by letter, or in person.

Another way to prepare for a job interview is to learn about the agency or business. Also learn about the position itself. Write down questions you may have. Employers want to hire people who are interested in their businesses.

Carefully choose what you will wear to the interview. Your grooming and clothes will make an impression. Be sure it is a good one. Wear clothes that are one step more formal than what you would wear on the job. For example, if you interview for a child care position, slacks, a nice shirt or blouse (no lettering or inappropriate designs), and flat-heeled shoes are often appropriate. All clothing must be clean and neat. Jeans are likely to be out of place.

Think about questions the interviewer might ask you. Have possible responses in mind. Some questions may be general, such as "Tell me about yourself." Others may be more specific. For example, an interviewer might ask you to describe previous work experience or why you are interested in this job. The interviewer may give you a hypothetical job situation and ask you how you might deal with it. Practicing for the interview with a family member, friend, or in front of a mirror can help build your confidence and help you feel more relaxed.

Know where to go for your interview. Many businesses have personnel departments in separate buildings. Verify the time and date of the interview. Know the name of the person you are to see. Write the name on a note card to carry with you. Allow plenty of time for travel. Plan to arrive a few minutes early. Take your résumé and a pen to fill out an application form. Do not take anyone with you.

Be sure to remove or put away any items that may distract your attention during the interview. For example, put away keys or coins. Turn off your cell phone and other electronic devices before you reach the site. Do not have gum, candy, or even breath mints in your mouth. Do not get out any of these items until you have left the building.

Begin the interview with a firm handshake and a friendly greeting, 22-24. Do not sit until asked to do so. Sit up straight.

22-24 A firm handshake is beneficial when greeting a potential employer.

Look directly at the interviewer. Listen carefully to the questions the interviewer asks you. Respond positively, concisely, and honestly. Show you are enthusiastic about the position. Speak slowly and clearly, using good grammar. Answer questions verbally rather than merely nodding your head.

When the interviewer asks if you have any questions, the interview is nearing an end. This is your time to ask questions. A thoughtful question about the business or the position can indicate your interest. Questions about wages are not appropriate until you receive a job offer.

After answering your questions, the interviewer may offer you the job. In most cases, the interviewer needs time to decide. He or she may indicate that you will receive a call, or give you directions to call by a certain date. If not, ask when you may inquire about the job. Before you leave, thank the interviewer for taking time to meet with you.

Interview Follow-Up

When your interview is over, your interview responsibilities do not end. Within a day of the interview, write a follow-up letter thanking the interviewer for his or her time. This letter will help remind the interviewer of your interest in the job. Use a business-letter format. As with all correspondence, be sure to use correct spelling, grammar, and punctuation.

If you receive a job offer, let the employer know as soon as possible whether you will accept the position. At this point, the employer will also give you information about wages and benefits, such as health insurance, sick pay, vacation pay, and retirement programs. If you do not receive this information with the job offer, it is appropriate to ask about it. Think about the position requirements and whether your knowledge, skills, and abilities are a good fit. Politely thank the employer for offering you the position. Express appreciation for the interview even if you decide not to accept the job.

Do not be discouraged if you do not get the job. Instead, review the interview mentally and note where you can improve. This will prepare you for the next interview. Eventually, you will find the right job.

Summing It Up

- Many career opportunities exist for working directly with children and families and those working on behalf of children and families.

- Before making a career decision, learn about the key trends job outlook for a career area.

- People who enter a child and family services career must have certain personal traits that suit these careers.

- Knowing your interests, aptitudes, and abilities is essential before making career plans.

- Strengthening your workplace knowledge, skills, and attitudes increases your employment opportunities.

- You can prepare for future roles now by making a career plan, joining student organizations, and enrolling in work-based learning programs.

- Carefully planning your job search will help you find employment that is satisfying and meets your goals.

Recalling the Facts

1. What is the difference between a *job* and a *career*?

2. List four careers in which people work directly with children, parents, or families.

3. Contrast a parent educator with a teacher educator.

4. Describe two pros and two cons of operating your own business.

5. Identify two key trends that impact job outlook for careers related to children, parents, and families.

6. List six personal traits necessary for working with children.

7. Explain why you should consider your interests, aptitudes, and abilities in career planning.

8. What academic skills do all employers look for in employees?

9. What is the difference between *teamwork* and *leadership*?

10. Name three desirable employee qualities in the workplace.

11. Contrast *short-term* and *long-term* goals for career planning.

12. How can the career clusters help you plan for your career?

13. What critical skills can you develop by joining a student organization?

14. What are four sources of job leads?

Applying New Skills

1. **Newspaper search.** Scan a newspaper's classified ads section online or in print and list job opportunities in child and family services careers. Make a list of those jobs that interest you most.

2. **Research.** Investigate community colleges and universities in your area that offer courses or degrees that lead to careers related to children, parents, and families. Share your findings with the class.

3. **Interview.** Interview an employer in child and family services about what he or she wants in an employee. After the interview, contrast the interview content with that of this text's discussion of employability skills.

4. **Role-play.** Role-play a job interview. Video-record the interview and evaluate the results.

5. **Picture wall.** Create a picture wall showing appropriate dress for entry-level and professional careers related to children, parents, and families.

Thinking Critically

1. In a small group, brainstorm ideas for a child-related entrepreneurship. Choose one idea and draw conclusions about how you could start this business.

2. Compare and contrast organizations and activities in your school and community in which you can develop leadership skills, become an effective team member, and improve your communication skills. Which options offer the best opportunities to learn and improve these skills?

Linking Academics

1. **Social Studies.** Review the rules of parliamentary procedure. Conduct a mock meeting in your classroom using these rules.

2. **Writing.** In 15 sentences or less, summarize the benefits of *work-based learning programs*. What types of programs are available to high school students?

3. **Technology.** Investigate the procedure for preparing an electronic résumé. As a practice exercise, create an electronic résumé and cover letter and e-mail it to your teacher or parent.

Appendix A
Erikson's Theory of Personality Development

Stage	Approximate Age	Step Toward Stable Personality	Step Toward Unstable Personality
1	Birth to age 2	Trust	Mistrust

Characteristics: The task of infancy and the first year of the toddlerhood is developing a sense of *basic trust* in one's environment and in those who provide care. What helps these very young children develop a sense of trust? Learning to trust the environment occurs when the child experiences sameness in day-to-day happenings. Although some of the sameness is created by natural laws, such as objects fall, others occur due to household routines. Trust in the parents occurs when there are quality interactions—holding, cuddling, smiling at, and speaking to—between parent and child. Feelings of trust set the stage for the child's lifelong expectation that the world is a wonderful place and that he or she is lovable.

When inconsistency occurs and parents fail to give attention and stimulation, the child becomes fearful and lacks self-confidence. *Mistrust* arises and results in suspicion of others and low self-esteem.

Stage	Approximate Age	Step Toward Stable Personality	Step Toward Unstable Personality
2	Ages 2 and 3	Autonomy	Shame and doubt

Characteristics: As toddlers learn to walk and talk, they develop a mind and will of their own. To develop autonomy, toddlers must be given choices and opportunities for mastery. Having clear limits allows toddlers to achieve and be happy with their own accomplishments. Autonomy at this stage is a foundation for later self-identity.

How do toddlers develop shame and doubt? Children who are not allowed to make decisions or explore, learn to doubt their ability to control anything in their world. These children feel shame because their parents may be impatient or use harsh discipline.

Stage	Approximate Age	Step Toward Stable Personality	Step Toward Unstable Personality
3	Ages 4 and 5	Initiative	Guilt

Characteristics: Preschool children have much energy. They show *initiative* (undertake activities) by exploring their physical and social worlds. They try to master new skills, attempt to learn new information, and put plans into action. Parents set rules and reinforce acceptable behavior.

If parents punish too often or too harshly for mistakes, children learn it is safer not to show initiative. Children begin to think their physical activity (such as wiggling too much or breaking something while helping) is bad, "tall tales" are lies, fantasy play is silly, and failure to complete a task is irresponsible. These feelings lead to *guilt*, and an "I can't" attitude.

Stage	Approximate Age	Step Toward Stable Personality	Step Toward Unstable Personality
4	Ages 6 to 11	Industry	Inferiority

Characteristics: As children enter the school years, they are expected to master what the culture feels is needed for adult life, such as reading, writing, math, and computer literacy. Families try to teach a sense of duty in contributing to the family system. Children show much industry, especially in the early school years. They are often competitive with peers and hope to be best in some effort.

Problems occur when children feel they will not be able to do enough to please others, especially their parents. They fear they will not be as good as their peers in some area they believe to be important. They feel tension between wanting to grow up and wanting to stay a child. Inferiority develops when they feel their best efforts are not good enough.

Stage	Approximate Age	Step Toward Stable Personality	Step Toward Unstable Personality
5	Ages 12 to 18	Identity	Role confusion

Characteristics: Teens confront the question, "Who am I?" The teen forms ideas about how things should be within himself or herself, within the family system, and within all other relationships. By resolving the issues of the previous stages, the teen is able to get a clear *identity* of who he or she is, what types of attitudes are important, and what is valued. Career roles are the focus of this stage.

If others cannot confirm that teens are who they think they are, *role confusion* results. These teens are uncertain who they are and where they are headed.

Stage	Approximate Age	Step Toward Stable Personality	Step Toward Unstable Personality
6	Early adulthood	Intimacy	Isolation

Characteristics: Having an idea of whom one is and where one is headed in life allows the young adult to "lose and find him- or herself in another." The young adult trusts he or she can surrender the self (the identity) to another person and to the relationship. The person is able to develop *intimacy* with another.

If intimacy is not learned, then a sense of *isolation occurs. The person feels others cannot be trusted in a close, intimate way.*

Stage	Approximate Age	Step Toward Stable Personality	Step Toward Unstable Personality
7	Middle age	Generativity	Stagnation

Characteristics: This is a long stage (24 to 54 years). During this period *generativity* (productivity) may be in the forming of a family system and/or in achievement in one's career. Erikson said that adults are now interested in contributing to the next generation even if caring involves sacrifice.

Those adults who fail to establish a sense of caring for others or are not involved in creative production become concerned only with self. This is called *stagnation* or *self-absorption*.

Stage	Approximate Age	Step Toward Stable Personality	Step Toward Unstable Personality
8	Late adulthood	Integrity	Despair

Characteristics: As adults approach their older years, they look back on their life. If they believe their life has been unique and meaningful, they see a picture of a life well spent. They feel a sense of satisfaction. *Integrity* (the state of being complete) has been achieved.

A sense of *despair* comes from a feeling of regret about the way one's life was lived. The person often says, "If only_____." This feeling of incompleteness makes one fear the end of life.

Appendix B
Piaget's Stages of Intellectual Development

1. Sensorimotor	
Age: Birth to 2 years	**Characteristics:** Children use their senses and motor activities to explore their world. They learn through sensory input (how things look, sound, feel, taste, and smell) and actions with objects (shake, hit, roll, push, pull, and drop).
1A: Exercising the Reflexes	
Age: Birth to 1 month	**Characteristics:** Newborns practice with five reflexes: sucking, grasping, looking, hearing, and vocalizing. With exercise, the reflexes become stable and begin to be used to meet needs.
1B: Primary Circular Reactions	
Age: 1 to 4 months	**Characteristics:** Babies learn by chance to do things that involve their bodies, such as opening and closing their hands. Because the actions bring pleasure, babies repeat the actions many times over many days.
1C: Secondary Circular Reactions	
Age: 4 to 8 months	**Characteristics:** Babies learn by chance to do things that involve objects, such as shaking a rattle. Babies notice the sound. At some point, babies see the connection between their actions (shaking) and the responses (sound). This brings pleasure. They begin to do this action over and over. Each time they get the same response.
1D: Coordination of Secondary Circular Reactions	
Age: 8 to 12 months	**Characteristics:** Babies now have a motor goal in mind. They "think" of a way to achieve a goal. To achieve the goal, they combine two or more actions they have learned in the past but never combined. For example, opening a cabinet door to get an object or pushing a footstool out of the way to get to a favorite toy becomes a new goal.
1E: Tertiary Circular Reactions	
Age: 12 to 18 months	**Characteristics:** Toddlers now vary their actions to achieve a goal. For example, a toddler trying to put a triangular prism through the triangular hole in a sorting box would now rotate the prism until it would fit. Piaget referred to the child's actions as experiments in order to see.
1F: Mental Representation	
Age: 18 months to 2 years	**Characteristics:** Toddlers spend a great deal of time tracing the contours of objects with hands and eyes until they have constructed mental drawings of objects. Toddlers now have "picture-like" symbols in their head. Toddlers can also "think" in advance of acting on an object. They can imagine a few solutions to achieving their goal, decide on what they think is the "best" way to solve their problem, and then try it.

2. Preoperational	
Age: 2 to 7 years	**Characteristics:** Young children very gradually develop the ability to do mentally what was done earlier by physically acting on objects. Because young children are not able to think in a completely logical way, Piaget called this stage preoperational or before logical thought. Although children do not yet have full-fledged logical thinking, mental reasoning is emerging and some stable concepts are being formed. The preoperational stage is divided into these two substages: the *preconceptual phase* and the *intuitive phase*.
2A: Preconceptual Phase	
Age: 2 to 4 years	**Characteristics:** The older toddler and young child gain the ability to represent through symbols an object or person that is not present. The child's mental world can be seen through symbols used in language, art, and pretend play. These children have many limitations in their thinking including their collections of disorganized images about their world. These images are called preconcepts. Thus, Piaget named this substage the preconceptual phase.
2B: Intuitive Phase	
Age: 4 to 6 or 7 years	**Characteristics:** Older preschool and younger school-age children still are not logical thinkers. They are swayed by how things appear. Perceptions are sometimes correct, but are often faulty. Children of this age are sure of their "knowledge" but are unaware of how they know what they know.
3. Concrete Operations	
Age: 7 to 13 years.	**Characteristics:** School-age children begin to use logic, rather than perception, in thinking how events and objects can be changed. Yet, school-age children can only use logical reasoning with information they can see or they can imagine; that is, the information must be concrete (real) to them.
4. Formal Operations	
Age: 13 years and beyond	**Characteristics:** Teens and adults continue to use logic, but are slowly released from concrete thinking ("what is") to hypothetical ("what if") thinking. Because formal operational thinking requires specific learning experiences, not all teens or adults think in this most advanced way.

Appendix C
Immunization Schedules

Recommended Immunization Schedule for Persons Aged 0–6 Years—UNITED STATES • 2008

For those who fall behind or start late, see the catch-up schedule

Vaccine ▼ Age ►	Birth	1 month	2 months	4 months	6 months	12 months	15 months	18 months	19–23 months	2–3 years	4–6 years
Hepatitis B[1]	HepB	HepB		see footnote 1	HepB						
Rotavirus[2]			Rota	Rota	Rota						
Diphtheria, Tetanus, Pertussis[3]			DTaP	DTaP	DTaP	see footnote 3	DTaP				DTaP
Haemophilus influenzae type b[4]			Hib	Hib	Hib[4]	Hib					
Pneumococcal[5]			PCV	PCV	PCV	PCV				PPV	
Inactivated Poliovirus			IPV	IPV	IPV						IPV
Influenza[6]					Influenza (Yearly)						
Measles, Mumps, Rubella[7]						MMR					MMR
Varicella[8]						Varicella					Varicella
Hepatitis A[9]						HepA (2 doses)				HepA Series	
Meningococcal[10]										MCV4	

Range of recommended ages

Certain high-risk groups

This schedule indicates the recommended ages for routine administration of currently licensed childhood vaccines, as of December 1, 2007, for children aged 0 through 6 years. Additional information is available at www.cdc.gov/vaccines/recs/schedules. Any dose not administered at the recommended age should be administered at any subsequent visit, when indicated and feasible. Additional vaccines may be licensed and recommended during the year. Licensed combination vaccines may be used whenever any components of the combination are indicated and other components of the vaccine are not contraindicated and if approved by the Food and Drug Administration for that dose of the series. Providers should consult the respective Advisory Committee on Immunization Practices statement for detailed recommendations, including for **high-risk conditions:** http://www.cdc.gov/vaccines/pubs/ACIP-list.htm. Clinically significant adverse events that follow immunization should be reported to the Vaccine Adverse Event Reporting System (VAERS). Guidance about how to obtain and complete a VAERS form is available at www.vaers.hhs.gov or by telephone, 800-822-7967.

See the Centers for Disease Control (www.cdc.gov) for further information.

Recommended Immunization Schedule for Persons Aged 7–18 Years—UNITED STATES • 2008

For those who fall behind or start late, see the green bars and the catch-up schedule

Vaccine ▼ Age ▶	7–10 years	11–12 years	13–18 years
Diphtheria, Tetanus, Pertussis[1]	see footnote 1	Tdap	Tdap
Human Papillomavirus[2]	see footnote 2	HPV (3 doses)	HPV Series
Meningococcal[3]	MCV4	MCV4	MCV4
Pneumococcal[4]	PPV		
Influenza[5]	Influenza (Yearly)		
Hepatitis A[6]	HepA Series		
Hepatitis B[7]	HepB Series		
Inactivated Poliovirus[8]	IPV Series		
Measles, Mumps, Rubella[9]	MMR Series		
Varicella[10]	Varicella Series		

Range of recommended ages

Catch-up immunization

Certain high-risk groups

This schedule indicates the recommended ages for routine administration of currently licensed childhood vaccines, as of December 1, 2007, for children aged 7–18 years. Additional information is available at www.cdc.gov/vaccines/recs/schedules. Any dose not administered at the recommended age should be administered at any subsequent visit, when indicated and feasible. Additional vaccines may be licensed and recommended during the year. Licensed combination vaccines may be used whenever any components of the combination are indicated and other components of the vaccine are not contraindicated and if approved by the Food and Drug Administration for that dose of the series. Providers should consult the respective Advisory Committee on Immunization Practices statement for detailed recommendations, including for **high risk conditions:** http://www.cdc.gov/vaccines/pubs/ACIP-list.htm. Clinically significant adverse events that follow immunization should be reported to the Vaccine Adverse Event Reporting System (VAERS). Guidance about how to obtain and complete a VAERS form is available at www.vaers.hhs.gov or by telephone, 800-822-7967.

Glossary

A

abilities. Skills that are learned and developed. (22)

abstinence. Refraining from sexual intercourse. (17)

accreditation. A credential ensuring the program meets the highest standards as set by a specific professional group. (20)

acne. A skin disorder involving inflammation of skin glands that is characterized by blackheads and pimples. (17)

active listening. Hearing the total message, verbal and nonverbal, and making responses to promote mutual understanding. (5)

adolescence. A time of change in which people move from the dependency of childhood to the independence of adulthood. (17)

adoption. The legal process of transferring a child's parental relationship from his or her birthparents to adoptive parents. (2)

adoptive families. Adoptive parents and one or more adopted children. (2)

afterbirth stage. Third and final stage of labor. (11)

aggression. An action that results in physical or emotional injury to a person or animal or damage to property. (5)

AIDS (acquired immunodeficiency syndrome). Disease that breaks down a person's immune system. (8)

alternatives. Available options from which you can choose. (3)

amniocentesis. Prenatal test, usually given between weeks 14 and 16, in which a sample of amniotic fluid is drawn and tested for congenital disorders. (9)

amniotic fluid. Fluid that surrounds the baby in the uterus. (8)

anabolic steroids. Synthetic hormone drugs that mimic the action of the natural male sex hormone, testosterone. (17)

anemia. Iron deficiency in the blood. (9)

Apgar test. A test that is used at birth (and then again five minutes later) to evaluate a baby's overall physical condition. (11)

apprenticeships. Specialized job-training programs in a craft, trade, or any career offered in the high school. (22)

aptitudes. Natural talents. (22)

artificial insemination. Procedure to promote conception in which a doctor places sperm-containing semen directly in the upper part of a woman's vagina or uterus. (7)

associative play. A stage of play in which preschoolers associate with other children, but do not form group goals for play. (15)

attachment. The lasting emotional relationship that begins in infancy and ties the child to his or her parents and later to other important people. (4)

attention deficit disorder (ADD). A disorder that includes symptoms of distraction and inattention that are more frequent and severe than those of others at a similar developmental level. (21)

attention deficit hyperactivity disorder (ADHD). A disorder that includes symptoms of ADD along with over or uncontrollable activity. (21)

au pair. A young person who comes from another country to live with and provide child care for a family. (20)

authoritarian. Parenting style in which behavior expectations, or standards, are set very high by parents. They expect their children to follow these expectations without question. (5)

autism spectrum disorder (ASD). A group of complex developmental disorders that involve problems with communication, social relationships, and repetitive routines or behaviors. (21)

autonomy. Independence. (14)

B

babbling. Repeated vocalizing, or speech, in which babies add consonant sounds to vowels. (13)

baby talk. Regression to language expressions used as older infant or young toddler. (15)

babysitting. Occasional in-home care. (20)

behavior disorders. A wide variety of social and emotional problems ranging from mild to severe that impairs a person's ability to function normally. (21)

behavioral reflections. Nonjudgmental statements regarding some aspect of a child's (or person's) behavior. (5)

bilingualism. Knowing and speaking two languages. (15)

birth center. Nonhospital facility that provides prenatal care and delivery services. (10)

birthing room. Special room in a hospital where a woman can labor, deliver, recover, and rest. (10)

birth plan. Plan that combines all parental expectations about labor and delivery. (10)

blastocyst. Hollow ball of cells that forms as the zygote divides. (8)

body image. How a person views his or her body and its functions. (13)

bonding. The loving feeling parents have for their child. (11)

Brazelton scale. A newborn assessment that can identify nonemergency problems with the baby's movement, reflexes, responses, and general state. (11)

breech. When the baby's buttocks or feet settle into the mother's pelvic area for birth. (11)

bullying. Occurs when one or more people inflict physical, verbal, or emotional abuse on another person. (19)

C

career. A series of related jobs and work experiences. (22)

career clusters. Sixteen broad groupings of occupational and career specialties. (22)

career plan. A program of study to reach a desired career goal. (22)

certified-nurse midwife. Nurse practitioner who has extensive training and experience in providing prenatal care and delivering babies. (9)

cesarean delivery. Major surgery in which a baby is delivered through incisions in the mother's abdomen and uterus. (11)

character. Principles, concepts, and beliefs that a person holds and uses as a guide for living. (6)

child abuse. Nonaccidental injury or pattern of injuries to a child for which there is no reasonable explanation. (19)

Child care resource and referral agencies (CCR&Rs). Service agencies that provide information to parents who are looking for any type of child care. (20)

child neglect. Failing to provide for a child's basic needs. (19)

child support payments. Payments one parent makes to the custodial parent to help meet the children's financial needs. (18)

chorionic villi sampling. Prenatal test, usually given in 10th week, that involves removing a sample of the amnio-chorionic membrane to check for congenital disorders. (9)

chromosome. Threadlike structure that contains hereditary information. (7)

circumcision. Surgical removal of the male's foreskin, a skin flap that covers the head of the penis. (11)

classification. The process of putting a person, object, or event in a group or category according to one or more common characteristics. (16)

cliques. Small exclusive groups of friends of the same or mixed gender. (17)

closed adoption. No contact between the birthparents and the adoptive family. (7)

closed toys. Toys that work only one way and limit creativity. (14)

codependency. A psychological condition in which a person is controlled or manipulated by another with an addiction. (19)

colic. Inconsolable crying that cannot be comforted or soothed. (12)

colostrum. Thick, yellowish liquid in the mother's breasts that nourishes the baby until the mother's milk supply is established. (10)

communicable. Diseases that are transmittable through coughs, sneezes, and contact with bodily fluids. (21)

communication. Any means by which people send and receive messages. (5)

conception. Fertilization of a mature egg by a male sperm. (7)

conformity. To be similar in manner, character, and conduct. (16)

congenital disorders. Disorders that people are born with that result from heredity. (7)

conscience. Inner sense of moral goodness that drives a person's conduct, intentions, or character. (6)

consequences. The results of alternatives, some of which are good and others are not. (3)

conservation. The understanding that certain properties remain the same even if they change in appearance. (16)

contraception. The deliberate prevention of pregnancy, or birth control. (7)

contractions. Pains felt during labor when the muscles of the uterus contract to open the cervix. (11)

cooing. One-syllable, vowel-like sounds such as ooh, ah, and aw. (13)

cooperative child care. A type of ownership in which parents join together to provide care and services for their children. (20)

cooperative education. A combination of classroom training and paid, on-the-job training in a certain occupation. (22)

cooperative play. A form of play in which older preschoolers join forces to form group goals for play. (15)

cradle cap. A condition in which a scaly crust appears on a baby's scalp. (12)

crawling. Pulling with the arms while the abdomen remains on the floor. (13)

creativity. Producing a new or original idea, product, or process. (16)

creeping. Moving on the hands and knees. (13)

crisis. An unforeseen situation that demands adjustment by all family members. (19)

cultural bias. Belief that a person's own cultural or ethnic group is better than any other. (6)

cultural traditions. Customs, beliefs, and behaviors that are shared by members of a cultural or ethnic group. (1)

custody. The right and responsibility to raise a child and make decisions about the child's care, upbringing, and overall welfare within the framework given by the court. (18)

cyberbullying. Involves verbal and emotional bullying through online e-mail or chat rooms. (19)

D

dedication. A deep level of continued commitment. (1)

delay of gratification. The postponement of an immediate reward for an even greater reward. (4)

delivery stage. Second stage of labor. (11)

democratic. Parenting style in which parents set behavioral limits, but also allow freedom within those limits. Parents also talk with their children about reasons behind the limits or standards. (5)

development. A change in function as a result of growth; progress in skills and abilities. (4)

developmentally appropriate practice (DAP). An attempt to make all aspects of a program fit each child's development. (20)

developmental screening. A test that can identify possible developmental delay. (15)

diaper rash. A skin irritation caused by bacteria that build up on the warm, moist skin in the diaper area. (12)

dilation stage. First stage of labor. (11)

diversity. The condition of differing from one another. (1)

dual-career families. Families in which both spouses work outside the home. (3)

dysfunctional family. A family that cannot function properly because of certain overwhelming problems. (19)

E

eating disorders. Real medical illnesses with complex emotions and behaviors that involve abnormal eating patterns and concerns with weight and body image. (17)

egg (ovum). The female sex cell. (7)

egocentric. Toddler inability to see things from the perspective of others. (14)

embryo. Developing baby from two weeks after conception until the eighth week of pregnancy. (8)

emergency care. Treatment of life-threatening injuries. (21)

emotional development. Recognizing feelings or emotions such a love, hate, fear, happiness, or anger. (4)

emotional neglect. Failure to provide children with love and affection. (19)

empathy. Sensitivity to the feelings, thoughts, or experiences of others. (6)

endometrium. Inner lining of the uterus. (7)

entrepreneur. A person who owns and operates his or her business. (22)

enuresis. Bedwetting problem in children over age 3 that may have physical or psychological causes. (15)

environment. Everything in a person's surroundings. (4)

epidural. Regional anesthetic that can be injected into the epidural space during labor. (11)

episiotomy. Small cut in the opening of the birth canal to allow more room for the baby to be delivered. (11)

ethnic groups. Groups of people with a common racial, national, tribal, religious, or cultural origin or background. (1)

ethnic identity. The way a person views himself or herself as a member of a particular ethnic group. (1)

euphemism. The substitution of a pleasant word for one that sounds unpleasant, such as death. (18)

extended family. A family that includes all the relatives in a family, such as grandparents, aunts, uncles, and cousins. (2)

eye-hand coordination. The ability to move the hands in the direction that the eyes see. (13)

F

failure to thrive. A condition in which children do not meet the normal milestones in weight gain, increase in height, or in brain development. (19)

fallopian tubes. Narrow tubes that lie close to the ovaries and connect to the uterus. (7)

family. A group of two or more people who are related by birth, marriage, adoption, or other circumstances. (2)

Family and Medical Leave Act (FMLA). Law that allows eligible employees (in companies with over 50 employees) to take up to 12 weeks of unpaid leave for certain family situations. (10)

Family, Career and Community Leaders of America, Inc. (FCCLA). The national career and technical high school student organization with the family as its focus. (22)

family-centered childbirth. Childbirth method based on the belief childbirth affects the family as a unit. (11)

family functions. The responsibilities a family has for its members and how the family carries out these responsibilities. (2)

family life cycle. The stages of family development that expand and contract over a period of time from marriage to old age. (2)

family planning. A couple's decisions about their reproductive capabilities including number, timing, and spacing of children. (7)

fetal alcohol syndrome (FAS). A condition that includes physical and mental disabilities common among the babies of mothers who drink alcohol heavily during pregnancy. (9)

fetus. Developing baby from the ninth week of pregnancy until birth. (8)

fine-motor skills. Skills that involve the use of smaller body muscles, such as those in the hands, fingers, feet, and toes. (13)

finger foods. Foods eaten with the fingers, such as cooked and diced fruits and vegetables. (13)

first aid. Treatment of injuries that are not life threatening. (21)

flexibility. Being ready and able to adapt to new and different circumstances. (1)

fontanel. The soft spot on a newborn's head. (12)

for-profit. Program that operates as a business with owners using the profits as they see fit. (20)

foster family. A family that provides temporary, substitute care for children who need it. (2)

G

gender constancy. Understanding that despite outward changes or desire, gender does not change. (15)

gender identity. Understanding the concept that people are either male or female. (14)

gender role. A person's behaviors, attitudes, and beliefs about men and women in society, acquired by watching the same-gender parent. (2)

gender-role identification. Behaving in ways consistent with gender and cultural rules. (16)

gender stability. Understanding that boys become men and girls become women. (15)

gene. Basic unit of heredity. (7)

genetic counseling. Scientific information and advice about heredity. (7)

gestational diabetes. Pregnancy-related high blood glucose (blood sugar). (8)

gifted and talented. Children who show outward signs of high achievement or potential for high achievement in such areas as intellectual, creative, artistic, or leadership ability. (21)

goal. A direction or end to which you work. (3)

gross-motor skills. Skills that involve the use of large muscles, such as the trunk, neck, arm, and leg muscles. (13)

growth. An increase in size, strength, and ability that begins with pregnancy and continues through adulthood. (4)

guardians. Unrelated adults who raise children, but never legally adopt them. (2)

guidance. The act of directing and influencing a person toward a particular end. (4)

guilt. Ability to self-criticize or have remorse. (6)

H

hereditary. Something genetically passed from parent to child. (3)

heritage. All that has been passed down through the generations. (1)

high-risk behaviors. Risky actions in which teens often know the dangers, but believe they are exempt from the risks. (17)

HIV (human immunodeficiency virus). Virus that enters a person's body and slowly begins to destroy the immune system. (8)

homicide. The intentional taking of another's life. (17)

I

identification. Children unconsciously adopt the behavior patterns of people they like and admire. (4)

"I" messages. Messages that describe a thought, feeling, or other experience in the singular, first-person manner. They give the responsibility to a problem to the speaker. (5)

imitation. When children copy the behavior of others. (4)

immunizations. Treatments that prevent people from developing certain diseases. (13)

incest. Sexual activity between people who are closely related that is forbidden by law. (19)

inclusion. The practice of placing children with disabilities and children without disabilities in the same classroom for learning. (21)

infant. A baby less than 1 year of age. (13)

infant mortality rate. The rate of infant deaths per 1000 live births. (3)

infections. Illnesses caused by pathogens, such as viruses, bacteria, or parasites. (21)

infertility. Inability to conceive despite having intercourse regularly for at least one year. (7)

in-home care. Care in which the caregiver provides care in the child's home. (20)

integrity. Firm adherence to a code of moral values. (6)

intellectual development. The changes in a person's thinking, intelligence, and language. (4)

interests. Activities that appeal to a person over a period of time. (22)

internships. School programs that offer paid or unpaid supervised work experience to learn about specific jobs or careers. (22)

in vitro fertilization. Procedure to promote conception that involves removing eggs from a woman's ovaries, fertilizing them with a man's sperm in a glass dish, and then placing the fertilized eggs in the woman's uterus. (7)

J

job. Work experience a person does for money. (22)

job shadowing. Learning about a job by following an employee as he or she works. (22)

job sharing. Work situation in which two employees share one job, each working part-time. (10)

joint custody. Both parents keep their parenting rights and responsibilities. (18)

L

Lamaze. A prepared childbirth method in which parents attend weekly classes to learn what to expect in the final stages of pregnancy and during labor and delivery. (11)

leadership. The ability to direct and influence others to achieve goals. (22)

learning disability. A disorder in one or more psychological processes involving the use of spoken and written language. (21)

Leboyer method. Childbirth method that focuses on the birth experience of the baby; it makes the birth process less shocking and more comforting for the baby. (11)

licensing. A document that ensures a child care facility has been inspected and meets basic standards. (20)

life skills. The routine eating, dressing, and grooming skills children must learn for self-care. (14)

lifestyle. A way of living. (2)

lisping. The mispronunciation of words by dropping or distorting letter sounds, usually consonants. (15)

locomotor skills. Gross-motor skills that involve moving from place to place. (15)

logical consequences. Consequences parents establish for misbehavior that show a direct link between the misbehavior and the consequence. (5)

long-term goals. Goals that you want to accomplish later, perhaps years from now. (3)

M

maturation. The orderly sequence of developmental changes shaped by human genes. (4)

menarche. The first menstrual period for females. (17)

menstruation. Monthly discharge of the endometrium from the uterus through the vagina when fertilization does not occur. (7)

miscarriage. Natural ending of pregnancy before the fifth month. (8)

mitten grasp. A grasp in which the palm and fingers oppose the thumb. (13)

moral development. A gradual process that reflects a child's understanding of the difference between right and wrong. (1)

morality. Conformity to the ideals of right human conduct. (6)

moral judgments. How a person reasons or thinks about rules for ethical conduct. (6)

morals. Beliefs people have that help them distinguish between right and wrong. (1)

motor skills. Skills that require the movement and control of certain muscles. (13)

multicultural. Including people of more than one culture. (6)

MyPyramid. A food guidance system developed by the U.S. Departments of Agriculture and Health and Human Services to promote healthy eating and physical activity. (9)

myth. Story or notion used to explain certain traditions, practices, or beliefs that are often half-truths and sometimes based on false thinking. (1)

N

nanny. A specially trained child care provider who may or may not live in the family's home. (20)

natural consequences. The common results of misbehavior. (5)

negative reinforcement. A response that makes repeating a behavior less likely. (4)

Neonatal Intensive Care Unit (NICU). Intensive care area for newborns that require emergency care; has special equipment (machines, monitors, and incubators) and medical staff to help babies survive. (11)

neonate. Meaning newborn, a name for the baby from birth to one month. (11)

not-for-profit. Program that operates as a service to parents and uses profits to run the program. (20)

nuclear family. A family that includes a husband, wife, and the children they have together. (2)

nurturance. Loving care and attention. (1)

O

object permanence. An understanding of the concept that people and objects still exist even when they cannot be seen, heard, or touched. (13)

obstetrician. Doctor who specializes in providing medical care for pregnant women and delivering babies. (9)

open adoption. Some degree of contact between birthparents and adoptive parents. (7)

open communication. Sharing of thoughts and feelings between a parent and a child (or between any two people). (5)

open toys. Toys that allow children to use their imaginations and creative-thinking skills to devise new play activities. (14)

ovaries. A female's almond-shaped organs that store the immature egg cells. (7)

ovulation. Process through which one of the female's ovaries usually releases a mature egg about once a month. (7)

P

parallel play. A form of play in which children play alongside each other in the same activity without interacting. (14)

parent. A person who gives birth to offspring and brings up and cares for a child. (1)

parent educator. A person who teaches parenting or child development to adults. (22)

parental leave. Paid or unpaid leave from work to tend to parenting duties. (10)

parenthood. The role of parenting in society that involves legal rights and responsibilities. (1)

parenting. The act or process of raising a child. (1)

parenting style. The ways of parenting influenced by parental values about what is important in childrearing. (5)

parliamentary procedure. A set of rules for making decisions and conducting business in an orderly manner. (22)

partner abuse. Any physical, emotional, sexual, stalking, or economic abuse of a partner. (19)

pediatrician. Doctor who specializes in providing medical care for infants and children through the young-adult years. (10)

peer violence. Violence directed at a person by someone in the same peer group. (19)

perceptual thinking. Intuitive thinking based on how things appear. (15)

permanency planning. Plans for and legal decisions about a foster child's future that often result in children waiting a long time for parents. (18)

permissive. Parenting style in which parents allow children to make their own decisions with very few, if any, limits, guidance, or consistent discipline. (5)

perseverance. Setting and pursuing worthwhile goals and seeing them through to completion. (6)

phobias. Extreme fears out of proportion to the threat. (16)

physical development. The biological changes in a person. (4)

physical disability. A limitation of a person's body or its function. (21)

physical neglect. Failure to provide food, clothing, shelter, medical care, education, and supervision for a child. (19)

picture books. Books that contain only pictures, have pictures that dominate the text, or have words and pictures that are equally important. (14)

pincer grasp. Grasping objects between the thumb and index finger. (13)

placenta. A special organ that allows nutrients, oxygen, and water to pass from mother to baby. It also allows the baby's waste products to pass to the mother for elimination. (8)

play groups. Informal groups in which parents exchange child care services and arrange for their children to play together. (20)

portfolio. A collection of materials that document achievements over time. (22)

positive discipline. The process of intentionally teaching and training a child to behave in appropriate ways. (4)

positive reinforcement. A response that makes repeating a behavior more likely. (4)

postpartum depression. A serious mood disorder that follows childbirth. (11)

postpartum period. A period of time that begins when the baby is born and lasts about six weeks. (11)

preconcepts. According to Piaget, these are toddler concepts and reasoning that are illogical and confused. (14)

pregnancy. Time during which a fertilized egg grows and develops into a human being inside the mother's body. (8)

pregnancy-induced hypertension (PIH). Pregnancy-related high blood pressure. (8)

prejudice. Unfair judgments or opinions about people of another group. (6)

prelogical. Illogical and irrational thinking that occurs during the toddler years, according to Piaget. (14)

prenatal care. Special care a woman and her developing baby need during pregnancy. (9)

prenatal development. Development that occurs between conception and birth. (8)

preoperational stage. The stage before logical thought and advanced reasoning. (14)

prepared childbirth. Birth method in which both parents learn about the birth process. (10)

preschooler. A child ages 3 through 5 years. (15)

primary caregiver. Person who spends the most time with the baby. (10)

problem ownership. Communication technique that defines who owns a problem—the child, the parent, or both. (5)

puberty. The process through which the body becomes capable of reproduction. (16)

punishment. A penalty for something a person has done wrong. (4)

Q

quality rating systems (QRSs). The use of various quality standards, such as licensing, accreditation, financing, and parent education, to rate a child care program. (20)

R

realistic expectations. Knowledge of developmental skills children have at a certain age that helps parents provide an atmosphere for growth and learning. (1)

reciprocity. Behavior that occurs when people treat others in the same way they want to be treated; involves mutual give and take. (6)

reflexes. Automatic reactions to certain stimuli. (12)

registration. A document indicating a caregiver has informed the state about the family child care program and in turn receives state information on good practices. Program does not receive inspection. (20)

resilient. Able to recover. (18)

responsibility. A sense of duty to accept and meet obligations without reminder or direction. (6)

résumé. A document that contains detailed information about your education, work experience, and qualifications for employment. (22)

reversibility. The principle that any process done on an object can be undone—in actuality or through mental thought—to restore it to its original form. (16)

Rh factor disorder. A condition that occurs when an Rh- mother gives birth to an Rh+ baby. (8)

role. A set of behaviors related to a certain function you assume in life. (1)

rubella. Virus that can impact pregnancy, also called German measles. (8)

S

self-care children. Children who meet their own needs after school until their parents return home. (16)

self-concept. The mental image a person has of himself or herself. (5)

self-control. The ability of a person to govern his or her actions, impulses, and desires. (4)

self-demand feeding. Feeding the baby when he or she is hungry. (12)

self-discipline. Judging what is right or wrong and behaving appropriately. (5)

self-esteem. How a person feels about his or her self-concept. (5)

sensorimotor stage. Piaget's first stage of development in which the infant learns through the senses and motor skills. (12)

separation anxiety. A fear that occurs when babies cannot see their parents. (13)

seriation. The ability to arrange items in a logical order, such as short to long, long to short, light to dark colors, or more to less. (16)

sexual maturity. A time by which females begin ovulation and males have a sufficient number of sperm for fertility. (17)

sexually transmitted infections (STIs). Conditions and infections that pass from one person to another through sexual contact. (8)

Shaken Baby Syndrome (SBS). A form of physical abuse in which a caregiver violently shakes an infant or small child, causing injury or death. (19)

short-term goals. Goals you hope to accomplish soon, within a few days or months. (3)

sibling rivalry. Sibling jealousy of and competition for parental attention. (15)

single-parent family. A family that includes one parent and his or her biological or adopted children. (2)

social competence. Knowing and using social skills in all social settings (school, work, and social events). (5)

social development. The changes in a person's relationships with other people. (4)

socializers. Family and nonfamily members, as well as all aspects of the environment, that transmit knowledge, skills, and traits to others and enable them to be fit for society. (4)

socioeconomic status. A family's position within society based on social and economic factors. (2)

sole custody. Custody granted to one parent when a judge determines that joint custody will likely produce further conflict. (18)

sperm. The male sex cell. (7)

spermarche. The first ejaculation for males. (17)

sphincter muscles. The ringlike muscles that control the openings to the bladder and rectum. (14)

stepfamily. A family that includes a married couple and the children one or both of them brings from a previous relationship to the new family. (2)

stereotypes. Widely held beliefs that all members of a group are alike and share the same characteristics. (6)

stillbirth. Natural ending of pregnancy after the fifth month. (8)

stranger anxiety. A fear of strangers that relates to attachment. (13)

stress. The tension caused by a condition or situation that demands a mental or physical adjustment. (1)

stressors. Anything that causes stress. (12)

structure. Behavioral limits (home rules) that teach children how to get along in the world. Personal boundaries that do not infringe on the needs and rights of others, experiences that promote self-worth, and experiences that offer a sense of safety and security are part of structure. (1)

stuttering. An involuntary disruption in speech in which words are prolonged, repeated, or tough to get out. (15)

substance abuse. The use of any substance that can cause addiction. (19)

sudden infant death syndrome (SIDS). A syndrome in which a seemingly healthy infant dies without warning. (9)

support group. A group of people who share a similar problem or concern. (4)

support system. People, institutions, and organizations parents turn to in times of need. (4)

T

teachable moments. Spontaneous learning experiences that parents can use to introduce new ideas to their toddlers. (14)

teacher. An adult whose primary responsibility is for a group of children. (22)

teamwork. Working with other people to achieve common goals. (22)

temperaments. Tendencies to react emotionally in certain ways to events. (4)

testes. Male reproductive glands that produce sperm. (7)

time-out. Period of time used by parents to withdraw their misbehaving children from an activity or the presences of others. (5)

toddler. A child between 13 and 35 months of age. (14)

toilet learning. The process of children gaining control of bladder and bowel functions and successfully using the toilet. (14)

toilet talk. Talking about bodily functions in playful ways by preschoolers. (15)

traditional childbirth. Childbirth method in which attention focuses on health of mother and baby and on the woman's comfort; anesthetics are given as needed, and the baby's health is monitored. (11)

trimester. Period of three months. (8)

U

ultrasound test. Prenatal test that uses sound waves to create a "map" of the fetus, showing fetal position and development. (9)

umbilical cord. Flexible cord that contains blood vessels and connects the baby to the placenta. (8)

unconditional love. Love that sets no conditions or boundaries. (1)

unintentional injuries. Accidental and preventable injuries. (21)

uterus. Hollow, muscular organ that holds the baby during pregnancy. (7)

V

values. The ideals and beliefs about what is important and how to act on them. (2)

vas deferens. Long, narrow tube through which sperm travel into the man's body to the ejaculatory duct. (7)

visitation rights. The right to visit the children during certain specified times and under certain conditions. (18)

voluntary motor movements. Motions learned and done at will. (12)

W

weaning. Phasing out the taking of milk from breast or bottle. (13)

"we" messages. Similar to "I" messages, but imply that two or more people are jointly involved and affected by a problem situation. (5)

window of opportunity. A sensitive period in which a person's capacity to develop a certain skill peaks. (13)

"win/win" method. Problem-solving approach in which parent and child work together to solve a problem. (5)

work-based learning programs. School programs that help students get firsthand experiences in the world of work. (22)

Y

"you" messages. Messages that place all the blame for a problem on others, creating defensiveness and resistance. (5)

Z

zygote. The new cell that forms when the nuclei of the sperm and egg merge into one nucleus. (7)

Photo Credits

6-7   David Hopper
6-9   Cholla
8-5   Illustrations courtesy of the March of Dimes, ©2007
10-3   Provena Mercy Medical Center
11-4   Women's Center Hospital
12-3   Nancy Henke-Konopasek
12-5   Monica Wilson
12-9   Cholla
12-10   Cholla
13-2   Cholla
13-3   Cholla
13-4   Cholla
13-5   Cholla
12-7   Cholla
14-6   Susan Fincher
14-20   Cholla
15-2   Pam Ryder
15-5   Cholla
15-7   Nancy Henke-Konopasek

15-22   Cholla
16-2   David Hopper
16-7   Cholla
16-18   Cholla
16-20   Cholla
17-10   Thornridge High School
18-1   David Hopper
18-8   Pam Ryder
20-2   Pam Ryder
20-4   Todd Scheffers
21-3   Bristol-Meyers Squibb Co.
21-10   Eisenhower Elementary, Gaye Yvonne Kuechenmeister
21-16   Barrier Free Environments
21-14   Mississippi Dept. of Economic and Community Development
22-1   Pam Ryder
22-3   The Crayon Club, Cholla
22-20   Family, Career and Community Leaders of America, Inc. (FCCLA)

Index